Global Politics

Palgrave Foundations Series

A series of introductory texts across a wide range of subject areas to meet the needs of today's lecturers and students

Foundations texts provide complete yet concise coverage of core topics and skills based on detailed research of course requirements suitable for both independent study and class use – the firm foundation for future study.

Published

A History of English Literature (third edition)
Biology
British Politics (second edition)
Chemistry (fourth edition)
Communication Studies
Contemporary Europe (third edition)
Economics for Business
European Union Politics
Foundations of Marketing
Global Politics (second edition)
Modern British History
Nineteenth-Century Britain
Philosophy
Physics (third editon)
Politics (fourth edition)
Theatre Studies

Global Politics

Second Edition

ANDREW HEYWOOD

First edition 2011
Second edition 2014
Reprinted with minor changes in 2015
Published by
PALGRAVE

Palgrave Macmillan in the UK is an imprint of Macmillan Publishers Limited, registered in England, company number 785998, of 4 Crinan Street, London, N1 9XW.

Palgrave Macmillan in the US is a division of St Martin's Press LLC, 175 Fifth Avenue, New York, NY 10010.

Palgrave is the global imprint of the above companies and is represented throughout the world.

Palgrave® and Macmillan® are registered trademarks in the United States, the United Kingdom, Europe and other countries.

ISBN 978-1-137-34926-2

This book is printed on paper suitable for recycling and made from fully managed and sustained forest sources. Logging, pulping and manufacturing processes are expected to conform to the environmental regulations of the country of origin.

A catalogue record for this book is available from the British Library.

A catalog record for this book is available from the Library of Congress.

Printed in China

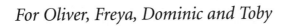

For Oliver, Freya, Dominic and Toby

Brief Contents

Contents

List of Illustrative Material

Debating

Focus on

Deconstructing

Concepts

Key events

Figures

Tables

Maps

Featured thinkers

Preface to the Second Edition

The second edition of this book remains faithful to the approach to international relations and world affairs adopted in the first edition, in that it treats 'the global' and 'the international' not as rival, but as complementary, modes of understanding. Such an approach acknowledges that states and national governments continue to play a major role on the world stage, while also accepting that, over a significant range of issues, states now operate in a context of global interdependence. The choice of *Global Politics* as the title of the book reflects the fact that both what goes on *within* states and what goes on *between* states impact on one another to a greater degree than before, and that an increased range of political interactions no longer take place simply in and through the state.

The new edition has been comprehensively updated to take account of the ever-evolving field of global politics, both in the body of the text and through the inclusion of new boxed material (especially revised 'Politics in Action' features). In addition, two more substantial changes have been made. The first is the inclusion of a second chapter on theory, Chapter 21, Why Theory Matters. Whereas Chapter 3, Theories of Global Politics, provides an introduction to key substantive theories, the new chapter focuses more on how, and how far, theory contributes to our understanding of global politics. Although the new chapter addresses metatheoretical issues to do with ontology, epistemology, and so on, it seeks to avoid getting lost in abstract debate, attempting instead to de-mystify theory, in part by relating it to 'real-world' examples and the substance of global politics. As the new chapter draws together themes and issues that emerge at various points in the book, it is placed towards the end, allowing it also to be used to stimulate further, and deeper, reflection on matters related to theory. The second major change is that Chapter 7, The Nation in a Global Age, has been revised to include more extensive coverage of the issue of international migration, including an examination of its economic impact. To allow this to happen, the section on 'Multiculturalism and Hybridity', formerly in Chapter 7, has been relocated to Chapter 8, Identity, Culture and Challenges to the West, where it, anyway, fits better.

GUIDE TO THE KEY FEATURES

The pedagogical features found in this book allow important events, concepts and theoretical issues to be examined in greater depth or detail, whilst also maintaining the flow of the main body of the text. They are, moreover, designed to encourage readers to think critically and independently about the key issues of global politics.

Each chapter starts with a **Preview** that outlines the major themes and a series of questions that highlight the central themes and issues addressed in the chapter. At the end of each chapter there is a **Summary** of its major points, a list of **Questions for discussion**, and suggestions for **Further reading**. Additional material is provided throughout the text in the form of glossary panels and boxed information. These boxes are comprehensively cross-referenced throughout the text. The most significant features are the following:

Approaches boxes outline important theoretical approaches to a central theme under discussion, providing in each case realist, liberal and critical views of the theme or issue.

Global politics in action boxes examine major events in global politics and reflect on how they contribute to our understanding of world affairs.

Global actors boxes consider the nature of key actors on the world stage and reflect on their impact and significance.

Debating boxes examine major controversies in global politics and highlight arguments for and against a particular proposition.

Deconstructing boxes examine the internal structure of key terms to uncover the biases and 'hidden' meanings they embody.

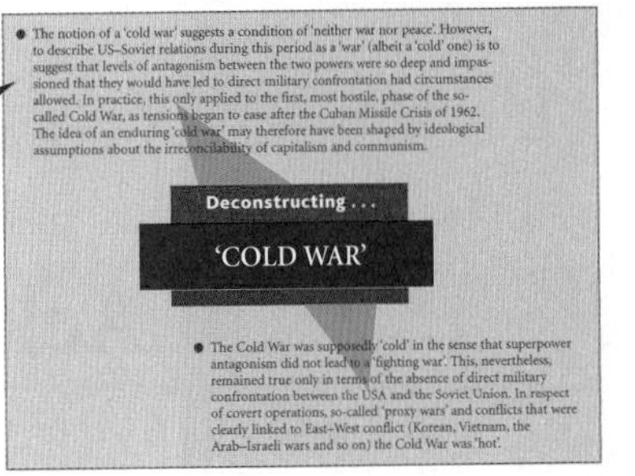

Key theorists provide brief biographical material of key figures or major thinkers, some of these boxes group together a number of influential theorists in a related area.

Definitions of **key terms** and explanations of **key concepts** are found in the margin of the text.

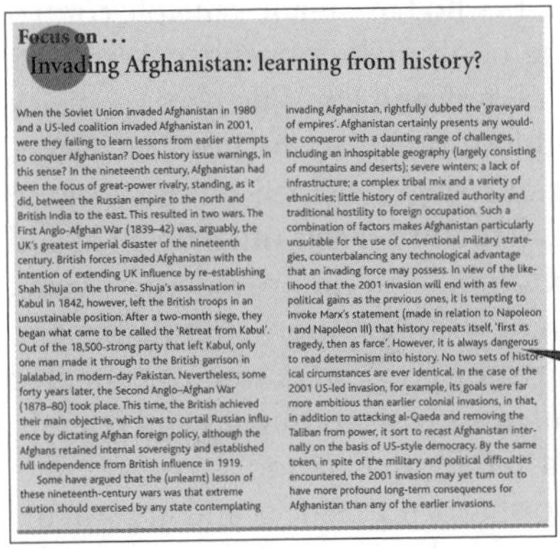

Focus boxes give either further insight into theoretical issues or provide additional material about topics under discussion.

Key events boxes provide a brief overview of significant events or developments in a particular area.

The **companion website** features a password-protected instructor area plus a freely accessible student site including additional **key-feature boxes**, a searchable **glossary**, **self-test** questions, **web links**, **update materials**, and suggested **additional reading**. It is available at: www.palgrave.com/politics/global.

KEY THEORISTS IN THE SOCIOLOGY OF GLOBALIZATION

Manuel Castells (born 1942)
A Spanish sociologist, Castells is especially associated with the idea of information society and communications research. He suggests that we live in a 'network society', in which territorial borders and traditional identities have been undermined by the power of knowledge flows. Castells thus emphasizes the 'informational' basis of network society, and shows how human experience of time and space have been transformed. His works include *The Rise of the Network Society* (1996), *The Internet Galaxy* (2004) and *Communication Power* (2009).

Ulrich Beck (born 1944)
A German sociologist, Beck's work has examined topics as wide-ranging as the new world of work, the perils of globalization, and challenges to the global power of capital. In *The Risk Society* (1992), he analyzed the tendency of the globalizing economy to generate uncertainty and insecurity. *Individualization* (2002) (written with his wife, Elizabeth) champions rights-based individualization against free-market individualism. In *Power in the Global Age* (2005), Beck explored how the strategies of capital can be challenged by civil society movements.

Roland Robertson (born 1938)
A UK sociologist and one of the pioneers in the study of globalization, Robertson's psycho-social view of globalization portrays it as 'the compression of the world and the intensification of the consciousness of the world as a whole'. He has drawn attention to both the process of 'relativization' (when local cultures and global pressures mix) and the process of 'glocalization' (through which global pressures are forced to conform to local conditions). Robertson's key work in this field is *Globalization: Social Theory and Global Culture* (1992).

Saskia Sassen (born 1949)
A Dutch sociologist, Sassen is noted for her analyses of globalization and international human migration. In *The Global City* (2001), she examined how cities such as New York, London and Tokyo have become emblematic of the capacity of globalization to create contradictory spaces, characterized by the relationship between the employees of global corporations and the vast population of the low-income 'others' (often migrants and women). Sassen's other works include *The Mobility of Capital and Labour* (1988) and *Territory, Authority, Rights* (2006).

Jan Aart Scholte (born 1959)
A Dutch sociologist and globalization theorist, Scholte argues that globalization is best understood as a reconfiguration of social geography marked by the growth of transplanetary and supraterritorial connections between people. Although by no means a critic of the 'supraterritorialism' that globalization brings about, he highlights the tendency of 'neoliberalist globalization' to heighten insecurities, exacerbate inequalities and deepen democratic deficits. Scholte's main works include *International Relations of Social Change* (1993) and *Globalization: A Critical Introduction* (2005).

Zygmunt Bauman (born 1925)
A Polish sociologist, Bauman's interests range from the nature of intimacy to globalization, and from the Holocaust to reality television programmes such as *Big Brother*. Sometimes portrayed as the prophet of postmodernity, he has highlighted trends such as the emergence of new patterns of deprivation and exclusion, the psychic corruption of consumer society, and the growing tendency for social relations to have a 'liquid' character. Bauman's main writings include *Modernity and the Holocaust* (1994), *Globalization* (1998) and *Liquid Modernity* (2000).

Deconstructing . . .

'COLD WAR'

● The notion of a 'cold war' suggests a condition of 'neither war nor peace'. However, to describe US–Soviet relations during this period as a 'war' (albeit a 'cold' one) is to suggest that they would have led to direct military confrontation had circumstances allowed. In practice, this only applied to the first, most hostile, phase of the so-called Cold War, as tensions began to ease after the Cuban Missile Crisis of 1962. The idea of an enduring 'cold war' may therefore have been shaped by ideological assumptions about the irreconcilability of capitalism and communism.

● The Cold War was supposedly 'cold' in the sense that superpower antagonism did not lead to a 'fighting war'. This, nevertheless, remained true only in terms of the absence of direct military confrontation between the USA and the Soviet Union. In respect of covert operations, so-called 'proxy wars' and conflicts that were clearly linked to East–West conflict (Korean, Vietnam, the Arab–Israeli wars and so on) the Cold War was 'hot'.

CONCEPT

Security dilemma
Security dilemma describes a condition in which actions taken by one actor to improve national security are interpreted as aggressive by other actors, thereby provoking military counter-moves. This reflects two component dilemmas (Booth and Wheeler 2008). First, there is a dilemma of *interpretation* – what are the motives, intentions and capabilities of others in building up military power? As weapons are inherently ambiguous symbols (they can be either defensive or aggressive), there is irresolvable uncertainty about these matters. Second, there is a dilemma of *response* – should they react in kind, in a militarily confrontational manner, or should they seek to signal reassurance and attempt to defuse tension?

a state is, the more secure it is likely to be. This focus on military security nevertheless draws states into dynamic, competitive relationships with one another, based on what is called the 'security dilemma'. This is the problem that a military build-up for defensive purposes by one state is always liable to be interpreted by other states as potentially or actually aggressive, leading to retaliatory military build-ups and so on. The security dilemma gets to the very heart of politics amongst states, making it the quintessential dilemma of international politics (see p. 000). Permanent insecurity between and amongst states is therefore the inescapable lot of those who live in a condition of anarchy.

However, the state-centric ideas of national security and an inescapable security dilemma have also been challenged. There is, for example, a long-established emphasis within liberal theory on collective security (see p. 000), reflecting the belief that aggression can best be resisted by united action taken by a number of states. Such a view shifts attention away from the idea of 'national' security towards the broader notion of '**international**' **security** (Smith 2010). Furthermore, the security agenda in modern global politics has changed in a number of ways. These include, on the one hand, the expansion of 'zones of peace' in which the tensions and incipient conflicts implied by the security dilemma appear to be absent. Thus 'security regimes' or 'security communities' have developed to manage disputes and help to avoid war, a trend often associated with growing economic interdependence (linked to globalization) and the advance of democratization. On the other hand, September 11 and the wider threat of terrorism has highlighted the emergence of new security challenges that are particularly problematical because they arise from non-state actors and exploit the greater interconnectedness of the modern world. International security may therefore have given way to 'global' security. A further development has been the trend to rethink the concept of security at a still deeper level, usually linked to the notion of 'human security' (see p. 000). Interest in human security has grown both because the decline of inter-state war in the post-Cold War means that the threat from violent conflict now usually occurs *within* states, coming from civil war, insurrection and civic strife, and because of the recognition that in the modern world people's safety and survival is often put at risk more by non-military threats (such as environmental destruction, disease, refugee crises and resource scarcity), than it is by military threats.

Justice
Realist theorists have traditionally viewed justice as a largely irrelevant issue in international or global politics. Relations between states should be determined by hard-headed judgements related to the national interest, not by ethical considerations. Liberals, by contrast, insist that international politics and morality should go hand in hand, amoral power politics being a recipe for egoism, conflict and violence. Traditionally, however, they have defended the idea of 'international' justice based on principles that set out how nation-states should behave towards one another. Respect for state sovereignty and the norm of non-interference in the affairs of other states, seen as guarantees of national independence and political freedom, are clearly an example of this. Such thinking is also reflected in 'just war' theory (see p. 000). This is the idea that

● **international security**
conditions in which the mutual survival and safety of states is secured through measures taken to prevent or punish aggression, usually within a rule-governed international order.

● **Security regime** A framework of cooperation amongst states and other actors to ensure the peaceful resolution of conflict (see international regime, p. 00).

Focus on . . .

Invading Afghanistan: learning from history?

When the Soviet Union invaded Afghanistan in 1980 and a US-led coalition invaded Afghanistan in 2001, were they failing to learn lessons from earlier attempts to conquer Afghanistan? Does history issue warnings, in this sense? In the nineteenth century, Afghanistan had been the focus of great-power rivalry, standing, as it did, between the Russian empire to the north and British India to the east. This resulted in two wars. The First Anglo-Afghan War (1839–42) was, arguably, the UK's greatest imperial disaster of the nineteenth century. British forces invaded Afghanistan with the intention of extending UK influence by re-establishing Shah Shuja on the throne. Shuja's assassination in Kabul in 1842, however, left the British troops in an unsustainable position. After a two-month siege, they began what came to be called the 'Retreat from Kabul'. Out of the 18,500-strong party that left Kabul, only one man made it through to the British garrison in Jalalabad, in modern-day Pakistan. Nevertheless, some forty years later, the Second Anglo-Afghan War (1878–80) took place. This time, the British achieved their main objective, which was to curtail Russian influence by dictating Afghan foreign policy, although the Afghans retained internal sovereignty and established full independence from British influence in 1919. Some have argued that the (unlearnt) lesson of these nineteenth-century wars was that extreme caution should exercised by any state contemplating

invading Afghanistan, rightfully dubbed the 'graveyard of empires'. Afghanistan certainly presents any would-be conqueror with a daunting range of challenges, including an inhospitable geography (largely consisting of mountains and deserts); severe winters; a lack of infrastructure; a complex tribal mix and a variety of ethnicities; little history of centralized authority and traditional hostility to foreign occupation. Such a combination of factors makes Afghanistan particularly unsuitable for the use of conventional military strategies, counterbalancing any technological advantage that an invading force may possess. In view of the likelihood that the 2001 invasion will end with as few political gains as the previous ones, it is tempting to invoke Marx's statement (made in relation to Napoleon I and Napoleon III) that history repeats itself, 'first as tragedy, then as farce'. However, it is always dangerous to read determinism into history. No two sets of historical circumstances are ever identical. In the case of the 2001 US-led invasion, for example, its goals were far more ambitious than earlier colonial invasions, in that, in addition to attacking al-Qaeda and removing the Taliban from power, it sort to recast Afghanistan internally on the basis of US-style democracy. By the same token, in spite of the military and political difficulties encountered, the 2001 invasion may yet turn out to have more profound long-term consequences for Afghanistan than any of the earlier invasions.

KEY EVENTS . . .

Advances in communication technology

1455	Gutenberg Bible is published, initiating the printing revolution through the first use of removable and reusable type.
1837	The telegraph is invented, providing the first means of substantially superterritorial communication.
1876	The telephone is invented by Alexander Graham Bell, although the first telephone device was built in 1861 by the German scientist Johann Philip Reis.
1894	The radio is invented by Guglielmo Marconi, with a transatlantic radio signal being received for the first time in 1901.
1928	Television is invented by John Logie Baird, becoming commercially available in the late 1990s and reaching a mass audience in the 1950s and 1960s.
1936	First freely programmable computer is invented by Konrad Zuse.
1957	The Soviet Sputnik 1 is launched, initiating the era of communications satellites (sometimes called SATCOM).
1962	'Third generation' computers, using integrated circuits (or microchips), started to appear (notably NASA's Apollo Guidance Computer).
1969	Earliest version of the Internet developed, in the form of the ARPANET link between the University of California and the Stanford Research Institute, with electronic mail, or email, being developed three years later.
1991	Earliest version of the World Wide Web becomes publicly available as a global information medium through which users can read and write via computers connected to the Internet.
1995	Digitalization is introduced by Netscape and the Web, substantially broadening access to the Internet and the scope of other technologies.

Global Politics, Second Edition
by Andrew Heywood

Welcome to the companion website for Global Politics

This revised, updated, and considerably expanded new edition provides a systematic introduction to the theory and practice of contemporary international relations. Including pedagogical features highlighting key theorists and concepts, this text clarifies the fundamental debates and issues at stake in global political affairs.

About this site

Acknowledgements

Although this book has a single author, it is certainly not the product of a single person's work. I have been especially fortunate in my publisher at Palgrave Macmillan, Steven Kennedy, who suggested that I should write the book in the first place and who has been closely involved at every stage in its production and subsequent development. He has been a constant source of enthusiasm, encouragement, good advice and good humour. Others who have made valuable contributions to the design and production of the book include Stephen Wenham, Helen Caunce, Maddy Hamey-Thomas, Keith Povey and Ian Wileman. Feedback from Jacqui True, Garrett Wallace Brown and four other, anonymous reviewers, who commented on the first edition at various stages, helped significantly in strengthening its contents and, sometimes, its structure. Their often detailed and always thoughtful criticisms and suggestions not only improved the overall quality of the book, but also made the process of writing it more stimulating and enjoyable. I would also like to thank the anonymous reviewers who commented on the second edition as it took shape. Discussions with colleagues and friends, particularly Karon and Doug Woodward, Rita and Brian Cox and Barry and Kate Taylor, and with my brother David, helped to sharpen the ideas and arguments developed in the book. However, my most heartfelt thanks go, as ever, to my wife Jean, with whom this book, as my previous books, has been produced in partnership. She took sole responsibility for the preparation of the typescript, and was a regular source of advice on both style and content. This book is dedicated to my grandchildren, for whom (and for much else) I would like to thank my sons Mark and Robin, and my daughters-in-law Jessie and Helen.

ANDREW HEYWOOD

Copyright Acknowledgements

354, 415, 450, 521; Saltzman Institute for War and Peace Studies (Columbia University), p. 63; The People's History Museum, p. 73; Ohio State University, p. 77; Ann Tickner, p. 78; The Institute for Global Leadership, Tufts University, p. 83; Library of Congress, pp. 88, 189, 445; Immanuel Wallerstein, p. 104; Soros Fund Management LLC, p. 110 (George Soros); Dan Deitch, p. 110 (Paul Krugman); Herman Daly, p. 110 (Herman Daly); Robert Cox, p. 124; Roland Robertson, p. 148 (Roland Robertson); A. Rusbridger, p. 148 (Saskia Sassen); Bill Brydon, p. 148 (Jan Aart Scholte); Grzegorz Lepiarz, p. 148 (Zygmunt Bauman); Naomi Klein, p. 150; David Gellner, p. 169; Benedict Anderson, p. 169; The Library of the London School of Economics and Political Science, p. 220; Tom Fitzsimmons, p. 222; John Mearsheimer, p. 241; Mary Kaldor, p. 257; Dvora Lewy, p. 257 (Martin van Creveld); Center for a New American Security, p. 257 (David Kilkullen); Jon R. Friedman, p. 265; Columbia Law School (photo by Jon Roemer), p. 384 (Jagdish Bhagwati); Susan George, p. 384; The Earth Institute, p. 375 (Jeffrey Sachs); Janet Biehl, p. 411 (Murray Bookchin); Rachel Basso, p. 411 (Carolyn Merchant); Vandana Shiva, p. 411 (Vandana Shiva); Jean Bethke Elshtain, p. 435 (Jean Bethke Elshtain); Courtesy of IDCE Department at Clark University, p. 435 (Cynthia Enloe); Courtesy of Woodrow Wilson School of Public and International Affairs (Princeton University), p. 442; International Political Science Association, p. 494; Peter Haas, p. 494 (Ernst Haas); Audiovisual Library of the European Commission (©European Union, 2010), p. 502; The Elliott School of International Affairs (The George Washington University), p. 527; Francis Fukuyama, p. 539; Jon Chase/Harvard Staff Photographer, p. 540; Mary Bull, p. 543 (Hedley Bull); Gabriele Wight, p. 543 (Martin Wight); Terry Nardin, p. 543 (Terry Nardin).

The author and publishers would like to thank the following who have kindly given permission for the use of other copyright material:

Palgrave Macmillan and The Guilford Press, *Map 7.1 Global migratory flows since 1973*, which originally appeared as *Map 1.1 Global migratory flows from 1973* in *The Age of Migration*, Castles and Miller, 2009 (now Castles *et al.* 2013).

Palgrave Macmillan, *Map 20.1 Europe and EU membership*, which originally appeared as *Map of member states and applicant states of the European Union* in *European Union Enlargement*, Nugent (ed.), 2004.

Palgrave Macmillan, *Table 19.1 Competing models of global politics*, which originally appeared as *Table 12.1 Four models of international relations in international organization*, Rittberger *et al.*, 2012.

Every effort has been made to contact all copyright-holders, but if any have been inadvertently omitted the publishers will be pleased to make the necessary arrangement at the earliest opportunity.

CHAPTER 1

Introducing Global Politics

'Only connect!'

E. M. FORSTER, *Howards End* (1910)

PREVIEW

How should we approach the study of world affairs? How is the world best understood? World affairs have traditionally been understood on the basis of an *international* paradigm. In this view, states (often understood as 'nations', hence 'international') are taken to be the essential building blocks of world politics, meaning that world affairs boil down, essentially, to the relations between states. This suggests that once you understand the factors that influence how states interact with one another, you understand how the world works. However, since the 1980s, an alternative *globalization* paradigm has become fashionable. This reflects the belief that world affairs have been transformed in recent decades by the growth of global interconnectedness and interdependence. In this view, the world no longer operates as a disaggregated collection of states, or 'units', but rather as an integrated whole, as 'one world'. Global politics, as understood in this book, attempts to straddle these rival paradigms. It accepts that it is equally absurd to dismiss states and national government as irrelevant in world affairs as it is to deny that, over a significant range of issues, states now operate in a context of global interdependence. However, in what sense is politics now 'global'? And how, and to what extent, has globalization reconfigured world politics? Our understanding of global politics also needs to take account of the different theoretical 'lenses' though which the world has been interpreted; that is, different ways of *seeing* the world. What, in particular, is the difference between mainstream perspectives on global politics and critical perspectives? Finally, the world stubbornly refuses to stand still. Global politics is therefore an arena of ongoing and, many would argue, accelerating change. And yet, certain aspects of global politics appear to have an enduring character. What is the balance between continuity and change in global politics?

KEY ISSUES

- How do 'the global' and 'the international' complement one another?
- How have the contours of world politics changed in recent years?
- What have been the implications of globalization for world politics?
- How do mainstream approaches to global politics differ from critical approaches?
- How has global politics changed in recent years in relation to the issues of power, security and justice?

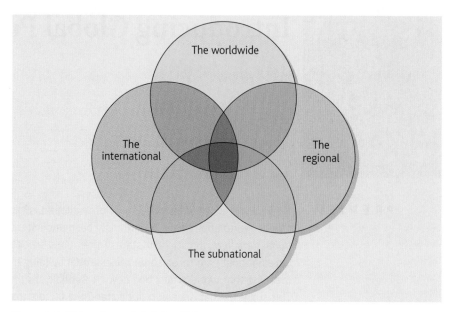

Figure 1.1 **Dimensions of global politics**

FROM 'THE INTERNATIONAL' TO 'THE GLOBAL'?

The aim of this book is to provide an up-to-date, integrated and forward-looking introduction to international relations/ global politics (see p. 3). It seeks to be genuinely global while not ignoring the international dimension of world affairs, accepting that 'the global' and 'the international' complement one another and are not rival or incompatible modes of understanding. In this view, global politics encompasses not just politics at the 'global' level – that is, world-wide processes, systems and institutional frameworks – but politics at, and, crucially, across, *all* levels – the worldwide, the regional, the national and the subnational (see Figure 1.1). Such an approach reflects the fact that while, over an increasing range of issues, **states** interact with one another in conditions of global interdependence, they nevertheless remain the key actors on the world stage.

However, if the international paradigm, in which world affairs boil down, essentially, to relations between and among states, no longer constitutes an adequate basis for understanding, what has changed, and how profound have these changes been? How have the contours of world politics changed in recent years? The most significant changes have been the following:

- The emergence of new global actors
- The growth of interdependence and interconnectedness
- The erosion of the domestic/international divide
- The rise of global governance.

● **State**: A political association that enjoys sovereign jurisdiction within defined territorial borders.

Focus on ...
Defining global politics?

What does it mean to suggest that politics has 'gone global'? How does 'global' politics differ from 'international' politics? The term 'global' has two meanings. In the first, global means *worldwide*, having planetary (not merely regional or national) significance. The globe is, in effect, the world. Global politics, in this sense, refers to politics that is conducted at a global rather than a national or regional level. It therefore focuses primarily on the work of organizations such as the United Nations (UN) and the World Trade Organization (WTO), which have a near universal membership, and on issues (such as the environment and the economy) where interconnectedness has gone so far that events and developments affect, actually or potentially, all parts of the world and so all people on the planet.

In the second meaning (the one used in this book), global means *comprehensive*; it refers to *all* elements within a system, not just to the system as a whole. While such an approach acknowledges that a significant (and, perhaps, growing) range of political interactions now takes place at the global level, it rejects the idea that the global level has, in any sense, *transcended* politics at the national, local or, for that matter, any other level. In particular, the advent of global politics does not imply that international politics should be consigned to the dustbin of history. This is important because the notion that politics has been caught up in a swirl of interconnectedness that effectively absorbs all of its parts, or 'units', into an indivisible, global whole, is difficult to sustain.

From state-centrism to the mixed-actor model?

World politics has conventionally been understood in international terms. Although the larger phenomenon of patterns of conflict and cooperation between and among territorially-based political units has existed throughout history, the term 'international relations' was not coined until the UK philosopher and legal reformer, Jeremy Bentham (1748–1832), used it in his *Principles of Morals and Legislation* ([1789] 1968). Bentham's use of the term acknowledged a significant shift: that, by the late eighteenth century, territorially-based political units were coming to have a more clearly national character, making relations between them appear genuinely 'inter-national'. However, although most modern states are either nation-states (see p. 168) or aspire to be nation-states, it is their possession of statehood rather than nationhood that allows them to act effectively on the world stage. 'International' politics should thus, more properly, be described as 'inter-state' politics. But what is a state? As defined by the 1933 Montevideo Convention on the Rights and Duties of States, a state must possess four qualifying properties: a defined territory, a permanent population, an effective government, and the 'capacity to enter into relations with other states'. In this view, states, or countries (the terms can be used interchangeably in this context); are taken to be the key actors on the world stage, and perhaps the only ones that warrant serious consideration. This is why the conventional approach to world politics is seen as **state-centric**, and why the international system is often portrayed as a **state-system**. The origins of this view of international politics are usually traced back to the Peace of Westphalia (1648), which established sovereignty (see p. 4) as the distinguishing feature of

● **State-centrism**: An approach to political analysis that takes the state to be the key actor in the domestic realm and on the world stage.

● **State-system**: A pattern of relationships between and amongst states that establishes a measure of order and predictability (see p. 5).

CONCEPT

Sovereignty

Sovereignty is the principle of supreme and unquestionable authority, reflected in the claim by the state to be the sole author of laws within its territory. *External* sovereignty (sometimes called 'state sovereignty' or 'national sovereignty') refers to the capacity of the state to act independently and autonomously on the world stage. This implies that states are legally equal and that the territorial integrity and political independence of a state are inviolable. *Internal* sovereignty refers to the location of supreme power/authority within the state. The institution of sovereignty is nevertheless developing and changing, both as new concepts of sovereignty emerge ('economic sovereignty', 'food sovereignty' and so on) and as sovereignty is adapted to new circumstances ('pooled sovereignty', 'responsible sovereignty' and so forth).

the state. State sovereignty thus became the primary organizing principle of international politics.

However, the state-centric approach to world politics has become increasingly difficult to sustain. This has happened, in part, because it is no longer possible to treat states as the only significant actors on the world stage. Transnational corporations (TNCs) (see p. 94), non-governmental organizations (NGOs) (see p. 10) and a host of other non-state bodies have come to exert influence. In different ways and to different degrees, groups and organizations ranging from al-Qaeda (see p. 301), the anti-capitalist movement (see p. 74) and Greenpeace to Google (see p. 146), General Motors and the Papacy contribute to shaping world politics. Since the 1970s, indeed, pluralist theorists have advocated a **mixed-actor model** of world politics. However, although it is widely accepted that states and national governments are merely one category of actor amongst many on the world stage, they may still remain the most important actors. No TNC or NGOs, for instance, can rival the state's coercive power, either its capacity to enforce order within its borders or its ability to deal militarily with other states. (The changing role and significance of the state are examined in depth in Chapter 5.)

From independence to interdependence?

To study international politics traditionally meant to study the implications of the international system being divided into a collection of states. Thanks to sovereignty, these states were, moreover, viewed as independent and autonomous entities. This state-centric approach has often been illustrated through the so-called 'billiard ball model', which dominated thinking about international relations in the 1950s and later, and was particularly associated with realist theory. This suggested that states, like billiard balls, are impermeable and self-contained units, which influence each other through external pressure. Sovereign states interacting within the state-system are thus seen to behave like a collection of billiard balls moving over the table and colliding with each other, as in Figure 1.2. In this view, interactions between and amongst states, or 'collisions', are linked, in most cases to military and **security** matters, reflecting the assumption that power and survival are the primary concerns of the state. International politics is thus orientated mainly around issues of war and peace,

● **Mixed-actor model**: The theory that, while not ignoring the role of states and national governments, international politics is shaped by a much broader range of interests and groups.

● **Security**: To be safe from harm, the absence of threats; security may be understood in 'national', 'international', 'global' or 'human' terms.

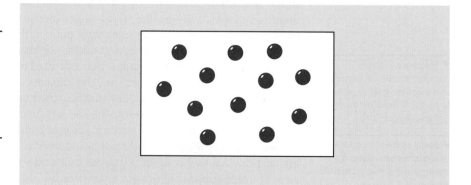

Figure 1.2 Billiard ball model of world politics

Focus on . . .
The Westphalian state-system

The Peace of Westphalia (1648) is commonly said to mark the beginning of modern international politics. The Peace was a series of treaties that brought an end to the Thirty Years War (1618–48), which consisted of a series of declared and undeclared wars throughout central Europe involving the Holy Roman Empire and various opponents, including the Danes, the Dutch and, above all, France and Sweden. Although the transition occurred over a much longer period of time, these treaties helped to transform a medieval Europe of overlapping authorities, loyalties and identities into a modern state-system. The so-called 'Westphalian system' was based on two key principles:

- States enjoy sovereign jurisdiction, in the sense that they have independent control over what happens within their territory (all other institutions and groups, spiritual and temporal, are therefore subordinate to the state).
- Relations between and among states are structured by the acceptance of the sovereign independence of all states (thus implying that states are legally equal).

with **diplomacy** and possibly military action being the principal forms of state interaction.

The billiard ball model of world politics implies that patterns of conflict and cooperation within the international system are largely determined by the distribution of power among states. Thus, although state-centric theorists acknowledged the formal, legal equality of states, each state being a sovereign entity, they also recognized that some states are more powerful than others, and, indeed, that strong states may sometimes intervene in the affairs of weak ones. In effect, not all billiard balls are the same size. This is why the study of international politics has conventionally given particular attention to the interests and behaviour of so-called 'great powers' (see p. 6).

The billiard ball model has nevertheless come under pressure as a result of growing interdependence (see p. 7) and interconnectedness. Tasks such as promoting economic growth and prosperity, tackling global warming, halting the spread of weapons of mass destruction and coping with pandemic diseases are impossible for any state to accomplish on its own, however powerful it might be. States, in these circumstances, are forced to work together, relying on collective efforts and energies. For Keohane and Nye (1977), such a web of relationships has created a condition of 'complex interdependence', in which states are drawn into cooperation and integration by forces such as closer trading and other economic relationships. This is illustrated by what has been called the 'cobweb model' of world politics (see Figure 1.3). Nevertheless, such thinking can be taken too far. For one thing, there are parts of the world, not least the Middle East, where states clearly remain enmeshed in military-strategic conflict, suggesting both that the billiard ball model is not entirely inaccurate and that levels of interdependence vary greatly across the globe. For another, interdependence is by no means always associated with trends towards peace, cooperation and integration. Interdependence may be asymmetrical rather than

● **Diplomacy**: A process of negotiation and communication between states that seeks to resolve conflict without recourse to war; an instrument of foreign policy.

Great power

A great power is a state deemed to rank amongst the most powerful in a hierarchical state-system. The criteria that define a great power are subject to dispute, but four are often identified. (1) Great powers are in the first rank of military prowess, having the capacity to maintain their own security and, potentially, to influence other powers. (2) They are economically powerful states, although (as Japan shows) this is a necessary but not a sufficient condition for great power status. (3) They have global, and not merely regional, spheres of interest. (4) They adopt a 'forward' foreign policy and have actual, and not merely potential, impact on international affairs (during its isolationist phase, the USA was thus not a great power).

● **Globalization**: The emergence of a complex web of interconnectedness that means that our lives are increasingly shaped by events that occur, and decisions that are made, at a great distance from us (see p. 8).

● **Transnationalism**: Political, social, economic or other forms that transcend or cut across national borders

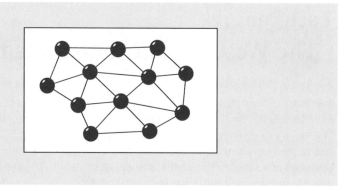

Figure 1.3 **Cobweb model of world politics**

symmetrical, in which case it can lead to domination and conflict rather than peace and harmony.

From the domestic/international divide to transnationalism?

One of the key implications of approaching study from the perspective of 'the international' is that politics has a distinct spatial or territorial character. In short, borders and boundaries matter. This applies especially in the case of the distinction between *domestic* politics, which is concerned with the state's role in maintaining order and carrying out regulation within its borders, and *international* politics, which is concerned with relations between and among states. In that sense, sovereignty is a 'hard shell' that divides the 'inside' of politics from the 'outside'. This domestic/international, or 'inside/outside', divide also separates what have conventionally been seen as two quite different spheres of political interaction. Whereas politics 'inside' has an orderly and regulated character, stemming from the ability of the state within the domestic sphere to impose rule from above, order of this kind is absent from politics 'outside', in that there is no authority in the international sphere higher than the sovereign state. According to John Agnew (1994), such thinking had created a 'territorial trap' within the discipline of international relations, reflected in three assumptions. First, the state is a clearly bounded territorial space. Second, domestic and foreign affairs are entirely different realms. Third, states are 'containers' of society, implying that the boundaries of the state coincide with the boundaries of society.

Such an emphasis on borders and clear territorial divisions have nevertheless come under pressure as a result of recent trends and developments, not least those associated with **globalization**, as discussed in the next main section. In particular, there has been a substantial growth in cross-border flows and trans-actions – movements of people, goods, money, information and ideas. This has created the phenomenon of **transnationalism**. As state borders have become increasingly 'porous', the conventional domestic/international, or 'inside/ outside' divide has become more difficult to uphold. This can be illustrated by both the substantially greater vulnerability of domestic economies to events that take place elsewhere in the world (as demonstrated by the wide-ranging impact

CONCEPT

Interdependence

Interdependence refers to a relationship between two parties in which each is affected by decisions that are taken by the other. Interdependence implies mutual influence, even a rough equality between the parties in question, usually arising from a sense of mutual vulnerability. Interdependence, then, is usually associated with a trend towards cooperation and integration in world affairs. Keohane and Nye (1977) advanced the idea of 'complex interdependence' as an alternative to the realist model of international politics. This highlighted the extent to which (1) states have ceased to be autonomous international actors; (2) economic and other issues have become more prominent in world affairs; and (3) military force has become a less reliable and less important policy option.

● **Anarchy**: Literally, without rule; the absence of a central government or higher authority, sometimes, but not necessarily, associated with instability and chaos.

● **Self-help**: A reliance on internal or inner resources, often seen as the principal reason states prioritize survival and security.

● **Balance of power**: A condition in which no one state predominates over others, tending to create general equilibrium and curb the hegemonic ambitions of all states (see p. 262).

of the 2007–09 global financial crisis) and by the wider use of digital technologies that enable people to communicate with one another through means (such as mobile phones and the Internet) that national governments find difficult to control. It is also notable that issues that are becoming more prominent in world affairs, such as environmental politics and human rights (see p. 311), tend to have an intrinsically transnational character. However, claims that the modern world is effectively 'borderless' are manifestly absurd, and, in some ways, territorial divisions are becoming more important, not less important. This is evident, for instance, in the greater emphasis on national or 'homeland' security in many parts of the world since the terrorist attacks of September 11, and in attempts to constrain international migration by strengthening border and other immigration controls.

From international anarchy to global governance?

A key assumption of the traditional approach to international politics has been that the state-system operates in a context of **anarchy**. This reflects the notion that there is no higher authority than the state, meaning that external politics operates as an international 'state of nature', a pre-political society. The implications of international anarchy are profound. Most importantly, in the absence of any other force attending to their interests, states are forced to rely on **self-help**. If international politics operates as a 'self-help system', the power-seeking inclinations of one state are only tempered by competing tendencies in other states, suggesting that conflict and war are inevitable features of the international system. In this view, conflict is only constrained by a **balance of power**, developed either as a diplomatic strategy by peace-minded leaders or occurring through a happy coincidence. This image of anarchy has been modified by the idea that the international system operates more like an 'international society' (see p. 9). Hedley Bull ([1977] 2012) thus advanced the notion of an 'anarchical society', in place of the conventional theory of international anarchy.

However, the idea of international anarchy, and even the more modest notion of an 'anarchical society', have become more difficult to sustain because of the emergence, especially since 1945, of a framework of global governance (see p. 462) and sometimes regional governance. This is reflected in the growing importance of organizations such as the United Nations, the International Monetary Fund (IMF) (see p. 475), the World Trade Organization (WTO) (see p. 537), the European Union (see p. 509) and so on. The growing number and significance of international organizations has occurred for powerful and pressing reasons. Notably, they reflect the fact that states are increasingly confronted by **collective dilemmas**, issues that are particularly taxing because they confound even the most powerful of states when acting alone. This first became apparent in relation to the development of technologized warfare and particularly the invention of nuclear weapons, but has since been reinforced by challenges such as financial crises, climate change, terrorism, crime, migration and development. Such trends, nevertheless, have yet to render the idea of international anarchy altogether redundant. While international organizations have undoubtedly become significant actors on the world stage, competing, at times, with states and other non-state actors, their impact should not be exaggerated. Apart from anything else, they are, to a greater or lesser extent, the creatures of their members: they

CONCEPT

Globalization

Globalization is the emergence of a complex web of interconnectedness that means that our lives are increasingly shaped by events that occur, and decisions that are made, at a great distance from us. The central feature of globalization is therefore that geographical distance is of declining relevance and that territorial borders, such as those between nation-states, are becoming less significant. By no means, however, does globalization imply that 'the local' and 'the national' are subordinated to 'the global'. Rather, it highlights the *deepening* as well as the *broadening* of the political process, in the sense that local, national and global events (or perhaps local, regional, national, international and global events) constantly interact.

● **Collective dilemma**: A problem that stems from the interdependence of states, meaning that any solution must involve international cooperation rather than action by a single state.

● **Globality**: A totally interconnected whole, such as the global economy; the end-state of globalization.

● **Globalism**: An ideological project committed to the spread of globalization, usually reflecting support for the values and theories of free-market capitalism.

can do no more than their member states, and especially powerful states, allow them to do.

GLOBALIZATION AND ITS IMPLICATIONS

No development has challenged the conventional state-centric image of world politics more radically than the emergence of globalization. Globalization, indeed, can be seen as the buzz word of our time. Amongst politicians, for instance, the conventional wisdom is that the twenty-first century will be the 'global century'. But what actually is 'globalization'? Is it actually happening, and, if so, what are its implications?

Explaining globalization

Globalization is a complex, elusive and controversial term. It has been used to refer to a process, a policy, a marketing strategy, a predicament or even an ideology. Some have tried to bring greater clarity to the debate about the nature of globalization by distinguishing between globalization as a *process* or set of processes (highlighting the dynamics of transformation or change, in common with other words that end in the suffix '-ization', such as modernization) and **globality** as a *condition* (indicating the set of circumstances that globalization has brought about, just as modernization has created a condition of modernity) (Steger 2003). Others have used the term **globalism** to refer to the *ideology* of globalization, the theories, values and assumptions that have guided or driven the process (Ralston Saul 2009). The problem with globalization is that it is not so much an 'it' as a 'them': it is not a single process but a complex of processes, sometimes overlapping and interlocking but also, at times, contradictory and oppositional. It is therefore difficult to reduce globalization to a single theme. Nevertheless, the various developments and manifestations that are associated with globalization, or indeed globality, can be traced back to the underlying phenomenon of interconnectedness. Globalization, regardless of its forms or impact, forges connections between previously unconnected people, communities, institutions and societies. Held *et al.* (1999) thus defined globalization as 'the widening, intensifying, speeding up, and growing impact of world-wide interconnectedness'.

The interconnectedness that globalization has spawned is multidimensional and operates through distinctive economic, cultural and political processes. In other words, globalization has a number of dimensions or 'faces'. Although globalization theorists have championed particular interpretations of globalization, these are by no means mutually exclusive. Instead, they capture different aspects of a complex and multifaceted phenomenon. Globalization has been interpreted in three main ways:

● *Economic* globalization (see p. 98) is the process through which national economies have, to a greater or lesser extent, been absorbed into a single global economy (examined in greater depth in Chapter 4).
● *Cultural* globalization (see p. 151) is the process whereby information, commodities and images that have been produced in one part of the world enter into a global flow that tends to 'flatten out' cultural differences

between nations, regions and individuals (discussed more fully in Chapter 6).

- *Political* globalization (see p. 122) is the process through which policy-making responsibilities have been passed from national governments to international organizations (considered in greater detail in Chapter 5).

Globalization: myth or reality?

Is globalization actually happening? Although globalization may be the buzz word of our time, there has been intense debate about its impact and significance. No sooner had (roughly by the mid-1990s) academics and other social commentators seemed to agree that globalization was 'changing everything', than it became fashionable (in the early 2000s) to proclaim the 'end of globalization', or the 'death of globalism' (Bisley 2007). The most influential attempt to outline the various positions on this globalization debate was set out by Held *et al.* (1999). They distinguished between three positions:

- The hyperglobalists
- The sceptics
- The transformationalists.

The hyperglobalizers are the chief amongst 'the believers' in globalization. **Hyperglobalism** portrays globalization as a profound, even revolutionary set of economic, cultural, technological and political shifts that have intensified since the 1980s. Particular emphasis, in this view, is placed on developments such as the digital revolution in information and communications, the advent of an integrated global financial system and the emergence of global commodities that are available almost anywhere in the world. Indeed, hyperglobalism is often based on a form of technological determinism, which suggests that the forces creating a single global economy became irresistible once the technology that facilitates its existence was available. The chief image of hyperglobalism is captured in the notion of a 'borderless world' (discussed in more detail in Chapter 22), which suggests that national borders and, for that matter, states themselves have become irrelevant in a global order increasingly dominated by transnational forces. 'National' economic strategies are therefore virtually unworkable in a global context. Resistance to the dictates of global markets is both damaging – countries prosper to the extent that their economies are integrated into the global economy – and ultimately futile. Hyperglobalizers therefore have a strongly positive attitude towards globalization, usually assuming that, in marking the triumph of markets over the state, it is associated with economic dynamism and growing worldwide prosperity.

Nevertheless, hyperglobalism offers an unbalanced and exaggerated view of globalization, in at least two senses. First, it overstates the extent to which policy-makers have been dominated by 'irresistible' economic and technological forces, underestimating the importance of values, perceptions and ideological orientations. Second, the images of the 'end of sovereignty' and the 'twilight of the nation-state' can be said to feature amongst the myths of globalization (sometimes called 'globalony'). Although states may increasingly operate in post-sovereign conditions, in a context of interdependence and permeability, their role

---

CONCEPT

International society

The term 'international society' suggests that relations between and amongst states are conditioned by the existence of norms and rules that establish the regular patterns of interaction that characterize a 'society'. Such a view modifies the realist emphasis on power politics and international anarchy by suggesting the existence of a 'society of states' rather than simply a 'system of states'. This implies both that international relations are rule-governed, and that these rules help to maintain international order. The chief institutions that generate cultural cohesion and social integration are international law (see p. 399), diplomacy and the activities of international organizations (see p. 440).

● **Hyperglobalism**: The view that new, globalized economic and cultural patterns became inevitable once technology such as computerized financial trading, satellite communications, mobile phones and the Internet became widely available.

GLOBAL ACTORS . . .

NON-GOVERNMENTAL ORGANIZATIONS

A non-governmental organization (NGO) is a private, non-commercial group or body which seeks to achieve its ends through non-violent means. The World Bank (see p. 380) defines NGOs as 'private organizations that pursue activities to relieve suffering, promote the interests of the poor, protect the environment, provide basic social services, or undertake community development'. Very early examples of such bodies were the Society for the Abolition of the Slave Trade (formed by William Wilberforce in 1787) and the International Committee of the Red Cross, founded in 1863. The first official recognition of NGOs was by the United Nations (UN) in 1948, when 41 NGOs were granted consultative status following the establishment of the Universal Declaration of Human Rights (indeed, some NGO activists believe that only groups formally acknowledged by the UN should be regarded as 'true' NGOs). A distinction is often drawn between operational NGOs and advocacy NGOs:

- *Operational* NGOs are those whose primary purpose is the design and implementation of development-related projects; they may be either relief-orientated or development-orientated, and they may be community-based, national or international.
- *Advocacy* NGOs exist to promote or defend a particular cause; they are sometimes termed 'promotional pressure groups' or 'public interest groups'.

Significance: Since the 1990s, the steady growth in the number of NGOs has become a veritable explosion. By 2012, over 3,500 groups had been granted consultative status by the UN, with estimates of the total number of international NGOs usually exceeding 40,000. If national NGOs are taken into account, the number grows enormously: the USA has an estimated 2 million NGOs; Russia has 65,000 NGOs; and Kenya, to take one developing country alone, has about 2,400 NGOs coming into existence each year. The major international NGOs have developed into huge organizations. For example, Care International, dedicated to the worldwide reduction of poverty, controls a budget worth more than 100m dollars, Greenpeace has a membership of 2.5m and a staff of over 1,200, and Amnesty International is better resourced than the human rights arm of the UN.

There can be little doubt that major international NGOs and the NGO sector as a whole now constitute significant actors on the global stage. Although lacking the economic leverage that TNCs can exert, advocacy NGOs have proved highly adept at mobilizing 'soft' power and popular pressure. In this respect, they have a number of advantages. These include that leading NGOs have cultivated high public profiles, often linked to public protests and demonstrations that attract eager media attention; that their typically altruistic and humanitarian objectives enable them to mobilize public support and exert moral pressure in a way that conventional politicians and political parties struggle to rival; and that, over a wide range of issues, the views of NGOs are taken to be both authoritative and disinterested, based on the use of specialists and academics. Operational NGOs, for their part, have come to deliver about 15 per cent of international aid, often demonstrating a greater speed of response and level of operational effectiveness than governmental bodies, national or international, can muster. Relief- and development-orientated NGOs may also be able to operate in politically sensitive areas where national governments, or even the UN, would be unwelcome.

Nevertheless, the rise of the NGO has provoked considerable political controversy. Supporters of NGOs argue that they benefit and enrich global politics. They counter-balance corporate power, challenging the influence of TNCs; democratize global politics by articulating the interests of people and groups who have been disempowered by the globalization process; and act as a moral force, widening people's sense of civic responsibility and even promoting global citizenship. In these respects, they are a vital component of emergent global civil society (see p. 156). Critics, however, argue that NGOs are self-appointed groups that have no genuine democratic credentials, often articulating the views of a small group of senior professionals. In an attempt to gain a high media profile and attract support and funding, NGOs have been accused of making exaggerated claims, thereby distorting public perceptions and the policy agenda. Finally, in order to preserve their 'insider' status, NGOs tend to compromise their principles and 'go mainstream', becoming, in effect, deradicalized social movements. (The impact and significance of NGOs is examined further in Chapter 6.)

Focus on . . .
Definitions of globalization

- '[T]he intensification of worldwide social relations that link distant localities in a way that local happenings are shaped by events occurring many miles away and vice versa' (Giddens 1990)
- 'The integration of national economies into the international economy through trade, direct foreign investment, short-term capital flows, international flows of workers and humanity generally, and flows of technology' (Bhagwati 2004)

- 'The processes through which sovereign nation-states are criss-crossed and undermined by transnational actors with varying prospects of power, orientations, identities and networks' (Beck 2000)
- 'A process (or set of processes) which embody the transformation of the spatial organization of social relations and transactions' (Held et al. 1999)
- 'A reconfiguration of social geography marked by the growth of transplanetary and supraterritorial connections between people' (Scholte 2005)

and significance has altered rather than become irrelevant. States, for example, have become 'entrepreneurial' in trying to develop strategies for improving their competitiveness in the global economy, notably by boosting education, training and job-related skills. They are also more willing to 'pool' sovereignty by working in and through international organizations such as regional training blocs and the WTO. Finally, the advent of global terrorism and intensifying concern about migration patterns has re-emphasized the importance of the state in ensuring homeland security and in protecting national borders. (The implications of globalization for the state are examined more fully in Chapter 5.)

The sceptics, by contrast, have portrayed globalization as a fantasy and dismissed the idea of an integrated global economy. They point out that the overwhelming bulk of economic activity still takes place within, not across, national boundaries, and that there is nothing new about high levels of international trade and cross-border capital flows (Hirst and Thompson 1999). Sceptics have, further, argued that globalization has been used as an ideological device by politicians and theorists who wish to advance a market-orientated economic agenda. The globalization thesis has two major advantages in this respect. In the first place, it portrays certain tendencies (such as the shift towards greater flexibility and weaker trade unions, controls on public spending and particularly welfare budgets, and the scaling down of business regulation) as inevitable and therefore irresistible. Second, it suggests that such shifts are part of an impersonal process, and not one linked to an agent, such as big business, whose interests might be seen to be served by globalizing tendencies. However, although such scepticism has served to check the over-boiled enthusiasm of earlier globalization theorists, it is difficult to uphold the idea of 'business as normal'. Goods, capital, information and people do move around the world more freely than they used to, and this has inevitable consequences for economic, cultural and political life.

Falling between the hyperglobalizers and the sceptics, the 'transformationalist' stance offers a middle-road view of globalization. It accepts that profound changes have taken place in the patterns and processes of world politics without

APPROACHES TO . . .

GLOBALIZATION

Realist view

Realists have typically adopted a sceptical stance towards globalization, seeing it more in terms of intensifying economic interdependence (that is, 'more of the same') rather than the creation of an interlocking global economy. Most importantly, the state continues to be the dominant unit in world politics. Instead of being threatened by globalization, the state's capacity for regulation and surveillance may have increased rather than decreased. However, realists are not simply globalization deniers. In assessing the nature and significance of globalization, they emphasize that globalization and the international system are not separate, still less rival, structures. Rather, the former should be seen as a manifestation of the latter. Globalization has been made *by* states, *for* states, particularly dominant states. Developments such as an open trading system, global financial markets and the advent of transnational production were all put in place to advance the interests of western states in general and the USA in particular. Furthermore, realists question the notion that globalization is associated with a shift towards peace and cooperation. Instead, heightened economic interdependence is as likely to breed 'mutual vulnerability', leading to conflict rather than cooperation.

Liberal view

Liberals adopt a consistently positive attitude towards globalization. For economic liberals, globalization reflects the victory of the market over 'irrational' national allegiances and 'arbitrary' state borders. The miracle of the market is that it draws resources towards their most profitable use, thus bringing prosperity to individuals, families, companies and societies. The attraction of economic globalization is therefore that it allows markets to operate on a global scale, replacing the 'shallow' integration of free trade and intensified interdependence with the 'deep' integration of a single global economy. The increased productivity and intensified competition that this produces benefits all the societies that participate within it, demonstrating that economic globalization is a positive-sum game, a game of winners and winners. Liberals also believe that globalization brings social and political benefits. The freer flow of information and ideas around the world both widens opportunities for personal self-development and creates more dynamic and vigorous societies. Moreover, from a liberal standpoint, the spread of market capital-ism is invariably associated with the advance of liberal democracy, economic freedom breeding a demand for political freedom. For liberals, globalization marks a watershed in world history, in that it ends the period during which the nation-state was the dominant global actor, world order being determined by an (inherently unstable) balance of power. The global era, by contrast, is characterized by a tendency towards peace and international cooperation as well as by the dispersal of global power, in particular through the emergence of global civil society (see p. 156) and the growing importance of international organizations.

Critical views

Critical theorists have adopted a negative or oppositional stance towards globalization. Often drawing on an established socialist or specifically Marxist critique of capitalism, this portrays the essence of globalization as the establishment of a global capitalist order. (Indeed, Marx (see p. 72) can be said to have prefigured much 'hyperglobalist' literature, in having highlighted the intrinsically transnational character of the capitalist mode of production.) Like liberals, critical theorists usually accept that globalization marks a historically significant shift, not least in the relationship between states and markets. States have lost power over the economy, being reduced to little more than instruments for the restructuring of national economies in the interests of global capitalism. Globalization is thus viewed as an uneven, hierarchical process, characterized both by the growing polarization between the rich and the poor, explained by world-systems theorists in terms of a structural imbalance between 'core' and 'peripheral' areas in the global economy, and by a weakening of democratic accountability and popular responsiveness due to burgeoning corporate power. Feminist analysts have sometimes linked globalization to growing gender inequalities, associated, for example, with the disruption of small-scale farming in the developing world, largely carried out by women, and growing pressure on them to support their families by seeking work abroad, leading to the 'feminization of migration'. Postcolonial theorists, for their part, have taken particular exception to cultural globalization, interpreted as a form of western imperialism which subverts indigenous cultures and ways of life and leads to the spread of soulless consumerism.

its established or traditional features having been swept away altogether. In short, much has changed, but not everything. This has become the most widely accepted view of globalization, as it resists both the temptation to over-hype the process and to debunk it. Major transformations have nevertheless taken place in world politics. These include the following:

- The *breadth* of interconnectedness has not only stretched social, political, economic and cultural activities across national borders, but also, potentially, across the globe. Never before has globalization threatened to develop into a *single* worldwide system.
- The *intensity* of interconnectedness has increased with the growing magnitude of transborder or even transworld activities, which range from migration surges and the growth of international trade to the greater accessibility of Hollywood movies or US television programmes.
- Interconnectedness has *speeded up*, not least through the huge flows of electronic money that move around the world at the flick of a computer switch, ensuring that currency and other financial markets react almost immediately to economic events elsewhere in the world.

LENSES ON GLOBAL POLITICS

However, making sense of global politics also requires that we understand the theories, values and assumptions through which world affairs have been interpreted. How do different analysts and theorists *see* the world? What are the key 'lenses' on global politics? The theoretical dimension of the study of global politics has become an increasingly rich and diverse arena in recent decades. The substantive ideas of the growing range of theoretical traditions are examined in Chapter 3, while issues to do with the nature and purpose of theory are considered in Chapter 21. This introduction, nevertheless, attempts to map out broad areas of debate among the traditions, in particular by distinguishing between 'mainstream' perspectives and 'critical' perspectives.

Mainstream perspectives

The two mainstream perspectives on global politics are realism and liberalism. What do they have in common, and in what sense are they 'mainstream'? Realism and liberalism can be viewed as mainstream perspectives in the sense that they, in their various incarnations, have dominated conventional academic approaches to the field of international politics since its inception. Realist and liberal theories have two broad things in common. In the first place, they are both grounded in **positivism**. This suggests that it is possible to develop objective knowledge, through the capacity to distinguish 'facts' from 'values'. In short, it is possible to compare theories with the 'real world', the world 'out there'. Robert Cox (1981) thus describes such theories as 'problem-solving theories', in that they take the world 'as it is' and endeavour to think through problems and offer prudent advice to policy-makers trying to negotiate the challenges of the 'real world'. (These issues are discussed in greater detail in pp. 527–30.) Second, realist and liberal theorists share similar concerns and address similar issues, meaning that they, in effect, talk to, rather than past, one another. In particular,

● **Positivism**: The theory that social and indeed all forms of enquiry should conform to the methods of the natural sciences (see p. 526).

Thomas Hobbes (1588–1679)

English political philosopher. Hobbes was the son of a minor clergyman who subsequently abandoned his family. Writing at a time of uncertainty and civil strife, precipitated by the English Revolution, Hobbes developed the first comprehensive theory of nature and human behaviour since Aristotle. His classic work, *Leviathan* (1651) discussed the grounds of political obligation and undoubtedly reflected the impact of the Civil War. Based on the assumption that human beings seek 'power after power', it provided a realist justification for absolutist government as the only alternative to the anarchy of the 'state of nature', in which life would be 'solitary, poor, nasty, brutish and short'. Hobbes' emphasis on the state as an essential guarantor of order and security has led to a revived interest in his ideas since 9/11.

the core concern of both realism and liberalism is the balance between conflict and cooperation in state relations. Although realists generally place greater emphasis on conflict, while liberals highlight the scope for cooperation, neither is unmindful of the issues raised by the other, as is evidenced in the tendency, over time, for differences between realism and liberalism to have become blurred (see Closing the realist–liberal divide? p. 68). Nevertheless, important differences can be identified between the realist and liberal perspectives.

How do realists see global politics? Deriving from ideas that can be traced back to thinkers such as Thucydides (see p. 249), Sun Tzu, author of *The Art of War*, Machiavelli (see p. 58) and Thomas Hobbes, the realist vision is pessimistic: international politics is marked by constant power struggles and conflict, and a wide range of obstacles standing in the way of peaceful cooperation. Realism is grounded in an emphasis on **power politics**, based on the following assumptions:

Realism

- Human nature is characterized by selfishness and greed.
- Politics is a domain of human activity structured by power and coercion.
- States are the key global actors.
- States pursue self-interest and survival, prioritizing security above all else.
- States operate in a context of anarchy, and thus rely on self-help.
- Global order is structured by the distribution of power (capabilities) among states.
- The balance of power is the principal means of ensuring stability and avoiding war.
- Ethical considerations are (and should be) irrelevant to the conduct of foreign policy.

● **Power politics**: An approach to politics based on the assumption that the pursuit of power is the principal human goal; the term is sometimes used descriptively.

● **Internationalism**: The theory or practice of politics based on cooperation or harmony among nations, as opposed to the transcendence of national politics (see p. 67).

By contrast, how do liberals see global politics? Liberalism offers a more optimistic vision of global politics, based, ultimately, on a belief in human rationality and moral goodness (even though liberals also accept that people are essentially self-interested and competitive). Liberals tend to believe that the principle of balance or harmony operates in all forms of social interaction. As far as world politics is concerned, this is reflected in a general commitment to **internationalism**, as reflected in Immanuel Kant's (see p. 15) belief in the possibility of

liberalism

Immanuel Kant (1724–1804)

German philosopher. Kant spent his entire life in Königsberg (which was then in East Prussia), becoming professor of logic and metaphysics at the University of Königsberg in 1770. His 'critical' philosophy holds that knowledge is not merely an aggregate of sense impressions; it depends on the conceptual apparatus of human understanding. Kant's political thought was shaped by the central importance of morality. He believed that the law of reason dictated categorical imperatives, the most important of which was the obligation to treat others as 'ends', and never only as 'means'. Kant's most important works include *Critique of Pure Reason* (1781), *Idea for a Universal History with a Cosmopolitan Purpose* (1784) and *Metaphysics of Morals* (1785).

'universal and perpetual peace'. The liberal model of global politics is based on the following key assumptions:

- Human beings are rational and moral creatures.
- History is a progressive process, characterized by a growing prospect of international cooperation and peace.
- Mixed-actor models of global politics are more realistic than state-centric ones.
- Trade and economic interdependence make war less likely.
- International law helps to promote order and fosters rule-governed behaviour among states.
- Democracy is inherently peaceful, particularly in reducing the likelihood of war between democratic states.

Critical perspectives

Since the late 1980s, the range of critical approaches to world affairs has expanded considerably. Until that point, Marxism had constituted the principal alternative to mainstream realist and liberal theories. What made the Marxist approach distinctive was that it placed its emphasis not on patterns of conflict and cooperation between states, but on structures of economic power and the role played in world affairs by international capital. It thus brought international political economy, sometimes seen as a sub-field within IR, into focus. However, hastened by the end of the Cold War, a wide range of 'new voices' started to influence the study of world politics, notable examples including social constructivism, critical theory, poststructuralism, postcolonialism, feminism and green politics. What do these new critical voices have in common, and in what sense are they 'critical'? In view of their diverse philosophical underpinnings and contrasting political viewpoints, it is tempting to argue that the only thing that unites these 'new voices' is a shared antipathy towards mainstream thinking. However, two broad similarities can be identified. The first is that, albeit in different ways and to different degrees, they have tried to go beyond the positivism of mainstream theory, emphasizing instead the role of consciousness in shaping social conduct and, therefore, world affairs. These so-called post-positivist theories are therefore 'critical' in that they not only take issue with the conclusions of mainstream theory, but also subject these theories themselves to critical scrutiny, exposing biases that operate within them and examining their implications. The second similarity is linked to the first: critical persepectives are 'critical' in that, in their different ways, they oppose the dominant forces and interests in modern world affairs, and so contest the global status quo by (usually) aligning themselves with marginalized or oppressed groups. Each of them, thus, seeks to uncover inequalities and asymmetries that mainstream theories tend to ignore.

However, the inequalities and asymmetries to which critical theorists have drawn attention are many and various:

- Neo-Marxists (who encompass a range of traditions and tendencies that in fact straddle the positivist–post-positivist divide) highlight inequalities in the global capitalist system, through which developed countries or areas, sometimes operating through TNCs or linked to 'hegemonic' powers such as the USA, dominate and exploit developing countries or areas.
- Constructivism is not so much a substantive theory as an analytical tool. In arguing that people, in effect, 'construct' the world in which they live, suggesting that the world operates through a kind of 'inter-subjective' awareness, constructivists have thrown mainstream theory's claim to objectivity into question.
- Poststructuralists emphasize that all ideas and concepts are expressed in language which itself is enmeshed in complex relations of power. Influenced particularly by the writings of Michel Foucault, poststructuralists have drawn attention to the link between power and systems of thought using the idea of a 'discourse of power'.
- Feminists have drawn attention to systematic and pervasive structures of gender inequality that characterize global and, indeed, all other forms of politics. In particular, they have highlighted the extent to which mainstream, and especially realist, theories are based on 'masculinist' assumptions about rivalry, competition and inevitable conflict.
- Postcolonialists have emphasized the cultural dimension of colonial rule, showing how western cultural and political hegemony over the rest of the world has been preserved despite the achievement of formal political independence across almost the entire developing world.
- Green politics, or ecologism, has focused on growing concerns about environmental degradation, highlighting the extent to which this has been a by-product of industrialization and an obsession with economic growth, supported by systems of thought that portray human beings as 'masters over nature'.

CONTINUITY AND CHANGE IN GLOBAL POLITICS

Finally, global politics is an ever-shifting field, with, if anything, the pace of change accelerating over time. Recent decades have witnessed momentous

Michel Foucault (1926–84)

French philosopher and radical intellectual. The son of a prosperous surgeon, Foucault had a troubled youth in which he attempted suicide on several occasions and struggled to come to terms with his homosexuality. His work, which ranged over the history of madness, of medicine, of punishment, of sexuality and of knowledge itself, was based on the assumption that the institutions, concepts and beliefs of each period are upheld by 'discourses of power'. This suggests that power relations can largely be disclosed by examining the structure of 'knowledge', since 'truth serves the interests of a ruling class or the prevailing power-structure'. Foucault's most important works include *Madness and Civilization* (1961), *The Order of Things* (1966) and *The History of Sexuality* (1976).

events such as the end of the Cold War, the collapse of the Soviet Union, the September 11 terrorist attacks on the USA and the global financial crisis of 2007–09. While these and other events have changed the contours of global politics, sometimes radically, certain features of world affairs have proved to be of more enduring significance. This can be illustrated by examining the balance between continuity and change in three key aspects of world politics:

- Power
- Security
- Justice.

Power

All forms of politics are about power. Indeed, politics is sometimes seen as the study of power, its core theme being: who gets what, when, how? Modern global politics raises two main questions about power. The first is about where power is located: who has it? During the Cold War era, this appeared to be an easy question to answer. Two 'superpowers' (see p. 38) dominated world politics, dividing the global system into rival 'spheres of influence'. East–West conflict reflected the existence of a bipolar world order, marked by the political, ideological and economic ascendancy, respectively, of the USA and the Soviet Union. The end of the Cold War has precipitated a major debate about the shifting location of global power. In one view, the fall of communism and the disintegration of the Soviet Union left the USA as the world's sole superpower, meaning that it had been transformed into a global **hegemon**. Such a view also took account of the extent to which the USA was the architect, and chief beneficiary, of the process of globalization, as well as the possessor of enormous 'structural' power (see pp. 218–20), its pivotal position within institutions such as the UN, the WTO, IMF and World Bank giving it disproportional influence over the frameworks within which states relate to one another and decide how things shall be done.

However, alternative views about the shifting configuration of global power suggest that it is becoming more fragmented and pluralized. For example, power

● **Hegemon**: A leading or paramount power.

*NGOs

may have shifted away from states generally through the growing importance of non-state actors and the increased role played by international organizations. Furthermore, globalization may have made power more diffuse and intangible, increasing the influence of global markets and drawing states into a web of economic interdependence that substantially restricts their freedom of manoeuvre. A further dimension of this traces the implications for global power of the rise of emerging states, such as China, India and Brazil, as well as the impact of a resurgent Russia, sometimes collectively known as the BRICs (see p. 463). In this view, the bipolar Cold War world order is in the process of being replaced by a multipolar world order. (The changing nature of global order is examined more closely in Chapter 9.) Power has also been pluralized through the capacity of new technology to alter power balances both within society and between societies, often empowering the traditionally powerless. For example, advances in communications technology, particularly the use of mobile phones and the Internet, have improved the tactical effectiveness of loosely organized groups, ranging from terrorist bands to protest groups and social movements. Al-Qaeda's influence on world politics since September 11 has thus been out of all proportion to its organizational and economic strength, because modern technology, in the form of bombs and airplanes, has given its terrorist activities a global reach.

The second debate is about the changing nature of power. This has, arguably, occurred because, due to new technology and in a world of global communications and rising literacy rates and educational standards, 'soft' power is becoming as important as 'hard' power in influencing political outcomes. As discussed in Chapter 9, soft power is power as *attraction* rather than *coercion*, the ability to influence others by persuading them to follow or agree to norms and aspirations, as opposed to using threats or rewards. This has, for instance, stimulated a debate about whether military power is now redundant in global politics, especially when it is not matched by 'hearts and minds' strategies. In addition, the near-ubiquitous spread of television and the wider use of satellite technology mean that pictures of devastation and human suffering, whether caused by warfare, famine or natural disaster, are shared across the globe almost instantly. This means, amongst other things, that the behaviour of governments and international organizations is influenced as never before by public opinion around the world.

Security

Security is the deepest and most abiding issue in politics. At its heart is the question: how can people live a decent and worthwhile existence, free from threats, intimidation and violence? Security has usually been thought of as a particularly pressing issue in international politics because, while the domestic realm is ordered and stable, by virtue of the existence of a sovereign state, the international realm is anarchical and therefore threatening and unstable. For realists, as the most important actors in the international system are states, security is primarily understood in terms of 'national' security. As, in a world of self-help, all states are under at least potential threat from all other states, each state must have the capacity for self-defence. National security therefore places a premium on military power, reflecting the assumption that the more militarily powerful

CONCEPT

Security dilemma

Security dilemma describes a condition in which actions taken by one actor to improve national security are interpreted as aggressive by other actors, thereby provoking military counter-moves. This reflects two component dilemmas (Booth and Wheeler 2008). First, there is a dilemma of *interpretation* – what are the motives, intentions and capabilities of others in building up military power? As weapons are inherently ambiguous symbols (they can be either defensive or aggressive), there is irresolvable uncertainty about these matters. Second, there is a dilemma of *response* – should they react in kind, in a militarily confrontational manner, or should they seek to signal reassurance and attempt to defuse tension?

● **International security**: Conditions in which the mutual survival and safety of states is secured through measures taken to prevent or punish aggression, usually within a rule-governed international order.

● **Security regime**: A framework of cooperation amongst states and other actors to ensure the peaceful resolution of conflict (see international regime, p. 71).

a state is, the more secure it is likely to be. This focus on military security nevertheless draws states into dynamic, competitive relationships with one another, based on what is called the 'security dilemma'. This is the problem that a military build-up for defensive purposes by one state is always liable to be interpreted by other states as potentially or actually aggressive, leading to retaliatory military build-ups and so on. The security dilemma gets to the very heart of politics amongst states, making it the quintessential dilemma of international politics (Booth and Wheeler 2008). Permanent insecurity between and amongst states is therefore the inescapable lot of those who live in a condition of anarchy.

However, the state-centric ideas of national security and an inescapable security dilemma have also been challenged. There is, for example, a long-established emphasis within liberal theory on collective security (see p. 447), reflecting the belief that aggression can best be resisted by united action taken by a number of states. Such a view shifts attention away from the idea of 'national' security towards the broader notion of **'international' security** (Smith 2010). Furthermore, the security agenda in modern global politics has changed in a number of ways. These include, on the one hand, the expansion of 'zones of peace' in which the tensions and incipient conflicts implied by the security dilemma appear to be absent. Thus **'security regimes'** or 'security communities' have developed to manage disputes and help to avoid war, a trend often associated with growing economic interdependence (linked to globalization) and the advance of democratization. On the other hand, September 11 and the wider threat of terrorism has highlighted the emergence of new security challenges that are particularly problematical because they arise from non-state actors and exploit the greater interconnectedness of the modern world. International security may therefore have given way to 'global' security. A further development has been the trend to rethink the concept of security at a still deeper level, usually linked to the notion of 'human security' (see p. 430). Interest in human security has grown both because the decline of inter-state war in the post-Cold War means that the threat from violent conflict now usually occurs *within* states, coming from civil war, insurrection and civic strife, and because of the recognition that in the modern world people's safety and survival is often put at risk more by non-military threats (such as environmental destruction, disease, refugee crises and resource scarcity), than it is by military threats.

Justice

Realist theorists have traditionally viewed justice as a largely irrelevant issue in international or global politics. Relations between states should be determined by hard-headed judgements related to the national interest, not by ethical considerations. Liberals, by contrast, insist that international politics and morality should go hand in hand, amoral power politics being a recipe for egoism, conflict and violence. Traditionally, however, they have defended the idea of 'international' justice based on principles that set out how nation-states should behave towards one another. Respect for state sovereignty and the norm of non-interference in the affairs of other states, seen as guarantees of national independence and therefore political freedom, are clearly an example of this. Such thinking is also reflected in 'just war' theory (see p. 264). This is the idea that the

September 11 and global security

Events: On the morning of 11 September 2001, a coordinated series of terrorist attacks were launched against the USA using four hijacked passenger jet airliners (the events subsequently became known as September 11, or 9/11). Two airliners crashed into the Twin Towers of the World Trade Centre in New York, leading to the collapse first of the North Tower and then the South Tower. The third airliner crashed into the Pentagon, the headquarters of the Department of Defence in Arlington, Virginia, just outside Washington DC. The fourth airliner, believed to be heading towards either the White House or the US Capitol, both in Washington DC, crashed in a field near Shanksville, Pennsylvania, after passengers on board tried to seize control of the plane. There were no survivors from any of the flights. A total of 2,995 people were killed in these attacks, mainly in New York City. In a videotape released in October 2001, responsibility for the attacks was claimed by Osama bin Laden, head of the al-Qaeda (see p. 301) organization, who praised his followers as the 'vanguards of Islam'.

Significance: September 11 has sometimes been described as 'the day the world changed'. This certainly applied in terms of its consequences, notably the unfolding 'war on terror' and the invasions of Afghanistan and Iraq and their ramifications. It also marked a dramatic shift in global security, signalling the end of a period during which globalization and the cessation of superpower rivalry appeared to have been associated with a diminishing propensity for international conflict. Globalization, indeed, appeared to have ushered in new security threats and new forms of conflict. For example, 9/11 demonstrated how fragile national borders had become in a technological age. If the world's greatest power could be dealt such a devastating blow to its largest city and its national capital, what chance did other states have? Further, the 'external' threat in this case came not from another state, but from a terrorist organization, and one, moreover, that operated more as a global network than a nationally-based organization. The motivations behind the attacks were also not conventional ones. Instead of seeking to conquer territory or acquire control over resources, the 9/11 attacks were carried out in the name of a religiously-inspired ideology, militant Islamism (see p. 205), and aimed at exerting a symbolic, even psychic, blow against the cultural, political and ideological domination of the West. This led some to see 9/11 as evidence of an emerging 'clash of civilization'

(see p. 196), even as a struggle between Islam and the West.

However, rather than marking the beginning of a new era in global security, 9/11 may have indicated more a return to 'business as normal'. In particular, the advent of a globalized world appeared to underline the vital importance of 'national' security, rather than 'international' or 'global' security. The emergence of new security challenges, and especially transnational terrorism, re-emphasized the core role of the state in protecting its citizens from external attack. Instead of becoming progressively less important, 9/11 gave the state a renewed significance. The USA, for example, responded to 9/11 by undertaking a substantial build-up of state power, both at home (through strengthened 'homeland security') and abroad (through increased military spending and the invasions of Afghanistan and Iraq). A unilateralist tendency also became more pronounced in its foreign policy, as the USA became, for a period at least, less concerned about working with or through international organizations of various kinds. Other states affected by terrorism have also exhibited similar tendencies, marking a renewed emphasis on national security sometimes at the expense of considerations such as civil liberties and political freedom. In other words, 9/11 may demonstrate that state-based power politics is alive and kicking.

CONCEPT

Cosmopolitanism

Cosmopolitanism literally means a belief in a *cosmopolis* or 'world state'. *Moral* cosmopolitanism is the belief that the world constitutes a single moral community, in that people have obligations (potentially) towards all other people in the world, regardless of nationality, religion, ethnicity and so forth. All forms of moral cosmopolitanism are based on a belief that every individual is of equal moral worth, most commonly linked to the doctrine of human rights. *Political* cosmopolitanism ('legal' or 'institutional' cosmopolitanism) is the belief that there should be global political institutions, and possibly a world government (see p. 464). However, most modern political cosmopolitans favour a system in which authority is divided between global, national and local levels (Brown and Held 2010).

use of violence through war can only be justified if the reasons for war and the conduct of war conform to principles of justice.

However, the growth of interconnectedness and interdependence has extended thinking about morality in world affairs, particularly through an increasing emphasis on the notion of 'global' or 'cosmopolitan' justice. The idea of global justice is rooted in a belief in universal moral values, values that apply to all people in the world regardless of nationality and citizenship. The most influential example of universal values is the doctrine of international human rights. Such cosmopolitanism has shaped thinking on the issue of global distributive justice, suggesting, for instance, that rich countries should give more foreign aid, and that there should be a possibly substantial redistribution of wealth between the world's rich and the world's poor. The utilitarian philosopher Peter Singer (1993) argued that the citizens and governments of rich countries have a basic obligation to eradicate absolute poverty in other countries on the grounds that (1) if we can prevent something bad without sacrificing anything of comparable significance, we ought to do it, and (2) absolute poverty is bad because it causes suffering and death. For Pogge (2008), the obligation of rich countries to help poor countries stems not from the simple existence of poverty and our capacity to alleviate it, but from the *causal* relationship between the wealth of the rich and the poverty of the poor. The rich have a duty to help the poor because the international order is structured so as to benefit some people and areas at the expense of others. Similar ideas are implied by neo-colonial and world-system theories of global poverty, as examined in Chapter 15. Similarly, ideas have been developed about global environmental justice. These, for instance, reflect on issues such as protecting the natural environment for the benefit of future generations, the disproportionate obligation of rich countries to tackle climate change because they largely created the problem in the first place, and the idea that any legally binding emissions targets should be structured on a per capita basis, rather than a country basis, so as not to disadvantage states with large populations (and therefore the developing world generally). These ideas are discussed further in Chapter 16.

USING THIS BOOK

Global politics is, by its nature, an overlapping and interlocking field. The material encountered in this book stubbornly resists compartmentalization, which is why, throughout, there is regular cross-referencing to related discussions that occur in other chapters and particularly to relevant boxed material found elsewhere. Nevertheless, the book develops by considering what can be thought of as a series of broad issues or themes.

The first group of chapters is designed to provide background understanding for the study of global politics.

- This chapter has examined the nature of global politics and considered the developments that make a global politics approach to world affairs appropriate, as well as providing an introduction to contrasting mainstream and critical perspectives on global politics.
- Chapter 2 examines the historical context of modern global politics, particularly by looking at key developments in world history during the twentieth and twenty-first centuries.

- Chapter 3 provides an account of the key theoretical approaches to global politics, thus considering mainstream perspectives and critical perspectives in greater depth, as well as the implications of global thinking.

The next group of chapters discusses the various transformations that have occurred, and are occurring, as a result of the globalization of world politics.

- Chapter 4 discusses the nature, extent and implications of economic globalization, and considers, amongst other things, the crisis tendencies within modern global capitalism.
- Chapter 5 examines the role and significance of the state in a global age, as well as the nature of foreign policy and how foreign policy decisions are made.
- Chapter 6 considers the social and cultural implications of globalization and whether or not it is possible to talk of an emergent global civil society.
- Chapter 7 examines the ways in which nations and nationalism have been shaped and reshaped in a global world, focusing on ways in which nationalism has been both weakened and strengthened.
- Chapter 8 examines the politics of identity and the growth of cultural conflict in a global age, particularly in the form of challenges to the politico-cultural domination of the West, especially from political Islam.

The following group of chapters considers the broad themes of global order and conflict.

- Chapter 9 looks at the nature of global power and the changing shape of twenty-first century global order, as well as at the implications of such changes for peace and stability.
- Chapter 10 examines how and why wars occur, the changing nature of warfare, and how, and how successfully, war has been justified.
- Chapter 11 considers the nature and implications of nuclear proliferation, and examines the prospects for non-proliferation and nuclear disarmament.
- Chapter 12 discusses the nature of terrorism, the various debates that have sprung up about its significance and the strategies that have been used to counter it.

The next group of chapters focuses on various issues to do with the theme of global justice.

- Chapter 13 considers the nature and significance of international human rights, how, and how effectively, they have been protected, and debates about humanitarian intervention and its implications.
- Chapter 14 addresses the issue of international law, in particular examining the changing nature and significance of international law in the modern period.
- Chapter 15 considers the issues of global poverty and inequality, and also looks at development and the politics of international aid.
- Chapter 16 focuses on global environmental issues, and examines the challenge of climate change in depth.

- Chapter 17 discusses feminist approaches to global politics and how gender perspectives have changed thinking about war, security and other matters.

The following group of chapters considers attempts to address global or transnational issues through the construction of intergovernmental or supranational institutions.

- Chapter 18 examines the nature and growth of international organizations, and looks in particular at the role and effectiveness of the United Nations.
- Chapter 19 discusses the idea of global governance and examines its development in the economic sphere through the evolution of the Bretton Woods system.
- Chapter 20 focuses on the causes and significance of regionalism, focusing especially on the nature and significance of the European Union.

The final group of chapters reflects on broad themes that have been addressed at various points in the book.

- Chapter 21 considers how, and how far, theory contributes to our understanding of global politics, and, in the process, examines key debates about the nature and purpose of theory.
- Chapter 22 provides a conclusion to the book by reviewing and evaluating various images of the global future and reflecting on whether attempts to predict the future are ultimately futile.

SUMMARY

- Global politics is based on a comprehensive approach to world affairs that takes account not just of political developments at a global level, but also at and, crucially, across, all levels – global, regional, national, sub-national and so on. In that sense, 'the global' and 'the international' complement one another and should not be seen as rival or incompatible modes of understanding.

- 'International' politics has been transformed into 'global' politics through a variety of developments. New actors have emerged from the world stage alongside states and national governments. Levels of interconnectedness and interdependence in world politics have increased, albeit unevenly. And international anarchy has been modified by the emergence of a framework of regional and global governance.

- Globalization is the emergence of a complex web of interconnectedness that means that our lives are increasingly shaped by events that occur, and decisions that are made, at a great distance from us. Distinctions are commonly drawn between economic globalization, cultural globalization and political globalization. However, there are significant debates about whether globalization is actually happening and how far it has transformed world politics.

- The two mainstream perspectives on global politics are realism and liberalism; these are both grounded in positivism and focus on the balance between conflict and cooperation in state relations, even though they offer quite different accounts of this balance. Critical perspectives, by contrast, tend to adopt a post-positivist approach to theory and contest the global status quo by aligning themselves with the interests of marginalized or oppressed groups.

- Global politics is an ever-shifting field, with, if anything, the pace of change accelerating over time. Debates have emerged about the changing nature of power and the shifting configuration of global power, about whether national security has been displaced by international, global or even human security, and about the extent to which justice now has to be considered in cosmopolitan or global terms.

Questions for discussion

- How does 'global' politics differ from 'international' politics?
- In what ways is the international dimension of politics still important?
- To what extent have non-state actors come to rival states and national governments on the world stage?
- Does interdependence always lead to cooperation and peace, or can it generate conflict?
- Which definition of globalization is most persuasive, and why?
- Has the impact and significance of globalization been exaggerated?
- What are the key differences between mainstream and critical approaches to global politics?
- Over what do realist and liberal theorists disagree?
- To what extent has global power become more diffuse and intangible in recent years?
- Why has there been growing interest in the notion of 'human' security?
- Does the idea of 'global' justice make sense?

Further reading

Brown, C. and K. Ainley, *Understanding International Relations* (2009). A highly readable and thought-provoking introduction to the theory and practice of international relations.

Hay, C. (ed.), *New Directions in Political Science: Responding to the Challenges of an Interdependent World* (2010). A series of astute reflections on the nature, extent and implications of global interdependence.

Held, D. and A. McGrew, *Globalization/Anti-globalization: Beyond the Great Divide* (2007). A comprehensive and authoritative survey of contemporary political and intellectual debates over globalization.

Scholte, J. A., *Globalization: A Critical Introduction* (2005). An excellent and accessibly written account of the nature of globalization and of its various implications.

ONLINE RESOURCES AVAILABLE

Links to relevant web resources can be found on the *Global Politics* website

CHAPTER 2

Historical Context

'*Those who cannot remember the past are condemned to repeat it.*'

GEORGE SANTAYANA, *Life of Reason* (1905–6)

PREVIEW   Politics and history are inextricably linked. In a simple sense, politics is the history of the present while history is the politics of the past. An understanding of history therefore has two benefits for students of politics. First, the past, and especially the recent past, helps us to make sense of the present, by providing it with a necessary context or background. Second, history can provide insight into present circumstances (and perhaps even guidance for political leaders), insofar as the events of the past resemble those of the present. History, in that sense, 'teaches lessons'. In the aftermath of 9/11, President George W. Bush thus justified the 'war on terror' in part by pointing to the failure of the policy of 'appeasement' in the 1930s to halt Nazi expansionism. The notion of 'lessons of history' is a debatable one, however; not least because history itself is always a debate. What happened, and why it happened, can never be resolved with scientific accuracy. History is always, to some extent, understood through the lens of the present, as modern concerns, understandings and attitudes help us to 'invent' the past. And it is also worth remembering Zhou Enlai (Chou En-lai), then Premier of the People's Republic of China, who replied, when asked in the 1960s about the lessons of the 1789 French Revolution, that 'it is too early to say'. Nevertheless, the modern world makes little sense without some understanding of the momentous events that have shaped world history, particularly since the advent of the twentieth century. What do the events that led up to the outbreak of World War I and World War II tell us about the causes of war, and what does the absence of world war since 1945 tell us about the causes? In what sense were years such as 1914, 1945 and 1990 watersheds in world history? What does world history tell us about the possible future of global politics?

KEY ISSUES
- What developments shaped world history before the twentieth century?
- What were the causes and consequences of World War I?
- What factors resulted in the outbreak of the World War II?
- What were the causes and consequences of the 'end of empire'?
- Why did the Cold War emerge after 1945, and how did it end?
- What are the major factors that have shaped post-Cold War world history?

CONCEPT

The West

The term 'the West' has two overlapping meanings. In a general sense, it refers to the cultural and philosophical inheritance of Europe, which has often been exported through migration or colonialism. The roots of this inheritance lie in Judeo-Christian religion and the learning of 'classical' Greece and Rome, shaped in the modern period by the ideas and values of liberalism. In a narrower sense, fashioned during the Cold War, 'the West' meant the USA-dominated capitalist bloc, as opposed to the USSR-dominated East. The relevance of the latter meaning was weakened by the end of the Cold War, while the value of the former meaning has been brought into question by political and other divisions amongst so-called western powers.

MAKING OF THE MODERN WORLD

From ancient to modern

The beginning of world history is usually dated from the establishment of a succession of ancient civilizations in place of the hunter-gatherer communities of earlier times. Mesopotamia, located between the rivers Tigris and Euphrates in the area of modern day Iraq, is often portrayed as the 'cradle of civilization', with three major civilizations arising there from around 3500 to 1500 BCE (Before the Common Era, notionally determined by the birth of Jesus) – the Sumerian, the Babylonian and the Assyrian. The other early civilization developed in Ancient Egypt, along the course of the Nile, and this endured for around three and a half thousand years, only ending with the rise of the Roman Empire. The two key features of these early civilizations were agriculture, which allowed for permanent settlement and the emergence of urban life, and the development of writing, which occurred from around 3000 BCE (the earliest forms being Mesopotamian cuneiform and Egyptian hieroglyphics). The beginnings of Chinese civilization date from the establishment of the Shang Dynasty in around 1600 BCE, corresponding to the emergence of the Bronze Age. After the Warring States period, 403–221 BCE, China (see p. 238) was eventually unified under the Ch'in (from which the name comes). The earliest civilization in South Asia emerged in the Indus River valley, in what is now Pakistan, and flourished between 2600 and 1900 BCE. Ancient India, which stretched across the plains from the Indus to the Ganges, extending from modern-day Afghanistan to Bangladesh, began around 500 BCE with the birth of the 'golden age' of classical Hindu culture, as reflected in Sanskrit literature.

The period generally known as 'classical antiquity', dating from around 1000 BCE, witnessed the emergence of various civilizations in the area of the Mediterranean Sea. Starting with the growth of Etruscan culture and the spread of Phoenician maritime trading culture, the most significant developments were the emergence of Ancient Greece and Ancient Rome. Ancient Greece, often viewed as the foundational culture of western civilization, developed through the extension of Greek settlements throughout the eastern Mediterranean during the period 800–600 BCE, with colonies being formed in Asia Minor as well as in the southern parts of the Balkans. Ancient Rome flourished once the Roman monarchy was overthrown in 509 BCE, creating an oligarchic republic that developed into a vast empire, which extended from the eastern Mediterranean across North Africa and included most of Europe.

However, the classical world gradually descended into crisis, reaching its height during the fifth century. This crisis was caused by the eruption of mounted nomadic peoples into the great crescent of ancient civilizations which stretched from the Mediterranean to China, ushering in the 'Dark Ages'. It affected not merely the Greeks and the Romans, but all the established civilizations of Eurasia. Only China coped successfully with the invaders, but even here their appearance saw a period of political fragmentation only ended by the Sui Dynasty in 589. Europe was affected by the 'barbarian' invasions, and later settlement, of the Germanic and Slav peoples during the fifth and sixth centuries, with a further wave of invasions coming in the ninth and tenth centuries from the Vikings, Magyars and Saracens. The most significant of these primitive nomadic peoples were, nevertheless, the Mongols, who emerged from the depths of Asia to create, between 1206 and 1405, an empire of unequal scope and range. The Mongol Empire stretched from the eastern frontiers of Germany and from the Arctic Ocean to Turkey and the Persian Gulf. Its impact on world history was profound. The political organization of Asia and large parts of Europe was altered; whole peoples were uprooted and dispersed, permanently changing the ethnic character of many regions (not least through the wide dispersal of the Turkic peoples across western Asia); and European access to Asia and the Far East became possible again.

Rise of the West

In a process which commenced around 1500, a single, originally European-based civilization became the world's dominant civilization. Non-western societies increasingly came to model themselves on the economic, political and cultural structure of western societies, so much so that **modernization** came to be synonymous with westernization. This period started with the so-called 'age of discovery', or the 'age of exploration'. From the early fifteenth century and continuing into the early seventeenth century, first Portuguese ships, then Spanish and finally British, French and Dutch ships set out to discover the New World. This process had strong economic motivations, starting with the desire to find a direct route to India and East Asia in order to obtain spices, and leading to the establishment of trading empires focused on tea, cane sugar, tobacco, precious metals and slaves (some 8 to 10.5 million Africans were forcibly transported to the Americas). The rise of the West (see p. 26) nevertheless had crucial political, socio-economic and cultural manifestations.

In political terms, the rise of the West was associated with the establishment, during the sixteenth and seventeenth centuries, of sovereign states with strong central governments. This occurred particularly through the Peace of Westphalia (1648), which brought an end to the Thirty Years War, the most barbaric and devastating war in European history up to the two world wars of the twentieth century. The advent of sovereign statehood fostered in Europe a level of social and political stability that favoured technological innovation and economic development. The socio-economic dimension of the rise of the West lay in the breakdown of **feudalism** in Europe and the growth, in its place, of a market or capitalist society. This, most importantly, stimulated the growth of industrialization, which started in mid-eighteenth-century Britain (the 'workshop of the world') and spread during the nineteenth century to North America and throughout western and central Europe. Industrialized states acquired massively enlarged productive capacities, which contributed, amongst other things, to their military strength. The advance of agricultural and industrial technology also contributed to improving diets and rising living standards, which, over time, had a massive impact on the size of the world's population (see Figure 2.1).

In cultural terms, the rise of the West was fostered by the **Renaissance,** which, beginning in Italy in the late Middle Ages, reshaped European intellectual life in areas such as philosophy, politics, art and science. This, in turn, helped to fuel interest in and curiosity about the wider world and was associated with the rise of science and the growth of commercial activity and trade. The **Enlightenment**, which reached its height in the late eighteenth century, imbued western intellec-

● **Modernization**: The process though which societies become 'modern' or 'developed', usually implying economic advancement, technological development and the rational organization of political and social life.

● **Feudalism**: A system of agrarian-based production that is characterized by fixed social hierarchies and a rigid pattern of obligations.

● **Renaissance**: From the French, literally meaning 'rebirth'; a cultural movement inspired by revived interest in classical Greece and Rome that saw major developments in learning and the arts.

● **Enlightenment, the**: An intellectual movement that challenged traditional beliefs in religion, politics and learning in general in the name of reason and progress.

CONCEPT

Imperialism

Imperialism is, broadly, the policy of extending the power or rule of the state beyond its boundaries, typically through the establishment of an empire. In its earliest usage, imperialism was an ideology that supported military expansion and imperial acquisition, usually by drawing on nationalist and racialist doctrines. In its traditional form, imperialism involves the establishment of formal political domination or colonialism (see p. 186), and reflects the expansion of state power through a process of conquest and (possibly) settlement. Modern and more subtle forms of imperialism may nevertheless involve economic domination without the establishment of political control, or what is called 'neo-colonialism'.

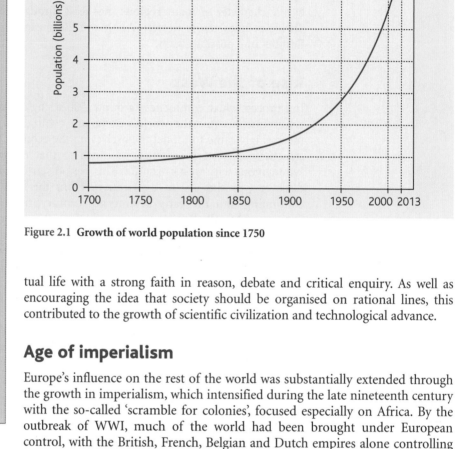

Figure 2.1 **Growth of world population since 1750**

tual life with a strong faith in reason, debate and critical enquiry. As well as encouraging the idea that society should be organised on rational lines, this contributed to the growth of scientific civilization and technological advance.

Age of imperialism

Europe's influence on the rest of the world was substantially extended through the growth in imperialism, which intensified during the late nineteenth century with the so-called 'scramble for colonies', focused especially on Africa. By the outbreak of WWI, much of the world had been brought under European control, with the British, French, Belgian and Dutch empires alone controlling almost one-third of the world's population (see Map. 2.1). The **belle époque** was accompanied by the establishment of levels of economic globalization that are comparable with those of the contemporary period. International trade, expressed as a proportion of the world's aggregate GDP, was as great in the late nineteenth century as it was in the late twentieth century. Indeed, the UK, the world's foremost imperial power during this era, was more dependent on trade than any contemporary state, including the USA (see p. 46).

This period was also characterized by substantial cross-border migration flows that peaked in the period between 1870 and 1910. Immigration into the USA rose steadily from the mid-nineteenth century onwards, coming mainly from Germany and Ireland, but also from the Netherlands, Spain, Italy, the Scandinavian countries and Eastern Europe. Canada, Australia and South Africa also attracted large numbers of migrants from the poorest parts of Europe and some parts of Asia. These relatively rapid flows of goods, capital and people were, in turn, facilitated by technological advances in transport and communications,

● **Belle époque**: From the French, literally meaning 'beautiful era'; a period of peace and prosperity in Europe between the late nineteenth century and the outbreak of WWI was seen as a 'golden age'.

notably the development of steam-powered shipping, the spread of the railroads and the invention and commercial application of the telegraph. These made the nineteenth century the first truly universal era in human society (Bisley 2007). However, this period of what Scholte (2005) called 'incipient globalization' came to an abrupt end with the outbreak of WWI, which brought the 'golden age of free trade' to an end and led to a return to economic nationalism and a backlash against immigration. In a warning for the contemporary global era, some have even interpreted the outbreak of WWI as a consequence of *belle époque* globalization, in that it brought the European states into conflict with one another as they struggled for resources and prestige in a shrinking world.

THE 'SHORT' TWENTIETH CENTURY: 1914–90

Origins of World War I

The outbreak of war in 1914 is often seen as the beginning of the 'short' twentieth century (Hobsbawm 1994), the period during which world politics was dominated by the ideological struggle between capitalism and communism, and which ended in 1989–91. WWI has been described as the most significant war in world history. It was the first example of **total war**, meaning that domestic populations and the patterns of civilian life (the 'home front') were more profoundly affected than by earlier wars. The war was also genuinely a 'world' war, not only because, through the involvement of Turkey, fighting extended beyond Europe into the Middle East, but also because of the recruitment of armies from across the **empires** of Europe and the participation of the USA. WWI was the first 'modern' war, in the sense of being industrialized – it witnessed the earliest use of, for example, tanks, chemical weapons (poison gas and flame-throwers) and aircraft, including long-range strategic bombing. Some 65 million men were mobilized by the various belligerents, over 8 million of whom died, while about 10 million civilians were killed in the war itself or perished in the epidemic of Spanish influenza that broke out in the winter of 1918–19.

WWI was precipitated by the assassination, in June 1914, of Archduke Franz Ferdinand, nephew of the Austrian Emperor, by the Black Hand, a group of Serbian nationalists. This precipitated declarations of war by Austria-Hungary and Russia (see p. 187), which, thanks to a system of alliances that had been constructed over the previous decade, led to a wider war between the Triple Alliance (Britain, France and Russia) and the Central Powers (Germany and Austria-Hungary). Other states were drawn into the conflict, notably Turkey (1914) and Bulgaria (1915) on the side of the Central Powers, and Serbia, Belgium, Luxembourg, Japan (all in 1914), Italy (1915), Rumania, Portugal (1916), Greece and, most significantly, the USA (1917) on the side of the Allied Powers. The eventual victory of the Allies was probably accounted for by their greater success, perhaps linked to their democratic systems, in mobilizing manpower and equipment; by their earlier and more effective use of mechanized warfare; and, ultimately, by the entry of the USA into the war. However, there was, and remains, considerable debate about the origins of the war. The main causes that have been linked to the outbreak of WWI are the following:

● **Empire**: A structure of domination in which diverse cultures, ethnic groups or nationalities are subject to a single source of authority.

● **Total war**: A war involving all aspects of society, resulting from large-scale conscription, the gearing of the economy to military ends, and the mass destruction of enemy targets, civilian and military.

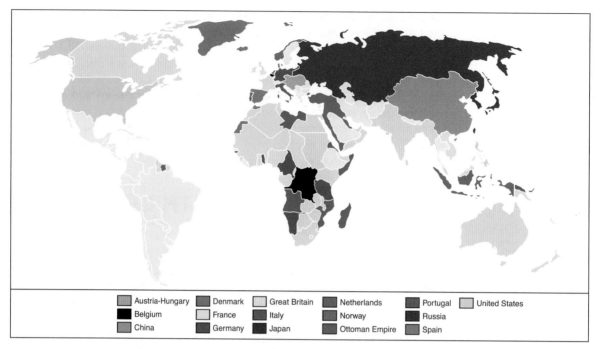

Austria-Hungary	Denmark	Great Britain	Netherlands	Portugal	United States
Belgium	France	Italy	Norway	Russia	
China	Germany	Japan	Ottoman Empire	Spain	

Map 2.1 Colonial holdings, circa 1914

- The 'German problem'
- The 'Eastern question'
- Imperialism
- Nationalism.

The 'German problem' draws attention to a phenomenon that has many and diverse interpretations. Realist theorists, who believe that the basic inclination of states towards the acquisition of power and the pursuit of national interest can only be constrained by a balance of power (see p. 274), argue that Europe's instability stemmed from a structural imbalance which had resulted from the emergence, through the unification of Germany in 1871, of a dominant power in central Europe. This imbalance encouraged Germany's bid for power, reflected, for instance, in its desire for colonies (Germany's 'place in the sun') and in growing strategic and military rivalry with Britain, especially in terms of naval power. Alternative interpretations of the 'German problem', however, tend to locate the source of German expansionism in the nature of its imperial regime and in the annexationist ambitions of its political and military elites. The most famous expression of this was in the writings of the German historian Fritz Fischer (1968), who emphasized the role of *Weltpolitik*, or 'world policy', in shaping Germany's aggressive and expansionist foreign policy during the reign of Kaiser Wilhelm II, 1888–1918. This view, in effect, blames Germany (or at least its political leaders) for the outbreak of WWI, something which the Allies expressed through the 'war guilt' clause of the Treaty of Versailles (1919).

The fact that WWI broke out in the Balkans and initially involved declarations of war by Russia and Austria-Hungary highlights the significance of the so-called

HISTORY

Realist view

Realists believe that history tends to have an enduring character. From their perspective, similarities between historical eras are always more substantial than the differences. In particular, power politics, conflict and the likelihood of war (though, by no means, endless war) are inescapable facts of history. History, if you like, does not 'move forward'; rather, it repeats itself, endlessly. This happens for at least three reasons. First, human nature does not change: humans are egotistical and power-seeking creatures, given to lusts and impulses that cannot be restrained by reason or moral considerations. Changes in terms of cultural, technological and economic progress do not change these 'facts of life'. Second, history is shaped by self-interested political units of one kind or another. These political units may take different forms in different historical periods – tribes, empires, city-states, nation-states and so on – but their basic behaviour in terms of rivalry (potentially or actually) with other political units never changes. Third, anarchy is an enduring fact of history, an assumption sometimes referred to as 'anarcho-centrism'. Despite long periods of domination by various civilizations, empires, great powers or super-powers, none has managed to establish global supremacy. The absence of world government (see p. 457) ensures that every historical period is characterized by fear, suspicion and rivalry, as all political units are forced, ultimately, to rely on violent self-help.

Liberal view

The liberal view of history is characterized by a belief in progress: history marches forwards as human society achieves higher and higher levels of advancement. The assumption that history moves from the 'dark' to the 'light' is based, above all, on a faith in reason. Reason emancipates humankind from the grip of the past and the weight of custom and tradition. Each generation is able to advance beyond the last as the stock of human knowledge and understanding progressively increases. In international affairs, progress involves a transition from power-seeking behaviour, in which aggression and violence are routinely used as tools of state policy, to a condition characterized by cooperation and peaceful co-existence, brought about by economic interdependence, the emergence of an international rule of law and the advance of democracy. Such thinking has a utopian dimension, in that it emphasizes the possibility of 'perpetual peace' (Kant) and suggests, following Fukuyama (see p. 539) that the worldwide victory of liberal democracy would amount to the 'end of history'. However, the scope and degree of liberal optimism about the future has fluctuated over time. Whilst liberalism flourished both in the period after WWI and following the collapse of communism in the early 1990s, it was distinctly muted in the post-1945 period and also became so in the aftermath of September 11.

Critical views

The most influential critical approaches to history have developed out of Marxism. The Marxist theory of history – often portrayed as 'historical materialism – emphasizes that the primary driving forces in history are material or economic factors. In Marx's view, history moves forwards from one 'mode of production' to the next, working its way through primitive communism, slavery, feudalism and capitalism and eventually leading to the establishment of a fully communist society, history's determinant end point. Each of these historical stages would collapse under the weight of their internal contradictions, manifest in the form of class conflict. However, communism would mark the end of history because, being based on common ownership of wealth, it is classless. Although orthodox Marxists sometimes interpreted this as a form of economic determinism. Frankfurt School critical theorists, such as Robert Cox (see p. 124), have rejected determinism in allowing that, in addition to the material forces of production, states and relations among states can also influence the course of history. Nevertheless, such essentially class-based theories have been rejected by poststructuralists, social constructivists and feminists. Poststructuralists have often followed Foucault (see p. 17) in employing a style of historical thought called 'genealogy', attempting to expose hidden meanings and representations in history that serve the interests of domination and exclude marginalized groups and peoples. Social constructivists criticise materialism in emphasizing the power of ideas, norms and values to shape world history. Feminists, for their part, have sometimes highlighted continuity, by portraying patriarchy (see p. 424) as a historical constant, found in all historical and contemporary societies.

'Eastern question'. The 'Eastern question' refers to the structural instabilities of the Balkans region in the late nineteenth and early twentieth centuries. These instabilities resulted from a power vacuum which occurred through the territorial and political decline of the Ottoman Empire, which had once covered the Middle East, much of south-eastern Europe and parts of North Africa. This meant that the Balkans, a region consisting of a complex pattern of ethnic and religious groupings which, by the late nineteenth century, were increasingly animated by nationalist aspirations, sparked the expansionist ambitions of two of Europe's traditional great powers, Russia and Austria-Hungary. But for this, the assassination of the Austrian archduke Franz Ferdinand in June 1914 may have remained a localized incident. As it was, it led to war between Russia and Austria-Hungary, which turned into a continent-wide war and eventually a world war.

Wider explanations of the outbreak of WWI have drawn attention to developments such as the advent of imperialism and the impact of nationalism. As discussed earlier, the late nineteenth century had witnessed a remarkable period of colonial expansion and particularly a 'scramble for Africa'. Marxist historians have sometimes followed V. I. Lenin in viewing imperialism as the core explanation for world war. Lenin (1916) portrayed imperialism as the 'highest' stage of capitalism, arguing that the quest for raw materials and cheap labour abroad would lead to intensifying colonial rivalry amongst capitalist powers, eventually precipitating war. However, critics of Lenin's Marxist interpretation of WWI have argued that, in interpreting imperialism as essentially an economic phenomenon, he failed to take account of a more powerful force in the form of nationalism. From the late nineteenth century onwards, nationalism had become enmeshed with militarism and **chauvinism**, creating growing support for expansionist and aggressive foreign policies amongst both political elites and the general public. In this view, the spread of chauvinist or expansionist nationalism both fuelled 'new' imperialism and created intensifying international conflict, eventually leading to war in 1914.

Road to World War II

World War I was meant to be the 'war to end all wars', and yet within a generation a second world war broke out. World War II was the world's biggest military confrontation. Over 90 million combatants were mobilized with estimates of the war dead, including civilians, ranging from 40 to 60 million. The war was more 'total' than WWI, in that the proportion of civilian deaths was much greater (due to indiscriminate air attacks and the murderous policies of the Nazi regime, particularly towards Jewish people), and the level of disruption to domestic society was more intense, with economies being restructured to support the war effort. The reach of warfare during WWII was also truly global. The war started as a European war with the invasion of Poland on 1 September 1939 by Nazi Germany and the Soviet Union, leading, within days, to the UK and France declaring war on Germany. Denmark, Norway, Belgium and the Netherlands were engulfed in war through Germany's *Blitzkrieg* ('lightning war') attacks in 1940. In 1941, an Eastern Front opened up through the German invasion of Yugoslavia, Greece and, most crucially, Russia. The war in Asia was precipitated by the Japanese attack on the US military base at Pearl Harbor in Hawaii on 7 December 1941, which also drew the USA into the war against Germany and Italy and resulted in fighting in Burma and

● **Chauvinism**: An uncritical and unreasoned dedication to a cause or group, typically based on a belief in its superiority, as in 'national chauvinism'.

World history, 1900–45

1900–1	Boxer Rebellion in China		**1933**	Hitler becomes Chancellor of Germany
1904–5	Russo-Japanese War		**1934**	Mao Zedong begins the Long March
1914	World War I begins			
1915	Armenian genocide		**1935**	Italy invades Abyssinia (Ethiopia)
1917	Russian Revolution creates world's first communist state		**1936**	Germany reoccupies the Rhineland
			1938	*Anschluss* with Austria
1919	Treaty of Versailles		**1938**	Munich Agreement
1922	Mussolini seizes power in Italy		**1939**	World War II begins
1929	Wall Street Crash (October); Great Depression begins		**1941**	Japanese attack on Pearl Harbor
1929	Stalin begins forced collectivization in Soviet Union		**1942–3**	Battle of Stalingrad
			1942–5	Holocaust extermination campaign
1930	Japan invades Manchuria			
1932	F.D. Roosevelt elected US President; the New Deal starts		**1945**	End of WWII in Europe (May) and against Japan (September)

across much of South-east Asia and the Pacific. The war also spread to North Africa from 1942 onwards. The war in Europe ended in May 1945 with the capitulation of Germany, and the war in Asia ended in August 1945, following the dropping of atomic bombs on Hiroshima and Nagasaki.

The factors that were decisive in determining the outcome of WWII were the involvement of the USSR and the USA. War against Russia forced Germany to fight on two fronts, with the Eastern Front attracting the bulk of German manpower and resources. Following the Battle of Stalingrad in the winter of 1942–3, Germany was forced into a draining but remorseless retreat. The involvement of the USA fundamentally affected the economic balance of power by ensuring that the resources of the world's foremost industrial power would be devoted to ensuring the defeat of Germany and Japan. However, the origins of WWII have been a subject of even greater historical controversy than the origins of WWI. The main factors that have been associated with the outbreak of WWII have been:

- The WWI peace settlements
- The global economic crisis
- Nazi expansionism
- Japanese expansionism in Asia.

E. H. Carr (1892–1982)

British historian, journalist and international relations theorist. Carr joined the Foreign Office and attended the Paris Peace Conference at the end of WWI. Appointed Woodrow Wilson Professor of International Politics at the University College of Wales at Aberystwyth in 1936, he later became assistant editor of *The Times* of London before returning to academic life in 1953. Carr is best known for *The Twenty Years' Crisis, 1919–1939* (1939), a critique of the entire peace settlement of 1919 and the wider influence of 'utopianism' on diplomatic affairs, especially a reliance on international bodies such as the League of Nations. He is often viewed as one of the key realist theorists, drawing attention to the need to manage (rather than ignore) conflict between 'have' and 'have-not' states. Nevertheless, he condemned cynical realpolitik for lacking moral judgement. Carr's other writing includes *Nationalism and After* (1945) and the quasi-Marxist 14-volume *A History of Soviet Russia* (1950–78).

Many historians have seen WWII as, in effect, a replay of WWI, with the Treaty of Versailles (1919) marking the beginning of the road to war. In this sense, the years 1919–39 amounted to a 'twenty-year truce'. Critics of Versailles tend to argue that it was shaped by two incompatible objectives. The first was the attempt to create a liberal world order by breaking up the European empires and replacing them with a collection of independent nation-states policed by the League of Nations, the world's first attempt at global governance (see p. 462). The second, expressed in particular by France and the states neighbouring Germany, was the desire to make Germany pay for the war and to benefit territorially and economically from its defeat. This led to the 'war guilt' clause, the loss of German territory on both western and eastern borders, and to the imposition of **reparations**. Although it set out to redress the European balance of power, Versailles therefore made things worse. Realists have often followed E.H. Carr in arguing that a major cause of the 'twenty-year crisis' that led to war in 1939 was wider faith in 'utopianism', or liberal internationalism. This encouraged the 'haves' (the WWI victors) to assume that international affairs would in future be guided by a harmony of interests, inclining them to disregard bids for power by the 'have-nots' (in particular Germany and Italy).

The second major factor that helped to foster intensifying international tension in Europe was the global economic crisis, 1929–33. Sparked by the Wall Street Crash of October 1929, this highlighted both the higher level of interconnectedness of the global economy (through its rapid spread across the industrialized world) and the structural instability of its financial systems in particular. The main political impact of the economic crisis was a rise in unemployment and growing poverty, which, in politically unstable states such as Germany, invested radical or extreme political solutions with greater potency. Economically, the crisis resulted in the abandonment of free trade in favour of protectionism and even in **autarky**, the turn to economic nationalism helping to fuel the rise of political nationalism and international distrust.

However, the main controversies surrounding the origins of WWII concern the role and significance of Nazi Germany. Historians have disagreed about both the importance of ideology in explaining the outbreak of war (can German

● **Reparations**: Compensation, usually involving financial payments or the physical requisition of goods, imposed by victors on vanquished powers either as punishment or as a reward.

● **Autarky**: Economic self-sufficiency, often associated with expansionism and conquest to ensure the control of economic resources and reduce economic dependency on other states.

Focus on ...
Hitler's war?

The debate about Hitler's personal responsibility for WWII has been particularly intense. Those who subscribe to the 'Hitler's war' thesis emphasize the clear correlation between the three aims he set out for Germany in *Mein Kampf* (1924) and unfolding Nazi expansionism in the 1930s. Hitler's 'war aims' were, first, to achieve a Greater Germany (achieved through the incorporation of Austria and the Sudetan Germans into the Third Reich); second, the expansion into eastern Europe in search of *lebensraum* or 'living space' (achieved through the invasion of Russia); and third, a bid for world power through the defeat of the major sea empires, Britain and USA. This view is also supported by the fact that Nazi Germany operated, in effect, as Hitler's state, with power concentrated in the hands of a single, unchallengeable leader.

On the other hand, opponents of this view have emphasized the limitations of the 'great man' theory of history (in which history is seen to be 'made' by leaders acting independently of larger political, social and economic forces). Marxist historians, for example, have drawn attention to the extent to which Nazi expansionism coincided with the interests of German big business. Others have drawn attention to miscalculation on the part of both Hitler and those who sought to contain Nazi aggression. The chief culprits here are usually identified as a lingering belief in liberal internationalism across much of Europe, which blinded statesmen generally to the realities of power politics, and the UK's policy of **appeasement**, which encouraged Hitler to believe that he could invade Poland without precipitating war with the UK and eventually the USA.

● **Appeasement**: A foreign policy strategy of making concessions to an aggressor in the hope of modifying its political objectives and, specifically, avoiding war.

● **Social Darwinism**: The belief that social existence is characterized by competition or struggle, 'the survival of the fittest', implying that international conflict and probably war are inevitable.

aggression and expansionism be explained largely in terms of the rise of fascism and, specifically, Nazism?) and the extent to which the war was the outcome of the aims and deliberate intentions of Adolf Hitler. German foreign policy certainly became more aggressive after Hitler and the Nazis came to power in 1933. The Rhineland was occupied in 1936, Austria was annexed in 1938, the Sudetenland portion of Czechoslovakia was occupied and the rest of Czechoslovakia invaded in 1938–9, then Poland was invaded in September 1939. Moreover, the fact that fascist and particularly Nazi ideology blended **social Darwinism** with an extreme form of chauvinist nationalism appeared to invest Hitler's Germany with a sense of messianic or fanatical mission: the prospect of national regeneration and the rebirth of national pride through war and conquest. Others, on the other hand, have argued that Nazi foreign policy was dictated less by ideology and more by either geopolitical factors or by a political culture that was shaped by the nineteenth-century unification process. From this perspective, there was significant continuity between the foreign policy goals of the Nazi regime and the preceding Weimar Republic (1919–33) and early Wilhelmine Germany, the turn to aggressive expansion in the 1930s being explicable more in terms of opportunity than ideology.

However, unlike WWI, WWII did not originate as a European war which spilled over and affected other parts of the world; important developments took place in Asia, notably linked to the growing power and imperial ambition of Japan. In many ways, the position of Japan in the interwar period resembled that of Germany before WWI: the growing economic and military strength of a single state upset the continental balance of power and helped to fuel expansionist

CONCEPT

Third World

The term 'Third World' drew attention to the parts of the world that, during the Cold War, did not fall into the capitalist so-called 'First World' or the communist so-called 'Second World'. The less-developed countries of Africa, Asia and Latin America were 'third' in the sense that they were economically dependent and often suffered from widespread poverty. The term also implied that they were 'non-aligned', the Third World often being the battleground on which the geopolitical struggle between the First and Second Worlds was conducted. The term Third World has gradually been abandoned since the 1970s due to its pejorative ideological implications, the receding significance of a shared colonial past, and economic development in Asia in particular.

tendencies. Japan's bid for colonial possessions intensified in the 1920s and 1930s, in particular with the occupation of Manchuria in 1931 and the construction of the puppet state of Manchukuo. In 1936, Japan joined with Germany and Italy to form the Anti-Comintern Pact which developed into a full military and political alliance, the 'Pact of Steel', in 1939 and eventually the Tripartite Pact in 1940. However, expansionism into Asia brought growing tension between Japan and the UK and the USA. Calculating that by 1941 its naval forces in the Pacific had achieved parity with those of the USA and the UK, and taking advantage of the changing focus of the war once Germany had invaded Russia in June 1941, Japan decided deliberately to provoke confrontation with the USA through the pre-emptive strike on Pearl Harbor. By drawing the USA into WWII, this act also effectively determined its outcome.

End of Empires

The year 1945 was a turning point in world history in a number of respects. These include that it instigated a process of decolonization that witnessed the gradual but dramatic disintegration of the European empires. Not only did 'end of empire' symbolize the larger decline of Europe, but it also set in train, across much of Asia, Africa and the Middle East in particular, political, economic and ideological developments that were going to have profound implications for global politics.

The process whereby European control of overseas territories and peoples was gradually dismantled had begun after WWI. Germany was forced to give up its colonies and the British dominions were granted virtual independence in 1931. However, the process accelerated greatly after WWII through a combination of three factors. First, the traditional imperial powers (especially the UK, France, Belgium and The Netherlands) were suffering from 'imperial over-reach' (Kennedy 1989). Second, a decisive shift against European colonialism had occurred in the diplomatic context as a result of the ascendancy of the USA over Western Europe and the capitalist West in general. US pressure to dismantle imperialism became more assertive after WWII and more difficult to resist. Third, resistance to colonialism across Asia, Africa and Latin America became fiercer and more politically engaged. This occurred, in part, through the spreading influence in what came to be known as the Third World of two sets of western ideas: nationalism and Marxism–Leninism. In combination, these created a potent form of anti-colonial nationalism across much of the Third World in pursuit of 'national liberation', implying not only political independence, but also a social revolution, offering the prospect of both political and economic emancipation.

The end of the British Empire, which had extended across the globe and, at its greatest extent after WWI, extended over 600 million people, was particularly significant. India was granted independence in 1947, followed by Burma and Sri Lanka in 1948, and Malaya in 1957, with the UK's African colonies achieving independence in the late 1950s and early 1960s. By 1980, when Zimbabwe (formerly Rhodesia) achieved independence, the end of the British Empire had brought 49 new states into existence. Although the UK had confronted military resistance in Malaya and Kenya in particular, the logic of inevitable decolonization was accepted, meaning that the process was generally peaceful. This

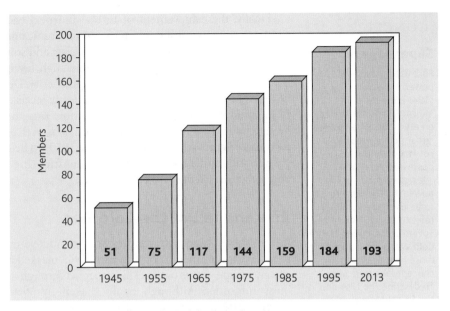

Figure 2.2 **Growth of membership of the United Nations, 1945 to present**

contrasted with French experience, where a greater determination to retain her imperial status resulted in a prolonged and ultimately fruitless war to resist Vietnamese independence, 1945–54, and the similarly fruitless Algerian War of Independence, 1954–62. The final major European empire to be dismantled was that of Portugal, which occurred following the overthrow of the military dictatorship in Lisbon in 1974. Africa's final colony, Namibia (formerly known as South West Africa), achieved independence in 1990, once South Africa accepted that it could not win its war against national liberation forces.

It may be possible to argue that the implications of decolonization were more profound than those of the Cold War, and it certainly had an impact over a longer period of time. In the first place, the early decades after WWII witnessed the most dramatic and intense process of state construction in world history. European decolonization in the Third World more than tripled the membership of the UN, from about 50 states in 1945 to over 150 states by 1978 (see Figure 2.2). This meant that the European state-system that had originated in the seventeenth century became a truly global system after 1945. However, the end of empire also significantly extended the reach of superpower influence, highlighting the fact that decolonization and the Cold War were not separate and distinct processes, but overlapping and intertwined ones. The developing world increasingly became the battleground on which the East–West conflict was played out. In this way, the establishment of a global state-system, and the apparent victory of the principle of sovereign independence, coincided with a crucial moment in the advance of globalization: the absorption of almost all parts of the world, to a greater or lesser extent, into rival power blocs. This process not only created a web of strategic and military interdependence, but also resulted in higher levels of economic and cultural penetration of the newly independent states.

Finally, the achievement of formal independence had mixed consequences for developing world states in terms of economic and social development. In the case of the so-called 'tiger' economies of East and southeast Asia and many of the oil producing states of the Gulf region, high levels of growth were achieved, banishing poverty and bringing wider prosperity. Despite the political upheavals of the Mao period in China, 1949–75, steady levels of economic growth laid the foundation for the subsequent transition to a market economy and rising growth rates from the 1980s onwards. However, many other areas were less fortunate. Across what started from the 1970s to be called the 'global South' (see p. 367), and most acutely in sub-Saharan Africa (the 'Fourth World'), widespread and sometimes acute poverty persisted.

Rise and fall of the Cold War

If the 'short' twentieth century was characterized by the ideological battle between capitalism and communism, 1945 marked a dramatic shift in the intensity and scope of this battle. This occurred through an important transformation in world order. Although badly shaken by WWI and having experienced economic decline relative in particular to the USA, Europe and European powers had been the major forces shaping world politics in the pre-1939 world. The post-1945 world, however, was characterized by the emergence of the USA and the USSR as 'superpowers', predominant actors on the world stage, apparently dwarfing the 'great powers' of old. The superpower era was characterized by the Cold War, a period marked by tensions between an increasingly US-dominated West and a Soviet-dominated East. The multipolarity (see p. 237) of the pre-WWII period thus gave way to Cold War bipolarity (see p. 223).

The first phase of the Cold War was fought in Europe. The division of Europe that had resulted from the defeat of Germany (the Soviet Red Army having advanced from the east and the USA, the UK and their allies having pushed forward from the west) quickly became permanent. As Winston Churchill put it in his famous speech in Fulton, Missouri in 1946, an 'iron curtain' had descended between East and West, from Lübeck in Northern Germany to Trieste in the Adriatic. Some trace back the start of the Cold War to the Potsdam Conference of 1945, which witnessed disagreements over the division of Germany and Berlin into four zones, while others associate it with the establishment of the so-called 'Truman Doctrine' in 1947, whereby the USA committed itself to supporting 'free people', later instigating the Marshall Plan, which provided economic support for the rebuilding of war-torn Europe in the hope that it would be able to resist the appeal of communism. The process of division was completed in 1949 with the creation of the 'two Germanys' and the establishment of rival military alliances, consisting of the North Atlantic Treaty Organization (NATO) and, in 1955, the Warsaw Pact. Thereafter, the Cold War became global. The Korean War (1950–53) marked the spread of the Cold War to Asia following the Chinese Revolution of 1949. However, how did the Cold War start in the first place?

There is a little controversy over the broad circumstances that led to the Cold War: in line with the assumptions of realist theorists, superpower states provided an irresistible opportunity for aggrandizement and expansion which made rivalry between the world's two superpowers virtually inevitable. In the case of the USA and the Soviet Union, this rivalry was exacerbated by their common

● The notion of a 'cold war' suggests a condition of 'neither war nor peace'. However, to describe US–Soviet relations during this period as a 'war' (albeit a 'cold' one) is to suggest that levels of antagonism between the two powers were so deep and impassioned that they would have led to direct military confrontation had circumstances allowed. In practice, this only applied to the first, most hostile, phase of the so-called Cold War, as tensions began to ease after the Cuban Missile Crisis of 1962. The idea of an enduring 'cold war' may therefore have been shaped by ideological assumptions about the irreconcilability of capitalism and communism.

Deconstructing . . .

'COLD WAR'

● The Cold War was supposedly 'cold' in the sense that superpower antagonism did not lead to a 'fighting war'. This, nevertheless, remained true only in terms of the absence of direct military confrontation between the USA and the Soviet Union. In respect of covert operations, so-called 'proxy wars' and conflicts that were clearly linked to East–West conflict (Korean, Vietnam, the Arab–Israeli wars and so on) the Cold War was 'hot'.

geopolitical interests in Europe and by a mutual deep ideological distrust. Nevertheless, significant debates emerged about responsibility for the outbreak of the Cold War, and these were closely linked to the rivalries and ideological perceptions that helped to fuel the Cold War itself. The traditional, or 'orthodox', explanation for the Cold War lays the blame firmly at the door of the Soviet Union. It sees the Soviet stranglehold over Eastern Europe as an expression of long-standing Russian imperial ambitions, given renewed impetus by the Marxist–Leninist doctrine of worldwide class struggle leading to the establishment of international communism.

A 'revisionist' interpretation of the Cold War was nevertheless developed that attracted growing support during the Vietnam War (1964–75) from academics such as Gabriel Kolko (1985). This view portrayed Soviet expansionism into Eastern Europe as defensive rather than aggressive, motivated essentially by the desire for a **buffer zone** between itself and a hostile West, and a wish to see a permanently weakened Germany. Various 'post-revisionist' explanations have also been developed. Some of these acknowledge the hegemonic ambitions of both superpowers, arguing that the Cold War was the inevitable consequence of a power vacuum that was a product of the defeat of Germany and Japan as well as the exhaustion of the UK (Yergin 1980). Alternative explanations place a heavier emphasis on misunderstanding and missed opportunities. For example, there had

● **Buffer zone**: An area, state or collection of states located between potential (and more powerful) adversaries, reducing the likelihood of land-based attack in particular.

Debating . . .
Was the Cold War inevitable?

There is always a tendency to read inevitability into historical events: they happened because they *had* to happen; history has a predestined course. In the case of the Cold War, this debate has raged with a particular passion, because it is linked to rival theories about the factors that drive world politics. Is history shaped by irresistible political or ideological forces, or is it, all too often, a product of misperceptions and miscalculations?

YES

Dynamics of bipolarity. Realist theorists have argued that the Cold War is best understood in terms of power politics and the nature of the international system. In this view, states are primarily concerned with their own survival and therefore prioritize military and security concerns. However, their ability to pursue or maintain power is determined by the wider distribution of power within the international system. What made the Cold War inevitable was that after WWII the defeat of Germany, Japan and Italy and the long-term decline of victorious states such as the UK and France created a bipolar world order in which the USA and the Soviet Union had predominant influence. The shape of global politics in the post-WWII era was therefore clear. Bipolarity meant that rivalry and hostility between the USA and the Soviet Union was inevitable, as each sought to consolidate and, if possible, expand its sphere of influence. This led to growing enmity between a US-dominated West and a Soviet-dominated East. A world of multiple great powers had given way to a world dominated by two superpowers, and peace and cooperation between these superpowers was impossible.

The ideological 'long war'. An alternative version of Cold War inevitability portrays ideology as the irresistible driving force. In this view, the Cold War was essentially an expression of the global ideological struggle between capitalism and communism that emerged in the nineteenth century but assumed more concrete form after the Russian Revolution of 1917. Antagonism between capitalism and communism derives from the fact that they represent incompatible modes of economic organization; in effect, competing visions of the future. The Cold War was therefore a battle between the capitalist West and the communist East, the USA and the Soviet Union being merely the instruments through which it was fought. The Cold War, thus, became inevitable once fascism had been vanquished in 1945, leaving global politics to be structured by East–West conflict.

NO

Western misperceptions about the Soviet Union. The Cold War was not dictated by either bipolarity or ideology, but came about through a process of mistake, miscalculation and misinterpretation. Both key actors blundered in missing opportunities for peace and co-operation; instead, escalating misperception created a mentality of 'bombs, dollars and doctrines' that made mutual suspicion and ingrained hostility seem unavoidable. Western misperceptions about the Soviet Union were based on the assumption that Soviet foreign policy was determined by ideology rather than territorial security. The Soviet Union's primary concerns were permanently to weaken Germany and to create a buffer zone of 'friendly' states in Eastern Europe. However, by 1946–7, US policy analysts were starting to see the creation of the Soviet bloc as either an expression of deep-seated Russian imperial ambitions or as a manifestation of the Marxist–Leninist doctrine of worldwide class struggle. Key figures in the Truman administration came to believe that they were confronting a Soviet Union bent on pursuing world revolution, and increasingly acted accordingly.

Soviet misperceptions about the West. The Soviet Union, particularly under Stalin, was influenced by a deep distrust of the West, borne out of inter-war fears about 'capitalist encirclement'. Paralleling western misperceptions, Soviet leaders believed that US foreign policy was guided more by ideological considerations, particularly anti-communism, than by strategic concerns. Thus, the USA's rapidly reducing military presence in Europe (US forces from 3.5 million in May 1945 to 400,000 the following March, and eventually to 81,000) had little or no impact on Soviet policy-makers, who failed to understand that the USA genuinely wanted cooperation after WWII, albeit on its own terms. The mutual interest that the Soviet Union and the USA had in establishing a possible long-term relationship (based on a shared desire to reduce their defence burden and plough resources instead into domestic reconstruction) thus proved to be insufficiently strong to contain the drift towards fear and antagonism.

KEY EVENTS . . .

The Cold War period

1945	United Nations created (June)		**1962**	Cuban Missile Crisis	
1945	Hiroshima and Nagasaki atomic bomb attacks (August)		**1967**	Six Day War	
1946	Nuremberg and Tokyo war crimes trials begin		**1968**	Soviet invasion of Czechoslovakia	
1947	Truman Doctrine announced (April)		**1969**	Apollo 11 lands on the moon	
1947	Marshall Plan introduced (June)		**1971**	Communist China joins the UN	
1948–9	Berlin Blockade/Airlift		**1973**	Oil crisis	
1949	Soviet atomic bomb explosion (August)		**1977**	Economic reforms begin in China	
1949	Chinese Revolution (October)		**1979**	Islamic Revolution in Iran	
1950–3	Korean War		**1979**	Soviet Union invades Afghanistan	
1955–75	Vietnam War		**1980–8**	Iran–Iraq War	
1956	Soviet invasion of Hungary		**1985**	Gorbachev becomes Soviet leader	
1961	Berlin Wall is erected		**1989**	Berlin Wall falls (November 9) (see p. 43)	
1961	Yuri Gagarin first person in space		**1990**	CSCE meeting formally ends the Cold War (November)	
			1991	Collapse of the Soviet Union (December)	

● **Brinkmanship**: A strategy of escalating confrontation even to the point of risking war (going to the brink) aimed at persuading an opponent to back down.

● **Mutually Assured Destruction (MAD)**: A condition in which a nuclear attack by either state would only ensure its own destruction, as both possess an invulnerable second-strike capacity.

been early signs of hope in President Roosevelt's belief in peaceful cooperation under the auspices of the newly-created United Nations, and also in Stalin's distinctly discouraging attitude towards Tito in Yugoslavia and Mao in China.

The Cold War was not a period of consistent and unremitting tension: it went through 'warmer' and 'cooler' phases, and at times threatened to become a 'hot' war. The Cuban Missile Crisis of 1962 was probably the moment at which direct confrontation between the superpowers came closest to happening. The fact that this exercise in **brinkmanship** ended peacefully perhaps demonstrated the effectiveness of the condition of **Mutually Assured Destruction** in preventing tension between the superpowers developing into military confrontation. However, the bipolar model of the Cold War became increasingly less accurate from the 1970s onwards. This was due, first, to the growing fragmentation of the communist world (notably, the deepening enmity between Moscow and Beijing), and second, to the resurgence of Japan and Germany as 'economic superpowers'. This was reflected in the emerging multipolarity of the 1963–71 period and, more clearly, to the era of **détente** between East and West, 1972–80. *Détente* nevertheless ended with the advent of the 'Second' Cold War in 1980, which was a product of the Reagan administration's military build-up and more assertively anti-communist and anti-Soviet foreign policy.

However, when the Cold War came to an end, the end was dramatic, swift and quite unexpected. Over 70 years of communism collapsed in just two years, 1989–91, and where communist regimes survived, as in China, a process of radical change was taking place. During the momentous year of 1989, communist rule in Eastern Europe was rolled back to the borders of the Soviet Union; in 1990 the CSCE Paris Conference formally announced the end of the Cold War; and in 1991, the Soviet Union itself collapsed. Nevertheless, debate about the end of the Cold War is mired in as much ideological controversy as the debate about its origins (see p. 40). The range of factors that have been associated with the collapse of communism and the end of the Cold War include the following:

- The structural weaknesses of Soviet-style communism
- The impact of Gorbachev's reform process
- US policy and the 'Second' Cold War
- Economic and cultural globalization.

Some have argued that the collapse of communism was an accident waiting to happen, the inevitable outcome of structural flaws that doomed Soviet-style regimes to inevitable collapse more effectively than the contradictions identified by Marx as the fatal flaw of the capitalist system. These weaknesses were of two kinds, economic and political. The economic weaknesses were linked to the inherent failings of central planning. Centrally planned economies proved to be less effective than capitalist economies in delivering general prosperity and producing modern consumer goods. Eruptions of political discontent in 1980–91 were thus, in significant measure, a manifestation of economic backwardness and expressed a desire for western-style living standards and consumer goods. The political weaknesses derived from the fact that communist regimes were structurally unresponsive to popular pressure. In particular, in the absence of competitive elections, independent interest groups and a free media, single-party communist states possessed no mechanisms for articulating political discontent and initiating dialogue between rulers and the people. There is little doubt that, in addition to economic frustration, the popular protests of the 1989–91 period articulated demand for the kind of civil liberties and political rights that were seen as being commonplace in the liberal-democratic West.

Although structural weaknesses may explain communism's susceptibility to collapse they do not explain either its timing or its swiftness. How did economic and political frustration accumulated over decades spill over and cause the downfall of regimes in a matter of months or even weeks? The answer lies in the impact of the reforms that Mikhail Gorbachev introduced in the Soviet Union from 1985 onwards. There were three key aspects of the reform process. The first, based on the slogan **perestroika**, involved the introduction of elements of market competition and private ownership to tackle the long-term deficiencies of Soviet central planning, drawing on earlier experiments in 'market socialism', particularly in

● **Détente**: (French) Literally, loosening; the relaxation of tension between previously antagonistic states, often used to denote a phase in the Cold War.

● **Perestroika**: (Russian) Literally, 'restructuring'; used in the Soviet Union to refer to the introduction of market reforms to a command or planned economy.

GLOBAL POLITICS IN ACTION . . .

Fall of the Berlin Wall

Events: On 9 November 1989, a weary East German government spokesman announced that travel restrictions would be lifted. Flustered and subjected to further questioning, he then stated that this would take effect 'immediately'. The effect of the announcement was electric. Inspired by the heady excitement that had been generated by the collapse of communist regimes in Poland and Hungary and by weekly mass demonstrations in Leipzig and, on a smaller scale, in other major East German cities, West and East Berliners rushed to the Wall. A euphoric party atmosphere rapidly developed, with people dancing on top of the Wall and helping each other over in both directions. By the

morning of November 10, the dismantling of the Berlin Wall, the chief symbol of the Cold War era, had begun. Over the following days and weeks, the borders between the two Germanies and the two parts of Berlin were increasingly opened up. Just as the fall of the Berlin Wall had been inspired by events elsewhere in Eastern Europe, it, in turn, proved to be a source of inspiration. Communist rule collapsed in Czechoslovakia in December, and in Romania rioting first forced the Communist leader Ceaușescu and his wife Elena to flee by helicopter, before they were captured and summarily executed on Christmas Day.

Significance: The fall of the Berlin Wall was the iconic moment in the momentous year of 1989, which witnessed the Eastern Europe Revolutions that effectively rolled back the boundaries of communism to the borders of the Soviet Union and ignited a process of reform that affected the entire communist world. The year 1989 is widely, and with justification, viewed as one of the most significant dates in world history, ranking alongside 1648 (the birth of the European state-system), 1789 (the French Revolution), 1914 (the outbreak of WWI) and 1945 (the end of WWII and the beginning of the Cold War). The momentum generated in 1989 led directly to a series of world-historical events. First, Germany was reunified in 1990, starting a process through which Europe would be reunified through the subsequent eastward expansion of

the EU (see p. 505) and, to some extent, NATO. Also in 1990, representatives of the Warsaw Pact and NATO, the military faces of East–West confrontation, met in Paris formally to declare an end to hostilities, officially closing the book on the Cold War. Finally, in December 1991, the world's first communist state, the Soviet Union, was officially disbanded.

For Francis Fukuyama, 1989 marked the 'end of history', in that the collapse of Marxism-Leninism as a world-historical force meant that liberal democracy had emerged as the sole viable economic and political system world-wide (for a fuller discussion of the 'end of history' thesis, see p. 539). For Philip Bobbitt (2002), the events precipitated by 1989 marked the end of the 'long war' between liberalism, fascism and communism to define the constitutional form of the nation-state. Nevertheless, some have questioned the historical significance of 1989, as represented by the fall of the Berlin Wall. This has been done in two ways. First, it is possible to argue that there is significant continuity between the pre- and post-1989 periods, in that both are characterized by the hegemonic position enjoyed by the USA. Indeed, 1989 may simply mark a further step in the USA's long rise to hegemony. Second, 1989–91 may have marked only a temporary weakening of Russian power, which, as Russia emerged from the crisis years of the 1990s and started to reassert its influence under Putin, led to the resumption of Cold War-like rivalry with the USA.

Yugoslavia. However, economic restructuring under Gorbachev had disastrous consequences: it replaced an inefficient but still functioning planned economy with one that barely functioned at all. The second aspect of the reform process involved the dismantling of restrictions on the expression of opinion and political debate, under the slogan of **glasnost**. However, *glasnost* merely gave a political voice to Gorbachev's opponents – hard-line communists who opposed any reforms that might threaten the privileges and power of the party-state elite, as well as radical elements that wished to dismantle the apparatus of central planning and communist rule altogether. Gorbachev thus became increasingly isolated and retreated from 'reform communism' into more radical changes, including the formal abandonment of the Communist Party's monopoly of power. The third, and crucial, aspect of Gorbachev's reforms was a new approach to relations with the USA and Western Europe, the basis of which was the abandonment of the **Brezhnev doctrine**. Its replacement, the so-called 'Sinatra doctrine', allowing the states of Eastern Europe to 'do it their way', meant that Gorbachev and the Soviet Union refused to intervene as, one after another, communist regimes collapsed in 1989–90, symbolized by the fall of the Berlin Wall.

Alternative explanations of the end of the Cold War draw attention away from internal developments within the Soviet Union and the communist bloc in general, and focus instead on the changing context within which communism operated. The chief external factors contributing to the collapse of communism were the policies of the Reagan administration in the USA and the advance of economic and cultural globalization. The Reagan administration's contribution to this process was in launching the 'Second Cold War' by instigating a renewed US military build-up in the 1980s, particularly in the form of the Strategic Defense Initiative (SDI) (the 'star wars' initiative) of 1983. Whether intended or not, this drew the Soviet Union into an arms race (see p. 272) that its already fragile economy could not sustain, helping provoke economic collapse and increase the pressure for reform. The contribution of economic globalization was that it helped to widen differential living standards between the East and the West. While the progressive internationalization of trade and investment helped to fuel technological and economic development in the US-dominated West from the 1970s onwards, its exclusion from global markets ensured that the Soviet-dominated East would suffer from economic stagnation. Cultural globalization contributed to the process through the spread of radio and television technology, helping ideas, information and images from an apparently freer and more prosperous West to penetrate the more developed communist societies, particularly those in Eastern Europe. This, in turn, further fuelled discontent and bred support for western-style economic and political reforms.

THE WORLD SINCE 1990

A 'new world order'?

The birth of the post-Cold War world was accompanied by a wave of optimism and idealism. The superpower era had been marked by East–West rivalry that extended across the globe and led to a nuclear build-up that threatened to destroy the planet. As communism collapsed in Eastern Europe, and Soviet power was in retreat both domestically and internationally, President Bush (Snr) of the USA

● *Glasnost*: (Russian) Literally, 'openness'; used in the Soviet Union to refer to freedom of expression within the context of a one-party communist state.

● **Brezhnev doctrine**: The doctrine, announced by Leonid Brezhnev in 1968, that Warsaw Pact states only enjoyed 'limited sovereignty', justifying possible Soviet intervention.

proclaimed the emergence of a 'new world order'. Although the idea of a 'new' world order often lacked clear definition, it undoubtedly expressed quintessentially liberal hopes and expectations. Whereas the Cold War had been based on ideological conflict and a balance of terror, the end of superpower rivalry opened up the possibility of 'liberal peace', founded on a common recognition of international norms and standards of morality. Central to this emerging world order was the recognition of the need to settle disputes peacefully, to resist aggression and expansionism, to control and reduce military arsenals, and to ensure the just treatment of domestic populations through respect for human rights (see p. 311). As 'end of history' theorists such as Francis Fukuyama (1989, 1991) argued, all parts of the world would now irresistibly gravitate towards a single model of economic and political development, based on liberal democracy.

The post-Cold War world order appeared to pass its first series of major tests with ease, helping to fuel liberal optimism. Iraq's annexation of Kuwait in August 1990 led to the construction of a broad western and Islamic alliance that, through the Gulf War of 1991, brought about the expulsion of Iraqi forces. The disintegration of Yugoslavia in 1991, which precipitated war between Serbia and Croatia, saw the first use of the Conference on Security and Co-operation in Europe (CSCE) (renamed the Organization for Security and Co-operation in Europe (OSCE) in 1994) as a mechanism for tackling international crises, leading to hopes that it would eventually replace both the Warsaw Pact and NATO. Although the CSCE had been effectively sidelined by superpower hostility since its creation at the Helsinki Conference of 1975, it was the CSCE heads of government meeting in Paris in November 1990 that produced the treaty that brought a formal end to the Cold War. However, the early promise of international harmony and cooperation quickly proved to be illusory as new forms of unrest and instability rose to the surface.

Stresses within the new world order were generated by the releasing of tensions and conflicts that the Cold War had helped to keep under control. The existence of an external threat (be it 'international communism' or '**capitalist encirclement**') promotes internal cohesion and gives societies a sense of purpose and identity. To some extent, for instance, the West defined itself through antagonism towards the East, and *vice versa*. There is evidence that, in many states, the collapse of the external threat helped to unleash centrifugal pressures, usually in the form of racial, ethnic and regional tensions. This occurred in many parts of the world, but in particular in eastern Europe, as demonstrated by the break-up of Yugoslavia and prolonged bloodshed amongst Serbs, Croats and Muslims. The Bosnian War (1992–95) witnessed the longest and most violent European war in the second half of the twentieth century. Far from establishing a world order based on respect for justice and human rights, the international community stood by former Yugoslavia and, until the Kosovo crisis of 1999, allowed Serbia to wage a war of expansion and perpetrate genocidal policies reminiscent of those used in WWII. Nevertheless, these early trends, hopeful and less hopeful, in post-Cold War world history were abruptly disrupted by the advent of global terrorism in 2001.

9/11 and the 'war on terror'

For many, the September 11 terrorist attacks on New York and Washington (see p. 20) were a defining moment in world history, the point at which the true

● **Capitalist encirclement**: The theory, developed during the Russian Civil War (1918–21), that capitalist states were actively engaged in attempts to subvert the Soviet Union in order to bring down communism.

GLOBAL ACTORS . . .

THE UNITED STATES OF AMERICA

Type: State • **Population:** 315.5 m • **GDP per capita:** $49,601 • **HDI ranking:** 3/187
Capital: Washington, DC

The United States of America was established as a federal republic in 1787, through the adoption of the US Constitution. It was formed by 13 former British colonies that had founded a confederation after the 1776 War of Independence. The nineteenth century was characterized by the establishment of the territorial integrity of the USA as it exists today. By 1912, all 48 states of the continuous land mass of the USA had been created (Hawaii and Alaska were added in 1959). The USA is a liberal democracy (see p. 189) comprising:

- The Congress, composed of the House of Representatives and the Senate (two senators represent each state, regardless of size)
- The presidency which heads the executive branch of government
- The Supreme Court, which can nullify laws and actions that run counter to the Constitution.

As the US system of government is characterized by a network of constitutional checks and balances, deriving from federalism and a separation of powers between the legislature, executive and judiciary, it is susceptible to 'government gridlock'. For example, treaties need to be both signed by the president and ratified by the Senate, and although the president is the commander-in-chief, only Congress can declare war.

Significance: The USA's rise to global hegemony started with its economic emergence during the nineteenth century. By 1900, the USA had overtaken the UK as the world's leading industrial country, producing around 30 per cent of the world's manufactured goods. However, burgeoning economic power was only gradually expressed in international self-assertiveness, as the USA abandoned its traditional policy of isolationism. This process was completed in 1945, when the USA emerged as a superpower, commanding unchallengeable military and economic might and exerting influence over the whole of the capitalist West. The USA's rise to global hegemony came about both because the collapse of the Soviet Union in 1991 left the USA as the world's sole superpower, a hyperpower, and because of close links between the USA and 'accelerated' globalization (so much so that globalization is sometimes viewed as a process of 'Americanization'). US power in the post-Cold War era was bolstered by massively increased defence spending, giving the USA an unassailable lead in high-tech military equipment in particular and, as its response to September 11 demonstrated, making the USA the only country that can sustain military engagements in more than one part of the world at the same time.

However, US power has a paradoxical character. For example, although the USA's military dominance cannot be doubted, its political efficacy is open to question. September 11 thus demonstrated the vulnerability of the USA to new security threats, in this case transnational terrorism. The launch of the 'war on terror' as a response to September 11 also highlighted the limits of US power and was, in some senses, counter-productive. Although the invasions of Afghanistan in 2001 and Iraq in 2003 were quickly successful in removing the targeted regimes, both wars developed into protracted and highly complex counter-insurgency wars that proved to be difficult to 'win' in the conventional sense. Moreover, the general tendency of the Bush administration towards unilateralism and, in particular, its approach to the 'war on terror' damaged the USA's 'soft' power and bred resentment, particularly within the Muslim world. The need to work within a multilateral framework in a more interdependent world has been recognized by shifts that have occurred in US foreign affairs under President Obama since 2008. Perhaps the most significant challenge to US power, however, is the rise of so-called 'emerging states', and particularly China. Warnings about the decline of US hegemony date back to the 1970s and 1980s, when events such as defeat in the Vietnam War and economic decline relative to Japan and Germany were interpreted as evidence of 'imperial over-reach'. The rise of China is nevertheless much more significant, in that it perhaps suggests the emergence of a new global hegemon, with China set to overtake the USA in economic terms during the 2020s.

nature of the post-Cold War era was revealed and the beginning of a period of unprecedented global strife and instability. On the other hand, it is possible to exaggerate the impact of 9/11. As Robert Kagan (2004) put it, 'America did not change on September 11. It only became more itself'. A variety of theories have been advanced to explain the advent of global or transnational terrorism. The most influential and widely discussed of these has been Samuel Huntington's (see p. 540) theory of a 'clash of civilizations'. Huntington (1996) suggested that twenty-first century conflict will not primarily be ideological or economic but rather cultural, conflict between nations and groups from 'different civilizations'. In this light, September 11 and the so-called 'war on terror' that it unleashed could be seen as evidence of an emerging 'civilizational' struggle between the West and Islam. Such a view suggests that the origins of global terrorism lie in arguably irreconcilable tensions between the ideas and values of western liberal democracy and those of Islam, particularly Islamic fundamentalism. Islamic fundamentalists wish to establish the primacy of religion over politics. However, the view that global terrorism is essentially a religious or civilizational issue ignores the fact that radical or militant Islam developed in the twentieth century in very specific political and historical circumstances, linked to the tensions and crises of the Middle East in general and the Arab world in particular. The key factors that have contributed to political tension in the Middle East include the following:

- The inheritance from colonialism
- Conflict between Israel and the Palestinians
- The 'curse' of oil
- The rise of political Islam.

Political instability in the Middle East can be traced back to the final demise of the Ottoman Empire in 1918. This led to the establishment of UK and French 'mandates' (trusteeships) over Syria, Lebanon, Palestine and what became Iraq. Western colonialism had a number of debilitating implications for the region. It bred a sense of humiliation and disgrace, particularly as it led to the dismantling of traditional Muslim practices and structures including *Shari'a* law; it resulted in political borders that reflected the interests of western powers and showed no regard for the facts of history, culture and ethnicity; and authoritarian and corrupt government was installed, based on pro-western 'puppet' rulers. Although the mandates were gradually given up during the 1930s and 1940s, western influences remained strong and the inheritance of colonialism was difficult to throw off.

The establishment, in 1947, of the state of Israel was perceived by the surrounding newly-independent Arab states as an extension of western colonialism, the creation of a western outpost designed to weaken the Arab world, defeat in a succession of Arab–Israeli wars merely deepening the sense of frustration and humiliation across the Arab world. The political and symbolic impact of the 'Palestine problem' – the displacement of tens of thousands of Palestinian Arabs after the 1948 war and establishment of 'occupied territories' after the Six-Day War in 1968 – is difficult to overestimate, particularly across the Arab world but also in many other Muslim states. In addition to breeding a festering sense of resentment against western influences that are seen to be embodied in the state of Israel, it also made it easier for corrupt and complacent military dictatorships to come to power and remain in power, knowing that they could always use the issue of Israel and Palestine to mobilize popular support.

On the face of it, the idea that the possession of the world's largest oil reserves could be a source of political tension and instability strains credibility. However, oil can be viewed as a 'curse' on the Middle East in at least two senses. First, in providing regimes in the Middle East with a secure and abundant source of revenue, it reduced the pressure for domestic political reform, thereby helping entrench complacent and unresponsive government. Oil revenues were also some-times used to build up extensive military-security apparatus, which were used to repress political opponents and contain discontent. Monarchical **autocracy** and military dictatorship thus remained deeply entrenched in the Middle East. The second drawback of oil was that it guaranteed the continuing involvement in the Middle East of western political and corporate interests, concerned to ensure access to oil resources and, until the Organization of Petroleum Exporting Countries (OPEC) succeeded in tripling the price of crude oil in the early 1970s, keeping oil prices low. Together with the fact that the Middle East was also an important arena for Cold War antagonism, this helped to fuel anti-westernism and sometimes, more specifically, anti-Americanism. While anti-westernism was expressed during the 1960s and 1970s in the form of Arab socialism, from the 1980s onwards it increasingly took the form of religious fundamentalism.

Political Islam, a militant and uncompromising form of Islam that sought political and spiritual regeneration through the construction of an Islamic state, gained impetus from the potent mix of national frustration, political repression, cultural disjunction and the social frustrations of both the urban poor and young intellectuals in the twentieth-century Middle East. In its earliest form, the Muslim Brotherhood (see p. 206), it moved from being a non-violent, puritani-cal movement to one that increasingly advocated violence in order to resist all 'foreign' ideologies and construct a pure Islamic state. The profile and influence of political Islam was substantially strengthened by the Iranian Revolution of 1979, which brought the hard-line Shia cleric Ayatollah Khomeini (see p. 198) to power. Thereafter, radical Islamic groups such as Hamas and Hezbollah ('Party of God') tended to displace secular-based groups, like the Palestine Liberation Organization (PLO), in leading the struggle against Israel and what was seen as western imperialism. Al-Qaeda (see p. 301), which emerged out of the Islamic fundamentalist resistance fighters who fought against the Soviet invasion of Afghanistan, 1979–86, has developed into the foremost exponent of global terrorism, increasingly mounting direct attacks on US targets. Through 9/11, al-Qaeda not only demonstrated the new global reach of terrorism but also that, in the twenty-first century, war can be fought by non-state actors, including loosely-organized terrorist networks, as well as by states.

After 9/11, the USA's approach to the 'war on terror' quickly started to take shape. Its opening act, launched in November 2001, was the US-led military assault on Afghanistan that toppled the Taliban regime within a matter of weeks. Because the Taliban was so closely linked to al-Qaeda and had provided Osama bin Laden and his followers with a base, this war attracted broad international support and became only the second example in which the United Nations endorsed military action (the first one being the Korean War). Influenced by the ideas of neoconservatism (see p. 233), the strategy of the Bush administration was geared to a larger restructuring of global politics, based on the need to

● **Autocracy**: Literally, rule by a single person; the concentration of political power in the hands of a single ruler, typically a monarch.

KEY EVENTS . . .

The post-Cold War period

1991	Gulf War (January–February)		**2001**	US-led invasion of Afghanistan (October)
1992	Civil war breaks out in former Yugoslavia		**2002**	International Criminal Court established
1993	European Union created		**2003**	US-led invasion of Iraq (March)
1994	Rwandan genocide (April–July)		**2006**	North Korea tests nuclear weapon
1994	Apartheid ends in South Africa (September)		**2008**	Russia invades Georgia
1996	Taliban seize power in Afghanistan		**2007–9**	Global financial crisis
1997–8	Asian financial crisis		**2010**	Birth of the Arab Spring (December) (see p. 211)
1998	India and Pakistan test nuclear weapons		**2010–13**	Eurozone crisis
1999	Kosovo War		**2011**	Libyan civil war (see p. 331)
2001	September 11 terrorist attacks on the USA (see p. 20)		**2011**	Syrian civil war begins
			2013	Egyptian coup d'état (July)

address the problem of 'rogue' states (see p. 231) by promoting democracy, if necessary through pre-emptive military strikes (see p. 232). In January 2002, President Bush identified Iraq, Iran and North Korea as part of an 'axis of evil', later expanding this to include Cuba, Syria and Libya (later dropped from this list). However, it was becoming clear that 'regime change' in Saddam Hussein's Iraq was the administration's next objective, supposedly providing the basis for the larger democratic reconstruction of the larger Arab world. This led to the 2003 Iraq war, fought by the USA and a 'coalition of the willing'.

Although the initial goals of military intervention in Afghanistan and Iraq were speedily accomplished (the removal of the Taliban and the overthrow of Saddam and his Ba'athist regime, respectively), the pursuit of the 'war on terror' became increasingly problematical. Both the Afghan and Iraq wars turned into protracted counter-insurrection struggles, highlighting the difficulties involved in modern asymmetrical warfare (discussed in Chapter 10). Despite improvements to the security position in Iraq in particular, the establishment of civic order and the longer-term processes of state-building and even nation-building have proved to be complex and challenging. Moreover, the US policy of using military intervention in order to 'promote democracy' was widely viewed as an act of imperialism across the Muslim world, strengthening anti-westernism and anti-Americanism. The fear therefore was that the 'war on terror' had become

Focus on ...
Invading Afghanistan: learning from history?

When the Soviet Union invaded Afghanistan in 1980 and a US-led coalition invaded Afghanistan in 2001, were they failing to learn lessons from earlier attempts to conquer Afghanistan? Does history issue warnings, in this sense? In the nineteenth century, Afghanistan had been the focus of great-power rivalry, standing, as it did, between the Russian empire to the north and British India to the east. This resulted in two wars. The First Anglo-Afghan War (1839–42) was, arguably, the UK's greatest imperial disaster of the nineteenth century. British forces invaded Afghanistan with the intention of extending UK influence by re-establishing Shah Shuja on the throne. Shuja's assassination in Kabul in 1842, however, left the British troops in an unsustainable position. After a two-month siege, they began what came to be called the 'Retreat from Kabul'. Out of the 18,500-strong party that left Kabul, only one man made it through to the British garrison in Jalalabad, in modern-day Pakistan. Nevertheless, some forty years later, the Second Anglo–Afghan War (1878–80) took place. This time, the British achieved their main objective, which was to curtail Russian influence by dictating Afghan foreign policy, although the Afghans retained internal sovereignty and established full independence from British influence in 1919.

Some have argued that the (unlearnt) lesson of these nineteenth-century wars was that extreme caution should exercised by any state contemplating invading Afghanistan, rightly dubbed the 'graveyard of empires'. Afghanistan certainly presents any would-be conqueror with a daunting range of challenges, including an inhospitable geography (largely consisting of mountains and deserts); severe winters; a lack of infrastructure; a complex tribal mix and a variety of ethnicities; little history of centralized authority; and traditional hostility to foreign occupation. Such a combination of factors makes Afghanistan particularly unsuitable for the use of conventional military strategies, counterbalancing any technological advantage that an invading force may possess. In view of the likelihood that the 2001 invasion will end with as few political gains as the previous ones, it is tempting to invoke Marx's statement (made in relation to Napoleon I and Napoleon III) that history repeats itself, 'first as tragedy, then as farce'. However, it is always dangerous to read determinism into history. No two sets of historical circumstances are ever identical. In the case of the 2001 US-led invasion, for example, its goals were far more ambitious than earlier colonial invasions, in that, in addition to attacking al-Qaeda and removing the Taliban from power, it sort to recast Afghanistan internally on the basis of US-style democracy.

counter-productive, threatening to create, rather than resolve, the clash of civilizations that was fuelling Islamist terrorism.

Shifts in the Bush administration's approach to the 'war on terror' were evident from 2004 onwards, especially in attempts to increase the involvement of the UN, but more significant changes occurred after President Obama came to office in 2009. These involved, in the first place, a reduced emphasis on the use of military power and a greater stress on building up the USA's 'soft' power. A phased withdrawal of US troops from Iraq was started and Iraqi forces assumed responsibility for security in towns and cities in 2009, with a commitment being given to end the combat mission in Afghanistan by the end of 2014. Important overtures were also made to the Muslim world in general and, more specifically, to Iran (in view of its strengthened influence, not least over Iraq, and the belief that it was trying to acquire nuclear weapons), calling for a strengthening of cross-cultural understanding and recognizing the mistakes of the past. The Obama administration's strategy also attempted to give greater attention to the causes of terrorism and not merely its manifestations, addressing long-standing sources of resentment and grievance, most importantly through bolder international pressure to resolve the Palestinian problem. Progress with this, however, has been slow.

Shifting balances within the global economy

There is no settled view about exactly when the modern phase of 'accelerated' globalization began. The idea that economic globalization (see p. 98) was happening was only widely accepted during the 1990s. However, the origins of contemporary globalization can be traced back to the general shift in economic priorities following the collapse of the Bretton Woods system of 'fixed' exchange rates during 1968–72. The shift to floating exchange rates led to pressures for greater financial deregulation and converted the International Monetary Fund (IMF) (see p. 475) and the World Bank (see p. 380) to the ideas of the 'Washington consensus' (see p. 96), under which many parts of the developing world were encouraged to adopt 'structural adjustment' programmes, based on the rigorous (and sometimes disastrous) application of free-market policies. The emphasis on free-market priorities was most eagerly embraced during the 1980s by the Reagan administration in the USA and the Thatcher government in the UK. In this context, the collapse of communism, in 1989–91, had profound economic implications. Together with China's opening to foreign investment, it dramatically widened the parameters of international capitalism, transforming the western economic system into a genuinely global one. Nevertheless, 'shock therapy' market-based reforms had very different consequences in different parts of the post-communist world. In Russia, for example, they led to falling living standards and a steep decline in life expectancy, which provided the basis for a drift back towards authoritarian rule under Putin after 1999.

However, the balance has continued to shift within the new global economy. Economic globalization was intrinsically linked to the growing economic dominance of the USA. US influence over the IMF, GATT (replaced by the World Trade Organization (WTO) (see p. 537) in 1995) and the World Bank has been decisive in wedding these institutions to free-market and free-trade policies since the 1970s. As with the UK in the nineteenth century, free trade in the late twentieth and early twenty-first centuries has provided the USA both with new markets for its goods and sources of cheap labour and raw materials. By 2000, the USA controlled over 30 per cent of global economic output. The emergence of the USA as the most significant actor in the global economy was linked to the burgeoning power of transnational corporations (TNCs) (see p. 94), major firms with subsidiaries in several countries, which are therefore able to switch production and investment to take advantage of the most favourable economic and fiscal circumstances. By the turn of the century, TNCs accounted for 70 per cent of world trade, with nearly half of the world's biggest 500 corporations being based in the USA.

The benefits of global capitalism have not been equally distributed, however. In particular, during the 1990s much of Africa suffered rather than benefited from globalization, a disproportionate number of Africans remaining uneducated and undernourished, with the population also suffering disproportionately from diseases such as AIDS. The impact of TNCs on Africa has often, overall, been negative, leading, for example, to a concentration of agriculture on the production of 'cash crops' for export rather than meeting local needs. Other parts of the world have either suffered from the increased instability of a globalized financial system or have experienced declining growth rates through an unwillingness fully to engage with neoliberal or market reforms. The heightened instability of the global economy was demonstrated by the financial crisis in Mexico in 1995, the Asian financial crisis of 1997–98 which affected the 'tiger' economies of Southeast and East Asia, and the Argentine financial crisis of 1999–2002 which led to a severe contraction of the economy.

Twenty-first century trends in the global economy have been dominated by the rise of new economic powers, most importantly China, India and Brazil. In this light, the most significant development of the post-1945 period may turn out to be, not the rise and fall of the Cold War, or even the establishment of US economic and military hegemony (see p. 228), but the process of decolonization that laid the basis for the emergence of the superpowers of the twenty-first century. Some have suggested that if the nineteenth century was the 'European century', and the twentieth century was the 'American century', the twenty-first century may be the 'Asian century'. Since around 1980, when the effects of the transition from a command economy to a market economy started to become apparent, China has consistently achieved annual economic growth rates of more than 9 per cent. In 2011, China overtook Japan to become the world's second largest economy, and, if growth rates persist, it has been estimated that it will eclipse the economic might of the USA during the 2020s. Indian growth levels since the 1990s have only been marginally lower than those of China. The emergence of India as a major economic power can be traced back to the economic liberalization of the 1980s, which gave impetus to the expansion of the new technology sector of the economy and stimulated export-orientated growth.

In many ways, the global financial crisis of 2007–09 both reflected and gave further impetus to the shift in the centre of gravity of the global economy from West to East. Not only was this crisis precipitated by a banking crisis in the USA, and has brought, some argue, the US model of enterprise capitalism into question, but evidence of early economic recovery in China and India in particular showed the extent to which these countries and some of their small neighbours' economies have succeeded in 'de-coupling' themselves from the US economy. The changing face of the world economy is also evident in the plight of Europe, afflicted by debt, austerity and low growth, by contrast with the economic emergence of states such as Turkey, Indonesia, Nigeria and Vietnam. The prospects of these and other trends continuing as the twenty-first century unfolds are examined in Chapter 22.

SUMMARY

- The 'modern' world was shaped by a series of developments. These include the final collapse of ancient civilizations and the advent of the 'Dark Ages'; the growing dominance of Europe through the 'age of discovery' and, eventually, industrialization; and the growth of European imperialism.

- WWI was meant to be the 'war to end all wars' but, within a generation, WWII had broken out. The key factors that led to WWII include the WWI peace settlements, the global economic crisis of the 1930s, the programme of Nazi expansion, sometimes linked to the personal influence of Hitler, and the growth of Japanese expansionism in Asia.

- The year 1945 is commonly seen as a watershed in world history. It initiated two crucial processes. The first was the process of decolonization and the collapse of European empires. The second was the advent of the Cold War, giving rise to bipolar tensions between an increasingly US-dominated West and Soviet-dominated East.

- Cold War bipolarity came to an end through the Eastern European revolutions of 1989–91, which witnessed the collapse of the Soviet Union. This was a result of factors including the structural weakness of Soviet-style communism, the impact of Gorbachev's reform process, the advent of the 'Second Cold War' and the wider implications of economic and cultural globalization.

- 'Liberal' expectations about the post-Cold War period flourished briefly before being confounded by the rise of forms of ethnic nationalism and the growth of religious militancy. This especially applied in the form of 9/11 and the advent of the 'war on terror', which has sometimes been seen as a civilizational struggle between Islam and the West.

- Power balances within the global economy have shifted in important ways. While some have linked globalization to the growing economic dominance of the USA, others have argued that the global economy is increasingly multipolar, especially due to the rise of emerging economies.

Questions for discussion

- Why and how was Europe a dominant influence in the pre-1900 world?
- In what sense, and why, was Germany a 'problem' following its unification in 1871?
- Was WWII really a re-run of WWI?
- Would WWII have happened without Hitler?
- Was rivalry and tension between the USA and the Soviet Union inevitable after 1945?
- Did the Cold War help to make the world more peaceful and stable or less?
- Did anyone 'win' the Cold War?
- Why did hopes for a 'new' world order of international cooperation and peaceful co-existence prove to be so short-lived?
- Was 9/11 a turning point in world history?
- Is China in the process of eclipsing the USA as the most powerful force in global politics?
- Does history 'teach lessons', and is there any evidence that we learn from them?

Further reading

Cowen, N., *Global History: A Short Overview* (2001). A sweeping account of global history from the classical era through to the modern era.

Hobsbawm, E., *Globalization, Democracy and Terrorism* (2008). A short and lucid account of major trends in modern world history, taking particular account of developments in the Middle East.

Spellman, W., *A Concise History of the World Since 1945* (2006). An authoritative analysis of world history since the end of WWII.

Young, J. W. and G. Kent, *International Relations Since 1945: A Global History* (2004). A comprehensive account of international developments during the Cold War and after.

 ONLINE RESOURCES AVAILABLE

Links to relevant web resources can be found on the *Global Politics* website

CHAPTER 3

Theories of Global Politics

'Mad men in authority, who hear voices in the air, are distilling their frenzy from some academic scribbler of a few years back.'

J. M. KEYNES, *The General Theory* (1936)

PREVIEW

No one sees the world just 'as it is'. All of us look at the world through a veil of theories, presuppositions and assumptions. In this sense, observation and interpretation are inextricably bound together: when we look at the world we are also engaged in imposing meaning on it. This is why theory is important: it gives shape and structure to an otherwise shapeless and confusing reality. The most important theories as far as global politics is concerned have come out of the discipline of International Relations, which has spawned a rich and increasingly diverse range of theoretical traditions. The dominant mainstream perspectives within the field have been realism and liberalism, each offering a different account of the balance between conflict and cooperation in world affairs. Why do realists believe that global politics is characterized by unending conflict, while liberals have believed in the possibility of cooperation and enduring peace? And why have realist and liberal ideas become more similar over time? However, from the 1980s onwards, especially gaining impetus from the collapse of communism and the end of the Cold War, a series of new theoretical voices have emerged. These 'new voices' have substantially expanded the range of critical perspectives on world affairs, once dominated by the Marxist tradition. How have theories such as neo-Marxism, social constructivism, poststructuralism, feminism, postcolonialism and green politics cast a critical lens on global politics, and how do they differ from one another? Finally, the emergence of globalization has posed a series of new theoretical challenges, most significantly about the moral and theoretical implications of global interconnectedness. How is it possible to 'think globally'? In what ways and to what extent does global interconnectedness require that we re-think existing theories?

KEY ISSUES

- What is theory, and what forms does it take?
- Why have realists argued that world affairs should be understood in terms of power and self-interest?
- Why do liberals believe that world affairs are biased in favour of interdependence and peace?
- How have critical theorists challenged mainstream approaches to global politics?
- Are the similarities among critial theories greater than the differences?
- What are the empirical and moral implications of global interconnectedness?

WHAT IS THEORY?

This is the first of two chapters that focus on the issue of theory. Chapter 21 considers how, and how far, theory helps us make sense of the world. It both reflects on the importance of theory, and explores debates about the proper place of theory in the field of global politics. The present chapter, by contrast, provides an introduction to the key substantive theories of global politics, each of which constitutes a distinctive 'lens' on world affairs. But what is theory? Anything from a plan to a piece of abstract knowledge can be described as a 'theory'. In academic study, theory can, most broadly, be viewed as a kind of abstract or generalized thinking that seeks to explain, interpret or evaluate something. However, theory is a plural rather than singular phenomenon: it comes in a variety of shapes and forms.

In the first place, theory may serve quite different purposes. Three *types* of theory can thus be identified, as follows:

- *Explanatory theory*. Sometimes called 'descriptive' or 'empirical' theory, this helps to explain why, and under what circumstances, events happen or developments unfold. Explanatory theories embody generalized causal propositions, which can be tested against 'hard' evidence; that is, data that exists separately from our perception of it. Mainstream perspectives on global politics tend to use theory in this sense.
- *Interpretive theory*. Sometimes referred to as 'constitutive' theory, this imposes meaning on events or issues, attempting to understand, rather than explain, the world. Interpretive theory emphasizes that human reflection is a social process, and treats the 'real world' as a series of competing truths or interpretations. This is a stance most commonly associated with critical perspectives on global politics.
- *Normative theory*. Sometimes termed 'prescriptive' or 'political' theory, this prescribes values and standards of conduct; it deals with what *ought to be*, rather than with what *is*. However, all empirical theories of global politics are underpinned, at some level, by normative considerations. Normative theory also overlaps with interpretive theory, as the latter rejects the distinction between facts and values.

Second, theories differ in terms of their scope and scale (see Figure 3.1). The broadest theories of global politics are theoretical traditions (sometimes termed 'perspectives', 'discourses', 'schools of thought' 'world-views' or 'paradigms' (see p. 524)). Theoretical traditions are intellectual frameworks comprising interrelated values, theories and assumptions; they constitute broad approaches to the analysis of world affairs. Examples include realism, liberalism, Marxism/critical theory, feminism and so on. Each of these traditions can nevertheless be divided into a series of sub-traditions, or 'currents of thought'. For instance, realism encompasses **classical realism**, **neorealism** and, perhaps, post-neorealism, while liberalism comprises interdependence liberalism, **republican liberalism** and **liberal institutionalism**. Tensions between rival sub-traditions mean that there can sometimes be as much debate *within* a theoretical tradition as there is *between* traditions. Finally, there are concrete or specific theories, such as neorealist stability theory (see p. 57), world systems theory (see p. 374) and just war

---

- **Classical realism**: A form of realism that explains power politics largely in terms of human selfishness or egoism.

- **Neorealism**: A perspective on international politics that modifies the power politics model by highlighting the structural constraints of the international system; sometimes called 'new' or 'structural' realism.

- **Republican liberalism**: A form of liberalism that highlights the benefits of republican (rather than monarchical) government and, in particular, emphasizes the link between democracy and peace.

- **Liberal institutionalism**: An approach to study that emphasizes the role of institutions (both formal and informal) in the realization of liberal principles and goals.

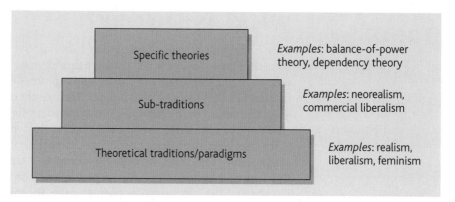

Figure 3.1 **Levels of theoretical analysis**

theory (see p. 264). While such theories are usually linked to a particular theoretical tradition, or a specific sub-tradition, others may resist becoming the 'property' of any single tradition.

REALISM

The key mainstream perspectives on global politics are realism and liberalism. As the discipline of international relations took shape following WWI, it drew particularly heavily on liberal ideas and theories, especially about the desirability of conducting international politics within a framework of moral and legal norms. From the late 1930s onwards, such liberal ideas were subject to increasing criticism by realist theorists, who highlighted what they saw as the inescapable realities of power politics. This established international relations as a 'divided discipline', a battleground between liberalism and realism, with the latter increasingly dominating the academic study of the subject from 1945 onwards. However, this so-called first 'great debate' within IR (see p. 516) has refused to stand still. By the 1970s, new versions of realism and liberalism had appeared, and, over time, the differences between these mainstream traditions have been blurred.

Realism (sometimes called 'political realism') claims to offer an account of world affairs that is 'realistic', in the sense that it is hard-headed and (as realists see it) devoid of wishful thinking and deluded moralizing. For realists, global politics is, first and last, about power and self-interest. This is why it is often portrayed as a 'power politics' model of international politics. As Hans Morgenthau (see p. 61) put it, 'Politics is a struggle for power over men, and whatever its ultimate aim may be, power is its immediate goal and the modes of acquiring, maintaining and demonstrating it determine the technique of political action'. The theory of power politics is based on two core assumptions (Donnelly 2000):

● **Egoism**: Concern for one's own interest or well-being, or selfishness; the belief that one's own interests are morally superior to those of others.

- People are essentially selfish and competitive, meaning that **egoism** is the defining characteristic of human nature.
- The state-system operates in a context of international anarchy, in that there is no authority higher than the sovereign state.

Focus on . . .
Neorealist stability theory: the logic of numbers?

From a neorealist perspective, bipolar systems tend towards stability and strengthen the likelihood of peace. This happens for the following reasons:

- The existence of only two great powers encourages each to maintain the bipolar system as, in the process, they are maintaining themselves.
- Fewer great powers means the possibilities of great-power war are reduced.
- The existence of only two great powers reduces the chances of miscalculation and makes it easier to operate an effective system of deterrence.
- Power relationships are more stable as each bloc is forced to rely on inner (economic and military) resources, external (alliances with other states or blocs) means of expanding power not being available.

On the other hand, multipolar systems tend to be inherently unstable, for the following reasons:

- A larger number of great powers increases the number of possible great-power conflicts.
- Multipolarity creates a bias in favour of fluidity and, perhaps, instability, as it leads to shifting alliances as great powers have external means of extending their influence.
- As power is more decentralized, existing great powers may be more restless and ambitious while weak states may be able to form alliances in order to challenge and displace existing great powers.

Such thinking was most prevalent during the Cold War, when it was used to explain the dynamics of the superpower era. Since then, it has become less fashionable to explain stability and conflict simply in terms of the structural dynamics of the international system.

The core theme of realist theory can therefore be summed up in the equation: egoism plus anarchy equals power politics. Some have suggested that this formulation betrays a basic theoretical fault line within realism, dividing it into two distinct schools of thought. One of these – classical realism – explains power politics in terms of egoism, while the other – neorealism, or structural realism – explains it in terms of anarchy. However, these alternative approaches reflect more a difference of emphasis within realism rather than a division into rival 'schools', as the central assumptions of realism are common to most realist theorists, even though they may disagree about which factors are ultimately the most important.

The key themes within realism are as follows:

- State egoism and conflict
- Statecraft and the national interest
- International anarchy and its implications
- Polarity, stability and the balance of power.

State egoism and conflict

In basing their theories of politics on a pessimistic, but allegedly 'realistic', model of human nature (see p. 59), classical realists have worked within a long and

Niccolò Machiavelli (1469–1527)

Italian politician and author. The son of a civil lawyer, Machiavelli's knowledge of public life was gained from a sometimes precarious existence in politically unstable Florence. As a servant of the republic of Florence, he was despatched on diplomatic missions to France, Germany and throughout Italy. After a brief period of imprisonment and the restoration of Medici rule, Machiavelli retired into private life and embarked on a literary career. His major work *The Prince*, written in 1513 but not published until 1531 and seen as the classic realist analysis of power politics, drew heavily on his first-hand observations of the statecraft of Cesare Borgia. *The Disourses*, written over a twenty-year period, nevertheless portray him as a republican. The adjective 'Machiavellian' (fairly or unfairly) subsequently came to mean 'cunning and duplicitous'.

established tradition of thought, which can be traced back to Thucydides' (see p. 249) account of the Peloponnesian War, and to Sun Tzu's classic work on strategy, *The Art of War*, written at roughly the same time in China. Other significant figures included Machiavelli and Thomas Hobbes (see p. 14). Machiavelli's theory of politics was based on a darkly negative model of a changeless human nature. In his view, humans are 'insatiable, arrogant, crafty and shifting, and above all malignant, iniquitous, violent and savage'. On this basis, Machiavelli argued that political life is always characterized by inevitable strife, encouraging political leaders to rule through the use of cunning, cruelty and manipulation. Hobbes's thinking was also based on a pessimistic view of human nature. He argued that humans are driven by non-rational appetites: aversions, fears, hopes and desires, the strongest of which is the desire for 'power after power'. As no single person or group is strong enough to establish dominance, and therefore a system of orderly rule, over society – a condition that Hobbes referred to as a '**state of nature**' – an ongoing civil war developed between all members of society. Life in this 'state of nature' would thus be 'solitary, poor, nasty, brutish and short'. According to Hobbes, the only way of escaping from the barbarity of such a society would be through the establishment of a sovereign and unchallengeable power; that is, by the creation of a state.

How did such thinking shape the understanding of international politics? In the first place, as realists accept that no form of world government (see p. 464) can ever be established, it meant that politics is conducted within what is, in effect, an international 'state of nature'. The international arena is therefore dangerous and uncertain, with order and stability always being the exception rather than the rule. Second, whereas Machiavelli and Hobbes were primarily concerned to explain the conduct of individuals or social groups, realist international theorists have been concerned, above all, with the behaviour of states. Realists view states as coherent and cohesive 'units', and regard them as the most important actors on the world stage. Realists' theories of international politics are thus firmly state-centric. Third, and crucially, the fact that states are composed of, and led by, people who are inherently selfish, greedy and power-seeking means that state behaviour cannot but exhibit the same characteristics. Human egoism therefore determines state egoism; or, as Morgenthau (1962) put

● **State of nature**: A society devoid of political authority and of formal (legal) checks on the individual.

HUMAN NATURE

Realist view

Human nature is the starting point for much realist analysis, so much so that classical realism has sometimes been portrayed as 'biological realism'. Influenced by thinkers such as Hobbes and Machiavelli, realists have embraced a theory of human nature that has three main features. First, the essential core of human nature is fixed and given, fashioned by 'nature' (biological or genetic factors) rather than by 'nurture' (the influence of education or social factors generally). Second, instinct ultimately prevails over intellect. Human beings are driven by non-rational appetites: aversions, fears, hopes and desires, the strongest of which is the desire to exercise power over others. Intellect and reason may guide us in pursuing these appetites, but they do not define them in the first place. Third, as human beings are essentially self-seeking and egoistical, conflict between and amongst them is an unavoidable fact of life. For classical realists, this human egoism determines state egoism, and creates an international system that is inevitably characterized by rivalry and the pursuit of the national interest. Hopes for international cooperation and even 'perpetual peace' are therefore a utopian delusion. However, assumptions about human nature are peripheral within neorealism, in which rivalry and conflict is explained in terms of the structure of the international system rather than the make-up of individuals and therefore of states.

Liberal view

Liberals have a broadly optimistic view of human nature. Humans are self-seeking and largely self-reliant creatures; but they are also governed by reason and are capable of personal self-development. This implies, on the one hand, that there is an underlying and unavoidable tendency towards rivalry and competition among individuals, groups and, in the international arena, states. However, on the other hand, this tendency towards rivalry is contained by an underlying faith in a harmony of interests (conflicts can and should be resolved) and by a preference for resolving conflict through discussion, debate and negotiation. Liberals therefore typically deplore the use of force and aggression; war, for example, is invariably seen as an option of the very last resort. In this view, the use of force may

be justified, either on the grounds of self-defence or as a means of countering oppression, but always and only after reason and argument have failed. By contrast with the realist image of humans as ruthless power-maximizers, liberals emphasize that there is a moral dimension to human nature, most commonly reflected in the doctrine of human rights. This moral dimension is grounded in a strong faith in reason and progress. Reason dictates that human beings treat each other with respect, guided by rationally-based rules and principles. It also emphasizes the scope within human beings for personal development – as individuals expand their understanding and refine their sensibilities – and thus for social progress.

Critical views

While both realists and liberals tend to believe that core aspects of human nature are unchanging and fixed at birth, critical theorists generally view human nature as 'plastic', moulded by the experiences and circumstances of social life. In the nurture–nature debate, they therefore tend to favour nurture. This has two key implications. First, it suggests a unifying vision of humans as social creatures, animated by a common humanity and, therefore, cosmopolitan moral sensibilities. Critical theorists, for example, are often willing to go further than liberal internationalists in endorsing a 'one world' vision, grounded in the ideas of global justice. The second implication of 'plasticity' is that it highlights the extent to which economic, political or cultural structures shape human identities, wants and perceptions. As Marxists have put it, social being determines consciousness. For social constructivists and poststructuralists, this may suggest that there is no such thing as 'human nature', in the sense of a set of abiding tendencies or dispositions that apply in all circumstances and all societies. Feminists usually embrace an androgynous model of human nature, implying that women and men share a common human nature and that gender differences are socially and culturally imposed. Difference feminists nevertheless hold that there are deep-rooted, and perhaps even essential, differences between women and men, such that men are disposed to competition and domination while women are naturally sympathetic and peaceful.

it, 'the social world [is] but a projection of human nature onto the collective plane'. Just as human egoism leads to unending conflict amongst individuals and groups, state egoism means that international politics is marked by inevitable competition and rivalry. As essentially self-interested actors, the ultimate concern of each state is for survival, which thereby becomes the first priority of its leaders. As all states pursue security through the use of military or strategic means, and where possible seek to gain advantage at the expense of other states, international politics is characterized by an irresistible tendency towards conflict.

Statecraft and the national interest

Although realism is often associated with the attempt to understand international politics from an objective or 'scientific' standpoint, it also acknowledges the impòrtant role played by **statecraft**. For example, in his analysis of the 'twenty-years crisis' that came between WWI and WWII, E. H. Carr (see p. 34) criticised the leading figures at the Paris Peace Conference of 1919–20 (see p. 62) for allowing 'wishing' to prevail over 'thinking'. By neglecting the importance of power in international politics, they had set the world on an inevitable course to further conflict. Morgenthau (1948) similarly placed an emphasis on the 'art of statecraft', arguing that the practical conduct of politics should nevertheless be informed by the 'six principles of political realism', spelled out as follows:

- Politics is governed by *objective laws* which have their root in human nature.
- The key to understanding international politics is the concept of interest defined in terms of *power*.
- The forms and nature of state power will vary in time, place and context but the concept of interest remains *consistent*.
- Universal *moral principles* do not guide state behaviour, although this does not rule out an awareness of the moral significance of political action.
- Moral aspirations are specific to a *particular* nation; there is no universally agreed set of moral principles.
- The political sphere is *autonomous*, meaning that the key question in international politics is 'How does this policy affect the power of the nation?'

The key guide to statecraft in the realist tradition is a concern about the **national interest**. This concern highlights the realist stance on political morality. Realism is commonly portrayed as essentially amoral, both because of its image of humans as lustful and power-seeking creatures and because of its insistence that ethical considerations should be strictly excluded from foreign policy decision-making. However, a normative emphasis also operates within realist analysis, in that the requirement that state policy should be guided by a hard-headed pursuit of the national interest suggests, ultimately, that the state should be guided by the well-being of its citizens. What realists reject, therefore, is not nationally-based conceptions of political morality, but universal moral principles that supposedly apply to all states in all circumstances. Indeed, from a realist perspective, one of the problems with the latter is that they commonly get in the

● **Statecraft**: The art of conducting public affairs, or the skills associated with it; statesmanship.

● **National interest**: Foreign policy goals, objectives or policy preferences that supposedly benefit a society as a whole (the foreign policy equivalent of the 'public interest') (see p. 135).

Hans Morgenthau (1904–80)

German-born, US international relations theorist. A Jewish refugee from Nazi Germany, Morgenthau arrived in the USA in 1937 and started an academic career which led to him being dubbed the 'Pope' of international relations. Morgenthau's *Politics Among Nations* (1948) was highly influential in the development of international relations theory. He set out to develop a science of 'power politics', based on the belief, clearly echoing Machiavelli and Hobbes, that what he called 'political man' is an innately selfish creature with an insatiable urge to dominate others. Rejecting 'moralistic' approaches to international politics, Morgenthau advocated an emphasis on 'realistic' diplomacy, based on an analysis of balance of power and the need to promote the national interest. His other major writings include *Scientific Man Versus Power Politics* (1946), *In Defence of the National Interest* (1951) and *The Purpose of American Politics* (1960).

way of the pursuit of the former. Calculations about the national interest, moreover, offer the surest basis for deciding when, where and why wars should be fought. Although realism is commonly associated with the idea of endless war, realists have often opposed war and aggressive foreign policy. In their view, wars should only ever be fought if vital national interests are at stake, the decision to wage war being based on something like a cost–benefit analysis of its outcomes in terms of strategic interests. Such thinking, for example, led Morgenthau and most US realists (except for Henry Kissinger, who was the National Security Advisor and later Secretary of State under Presidents Nixon and Ford, 1969–77) to oppose the Vietnam War. Realists were amongst the most trenchant critics of the 'war on terror' (see p. 230), thirty-four leading US realist scholars having publicly opposed the US military build-up against Iraq in 2002 (see p. 521).

Anarchy and its implications

From the 1970s onwards, new thinking within the realist tradition started to emerge, which was critical of 'early' or 'traditional' realism. The key text in this process was Kenneth Waltz's *The Theory of International Politics* (1979). For Waltz (see p. 63), theories about international politics could be developed on 'three levels of analysis – the human individual, the state and the international system'. In this light, the defect of classical realism was that it could not explain behaviour at a level above the state, which is a limitation of any endogenous, or 'inside-out', theory (one which explains behaviour in terms of 'the inside', the intentions or inclinations of key actors) (see Structure or agency? p. 76). Using **systems theory**, neorealism – or, more specifically, 'structural realism' – explains the behaviour of states in terms of the structure of the international system. As such, neorealism is an exogenous, or 'outside-in', theory (one in which the behaviour of actors is explained in terms of 'the outside', the context or structure in which they operate) of global politics. In shifting attention from the state to the international system, it places an emphasis on the implications of anarchy. The characteristics of international life stem from the fact that states (and other international actors) operate within a domain which has no formal central

• **Systems theory**: An approach to study that focuses on works of 'systems', explaining their operation and development in terms of reciprocal interactions amongst component parts.

Paris Peace Conference 1919–20

Events: In the aftermath of WWI, representatives of the Allies (the leading figures were
President Wilson (see p. 445) of the USA,
Clemenceau, the Prime Minister of France,
and Lloyd George, the UK Prime Minister)
met in Paris in January 1919 to arrange a
peace treaty with Germany. The result of
this was the Treaty of Versailles, signed in
June 1919, with a further series of treaties
later being signed with the other defeated
powers. Two main motivations lay behind
these treaties. The first, articulated by Wilson
and set out in his Fourteen Points (a peace
programme announced in a speech to
Congress in January 1918) was the desire to
institute a new international order, achieved
through a 'just peace' that would banish power politics for
ever. This resulted in the redrawing of the map of central
and eastern Europe in line with the principle of national
self-determination, leading to the creation of new states
such as Yugoslavia, Czechoslovakia and Poland. Wilson's
major contribution to the Versailles conference, however,
was the creation of the League of Nations. However, the
other major motivation, expressed in particular by
Clemenceau, was to punish Germany and strengthen
French security. This led to the large-scale disarmament of
Germany, the loss of German territory and the distribution
of its colonies as 'mandates' to various Allied powers, and
the imposition of the 'war guilt' clause.

Significance: Just twenty years after the Paris Peace
Conference, the world was plunged once again into total
warfare, WWII bringing even greater carnage and suffering than WWI. What had gone wrong? Why had the 'just
peace' failed? These questions have deeply divided generations of international relations theorists. Taking their
lead from E. H. Carr, realist theorists have often linked the
outbreak of war in 1919 to the 'idealist' or 'utopian' ideas
of the Paris peacemakers. By believing that WWI had
been caused by an 'old order' of rampant militarism and
multinational empires, they placed their faith in democracy, self-determination and international organizations.
In particular, they had failed to recognize that power politics is not the cause of war but the major way in which
war can be prevented. When Germany, blamed (with
dubious fairness) for the outbreak of WWI, re-emerged as
a major and ambitious military power, breaking, in the
process, many of the terms of the Treaty of Versailles, the

League of Nations stood by powerless to stop it. Liberal
statesmen and theorists had ignored the most basic fact
of international relations: as all states are ultimately
driven by self-interest, only power can be a constraint on
power; a reliance on law, morality and international
institutions will be of no avail. The wider acceptance of
such an analysis in the aftermath of WWII helped to
assure the growing ascendancy of realist theories over
liberal theories within the discipline of international
relations.

On the other hand, liberal internationalists have
pointed to the inconsistent application of liberal principles
at the Paris Peace Conference. The Treaty of Versailles was
never properly a 'liberal peace'. This was both because it
left many nationalistic conflicts unresolved, and sometimes worsened (especially through the loss of German
land to France and Czechoslovakia), and because, in
important respects, the desire to punish and permanently
weaken Germany took precedence over the quest for a
just peace. Arguably, the seeds of WWII were thus sowed
not by a reliance on 'utopian' principles, but by the fact
that Versailles was in many ways a 'victors' peace'. The
'mistreatment' of the defeated stored up massive griev-
ances that could only, over time, help to fuel hostile and
aggressive foreign policies. What is more, the much
vaunted League of Nations never lived up to its name, not
least because of the refusal of the world's most powerful
state, the USA, to enter. In that sense, the Paris Peace
Conference produced the worst of all worlds: it strengthened the currents of power politics in Europe while
persuading the victorious powers that power politics had
been abolished.

Kenneth Waltz (1924–2013)

US international relations theorist. Waltz's initial contribution to international relations, outlined in *Man, the State, and War* (1959), adopted a conventional realist approach and remains the basic starting point for the analysis of war. His *Theory of International Politics* (1979) was the most influential book on international relations theory of its generation, establishing Waltz as the successor to Morgenthau in the discipline. Ignoring human nature and the ethics of statecraft, Waltz used systems theory to explain how international anarchy effectively determines the actions of states, with change in the international system occurring through changes in the distribution of capabilities between and amongst states. Waltz's analysis was closely associated with the Cold War and the belief that bipolarity is more stable and provides a better guarantee of peace and security than does multipolarity.

authority. But how does this shape behaviour? And why, according to neorealists, does international anarchy tend towards conflict rather than cooperation?

Neorealists argue that international anarchy necessarily tends towards tension, conflict and the unavoidable possibility of war for three main reasons. In the first place, as states are separate, autonomous and formally equal political units, they must ultimately rely on their own resources to realise their interests. International anarchy therefore results in a system of '**self-help**', because states cannot count on anyone else to 'take care of them'. Second, relationships between and amongst states are always characterized by uncertainty and suspicion. This is best explained through the **security dilemma** (Booth and Wheeler 2008). Although self-help forces states to ensure security and survival by building up sufficient military capacity to deter other states from attacking them, such actions are always liable to be interpreted as hostile or aggressive. Uncertainty about motives therefore forces states to treat all other states as enemies, meaning that permanent insecurity is the inescapable consequence of living in conditions of anarchy. Third, conflict is also encouraged by the fact that states are primarily concerned about maintaining or improving their position relative to other states; that is, about making **relative gains**. Apart from anything else, this discourages cooperation and reduces the effectiveness of international organizations (see p. 440), because, although all states may benefit from a particular action or policy, each state is actually more worried about whether other states benefit more that it does.

Polarity, stability and the balance of power

However, the fact that states are inclined to treat other states as enemies does not inevitably lead to bloodshed and open violence. Rather, neorealists, in common with classical realists, believe that conflict can be contained by the balance of power, a key concept for all realist theorists. However, while classical realists treat the balance of power as a product of prudent statecraft, neorealists see it as a consequence of the structural dynamics of the international system, and specifically, of the distribution of power (or capacities) between and among states. In

● **Self-help**: A state's reliance on its own capacities and resources, rather than external support, to ensure security and survival.

● **Security dilemma**: The dilemma that arises from the fact that a build-up of military capacity for defensive reasons by one state is always liable to be interpreted as aggressive by other states (see p. 19).

● **Relative gains**: The position of states in relation to one another, reflected in the distribution of benefits and capabilities between and amongst them (see p. 443).

short, the principal factor affecting the likelihood of a balance of power, and therefore the prospect of war or peace, are the number of great powers (see p. 6) operating within the international system. Although neorealists believe that there is a general bias in the international system in favour of balance rather than imbalance (see To balance or to bandwagon? p. 242), world order is determined by the changing fate of great powers. This is reflected in an emphasis on **polarity**.

Neorealists have generally associated bipolar systems with stability and a reduced likelihood of war, while multipolar systems have been associated with instability and a greater likelihood of war. This inclined neorealists to view Cold War bipolarity (see p. 223) in broadly positive terms, as a 'long peace', but to warn about the implications of rising multipolarity (see p. 237) in the post-Cold War era (discussed in more detail in Chapter 9). Realists, nevertheless, disagree about the relationship between structural instability and the likelihood of war. For so-called **offensive realists**, as the primary motivation of states is the acquisition of power, if the balance of power breaks down (as it tends to in conditions of multipolarity), there is a very real likelihood that war will break out (Mearsheimer 2001). **Defensive realists**, on the other hand, argue that states tend to prioritize security over power, in which case states will generally be reluctant to go to war, regardless of the dynamics of the international system (Mastanduno 1991) (see Offensive or defensive realism? p. 240).

Assessing realism

Realism was so dominant within international relations during much of the post-WWII period that, when Waltz's *Theory of International Politics* (1979) was published, some claimed that, in neorealism, the discipline had found its 'master theory'. Amongst the reasons for realism's dominance was that the Cold War, characterized as it was by superpower rivalry and a nuclear arms race, made the politics of power and security appear to be undeniably relevant and insightful. Waltz (1986) was thus able to assert that realism identifies 'a small number of big and important things'. However, in a process that began during the 1970s and 1980s, but was significantly accelerated by the end of the Cold War, more and more aspects of world politics came to be shaped by developments that either ran counter to realist expectations or highlighted the limitations of realist analysis. These included the end of the Cold War itself (which realists failed to predict and struggled to explain (see p. 225)), the growing impact of non-state actors on world affairs, the advance of globalization and the increased significance of issues related to human rights. Realism's centrality within international relations therefore came under growing pressure. Not only was greater attention given to rival theoretical approaches, in the form of revived liberalism and 'new' critical voices such as constructivism (see p. 75), but a growing number of realists (sometimes called 'weak' or 'hedged' realists) sought to blend the core principles of realist analysis with a range of wider political possibilities.

Nevertheless, while the impulse to establish the overall explanatory priority of realism over rival traditions may have receded, the continued relevance of realist theory is rarely doubted, and few deny that realism should form part of the analytical toolkit of every serious student of international relations (Donnelly 2000). This applies, in part, because the acceptance that anarchy (albeit, perhaps, modified by other developments) remains a basic feature of

● **Polarity**: The existence within a system of one or more significant actors, or 'poles', which affect the behaviour of other actors and shape the contour of the system itself, determining its structural dynamics.

● **Offensive realism**: A form of structural realism that portrays states as 'power maximizers', as there is no limit to their desire to control the international environment.

● **Defensive realism**: A form of structural realism that views states as 'security maximizers', placing the desire to avoid attack above a bid for world power.

CONCEPT

Idealism

Idealism (sometimes called 'utopianism') (see p. 530) is an approach to international politics that stresses the importance of moral values and ideals, rather than power and the pursuit of the national interest. As a guide to foreign policy-making, idealism is essentially a variant of liberal internationalism: it reflects a strong optimism about the prospects for international peace, usually associated with a desire to reform the international system by strengthening international law (see p. 339) and embracing cosmopolitan ethics. However, idealism is not co-extensive with liberalism: idealism is broader and more nebulous than liberalism, and modern liberal theorizing is often disconnected from the idealist impulse.

● **Neoliberal institutionalism**: A school of thought within liberalism that emphasizes the scope for cooperative behaviour within the international system while not denying its anarchic character.

● **Democratization**: The transition from authoritarianism to liberal democracy, reflected in the granting of basic freedoms and political rights, the establishment of competitive elections and the introduction of market reforms.

world politics extends well beyond realism. Neorealist thinking about the structural dynamics of a self-help international system is, therefore, seldom dismissed out of hand. Moreover, in a range of areas realism continues to be in the forefront of contemporary debate. This can be seen in the case of debate, especially in the USA, about US foreign policy, as has been apparent over the 'war on terror' and especially the invasion of Iraq, and over how the USA should respond the rise of China (see p. 243). Since the 1990s, one of the clearest trends in realist theory has been the tendency to fuse systems analysis with a unit-level approach, giving rise to what has been called 'neoclassical realism' or 'post-neorealism' (Wohlforth 1993, Zakaria 1998). Greater openness to the insights of classical realism has, in particular, allowed renewed stress to be placed on the importance of statecraft. This underlines that the most enduring lesson taught by realist theory is perhaps that actions, however well-intentioned, may always have unintended consequences, implying that, where possible, international affairs should be approached with caution and prudence.

LIBERALISM

Liberalism has been the dominant ideological force shaping western political thought. Indeed, some portray liberalism as the ideology of the industrialized West and identify it with western civilization itself. Liberal ideas and theories had a considerable impact on the discipline of international relations as it took shape following WWI, although they drew on a much older tradition of so-called 'idealist' theorizing which dates back, via Kant's (see p. 15) belief in the possibility of 'universal and perpetual peace', to the Middle Ages and the ideas of early 'just war' thinkers such as Thomas Aquinas (see p. 261). Marginalized during the early post-1945 period due to the failure of the liberal-inspired Versailles Settlement and the ascendancy of realist thought, liberal ideas nevertheless attracted growing attention from the 1970s onwards, often in the form of so-called **neoliberal institutionalism**. This largely stripped liberalism of its idealist trappings. The end of the Cold War (sometimes seen as the 'liberal moment' in world affairs), the growing impact of globalization (see p. 8) and a new wave of **democratization** in the 1990s each gave liberal theory additional impetus.

The central theme of liberalism in all its forms is the notion of harmony or balance amongst competing interests. Individual, groups and, for that matter, states may pursue self-interest but a natural equilibrium will tend to assert itself. At a deeper level, competing interests complement one another; conflict is never irreconcilable. Just as, from a liberal perspective, natural or unregulated equilibrium tends to emerge in economic life (see Approaches to global political economy, p. 90), a balance of interests tends to develop amongst the states of the world, disposing liberals to believe in the possibility of peace and cooperation. However, it is important to note that the liberal paradigm is not clearly distinct from realism, as both of them share certain mainstream assumptions about how international politics works. Most significantly, liberals and realists both accept that world affairs are shaped, in important ways, by competition amongst states, implying that the international system is, and perhaps must always remain, decentralized. The difference, nevertheless, is that liberals assume that competition within this system is conducted within a larger framework of harmony. This inclines liberals to believe in internationalism (see p. 67) and to hold that realists substantially underestimate the scope for cooperation and integration within the decentralized state-system.

The key themes within liberal theory are as follows:

- Interdependence liberalism
- Republican liberalism
- Liberal institutionalism.

Interdependence liberalism

Liberal theories about interdependence (see p. 7) are grounded in ideas about trade and economic relations. Such thinking can be traced back to the birth of **commercial liberalism** in the nineteenth century, based on the classical economics of David Ricardo (1770–1823) and the ideas of the so-called 'Manchester liberals', Richard Cobden (1804–65) and John Bright (1811–89). The key theme within commercial liberalism was a belief in the virtues of **free trade**. Free trade has economic benefits, as it allows each country to specialize in the production of the goods and services that it is best suited to produce, the ones in which they have a 'comparative advantage'. However, free trade is no less important in drawing states into a web of economic interdependence that means that the material costs of international conflict are so great that warfare becomes virtually unthinkable. Cobden and Bright argued that free trade would draw people of different races, creeds and languages together in what Cobden described as 'the bonds of eternal peace'. Not only would free trade maintain peace for negative reasons (the fear of being deprived of vital goods), but it would also have positive benefits in ensuring that different peoples are united by shared values and a common commercial culture, and so would have a better understanding of one another. In short, aggression and expansionism are best deterred by the 'spirit of commerce'.

The stress on interdependence that is basic to commercial liberalism has been further developed by neoliberals into what Keohane and Nye (1977) called 'complex interdependence', viewed, initially at least, as an alternative theoretical model to realism. Complex interdependence reflects the extent to which peoples and governments in the modern world are affected by what happens elsewhere, and particularly by the actions of their counterparts in other countries. This applies not only in the economic realm, through the advance of globalization, but is also evident in relation to a range of other issues, including climate change, development and poverty reduction, and human rights (see p. 311). Such a view suggests that realism's narrow preoccupation with the military and diplomatic dimensions of international politics, the so-called '**high politics**' of security and survival, is misplaced. Instead, the international agenda is becoming broader with greater attention being given to the '**low politics**' of welfare, environmental protection and political justice. Relations between and amongst states have also changed, not least through a tendency for modern states to prioritize trade over war and through a trend towards closer cooperation or even integration, as, for instance, in the case of the European Union. Nevertheless, there has been disagreement amongst interdependence liberals about the significance of such trends. So-called 'strong' liberals believe that

● **Commercial liberalism**: A form of liberalism that emphasizes the economic and international benefits of free trade, leading to mutual benefit and general prosperity as well as peace amongst states.

● **Free trade**: a system of trade between states not restricted by tariffs or other forms of protectionism.

● **High politics**: Issue areas that are of primary importance, usually taken to refer to defence and foreign policy generally, and particularly to matters of state self-preservation.

● **Low politics**: Issue areas that are seen not to involve a state's vital national interests, whether in the foreign or the domestic sphere.

CONCEPT

Internationalism

Internationalism is the theory or practice of politics based on cooperation between states or nations. It is rooted in universalist assumptions about human nature that put it at odds with political nationalism, the latter emphasizing the degree to which political identity is shaped by nationality. However, internationalism is compatible with nationalism, in the sense that it calls for cooperation or solidarity *among* pre-existing nations, rather than for the removal or abandonment of national identities altogether. Internationalism thus differs from cosmopolitanism (see p. 21). Liberal internationalism is reflected in support for free trade and economic interdependence as well as a commitment to construct, or strengthen, international organizations.

● **Democratic peace thesis**: The notion that there is an intrinsic link between peace and democracy, in particular that democratic states do not go to war with one another.

qualitative changes have taken place in the international system which substantially modify the impact of anarchy, self-help and the security dilemma, creating an irresistible tendency towards peace, cooperation and integration (Burton 1972; Rosenau 1990). 'Weak' liberals, on the other hand, have come to accept neorealist assumptions, particularly about the implications of international anarchy, as the starting point for analysis, thereby highlighting the extent to which modern realist and liberal theory sometime overlap (Axelrod 1984; Stein 1990).

Republican liberalism

Like classical realism, the liberal perspective on international politics adopts an 'inside-out' approach to theorizing. Larger conclusions about international and global affairs are thus derived from assumptions about their basic elements. Although liberalism's stress on peace and international harmony contrasts sharply with the realist belief in power politics, the two perspectives are united in viewing states as essentially self-seeking actors. Each state therefore poses at least a potential threat to other states. However, unlike realists, liberals believe that the external behaviour of a state is crucially influenced by its political and constitutional make-up. This is reflected in a tradition of republican liberalism that can be traced back to Woodrow Wilson (see p. 445), if not to Kant. While autocratic or authoritarian states are seen to be inherently militaristic and aggressive, democratic states are viewed as naturally peaceful, especially in their dealings with other democratic states (Doyle 1986, 1995). The aggressive character of authoritarian regimes stems from the fact that they are immunized from popular pressure and typically have strong and politically powerful armies. As they are accustomed to the use of force to maintain themselves in power, force becomes the natural mechanism through which they deal with the wider world and resolve disputes with other states. Liberals, moreover, hold that authoritarian states are inherently unstable because they lack the institutional mechanisms for responding to popular pressure and balancing rival interests, and are so impelled towards foreign policy adventurism as a means of regime consolidation. If the support of the people cannot be ensured through participation and popular consent, 'patriotic' war may provide the only solution.

In this light, liberals have seen democracy as a guarantee of peace (see p. 69). The **democratic peace thesis** resurfaced with particular force in the aftermath of the collapse of communism, notably in the writings of Francis Fukuyama (see p. 539). In Fukuyama's view, the wider acceptance of liberal-democratic principles and structures, and the extension of market capitalism, amounted to the 'end of history' and also promised to create a more stable and peaceful global order. Liberals have claimed empirical as well as theoretical support for such beliefs, especially in the fact that there has never been a war between two democratic nation-states (even though wars have continued to take place between democracies and other states). They have also associated the general advance of democratization with the creation of 'zones of peace', composed of collections of mature democracies in places such as Europe, North America and Australasia, as opposed to the 'zones of turmoil' that are found elsewhere in the world (Singer and Wildavsky 1993). Nevertheless, republican liberalism has also been drawn into deep controversy, not least through the growth of so-called liberal interven-

Focus on . . .
Closing the realist–liberal divide?

Although realism and liberalism are commonly portrayed as antithetical theories of international politics – the one emphasizing egoism, power and conflict; the other, morality, peace and cooperation – the difference between them has tended to fade over time. One of the characteristic features of neoliberals is an acceptance of certain neorealist assumptions, making them, for instance, happier than 'traditional' liberals to explain state behaviour in terms of self-interest and to accept that the international system is essentially anarchical. Similarly, most modern realists are 'weak' or 'hedged' realists, in that they accept that international politics cannot be explained exclusively in terms of power, self-interest and conflict. The 'neo–neo debate' has therefore become an increasingly technical, rather than foundational, debate.

The idea that international politics is best explained in the light of both realist and liberal insights, recognizing the counter-balancing forces of conflict and cooperation, has been championed, since the 1960s, by theorists who subscribe to the notion of 'international society' (see p. 9), sometimes seen as the 'English School' of international relations. This view modifies the realist emphasis on power politics and international anarchy by suggesting the existence of a '*society* of states' rather than simply a '*system* of states', implying that international relations are rule-governed and that these rules help to maintain international order. The chief institutions that generate cultural cohesion and social integration are international law, diplomacy and the activities of international organizations. Hedley Bull ([1977] 2012) thus advanced the notion of an 'anarchical society', in place of the conventional realist idea of international anarchy. International society theory can be seen as a form of liberal realism.

tionism and the idea that democracy can and should be promoted through militarily imposed 'regime change'. This issue is examined in more detail in Chapter 9, in association with the 'war on terror'.

Liberal institutionalism

The chief 'external' mechanism that liberals believe is needed to constrain the ambitions of sovereign states is international organizations. This reflects the ideas of what is called liberal institutionalism. The basis for such a view lies in the 'domestic analogy', the idea that insight into international politics can be gained by reflecting on the structures of domestic politics. Taking particular account of social contract theory, as developed by thinkers such as Hobbes and John Locke (1632–1704), this highlights the fact that only the construction of a sovereign power can safeguard citizens from the chaos and barbarity of the 'state of nature'. If order can only be imposed 'from above' in domestic politics, the same must be true of international politics. This provided the basis for the establishment of the **rule of law**, which, as Woodrow Wilson put it, would turn the 'jungle' of international politics into a 'zoo'. The League of Nations was the first, if flawed, attempt to translate such thinking into practice. The United Nations (see p. 456) has attracted far wider support and established itself as a seemingly permanent feature of global politics. Liberals have looked to such bodies to establish a rule-governed international system that would be based on collective security (see p. 447) and respect for international law.

● **Rule of law**: The principle that law should 'rule', in the sense that it establishes a framework within which all conduct and behaviour takes place.

Debating ...
Is democracy a guarantee of peace?

The 'democratic peace' thesis, supported by most liberals, suggests that democracy and peace are linked, particularly in the sense that wars do not occur between democratic states. Realists and others nevertheless argue that there is nothing necessarily peaceful about democracy.

FOR

Zones of peace. Much interest in the idea of a 'democratic peace' derives from empirical analysis. As democracy has spread, 'zones of peace' have emerged, in which military conflict has become virtually unthinkable. This certainly applies to Europe (previously riven by war and conflict), North America and Australasia. History seems to suggest that wars do not break out between democratic states, although, as proponents of the democratic peace thesis accept, war continues to occur between democratic and authoritarian states.

Public opinion. Liberals argue that wars are caused by governments, not by the people. This is because it is citizens themselves who are likely to be war's victims: they are the ones who will do the killing and dying, and who will suffer disruption and hardship. In short, they have no 'stomach for war'. In the event of international conflict, democracies will thus seek accommodation rather than confrontation, and use force only as a last resort, and then only for purposes of self-defence.

Non-violent conflict resolution. The essence of democratic governance is a process of compromise, conciliation and negotiation, through which rival interests or groups find a way of living together rather than resorting to force and the use of naked power. This, after all, is the purpose of elections, parliaments, pressure groups and so on. Not only is it likely that regimes based on compromise and conciliation will apply such an approach to foreign policy as well as domestic policy, but governments unused to using force to resolve civil conflict will be less inclined to use force to resolve international conflicts.

Cultural bonds. Cultural ties develop amongst democracies because democratic rule tends to foster particular norms and values. These include a belief in constitutional government, respect for freedom of speech and guarantees for property ownership. The common moral foundations that underpin democratic government tend to mean that democracies view each other as friends rather than as foes. Peaceful coexistence amongst democracies therefore appears to be a 'natural' condition.

AGAINST

Democracies at war. The idea that democracies are inherently peaceful is undermined by continued evidence of wars between democratic and authoritarian states, something that most democratic peace theorists acknowledge. Moreover, empirical evidence to support the thesis is bedevilled by confusion over which regimes qualify as 'democracies'. If universal suffrage and multi-party elections are the core features of democratic governance, NATO's bombardment of Serb troops in Kosovo in 1999 and Russia's invasion of Georgia in 2008 are both exceptions to the democratic peace thesis. Moreover, the wars in Afghanistan and Iraq both demonstrate that democracies do not go to war only for purposes of simple self-defence.

States are states. Realist theorists argue the factors that make for war apply to democratic and authoritarian states alike. In particular, the constitutional structure of a state does not, and never can, alter the selfishness, greed and potential for violence that is simply part of human nature. Far from always opposing war, public opinion therefore sometimes impels democratic governments towards foreign policy adventurism and expansionism (European imperialism, WWI and perhaps the 'war on terror' each illustrate this). Realists, moreover, argue that the tendency towards war derives less from the constitutional make-up of the state and more from the fear and suspicion that are an unavoidable consequence of international anarchy.

Peace by other means. Although the division of the world into 'zones of peace' and 'zones of turmoil' may be an undeniable feature of modern world politics, it is far from clear that the difference is due only, or even chiefly, to democracy. For example, patterns of economic interdependence that result from free trade may be more effective in maintaining peace amongst democracies than popular pressures. Similarly, it may be more significant that mature liberal democracies are wealthy than that they are either liberal or democratic. In this view, war is an unattractive prospect for rich states because they have little impulse to gain through conquest and much to fear from the possibility of defeat.

Modern neoliberals have built on this positive approach to international organizations, practising what is usually called neoliberal institutionalism. Distancing themselves from the cosmopolitan dreams of some early liberals, they have instead explained growing cooperation and integration in functional terms, linked to self-interest. Institutions thus come into existence as mediators, to facilitate cooperation among states on matters of common interest. Whereas neorealists argue that such cooperation is always difficult and prone to break down because of the emphasis by states on 'relative' gains, neoliberals assert that states are more concerned with **absolute gains**. Instead of constantly engaging in one-upmanship, states are always willing to cooperate if they calculate that they will be better off in real terms as a result. Although neoliberals use such arguments to explain the origins and development of formal institutions, ranging from the World Trade Organization (WTO) (see p. 537) and the International Monetary Fund (IMF) (see p. 475) to regional economic blocs such as the European Union (see p. 509), they also draw attention to more informal institutions. In this, they embrace what has been called 'new' institutionalism, which defines institutions not so much as established and formal bodies, but, more broadly, as sets of norms, rules and 'standard operating procedures' that are internalized by those who work within them. This explains the stress within neoliberal theory on the role of international regimes.

Assessing liberalism

Interest in liberal theory revived from the 1970s onwards through the emergence of a series of trends in global politics that appeared to correspond closely with liberal thinking. The advance of globalization generated renewed interest in interdependence liberalism, particularly as liberal political economy was widely used to cast globalization in a positive light, associating it with economic dynamism and the prospect of worldwide prosperity. The wave of democratization that commenced in the late 1980s with the fall of communism stimulated a resurgence of republican liberalism, reviving debates that had originated in the aftermath of WWI about the link between democracy and peace. And the growing prominence of international organizations helped to establish neoliberal institutionalism as a major rival to neorealism, seemingly bearing out the possibility of 'cooperation under anarchy'. However, if there had been a 'liberal moment' in world affairs, it may not have extended far beyond the 1990s, as other trends emerged that seemed to defy liberal analysis. This, for instance, applied in the case of the growth of political Islam and the wider tendency towards religious revivalism. These developments clearly ran counter to the liberal belief that modernization and secularization march hand in hand, as religious belief is either weakened by the advance of rationalism, or is increasingly confined to the private sphere.

Further challenges to liberal theory have arisen due to its multifarious and complex character. Although the breadth of liberalism is commonly viewed as a strength, particularly by comparison with realism's narrow focus on issues of power, security and survival, it may bring the overall coherence of liberal theory into question. This occurs, in part, because liberalism's three main sub-traditions do not necessarily support one another, and may even be contradictory (Griffiths 2011). Thus, support for free trade and the integration of national

● **Absolute gains**: Benefits that accrue to states from a policy or action regardless of their impact on other states (see p. 443).

CONCEPT

International regime

A regime is a set of principles, procedures, norms or rules that govern the interactions of states and non-state actors in particular issue areas within international politics. As such, they are social institutions with either a formal or informal character. Examples of regimes include treaties, conventions, international agreements and international organizations. These now operate in a wide variety of issue areas, including economics, human rights, the environment, transport, security, policing, communications and so on. The greater significance of regimes reflects the growth of interdependence and the recognition that cooperation and coordination can bring absolute gains to all parties.

economies into a single, global economy (in line with interdependence liberalism) may, by allowing global markets and transnational corporations (see p. 94) to dictate to national governments, undermine the quality of domestic democracy (a core concern of republican liberalism). Other sources of tension within liberalism can also be identified. For example, the advance of globalization highlights divisions within liberal political economy between those who placed their faith in the untrammelled workings of global markets, and those who argue that global capitalism needs to be protected from itself through a framework of regulation. In the same way, the growth of international organizations exposes tensions within liberalism between its internationalist and its cosmopolitan tendencies. While liberal internationalists seek to use international organizations as a mechanism through which sovereign nation-states can cooperate, liberal cosmopolitans advocate supranational governance and may insist that the norm of state sovereignty is subordinated to the norm of human rights.

CRITICAL APPROACHES

Mainstream perspectives on international politics and world affairs have been challenged by a growing array of critical perspectives, many of which have only gained prominence since the late 1980s. Although these perspectives are often very different from one another, they tend to have two broad things in common. The first is that, with the exception of orthodox Marxism and most forms of green politics, they have, in their different ways, embraced a **post-positivist** approach that takes subject and object, and therefore theory and practice, to be intimately linked. (These issues are discussed more fully in Chapter 21). The second similarity is related to the first, and this is that critical perspectives seek to challenge the global status quo and the norms, values and assumptions on which it is based. In exposing inequalities and asymmetries that mainstream theories ignore, critical theorists therefore tend to view realism and liberalism as ways of concealing, or of legitimizing, the power imbalances of the established global system. Critical theories are thus emancipatory theories: they are dedicated to overthrowing oppression and thus consciously align themselves with the interests of exploited groups. Being politically engaged, it is sometimes difficult to reconcile critical theories with the tradition of dispassionate scholarship, although critical theorists would argue that this highlights the limitations of the latter rather than of the former. The key critical perspectives on global politics are as follows:

- Marxism, neo-Marxism and critical theory
- Constructivism
- Poststructuralism
- Feminism
- Green politics
- Postcolonialism.

Marxism, neo-Marxism and critical theory

Marxism has traditionally been viewed as the principal critical or radical alternative to mainstream realist and liberal thinking, although its impact on

● **Post-positivism**: An approach to knowledge that questions the idea of an 'objective' reality, emphasizing instead the extent to which people conceive, or 'construct'; the world in which they live.

Karl Marx (1818–83)

German philosopher, economist and political thinker, usually portrayed as the father of twentieth-century communism. After a brief career as a university teacher, Marx became increasingly involved in the socialist movement. Finally settling in London, he worked for the rest of his life as an active revolutionary and writer, supported by his friend and lifelong collaborator, Friedrich Engels (1820–95). At the centre of Marx's work was a critique of capitalism that highlights its transitory nature by drawing attention to systemic inequality and instability. Marx subscribed to a teleological theory of history that holds that social development would inevitably culminate in the establishment of communism. His classic work was the three-volume *Capital* ([1885, 1887, 1894] 1969); his best-known and most accessible work, with Engels, is the *Communist Manifesto* ([1848] 1976).

academic theorizing was always limited. However, Marxism is a very broad field, which encompasses, as far as international theory is concerned, two contrasting tendencies. The first of these gives primary attention to economic analysis, and is mainly concerned with exposing capitalism as a system of class oppression that operates on national and international levels. This applies to classical Marxism and to most forms of **neo-Marxism**. The second tendency places greater emphasis on the ideological and cultural dimension of oppression, and has come to embrace a post-positivist, and therefore post-Marxist, mode of theorizing. This applies to what has been called 'critical theory', as influenced by the ideas of Gramsci (see p. 73) and the so-called Frankfurt School.

From classical Marxism to neo-Marxism

The core of Marxism is a philosophy of history that outlines why capitalism is doomed and why socialism and eventually communism are destined to replace it. This philosophy is based on the 'materialist conception of history', the belief that economic factors are the ultimately determining force in human history. In Marx's view, history is driven forward through a dialectical process in which internal contradictions within each 'mode of production', reflected in class conflict, lead to social revolution and the construction of a new and higher mode of production. This process was characterized by a series of historical stages (slavery, feudalism, capitalism and so on) and would only end with the establishment of a classless communist society. For Marx, capitalist development nevertheless always had a marked transnational character, leading some to regard him as an early 'hyperglobalist' theorist. The desire for profit would drive capitalism to 'strive to tear down every barrier to intercourse' and to 'conquer the whole earth for its market' (Marx [1848] 1976). However, the implications of viewing capitalism as an international system were not fully explored until V. I. Lenin's *Imperialism: The Highest Stage of Capitalism* ([1916] 1970). Lenin portrayed imperialism as an essentially economic phenomenon, reflecting domestic capitalism's quest to maintain profit levels through the export of surplus capital. This, in turn, would bring major capitalist powers into conflict with one another, the resulting war (WWI) being essentially an imperialist war in the sense that it

● **Neo-Marxism**: An updated and revived form of Marxism that rejects determinism, the primacy of economics and the privileged status of the proletariat.

Antonio Gramsci (1891–1937)

Italian Marxist and social theorist. The son of a minor public official, Gramsci joined the Socialist Party in 1913, but switched to the newly-formed Italian Communist Party in 1921, being recognized as its leader by 1924. He was imprisoned by Mussolini in 1926, and remained incarcerated until his death. In *Prison Notebooks* (1970), written between 1929 and 1935, Gramsci sought to redress the emphasis within orthodox Marxism on economic or material factors. Rejecting any form of 'scientific' determinism, he stressed, through the theory of hegemony, the importance of political and intellectual struggle. Gramsci insisted that bourgeois hegemony could only be challenged at the political and intellectual level, through a 'counter-hegemonic' struggle, carried out in the interests of the proletariat and on the basis of socialist principles, values and theories.

was fought for the control of colonies in Africa, Asia and elsewhere. Such thinking was further developed by later Marxists, who focused on the '**uneven development**' of global capitalism.

Interest in Marxism was revived during the 1970s through the use of neo-Marxist theories to explain patterns of global poverty and inequality. **Dependency theory**, for example, highlighted the extent to which, in the post-1945 period, traditional imperialism had given way to neo-colonialism, sometimes viewed as 'economic imperialism' or, more specifically, 'dollar imperialism'. World-systems theory (see p. 374) suggested that the world economy is best understood as an interlocking capitalist system which exemplifies, at international level, many of the features that characterize national capitalism; that is, structural inequalities based on exploitation and a tendency towards instability and crisis that is rooted in economic contradictions. The world-system consists of interrelationships between the 'core', the 'periphery' and the 'semi-periphery'. Core areas such as the developed North are distinguished by the concentration of capital, high wages and high-skilled manufacturing production They therefore benefit from technological innovation and high and sustained levels of investment. Peripheral areas such as the less-developed South are exploited by the core through their dependency on the export of raw materials, subsistence wages and weak frameworks of state protection. Semi-peripheral areas are economically subordinate to the core but in turn take advantage of the periphery, thereby constituting a buffer between the core and the periphery. Such thinking about the inherent inequalities and injustices of global capitalism was one of the influences on the anti-globalization, or 'anti-capitalist', movement that emerged from the late 1990s onwards (see p. 74).

Critical theory

'Critical theory' (often called 'Frankfurt School critical theory', to distinguish it from the wider category of critical theories or perspectives) has developed into one of the most influential currents of Marxist-inspired international theory A major influence on critical theory has been the ideas of Antonio Gramsci. Gramsci (1970) argued that the capitalist class system is upheld not simply by

● **Uneven development**: The tendency within a capitalist economy for industries, economic sectors and countries to develop at very different rates due to the pressures generated by economic exploitation.

● **Dependency theory**: A neo-Marxist theory that highlights structural imbalances within international capitalism that impose dependency and underdevelopment on poorer states and regions.

GLOBAL ACTORS...

THE ANTI-CAPITALIST MOVEMENT

Type: Social movement

There is general agreement that the birth of the anti-capitalist movement (also known as the 'anti-globalization', 'anti-corporate', 'anti-neoliberal', 'global justice', 'alter-globalization' movement) can be traced back to the so-called 'Battle of Seattle' in November 1999, when some 50,000 activists forced the cancellation of the opening ceremony of a World Trade Organization meeting. This 'coming-out party' for the anti-capitalist movement provided a model for the 'new politics' of activist-based theatrical politics that has accompanied most subsequent international summits and global conferences. In some respects, the anti-capitalist movement exists on two levels. One level is strongly activist-orientated, and consists of a loosely-knit, non-hierarchically organized international coalition of (usually young) people and social movements, articulating the concerns of environmental groups, trade unions, religious groups, student groups, anarchists, revolutionary socialists, campaigners for the rights of indigenous people, and so on. On the other level, the anti-capitalist movement is expert-orientated, focused on a number of leading authors and key works, and involving, through their influence, a much wider range of people, many of whom are not directly involved in activism but sympathize generally with the movement's goals. Leading figures (but by no means 'leaders') include Noam Chomsky (see p. 235), Naomi Klein (see p. 150) and Noreena Hertz (2002).

Significance: It is very difficult to make judgements about the impact of social movements because of their typically broad, and sometimes nebulous, cultural goals. It would be absurd, for example, to write off the anti-capitalist movement as a failure, simply because of the survival, worldwide, of the capitalist system. Proponents of the anti-capitalist movement argue that it is the nearest thing to a counter-hegemonic force in modern global politics, its role being to expose and contest the discourses and practices of neoliberal globalization. It is rightfully described as a 'movement of movements', in that the inequalities and asymmetries generated by 'corporate' globalization are multiple. The anti-capitalist movement therefore provides a vehicle through which the disparate range of peoples or groups who have been marginalized or disenfranchised as a result of globalization can gain a political voice. In that sense, the movement is a democratic force, an uprising of the oppressed and seemingly powerless. The anti-globalization movement may be credited with having altered thinking on a wide range of transnational issues, even with having reshaped global political agendas. This can be seen in a heightened awareness of, for example, environmental issues, and especially global warming, the failings of market-based development and poverty-reduction strategies, and so forth. UN conferences and bodies such as the WTO, the World Bank and the IMF now operate within a political and intellectual climate that is different from the 1980s and 1990s, and the anti-capitalist movement has contributed significantly to this.

Criticisms of the anti-capitalist movement have sometimes been damning, however. Most seriously, it has been condemned for its failure to develop a systematic and coherent critique of neoliberal globalization or failure to outline a viable alternative. This reflects both the highly diverse nature of the anti-capitalist movement and the fact that its goals are not commonly incompatible. While a minority of its supporters are genuinely 'anti-capitalist', adopting a Marxist-style analysis of capitalism that highlights its inherent flaws, most groups and supporters wish merely to remove the 'worst excesses' of capitalism. Similarly, the anti-capitalist movement is divided over globalization itself. While some, such as nationalists, cultural activists and campaigners for the rights of indigenous people, object to globalization in principle, a large proportion of the movement's supporters wish only to break the link between globalization and neoliberalism (see p. 93), attempting to establish a form of alternative globalization, or 'alter-globalization'. Another serious division within the anti-capitalist movement is between those who link global justice to strengthened regulation at a national and global level, and anarchist elements who distrust government and governance (see p. 130) in all its forms.

CONCEPT

Constructivism

Constructivism is an approach to social and political analysis whose key assumption is that beliefs, norms and values play a crucial role in the construction of reality. The social and political world is therefore not a 'given' but an inherently inter-subjective domain. This implies that normative or ideational structures are at least as important as material structures in shaping world affairs, particularly as they affect actors' identities and, thus, their interests and actions. However, constructivist analysis can be *systemic* (focusing on the interaction of states in the international system), *unit-level* (focusing on how domestic social and legal norms shape the identities and interests of states) or *holistic* (focusing on the entire range of factors conditioning the identities and interests of states).

● **Hegemony**: The ascendancy or domination of one element of a system over others; for Marxists, hegemony implies ideological domination (see p. 228).

● **Theoretical reflexivity**: An awareness of the impact of the values and presuppositions that a theorist brings to analysis, as well as an understanding of the historical dynamics that have helped to fashion them.

unequal economic and political power, but by what he termed the '**hegemony**' of bourgeois ideas and theories. Hegemony means leadership or domination and, in the sense of ideological hegemony, it refers to the capacity of bourgeois ideas to displace rival views and become, in effect, the 'common sense' of the age. Gramsci's ideas have influenced modern thinking about the nature of world or global hegemony. Instead of viewing hegemony in conventional terms, as the domination of one military power over another, modern neo-Gramscians have emphasized the extent to which hegemony operates through a mixture of coercion and consent, highlighting the interplay between economic, political, military and ideological forces, as well as interaction between states and international organizations. Robert Cox (see p. 124) thus analyzed the hegemonic power of the USA not only in terms of its military ascendancy, but also in terms of its ability to generate broad consent for the 'world order' that it represents.

The other key influence on critical theory has been the thinking of the Frankfurt School, a group of Marxist-influenced theorists who worked at the Institute of Social Research, which was established in Frankfurt in 1923, relocated to the USA in the 1930s, and was re-established in Frankfurt in the early 1950s (the Institute was dissolved in 1969). The defining theme of critical theory is the attempt to extend the notion of critique to all social practices by linking substantive social research to philosophy. Leading 'first generation' Frankfurt thinkers included Theodor Adorno (1903–69), Max Horkheimer (1895–1973) and Herbert Marcuse (1898–1979); the leading exponent of the 'second generation' of the Frankfurt School was Jürgen Habermas. While early Frankfurt thinkers were primarily concerned with the analysis of discrete societies, later theorists, such as Cox (1981, 1987) and Andrew Linklater (1990, 1998), have applied critical theory to the study of international politics, in at least three ways. In the first place, critical theory underlines the linkage between knowledge and politics, emphasizing the extent to which theories and understandings are embedded in a framework of values and interests. This implies that, as all theorizing is normative, those who seek to understand the world should adopt greater **theoretical reflexivity**. Second, critical theorists have adopted an explicit commitment to emancipatory politics: they are concerned to uncover structures of oppression and injustice in global politics in order to advance the cause of individual or collective freedom. Third, critical theorists have questioned the conventional association within international theory between political community and the state, in so doing opening up the possibility of a more inclusive, and maybe even cosmopolitan, notion of political identity.

Constructivism

Constructivism (sometimes called 'social constructivism') has been the most influential post-positivist approach to international theory, gaining significantly greater attention since the end of the Cold War. The constructivist approach to analysis is based on the belief that there is no objective social or political reality independent of our understanding of it. Constructivists do not therefore regard the social world as something 'out there', in the sense of an external world of concrete objects; instead, it exists only 'inside', as a kind of inter-subjective awareness. In the final analysis, people, whether acting as individuals or as social groups, 'construct' the world in which they live and act according to those

Focus on . . .
Structure or agency?

Is global politics best explained in terms of 'structures' (the context within which action takes place) or in terms of 'agency' (the ability of human actors to influence events)? A variety of approaches to global politics have a structuralist character; that is, they adopt what can be called an 'outside-in' approach to understanding. The nature of these contexts varies, however. Neorealists (sometimes called 'structural realists') explain the behaviour of states in terms of the structure of the international system, while Marxists emphasize the crucial impact of international capitalism, sometimes seen as a 'world-system' by neo-Marxist theorists. Even liberals recognize the limitations imposed on individual states by the complex web of economic interdependence into which they have been drawn, particularly by the forces of globalization. One of the attractions of structuralism is that, by explaining human behaviour in terms of external, or exogenous, factors, it dispenses with the vagaries of human volition and decision-making, allowing theories to claim scientific precision. Its disadvantage, though, is that it leads to determinism, which rules out free will altogether.

Alternative theories that stress agency over structure subscribe to intentionalism or voluntarism, which assigns decisive explanatory importance to the self-willed behaviour of human actors. These theories have an 'inside-out' character: they explain behaviour in terms of the intentions or inclinations of key actors. These theories are therefore endogenous. Examples include 'classical' realism, which holds that the key to understanding international relations is to recognize that states are the primary actors on the world stage and that each state is bent on the pursuit of self-interest. Liberals are also inclined towards 'inside-out' theorizing, in that they stress the extent to which states' foreign policy orientation is affected by their constitutional make-up (and particularly whether they are democratic or authoritarian). Although intentionalism has the advantage that it reintroduces choice and the role of the human actor, its disadvantage is that it is 'reductionist': it reduces social explanation to certain core facts about major actors, and so understates the structural factors that shape human action. In the light of the drawbacks of both structuralism and intentionalism, critical theorists in particular have tried to go beyond the 'structure versus agency' debate, in acknowledging that, as no neat or clear distinction can be drawn between conduct and the context within which it takes place, structure and agency both influence each other (Hay 2002).

constructions. People's beliefs and assumptions become particularly significant when they are widely shared, especially when they serve to give a community or people a sense of identity and distinctive interests. As such, constructivist analysis highlights the missing dimension in the 'structure–agent' debate in global politics. Constructivism stands, in a sense, between 'inside-out' and 'outside-in' approaches, in that it holds that interactions between agents and structures are always *mediated* by 'ideational factors' (beliefs, values, theories and assumptions). These ideational factors affect both how agents see themselves and how they understand, and respond to, the structures within which they operate. However, this implies that constructivism is not so much a substantive theory, or set of substantive theories, as an analytical tool, an approach to understanding.

One of the most influential formulations of constructivism was Alexander Wendt's (see p. 77) assertion that 'anarchy is what states make of it'. This implies that state behaviour is not determined, as neorealists assert, by the structure of the international system, but by how particular states view anarchy. While some states may view anarchy as dangerous and threatening, others may see it as the

Alexander Wendt (born 1958)

German-born international relations theorist who has worked mainly in the USA. Wendt is a meta-theorist who has used constructivist analysis to provide a critique of both neorealism and neoliberalism. He accepts that states are the primary units of analysis for international political theory, but urges that states and their interests should not be taken for granted. The key structures of the state-system are 'inter-subjective' rather than material, in that states act on the basis of identities and interests that are socially constructed. Wendt therefore argues that neorealism and neoliberalism are defective because both fail to take account of the self-understandings of state actors. Wendt's key writings include 'The Agent-Structure Problem in International Relations Theory' (1987), 'Anarchy is What States Make of It' (1992) and *Social Theory of International Politics* (1999).

basis for freedom and opportunity. An 'anarchy of friends' is thus very different from an 'anarchy of enemies'. What is at stake here is not the objective circumstances that confront a state so much as a state's self-identity and how it views its fellow states. This can also be seen in relation to nations and nationalism. Nations are not objective entities, groups of people who happen to share a common cultural heritage; rather, they are subjective entities, defined by their members, through a particular set of traditions, values and sentiments. Constructivist analysis highlights the fluidity of world politics: as nation-states (see p. 168) and other key global actors change their perception of who or what they are, their behaviour will change. This stance may have optimistic or pessimistic implications. On the one hand, it leaves open the possibility that states may transcend a narrow perception of self-interest and embrace the cause of global justice, even cosmopolitanism. On the other hand, it highlights the possibility that states and other international actors may fall prey to expansionist and aggressive political creeds. However, critics of constructivism have argued that it fails to recognize the extent to which beliefs are shaped by social, economic and political realities. Ultimately, ideas do not 'fall from the sky' like rain. They are a product of complex social realities, and reflect an ongoing relationship between ideas and the material world.

Poststructuralism

Poststructuralism emerged alongside postmodernism (see p. 525), the two terms sometimes being used interchangeably. Poststructuralism emphasizes that all ideas and concepts are expressed in language which itself is enmeshed in complex relations of power. Influenced particularly by the writings of Michel Foucault (see p. 17), poststructuralists have drawn attention to the link between power and systems of thought using the idea of **discourse**, or 'discourses of power'. In crude terms, this implies that knowledge is power. However, in the absence of a universal frame of reference or overarching perspective, there exist only a series of competing perspectives, each of which represents a particular discourse of power. Such a view has sometimes been associated with Jacques Derrida's ([1967] 1976) famous formulation: 'There is nothing outside the text'.

● **Discourse**: Human interaction, especially communication; discourse may disclose or illustrate power relations.

J. Ann Tickner (born 1937)

A US academic and feminist international relations theorist. An exponent of stand-point feminism, Tickner has exposed ways in which the conventional study of international relations marginalizes gender, whilst also being itself gendered. Her best known book, *Gender in International Relations* (1992a), highlights the biases and limitations of the masculinized, geo-political version of national security, demonstrating that it may enhance rather than reduce the insecurity of individuals and showing how peace, economic justice and ecological sustainability are vital to women's security. Although she argues that gender relations shape the search for knowledge, Tickner's ultimate goal is to transcend gender by overcoming gender inequality. Her other works include *Hans Morgenthau's Principles of Political Realism: A Feminist Reformulation* (1988) and *Feminist Perspectives on 9/11* (2002).

Poststructural or postmodern thinking has exerted growing influence on international relations theory, especially since the publication of Der Derian and Shapiro's *International/Intertextual* (1989). Poststructuralism draws attention to the fact that any political event will always be susceptible to competing interpretations: 9/11 is an example of this. Not only is there, for poststructuralists, irreducible debate about whether 9/11 is best conceived as an act of terrorism, a criminal act, an act of evil, or an act of (possibly justified) revenge, but there is also uncertainty about the nature of the 'act' itself – was it the attacks themselves, the process of planning, the formation of al-Qaeda, the onset of US neo-colonialism, or whatever? In such circumstances, the classic poststructuralist approach to exposing hidden meanings in particular concepts, theories and interpretations is **deconstruction**. Critics, however, accuse postmodernism/poststructuralism of relativism, in that they hold that different modes of knowing are equally valid and thus reject the idea that even science can distinguish between truth and falsehood.

Feminism

Feminist theories have influenced the study of global politics in a number of ways (True 2009). 'Empirical' feminists have challenged the 'sexist' exclusion of women and women's issues from conventional analysis. From this point of view, conventional approaches to international politics focus almost exclusively on male-dominated bodies and institutions – governments and states, transnational corporations (TNCs) and nongovernmental organizations (NGOs) (see p. 10), international organizations and so on. The role of women, as, for instance, diplomats' wives, domestic workers, sex workers and suchlike, is therefore ignored, as are the often international and even global processes through which women are subordinated and exploited. 'Analytical' feminists, such as J. Ann Tickner, have exposed the extent to which the theoretical framework of global politics is based on **gender** biases that pervade its key theories and concepts, drawing at times on the ideas of constructivism and poststructuralism. The dominant realist paradigm of 'power politics' has been a particular object of criticism. Feminists have argued that the theory of power politics is premised on 'masculinist'

● **Deconstruction**: A close reading of philosophical or other texts with an eye to their various blindspots and/or contradictions.

● **Gender**: A social and cultural distinction between males and females, usually based on stereotypes of 'masculinity' and 'femininity' (see p. 423).

James Lovelock (born 1919)

UK atmospheric chemist, inventor and environmental thinker. Lovelock was recruited by NASA as part of its team devising strategies for identifying life on Mars, but he has subsequently worked as an independent scientist for over forty years. He adopts a holistic approach to science which rejects disciplinary distinctions and emphasizes instead interconnectedness. Lovelock is best known for the 'Gaia hypothesis', which proposes that the earth is best understood as a complex, self-regulating, living 'being'. This implies that the prospects for humankind are closely linked to whether the species helps to sustain, or to threaten, the planetary ecosystem. Lovelock was also the first person to alert the world to the worldwide presence of CFCs in the atmosphere. His chief works include *Gaia* (1979) and *The Ages of Gaia* (1989).

assumptions about rivalry, competition and inevitable conflict, arising from a tendency to see the world in terms of interactions amongst series of power-seeking autonomous actors. Analytical feminism is concerned not only to expose such biases, but also to champion alternative concepts and theories; for example, ones linking power not to conflict but to collaboration. Feminist theories and the implications of gender-based analysis are examined in greater detail in Chapter 17.

Green politics

Green politics, or ecologism, has had an impact on international theory since issues such as 'limits to growth' and the 'population time bomb' came on the political agenda in the 1970s. However, interest in it has increased substantially since the 1990s as a result of growing concern about climate change, often viewed as the archetypal global issue. The central theme of green politics is the notion of an intrinsic link between humankind and nature, sometimes linked to the 'Gaia hypothesis' (see p. 399) developed by James Lovelock. Green politics nevertheless encompasses a wide range of theoretical positions, with quite different implications for international affairs and global politics. Mainstream or reformist green thinking attempts to develop a balance between modernization and economic growth, on the one hand, and the need to tackle environmental degradation, on the other. Its key theme is the notion of 'sustainable development' (see p. 397), which, by linking environmental to economic goals, has exerted considerable influence on development theory, particularly in the global South.

Radical green theorists nevertheless go further. Some, for instance, argue that the balance between humankind and nature will only be restored by radical social change. For 'eco-socialists', the source of the environmental crisis is the capitalist economic system, which 'commodifies' nature and draws it into the system of market exchange. 'Eco-anarchists' advance an environmental critique of hierarchy and authority, arguing that domination over other people is linked to domination over nature. 'Eco-feminists' advance an environmental critique of male power, suggesting that domination over women leads to domination over nature. '**Deep ecologists**', for their part, argue that only 'paradigm change' – the

● **Deep ecology**: A green ideological perspective that rejects anthropocentrism and gives priority to the maintenance of nature; it is associated with values such as bio-equality, diversity and decentralization.

adoption of a radically new philosophical and moral perspective, based on radical **holism** rather than conventional mechanistic and atomistic thinking – will bring an end to environmental degradation. This, in effect, treats nature as an integrated whole, within which every species has an equal right to 'live and bloom' (Naess 1989). The nature and implications of green politics are discussed more fully in Chapter 16.

Postcolonialism

The final critical perspective on global politics is postcolonialism (see p. 200). Theorists of postcolonialism have tried to expose the cultural dimension of colonial rule, usually by establishing the legitimacy of non-western and some-times anti-western ideas, cultures and traditions. In one of the most influential works of postcolonial theory, Edward Said (see p. 204) developed the notion of 'orientalism' to highlight the extent to which western cultural and political hegemony over the rest of the world, but over the Orient in particular, had been maintained through elaborate stereotypical fictions that belittled and demeaned non-western people and culture. Examples of such stereotypes include images such as the 'mysterious East', 'inscrutable Chinese' and 'lustful Turks'. The cultural biases generated by colonialism do not only affect, and subjugate, former colonized people, however. They also have a continuing impact on western states, which assume the mantle of the 'international community' in claiming the authority to 'sort out' less favoured parts of the world. In this view, humanitarian intervention (see p. 326) can be seen as an example of **Eurocentrism**. Forcible intervention on allegedly humanitarian grounds and, for that matter, other forms of interference in the developing world, such as international aid, can therefore be viewed as a continuation of colonialism by other means. The ideas and theories of postcolonialism are discussed in greater depth in Chapter 8.

THINKING GLOBALLY

The acceleration of globalization from the 1980s onwards not only contributed to a reconfiguration of world politics, it also brought with it a series of new theoret-ical challenges. Not the least of these was the problem of conceptualizing the emerging condition of global interconnectedness, in which politics is increasingly enmeshed in a web of interdependences that operate both within, and across, worldwide, regional, national and subnational levels. How is it possible, in other words, to 'think globally'? And what are the implications of global thinking? Two challenges have emerged in particular. The first concerns the difficulties that global interconnectedness poses to empirical understanding: how can we make sense of a world in which everything affects everything else? The second concerns the normative implications of global interconnectedness: have wider social connections between people expanded the moral universe in which we live?

Challenge of interconnectedness

To what extent can established theories, both mainstream and critical, engage in global thinking? In many ways, this is indicated by the degree to which they are

● **Holism**: The belief that the whole is more than a collection of parts; holism implies that understanding is gained by recognizing the relationships amongst the parts.

● **Eurocentrism**: The application of values and theories drawn from European culture to other groups and peoples, implying a biased or distorted viewpoint.

Debating...
Do moral obligations extend to the whole of humanity?

At the heart of the idea of global justice is the notion of universal rights and obligations stretching across the globe, establishing 'justice beyond borders'. But what is the basis for such thinking, and how persuasive is it?

YES

Humans as moral creatures. The core feature of cosmopolitan ethics is the idea that the individual, rather than any particular political community, is the principal source of moral value. Most commonly, this is asserted through the doctrine of human rights, the notion that people are entitled to at least the minimal conditions for leading a worthwhile existence. These rights are fundamental and universal, in that they belong to people by virtue of their humanity and cannot be denied on grounds of nationality, religion, cultural identity or whatever. The doctrine of human rights therefore implies that there is but a single ethical community, and that is humankind. People everywhere are part of the same moral universe.

The globalization of moral sensibilities. The narrowing of moral sensibilities just to people within our own society is unsustainable in a world of increasing interconnectedness. Transborder information and communication flows, particularly the impact of television, mean that the 'strangeness' and unfamiliarity of people and societies on the other side of the globe has reduced substantially. News reports and especially pictures of, for instance, the 2004 Indian Ocean tsunami provoked massive outpourings of humanitarian concern in other parts of the world, helping to fund major programmes of emergency relief. Globalization therefore has an important, and irresistible, moral dimension.

Global citizenship. Moral obligations to people in other parts of the world stem, in important respects, from the fact that we affect their lives. We live in a world of global cause and effect. Purchasing decisions in one part of the world thus affect job opportunities, working conditions and poverty levels in other parts of the world. Whether we like it or not, we are morally culpable, in that our actions have moral implications for others. Such thinking draws on the utilitarian belief that we should act so as to achieve the greatest possible pleasure over pain in the world at large, each person's happiness or suffering counting equally. A basic moral principle for 'citizens of the world' would therefore be: do no harm.

NO

Morality begins at home. Communitarian theorists argue that morality only makes sense when it is locally-based, grounded in the communities to which we belong and which have shaped our lives and values. The simple fact is that people everywhere give moral priority to those they know best, most obviously their family and close friends and, beyond that, members of their local community and then those with whom they share a national or cultural identity. Not only is morality fashioned by the distinctive history, culture and traditions of a particular society, but it is difficult to see how our obligations can extend beyond those who share a similar ethical framework.

The agency problem. The idea of universal rights only makes sense if it is possible to identify who is obliged to do what in relation to the rights-bearers. If moral obligations fall on individual human beings, there is little that they, as individuals, could do in the event of, say, a natural disaster or a civil war. If our obligations are discharged through states and national governments, there is the problem that states have different capabilities. Citizens' and states' obligations may therefore become little more than a reflection of the wealth and power of their society. If universal obligations only make sense in a context of world government (see p. 464), in which global justice is upheld by supranational bodies, this creates the prospect of global despotism.

The virtues of self-help. Doctrines of universal rights and obligations are invariably used to argue that rich and successful parts of the world should, in some way, help poor and less fortunate parts of the world. However, such interference is often counter-productive: it promotes dependency and undermines self-reliance. Perhaps the main obligation we owe other peoples and other societies is to leave them alone. This may result in short-term moral costs but longer-term ethical benefits, in the form of societies better able to protect their citizens from suffering and hardship. State sovereignty may therefore make good moral sense as well as good political sense.

able to address the issue of globalization. The picture here is mixed. As far as realism is concerned, its core focus on unit-level analysis, taking the state to be the primary actor on the world stage, puts it starkly at odds with most of the claims made about globalization, especially the idea of an interlocking global economy. Thus, insofar as realists have addressed the issue of globalization, it is to deny that it is anything new or different: globalization is 'more of the same', a game played by states for states. The much vaunted 'interdependent world' is thus largely a myth, from a realist perspective. Liberals and neo-Marxists, on the other hand, have both been able, if not eager, to incorporate the phenomenon of globalization into their thinking. For liberals, the advent of globalization fitted in well to long-established ideas about economic interdependence and the virtues of free trade. Much 'hyperglobalist' theorizing, indeed, is based on liberal assumptions, especially about the tendency of the market to achieve long-term equilibrium, bringing with it both general prosperity and widening freedom. Adam Smith's (see p. 88) image of the 'invisible hand' of market competition can therefore be seen to provide the basis for a market-based, and unashamedly positive, model of global interconnectedness. Marxist and neo-Marxist theorists, similarly, found no difficulty in addressing the issue of globalization; Marx, after all, may have been the first economic thinker to have drawn attention to the transnational, and not merely international, character of capitalism. For neo-Marxists, economic globalization was really only a manifestation of the emergence of a capitalist world-system, or global capitalism. However, this image of globalization was clearly negative, characterized by growing divisions between 'core' areas and 'peripheral' areas. Thus, as debate emerged from the 1990s onwards over the benefits and burdens of growing global interconnectedness, these debates wore an essentially familiar face. Pro-globalization arguments drew largely from the pool of liberal ideas, while anti-globalization arguments were based significantly, though by no means exclusively, on neo-Marxist or quasi-Marxist thinking.

However, some argue that the challenges of global interconnectedness defy all established theories, and, in effect, require the development of an entirely new way of thinking. This is because the rise of complex forms of interconnectedness make it difficult, and perhaps impossible, to think any longer in conventional terms of 'cause' and 'effect'. In an interdependent world, the relationships between two or more factors, processes or variables are characterized by reciprocal causation, or mutual conditioning. Thus, if A, B and C are interdependent, then any change in B will result in a change in A and C; any change in A will result in a change in B and C; and any change in C will result in a change in A and B (Hay 2010). However, complexity does not stop there. The fact that any change in A changes not just B and C but also A itself, means that it becomes difficult to think in terms of 'A-ness', 'B-ness' or, indeed, in terms of 'thing-ness' in any sense. One of the first theorists to apply 'complexity science' to the study of politics and international affairs was James Rosenau (see p. 83). Taking account of the dynamics and consequences of globalization, but also moving beyond a globalization paradigm, Rosenau highlighted the emergence of an ever-shrinking world of uncertainty, change and complexity, which can best be understood as an endless series of '**distant proximities**'.

Complex interconnectedness arguably challenges the very basis of reasoning in the western tradition, which dates back to Aristotle's assertion that 'everything

● **Distant proximity**: A phenomenon, rooted in complexity, in which what seems to be remote also seems to be close-at-hand.

James Rosenau (1924–2011)

A US political scientist and international affairs scholar. A pioneer in the analysis of foreign policy decision-making, Rosenau came to focus on the dynamics and consequences of globalization, and on the wider phenomenon of increased complexity and uncertainty. In *Turbulence in World Politics* (1990), he investigated the new forces shaping world politics beyond the nation-state, including the rising importance of NGOs and the empowerment of individuals as actors in world politics. *Along the Domestic-Foreign Frontier* (1997) and *Distant Proximities* (2003) took this analysis further, by emphasizing how the increasing number of actors involved in events and the deepening degree of interdependence amongst them creates an environment that is dense with causal layers. His concept of 'fragmentation' attempted to capture dynamics that operate beyond globalization, notably localization and decentralization.

must either be or not be'. While this dualistic, or 'either/or' approach to thinking implies that the world can be understood in terms of linear, causal relationships, complex interconnectedness perhaps calls for an alternative holistic, non-dualistic and therefore non-linear, approach to understanding. Eastern thinking in general, and Buddhism in particular (by virtue of its stress on oneness, grounded in the belief that all concepts and objects are 'empty' of own-being) (Clarke 1997), are often seen as archetypal examples of a non-dualistic thinking; other attempts to think beyond 'either/or' distinctions include 'fuzzy thinking' (Kosko 1994), deep ecology (Capra 1996) and systems thinking (Capra 2003). But where does non-linearity or non-dualist thinking lead us? One of its key implications is that, as patterns of causal relationships become increasingly difficult to identify, events take on a random and seemingly arbitrary character. This is highlighted by chaos theory (see p. 84), which describes systems whose behaviour is difficult to predict because they consist of so many variables or unknown factors. Chaos tendencies may, for instance, be evident in the inherent instability of global financial markets (Soros 2000) and in a general tendency towards risk and uncertainty in society at large (Beck 1992).

Cosmopolitanism

Global interconnectedness does not merely challenge us in terms of how we understand the world, but also, perhaps, in terms of our moral relationships. The advance of globalization has undoubtedly had an ethical dimension, in that it has renewed interest in forms of cosmopolitanism, often expressed through growing interest in ideas such as global justice or world ethics (Dower 1998; Caney 2005). As the world has 'shrunk', in the sense of people having a greater awareness of other people living in other countries, often at a great distance from themselves, it has become more difficult to confine their moral obligations simply to a single political society. The more they know, the more they care. For cosmopolitan theorists, this implies that the world has come to constitute a single moral community. People thus have obligations (potentially) towards all

CONCEPT

Chaos theory

Chaos theory emerged in the 1970s as a branch of mathematics that sought an alternative to linear differential equations. Linearity implies a strong element of predictability (for example, how a billiard ball will respond to being hit by another billiard ball). In contrast, chaos theory examines the behaviour of non-linear systems (such as weather systems), in which there are such a wide range of variable factors that the effect of a change in any of them may have a disproportionate, and seemingly random, effect on others. The classic example of this is the so-called 'butterfly effect': the idea that the mere flap of a butterfly's wing could cause a hurricane to occur on the other side of the globe.

other people in the world, regardless of nationality, religion, ethnicity and so forth (see p. 81). Such thinking is usually based on the doctrine of human rights. Pogge (2008) broke this rights-based cosmopolitanism into three elements. It believes in *individualism*, in that human beings, or persons, are the ultimate unit of moral concern. Second, it accepts *universality*, in the sense that individuals are of equal moral worth. Third, it acknowledges *generality*, in that it implies that persons are objects of concern for everybody, not just their compatriots. Other forms of moral cosmopolitanism have also been advanced, however. O'Neill (1996) thus used the Kantian notion that we should act on principles that we would be willing to apply to all people in all circumstances to argue that people have a commitment not to injure others and that this commitment has a universal scope. Singer (2002), on the other hand, argued that the ethics of globalization demand that we should act so as to reduce the overall levels of global suffering, thinking in terms of 'one world' rather than a collection of discrete countries or peoples.

Moral cosmopolitanism also has its critics, however. On the one hand, radical critics of cosmopolitanism reject ideas such as global justice or world ethics on the grounds that it is impossible to establish universal values that are binding on all people and all societies. This **cultural relativism** is often used to argue that human rights in particular are essentially a western ideal and therefore have no place in non-western cultures. From a broader perspective, cosmopolitanism is often contrasted with **communitarianism**. From the communitarian perspective, moral values only make sense when they are grounded in a particular society and a particular historical period. This implies that human beings are morally constituted to favour the needs and interests of those with whom they share a cultural and national identity. On the other hand, moderate critics accept that universal values such as human rights may make moral sense, but they nevertheless object to the priority that they are accorded within moral cosmopolitanism (Negal 2005). In this view, although the desire, for example, to reduce overall levels of global suffering may be laudable, this is accepted as an unreliable, indeed unrealistic, guide for day-to-day moral reasoning, which will inevitably be shaped by more personal and local concerns. Cosmopolitan ethics, therefore, may exist, but only on the basis of a 'thin' sense of moral connectedness, rather than the 'thick' sense of moral connectedness that emerges within nations and local communities (Walzer 1994).

● **Cultural relativism**: The view that matters of right or wrong are entirely culturally determined, usually implying that it is impossible to say that one culture is better or worse than another.

● **Communitarianism**: The belief that the self or person is constituted through the community, in the sense that individuals are shaped by the communities to which they belong (see p. 531).

SUMMARY

- The realist model of power politics is based on the combined ideas of human selfishness or egoism and the structural implications of international anarchy. While this implies a strong tendency towards conflict, bloodshed and open violence can be constrained by the balance of power. The key dynamics in the international system flow from the distribution of power (or capacities) between and among states.

- The central theme of the liberal view of international politics is a belief in harmony or balance. The tendency towards peace, cooperation and integration is by factors such as economic interdependence, brought about by free trade, the spread of democracy and the construction of international organizations. However, over time, liberalism (or neoliberalism) has become increasingly indistinct from realism.

- The key critical perspectives on global politics are Marxism in its various forms, social constructivism, post-structuralism, feminism, green politics and postcolonialism. In their different ways, these theories challenge norms, values and assumptions on which the global status quo is based. Critical theorists tend to view realism and liberalism as ways of concealing, or of legitimizing, the global power asymmetries.

- Many critical theorists embrace a post-positivist perspective that takes subject and object, and therefore theory and practice, to be intimately linked. Post-positivists question the belief that there is an objective reality 'out there', separate from the beliefs, ideas and assumptions of the observer. Reality is therefore best thought of in 'inter-subjective' terms.

- Increased levels of global interconnectedness, linked to accelerated globalization, has brought a series of new theoretical challenges. These include the difficulties that complexity poses to conventional linear thinking, the possibility that the world now constitutes a single moral community, and reduced value of theoretical paradigms.

Questions for discussion

- Does all politics boil down to power and the pursuit of self-interest?
- To what extent is realism a single, coherent theory?
- How do realists explain periods of peace and stability?
- Why do liberals believe that world affairs are characterized by balance or harmony?
- Is the 'democratic peace' thesis persuasive?
- Are states concerned more with relative gains or with absolute gains?
- Do mainstream theories merely legitimize the global status quo?
- Which of the critical perspectives on global politics is most 'critical'?
- Can any established theory cope with the challenges of complex interconnectedness?
- Does it make sense to think of the world as a single moral community?

Further reading

Bell, D. (ed.), *Ethics and World Politics* (2010). An excellent volume that discusses general perspectives of world politics and important ethical dilemmas.

Burchill, S. *et al.*, *Theories of International Relations* (2013). A systematic and comprehensive introduction to the main theoretical approaches in the study of international relations.

Capra, F., *The Hidden Connections* (2003). A thought-provoking analysis of human societies, corporations, nation-states and global capitalism from the perspective of systems theory.

Jackson, R. and G. Sørensen, *Introduction to International Relations: Theories and Approaches* (2012). An accessible, lucid and comprehensive introduction to the complexities of modern international thought.

 ONLINE RESOURCES AVAILABLE

Links to relevant web resources can be found on the *Global Politics* website

CHAPTER 4

The Economy in a Global Age

'Constant revolutionizing of production, uninterrupted disturbance of social conditions, everlasting uncertainty and agitation ... All that is solid melts into air.'

K. MARX and F. ENGELS, *The Communist Manifesto* (1848)

PREVIEW Economic issues have long been at the centre of ideological and political debate. For much of the nineteenth and twentieth centuries, the core battleground in politics was the contest between two rival economic models, capitalism and socialism. This nevertheless culminated in the victory of capitalism over socialism, registered in particular through the collapse of communism. As the market, private property and competition were accepted worldwide as the only viable ways of generating wealth, capitalism became global capitalism. However, capitalism did not cease to be politically contentious. In the first place, capitalism is not one system but many: different forms of capitalism have taken root in different parts of the world. How do these capitalisms differ, and what are the implications of these different forms of socio-economic organization? Moreover, a particular form of capitalist development has gained global ascendency since the 1980s, usually dubbed neoliberalism. What have been the chief consequences of the 'triumph' of neoliberalism? A further development has been a significant acceleration in the process of economic globalization, usually associated with the advance of neoliberalism. Has neoliberal globalization promoted prosperity and opportunity for all, or has it spawned new forms of inequality and injustice? These questions have become particularly pressing in the light of a tendency towards seemingly intensifying crises and economic instability. Are economic crises a price worth paying for long-term economic success, or are they a symptom of the fundamental failings of global capitalism?

KEY ISSUES
- What are the main types of capitalism in the modern world?
- Why has neoliberalism become dominant, and what are its chief implications?
- How can economic globalization best be explained?
- To what extent has the modern world economy been 'globalized'?
- Why does capitalism tend towards booms and slumps?
- What have recent economic crises told us about the nature of global capitalism?

CAPITALISM AND NEOLIBERALISM

Capitalisms of the world

The origins of **capitalism** can be traced back to seventeenth-century and eighteenth-century Europe, developing in predominantly feudal societies. Feudalism was characterized by agrarian-based production geared to the needs of landed estates, fixed social hierarchies and rigid patterns of obligation and duties. Capitalist practices initially took root in the form of commercial agriculture that was orientated towards the **market**, and increasingly relied on waged labour instead of bonded serfs. The market mechanism, the heart of the emerging capitalist system, certainly intensified pressure for technological innovation and brought about a substantial expansion in productive capacity. This was reflected in the 'agricultural revolution', which saw the enclosure of overgrazed common land and the increased use of fertilizers and scientific methods of production.

Nevertheless, the most significant development in the history of capitalism came with the industrial revolution, which developed from the mid-eighteenth century onwards, first in the UK but soon in the USA (see p. 46) and across much of Europe. Industrialization entirely transformed societies through the advent of mechanized and often factory-based forms of production, the increasing use of the **division of labour** and the gradual shift of populations from the land to the expanding towns and cities. In the process, industrialization massively expanded the productive capacity of capitalism, enabling industrial capitalism to emerge by the mid-nineteenth century as the dominant socio-economic system worldwide. The development of industrial capitalism also marked a key phase in the evolution of the world economy, in that it resulted in the export of **capital** from Europe to North America, South America and Asia, also leading to a sharpening of the division of labour between states and between different regions of the world. In these ways, as discussed later, the foundations of modern global capitalism were laid during the late nineteenth century. However, capitalism does not constitute just a single socio-economic form, but a variety of socio-economic forms (Brown 1995; Hall and Soskice 2001). It is possible to identify three types of capitalist system:

- Enterprise capitalism
- Social capitalism
- State capitalism.

Enterprise capitalism

Enterprise capitalism is widely seen, particularly in the Anglo-American world, as 'pure' capitalism; that is, as an ideal towards which other capitalisms are inevitably drawn (Friedman 1962). The home of enterprise capitalism is the USA and, despite its early post-1945 flirtation with Keynesian **social democracy**, the UK. Nevertheless, the principles of enterprise capitalism have been extended far beyond the Anglo-American world through the impact of economic globalization (see p. 98), which has gone hand-in-hand with the advance of **marketization**. Enterprise capitalism is based on the ideas of classical economists such as Adam Smith and David Ricardo (1772–1823), updated in the form of neoliberalism by modern

---

● **Capitalism**: A system of generalized commodity production in which wealth is owned privately and economic life is organized according to market principles.

● **Market**: A system of commercial exchange shaped by the forces of demand and supply, and regulated by the price mechanism.

● **Division of labour**: The process whereby productive tasks become separated and more specialized in order to promote economic efficiency.

● **Capital**: In a general sense, any 'asset', financial or otherwise; Marxists used the term to refer to accumulated wealth embodied in the 'means of production'.

● **Social democracy**: A moderate or reformist brand of socialism that favours a balance between the market and the state, rather than the abolition of capitalism.

● **Marketization**: The extension of market relationships, based on commercial exchange and material self-interest, across the economy and, possibly, society.

Adam Smith (1723–90)

Scottish economist and philosopher, usually seen as the founder of the 'dismal science' (economics). After holding the chair of logic and then moral philosophy at Glasgow University, Smith became tutor to the Duke of Buccleuch, which enabled him to visit France and Geneva and to develop his economic theories. *The Theory of Moral Sentiments* (1759) developed a theory of motivation that tried to reconcile human self-interestedness with unregulated social order. Smith's most famous work, *The Wealth of Nations* (1776), was the first systematic attempt to explain the workings of the economy in market terms, emphasizing the importance of the division of labour. Although he is often viewed as a free-market theorist, Smith was nevertheless aware of the limitations of the market.

theorists such as the Austrian economist and political philosopher, Friedrich von Hayek (1899–1992) and Milton Friedman (see p. 95). Its central feature is faith in the untrammelled workings of market competition, born out of the belief that the market is a self-regulating mechanism (or, as Adam Smith put it, an 'invisible hand'). This idea is expressed in Adam Smith's famous words: 'It is not from the benevolence of the butcher, the brewer or the baker, that we expect our dinner, but from their regard to their own interest'. In the USA, such free-market principles have helped to keep public ownership to a minimum, and ensure that welfare provision operates as little more than a safety net. US businesses are typically profit-driven, and a premium is placed on high productivity and labour flexibility. Trade unions are usually weak, reflecting the fear that strong labour organizations are an obstacle to profit maximization. The emphasis on growth and enterprise of this form of capitalism stems, in part, from the fact that productive wealth is owned largely by financial institutions, such as insurance companies and pension funds, that demand a high rate of return on their investments.

The undoubted economic power of the USA bears testament to the vigour of enterprise capitalism. Despite clear evidence of relative economic decline (whereas the USA accounted for half of the world's manufacturing output in 1945, this had fallen to less than one-fifth by 2007), the average productivity of the USA is still higher than Germany's or Japan's. The USA clearly enjoys natural advantages that enable it to benefit from the application of market principles, notably a continent-wide domestic market, a wealth of natural resources, and a ruggedly individualist popular culture, seen as a 'frontier ideology'. Enterprise capitalism also has serious disadvantages, however. Perhaps the most significant of these is a tendency towards wide material inequalities and social fragmentation. This is demonstrated in the USA by levels of absolute poverty that are not found, for example, in Europe, and in the growth of a poorly-educated and socially-dependent underclass.

Social capitalism

Social capitalism refers to a form of capitalism that took root in much of central and western Europe. Germany is its natural home but the principles of social capitalism were adopted in various forms in Austria, the Benelux countries, France and much of Scandinavia (van Kersbergen 1995). This economic form drew heavily on the flexible and pragmatic ideas of economists such as Friedrich List (1789–1846), an influential theorist of economic nationalism. The central theme of this capitalist model is the idea of a **social market**; that is, an attempt to marry the disciplines of market competition with the need for social cohesion and solidarity. This is reflected in an emphasis on long-term investment rather than short-term profitability. Business organization in what has been called Rhine-Alpine capitalism also differs from Anglo-American capitalism in that it is based on social partnership. Trade unions enjoy representation through works councils, and participate in annual rounds of wage negotiation that are usually industry-wide. This relationship is underpinned by comprehensive and well-funded welfare provisions that provide workers and other vulnerable groups with social guarantees.

The strengths of social capitalism were clearly demonstrated by the 'economic miracle' that transformed war-torn Germany into Europe's leading economic power by the 1960s. High and stable levels of capital investment, together with a strong emphasis on education and training, particularly in vocational and craft skills, enabled Germany to achieve the highest levels of productivity in Europe. However, the virtues of social capitalism are by no means universally accepted. One of its drawbacks is that, because it places a heavy stress on consultation, negotiation and consensus, it tends to lead to inflexibility and makes it difficult for businesses to adapt to market conditions (for example, economic globalization and intensified competition from East Asia, Latin America and elsewhere). Further strains are imposed by the relatively high levels of social expenditure required to maintain high-quality welfare provision. These push up taxes and so burden both employers and employees. Whereas supporters of social capitalism insist that the social and the market are intrinsically linked, its critics argue that social capitalism is nothing more than a contradiction in terms.

State capitalism

The term 'state capitalism' has been defined in a number of ways. For instance, Trotskyites used it to highlight the tendency of the Soviet Union under Stalin to use its control of productive power to oppress the working class, in a manner similar to capitalist societies. However, in its modern usage, state capitalism is more commonly used to describe capitalist economies in which the state plays a crucial directive role. These are often non-liberal capitalist societies. Hall and Soskice (2001) distinguished between 'liberal market economies', in which firms coordinate their activities on the basis of competitive market arrangements, and 'coordinated market economies', which depend heavily on non-market arrangements. Some aspects of state capitalism could be found in post-1945 Japan. This was the model that the East and South-east Asian 'tigers' eagerly adopted, and it has influenced emergent Chinese capitalism as well as, in some respects, Russian capitalism.

The distinctive character of state capitalism is its emphasis on cooperative, long-term relationships, for which reason it is sometimes called 'collective capitalism'. This allows the economy to be directed not by an impersonal price

● **Social market**: An economy that is structured by market principles and largely free from government interference, operating in a society in which cohesion is maintained through a comprehensive welfare system and effective welfare services.

GLOBAL POLITICAL ECONOMY

Realist view

Realist economic theory is firmly rooted in, and sometimes seen as being synonymous with 'economic nationalism' or 'mercantilism'. Mercantilism takes the state to be the most significant economic actor, highlighting the extent to which economic relations are determined by political power. In this view, markets are not 'natural' but exist within a social context largely shaped by the exercise of state power. As the state system is anarchical, the global economy tends to be characterized by conflict as states compete with each other for power and wealth in a zero-sum game. The classic mercantilist strategy is to build up a state's wealth, power and prestige by developing a favourable trading balance through producing goods for export while keeping imports low. The chief device for achieving this is protectionism. *Defensive* mercantilism is designed to protect 'infant' industries and weaker economies from 'unfair' competition from stronger economies, while *aggressive* mercantilism aims to strengthen the national economy in order to provide a basis for expansionism and war. The global economy has thus been fashioned by the interests of the most powerful states, sometimes through neo-colonialism but also through free trade arrangements that force weaker states to open up their markets. For some realists, a stable world economy requires the existence of a single dominant power, as implied by hegemonic stability theory (see p. 236).

Liberal view

Liberal economic theory is based on the belief that individuals, as rationally self-interested creatures, or 'utility maximizers', are the key economic actors (utility maximizers act to achieve the greatest pleasure over pain, calculated in terms of material consumption). In this light, businesses are an important means of organizing production and thus of generating wealth. In line with the deeper liberal belief in balance or harmony amongst competing forces, the key idea of economic liberalism is that an unregulated market economy tends towards long-run equilibrium (the price mechanism, the 'invisible hand' of the market, brings 'supply' and 'demand' into line with one another). From the perspective of classical liberal political economy, this implies a policy of *laissez-faire* (see p. 106), in which

the state leaves the economy alone, and the market is left to manage itself. Economic exchange via the market is therefore a positive-sum game, in that greater efficiency produces economic growth and benefits everyone. The global economy is thus characterized by cooperation as trading and other economic relationships promise to bring mutual benefit and general prosperity. This further implies a positive view of economic globalization, which is seen as the triumph of the market over 'irrational' impediments such as national borders. Such thinking has been taken furthest by neoliberalism (see p. 93). Since Keynes (see p. 108), however, an alternative tradition of liberal political economy has recognized that markets can fail or are imperfect, in which case they need to be managed or regulated on a national and global level.

Critical views

Critical approaches to the economy have been dominated by Marxism, which portrays capitalism as a system of class exploitation and treats social classes as the key economic actors. As class allegiances are taken to be more powerful than national loyalties, political economy always has an international dimension, in the Marxist view. In modern economic circumstances, the interests of the capitalist class, or bourgeoisie, are increasingly identified with those of transnational corporations (see p. 94), which are widely seen as more powerful than national governments, economics having primacy over politics. Capitalism therefore has inherently globalizing tendencies, an unceasing desire to expand regardless of national borders. The global economy is nevertheless characterized by conflict, stemming from the oppressive nature of the capitalist system itself. For some Marxists., this is expressed through imperialism (see p. 28) and the desire to secure raw materials and cheap labour. However, some neo-Marxists, following Wallerstein (see p. 104), have interpreted global capitalism as a world-system, which is structured by an exploitative relationship between so-called 'core' areas and 'peripheral' ones, and specifically between transnational corporations and the developing world. Others have adopted a neo-Gramscism approach that stresses the role of hegemony (see p. 228), highlighting the extent to which economic power and political power operate in tandem.

mechanism, but through what have been called 'relational markets'. An example of this is the pattern of interlocking share ownership that ensures that there is a close relationship between industry and finance in Japan, enabling Japanese firms to adopt strategies based on long-term investment rather than on short-space or medium-term profit. Firms themselves provide the social core of life in state capitalism. Workers (particularly male workers in larger businesses) are 'members' of firms in a way that does not occur in the USA or even social market Europe. In return for their loyalty, commitment and hard work, workers have traditionally expected lifetime employment, pensions, social protection and access to leisure and recreational opportunities. Particular stress is placed on teamwork and the building up of a collective identity, which has been under-pinned by relatively narrow income differentials between managers and workers. The final element in this economic mix is the government. Although East Asian levels of public spending and taxation are relatively low by international stan-dards (often below 30 per cent of GNP), the state has played a vital role in 'guiding' investment, research and trading decisions. The model here was undoubtedly the Ministry of International Trade and Industry (MITI), which oversaw the Japanese 'economic miracle' in the post-1945 period.

The Japanese version of state capitalism appeared to be highly successful in the early post-1945 period, accounting for Japan's ability to recover from war-time devastation to become the second largest economy in the world, and helping to explain the rise of the Asian 'tigers' (South Korea, Taiwan, Hong Kong, Singapore and so on). However, Japan's slowdown during the 1990s (the 'lost decade') and the Asian financial crisis of 1997 cast a darker shadow over state capitalism, highlighting its inflexibility and its failure to respond to the ever-changing pressures of the global economy. Moreover, a price had to be paid for Japan's economic success, in terms of heavy demands on workers and their fami-lies. Long hours and highly-disciplined working conditions can mean that indi-vidualism is stifled and work becomes the centrepiece of existence. In these circumstances, China (see p. 238) has become the standard-bearer for state capi-talism, having consistently achieved growth rates of about 9 per cent since the late 1980s, and having become the second largest economy in the world in 2010. China's mixture of burgeoning capitalism and Stalinist political control has been remarkably effective in delivering sustained economic growth, benefiting from a huge supply of cheap labour and massive investment in the economic infra-structure.

Russia's conversion to state capitalism occurred in the aftermath of the chaos and dislocation of the 1990s, when 'shock treatment' market reforms were introduced under Boris Yeltsin. From 1999 onwards, Vladimir Putin acted to reassert state power in both political and economic life, in part in order to wrest power back from the 'oligarchs', newly-rich business magnates who had been criticized for siphoning off wealth out of the country and for contributing to the 1998 Russian financial crisis. A key aspect of Putin's economic strategy was to exploit Russia's vast energy reserves, both as a motor for economic growth and to give Russia (see p. 181) greater leverage over neighbouring states and, indeed, over much of Europe. The strength of state capitalism derives from its pragmatism and flexibility, strong states being able to pursue economic priorities with a single-mindedness, even, at times, ruthlessness, that liberal democracies cannot match. Major infrastructural projects and economic

Focus on . . .
A Chinese economic model?

What is the source of China's remarkable economic success since the introduction of market reforms in the late 1970s? Is there such as thing as 'capitalism with Chinese characteristics'? China's economic model has a number of clear features. First, with a population of 1.3 billion, and with a historically unprecedented shift in people from the countryside to fast-expanding towns and cities, particularly on the eastern coast, China has benefited from a seemingly inexhaustible supply of cheap labour. Second, in common with Japan and the Asian 'tigers' before it, China has adopted an export-led growth strategy founded on manufacturing industry and the goal of becoming the 'workshop of the world'.

Third, a high savings ratio means that, unlike the USA and many western economies, investment in China largely comes from internal sources. This not only suggests that the Chinese banking system is more robust than those of the USA, the UK and other western states, but it also allows China to lend massively abroad. Such lending keeps China's currency cheap in relation to the US dollar, thereby boosting the competitiveness of Chinese exports. Fourth, economic success is underpinned by interventionist government, which, amongst other things, invests heavily in infra-structure projects and gears its foreign policy towards the goal of achieving resource security, guaranteeing

the supplies of oil, iron ore, copper, aluminium and many other industrial minerals that an ever-expanding economy desperately needs.

Nevertheless, the legitimacy of China's 'market Stalinism', and the allegiance of its fast-growing middle class and business elite, is closely linked to China's ability to keep expanding its GDP. A variety of factors threaten the Chinese economic model, or are forcing China to develop a new economic model. These include the fact that since the mid-2000s there have been signs of wage inflation in China, suggesting that cheap labour may not be in inexhaustible supply and putting at risk China's ability to undercut the rest of the world in manufacturing goods. An over-dependence on export markets creates the need to boost domestic consumption levels in China, particularly demonstrated by the global economic recession in 2008–9. However, increased domestic consumption may 'suck in' more imports, reducing China's currently strongly positive trade balance. Another threat derives from China's one-child policy, which is starting to become counter-productive as the size of China's working-age population is projected to fall sharply in the coming decades. The most serious challenge that China faces is, nevertheless, that there may be a fundamental contra-diction between the nature of its economic system and its political system (as discussed further in Chapter 9).

restructuring can thus be pursued more easily, and the vagaries of capital and currency markets have a reduced impact on economic decision-making. Some have even speculated that what has been called the 'Beijing consensus' (Ramo 2004) may be in the process of displacing the 'Washington consensus' (see p. 96). However, the major weakness of state capitalism is the contradiction between economic liberalism and non-liberal political arrangements. For example, critics have argued that China's version of state capitalism, based on a blend of market economics and one-party communist rule, is ultimately unsustainable, in that a widening of economic freedom must, sooner or later, generate pressure for a widening of political freedom (Hutton 2007). State capitalism will only constitute a viable alternative to western-based capitalist models if it is possible for market economics to prosper in the long term in the absence of political liberalism.

Neoliberalism

Neoliberalism (sometimes called 'neoclassical liberalism') is an updated version of classical liberalism. Its central theme is the idea that the economy works best when left alone by government, reflecting a belief in free market economics and atomistic individualism. While unregulated market capitalism delivers efficiency, growth and widespread prosperity, the 'dead hand' of the state saps initiative and discourages enterprise. In short, the neoliberal philosophy is: 'market: good; state: bad'. Key neoliberal policies include privatization, low public spending, deregulation, tax cuts (particularly corporate and direct taxes) and reduced welfare provision. The term neoliberalism is also used to describe modern developments in liberal international relations theory (as discussed in Chapter 3).

● **Market fundamentalism**: An absolute faith in the market, reflected in the belief that the market mechanism offers solutions to all economic and social problems.

● **Keynesianism**: A theory (developed by J. M. Keynes (see p. 108) or policy of economic management, associated with regulating aggregate demand to achieve full employment.

Triumph of neoliberalism

Since the 1980s, however, economic development has, to a greater or lesser extent in different parts of the world, taken on a neoliberal guise. Neoliberalism reflects the ascendancy of enterprise capitalism over rival forms of capitalism, its chief belief being a form of **market fundamentalism**. The 'neoliberal revolution' was, in fact, a counter-revolution: its aim was to halt, and if possible reverse, the trend towards 'big' government and state intervention that had characterized much of the twentieth century, and especially the early post-1945 period. The chief academic exponents of neoliberalism were Hayek and Friedman. A central object of their attack was **Keynesianism** and the 'tax and spend' policies that they claimed were responsible for the 'stagflation' of the 1970s (a combination of economic stagnation, and therefore rising unemployment, and high inflation (a general rise in the price level). The neoliberal solution was to 'roll back' the frontiers of the state and to give full, or at least a much fuller, rein to market forces.

The earliest experiment in neoliberalism was in Chile. Following the CIA-backed military coup that overthrew Salvador Allende in 1973, the newly-installed General Pinochet introduced sweeping market reforms on the advice of a group of US and US-trained free-market economists, the so-called 'Chicago boys' (reflecting the influence of Milton Friedman and the 'Chicago School'). Their influence subsequently spread to Brazil, Argentina and elsewhere in South America. During the 1980s, neoliberalism was extended to the USA and the UK, in the forms of 'Reaganism' (after President Reagan, 1981–89) and 'Thatcherism' (after Prime Minister Thatcher, 1979–90), with other countries such as Canada, Australia and New Zealand quickly following suit. The wider, and seemingly irresistible, advance of neoliberalism occurred during the 1990s through the influence of the institutions of global economic governance and the growing impact of globalization. During the 1980s, the World Bank (see p. 380) and International Monetary Fund (IMF) (see p. 475) were converted to the ideas of what later became know as the 'Washington consensus', which was aligned to the economic agenda of Reagan and Thatcher and focused on policies such as free trade, the liberalization of capital markets, flexible exchange rates, balanced budgets and so on. After the Eastern European revolutions of 1989–91, such thinking informed the 'shock therapy' transition from central planning to free-market capitalism in states such as Russia, Hungary and Poland, while free-market reforms were extended to many developing states through the imposition of 'structural adjustment' programmes (see p. 378).

Economic globalization supported the advance of neoliberalism in a number of ways. In particular, intensified international competition encouraged governments to deregulate their economies and reduce tax levels in the hope of attracting inward investment and preventing transnational corporations (TNCs) (see p. 94) from relocating elsewhere. Strong downward pressure was exerted on public spending, and particularly welfare budgets, by the fact that, in a context of heightened global competition, the control of inflation has displaced the maintenance of full employment as the principal goal of economic policy. Such pressures, together with the revived growth and productivity rates of the US economy and the relatively sluggish performance of other models of national capitalism, in Japan and Germany in particular, meant that by the late 1990s neoliberalism appeared to stand unchallenged as the dominant ideology of the

GLOBAL ACTORS . . .

TRANSNATIONAL CORPORATIONS

A transnational corporation, or TNC, is a company that controls economic activity in two or more countries. The parent company is usually incorporated in one state (the 'home'), with subsidiaries in others (the 'hosts'), although subsidiaries may be separately incorporated affiliates. Such companies are now generally referred to as *transnational* corporations rather than *multinational* corporations – as TNCs as opposed to MNCs – to reflect the extent to which their corporate strategies and processes transcend national borders rather than merely crossing them. Integration across economic sectors and the growing importance of intra-firm trade has allowed TNCs to operate as economies in their own right, benefiting from geographical flexibility, advantages in product innovation and the ability to pursue global marketing strategies.

Some early transnational corporations developed in association with the spread of European colonialism, the classic example being the East India Company, established in 1600. However, the period since 1945 has witnessed a dramatic growth in their number, size and global reach. The number of powerful companies with subsidiaries in several countries rose from 7,000 in 1970 to 38,000 in 2009. Initially, the spread of transnational production was a largely US phenomenon, linked to enterprises such as General Motors, IBM, Exxon Mobil and McDonalds. European and Japanese companies quickly followed suit, extending the TNC phenomenon across the global North. About 70 per cent of the world's leading 200 TNCs have parent companies that are based in just three countries – the USA, Germany and Japan – and 90 per cent are based in the developed world.

Significance: TNCs exert enormous economic power and political influence. Their economic significance is reflected in the fact that they account for about 50 per cent of world manufacturing production and over 70 per cent of world trade. TNCs often dwarf states in terms of their economic size. Based on a comparison between corporate sales and countries' GDP, 51 of the world's 100 largest economies are corporations; only 49 of them are countries. General Motors is broadly equivalent in this sense to Denmark; Wal-Mart is roughly the same size as Poland; and Exxon Mobil has the same economic weight as South Africa. However, economic size does not necessarily translate into political power or influence; states, after all, can do things that TNCs can only dream about, such as make laws and raise armies. What gives TNCs their strategic advantage over national governments is their ability to transcend territory through the growth of 'trans-border', even 'trans-global', communications and inter-actions, reflected, in particular, in the flexibility they enjoy over the location of production and invest-ment. TNCs can, in effect, shop around looking for circumstances that are conducive to profitability. They are likely to be drawn to states or areas that can offer, for instance, a stable political environment, low levels of taxation (especially corpo-rate taxation), low levels of economic and financial regulation, available supplies of cheap or well-skilled labour, weak trade unions and limited protection for labour rights, and access to markets prefer-ably composed of consumers with high disposable incomes. This creates a relationship of structural dependency between the state and TNCs whereby states rely on TNCs to provide jobs and capital inflows but can only attract them by provid-ing circumstances favourable to their interests.

Defenders of corporations argue that they bring massive economic benefits and that their political influence has been much exagger-ated: TNCs have been 'demonized' by the anti-globalization movement. From this perspective, TNCs have been successful because they have worked. Their two huge economic benefits are their efficiency and their high level of consumer responsive-ness. Greater efficiency has resulted from their historically unprece-dented ability to reap the benefits from economies of scale and from the development of new productive methods and the application of new technologies. The consumer respon-siveness of TNCs is demonstrated by their huge investment in research and development and product inno-vation. Critics nevertheless portray a much more sinister image of TNCs, arguing that they have accumulated excessive economic power, unac-ceptable levels of political influence, and created a 'brand culture' that pollutes the public sphere through the proliferation of commercial images and manipulates personal preferences.

Milton Friedman (1912–2006)

US academic and economist. A trenchant critic of Roosevelt's 'New Deal', and close associate of Friedrich Hayek, Friedman became professor of economics at the University of Chicago in 1948, founding the so-called 'Chicago School'. Friedman also worked as a *Newsweek* columnist and a US presidential adviser. He was awarded the Nobel prize for economics in 1976. A leading exponent of monetarism and free-market economics, Friedman was a powerful critic of Keynesian theory and 'tax and spend' government policies, helping to shift economic priorities during the 1970s and 1980s in the USA and the UK in particular. His major works, *Capitalism and Freedom* (1962) and, with his wife Rose, *Free to Choose* (1980), had a considerable impact on emerging neoliberal thinking.

'new' world economy. Only a few states, like China, were able to deal with neoliberal globalization on their own terms, limiting their exposure to competition by, for instance, holding down their exchange rate.

Implications of neoliberalism

The apparent global 'triumph' of neoliberalism has provoked considerable debate. For neoliberals and their supporters, the clearest argument in favour of market reforms and economic liberalization is that they have worked. The advance of neoliberalism coincided not only with three decades of growth in the USA and its renewed economic ascendancy (firmly burying, for example, predictions that had been widely made in the 1970s and 1980 that the USA was about to be eclipsed by Japan and Germany), but also three decades of growth in the world economy. In this light, neoliberalism was based on a new growth model that has clearly demonstrated its superiority over the Keynesian-welfarist orthodoxy of old. At the core of the neoliberal growth model are financial markets and the process of '**financialization**'. This was made possible by a massive expansion of the financial sector of the economy, explaining the growing importance of Wall Street, the City of London, Frankfurt, Singapore and elsewhere. In the process, capitalism was turned into 'turbo-capitalism', benefiting from greatly expanded monetary flows that were seeking an outlet in increased investment and higher consumption. Although this process involved a considerable growth of pubic and often private debt, this was thought to be sustainable due to the underlying growth that the debt fuelled. Other key features of the neoliberal growth model were a deeper integration of domestic economies into the global economy (and so an acceleration of economic globalization), the shift in many of the leading economies from manufacturing to services, and the enthusiastic introduction of new information technologies, often seen as the growth of the 'knowledge economy' (see p. 97).

Neoliberalism, nevertheless, has its critics. They have, for example, argued that in rolling back welfare provision and promoting an ethic of material self-interest ('greed is good'), neoliberalism struggles to maintain popular legitimacy as an economic doctrine because of its association with widening inequality and

● **Financialization**: The reconstruction of the finances of businesses, public bodies and individual citizens to allow them to borrow money and so raise their spending.

Focus on ...
The 'Washington consensus'

The term the 'Washington consensus' was coined by John Williamson (1990, 1993) to describe the policies that the international institutions based in Washington, the IMF and the World Bank, and the US Treasury Department, had come to favour for the reconstruction of economies in the developing world. Based on the 'orthodox' model of 'development as modernization' and drawing on the ideas of neoliberalism, the essence of the Washington consensus was 'stabilize, privatize and liberalize'. In its longer version, the Washington consensus favoured the following:

- Fiscal discipline (cutting public spending)

- Tax reform (cutting personal and corporate taxes)
- Financial liberalization (the deregulation of financial markets and capital controls)
- Floating and competitive exchange rates
- Trade liberalization (free trade)
- Openness to foreign direct investment
- Privatization

In the light of a backlash against such policies, and at times their failure, an 'augmented' Washington consensus has emerged that also stresses policies such as legal/political reform, anti-corruption, labour market flexibility and poverty reduction.

social breakdown. This led to a modification, although not a rejection, of the 'neoliberal revolution' in countries such as New Zealand, Canada and the UK during the 1990s, and even to a reappraisal of neoliberal priorities in the USA under President Obama from 2009 onwards. Moreover, the limitations of neoliberalism as a programme for development were exposed by the failure of many 'shock therapy' experiments in market reform, not only in the pioneering case of Chile, but also in the disappointing outcomes of many structural adjustment programmes in the developing world. In cases such as Russia, the growth of unemployment and inflation, and the deep insecurities unleashed by the 'shock therapy' application of neoliberal principles created a backlash against market reform and led to strengthened support for nationalist and authoritarian movements. A further problem is that neoliberalism's 'turbo' features may have less to do with the dynamism of the market or technological innovation than with the willingness of consumers to spend and borrow and the willingness of businesses to invest, making this economic model particularly vulnerable to the vagaries of financial markets and the shifts in consumer or business confidence. This is examined in greater depth later in this chapter in association with the crises of capitalism.

In the view of Robert Cox (see p. 124), neoliberalism, or what he calls 'hyper-liberal globalizing capitalism', is rooted in major contradictions and struggles, meaning that its dominance is destined to be challenged and eventually overthrown. These contradictions include the 'democratic deficit' that is generated by the 'internationalization of the state' (the tendency of the state to respond to the dictates of the global economy rather than public opinion), the growing pressure to protect the environment from the ravages caused by relentless economic growth, and the surrender of state authority to corporate financial and economic interests. A still darker interpretation of neoliberalism

Focus on . . .
A 'knowledge economy'?

How meaningful is the idea of a 'knowledge economy'? A knowledge economy (sometimes called the 'new' economy, or even the 'weightless' economy) is one in which knowledge is supposedly a key source of competitiveness and productivity, especially through the application of information and communication technology (ICT). Knowledge economies are sometimes portrayed as the economic expression of the transition from an industrial society to an information society. Proponents of the idea of a knowledge economy argue that it differs from a traditional economy in several ways. These include that, as knowledge (unlike other resources) does not deplete with use, knowledge economies are concerned with the economics of abundance, not the economics of scarcity. They substantially diminish the effect of location (and thereby accelerate globalization), as knowledge 'leaks' to where demand or rewards are highest, so disregarding national borders. Finally, they imply that profitability and high productivity are essentially linked to 'up-skilling' the workforce, rather than to the acquisition of 'hard' resources.

However, the image of the knowledge economy may be misleading. In the first place, modern technological advances linked to ICT may be nothing new: rapid and advanced technological change has always been a feature of industrial capitalism. Moreover, the link between the wider use of ICT and productivity growth has been questioned by some commentators. For example, the boost in productivity rates in the USA from the mid-1990s onwards may have been linked to factors other than investment in ICT, and there is little evidence that the increased use of ICT has boosted economic growth in other economies. Finally, knowledge-based production is largely confined to the developed North, and it is difficult to see wider access to ICT as the key development priority in the South. Africa, for example, may lag some fifteen years behind US levels of personal computer and Internet penetration, but it lags more than a century behind in terms of basic literacy and health care. Clean water, anti-malaria programmes, good schools and non-corrupt government are far higher priorities for the world's poor countries than improved access to mobile phones and the Internet.

has been developed by Naomi Klein (2008). In highlighting the rise of 'disaster capitalism', she drew attention to the extent to which the advance of neoliberalism has been implicated in 'shocks', states of emergency and crises of one kind or another, thus suggesting that the USA's foreign policy adventurism, from the overthrow of Allende to the 'war on terror', has been linked to the spread of neoliberalism. For many, the 2007–09 global financial crisis, discussed later in the chapter, exposed the underlying weaknesses of the neoliberal model.

ECONOMIC GLOBALIZATION
Causes of economic globalization

How can the emergence of economic globalization best be explained, and how far has it progressed? There is nothing new about economic globalization. The development of transborder and transnational economic structures has been a central feature of imperialism (see p. 28), and, arguably, the high point of economic globalization came in the late nineteenth century with the scramble of

Economic globalization

Economic globalization refers to the process whereby all national economies have, to a greater or lesser extent, been absorbed into an interlocking global economy. The OECD (1995) thus defined globalization as 'a shift from a world of distinct national economies to a global economy in which production is internationalized and financial capital flows freely and instantly between countries'. However, economic globalization should be distinguished from **internationalization**. The latter results in intensified interdependence between national economies ('shallow integration'), while the former marks a qualitative shift towards 'deep integration', transcending territorial borders through the construction of a consolidated global marketplace for production, distribution and consumption.

● **Internationalization**: The growth of relations and movements (for instance, of goods, money, people, messages and ideas) across borders and between states, creating higher levels of interdependence.

European states for colonies in Africa and Asia. Nevertheless, modern and past forms of globalization differ in important ways. Earlier forms of globalization, sometimes seen as 'proto-globalization', usually established transnational economic organizations on the back of expansionist political projects. Regardless of their spread and success, empires never succeeded in obliterating boundaries and borders, they merely readjusted them to the benefit of politically dominant powers, often establishing new boundaries between the 'civilized' world and the 'barbarian' one. In the case of the contemporary phenomenon of globalization, in contrast, the web of economic interconnectedness and interdependence has extended so far that it is possible, for the first time, to conceive of the world economy as a *single* global entity. This is the sense in which economic life has become 'borderless' (Ohmae 1990).

The modern globalized economy came into existence in the second half of the twentieth century. It was a product of two phases. The first phase, which lasted from the end of WWII to the early 1970s, was characterized by new arrangements for the management of the international financial system in the post-war period which became known as the Bretton Woods system (discussed in Chapter 19). Through a system of fixed exchange rates, regulation and support, Bretton Woods aimed to prevent a return to the 'beggar-thy-neighbour' economic policies that had contributed to the Great Depression of the 1930s and, in the process, helped to fuel political extremism and aggression. Together with the Marshall Plan, which provided US financial aid to Europe, in particular to support post-war reconstruction, and the wide adoption of Keynesian economic policies aimed at delivering sustained growth, the Bretton Woods system underpinned the so-called 'long boom' of the post-1945 period. In substantially expanding productive capacity and helping to fashion a consumerist form of capitalism, it laid the basis for the later 'accelerated' economic globalization.

Nevertheless, the collapse of Bretton Woods in the 1970s, allowing major currencies to float instead of staying fixed, initiated the second phase in the development of globalized capitalism. The Bretton Woods system had been based on the assumption that the world economy consisted of a series of inter-linked national economies: its purpose was to guarantee economic stability at the national level by regulating trading relations between and amongst nation-states. However, the breakdown of the system weakened national economies, in that the shift from fixed to floating exchange rates exposed national economies to greater competitive pressures. As a result, and in conjunction with others factors, such as the growing significance of transnational corporations, national economies were increasingly drawn into a web of interconnectedness. This economic interconnectedness achieved truly global dimensions in the 1990s thanks to the collapse of communism in eastern Europe and elsewhere and the opening up of the Chinese economy. However, although there may be broad agreement about the events through which the global economy came into existence, there is much more debate about the deeper forces and underlying dynamics that helped to shape, and perhaps determine, these events. These debates reflect competing perspectives on global political economy and contrasting positions on whether economic circumstances are best explained by structural factors, such as the organization of production, or by the free choices made by economic actors, be these states, firms or individuals.

In practice, complex economic developments such as the emergence of the global capitalist system are best explained through the dynamic relationship between structures and agents (O'Brien and Williams 2013). The most influential structuralist explanation of the emergence of a global economy is the Marxist argument that capitalism is an inherently universalist economic system. In short, globalization is the natural and inevitable consequence of the capitalist mode of production. As Marx (see p. 72) put it in the *Grundrisse* ([1857–58] 1971), the essence of capitalism is to 'pull down every local barrier to commerce' and, 'to capture the whole world as its market'. This occurs because the underlying dynamic of the capitalist system is the accumulation of capital, which, in turn, creates an irresistible desire to develop new markets and an unquenchable thirst for new and cheaper economic resources. According to Marxists, just as imperialism in the late nineteenth century had been fuelled by the desire to maintain profit levels, the acceleration of globalization from the late twentieth century onwards was a consequence of the end of the post-1945 'long boom' and the onset of a global recession in the 1970s.

Although liberals fiercely reject the critical Marxist view of capitalism, they nevertheless accept that globalization is fuelled by an underlying economic logic. In their case, this is linked not to the impulses of a capitalist enterprise but, in essence, to the content of human nature, specifically the innate and rational human desire for economic betterment. In this view, the global economy is merely a reflection of the fact that, regardless of their different cultures and traditions, people everywhere have come to recognize that market interaction is the best guarantee of material security and improved living standards. This is particularly expressed in the doctrine of free trade and the theory of competitive advantage, examined more closely in Chapter 19. As far as explaining when and how this inclination towards 'globality' started to be realized, liberals often emphasize the role of technological innovation. Technology, needless to say, has long played a role in facilitating transborder and even transworld connections between peoples – from the introduction of the telegraph (1857), to the telephone (1876) and the wireless (1895), the development of the aeroplane (1903), television (1926) and the liquid-fuelled rocket (1927), and the introduction of containerization in sea transport (1960s and 1970s). However, advances in information and communications technology (ICT) – notable examples include the invention of optical fibres in the late 1960s, and the introduction of commercial silicone chips in 1971 and of personal computers (PCs) in 1981 – have played a particularly important role in spurring progress towards globalization, especially by facilitating the development of global financial markets and the global administration of corporations. In the view of so-called 'hyperglobalists', globalized economic and cultural patterns, in effect, became inevitable once technologies such as computerized financial trading, mobile phones and the Internet became widely available.

Nevertheless, the global economy is not the creation of economic and technological forces alone; political and ideological factors also played a crucial part. Realist theorists, reviving the ideas of **mercantilism**, have countered the liberal and Marxist idea that globalization represents the final victory of economics over politics by emphasizing that, in crucial ways, the global economy is a product of state policy and institutional regulation. Far from having sidelined states, globalization may, in certain respects, be a device through which powerful

● **Mercantilism**: An economic philosophy, most influential in Europe from the fifteenth century to the late seventeenth century, which emphasizes the state's role in managing international trade and guaranteeing prosperity.

states, and especially the USA, have achieved their objectives. For example, the USA was instrumental in both the creation of the Bretton Woods system and its collapse. In this sense, globalization may be a response to the relative decline of the US economy in the 1970s and 1980s, the shift towards a more open and 'liberalized' trading system being a means of widening opportunities for US-based transnational corporations, thereby underpinning the health of the US economy. Indeed, much of this was achieved through, rather than in spite of, the institutions of economic governance that were constructed in the post-1945 period. The disproportionate influence that the USA exerts over the World Bank and the IMF, and the role played by the USA in transforming the General Agreement on Tariffs and Trade (GATT) into the more strongly pro-free-trade World Trade Organization (WTO), demonstrates the extent to which economic globalization was structured in line with US priorities, laid out through the Washington consensus.

Finally, these developments also have an ideological dimension. Unlike, for example, nineteenth-century imperialism, twentieth- and twenty-first-century globalization has not been brought about through coercion and explicit political domination. While liberals may argue that 'globalization by consent' – observed, for example, in an eagerness of states to join the WTO – reflects an underlying recognition of mutual economic benefit, critical theorists, who emphasize that the benefits of globalization are unequally shared, argue that this consent is manufactured through the spread of pro-market values and a culture of **consumerism** and materialism. In this view, the progress of economic globaliza-tion is underpinned by the advance of the ideology of neoliberalism which preaches both that there is no viable economic alternative to the global capitalist system and that the system is equitable and brings benefit to all.

How globalized is economic life?

Is economic globalization a myth or a reality? Have national economies effec-tively been absorbed into a single global system, or has nothing really changed: the world economy remains a collection of interlinked national economies? Two starkly contrasting positions are often adopted in this debate. On the one hand, hyperglobalists present the image of a 'borderless' global economy, in which the tendency for economic interaction to have a transborder or transworld character is irresistible, facilitated, even dictated, by advances in information and communication technologies (which are not now going to be *dis*invented). On the other hand, globalization sceptics point out that the demise of the national economy has been much exaggerated, and usually for ideological purposes: economic globalization is portrayed as advanced and irre-sistible in order to make a shift towards free market or neoliberal policies appear to be inevitable (Hirst and Thompson 1999). However, the choice between the model of a single global economy and a collection of more or less interdependent national economies is a misleading one. This is not to say that there is no such thing as the global economy, but that this image captures only part of a much more complex and differentiated reality. The world economy is better thought of as a 'globalizing' economy than as a 'global' economy: modern economic life is increasingly shaped by processes that have a regional and global, and not merely national, character. However, the significance of

● **Consumerism**: A psychological and cultural phenomenon whereby personal happiness is equated with the consumption of material possessions (see p. 153).

Debating...
Does economic globalization promote prosperity and opportunity for all?

As the ideological battle between capitalism and socialism has (apparently) been consigned to the dustbin of history, political debate has tended to focus instead on the impact of economic globalization. Should economic globalization be welcomed and embraced, or should it be resisted?

FOR

The magic of the market. From an economic liberal perspective, the market is the only reliable means of generating wealth, the surest guarantee of prosperity and economic opportunity. This is because the market, competition and the profit motive provide incentives for work and enterprise, and also allocate resources to their most profitable use. From this perspective, economic globalization, based on the transborder expansion of market economics, is a way of ensuring that people in all countries can benefit from the wider prosperity and expanded opportunities that only capitalism can bring.

Everyone's a winner. The great advantage of economic globalization is that it is a game of winners and winners. Although it makes the rich richer, it also makes the poor less poor. This occurs because international trade allows countries to specialize in the production of goods or services in which they have a 'comparative advantage', with other benefits accruing from the economies of scale that specialization makes possible. Similarly, transnational production is a force for good. TNCs, for instance, spread wealth, widen employment opportunities and improve access to modern technology in the developing world, helping to explain why developing world governments are usually so keen to attract inward investment. Economic globalization is thus the most reliable means of reducing poverty.

Economic freedom promotes other freedoms. Economic globalization does not just make societies richer. Rather, an open, market-based economy also brings social and political benefits. Social mobility increases as people are able to take advantage of wider working, career and educational opportunities, and the 'despotism' of custom and tradition is weakened as individualism and self-expression are given wider rein. Economic globalization is thus linked to democratization, the two processes coinciding very clearly in the 1990s. This occurs because people who enjoy wider economic and social opportunities soon demand greater opportunities for political participation, particularly through the introduction of multi-party elections.

AGAINST

Deepening poverty and inequality. Critics of globalization have drawn attention to the emergence of new and deeply entrenched patterns of inequality: globalization is thus a game of winners and losers. Critical theorists argue that the winners are TNCs and industrially advanced states generally, but particularly the USA, while the losers are in the developing world, where wages are low, regulation is weak or non-existent, and where production is increasingly orientated around global markets rather than domestic needs. Economic globalization is therefore a form of neo-colonialism: it forces poor countries to open up their markets and allow their resources to be plundered by rich states.

The 'hollowing out' of politics and democracy. Economic globalization diminishes the influence of national governments and therefore restricts public accountability. State policy is driven instead by the need to attract inward investment and the pressures generated by intensifying international competition. Integration into the global economy therefore usually means tax reform, deregulation and the scaling back of welfare. The alleged link between global capitalism and democratization is also a myth. Many states that have introduced market reforms and sought to integrate into the global economy have remained authoritarian if not dictatorial, conforming to the principles of state capitalism.

Corruptions of consumerist materialism. Even when economic globalization has succeeded in making people richer, it is less clear that it has improved, still less enriched, the quality of their lives. This is because it promotes an ethic of consumerism and material self-interest. Cultural and social distinctiveness is lost as people the world over consume the same goods, buy from the same stores and enjoy similar working practices and living conditions. This is particularly evident in the development of a 'brand culture', which pollutes public and personal spaces in order to create a culture of unthinking consumerism, even managing to absorb radical challenges to its dominance by turning them into consumer products (Klein 2001).

national, regional and global levels differs markedly in different economic sectors and types of activity, and, of course, in different parts of the world. Economic globalization is certainly not an 'even' process. Global interconnectedness has nevertheless increased in a number of ways. The most important of these include the following:

- International trade
- Transnational production
- Global division of labour
- Globalized financial system.

An increase in international trade has been one of the most prominent features of the world economy since 1945. Over this period, international trade has, on average, grown at double the rate of international production. Worldwide exports, for instance, grew from $629 million in 1960 to $7.3 trillion in 2003. Such trends were facilitated by the widely accepted link between trade and economic growth, exemplified by the success of export-orientated economies such as Germany and Japan from the 1950s onwards and the 'tiger' economies of East and South-east Asia from the 1970s onwards, and by a general trend towards free trade, punctuated briefly by a revival of protectionism in the 1970s. One of the novel features of international trade in the contemporary world economy is the increasing proportion of it that takes place within the same industry rather than between industries (which significantly heightens price competition) and the rise of **intra-firm trade**, made possible by the rise of TNCs. The growth of trade within firms, rather than between separate, individual firms, is one of the clearest signs of intensifying globalization. On the other hand, sceptics argue that trends in international trade are not a strong indication of the extent of globalization. For instance, there is little difference between modern levels of international trade and historical ones, and, with the exception of intra-firm trade, international trade promotes 'shallow' integration and greater interdependence, rather than a single globalized economy. Moreover, it is questionable whether the modern trading system has a truly global reach, in that around 80 per cent of world trade continues to take place between or among developed states, and most of this takes place within particular regions – in particular North America, Europe, and East and South-east Asia – rather than between different regions.

The issue of transborder production is closely linked to the growing importance of TNCs, which have come to account for most of the world's production and around half of world trade. Such corporations take advantage of global sourcing, through their ability to draw raw materials, components, investment and services from anywhere in the world. Crucially, they also have the advantage of being able to locate and relocate production in states or areas that are favourable to efficiency and profitability – for example, ones with cheap but relatively highly skilled sources of labour, or low corporation taxes and limited frameworks of workers' rights. Such trends, however, stop well short of a fully globalized system of production. Not only do most TNCs maintain strong links to their country of origin, and therefore only appear to be 'transnational' but, moreover, production continues overwhelmingly to be concentrated in the developed world.

● **Intra-firm trade**: Trade between two affiliates within the same company, or between a parent company and an affiliate.

Further evidence of economic globalization can be found in a strengthened global division of labour. Although this falls short of establishing a single, world labour market (as only an estimated 15 per cent of the world's workers are considered to be genuinely globally mobile), clearer patterns of economic specialization have become evident. In particular, high technology manufacturing has increasingly been concentrated in the developed world, while for many poorer states integration into the global economy means the production of agricultural goods or raw materials for export. Neo-Marxists and world-system theorists such as Immanuel Wallerstein (see p. 104) have argued that economic globalization is an uneven and hierarchical process, a game of winners and losers, which has seen economic power concentrated in an economic 'core' at the expense of the 'periphery'. These disparities also, to some extent, reflect differing levels of integration within the global economy, core areas or states being more fully integrated into the global economy, and thus reaping its benefits, while peripheral ones remain outside or at its margins.

The global financial system is often portrayed as the driving force behind economic globalization, even the foundation stone of the global economy. The global financial system was brought into existence through two processes. The first was the general shift towards deregulated financial markets in the 1970s and 1980s that followed the move to floating exchange rates with the collapse of Bretton Woods. This allowed money and capital to flow both within and between national economies with much greater ease. Then, in the 1990s, the application of new information and communication technologies to financial markets gave financial transactions a genuinely supraterritorial character, enabling transborder transactions to be conducted literally at 'the speed of thought'. An example of this is the emergence of transworld money, reflecting the fact that currencies have lost their national character in that they are traded across the globe and have values that are determined by global market forces. In 2012, approximately $5 trillion was traded each day in global currency markets. The impact of financial globalization on the stability of national economies as well as global capitalism has, nevertheless, been a matter of considerable debate.

Finally, it is important to remember that the conventional debate about the extent to which economic life has been globalized is conducted within narrow parameters, established by what is treated as productive labour and who are considered to be economically active. Despite the collapse of communism and the wider retreat of socialism, significant non-capitalist, or at least non-commercial, economic forms persist in many parts of the world. Feminist economists in particular have drawn attention to the vast, informal, 'invisible' economy that relies on unpaid labour, predominantly performed by women, in areas such housework, childcare, care for the elderly and small-scale farming. Especially important in the developing world, this economy operates on lines of exchange and material arrangements that are entirely outside global markets. It may, nevertheless, be responsible for feeding a substantial proportion of the world's population. For example, although home gardens managed by women occupy only 2 per cent of a household's farmland in eastern Nigeria, they account for about half of the farm's total output. In Indonesia, 20 per cent of household income and 40 per cent of domestic food supplies come from home gardens (Shiva 1999). An awareness of the significance of this 'invisible' economy has increasingly influenced the development strategies embraced by the United

Immanuel Wallerstein (born 1930)

US sociologist and pioneer of world-systems theory. Influenced by neo-Marxist dependency theory and the ideas of the French historian Fernand Braudel (1902–85), Wallerstein argues that the modern world-system is characterized by an international division of labour between the 'core' and the 'periphery'. Core regions benefit from the concentration of capital in its most sophisticated forms, while peripheral ones are dependent on the export of raw materials to the core, although fundamental contradictions will ultimately bring about the demise of the world-system. Wallerstein also traces the rise and decline of core hegemons (dominant powers) to changes in the world-system over time, arguing that the end of the Cold War marked the decline, not triumph, of the US hegemony. Wallerstein's key works include the three-volume *The Modern World System* (1974, 1980, 1989) and *Decline of American Power* (2003).

Nations and the World Bank, not least because of a realization that conventional, market-based development strategies can undermine the 'invisible' economy. Such issues are discussed in greater detail in Chapter 15.

GLOBAL CAPITALISM IN CRISIS

Explaining booms and slumps

The tendency towards booms, slumps and crises within a capitalist economy does not fit easily into classical liberal political economy. Economic liberalism is largely based on the assumption that market economies tend naturally towards a state of equilibrium, demand and supply coming into line with one another through the workings of the price mechanism – Adam Smith's 'invisible hand'. However, the history of capitalism, at both national and international levels, does not bear out this image of equilibrium and stability. Instead, capitalism has always been susceptible to booms and slumps, even violent fluctuations and crises. As early as 1720, the collapse of the so-called 'South Sea Bubble' (wildly speculative trading in the South Sea Company, a UK joint stock company granted a monopoly to trade in Spain's South American colonies), caused financial ruin for thousands of investors.

One factor that appears to be linked to economic fluctuations is war. Many of the most dramatic historical episodes of sustained **deflation** came in the aftermath of war. A sustained economic depression followed the American War of Independence, and, after the Congress of Vienna (1814–15) ended the Napoleonic Wars, Europe experienced decades of deflation, in which industrial investment was costly and many firms went bankrupt. In the mid-nineteenth century, the wars of unification in Italy and Germany, and the American Civil War, each produced immediate speculative bubbles, which then collapsed, leading to widespread bankruptcies and stock market crashes. WWI led to a brief reconstruction boom in 1919, before a collapse of the major western economies in 1920–21, with the Great Depression coming a decade later. In the post-1945

● **Deflation**: A reduction in the general level of prices, linked to a reduction in the level of economic activity in the economy.

era, the conflicts in Korea and Vietnam both produced inflationary surges, which initially reduced and then increased interest rates, which, in turn, created surges and declines in industrial investment. Linkages between war and economic performance stem from a variety of factors: the cost of financing unproductive military activity, the disruption of commerce, the freezing of capital movements, the cost of reconstruction, and so on.

However, other explanations of booms and slumps locate their source within the nature of the capitalist system itself. The classic example of this is found in Marx's analysis of capitalism. Marx was concerned not only to highlight the inherent instability of capitalism, based on irreconcilable class conflict, but also to analyze the nature of capitalist development. In particular, he drew attention to its tendency to experience deepening economic crises. These stemmed, in the main, from cyclical crises of over-production, plunging the economy into stagnation and bringing unemployment and immiseration to the working class. Each crisis would be more severe than the last, because, Marx calculated, in the long term the rate of profit would fall. This would eventually, and inevitably, produce conditions in which the proletariat, the vast majority in society, would rise up in revolution. Whatever its other advantages, the Marxist image of 'deepening' crises of capitalism, leading irresistibly towards the system's final collapse and replacement, has proved to be unsound. By contrast, capitalism has proved to be remarkably resilient and adaptable, capable of weathering financial and economic storms of various kinds, while also achieving long-term growth and expansion. This has occurred not least through the fact that capitalism's capacity for technological innovation has far outstripped Marx's expectations. Few therefore continue to see the tendency towards boom-and-bust cycles as a fatal flaw within capitalism, still less as a precursor of social revolution.

Amongst the most influential of non-Marxist theories were those developed by the Austrian economist and social theorist, Joseph Schumpeter (1883–1950). Building on Marx's theory of the capitalist **business cycle**, Schumpeter (1942) argued that capitalism existed in a state of ferment he dubbed 'creative destruction', with spurts of innovation destroying established enterprises and yielding new ones. The notion of creative destruction captures both the idea that it is entrepreneurs who drive economies, generating growth and, through successes and failures, setting business cycles in motion, and the idea that innovation is the main driver of wealth. However, Schumpeter himself was pessimistic about the long-term prospects for capitalism, arguing that the human and social costs of periodic slumps and the stifling of dynamism, creativity and individualism through the growth of elitism and state intervention would ultimately lead to capitalism's demise. Developments in the post-1945 period, and especially in the age of accelerated globalization and 'turbo-capitalism', nevertheless suggest that Schumpeter seriously underestimated capitalism's sustained appetite for creative destruction. More conventional academic economists tend to explain boom-and-bust cycles in terms of the factors determining business investment and its effects on the level of GDP. In such views, levels of business investment are inherently unstable because of factors such as the multiplier effect (the exaggerated impact of spending and investment as it ripples through the economy) and the accelerator principle (the hypothesis that levels of investment vary with changes to the rate of output).

● **Business cycle**: Regular oscillations in the level of business activity over time, sometimes called a 'trade cycle'.

CONCEPT

Laissez-faire

Laissez-faire (in French meaning literally 'leave to do') is the principle of non-intervention in economic affairs. It is the heart of the doctrine that the economy works best when left alone by government. The phrase originated with the Physiocrats of eighteenth-century France, who devised the maxim '*laissez faire est laissez passer*' (leave the individual alone, and let commodities circulate freely). The central assumption of *laissez-faire* is that an unregulated market tends naturally towards equilibrium. This is usually explained by the theory of 'perfect competition'. From this perspective, government intervention is seen as damaging unless it is restricted to actions that promote market competition, such as checks on monopolies and the maintenance of stable prices.

● **Recession**: A period of general economic decline that is part of the usual business cycle.

● **Beggar-thy-neighbour policies**: Policies pursued at the expense of other states that are believed to be in their own country's short-term national interest; most commonly used to describe protectionism.

Lessons of the Great Crash

The greatest challenge that international capitalism has faced was posed by the Great Depression of the 1930s, which was precipitated by the Wall Street Crash of 1929. From 1926, the USA experienced an artificial boom, fed by a rash of speculation and the expectation of ever-rising share prices. However, in 1929 confidence in the economy suddenly evaporated when signs appeared that the sale of goods was starting to decline. On 24 October 1929 ('Black Thursday'), a panic ensued on the stock market as 13 million shares changed hands in a single day. On 29 October, 16 million shares were sold. Banks subsequently failed, major businesses started to collapse and unemployment began to rise. As a severe economic depression in the USA spread abroad, affecting, to some degree, all industrialized states, the Great Crash became a Great Depression.

The Wall Street Crash is relatively easy to explain. As J. K. Galbraith argued in his classic *The Great Crash, 1929* ([1955] 2009), it was just 'another speculative bubble', albeit on an historically unprecedented scale. It was, he argued, an 'escape into make believe', fuelled by the belief that it is possible to get rich without effort and without work. That stock market crises have an impact on the 'real' economy is not a surprise, given the fact that falling stock values inevitably lead to a decline in business and consumer confidence, reducing the funds available for investment as well as domestic demand. However, does a **recession** have to become a fully-fledged depression? In the case of the Great Crash, two key mistakes were made. First, in view of a strong belief in 'rugged individualism' and the doctrine of *laissez-faire*, the Hoover administration responded to the Wall Street Crash by keeping public spending low and trying to achieve a balanced budget. Not only did this mean that the unemployed had to rely mainly on private charity (such as soup kitchens) for survival, but it also meant that, in withdrawing money from the economy, it helped to deepen, rather than cure, the crisis.

This lesson was most crucially taught by Keynes, whose *The General Theory of Employment, Interest and Money* ([1936]1963) challenged classical economic thinking and rejected its belief in a self-regulating market. Keynes argued that the level of economic activity, and therefore employment, is determined by the total amount of demand – aggregate demand – in the economy. This implied that governments could manage their economies through adjusting their fiscal policies, injecting demand into the economy in times of recession and high employment by either increasing public spending or reducing taxation. Unemployment could therefore be solved, not by the invisible hand of capitalism, but by government intervention, in this case by running a budget deficit, meaning that the government literally overspends. The first, if limited, attempts to apply Keynes's ideas were undertaken in the USA during Roosevelt's 'New Deal', but even then Roosevelt was unwilling to move away from the idea of a balanced budget, helping to explain why the Great Depression ran throughout the 1930s and only ended with the increase in military spending after the outbreak of WWII. Only in Germany did the Depression end earlier, and that was because rearmament and military expansion from the mid-1930s onwards served as a form of 'inadvertent Keynesianism'.

The second lesson of the Great Crash was that its economic impact was substantially deepened by the general trend towards **'beggar-thy-neighbour' policies**. In a context of economic decline, states in the late 1920s and through the

1930s took steps to maximize their exports while at the same time minimizing their imports. This was done in a variety of ways. First, fiscal deflation, through either or both reduced government spending and raised taxes, was used to reduce the demand for imports. The problem with this, as pointed out earlier, was that reduced levels of aggregate demand would affect the domestic economy just as much as it would affect imports. The second strategy was **devaluation**, in the hope that exports would become cheaper for overseas customers, while imports would become relatively more expensive, and less desirable. However, although countries that devalued earlier tended to recover from the Depression more quickly than the later devaluers did, competitive devaluations had a net deflationary effect and so deepened the economic crisis. Third, governments raised tariffs on imports, in the hope of protecting domestic industries and reducing unemployment, a policy that even Keynes favoured. However, the overall impact of beggar-thy-neighbour policies was self-defeating, and only served to deepen and prolong the Great Depression. Countries cannot maximize their exports while minimizing their imports, if all countries are trying to do the same thing. It was largely in an attempt to prevent the international economy being damaged in the post-1945 period by such policies that the Bretton Woods system was set up.

Modern crises and 'contagions'

During the early post-1945 period, western governments widely believed that the instabilities of the business cycle had been solved by the application of Keynesian principles, which seemed to offer a means of counteracting the tendency towards booms and slumps. However, the belief in Keynesianism declined after the 'stagflation' crisis of the 1970s, hastened by the subsequent revival of *laissez-faire* thinking in the guise of neoliberalism. This nevertheless did not cure, but rather accentuated, the fluctuations within the capitalist system, intensifying its tendency towards creative destruction. This is an important aspect of the development of a 'risk society'. In particular, greater instability was a direct result of the tendency towards 'financialization'.

Financial markets are always susceptible to fluctuations and instability as a result of speculative bubbles. However, the emergence of a globalized financial system has accentuated these tendencies, by leaving states more vulnerable and exposed to the vagaries of global markets. This has created what Susan Strange (1986) dubbed 'casino capitalism'. Massive amounts of 'mad money' surge around the world, creating the phenomenon of financial **contagion**. Such instabilities have been further accentuated by the fact that most modern financial growth has occurred in the form of purely money-dealing currency and security exchanges, such as so-called 'hedge funds', which are linked to profits from future, rather than actual, production, and 'derivatives', the value of which depend on the price of an underlying security or asset. Thus, although global financial flows can create artificial booms and slumps, as well as reap massive rewards for global speculators, they are, in a sense, one step removed from the performance of 'real' economies. The tendency for financial bubbles to form has also been linked to a 'bonus culture' that took root to varying degrees in banks and financial institutions across the world. The payment of massive bonuses incentivized short-term risk-taking, making banks and financial institutions more insecure and even vulnerable to collapse once the bubble burst.

● **Devaluation**: A reduction in the value of a currency relative to other currencies.

● **Casino capitalism**: A form of capitalism that is highly volatile and unpredictable because it is susceptible to speculatively-orientated lifts in finance capital.

● **Contagion**: The tendency of investors, alarmed by a crisis in one part of the world, to remove money from other parts of the world, thereby spreading panic well beyond the scope of the initial problem.

John Maynard Keynes (1883–1946)

British economist. Keynes's reputation was established by his critique of the Treaty of Versailles, outlined in *The Economic Consequences of the Peace* (1919). His major work, *The General Theory of Employment, Interest and Money* ([1936] 1963), departed significantly from neoclassical economic theories, and went a long way towards establishing the discipline now known as macroeconomics. By challenging *laissez-faire* principles, he provided the theoretical basis for the policy of demand management, which was widely adopted by western governments in the early post-WWII period. The last years of his life saw him devoting much of his efforts to shaping the nature of the post-war international monetary order through the establishment of the Bretton Woods system, including the IMF and the World Bank.

The economic instability of casino capitalism and its tendency towards financial crises has been demonstrated since the mid-1990s in Mexico, in East and South-east Asia, Brazil, Argentina and elsewhere. The Asian financial crisis was the most significant and far-reaching such crisis before the global financial crisis of 2008. The Asian crisis started in July 1997 when speculators in Thailand, anticipating that the government would have to devalue its currency, the baht, sold strongly, thereby turning their expectations into a reality. This led to a classic financial contagion, as similar speculative attacks were then mounted against Indonesia, Malaysia and South Korea, with Hong Kong, Taiwan and even China in danger of being drawn into the turmoil. As governments used up their entire foreign exchange reserves, economic output fell, unemployment increased and wages plummeted. At the end of 1997, the whole of South-east Asia was in the throes of a financial crisis that threatened to disrupt the stability of the entire global economy. Financial stability and, more gradually, economic recovery were brought about by the provision of bail-out funds by the IMF to Thailand, Indonesia and South Korea. However, this occurred at the cost of the liberalization of their financial systems, and therefore a reduction in domestic economic control. By contrast, Malaysia, which had resisted IMF pressure and instituted capital controls, was successful in preventing further rapid transborder capital flows. The crisis also demonstrated the disjuncture between the performance of financial markets and that of the 'real' economy, in that the Asian financial crisis occurred despite higher growth rates across much of East and South-east Asia between the early 1960s and the 1990s, and especially in the 'tiger' economies.

The 2007–09 global financial crisis and its implications

The global financial crisis started in the middle of 2007 with the onset of a **credit crisis**, particularly in the USA and the UK. However, this merely provided a background to the remarkable events of September 2008, when global capitalism appeared to teeter on the brink of the abyss, threatening to tip over into systemic failure. The decisive events took place in the USA. The two government-sponsored mortgage corporations, Fannie Mae and Freddie Mac, were baled out

● **Credit crisis**: A reduction in the general availability of loans (or credit), usually due to an unwillingness of banks to lend to one another.

Crises of modern global capitalism

1994–5	The Mexican economic crisis begins with the sudden devaluation of the Mexican peso and has an impact elsewhere in Latin America (the 'Tequila effect').
1997–8	The Asian financial crisis starts in Thailand with the collapse of the baht but spreads to most of South-east Asia and Japan, where currencies slump and stock markets crash.
1998	The Russian financial crisis sees the collapse of stock, bond and currency markets in a context of falling commodity prices in the wake of the Asian financial crisis.
1999–2002	The Argentine economic crisis begins with a loss of investor confidence in the Argentine economy in a context of falling GDP, leading to a flight of money away from the country.
2000	The Dot-com crisis sees the bursting of the 'dot-com bubble' after dramatic speculative rises in IT-related stocks since 1998.
2002	The Uruguay banking crisis witnesses a massive run on banks amid concerns about the Uruguayan economy linked to Argentina's economic meltdown.
2007–8	The US sub-prime mortgage crisis precipitates the global financial crisis.
2007–9	The global financial crisis
2010–13	The eurozone crisis (see p. 112)

by Federal authorities; Lehman Brothers, the 158-year old investment bank, succumbed to bankruptcy; the insurance giant AIG was only saved by a $85 billion government rescue package; while Wachovia, the fourth largest US bank, was bought by Citigroup, absorbing $42 billion of bad debt. Banking crises erupted elsewhere, and stock markets went into freefall worldwide, massively reducing share values and betokening the onset of a global recession which lasted, in most countries, until 2009, although much of Europe re-entered recession in 2011.

Debates about the implications of the global financial crisis of 2007–09 are closely linked to disagreement about its underlying causes. Was the crisis rooted in the US banking system, in Anglo-American enterprise capitalism, or in the nature of the capitalist system itself? At one level, the crisis was linked to inappropriate lending strategies adopted by US banks and mortgage institutions, the 'sub-prime' mortgage market. These high-risk loans to applicants with poor or non-existent credit histories were unlikely to be repaid, and when the scale of 'toxic debt' became apparent shockwaves ran through the US financial system and beyond. At a deeper level, however, the 'sub-prime' problem in the USA was merely a symptom of the defects and vulnerabilities of the neoliberal capitalism that has taken root in the USA, the UK and elsewhere, based on free markets and an under-regulated financial system. For George Soros (see p. 110), the crisis of

KEY CONTEMPORARY ECONOMIC THEORISTS

George Soros (born 1930)

A Hungarian-born stock market investor, businessman and philanthropist, Soros has been a critic of the market fundamentalist belief in natural equilibrium. He particularly emphasizes the role of reflexivity (the tendency for cause and effect to be linked, as actions 'bend back on' themselves) in showing why rational-actor economic models do not work. Soros's main works include *Open Society* (2000) and *The New Paradigm for Financial Markets* (2008).

Paul Krugman (born 1953)

A US economist and political commentator, Krugman's academic work has primarily focused on international economics. A neo-Keynesian, he has viewed expansionary fiscal policy as the solution to recession. Krugman criticized the Bush administration's tax cuts and widening deficit as unsustainable in the long run. His best-known works include *The Conscience of a Liberal* (2007) and *The Return of Depression Economics and the Crisis of 2008* (2008).

Dan Deitch © 2010

Ben Bernanke (born 1953)

A US economist and Chairman of the US Federal Reserve since 2006, Bernanke was instrumental in managing the USA's response to the 2007–09 global financial crisis. Bernanke's academic writings have focused largely on the economic and political causes of the Great Depression, highlighting, amongst other things, the role of the Federal Reserve and the tendency of banks and financial institutions to cut back significantly on lending. Bernanke's main work is *Essays on the Great Depression* (2004).

Herman Daly (born 1938)

A US ecological economist, Daly is best known for his theory of steady-state economics. This suggests that perpetual economic growth is neither possible nor desirable. Daly champions qualitatively-defined 'development' over quantitatively-defined 'growth' ('more of the same stuff'), and favours rich countries reducing their economic growth to free up resources and ecological space for use by the poor. His key works include *Steady-State Economics* (1973) and (with J. Cobb) *For the Common Good* (1990).

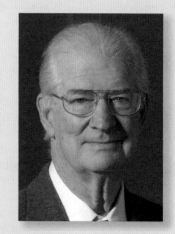

See also **Joseph Stiglitz** (see p. 474)

2007–09 reflected the failure of the market fundamentalism that had underpinned neoliberal economic thinking. Challenging the notion that markets operate rationally to ensure that resources are allocated to their most profitable use, Soros (2008) argued that deregulated financial markets had allowed a 'super-bubble' to develop over a period of some 25 years, taking the form of massive and unsustainable debt. When this super-bubble burst, many of the financial instruments (bonds, securities, derivatives and so on) that had been traded in ever-larger volumes were suddenly revealed to be almost valueless. Even an avowed supporter of *laissez-faire* capitalism such as the former Federal Reserve Board Chairman, Alan Greenspan, has noted the tendency of markets towards 'irrational exuberance', leading to an undue escalation in asset values.

The 2007–09 crisis was the first genuinely global crisis in the world economy since the stagflation crisis of the 1970s, and it gave rise to the most severe falls in global production levels since the Great Depression of the 1930s, later being dubbed the 'Great Recession'. As most major economies returned to growth in 2009, it appeared that the massive efforts quickly initiated by national governments and coordinated by the G-20 (see p. 121) had been successful. These had seen the recapitalizing of banks, substantial cuts in interest rates (monetary stimulus) and a boost to domestic demand by allowing spending to exceed taxation (fiscal stimulus). Above all, international action prevented a recurrence of the most serious mistake made in the aftermath of the 1929 Wall Street Crash: a resort to protectionism, which helped to ensure that a financial crisis turned into a deep and prolonged economic crisis. However, renewed and severe economic problems emerged from 2010 onwards, not least in the form of **sovereign debt crises** in a number of '**eurozone**'. economies. This suggested that, for western economies in particular, the global financial crisis may have triggered the beginning of an age of debt and austerity (see p. 112).

One of the most widely anticipated consequences of the financial crisis was that it would lead to a re-evaluation, and possibly a rejection, of the neoliberal model of globalization. This was, in part, because past major crises have led to significant changes in the management of the world economy. The Great Depression of the 1930s led, via Roosevelt's New Deal in the USA, to a shift in the post-1945 world in favour of Keynesianism, while the 'stagflation' crisis of the 1970s contributed to the abandonment of Keynesianism and the rise of neoliberalism. Nevertheless, there has been relatively little evidence of a shift of similar proportions in response to the 2007–09 Crash. For example, progress on the construction of a 'new Bretton Woods', widely mooted in the immediate aftermath of September 2008, which would re-orientate the institutions of global economic governance away from neoliberalism, has been slow. (The relationship between global economic governance during the Great Recession is discussed on p. 482.) The reasons for this may include the fact that political choice in such matters is constrained by the structural power of the interests most closely linked to neoliberal globalization – TNCs, the major banks, global markets and so forth – but it also reflects the intellectual and ideological failure of the political left (be it in the form of left-wing or centre-left political parties or the anti-capitalist movement (see p. 74)) to develop an alternative model of globalization that is both economically and politically viable. It is worth noting, however, that the full ideological significance of the Great Depression only became apparent in 1945, after almost a decade of mass unemployment and an intervening world war.

● **Sovereign debt crisis:** A structural imbalance in state finances that makes it impossible to repay, or re-finance, the national debt without assistance from a third party.

● **Eurozone:** The area of the EU within which the single currency (the euro) is used (in 2015, encompassing 19 member states).

GLOBAL POLITICS IN ACTION . . .

The West in an age of debt and austerity

Events: The dramatic events of September 2008 precipitated the steepest declines in global output since the 1930s. Although the world economy returned to modest growth in 2009, renewed economic problems emerged across much of the western world during 2010, in the form of escalating sovereign debt (sometimes called 'national debt' or 'government debt'). In some cases, this brought the creditworthiness of a country into question, as concerns over its ability to repay its loans pushed up interest rates to unsustainable levels and created the need for external intervention. Sovereign debt crises, often linked to banking crises, were most acute in the eurozone, where bail-outs were negotiated by the EU, the IMF and the European Central Bank for Greece (in 2010 and again in 2012), Ireland (in 2010), Portugal (in 2011), Spain (in 2012) and Cyprus (in 2013). Elsewhere, low growth and rising debt meant that states lost their prized AAA creditworthiness status; this, for instance, happened to the USA in 2011, France in 2012 and the UK in 2013. Either because of conditions attached to bail-outs, or because of wider anxieties about debt, many western states shifted economic policy away from fiscal stimulus (the initial, and orchestrated, response to the September 2008 crisis) to 'fiscal retrenchment' (reduced public spending or increased taxes), helping to initiate an 'age of austerity'.

Significance: The structural weaknesses of many western economies may have been exposed by the Great Recession, but they had deeper causes. These include a tendency, sometimes going back to the 1980s, to bring about growth by ever-higher levels of borrowing (in the form of mortgages, bank loans, credit cards and hire purchase, and so on), made possible by an inflated and under-regulated banking and financial sector. Moreover, some 30 years of growth in the world economy had allowed western governments to become complacent about sovereign debt, confident in the belief that growth would continue. This assumption was brutally destroyed by the Great Recession: as output plummeted, so did tax revenues, throwing the public finances into chaos with a resulting explosion of borrowing.

However, there is major debate about how the blight of debt should be addressed, and especially about the link between debt and austerity. The austerity approach, adopted across much of Europe, is based on the belief that if chronic indebtedness is the problem, the solution must be debt reduction, achieved, in particular, by cutting public spending. A failure to take the 'austerity medicine' risks passing on an escalating debt burden to future generations, and losing altogether the confidence of financial markets, making loans impossible to service. Quite simply, governments and general publics must (once again) get used to living within their means. Austerity, nevertheless, brings with it the problem that spending cuts and/or increased taxes take demand out of the economy, and so threatens to result in a 'lost decade' of economic stagnation and high unemployment. In this scenario, public finances remain in turmoil as low or zero growth results in declining tax revenues and stubbornly high public spending. A solution that makes sense for a family in debt may thus be self-defeating if applied to the economy as a whole, and disastrous (because of its impact on exports) if applied to a range of linked economies. The principal alternative to austerity is a neo-Keynesian strategy that, whilst accepting the long-term goal of a balanced budget, would maintain spending in the short- and perhaps medium-term on the infrastructure programmes in particular. This, broadly, is the approach adopted by the Obama administration in the USA. In such a strategy, the justification for continued or increased borrowing is that it will boost growth and, in due course, tax revenues, allowing the debt problem to be resolved as the economy revives. Critics, on the other hand, argue that neo-Keynesianism simply leaves government 'addicted to debt', unable or unwilling to carry out the 'rebalancing' that western economies have long needed to carry out.

The 2007–09 crisis may, nevertheless, come to be seen as a pivotal moment in the transfer of power in the global economy from the West to the East in general, and from the USA to China in particular. Not only had much of the growth in the world economy in the two decades preceding the financial crisis been generated by China, India, Brazil and other emerging economies, but their ability to produce massive quantities of cheap manufactured goods helped to conceal deeper structural economic defects in the developed world, in part by creating the impression that inflation had been 'cured'. In addition, China and many emerging economies weathered the storms of 2007–09 far better than did developed economies; China, for instance, experienced only a mild dip in its growth rate during this period. Emerging economies also entered the post-crisis period with the advantage that they usually had significant trade surpluses and were often major creditor countries, having bought much of the debt of the developed world. However, such shifts in the balance of economic power are occurring in a world that is more interdependent than ever before. Just as economic recovery in the USA is important to China, because China holds much of the USA's sovereign debt, so the developing world needs recovery in the developed world to provide a market for its manufacturing goods. Perhaps the key lesson of the crisis, then, is that it reminds us that in a globalized world no economy is an island.

SUMMARY

- Capitalism is a system of generalized commodity production in which wealth is owned privately and economic life is organized according to market principles. Enterprise capitalism, social capitalism and state capitalism nevertheless differ in relation to the balance within them between the market and the state.

- The advance of neoliberalism reflects the ascendance of enterprise capitalism over rival forms of capitalism. While supporters of neoliberalism claim that, in association with economic globalization, it is a reliable vehicle for generating global growth, its critics have associated it with widening inequality, financial crises and political 'shocks' of various kinds.

- Economic globalization is the process whereby all national economies have, to a greater or lesser extent, been absorbed into an interlocking global economy. However, there have been major debates about the extent to which economic life has been globalized as well as about the impact, for good or ill, of economic globalization.

- Despite its global success, capitalism has always been susceptible to booms and slumps. While Marxists have explained these crises in terms of an inherent tendency of capitalism towards over-production, Schumpeter drew attention to the business cycle, stemming from the disposition within capitalism towards 'creative destruction'.

- Modern crises and 'contagions' have derived from the trend – implicit, some argue, in neoliberal globalization – in favour of 'financialization'. This has created what has been dubbed 'casino capitalism', a highly volatile and unpredictable economic system that allows speculative bubbles to develop and then collapse, their impact extending, potentially, across the world.

- The origins of the global financial crisis of 2007–09 are hotly disputed, with disagreement about whether the crisis was rooted in the US banking system, in Anglo-American enterprise capitalism, or in the nature of the capitalist system itself. The crisis may have accelerated important shifts in global power, but it is far less clear that it will result in a major shift in favour of national or global financial regulation.

Questions for discussion

- What are the major strengths and weaknesses of enterprise capitalism?
- To what extent is capitalism compatible with a comprehensive welfare provision?
- Is state capitalism a contradiction in terms?
- Does China have a coherent economic model?
- To what extent are neoliberalism and economic globalization linked?
- What are the chief drivers of economic globalization?
- Is the idea of a global economy a myth?
- Are transnational corporations a force for good or for ill?
- Is capitalism inherently unstable and crisis-prone?
- What does the 2007–09 global financial crisis tell us about the nature of the modern world economy?

Further reading

Casey, T. (ed.), *The Legacy of the Crash* (2011). A wide-ranging collection of essays that examine the nature and consequences of the 2007–09 crisis and the differing political responses in the USA and the UK..

Harvey, D., *A Brief History of Neoliberalism* (2005). A concise and critical examination of the origins, spread and effects of neoliberalism.

O'Brien, R. and M. Williams, *Global Political Economy: Evolution and Dynamics* (2013). A lucid and comprehensive introduction to global political economy.

Ravenhill, J. (ed.), *Global Political Economy* (2011). A comprehensive and well-organized text in which leading experts examine the major issues of global political economy.

ONLINE RESOURCES AVAILABLE

Links to relevant web resources can be found on the *Global Politics* website

CHAPTER **5** # The State and Foreign Policy in a Global Age

'Traditional nation-states have become unnatural, even impossible units in a global economy.'

KENICHI OHMAE, *The End of the Nation State* (1996)

PREVIEW   The state has long been regarded as the most significant actor on the world stage, the basic 'unit' of global politics. Its predominance stems from its sovereign jurisdiction. As states exercise unchallengeable power within their borders, they operate, or should operate, as independent and autonomous entities in world affairs. However, the state is under threat, perhaps as never before. In particular, globalization, in its economic and political forms, has led to a process of state retreat, even fashioning what some have called the 'post-sovereign' state. Others, nevertheless, argue that conditions of flux and transformation underline the need for the order, stability and direction that (arguably) only the state can provide is greater than ever. Are states in decline, or are they in a process of revival? Globalizing trends have also had implications for the nature and processes of government. Once viewed as 'the brains' of the state, controlling the body politic from the centre, government has seemingly given way to 'governance', a looser and more amorphous set of processes that blur the distinction between the public and private realms, and often operate on supranational and subnational levels as well as the national level. Why and how has government been transformed into governance, and what have been the implications of this process? Finally, foreign policy is important as the mechanism through which, usually, national government manages the state's relations with other states and with international bodies, highlighting the role that choice and decision play in global politics. How are foreign policy decisions made, and what factors influence them?

KEY ISSUES

- Is sovereignty statehood compatible with a globalized world?
- Have nation-states been transformed into market or postmodern states?
- In what ways, and why, has the state become more important?
- To what extent has national government given way to multi-level governance?
- Is the concept of foreign policy any longer meaningful?
- What is the most persuasive theory of foreign policy decision-making?

STATES AND STATEHOOD IN FLUX

States and sovereignty

The state (see p. 118) is a historical institution: it emerged in fifteenth- and sixteenth-century Europe as a system of centralized rule that succeeded in subordinating all other institutions and groups, temporal and spiritual. The Peace of Westphalia (1648) is usually taken to have formalized the modern notion of statehood. By establishing states as sovereign entities, it made states the principal actors on the world stage. International politics was thus thought of as a 'state system'. The state system gradually expanded from Europe into North America, then, during the nineteenth century, into South America and Japan, becoming a truly global system in the twentieth century, largely thanks to the process of decolonization in Asia, Africa, the Caribbean and the Pacific. In the twenty-first century, statehood appears to be more popular and sought-after than ever before. In 2013, the United Nations recognized 193 states, compared with 50 in 1945, and there are a number of 'unrecognized' states waiting in the wings, including the Vatican (the Holy See), Taiwan, Kosovo and Northern Cyprus. The list of potential candidates for statehood is also impressive: Palestine, Kurdistan, Quebec, Chechnya, Western Sahara, Puerto Rico, Bermuda, Greenland and Scotland, to name but a few. However, what is a state, and what are the key features of statehood?

States have a dualistic structure, in that they have two faces, one looking outwards and the other looking inwards (Cerny 2010). The outward-looking face of the state deals with the state's relations with other states and its ability to provide protection against external attack. The classic definition of the state in international law is found in the Montevideo Convention on the Rights and Duties of the State (1933). According to Article 1 of the Montevideo Convention, the state has four features:

● A defined territory
● A permanent population
● An effective government
● The capacity to enter into relations with other states.

The Montevideo Connection advances a 'declaratory' theory of the state, in which states become states by virtue of meeting the minimal criteria for statehood, as opposed to a '**constitutive' theory of the state**. Even without recognition, the state has the right to defend its integrity and independence, to provide for its conservation and prosperity, and consequently to organize itself as it sees fit (Article 3).

The inward-looking face of the state deals with the state's relations with the individuals and groups that live within its borders and its ability to maintain domestic order. From this perspective, the state is usually viewed as an instrument of domination. The German sociologist Max Weber (1864–1920) thus defined the state in terms of its monopoly of the means of 'legitimate violence'. Joseph Schumpeter (1954) complemented this definition by pointing out that the state also has a monopoly of the right to tax citizens. In view of the state's dual structure, what can be called 'statehood' can be seen as the capacity both to protect against external attack and to maintain domestic order, and to do them simultaneously (Brenner 2004).

● **The constitutive theory of the state**: The theory that the political existence of a state is entirely dependent on its recognition by other states.

However, although not explicitly mentioned in the Montevideo Convention's list of state features, or in Weber's notion of a monopoly of the legitimate use of violence, the underlying character of the state is established by a single core characteristic: **sovereignty**. In the final analysis, states are states because they are capable of exercising sovereign jurisdiction within defined territorial borders, and so are autonomous and independent actors. In the billiard ball model of world politics, adopted by realist theorists, states are the billiard balls that collide with one another while sovereignty is the hard and impenetrable outer shell of the ball which enables it to withstand the impact of the collision. The first major theorist of sovereignty was the French political philosopher Jean Bodin (1530–96). He defined sovereignty as 'the absolute and perpetual power of a common wealth'. In his view, the only guarantee of political and social stability is the existence of a sovereign with final law-making power; in that sense, law reflects the 'will' of the sovereign. For Thomas Hobbes (see p. 14), the need for sovereignty arose from the self-seeking and power-interested nature of human beings, which meant that, in the absence of a sovereign ruler – that is, in a 'state of nature' – life would degenerate into a war of all against all, in which life would be 'solitary, poor, nasty, brutish and short'. He therefore defined sovereignty as a monopoly of coercive power and advocated that it be vested in the hands of a single ruler (whether this was a monarch, his preferred form of government, or an oligarchic group or even a democratic assembly). However, in line with the dual structure of the state, sovereignty can be understood in internal or external senses.

The concept of **internal sovereignty** refers to the location of power or authority *within* a state, and has been crucial to the development of state structures and systems of rule. Where, within a political system, should final and ultimate authority be located? Early thinkers, as already noted, were inclined to the belief that sovereignty should be vested in the hands of a single person, a monarch. Absolute monarchs described themselves as 'sovereigns', and could, as did Louis XIV of France in the seventeenth century, declare that they *were* the state. The most radical departure from this absolutist notion of sovereignty came in the eighteenth century with the Swiss political philosopher Jean-Jacques Rousseau's rejection of monarchical rule in favour of the notion of popular sovereignty. For Rousseau, ultimate authority was vested in the people themselves, expressed in the idea of the 'general will'. The doctrine of popular sovereignty has often been seen as the basis of the modern theory of democracy, inspiring, amongst other things, the liberal-democratic idea that the sole legitimate source of political authority is success in regular, fair and competitive elections. Nevertheless, some liberal thinkers warn that the concept of internal sovereignty is always tainted by its absolutist origins, arguing that the idea of an absolute and final source of authority is difficult to reconcile with the reality of diffused power and pluralist competition found within the modern democratic state. A state may, however, be considered sovereign over its people and territory despite the fact that there may be disputes or even confusion about the internal location of sovereign power. This is the notion of **external sovereignty**.

External sovereignty defines a state's relationship to other states and international actors. It establishes the state's capacity to act as an independent and autonomous entity in world affairs. As such, it is the form of sovereignty that is of crucial importance for global politics. External sovereignty, for example, provides the basis for international law (see p. 339). Not only does the United

● **Sovereignty**: The principle of absolute and unlimited power; the absence of a higher authority in either domestic or external affairs (see p. 4).

● **Internal sovereignty**: The notion of a supreme power/authority within the state, located in a body that makes decisions that are binding on all citizens, groups and institutions within the state's borders.

● **External sovereignty**: The absolute and unlimited authority of the state as an actor on the world stage, implying the absence of any higher authority in external affairs.

CONCEPT

The state

The state is a political association that establishes sovereign jurisdiction within defined territorial borders. In political theory, the state is usually defined in contrast to civil society: it encompasses institutions that are recognizably 'public' in that they are responsible for the collective organization of communal life, and are funded through taxation (the institutions of government, the courts, the military, nationalized industries, social security system, and so forth). In international politics, however, the state is usually defined from an external perspective, and so embraces civil society. In this view, a state is characterized by four features: a defined territory, a permanent population, an effective government and sovereignty. This means, in effect, that a state is equivalent to a country.

Nations (UN) operate according to the principle of sovereign equality, allowing all states equal participation in international relations through membership of the General Assembly, but, most importantly, external sovereignty guarantees that the territorial integrity and political independence of each state is inviolable. Similarly, many of the deepest divisions in world politics involve disputed claims to external sovereignty. The Arab–Israeli conflict, for instance, turns on the question of external sovereignty. The Palestinians have long sought to establish a homeland and, ultimately, a sovereign state in territory claimed by Israel (see p. 119); in turn, Israel has traditionally seen such demands as a challenge to its own sovereignty.

Nevertheless, the notion of external sovereignty has been the subject of growing controversy, with questions being raised about both its moral implications and its practical significance. Moral concerns have been raised because external sovereignty appears to allow states to treat their citizens however they please, including, possibly, subjecting them to abuse, torture and perhaps even genocide (see p. 333). There is therefore tension between the principle of external sovereignty and the doctrine of human rights (see p. 311), and indeed any global or cosmopolitan standard of justice. This tension has been particularly evident in relation to the issue of humanitarian intervention (see p. 326), as discussed in Chapter 13. Concerns about the practical significance of external sovereignty have also become more acute. In a sense, the disparity in power between and amongst states has always raised questions about the meaningfulness of sovereignty, powerful states being able, sometimes routinely, to infringe on the independence and autonomy of weaker states. However, a range of modern developments have put states under pressure perhaps as never before, leading to predictions about the 'end of sovereignty' and even the 'twilight of the state'. The most important of these are linked to the advance of globalization (see p. 8).

The state and globalization

The rise of globalization has stimulated a major debate about the power and significance of the state in a globalized world. Three contrasting positions can be identified. In the first place, some theorists have boldly proclaimed the emergence of 'post-sovereign **governance**' (Scholte 2005), suggesting that the rise of globalization is inevitably marked by the decline of the state as a meaningful actor. In the most extreme version of this argument, advanced by so-called 'hyperglobalists', the state is seen to be so 'hollowed out' as to have become, in effect, redundant. Realists, on the other hand, tend to deny that globalization has altered the core feature of world politics, which is that, as in earlier eras, sovereign states are the primary determinants of what goes on within their borders, and remain the principal actors on the world stage. Between these two views, however, is a third position, which acknowledges that globalization has brought about qualitative changes in the role and significance of the state, and in the nature of sovereignty, but emphasizes that these have transformed the state, rather than simply reduced or increased its power.

It is very difficult to argue that the state and sovereignty have been unaffected by the forces of globalization. This particularly applies in the case of the territorial jurisdiction of the state. The traditional theory of sovereignty was based on the idea that states had supreme control over what took place within their

● **Governance**: Broadly, the various ways in which social life is coordinated, of which government is merely one (see p. 130).

GLOBAL POLITICS IN ACTION . . .

The Palestinian quest for statehood

Events: In September 2011, Mahmoud Abbas, the chairman of the Palestine Liberation Organization (PLO), submitted a formal request for Palestine's admittance as a full-member state into the United Nations. The following month, the executive committee of UNESCO backed this bid in a 107–14 vote. In November 2012, the General Assembly of the UN voted overwhelmingly to recognize Palestine as a 'non-member observer state', giving Palestine access to other UN bodies, including the International Criminal Court. The emergence of a national consciousness amongst Palestinian Arabs can be traced back to a pre-WWI reaction against increasing Jewish immigration into Palestine (then loosely part of the Ottoman Empire), which was strengthened during WWI by British encouragement for Arab nationalism.

The establishment of the state of Israel in 1948 meant that the majority of Arab Palestinians became refugees, a problem exacerbated by the 1967 Six-Day War, after which Sinai, the Gaza Strip, the West Bank and the Golan Heights were occupied by Israel. The Oslo Accords of 1993, the first face-to-face meeting between the PLO and the government of Israel, prepared the way for the establishment in 1996 of the Palestinian National Authority, which assumed governmental authority, but not sovereignty, for the West Bank and the Gaza Strip.

Significance: The Palestinian quest for statehood has both legal and political dimensions. The legal status of Palestine is a matter of controversy and some confusion. The founding of the PLO in 1964, uniting a disparate collection of Palestinian Arab groups, did much to strengthen the notion of the Palestinians as a nation or people, separate from the larger Arab people and from existing states, such as Jordan, Egypt, Syria and Lebanon. However, it was not until the establishment of the Palestinian Authority that the Palestinians could be said to have a defined territory and an effective government, albeit one that lacked *de jure* and *de facto* sovereignty. The status of Palestine crucially underlines the role of the UN in establishing statehood through formal recognition. Palestine's transition from being a 'non-state entity' with an observer status in the UN General Assembly (granted in 1974) to being a 'non-member observer state' has not been endorsed by the UN Security Council and falls short of full membership of the UN, and thus full statehood.

Nevertheless, as of April 2013, 132 of the UN's 193 members had recognized the existence of the state of Palestine.

The political dimension of Palestinian statehood is substantially more important, however. The 'Palestinian problem' lies at the heart of the Arab–Israeli conflict and has poisoned the politics of the Middle East for decades. It is thus difficult to imagine meaningful progress in building mutual respect and understanding between the West and Islam, especially the Arab world, without improved relations between Israel and the Palestinians. Those who support Palestine's quest for statehood usually view the so-called 'two-state' solution as the only viable solution to the Israeli–Palestinian conflict. In this view, the continuing denial of the Palestinians' right to sovereign independence can only strengthen political extremism, hostility towards Israel and, probably, violence. However, the creation of a Palestinian state may be difficult to achieve in practical terms. Not only is the Palestinian Authority divided territorially and politically (Hamas, the Palestinian militant group, controls the Gaza Strip, while the Fatah wing of the PLO governs the West Bank), but if a Palestinian state were constructed in line with the 1967 borders, this would mean that some 500,000 Israelis would be defined as living in another country. Many in Israel, nevertheless, have deeper reservations about the 'two-state' solution. For them, implacable Palestinian hatred of the state of Israel would mean that a sovereign Palestinian state would pose an ongoing, and intolerable, threat to the security and survival of Israel itself.

borders, implying that they also controlled what crossed their borders. However, developments such as the rise of international migration and the spread of cultural globalization (see p. 151) have tended to make state borders increasingly 'permeable'. This can be seen in the growth of cross-border communications and information flows through, for instance, radio, satellite television, mobile telephones and the Internet, which occur both at a speed and in quantities that defy the capacity of any state to detect them, still less effectively control them. Most of the discussion about the changing nature and power of the state has, nevertheless, concerned the impact of economic globalization (see p. 98). One of the central features of economic globalization is the rise of '**supraterritoriality**', reflected in the declining importance of territorial locations, geographical distance and state borders. An increasing range of economic activities take place within a 'borderless world' (Ohmae 1990). This is particularly clear in relation to financial markets that have become genuinely globalized, in that capital flows around the world seemingly instantaneously, meaning, for instance, that no state can be insulated from the impact of financial crises that take place in other parts of the world. It is also evident in the changing balance between the power of territorial states and 'de-territorialized' transnational corporations, which can switch investment and production to other parts of the world if state policy is not conducive to profit maximization and the pursuit of corporate interests. Globalization, furthermore, has been closely associated with a trend towards regionalization, reflected in the growing prominence of regional trading blocs such as the European Union (EU) and the North American Free Trade Agreement (NAFTA).

If borders have become permeable and old geographical certainties have been shaken, state sovereignty, at least in its traditional sense, cannot survive. This is the sense in which governance in the twenty-first century has assumed a genuinely post-sovereign character. It is difficult, in particular, to see how **economic sovereignty** can be reconciled with a globalized economy. Sovereign control over economic life was only possible in a world of discrete national economies; the tendency of national economies to be incorporated to a greater or lesser extent into a single globalized economy renders economic sovereignty meaningless. As Susan Strange (1996) put it, 'where states were once masters of markets, now it is the markets which, on many issues, are the masters over the governments of states'. However, the rhetoric of a 'borderless' global economy can be taken too far. For example, there is evidence that, while globalization may have changed the strategies that states adopt to ensure economic success, it has by no means rendered the state redundant as an economic actor. As discussed later in this section, states retain a vital role in bringing about economic modernization. At the very least, there is a growing recognition that market-based economies can only operate effectively within a context of legal and social order that only the state can provide. Moreover, although states, when acting separately, may have a diminished capacity to control transnational economic activity, they retain the facility to do so through macro frameworks of economic regulation, as provided by the G-20, the World Trade Organization (WTO), (see p. 537) and the International Monetary Fund (IMF)(see p. 475).

The power and significance of the state has undoubtedly been affected by the process of political globalization (see p. 122). However, its impact has been complex and, in some ways, contradictory. On the one hand, international

● **Supraterritoriality**: A condition in which social life transcends territory through the growth of 'transborder' and 'transglobal' communications and interactions.

● **Economic sovereignty**: The absolute authority of the state over how economic life is conducted within its borders, involving independent control of fiscal and monetary policies, and trade and capital flows.

GLOBAL ACTORS . . .

GROUP OF TWENTY

Type: International economic forum • **Established:** 1999 • **Membership:** 20 countries

The Group of Twenty (G-20) Finance Ministers and Central Bank Governors was established in 1999 in response both to the financial crises of the late 1990s and a growing recognition that key emerging states were not adequately included in the core of global economic discussion and governance. There are no formal criteria for G-20 membership and the composition of the group has remained unchanged since it was established (Argentina, Australia, Brazil, Canada, China, France, Germany, India, Indonesia, Italy, Japan, Mexico, Russia, Saudi Arabia, South Africa, South Korea, Turkey, the UK, the USA and the EU). The group includes most, but not all, the leading economies in the world, thereby comprising, collectively, around 90 per cent of world GNP, but factors such as geographical balance (members are drawn from all continents) and population representation (about two-thirds of the global population is represented) also played a major part. Like the G-7/8 (see p. 472), the G-20 operates as an informal forum to promote dialogue between finance ministers, central bankers and heads of government, with no permanent location and no permanent staff of its own. However, at its Pittsburgh Summit in September 2009, heads of government agreed to provide the G-20 with wider resources and a permanent staff. Within the G-20, each member has one voice, regardless of its economic strength or population size.

Significance: In its early years, the G-20 was a relatively peripheral body, certainly less significant than the G-8. This, however, changed with the outbreak of the global financial crisis in 2007–09. Developed states, recognizing that their economic fate depended largely on a globally-coordinated response to the crisis, were eager to join with developing states, and saw the G-20 as the forum for doing this. The G-8, by contrast, suddenly appeared to be hopelessly antiquated, particularly as it excluded the emerging economies of China, India, South Africa, Mexico and Brazil. The G-20's growing stature was underlined by the fact that the global response to the crisis largely emerged out of its Washington and London summits, in November 2008 and April 2009, respectively. At the heart of this response was the agreement by G-20 members to contribute $500 billion to a programme of global reflation. A start was also made on reforming the institutions of global economic governance by the agreement to expand the IMF's borrowing programme and by urging that voting shares on the IMF and the World Bank be rebalanced to boost the representation of the developing world. At the Pittsburgh summit, it was decided that the G-20 would replace the G-8 as the main forum for promoting international economic cooperation.

The rise of the G-20 has been heralded as marking a potentially historic shift. Its high degree of inclusion and representativeness may indicate the emergence of a new institutional world order that better reflects current economic realities and thereby enjoys greater global legitimacy. By comparison, the G-8, the IMF, the World Bank and the UN (through the Security Council) concentrate global decision-making in the hands of just a few states. The G-20 has, nevertheless, also attracted criticism. First, its prominence may be temporary and specifically linked to the peculiarities of a global financial crisis in which developed and developing states recognized that they were 'in the same boat'. Developing a globally-coordinated response over issues such as climate change and world trade, where the interests of the developed and developing worlds often diverge, may be much more difficult. Second, the G-20, even transformed into a permanent body, remains toothless. It castigates countries judged to be behaving irresponsibly, condemns weak financial regulation at national and global levels, and takes a stance on matters such as bankers' bonuses, but it lacks the capacity to impose its will, still less to punish transgressors. Third, although the G-20 clearly provides better representation than the G-8, its membership is selected arbitrarily and excludes some rich states and all the world's poorest states. The G-20's key players are also firmly wedded to a mainstream economic philosophy that favours the market and globalization, albeit a more regulated form of globalization.

CONCEPT

Political globalization

Political globalization refers to the growing importance of international organizations. These are organizations that are transnational in that they exert influence not within a single state, but within an international area comprising several states. However, the nature of political globalization and its implications for the state varies depending on whether it is modelled on the principle of intergovernmentalism (see p. 466) or supranationalism (see p. 465). Intergovernmental international organizations provide a mechanism that enables states, at least in theory, to take concerted action without sacrificing sovereignty. Supranational bodies, on the other hand, are able to impose their will on states. Most commentators nevertheless accept that political globalization lags markedly behind economic and cultural forms of globalization.

● **Pooled sovereignty**: The combined sovereignty of two or more states; 'pooling' sovereignty implies gaining access to greater power and influence than state/national sovereignty.

● **Collectivized state**: A state that seeks to abolish private enterprise and sets up a centrally planned, or 'command', economy.

bodies such as the UN (see p. 456), the EU (see p. 509), NATO (see p. 259) and the WTO have undermined the capacity of states to operate as self-governing units. It is clear, for instance, that membership of the EU threatens state power, because a growing range of decisions (for example, on monetary policy, agricultural and fisheries policies, and the movement of goods and people within the EU) are made by European institutions rather than by member states. The range and importance of decisions that are made at an intergovernmental or supranational level has nevertheless undoubtedly increased, forcing states either to exert influence through regional or global bodies, or to operate within frameworks established by them. The WTO, for instance, operates as the judge and jury of global trade disputes and serves as a forum for negotiating trade deals between and among its members. Such tendencies reflect the fact that in an interconnected world, states have a diminishing capacity to act alone, because they are increasingly confronted by challenges and threats that have a transnational if not a global dimension.

On the other hand, political globalization opens up opportunities for the state as well as diminishing them. Working through international organizations and regimes (see p. 71) may expand the capacities of the state, allowing them to continue to extend their influence within a globalized and interconnected world. This occurs when states 'pool' their sovereignty. The notion of **pooled sovereignty** has been most explicitly developed in relation to the EU, but could just as well be applied to any other international organization. By 'pooling' sovereignty, member states transfer certain powers from national governments to EU institutions, thereby gaining access to a larger and more meaningful form of sovereignty. In this view, sovereignty is not a zero-sum game: the pooled sovereignty of the EU is, at least potentially, greater than the combined national sovereignties that compose it, because, in this case, a regional body is able to exert greater influence in a globalized world than the member states could if each acted individually.

State transformation

Globalizing tendencies have not only cast doubt over the continued relevance of the principle of state sovereignty, but also, arguably, reshaped the nature and role of the state itself. As a historical institution, the state has undergone a variety of transformations. The rise of nationalism from the early nineteenth century onwards led to the creation of the nation-state (see p. 168), which allied the state as a system of centralized rule to nationhood as a source of social cohesion and political legitimacy. Thereafter, the quest for national self-determination became the principal motor behind state construction (as discussed in Chapter 7). For much of the twentieth century, the state was characterized by its expanding social and economic role. The most extreme example of this was the development of **collectivized states**, which attempted to bring the entirety of economic life under state control. The best examples of such states were in orthodox communist countries such as the Soviet Union and throughout Eastern Europe. States in the capitalist world nevertheless also demonstrated a marked tendency towards economic and social intervention, albeit of a more modest kind. In their case, this involved the adoption of Keynesian strategies of economic management and a strengthening of social protection, leading to the development of the **welfare state**. The ability to deliver prosperity and to protect citizens from social deprivation thus became the principal source of legitimacy in most states.

Since the 1980s, however, many commentators have drawn attention to the progressive 'hollowing out' of the state, giving rise, allegedly, to a new state form. This has been variously described as the 'competition' state, the 'market' state (Bobbitt 2002) and the 'postmodern' state (Cooper 2004). The most common explanation for this has been the changed relationship between the state and the market that has been brought about by the pressures generated by economic globalization. This is reflected in the general trend towards neoliberalism (see p. 93), most dramatically demonstrated by the transition from collectivized to market-based economies in former communist countries during the 1990s, but it was also evident, to some degree, across the globe through the adoption of policies of privatization, deregulation and the 'rolling back' of welfare provision. Globalization can be seen to have promoted such developments in at least three ways. First, a greater exposure to global markets has encouraged many countries to adopt strategies designed to attract foreign capital and inward investment, namely policies of financial and economic deregulation. Second, intensified foreign competition forced countries to keep wage levels low and to promote labour flexibility, which meant scaling down welfare costs and other impediments to international competitiveness. Third, TNCs acquired growing influence at the expense of the state, by virtue of the ease with which they are able to relocate production and investment in a globalized economy if state policy is insufficiently responsive to corporate interests.

However, the changed relationship between markets and states may not simply mean a *reduced* role for the state but, rather, a *different* role for the state. The state may have been transformed, not eclipsed altogether (Sørensen 2004). Robert Cox (see p. 124) has argued that the growing global organization of production and finance had transformed conventional conceptions of government and society, leading to the 'internationalization of the state'. This is the process whereby national institutions, policies and practices become little more than an instrument for restructuring national economies in line with the dynamics of the global capitalist economy. Although this implies that states have lost substantial power over the economy, the process of economic globalization nevertheless requires a political framework that is provided by the state, notably in the form of the 'military-territorial power of an enforcer' (Cox 1994). In the modern global economy, this role has largely been assumed by the USA.

Bob Jessop (2002) described the advent of a more market-orientated state in terms of a move away from the 'Keynesian welfare national state', towards what he called the 'Schumpeterian competition state'. The **competition state** is a state that aims to secure economic growth within its borders by securing competitive advantages in the wider global economy. Competition states are distinguished by the recognition of the need to strengthen education and training as the principal way of guaranteeing economic success in the new technology-dependent economy, and this approach was adopted by the Asian 'tiger' economies from the 1970s onwards. Although they attempt to increase market responsiveness by promoting entrepreneurialism and labour flexibility, competition states are also aware of the need to combat social exclusion and bolster the moral foundations of society. To some extent, the advance of the competition state is evident in a

● **Welfare state**: A state that takes prime responsibility for the social welfare of its citizens, discharged through a range of social security, health, education and other services (albeit different in different counties).

● **Competition state**: A state that pursues strategies to ensure long-term competitiveness in the globalized economy.

Robert Cox (born 1926)

Canadian international political economist and leading exponent of critical theory. Cox worked in the International Labour Organization (ILO), before, in the early 1970s, taking up an academic career. Cox adopted a 'reflexive' approach to theory, in which theories are firmly linked to their context and subject. In his seminal work, *Production, Power, and World Order: Social Forces in the Making of History* (1987), he examined the relationship between material forces of production, ideas and institutions in three periods: the liberal international economy (1789–1873); the era of rival imperialisms (1873–1945); and the neoliberal world order (post-1945). His writing examines issues such as the implications of globalization and the nature of US global hegemony, in part to highlight the prospects for counter-hege-monic social forces. Cox's other major writings include (with H. Jacobson) *The Anatomy of Influence* (1972) and (with Timothy J. Sinclair) *Approaches to World Order* (1996).

wider shift from so-called 'demand-side' economics (which encourages consumers to consume, by, for instance, Keynesian reflation) to 'supply-side' economics (which encourages producers to produce, by, for example, improved education and training, labour flexibility and deregulation).

The notion of the 'postmodern state' has been associated in particular with the writings of Robert Cooper (2004). In Cooper's analysis, the post-Cold War world is divided into three parts, each characterized by a distinctive state struc-ture – the 'pre-modern', 'modern' and 'postmodern' worlds. The postmodern world is a world in which force has been rejected as a means of resolving disputes, order being maintained instead through a respect for the rule of law and a willingness to operate through multilateral institutions. Security in such a world is based on transparency, mutual openness, interdependence and, above all, a recognition of mutual vulnerability. The states appropriate to such a world, 'postmodern' states, are more pluralist, more complex and less centralized than the bureaucratic 'modern' states they have replaced, and they also tend to be less nationalistic, allowing, even encouraging, multiple identities to thrive. Postmodern states are characterized by both the wider role played by private organizations in the processes of governance and the fact that government's role is increasingly orientated around the promotion of personal development and personal consumption. As Cooper (2004) put it, 'Individual consumption replaces collective glory as the dominant theme of national life'. In terms of their external orientation, postmodern states are distinguished by their unwarlike character, reflected in the application of moral consciousness to international relations and a rejection of the balance of power (see p. 262) as unworkable in the post-Cold War era. On this basis, the only clear examples of postmodern states are found in Europe, with the EU perhaps being an example of a postmod-ern proto-state.

However, the plight of the state is most serious in the case of the 'pre-modern' world. Cooper portrayed this as a world of post-imperial chaos, in which such state structures as exist are unable to establish (in Weber's words) a legitimate

THE STATE

Realist view

Realists tend to view states from the outside; that is, from the perspective of the international system. Above all, they take states to be unitary and coherent actors; indeed, they are commonly portrayed as the basic 'units' of the international system. Their unitary and cohesive character derives from the fact that, regardless of their domestic make-up, state leaders speak and act on behalf of their respective states and can deploy their populations and resources as they wish or choose. State behaviour is determined by a single, overriding motive – 'the wish to survive' (Waltz 2002) – although realists disagree about whether this implies merely a defensive desire to avoid invasion and attack or an aggressive wish to maximize power and achieve domination (see Offensive or defensive realism? p. 240). The social, constitutional, political and social composition of the state is therefore irrelevant to its external behaviour. In this sense, the state is a 'black box'. Neorealists in particular insist that states differ only in terms of their 'capabilities', or power resources (there are great powers (see p. 6), minor powers and so on). All realists never-theless agree that the state is the dominant global actor; hence they adopt a state-centric view of global politics. For example, from a realist perspective, globalization and the state are not separate or, still less, opposing forces: rather, globalization has been created by states and thus exists to serve their interests. Other actors thus only exert influence to the extent that the state allows.

Liberal view

Liberals believe that the state arises out of the needs of society and reflects the interests of individual citizens. 'Social contract theory' suggests that the state was established through an agreement amongst citizens to create a sovereign power in order to escape from the chaos and brutality of the 'state of nature' (a stateless, or pre-political, society). The core role of the state is thus to ensure order by arbitrating between the competing individuals and groups in society. The state thus acts as a referee or umpire. This implies that changes in the structure of society can and will alter the role and power of the state. Liberals, as a result,

have been less willing than realists to view the state as the dominant global actor, usually adopting instead a mixed-actor model of world politics. Indeed, liberals have generally accepted that globalization has been marked by the decline of the state (and perhaps the transition from nation-states to 'postmodern' or 'market' states), as power has shifted away from the state and towards, in particular, global markets and transnational corporations (TNCs) (see p. 94), but also to individuals. Furthermore, liberals insist that the constitutional and political make-up of the state has a crucial impact on its external behaviour. In particular, republican liberals argue that democratic states are inherently more peaceable than non-democratic states (Doyle 1986).

Critical views

Critical theorists reject both realist state-centrism and liberal assertions about the retreat of the state, but they do so in different ways. Neo-Marxists and post-Marxist theorists may have abandoned the orthodox Marxist belief that the (capitalist) state is merely a reflection of the class system, but they continue to argue that state structures and, for that matter, world orders are grounded in social relations. The mutual dependence between markets and states has in fact intensified as a result of globalization, leading to what Cox (1993) called the 'internationalization of the state'. Social constructivists deny that the state has a fixed and objective character; rather, the identity of the state is shaped by a variety of historical and sociological factors, and these, in turn, inform the interests of the state and its actions. Wendt (1999), for example, distin-guished between the social identity of the state (shaped by the status, role or personality that international society ascribes to a state) and its corporate identity (shaped by internal material, ideological and cultural factors). Feminist theorists have been ambivalent about the state. While liberal feminists have believed that it is possible to reform the state from within, by increasing female representation at all levels, radical feminists have highlighted structural links between the state and the system of male power, believing that the state has an intrinsically patriarchal character.

CONCEPT

Failed state

A failed state is a state that is unable to perform its key role of ensuring domestic order by monopolizing the use of force within its territory. Examples of failed states in recent years include Cambodia, Haiti, Rwanda, Liberia and Somalia. Failed states are no longer able to operate as viable political units, in that they lack a credible system of law and order, often being gripped by civil war or warlordism. They are also no longer able to operate as viable economic units, in that they are incapable of providing for their citizens and have no functioning infrastructure. Although relatively few states collapse altogether, a much larger number barely function and are dangerously close to collapse.

monopoly of the use of force, thus leading to endemic **warlordism**, widespread criminality and social dislocation. Such conditions do not apply consistently to the developing world as a whole, however. In cases such as India, South Korea and Taiwan, developing world states have been highly successful in pursuing strategies of economic modernization and social development. Others, nevertheless, have been distinguished by their weakness, sometimes being portrayed as 'weak' states, 'quasi-states' or 'failed states'. Most of the weakest states in the world are concentrated in sub-Saharan Africa, classic examples being Somalia, Sierra Leone, Liberia and the Democratic Republic of the Congo. These states fail the most basic test of state power: they are unable to maintain domestic order and personal security, meaning that civil strife and even civil war become almost routine. Failed states are nevertheless not just a domestic problem. They often have a wider impact through, for instance, precipitating refugee crises, providing a refuge for drug dealers, arms smugglers and terrorist organizations, generating regional instability, and provoking external intervention to provide humanitarian relief and to keep the peace.

The failure of such states stems primarily from the experience of colonialism, which, when it ended (mainly in the post-1945 period) bequeathed formal political independence to societies that lacked an appropriate level of political, economic, social and educational development to function effectively as separate entities. As the borders of such states typically represented the extent of colonial ambition rather than the existence of a culturally cohesive population, postcolonial states also often encompassed deep ethnic, religious and tribal divisions. Failed states are thus failed, postcolonial states. Nevertheless, colonialism does not, on its own, explain the weakness or failure of the postcolonial state. Other sources of state failure include internal factors, such as the existence of social elites, backward institutions and parochial value systems which block the transition from pre-industrial, agrarian societies to modern industrial ones, and external factors, notably the impact of TNCs and neo-colonialism.

Return of the state

Discourse about the state in the early twenty-first century has been dominated by talk of retreat or decline. State sovereignty is routinely dismissed as an irrelevance and states are viewed as dinosaurs waiting to die. The reality is more complex, however. Realist and other state-centric commentators argue that the impact of globalization in its economic, cultural and political forms has always been exaggerated: states remain the decisive political actors. Nevertheless, a number of developments in recent years have helped to strengthen the state and to underline its essential importance. What explains the return of the state? In the first place, the state's unique capacity to maintain domestic order and protect its citizens from external attack has been strongly underlined by new security challenges that have emerged in the twenty-first century, notably those linked to transnational terrorism (see p. 294). This underlines what Bobbitt (2002) viewed as a basic truth: 'The State exists to master violence'; it is therefore essentially a 'warmaking institution'. The decline in military expenditure that occurred at the end of the Cold War, the so-called 'peace dividend', started to be reversed in the late 1990s, with global military expenditure rising steeply after the 9/11 terrorist attacks and the launch of the 'war on terror'. The USA with its massive military

● **Warlordism**: A condition in which locally-based militarized bands vie for power in the absence of a sovereign state.

Focus on . . .
Problems of state-building

Why is the process of state-building often so difficult? What challenges does successful state-building have to overcome? At least three significant challenges stand out. The first is that new or reformed institutions and structures have to be constructed in a context of often deep political and ethnic tension and endemic poverty. For example, in Afghanistan, a country in which no internal or external power has ever long held sway, there are 50 ethnic or sub-tribal groups, 34 languages and 27 million people, together with widespread internecine feuds and counter-feuds. The task of developing a unifying national leadership in such a context is therefore highly problematical.

Second, indigenous leadership and new institutions need to enjoy a significant measure of legitimacy. This is why state-building is invariably linked to the promo-

tion of 'good governance', with the eradication of corruption being a key goal. However, the democratization that 'good governance' implies may make the task of state-building more difficult, not least by bringing ethnic and other tensions to the surface and by exposing the flaws and failings of emergent institutions. Finally, state-building may involve the imposition of an essentially western model of political organization unsuited to the needs of developing countries that are more accustomed to traditional tribal models of governance in which interdependent groups are united by a shared ethnic identity. If the western assumption that the state is a universal institution, the only viable alternative to chaos and brutality, is unfounded, then the task of state-building may be doomed.

budget has been the principal determinant of the current world trend, but military spending has also grown significantly in China, France, the UK, Russia and elsewhere. Moreover, many countries have taken steps to strengthen the inviolability of the state as a territorial unit by imposing tighter border controls. Counter-terrorism strategies have often meant that states have assumed wider powers of surveillance, control and sometimes detention, even becoming 'national security states'.

Second, although the days of command-and-control economic management may be over, the state has sometimes reasserted itself as an agent of modernization. The myth of neoliberalism is that prosperity and growth are purely a result of the dynamism of the market. In fact, market economies can only operate successfully in conditions of legal and social order that only states can guarantee. This applies particularly in the case of the rule of law and the enforcement of property rights, without which economic activity would end up being determined by threats, bribes and the use of violence. Beyond this, however, modernizing states develop and implement strategies to ensure long-term economic success. 'Competition states' do this by improving education and training in order to boost productivity and by providing support for key export industries. States such as China and Russia each modernized their economies by making significant concessions to the market, but an important element of state control has been retained or re-imposed (these developments are examined in more detail in Chapter 3 in relation to state capitalism). On a wider level, the state's vital role in economic affairs was underlined by the 2007–09 global financial crisis. Although the G-20 may have provided states with a forum to develop a

Debating . . .
Is state sovereignty now an outdated concept?

State sovereignty has traditionally been viewed as the core principle of the international system. However, while some argue that globalization and other developments have changed the international system fundamentally, others suggest that the basic contours of the international system remain essentially unchanged.

YES

Permeable borders. State borders, the traditional guarantee of territorial sovereignty, are permeable in that they have increasingly been penetrated by external forces. These include international tourism and the movement of knowledge and information via the Internet. Global financial markets and transnational capital flows mean that economic sovereignty has become redundant. If the conventional domestic/international divide is increasingly difficult to sustain, states are no longer meaningful territorial units.

Rise of non-state actors. States are no longer the only, or necessarily the dominant, actors on the world stage. Transnational corporations (TNCs) wield greater financial power than many states, and can effectively dictate state policy through their ability to relocate production and investment at ease in a globalized economy. Non-governmental organizations (NGOs) such as Greenpeace and Amnesty International exert global influence. And state security is as likely to be threatened by global terrorist organizations such as al-Qaeda as it is by other states.

Collective dilemmas. In modern circumstances, states are increasingly confronted by collective dilemmas, issues that are particularly taxing because they confound even the most powerful of states when acting alone. Quite simply, global problems require global solutions. An increasing range of issues have acquired a collective or even global character – climate change, terrorism, transnational crime, pandemic diseases, international migration and so on. Only international organizations, not supposedly sovereign states, can tackle these.

International human rights. Respect for state sovereignty has been eroded by the growing belief that there are standards of conduct to which all states should conform as far as the treatment of their domestic populations is concerned. Such a view is usually based on a belief in human rights (see p. 311), and the idea that the fundamental individual rights are morally superior to the state's right to independence and autonomy. This is evident in shifts in international law (examined in Chapter 14), and in the wider acceptance of humanitarian intervention (see p. 326).

NO

Myth of the 'borderless world'. The image that world politics is dominated by transnational processes that elude state control is, at best, a gross exaggeration. For example, national economies have not simply been absorbed into a 'borderless' global economy, as much more economic activity takes place within state borders than it does across state borders. Furthermore, it is misleading to suggest that globalizing trends necessarily disempower states. Instead, states *choose* to engage in the global economy and do so for reasons of national self-interest.

States remain dominant. Although states are merely one actor amongst many on the world stage, they remain the most important actor. States exercise power in a way and to an extent that no other actor can. In particular, using the administrative processes of government and relying on unchallengeable coercive power, their control over what happens within their territories is rarely challenged. Only a tiny proportion of states, those classified as 'failed' or 'weak' states, have effectively lost control over what happens within their borders.

Pooled sovereignty. The advance of political globalization and the emergence of a framework of global governance have not brought about an erosion of sovereignty. Rather, they expand the opportunities available to states, particularly for achieving the benefits of cooperation. International organizations are bodies that are formed by states, for states; they are invariably used by states as tools to achieve their own ends. Indeed, by working together, states are able to pool their sovereignty, gaining greater capacity and influence than they would have possessed working alone.

Enduring attraction of the nation-state. There seems little likelihood that states will lose their dominance so long as they continue to enjoy the allegiance of the mass of their citizens. As most states are nation-states, this is ensured by the survival of nationalism as the world's most potent ideological force. Rival doctrines such as cosmopolitanism and allegiances based, for instance, on religion, culture or ethnicity are of minor significance compared with nationalism.

coordinated global response, the massive packages of fiscal and other interventions that were agreed were, and could only have been, implemented by states. Indeed, some have seen the crisis as marking the watershed between three decades of anti-statist neoliberal globalization and a new era of regulated globalization, in which states, through international organizations or sometimes acting alone, play a more active economic role.

Finally, there has been a growing recognition of the role of the state in promoting development. This is reflected in an increased emphasis on **state-building** as a key aspect of the larger process of peace-building (see p. 452). The provision of humanitarian relief and the task of conflict resolution become almost insuperably difficult in the absence of a functioning system of law and order. The wider acceptance of humanitarian intervention since the early 1990s has meant that ordered rule is often provided, initially at least, by external powers. However, this does not constitute a long-term solution. As examples such as Somalia, Iraq and Afghanistan demonstrate, externally-imposed order is only sustainable for a limited period of time, both because the economic and human cost to the intervening powers may be unsustainable in the long-run, and because, sooner or later, the presence of foreign troops and police provokes resentment and hostility. Foreign intervention has therefore come, over time, to focus increasingly on the construction of effective indigenous leadership and building legitimate national institutions, such as an army, a police force, a judiciary, a central bank, government departments, local administration, a tax collection agency and functioning education, transport, energy and healthcare systems. The process of state-building is nevertheless often profoundly difficult.

NATIONAL GOVERNMENT TO MULTI-LEVEL GOVERNANCE

From government to governance

● **State-building**: The construction of a functioning state through the establishment of legitimate institutions for the formulation and implementation of policy across key areas of government.

● **Good governance**: Standards for the process of decision-making in society, including (according to the UN) popular participation, respect for the rule of law, transparency, responsiveness and accountability.

● **Hierarchy**: An organization that is based on graded ranks and a clear and usually top-down authority structure.

Changes to the role and significance of the state have also had important implications for the nature and functioning of government. Government refers to the formal and institutional processes which operate at the national level to maintain order and facilitate collective action. Its central feature is the ability to make collective decisions and the capacity to enforce them. Since the 1980s, however, it has become increasingly fashionable for international theorists and political analysts to talk more in terms of 'governance' (see p. 130) rather than 'government', with terms such as 'global governance' (see p. 462), '**good governance**' and 'corporate governance' becoming commonplace. The so-called 'governance turn' in the study of international and domestic politics has been a consequence of a variety of developments. At the heart of these is the growing redundancy of the traditional notion of government as a **hierarchy** or collection of hierarchies. For Max Weber (1948), hierarchy, in the form of what he termed bureaucracy, was the typical form of organization in modern industrialized societies. It was typified by the existence of fixed and official areas of jurisdiction, clear laws or rules, and a firmly ordered hierarchy based on an established chain of command. The virtue of such a command-and-control system was supposedly its rationality: bureaucratization, according to Weber, reflected the advance of a reliable,

CONCEPT

Governance

'Governance' is a broader term than 'government'. Although it still has no settled or agreed definition, it refers, in its wider sense, to the various ways through which social life is co-ordinated. Governance is therefore a process (or a complex of processes), its principal modes including markets, hierarchies and networks. Although government may be involved in governance, it is possible to have 'governance without government'. Governance is typified by a blurring of the state/society distinction (private bodies and institutions work closely with public ones) and the involvement of a number of levels or layers (potentially local, provincial, national, regional and global). The processes through which international affairs are coordinated are increasingly referred to as 'global governance'.

predictable and, above all, efficient means of social organization. Bureaucracies or hierarchies thus developed in the military and the police, in schools and universities, and throughout the modern state in the growth of government departments and executive agencies. Similarly, the emergence of capitalist economies generating pressure for greater economic efficiency made large-scale corporations the dominant form of business organization in the twentieth century.

The shift from government to governance is a political reflection of the advent of more fluid and differentiated societies (as discussed in Chapter 6). Top-down authority structures have, in this context, been exposed as ineffective, unresponsive and perhaps redundant. The advent of governance thus parallels economic trends which have seen a transition from 'Fordist' models of business organization, based on large-scale mass production, to 'post-Fordist' ones (see p. 141) that emphasize flexibility, innovation and decentralized decision-making. Pressure to adjust the way governments behave and how governing is carried out came from a variety of sources. These include the fiscal crisis of the state that was precipitated by the end of the 'long boom' and the down-turn of the global economy in the 1970s. Whereas sustained economic growth in the 1950s and 1960s had underwritten, in developed societies at least, an expansion in the welfare and social responsibilities of the state, helping to strengthen faith in the efficacy of government, reduced tax revenues created a mismatch between people's expectations of government and what government could actually deliver. Governments had either to reduce popular expectations of government or to find new and more imaginative ways of delivering government services more cheaply and efficiently. A further set of pressures were generated in the 1980s and 1990s by the ideological shift towards free-market or neoliberal priorities. Pursued most radically through Reaganism in the USA and Thatcherism in the UK but affecting almost all societies to some degree, this set out to dismantle 'big government' in the belief that the economy worked best when regulated by market forces and that the individual should be liberated from the tyranny of the 'nanny state'. Economic globalization has also played a major role in this process. The integration of national economies to a greater or lesser degree into a single global economy has exposed all countries to intensified competitive pressures, creating a 'race to the bottom' as governments seek to attract or retain private investment by cutting taxes, deregulating economic life and promoting more flexible labour markets.

How have governments adapted themselves in the light of these circumstances? The shift to a governance mode of governing has been evident in at least three, albeit related developments. First, the role of government has been redefined and in some senses narrowed. Instead of 'rowing' (that is, administering and delivering services), the tasks of government have increasingly been confined to 'steering' (that is, setting targets and strategic objectives). This, in part, acknowledges the inefficiency and unresponsiveness of traditional public administration by comparison in particular with private businesses or 'third sector' bodies such as charities, community groups and NGOs (see p. 10). In the USA, where such ideas were born and most enthusiastically embraced, the shift in responsibility for 'rowing' has been described as 'reinventing government' (Osborne and Gaebler 1992). Second, there has been a significant blurring of the distinction between government and markets and thus between the public and private realms. This has happened in a variety of ways: for example, through the 'contracting out' of public services or full-scale privatization, by the growth in public–private partnerships and the introduction of 'internal markets' in public service delivery, and by the introduction into the public sector of private sector management styles and structures through the so-called 'new public management'. Third, there has been a shift from hierarchies to networks within the processes of government, which has led Castells (1996) to proclaim the emergence of a 'network state' alongside the 'network society' and the 'network corporation'. For instance, the tasks of developing and sometimes implementing policy have increasingly been transferred from hierarchical departments to **policy networks**, as networks have proved to be particularly effective in facilitating the exchange of and coordinating social life in a context of increasing complexity.

Multi-level governance

The transition from government to governance is reflected not only in the more complex ways through which social life is now coordinated within modern societies – for example, through a wider role for markets and networks and the weakening of the public–private divide – but it is also evident in the 'stretching' of government across a number of levels. In other words, government can no longer be thought of as a specifically national activity which takes place within discrete societies. This has led to the phenomenon of '**multi-level governance**'. Policy-making responsibility has both been 'sucked up' and 'drawn down', creating a complex process of interactions (see Figure 5.1). The 'sucking up' of policy-making responsibility has occurred through the advent of political globalization and the growing importance of regional and global governance, as discussed earlier.

The 'drawing down' of policy-making responsibilities reflects a process of **decentralization**. For much of the twentieth century, most states exhibited a

● **Policy network**: A systematic set of relationships between political actors who share a common interest or general orientation in a particular area.

● **Multi-level governance**: A pattern of overlapping and interrelated public authority that stems from the growth, or growing importance, of supranational and subnational bodies.

● **Decentralization**: The expansion of local autonomy through the transfer of powers and responsibilities away from national bodies.

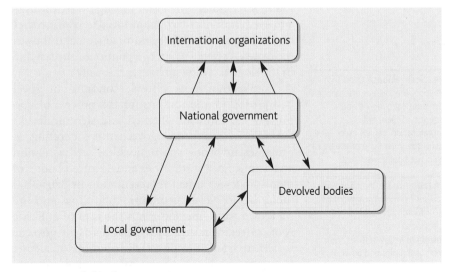

Figure 5.1 **Multilevel governance**

distinct trend towards centralization, largely as a consequence of their expanding economic and social roles. Central government has clear advantages over peripheral bodies in terms of its ability to manage the economy and deliver a widening range of public services, not least because of its significantly greater fiscal capacity. However, since about the 1960s this trend has often been reversed, giving way to a countervailing tendency towards **localization**. In many cases, this has been reflected in the growth or strengthening of peripheral or sub-national political bodies. For example, on achieving independence in 1947, India adopted a US-style federal system rather than a UK-style unitary one. As part of its transition to democratic government following the death of General Franco in 1975, Spain adopted a system of **devolution**, which led to the creation of 17 autonomous communities, each based on an elected assembly invested with broad control of domestic policy. In 1982, France developed its strategy of 'functional regionalism' into a fully-fledged system of regional government, based on 22 directly-elected regional councils. In the UK, the introduction of devolution in the late 1990s led to the creation of a Scottish Parliament, a Welsh Assembly and a Northern Ireland Assembly, and the emergence of a form of quasi-federalism (see p. 133).

Although localization may appear to be the antithesis of globalization, the two processes are closely, and perhaps intrinsically linked, as reflected in the notion of 'glocalization' (Robertson 1992). One of the key driving forces of localization has been the rise of cultural and ethnic politics, itself linked to the declining purchase of classical nationalism. In the late 1960s and early 1970s, secessionist groups and forms of ethnic nationalism sprang up in many parts of western Europe and North America. This was most evident in Quebec in Canada, Scotland and Wales in the UK, Catalonia and the Basque area in Spain, Corsica in France, and Flanders in Belgium. It created pressure for political decentralization, and sometimes, precipitated major constitutional upheavals. Similar manifestations of ethnic assertiveness were evident among the Native Americans in Canada and the USA, the Aboriginal peoples in Australia, and the Maoris in New Zealand. Other examples of localization include the tendency towards religious revivalism, through which Muslims, Christians, Hindus, Jews and even Buddhists have 'gone local' to reaffirm their faith through the adoption of fundamentalist beliefs and practices, and the stress within the anti-capitalist movement (see p. 74) on the politics of protest and political activism, reflected in the slogan: 'Think globally, act locally'.

Localization, in its cultural, economic but especially in its political form, has had profound implications for the process of governance, making the policy process yet more fragmented and decentralized. The EU provides the best example of multi-level governance, operating as it does through complex processes involving sub-national as well as national and supranational levels and actors. Local authorities and devolved bodies often bypass national governments and seek direct representation in Brussels, strengthening their involvement in EU-level economic planning and infrastructure development. Moreover, since the late 1980s the idea of a 'Europe of the Regions' has taken root, as regional and provincial levels of government have lobbied for, and benefited from, the direct distribution of aid from the European Regional Development Fund. Over time, regional aid has eclipsed agriculture as the largest single area of EU spending.

● **Localization**: A trend that favours the local as the basis for political action, cultural identity or economic organization, usually associated with the growing importance of sub-national governance.

● **Devolution**: The transfer of power from central government to subordinate regional or provincial institutions that have no share in sovereignty; their responsibilities and powers being derived entirely from the centre

Federalism

Federalism (from the Latin *foedus*, meaning 'pact', or 'covenant') refers to legal and political structures that distribute power between two distinct levels of government, neither of which is subordinate to the other. Its central feature is therefore the principle of **shared sovereignty**. 'Classical' federations are few in number: the USA, Switzerland, Belgium, Canada and Australia. However, many more states have federal-type features. Most federal, or federal-type, states were formed by the coming together of a number of established political communities; they are often geographically large and may have culturally diverse populations. Federalism may nevertheless also have an international dimension, providing the basis, in particular, for regional integration, as in the case of 'European federalism' (discussed in Chapter 20).

● **Shared sovereignty**: A constitutional arrangement in which sovereignty is divided between two levels of government, each exercising supreme and autonomous control over a specific range of issues.

● **Foreign**: (from the Latin *foris* meaning 'outside') Dealing or concerned with another country, area or people; implies strange or not familiar.

FOREIGN POLICY

End of foreign policy?

The making of foreign policy has traditionally been regarded as one of the key features of international politics. It reflects the importance of statecraft as an activity through which national governments manage their relations with other states and international bodies. Indeed, foreign policy-making has sometimes been thought of as a noble activity, seen as 'high' politics in that it deals with issues of sovereignty and security – in fact, the very survival of the state – as opposed to the 'low' politics of economics and other less important state activities. However, recent developments have called the concept of 'foreign policy' into question, certainly casting doubt on the conventional notion of foreign policy as a discrete activity, engaged in at a senior political level and involving formal diplomatic interactions between and amongst states. These pressures have came from various directions. In the first place, the emergence of neorealism in the late 1970s appeared to suggest that foreign policy, and indeed the wider process of decision-making in international politics, was simply no longer relevant. In the view of Kenneth Waltz (see p. 63) and others, state behaviour could essentially be explained through the power balances that shape the international system. As systemic factors were seen as decisively important, little or no role discretion was left to foreign policy actors, such as heads of government, foreign ministers, defence ministers, leading diplomats and so forth. The 'logic of anarchy' explained everything.

Further pressures have been generated by the advance of globalization and the growth of 'complex interdependence' (see p. 7). These developments dramatically widened and deepened the scope of the interactions between and amongst states. As the distinctions between home and abroad, inside and outside, and 'high' and 'low' politics became perhaps hopelessly blurred, the divide between '**foreign**' politics and 'domestic' politics became increasingly difficult to sustain. If the notion of 'the foreign' is meaningless, can foreign policy any longer exist? The matter was made yet more problematical by the fact that globalizing trends have also been associated with the advent of post-sovereign governance and the burgeoning importance of non-state actors: TNCs, NGOs, terrorist groups, international organizations and so on. At the very least, this means that foreign policy can no longer be thought of simply as 'what states do to, or with, other states'.

Nevertheless, the study of foreign policy remains a worthwhile activity, for at least two reasons. First, although the foreign/domestic divide may have become blurred, it has not been rendered redundant. The simple fact is that the world is still more separated into distinctive communities than it is a single, homogenizing entity (Hill 2003). How these communities attempt to manage the relations between and among them therefore continues to be an interesting and important issue. Second, foreign policy highlights the crucial interplay between structure and agency, emphasizing that events can neither be explained entirely through 'top-down' systemic pressures nor entirely through 'bottom-up' individual decision-making (see Structure or agency? p. 76). In so doing, foreign policy underlines the crucial significance of a sphere of decision, choice and intentionality within global politics.

CONCEPT

Foreign policy

Public policy lays out courses of action for government and its various agencies. Foreign policy refers, broadly, to attempts by governments to influence or manage events outside the state's borders, usually, but not exclusively, through their relations with foreign governments. Foreign policy-making involves the establishment of goals and the selection of means to achieve them. In view of the increased interpenetration of domestic and foreign affairs in modern global politics, the term 'external relations' is sometimes preferred to foreign policy, allowing for interactions that take place on multiple levels and which involve multiple actors. At the very least, the realm of foreign policy can no longer be confined simply to relations between foreign ministers/ ministries or between national diplomatic services.

How decisions are made

The making of decisions, and specifically of bundles of decisions, is clearly central to the policy process. Although policy-making also relates to the acts of initiation and implementation, the making of decisions and reaching of conclusions is usually seen as its key feature. However, it may be difficult to establish how and why decisions are made. In foreign policy-making a levels-of-analysis is commonly adopted, in line with the three levels at which Waltz (1959) analyzed the causes of war:

● The level of the *individual* decision-maker (involving personal priorities, psychological and cognitive dispositions and so on)
● The *nation-state* level (involving the nature of the state, type of government, bureaucratic structure and so on)
● The *systemic* level (involving power balances within the international system, the web of state interdependence, dynamics of global capitalism and so on).

Nevertheless, a number of general theories of political decision-making have been advanced. The most important of these are rational actor models, incremental models, bureaucratic organization models, and cognitive processes and belief-system models.

Rational actor models

Decision-making models that emphasize human rationality have generally been constructed on the basis of economic theories that have themselves been derived from utilitarianism. Developed by thinkers such as Anthony Downs (1957), these theories are usually based on the notion of 'economic man', a model of human nature that stresses the self-interested pursuit of material satisfaction, calculated in terms of utility (use-value; the balance of pleasure over pain). In this light, decisions can be seen to be reached using the following procedures:

● The nature of the problem is identified.
● An objective or goal is selected on the basis of an ordering of individual preferences.
● The available means of achieving this objective are evaluated in terms of their effectiveness, reliability, costs and so on.
● A decision is made through the selection of the means most likely to secure the desired end.

This type of process assumes both that clear-cut objectives exist, and that human beings are able to pursue them in a rational and consistent manner. The best example of such an approach to decision-making is found in the use of cost–benefit analysis in the making of business decisions. In line with the goal of profit maximization, business people make decisions that will ensure the least possible cost and the greatest possible benefit, both calculated in monetary terms. Realist theorists make similar assumptions about decision-making in

CONCEPT

National interest

In broad terms, the national interest refers to foreign policy goals, objectives or policy preferences that benefit a society as a whole (the foreign policy equivalent of the 'public interest'). The concept is often vague and contested, however. It is most widely used by realist theorists, for whom it is defined by the structural implications of international anarchy and so is closely linked to national security, survival and the pursuit of power. For decision-making theorists, the national interest refers to the strategies and goals pursued by those responsible for the conduct of foreign policy, although this may mean that it degenerates into mere rhetoric. Alternatively, it may refer to foreign policy goals that have been endorsed through the democratic process.

international politics. In their view, foreign policy is guided by a single overriding goal: the pursuit of vital national interests, understood, at minimum, as ensuring state survival, and beyond that the pursuit of power to enable the state to achieve its national ambitions. This may be dictated by system-level pressures (as neorealists suggest) or by egoistical pressures that operate in and through the state itself (as classical realists argue); either way, it implies that the role of individual decision-makers is largely restricted to the selection of the best means of achieving a pre-determined end.

The rational actor model is attractive, in part, because it reflects how most people believe decisions *should* be made. Certainly, politicians and others are strongly inclined to portray their actions as both goal-orientated and the product of careful thought and deliberation. When examined more closely, however, rational calculation may not appear to be a particularly convincing model of decision-making. In the first place, in practice, decisions are often made on the basis of inadequate and sometimes inaccurate information. Such difficulties encouraged Herbert Simon (1983) to develop the notion of 'bounded rationality'. This acknowledges that, as it is impossible to analyze and select all possible courses of action, decision-making is essentially an act of compromising between differently valued and imprecisely calculated outcomes. Simon described this process as 'satisficing'. The second problem with rational actor models is that they ignore the role of perception; that is, the degree to which actions are shaped by beliefs and assumptions about reality, rather than by reality itself. Little or no importance is thus attached to individual and collective psychology or to the values and ideological leanings of decision-makers.

Incremental models

Incrementalism is often portrayed as the principal alternative to rational decision-making. David Braybrooke and Charles Lindblom (1963) termed this model 'disjointed incrementalism', neatly summed up by Lindblom (1959) as the 'science of muddling through'. This position holds that, in practice, decisions tend to be made on the basis of inadequate information and low levels of understanding, and this discourages decision-makers from pursuing bold and innovative courses of action. Policy-making is therefore a continuous, exploratory process: lacking overriding goals and clear-cut ends, policy-makers tend to operate within an existing pattern or framework, adjusting their position in the light of feedback in the form of information about the impact of earlier decisions. Indeed, incrementalism may suggest a strategy of avoidance or evasion, policy-makers being inclined to move away from problems, rather than trying to solve them.

Lindblom's case for incrementalism is normative as well as descriptive. In addition to providing a perhaps more accurate account of how decisions are made in the real world, he argued that this approach also has the merit of allowing for flexibility and the expression of divergent views. 'Muddling through' at least implies responsiveness and flexibility, consultation and compromise. However, the model is clearly best suited to situations in which policy-makers are more inclined towards inertia rather than innovation. It thus explains the foreign policy trends of pro-status quo states more easily

● **Incrementalism**: The theory that decisions are made not in the light of clear-cut objectives, but through small adjustments dictated by changing circumstances.

than those that seek to revise or overturn the status quo. For example, incrementalism appears to explain the policy of appeasement, pursued by the UK and increasingly also France in the 1930s. This involved giving in to hostile demands from Hitler's Germany in the hope of avoiding war, but ended up emboldening Germany, if only by convincing Hitler that the western powers would never act to prevent Nazi expansionism. On the other hand, Nazi expansionism itself, the Japanese attack on Pearl Harbor in 1942, and, for that matter, more recent examples, such as the 2003 US invasion of Iraq, can hardly be described as incremental adjustments. Neorealists would further argue that the different foreign policy strategies of status-quo states and revisionist states can better be explained by the larger balance of power (see p. 262) than by an inclination amongst certain policy-makers to 'muddle through'. Finally, incrementalism places little or no emphasis on the role of beliefs and values, which may, for instance, have been a crucial factor driving foreign policy decision-making in Nazi Germany (see Hitler's war?, p. 35).

Bureaucratic organization models

Both rational actor and incremental models are essentially 'black box' theories of decision-making; neither pays attention to the impact that the structure of the policy-making process has on the resulting decisions. Operating on the nation-state level, bureaucratic or organizational models try, on the other hand, to get inside the black box by highlighting the degree to which process influences product. This approach was pioneered by Graham Allison (1971) in his examination of US and USSR decision-making during the Cuban Missile Crisis of 1962. Two contrasting, but related, models emerged from this study. The first, usually called the 'organizational process' model, highlights the impact on decisions of the values, assumptions and regular patterns of behaviour that are found in any large organization. Rather than corresponding to rational analysis and objective evaluation, decisions are seen to reflect the entrenched culture of the government department or agency that makes them. The second theory, the 'bureaucratic politics' model, emphasizes the impact on decisions of bargaining between personnel and agencies, each pursuing different perceived interests. This approach dismisses the idea of the state as a monolith united around a single view or a single interest, and suggests that decisions arise from an arena of contest in which the balance of advantage is constantly shifting.

Although these models undoubtedly draw attention to important aspects of decision-making, they also have their drawbacks. In the first place, the organizational process model allows little scope for political leadership to be imposed from above. It would be foolish, for example, to suggest that all decisions are shaped by organizational pressures and perceptions, for this would be to ignore the personal role played by, say, George W. Bush in initiating the 'war on terror', or Hitler's influence on Germany's decision to invade Poland. Second, it is simplistic to suggest, as the bureaucratic politics model does, that political actors simply hold views that are based on their own position and on the interests of the organizations in which they work. Although the aphorism 'where you stand depends on where you sit' may often be applicable, personal sympathies and individual goals cannot be altogether discounted. Finally, to explain decisions

Focus on . . .
Perception or misperception?

How are mistakes made in foreign policy? In particular, why do foreign policy-makers sometimes misinterpret or misunderstand the situations they are dealing with? Rational actor models of decision-making imply that policy blunders, when they occur, are primarily a consequence of inadequate or defective information. If decision-makers are able accurately to assess the costs and benefits of potential actions, they will usually select the one that best advances the national interest. Sadly, the history of international relations, and especially the frequency of war (which must damage the national interest of at least one side in the conflict), does not bear out this image of careful reasoning and dispassionate choice. A variety of factors that operate at the individual and small group levels of analysis may increase the likelihood of misperception. For example, time pressures often force policy-makers to 'rush to judgement', meaning that they may be disinclined to consider new or 'inconvenient' information and place unreasoned faith in information that supports a preferred course of action. Such pressures are exacerbated in a world of 24/7 news and current affairs, in which political leaders are expected to adopt a position on major events almost as soon as they happen. Crisis situations also compound such problems, meaning that policy is formulated in an atmosphere that is stressful and emotionally charged.

A further source of misperception stems from distorted images that actors have of themselves and of others. At one level, misperception is unavoidable because of the security dilemma (see p. 19), which systematically encourages policy-makers to over-estimate the aggressive intent of potential enemies, interpreting defensive actions as hostile ones. An exaggerated or distorted image of an opposing leader, regime, people or ideology can significantly increase the scale of misperception, leading either to over-reaction (for example, the escalation of the Cold War) or, at times, under-reaction (appeasement). Misperception is particularly common amongst small groups, where it may take on the characteristics of 'groupthink' (Janis 1982). This certainly occurs due to a tendency for leaders to select close advisers whose views correspond to their own, creating a tightly-knit 'in group'. Small groups, further, are prone to develop a sense of their own intellectual and moral superiority, sustained by stereotypes of their critics as weak, evil or stupid. Potential deviants within small groups often remain silent, rather than voicing their doubts or counter-arguments, as the strength of the group stems, in part, from an illusion of unanimity. Collective psychology thus inclines members to demonstrate their loyalty and commitment to a chosen path, rather than to 'rock the boat'.

entirely in terms of black box considerations is to fail to give any weight to the external pressures that emanate from the broader political, economic, cultural and ideological context.

Cognitive processes and belief-system models

Models of decision-making that place an emphasis on the role of cognitive processes and beliefs highlight the degree to which behaviour is structured by perception. What people see and understand is, to an extent, what their concepts and values allow them, or encourage them, to see and understand. This tendency is particularly entrenched because, in most cases, it is largely unconscious. Although decision-makers may believe that they are being

● **Ethnocentrism**: A mode of understanding in which the actions or intentions of other groups or peoples are understood through the application of values and theories drawn from the observer's own culture or experience.

● **Groupthink**: The phenomenon in which psychological and professional pressures conspire to encourage a group of decision-makers to adopt a unified and coherent position.

rational, rigorous and strictly impartial, their social and political values may act as a powerful filter, defining for them what is thinkable, what is possible, and what is desirable. Certain information and particular options are therefore not appreciated or even considered, while other pieces of information and other courses of action feature prominently in the calculus of decision-making. Indeed, Kenneth Boulding (1956) underlined the vital importance of this process by pointing out that, without a mechanism to filter information, decision-makers would simply be overwhelmed by the sheer volume of data confronting them.

However, there are different views about the origin and nature of this filtering process. Robert Jervis (1968, 1976), for instance, drew attention to evidence of consistent misperception (see p. 137) on the part of decision-makers in international affairs. In his view, this stemmed largely from **ethnocentrism**. The inclination of Anthony Eden and the UK government to view General Nasser as a 'second Hitler' during the 1956 Suez Crisis, and the tendency of the USA in 1959 to regard Fidel Castro as a Marxist revolutionary, may be examples of this phenomenon. Irving Janis (1982), on the other hand, suggested that many decisions in the field of international relations could be explained in terms of what he called '**groupthink**'. This helps to explain how and why contrary or inconvenient views may be squeezed out of consideration in the decision-making process.

Radical theorists, constructivists and feminists have each, in their different ways, highlighted the important role played by beliefs in the formulation of foreign policy. Radical theorists have tended to argue that senior policy-makers, both at a state level and within international organizations, are influenced by ideological biases that favour the interests of dominant economic and social groups. Capitalist economic structures are therefore seen as 'natural' and beneficial, meaning that free trade, market reforms and globalization are viewed in positive terms, with alternatives to them seldom being seriously considered. For Marxists, this is a reflection of ruling class ideology. Constructivists regard foreign policy-making as an intersubjective world, shaped more by ideas and identities than by supposedly objective facts. The interests that guide foreign policy do not therefore emerge out of the systemic pressures of the international system or from the nature of the state, but are fashioned by ideational processes at either a domestic or international level. In short, ideas and identities determine interests. Feminists, for their part, may argue that a preponderance of men amongst policy-makers ensures that the 'glue' of politics is provided by patriarchal ideas and values. This results in policy biases that help to sustain a system of male power, as discussed in Chapter 17.

SUMMARY

- The state has four key features: a defined territory, a permanent population, an effective government, and the capacity to enter into relations with other states. Its core feature, however, is sovereignty, the principle of absolute and unlimited power. There are, nevertheless, internal and external dimensions of sovereignty.
- Globalization has widely been seen to curtail state sovereignty, creating 'post-sovereign governance'. In particular, economic sovereignty has been compromised by transborder trading, capital and other flows. Some believe that such developments have transformed the nature of the state, giving rise to the 'competition' state, the 'market' state or the 'postmodern' state.
- Contrary to the 'declinist' literature, there is growing evidence of the return of state power. This has occurred as a response to new security threats, the increasing use of the state as an agent of economic modernization and through an emphasis on state-building as a means of promoting development.
- Changes in the environment in which the state operates have also, many claim, meant that government is being displaced by governance, implying a shift away from command-and-control and towards coordination. This trend has been associated with the 'stretching' of government across a number of levels, giving rise to multi-level governance.
- The making of foreign policy has traditionally been regarded as one of the key features of international politics, reflecting the importance of statecraft. However, some question whether foreign policy is any longer meaningful given factors such as the structural dynamics of the international system and the advance of globalization.
- A number of general theories of foreign policy decision-making have been advanced. The most important of these are rational actor models, incremental models, bureaucratic organization models and cognitive processes and belief-system models, although they are not necessarily incompatible.

Questions for discussion

- In what sense does the state have a dual structure?
- Why is sovereignty regarded as the core feature of the state?
- What are the major threats to external sovereignty?
- Is the notion of 'post-sovereign governance' meaningful?
- What are the implications for the state of the growth of international organizations?
- To what extent have globalizing tendencies reshaped the nature and role of the state?
- Is the 'return of the state' a myth or a reality?
- In what ways does governance differ from government?
- Is foreign policy-making best understood on an individual, national or systemic level?
- How has neorealism challenged the traditional conception of foreign policy?
- Why is it so difficult for foreign policy actors to make rational and balanced decisions?

Further reading

Bell, S. and A. Hindmoor, *Rethinking Governance: The Centrality of the State in Modern Society* (2009). A clear account of how modern states use a mixture of governance modes to address specific problems, which challenges the notion of the 'decentred' state.

Hay, C., M. Lister and D. Marsh (eds), *The State: Theories and Issues* (2006). An insightful collection that is international in scope and examines the nature of the state and the issue of state transformation.

Smith, S., A. Hadfield and T. Dunne (eds), *Foreign Policy: Theories, Actors, Cases* (2012). A collection of authoritative writings on the theory and practice of foreign policy, including useful case studies.

Sørensen, G., *The Transformation of the State: Beyond the Myth of Retreat* (2004). A systematic analysis that accepts the changing nature of statehood but stresses the state's continued importance in world affairs.

ONLINE RESOURCES AVAILABLE

Links to relevant web resources can be found on the *Global Politics* website

CHAPTER 6

Society in a Global Age

'There is no such thing as society. There are only individual men and women, and their families.'

MARGARET THATCHER, interview, 1987

PREVIEW

The study of international politics has conventionally paid little attention to social forces or social factors. 'States' rather than 'societies' were viewed as the principal actors on the world stage, and relations between and amongst them were thought to be determined by strictly political considerations (linked to power and security), not to sociological ones. In some ways, the advent of globalization accentuated this disregard for 'the social', as hyperglobalists in particular portrayed globalization as a strictly economic, or even technological, phenomenon. Both such views, however, fail to recognize the extent to which institutions such as the state and the economy are embedded in a network of social relationships, which both help to shape political and economic developments and are, in turn, shaped by them. Indeed, modern societies are changing as rapidly and as radically as modern economies. Key shifts include the changing nature of social connectedness, especially in the light of the rise of so-called 'post-industrial' societies and the massive growth in communications technology. Are 'thick' forms of social connectedness being replaced by 'thin' forms of connectedness? Furthermore, the advance of cultural globalization is reshaping social norms and values, especially, but by no means exclusively, in the developing world, not least through the spread of consumerism and the rise of individualism. What are the major drivers of this process, and is it leading to the spread of a global monoculture? Finally, the growth of transnational groups and global movements has led some to suggest that social relations and identities are in the process of being reshaped through the emergence of what has been dubbed 'global civil society'. Is there such a thing as global civil society, and what are its implications for the future shape of global politics?

KEY ISSUES

- What have been the social implications of the emergence of post-industrial societies and the communications revolution?

- Why have risk and insecurity become such prominent features of modern society?

- How, and to what extent, has globalization altered social norms and cultural beliefs?

- Why have NGOs and social movements grown in recent years?

- Is global civil society a force for good or for ill?

Fordism/post-Fordism

'Fordism' and 'post-Fordism' are used to explain the economic, political and cultural transformation of modern society by reference to the changing form and organization of production. Fordism refers to the large-scale mass production methods pioneered by Henry Ford in Detroit in the USA. Ford relied on mechanization and highly regimented production-line labour processes to produce standardized, relatively cheap products. Post-Fordism emerged as the result of the introduction of more flexible microelectronics-based machinery that gave individual workers greater autonomy and made possible innovations such as sub-contracting and batch production. Post-Fordism has been linked to decentralization in the workplace, social and political fragmentation, and a greater emphasis on choice and individuality.

● **Social class**: Broadly, a group of people who share a similar social and economic position, based either on their relationship to the means of production or on the income and status of their occupational group.

SOCIAL CONNECTEDNESS: THICK TO THIN?

What is a society? All societies are characterized by regular patterns of interaction; a 'society' is not just a collection of people who happen to occupy the same territorial area. Societies are fashioned out of a usually stable set of relationships between and among their members, involving a sense of 'connectedness', in the form of mutual awareness and at least a measure of cooperation. Warring tribes, for instance, cannot be viewed as a 'society', even though they may live in close proximity to one another and interact regularly. However, societies may exist on a number of different, and interconnected, levels. At a national or domestic level, particular countries are often referred to as societies, drawing attention to the capacity of a shared culture and political allegiances to inculcate a common sense of identity. Theorists of the so-called 'English School' have argued that society also has an international dimension, in that shared norms and values and regular patterns of interaction among states have created what they call 'international society' (see p. 9). At a still higher level, some have suggested that society has acquired a global dimension, in the form of 'world society' (Burton 1972) or 'global civil society' (see p. 156), as discussed in the final main section of this chapter.

However, the nature of society, and therefore of social connectedness, has changed significantly over time. Mainly applying to national or domestic societies, modern society appears to be characterized by a 'hollowing out' of social connectedness, a transition from the 'thick' connectedness of close social bonds and fixed allegiances to the 'thin' connectedness of more fluid, individualized social arrangements. Many aspects of these changes are associated with the social and cultural implications of globalization, which are examined in the next main section, but other aspects of it are linked to developments such as the advent of post-industrial society, the emergence of the 'information age', and a tendency towards uncertainty, insecurity and risk.

From industrialization to post-industrialism

Industrialization has been the most powerful factor shaping the structure and character of modern societies. It has contributed to a dramatic increase in geographical mobility through the process of urbanization (by the early 2000s, most of the world's then 6.3 billion people had come to live in towns and cities rather than in rural areas). The advance of industrialization also changed the structure of society, with the emergence of **social class** as the central organizing principle of society. Class divisions replaced the fixed social hierarchies of more traditional societies, usually linked to land ownership. In the process, however, the nature of social connectedness changed. One of the most influential attempts to covey this transition was undertaken by the German sociologist Ferdinand Tönnies (1855–1936). Tönnies distinguished between *Gemeinschaft*, or 'community', typically found in traditional societies and characterized by natural affection and mutual respect, and *Gesellschaft*, or 'association', the looser, artificial and contractual bonds typically found in urban and industrial societies.

Nevertheless, class solidarity remained a significant feature of most industrial societies, even though liberals and Marxists offered quite different accounts of the nature of class inequality (the former highlighted individual differences such as ability and the willingness to work, while the latter drew attention to structural divisions related to property ownership). Class loyalties, nevertheless, usually structured political allegiance: 'blue-collar' (or manual) workers generally supported left-wing parties, and 'white-collar' (or non-manual) workers usually supported right-wing parties. However, a further shift occurred from the 1960s onwards through the emergence of so-called '**post-industrial societies**'. One of the key features of such societies has been the process of de-industrialization, reflected in the decline of labour-intensive heavy industries such as coal, steel and shipbuilding. These tended to be characterized by a solidaristic culture rooted in clear political loyalties and, usually, strong union organization. By contrast, the expanding service sectors of the economy foster more individualistic and instrumentalist attitudes. Post-industrial societies are therefore characterized by growing **atomism** and the weakening of social connectedness. Piore and Sabel (1984) interpreted these changes as part of the shift from a Fordist to a post-Fordist era (see p. 141). The eclipse of the system of mass production and mass consumption, the chief characteristic of Fordism, has produced looser and more pluralized class formations.

The shrinkage of the traditional working class has led to the development of so-called 'two-thirds–one-third' societies, in which the two-thirds are relatively prosperous, a product of a marked tendency towards social levelling associated with mass education, rising affluence and consumerism (see p. 153). J.K. Galbraith (1992) highlighted this tendency in pointing to the emergence in modern societies, at least amongst the politically active, of a 'contented majority' whose material affluence and economic security encourages them to be politically conservative. In the process, debate about the nature of social inequality and poverty in modern societies has shifted from a concern about the working class and has focused instead on what is fashionably (but controversially) called the **underclass**. The underclass suffers less from poverty as it has been traditionally understood (deprivation of material necessities) and more from social exclusion, reflected in cultural, educational and social impediments to meaningful participation in the economy and society.

New technology and 'information society'

Technological change has always been closely linked to social change. For example, the introduction of industrial technology, through innovations such as steam power and the mechanization of heavy industries (iron and steel), led to rapid population growth and greatly increased social and geographical mobility, in the process significantly altering patterns of family, friendship and working relationships. This has certainly also applied to developments in information and communications technology, from the birth of printing through to what are sometimes called the three modern information revolutions. The first of these involved the development of the telegraph, telephone and radio; the second centred on television, early-generation computers and satellites; while the third witnessed the advent of the so-called 'new' media, notably mobile phones, cable and satellite television, cheaper and more powerful computers, and, most

● **Post-industrial society**: A society based on service industries, rather than on manufacturing industries, and accompanied by a significant growth in the white-collar workforce.

● **Atomism**: The tendency for society to be made up of a collection of self-interested and largely self-sufficient individuals, operating as separate atoms.

● **Underclass**: A poorly defined and politically controversial term that refers, broadly, to people who suffer from multiple deprivation (unemployment or low pay, poor housing, inadequate education and so on).

APPROACHES TO . . .

SOCIETY

Realist view

Realist theorists have given very little attention to society, in any sense of the term. This reflects the fact that the focus of their attention falls on the state, which they view as a 'black box', in that internal social, political, constitutional and, for that matter, cultural arrangements are irrelevant to its behaviour in the global system. As realists view states as robust, autonomous units that are capable of extracting resources from society and imposing their will on society, foreign policy is determined first and foremost by considerations of power and security. Moreover, relations between and amongst states are essentially 'strategic' rather than 'social': the international system is characterized by competition and struggle, not by regular patterns of social interaction that develop through the emergence of norms, shared values and a willingness to cooperate.

Liberal view

The liberal view of society is based on individualism (see p. 154). Liberals thus regard society not as an entity in its own right but as a collection of individuals. To the extent that society exists, it is fashioned out of voluntary and contractual agreements made by self-interested human beings. Pluralists, nevertheless, have drawn attention to the role of groups in articulating the diverse interests within society. However, whether society is understood simply as a collection of self-interested individuals or as a collection of competing groups, liberals hold that there is a general balance of interests in society that tends to promote harmony and equilibrium. This harmony is largely brought about through the state, which acts as a neutral arbiter amongst the competing interests and groups in society, so guaranteeing social order. This task also has implications for foreign policy, which may therefore be shaped by the different groups in society and the political influence they can exert. In this way, liberals accept that foreign policy decision-making may be society-centred, by contrast with the realist model of state-centrism. Liberals have typically welcomed the emergence of global civil society, seeing this as a way of pluralizing power and making intergovernmental decision-making more considered and popularly accountable. They also tend to assume that interactions among states have a significant social component, favouring the notion of

'international society' and believing that interactions among states and non-state actors tend to be structured by principles, procedures, norms or rules, often leading to the formation of international regimes (see p. 71).

Critical views

Critical approaches to society have been significantly influenced by social constructivism. Constructivists have placed sociological enquiry at the centre of global politics by emphasizing that identities and interests in world affairs are socially constructed. Social, cultural and historical factors are therefore of primary interest in affecting the behaviour of states and other actors. Whereas mainstream theorists view society as a 'strategic' realm, in which actors rationally pursue their various interests, constructivists view society as a 'constitutive' realm, the realm that makes actors who or what they are, shaping their identities and interests. However, constructivism is more an analytical tool that emphasizes the sociological dimension of academic enquiry than a substantive social theory, as advanced, for instance, by neo-Marxists and feminists.

Whereas orthodox Marxists explained society in terms of the class system, viewing the proletariat as an emancipatory force, neo-Marxists such as Frankfurt critical theorists have tended to place their faith in 'counter-cultural' social movements, such as the women's movement (see p. 422), the green movement and the peace movement. In this view, global civil society in general, or the 'anti-capitalist' movement (see p. 74) in particular, has sometimes been seen as a counter-hegemonic force. Feminists, for their part, have analyzed society primarily in terms of gender inequality, seeing all contemporary and historical societies as being characterized by patriarchy (see p. 424) and female subordination. However, there is significant disagreement within feminism about matters such as whether patriarchal society is shaped by biological or cultural factors, and the extent to which gender and class hierarchies are linked. From the perspective of green politics, society is either understood in mechanical terms, reflecting the disjuncture in conventional society between humankind and nature, or it is understood in terms of 'social ecology', reflecting natural harmony both amongst human beings and between humans and nature.

importantly, the **Internet**. The third information revolution has concerned the technologies of **connectivity**, and has been particularly significant. The extraordinary explosion that has occurred in the quantity of information and communication exchanges has marked, some argue, the birth of the 'information age' (in place of the industrial age), with society being transformed into an **'information society'** and the economy becoming a 'knowledge economy' (see p. 97).

The emergence of the 'new' media has given huge impetus to the process of globalization. Indeed, hyperglobalists subscribe to a kind of **technological determinism**, in that they argue that accelerated globalization became inevitable once such technologies became widely available. The clearest evidence of the globalizing tendencies of the new media is that national borders have become increasingly permeable (if not irrelevant) as far as communications are concerned. While the industrial age created new mechanisms for communicating at a national rather than a local level (via national newspapers, telephone systems, radio and television services and so on), the technologies of the information age are by their nature transnational – mobile phones, satellite television and the Internet (usually) operate regardless of borders. This, in turn, has facilitated the growth of transborder groups, bodies and institutions, ranging from non-governmental organizations (NGOs) (see p. 10) and transnational corporations (TNCs) (see p. 94) to international criminal organizations and global terrorist groups such as al-Qaeda (see p. 301). Not only do states struggle to control and constrain groups and organizations that have transborder structures, but they also have a greatly reduced capacity to control what their citizens see, hear and know. For instance, although states such as China, Burma and Iran have, at various times, tried to restrict transborder communications via mobile phones and the Internet, the pace of technological change is very likely to weaken such controls in the longer term. In 2000, US President Bill Clinton famously likened China's attempts to control the Internet to trying to nail Jell-O to the wall.

Not only have information societies brought about a historically unprecedented change in the *scope* of social connectedness (even giving it, at times, a transborder character); they have also altered the *nature* of social connectedness. More people are connected to more other people, but in different ways. One of the most influential attempts to explain this was advanced in Manuel Castells' (1996) notion of the 'network society'. Whereas the dominant mode of social organization in industrial societies had been hierarchy, more complex and pluralized information societies operate either on the basis of markets (reflecting the wider role of market economics as well as the impact of economic globalization (see p. 98)) or on the basis of looser and more diffuse **networks**. According to Castells, businesses increasingly function as 'network corporations'. Many TNCs, for instance, are organized as networks of franchises and subsidiaries. Similar trends can be witnessed in social and political life. For example, hierarchical bodies such as trade unions and pressure groups have increasingly lost influence through the emergence of network-based social movements, such as the anti-globalization movement and the environmental movement, and even terrorist organizations like al-Qaeda have adopted a network form of organization. The increased use of the 'new' media in general and the Internet in particular, especially facilitated by search engines such as the near-ubiquitous Google

● **Internet**: A global network of networks that connects computers around the world; 'virtual' space in which users can access and disseminate online information.

● **Connectivity**: A computer buzzword that refers to the links between one device (usually a computer) and others, affecting the speed, ease and extent of information exchanges.

● **Information society**: A society in which the crucial resource is knowledge/ information, its primary dynamic force being the process of technological development and diffusion.

● **Technological determinism**: A theory of history in which technological innovation and development is assumed to be the principal motor of social, economic or political change.

● **Network**: A means of co-ordinating social life through loose and informal relationships between people or organizations, usually for the purpose of knowledge dissemination or exchange.

KEY EVENTS . . .

Advances in communication technology

1455	Gutenberg Bible is published, initiating the printing revolution through the first use of removable and reusable type.
1837	The telegraph is invented, providing the first means of substantially superterritorial communication.
1876	The telephone is invented by Alexander Graham Bell, although the first telephone device was built in 1861 by the German scientist Johann Philip Reis.
1894	The radio is invented by Guglielmo Marconi, with a transatlantic radio signal being received for the first time in 1901.
1928	Television is invented by John Logie Baird, becoming commercially available in the late 1930s and reaching a mass audience in the 1950s and 1960s.
1936	First freely programmable computer is invented by Konrad Zuse.
1957	The Soviet Sputnik 1 is launched, initiating the era of communications satellites (sometimes called SATCOM).
1962	'Third generation' computers, using integrated circuits (or microchips), started to appear (notably NASA's Apollo Guidance Computer).
1969	Earliest version of the Internet developed, in the form of the ARPANET link between the University of California and the Stanford Research Institute, with electronic mail, or email, being developed three years later.
1991	Earliest version of the **World Wide Web** became publicly available as a global information medium through which users can read and write via computers connected to the Internet.
1995	Digitalization is introduced by Netscape and the Web, substantially broadening access to the Internet and the scope of other technologies.

(see p. 146), has also led to a boom in social networking and massively expanded popular access to information. Although the impact of such developments cannot be doubted, their social implications remain a matter of considerable controversy.

Risk, uncertainty and insecurity

Although the 'thinning' of social connectedness has had profound implications, the widening of its scope may be no less significant. People are exposed as never before to influences (people, events and processes) that are beyond the parameters of their face-to-face interactions, based on family, friends, work

● **World Wide Web**: A hypertext-based system that gives users of the Internet access to a collection of online documents stored on servers around the world; often simply called WWW or the Web.

GLOBAL ACTORS . . .

GOOGLE

Type of organization: Public corporation • **Founded:** 1998
Headquarters: Mountainview, California, USA • **Staff:** About 46,000 full-time employees

Google (the name originates from the mis-spelling of the word 'Googol', which refers to 10 to the power of 100) was founded in 1998 by Larry Page and Sergey Brin, while they were students at Stanford University. The company's remarkable growth derives from the fact that Google quickly became the world's predominant search engine (a tool designed to retrieve data and search for information on the World Wide Web). In 2011, an estimated 83 per cent of Internet searches worldwide were made using Google. Google has expanded rapidly through a strategy of acquisitions and partnerships, and it has also significantly diversified its products, which include email (Gmail), online mapping (Google Earth), customized home pages (iGoogle), video sharing (YouTube) and social networking sites. As well as developing into one of the most powerful brands in the world, Google has cultivated a reputation for environmentalism, philanthropy and positive employee relations. Its unofficial slogan is 'Don't be evil'.

Significance: Google's success as a business organization cannot be doubted. Its widespread use and ever-expanding range of products has helped to turn Google from a noun into a verb (as in 'to Google someone or something'), with young people sometimes being dubbed the 'Google generation'. However, Google's impact on culture, society and politics is a

matter of considerable debate. Supporters of Google argue that in facilitating access to websites and online data and information, Google has helped to empower citizens and non-state actors generally and has strengthened global civil society at the expense of national governments, international bureaucrats and traditional political elites. The oft-repeated truism that knowledge is power conventionally worked to the benefit of governmental bodies and political leaders. However, in the cyber age, easier and far wider access to news and information means that, for the first time, citizens and citizens' groups are privy to a quality and quantity of information that may sometimes rival that of government. NGOs, think-tanks, interest groups and protest movements have therefore become more effective in challenging the positions and actions of government, and may even displace government as an authoritative source of views and information about specialist subjects ranging from the environment and global poverty to public health and civil liberties. In this sense, Google and other search engines have turned the World Wide Web into a democratizing force.

On the other hand, Google and the bewildering array of knowledge and information available on the Internet have also been subject to criticism. The most significant drawback is the lack of quality control on the Internet: we cannot

be sure that what we read on the Internet is true. (Note, for example, the way Wikipedia entries can be hijacked for self-serving or mischievous purposes.) Neither can we always be certain, when we 'Google' for a particular piece of information, what the standpoint is of the website or blogger the search engine throws up. Linked to this is the fact that the Internet does not discriminate between good ideas and bad ones. It provides a platform for the dissemination not only of socially worthwhile and politically balanced views, but also of political extremism, racial and religious bigotry, and pornography of various kinds. A further danger has been the growth of a 'cult of information', whereby the accumulation of data and information becomes an end in itself, impairing the ability of people to distinguish between information, on the one hand, and knowledge, experience and wisdom on the other (Roszak 1994). The Google generation may therefore know more but have a gradually diminishing capacity to make considered and wise judgements. Such a criticism is linked to allegations that 'surfing' the Internet actually impairs people's ability to think and learn by encouraging them to skim and jump from one piece of information to the next, ruining their ability to concentrate. Google may therefore be making people stupid rather than better-informed (Carr 2008, 2010).

colleagues and so on. For Zygmunt Bauman (2000), the combination of the thinning and widening of social connectedness has changed every aspect of the human condition. Society has moved away from a 'heavy' or 'solid', hardware-based modernity to a 'light' or 'liquid' software-based modernity. What he calls 'liquid society' is characterized by the new remoteness and un-reachability of global processes coupled with the unstructured and under-defined, fluid state of people's everyday lives. This has, moreover, led to a substantial increase in the levels of uncertainty and insecurity in society: when everything is short-lived and nothing stands still, people feel anxious and are constantly on alert.

At a general level, the widening of connectedness fosters, in itself, greater risk, uncertainty and instability, because it expands the range of factors that influence decisions and events. As chaos theory (see p. 84) suggests, as more things influence more other things, not only do events have more far-reaching consequences, but these consequences also become more difficult to predict. An interconnected world thus assumes a random, unstable, even crisis-prone character. Ulrich Beck (1992) has taken this analysis further by suggesting that the prevalence of risk in modern societies reflects the transition from the 'first modernity', the period during which, at least in the West, the state could be relied on to provide democracy, economic growth and security, to the 'second modernity', a world 'beyond controllability'. One of the consequences of the emergence of what he calls 'risk societies' is the growth of **tragic individualization**. In industrial societies, political conflict was defined by the distribution of 'goods', typically goods or resources that were supplied by government, such as benefits, subsidies, jobs, healthcare and pensions. In risk societies, by contrast, political conflict is defined by the distribution of 'bads' – risks, threats or problems. Furthermore, these 'bads' are usually not *natural* catastrophes but *created* hazards; examples include pollution, industrial waste that is not easily disposed of, nuclear radiation, resource depletion and BSE (so-called 'mad cow disease').

Modern society is replete with 'manufactured' risks and instabilities of various kinds. The spread of industrialization and the dismantling of regulatory frameworks has created a range of environmental threats which do not respect borders and, indeed, may affect the entire world. Amongst the most obvious of these are the chemical pollution of rivers and lakes, ozone depletion, acid rain and climate change (examined in Chapter 16). The advance of economic globalization also means that economic conditions and livelihoods in one part of the world can be more easily affected by events that occur, or decisions that are taken, in other parts of the world. This applies, for instance, to investment or relocation decisions that are made by TNCs, and to the wider, and almost instantaneous, impact of stock market crashes in the globalized financial system (examined in Chapter 5, in connection with the crises of capitalism). Furthermore, levels of personal safety and security have been undermined by the spread of weapons of mass destruction and the growth in global terrorism (see p. 291). Wider access to chemical and biological weapons and to nuclear weapons has dramatically increased the threat to civilian populations of armed conflict between or within states, while terrorism, by its nature, poses a threat that is unpredictable and seemingly random.

● **Tragic individualization**: The condition in which the individual, through the failure of science, politics and other expert systems to manage risk, is forced to cope with the uncertainty of the global world by him or herself.

KEY THEORISTS IN THE SOCIOLOGY OF GLOBALIZATION

Manuel Castells (born 1942)

A Spanish sociologist, Castells is especially associated with the idea of information society and communications research. He suggests that we live in a 'network society', in which territorial borders and traditional identities have been undermined by the power of knowledge flows. Castells thus emphasizes the 'informational' basis of network society, and shows how human experience of time and space have been transformed. His works include *The Rise of the Network Society* (1996), *The Internet Galaxy* (2004) and *Communication Power* (2009).

Ulrich Beck (born 1944)

A German sociologist, Beck's work has examined topics as wide-ranging as the new world of work, the perils of globalization, and challenges to the global power of capital. In *The Risk Society* (1992), he analyzed the tendency of the globalizing economy to generate uncertainty and insecurity. *Individualization* (2002) (written with his wife, Elizabeth) champions rights-based individualization against free-market individualism. In *Power in the Global Age* (2005), Beck explored how the strategies of capital can be challenged by civil society movements.

Roland Robertson (born 1938)

A UK sociologist and one of the pioneers in the study of globalization, Robertson's psycho-social view of globalization portrays it as 'the compression of the world and the intensification of the consciousness of the world as a whole'. He has drawn attention to both the process of 'relativization' (when local cultures and global pressures mix) and the process of 'glocalization' (through which global pressures are forced to conform to local conditions). Robertson's key work in this field is *Globalization: Social Theory and Global Culture* (1992).

Saskia Sassen (born 1949)

A Dutch sociologist, Sassen is noted for her analyses of globalization and international human migration. In *The Global City* (2001), she examined how cities such as New York, London and Tokyo have become emblematic of the capacity of globalization to create contradictory spaces, characterized by the relationship between the employees of global corporations and the vast population of the low-income 'others' (often migrants and women). Sassen's other works include *The Mobility of Capital and Labour* (1988) and *Territory, Authority, Rights* (2006).

Jan Aart Scholte (born 1959)

A Dutch sociologist and globalization theorist, Scholte argues that globalization is best understood as a reconfiguration of social geography marked by the growth of transplanetary and supraterritorial connections between people. Although by no means a critic of the 'supraterritorialism' that globalization brings about, he highlights the tendency of 'neoliberalist globalization' to heighten insecurities, exacerbate inequalities and deepen democratic deficits. Scholte's main works include *International Relations of Social Change* (1993) and *Globalization: A Critical Introduction* (2005).

Zygmunt Bauman (born 1925)

A Polish sociologist, Bauman's interests range from the nature of intimacy to globalization, and from the Holocaust to reality television programmes such as *Big Brother*. Sometimes portrayed as the 'prophet of postmodernity', he has highlighted trends such as the emergence of new patterns of deprivation and exclusion, the psychic corruption of consumer society, and the growing tendency for social relations to have a 'liquid' character. Bauman's main writings include *Modernity and the Holocaust* (1994), *Globalization* (1998) and *Liquid Modernity* (2000).

GLOBALIZATION, CONSUMERISM AND THE INDIVIDUAL

Social and cultural implications of globalization

Globalization is a multidimensional process. Although it is often understood primarily in economic terms, linked to the establishment of an interlocking global economy, its social and cultural implications are no less important. Human societies, for instance, have traditionally had clear territorial foundations. People knew and interacted with others within their community and, to a lesser extent, with people from neighbouring communities. In short, geography and distance mattered. Globalization, however, has led to the rise of 'supraterritoriality' or '**deterritorialization**' (Scholte 2005), through which the constraints traditionally imposed by geography and distance have been substantially overcome. This process has occurred, most obviously, through improvements in the technologies of communication and transport. However, not only have mobile telephones, the Internet and air travel revolutionized our understanding of space, they have also transformed our notion of time, particularly through seemingly instantaneous information flows. In this light, David Harvey (1990, 2009) associated globalization with the phenomenon of '**time/space compression**', meaning that, for the first time, human interaction could take place outside the restrictions of both space and time. Time/space compression alters people's experience of the world in a variety of ways. For instance, it means that the speed of life is increasing, as, quite simply, events, transactions and travel happen more quickly.

The process of cultural globalization (see p. 151) has sometimes been seen to be yet more significant. In this view, the essence of globalization is the process whereby cultural differences between nations and regions are tending to be 'flattened out'. Such an approach to globalization links it to cultural **homogenization**, as cultural diversity is weakened or destroyed in a world in which we all watch the same television programmes, buy the same commodities, eat the same food, support the same sports stars, follow the antics of the same 'global celebrities', and so on. The chief factors fuelling cultural globalization have been the growth of TNCs, and especially global media corporations (such as AOL-Time Warner, News Corporation, Viacom, Disney, Vivendi Universal and Bertelsmann AG), the increasing popularity of international travel and tourism, and, of course, the information and communications revolution.

Many commentators portray cultural globalization as a 'top-down' process, the establishment of a single global system that imprints itself on all parts of the world; in effect, a global monoculture. From this perspective, cultural globalization amounts to a form of **cultural imperialism**, emphasizing that cultural flows are between unequal partners and are used as a means through which powerful states exert domination over weaker states. Some therefore portray cultural globalization as 'westernization' or, more specifically, as 'Americanization'. The image of globalization as homogenization is at best a partial one, however. Globalization often goes hand in hand with localization, regionalization and multiculturalism (see p. 192). The fear or threat of homogenization, especially when it is perceived to be imposed 'from above', or 'from outside', provokes cultural and political resistance. This can be seen in the resurgence of interest in

● **Deterritorialization**: The process through which social spaces can no longer be wholly mapped in terms of territorial places, territorial distance and territorial borders.

● **Time/space compression**: The idea that, in a globalized world, time and space are no longer significant barriers to communications and interaction.

● **Homogenization**: The tendency for all parts or elements (in this case, countries) to become similar or identical.

● **Cultural imperialism**: The displacement of an indigenous culture by the imposition of foreign beliefs, values and attitudes, usually associated with consolidating or legitimizing economic and/or political domination.

Naomi Klein (born 1970)

Canadian journalist, author and anti-corporate activist. Klein's *No Logo: Taking Aim at the Brand Bullies* (2000) is a wide-ranging critique of lifestyle branding and labour abuses, and discusses emerging forms of resistance to globalization and corporate domination. It has been described as 'the book that became part of the movement' but has had wider significance in provoking reflection on the nature of consumer capitalism and the tyranny of brand culture. In *Disaster Capitalism* (2008), she drew attention to the extent to which the advance of neoliberalism has been implicated in 'shocks', states of emergency and crises of one kind or another. Klein is a frequent and influential media commentator. She lives in Toronto but travels widely throughout North America, Asia, Latin America and Europe, supporting movements campaigning against the negative effects of globalization.

declining languages and minority cultures as well as in the spread of religious fundamentalism. Nevertheless, the two main ingredients of cultural globalization have been the spread of consumerism and the growth of individualism (see p. 154).

Consumerism goes global

Cultural globalization has most commonly been associated with the worldwide advance of a culture of consumer capitalism, sometimes seen as 'turbo-consumerism'. One aspect of this has been what is called 'Coca-Colonization', a process first highlighted by French communists in the 1950s. Coca-Colonization refers, on one level, to the emergence of global goods and global **brands** (Coca-Cola being a prime example) that have come to dominate economic markets in more and more parts of the world, creating an image of bland uniformity. However, at a deeper level, it also captures the psychological and emotional power that these brands have come to acquire through highly sophisticated marketing and advertising, allowing them to become symbols of freedom, youthfulness, vitality, happiness and so on. It is therefore a manifestation of what Marxists have called **commodity fetishism**. Consumerism has become one of the key targets of modern anti-corporate criticism, highlighted by Naomi Klein, amongst others, and it has been particularly emphasized by the green movement, as discussed in Chapter 16.

In one of the most influential accounts of trends in global consumerism, Benjamin Barber (2003) portrayed the emerging world as a 'McWorld'. McWorld is tied together by technology, ecology, communications and commerce, creating a 'shimmering scenario of integration and uniformity' in which people everywhere are mesmerized by 'fast music, fast computers, fast food – with MTV, McIntosh and McDonald's pressing nations into one commercially homogeneous theme park'. Alongside and reflecting such developments has been the increasing standardization of business organizations and practices, commonly referred to as '**McDonaldization**'. Underpinning the emergence of McWorld has been the seemingly relentless spread of materialist values, based on the notion of

● **Brand**: A symbolic construct, typically consisting of name, logo or symbol, which conveys the promise, 'personality' or image of a product or group of products.

● **Commodity fetishism**: The process whereby commodities are invested with symbolic and social significance, allowing them to exert sway over human beings.

● **McDonaldization**: The process whereby global commodities and commercial and marketing practices associated with the fast food industry have come to dominate more and more economic sectors (Ritzer 1993)

(see p. 26)

CONCEPT

Cultural globalization

Cultural globalization is the process whereby information, commodities and images produced in one part of the world enter into a global flow that tends to 'flatten out' cultural differences between nations, regions and individuals. Cultural globalization is closely linked to and emerged in association with economic globalization and the communication and information revolution. However, cultural globalization is a complex process that generates both homogenization, or cultural 'flattening', and polarization and diversity. The latter may occur both because cultural products spread more easily if they adapt to local traditions and understandings, and because perceived domination by foreign ideas, values and lifestyles can fuel the rise of ethnic, religious or national movements.

● **Americanization**: Either or both the politico-economic dominance of the USA, or the spread of American cultural values and practices to other parts of the world.

● **Community**: A principle or sentiment based on the collective identity of a social group, bonds of comradeship, loyalty and duty.

an intrinsic link between wealth and happiness. For many, these trends have a markedly western, and more specifically American character. The 'westernization' model of cultural globalization derives from the fact that the West (see p. 26) is the home of consumer capitalism and industrial society, and is backed up by the belief that the ethic of material self-seeking is a specifically western value, stemming as it does from western liberalism. The '**Americanization**' model of cultural globalization reflects the disproportionate extent to which the goods and images that dominate modern commerce and the media derive from the USA, meaning that the world is being taken over not just by consumer capitalism but by a very particular US model of consumer capitalism.

The trends associated with cultural globalization have by no means been universally condemned, however. For many, the advent of consumer culture and access to a wider range of goods and cultural products have broadened opportunities and provided an alternative to the narrow parochialism of traditional societies. Cultural globalization may, for instance, be compared favourably with insular nationalism. However, most interpretations of cultural globalization have been critical or pessimistic. At least three main lines of attack have been adopted. First, cultural globalization has been seen to serve the interests of economic or political domination. In this view, cultural globalization has been driven by the dominant interests in the new globalized economy – TNCs, the West generally and the USA in particular – and its role has been to shape values, appetites and lifestyles so as to ensure market penetration and the ascendancy of global capitalism. Second, cultural homogenization has been condemned as an assault on local, regional and national distinctiveness. A world in which everything looks the same and everyone thinks and acts in the same way is a world without a sense of rootedness and belonging. Third, consumerism and materialism have been condemned as a form of captivity, a form of manipulation that distorts values and denies happiness.

Rise of individualism

The trend towards 'thin' social connectedness and the pressures generated by globalization have combined in modern societies to place greater emphasis on the individual and, arguably, less emphasis on **community**. In many parts of the world, the notion of 'the individual' is now so familiar that its political and social significance, as well as its relatively recent origins, are often overlooked. In the traditional societies, there is typically little idea of individuals having their own interests or possessing personal and unique identities. Rather, people are seen as members of the social groups to which they belong: their family, village, tribe, local community and so on. Their lives and identities are largely determined by the character of these groups in a process that changes little from one generation to the next. The rise of individualism is widely seen as a consequence of the establishment of industrial capitalism as the dominant mode of social organization, first in western societies and, thanks to globalization, beyond. Industrial capitalism meant that people were confronted by a broader range of choices and social possibilities. They were encouraged, perhaps for the first time, to think for themselves, and to think of themselves in personal terms. A peasant, for example, whose family may always have lived and worked on the same piece of land, became a 'free man' and acquired some ability to choose who to work for, or

Focus on ...

Consumerism as captivity?

Is consumerism a source of personal gratification, even self-expression, or is it a form of manipulation and social control? The idea of consumerism as captivity would strike many people as simple nonsense – after all, no one is ever *forced* to shop! The desire for wealth and the pleasure derived from material acquisition are widely viewed as nothing more than an expression of human nature. What is more, such thinking is backed up by perfectly respectable social and economic theory. Utilitarianism, the most widely accepted tradition of moral philosophy, assumes that individuals act so as to maximize pleasure and minimize pain, these being calculated in terms of utility or use-value, usually seen as satisfaction derived from material consumption. The global spread of consumerist ethics is therefore merely evidence of deep-seated material appetites on the part of humankind.

Nevertheless, critiques of consumerism can be traced back to the Marxist notion of 'commodity fetishism' as a process through which objects came to have sway over the people who own or hope to acquire them. For Herbert Marcuse (1964), modern advertising techniques that allowed the manipulation of needs by vested interests were creating a 'one-dimensional society'. Modern marketing techniques have massively expanded this capacity for manipulation, not least through the development of a 'brand culture' (Klein 2000). The core theme of anti-consumerism is that advertising and marketing in their myriad forms create 'false' needs that serve the interests of corporate profit, often, in the process, undermining psychological and emotional well-being. By creating ever-greater material desires, they leave consumers in a constant state of dissatisfaction because, however much they acquire and consume, they always want more. Consumerism thus works not through the satisfaction of desires, but through the generation of new desires, keeping people in a state of constant neediness, aspiration and want. This is borne out by the emerging discipline of 'happiness economics' which suggests that once citizens enjoy fairly comfortable living standards (generally an annual income of around $20,000), more income brings little, if any, additional happiness (Layard 2006).

---

maybe the opportunity to leave the land altogether and look for work in the growing towns or cities. As individuals, people were more likely to be self-seeking, acting in accordance with their own (usually material) interests, and they were encouraged to be self-sufficient in the sense of taking responsibility for their economic and social circumstances. This gave rise to the doctrine of **economic individualism**.

However, there is deep disagreement over the implications of the spread of individualism. For many, the spread of individualism has profoundly weakened community and our sense of social belonging, perhaps implying that society in its conventional sense no longer exists. For instance, academic sociology largely arose in the nineteenth century as an attempt to explore the (usually negative) social implications of the spread of industrialization and urbanization, both of which had encouraged increasing individualism and competition. For Tönnies, this had led to the growth of so-called '*Gesellschaft*' relationships, which are artificial and contractual, reflecting the desire for personal gain rather than any meaningful social loyalty. Émile Durkheim (1858–1917) emphasized the degree to which the weakening of social codes and norms had resulted in the spread of 'anomie'; that is, feelings of isolation, loneliness and meaninglessness, which, in

● **Economic individualism**: The belief that individuals are entitled to autonomy in matters of economic decision-making; economic individualism is sometimes taken to be synonymous with private property and implies *laissez-faire* (see p. 106).

CONCEPT

Consumerism

Consumerism is a psychological and cultural phenomenon whereby personal happiness is equated with the consumption of material possessions. It is often associated with the emergence of a 'consumer society' or of 'consumer capitalism'. Consumer capitalism was shaped by the development of new advertising and marketing techniques that took advantage of the growth of the mass media and the spread of mass affluence. A consumer society is one that is organized around the consumption rather than the production of goods and services. Whereas 'productionist' societies emphasize the values of discipline, duty and hard work (the Protestant work ethic, for example), consumer societies emphasize materialism, hedonism and immediate rather than delayed gratification.

● **Social capital**: Cultural and moral resources, such as networks, norms and trust, that help to promote social cohesion, political stability and prosperity.

● **Social reflexivity**: The tendency of individuals and other social actors to reflect, more or less continuously, on the conditions of their own actions, implying higher levels of self-awareness, self-knowledge and contemplation.

Durkheim's ([1897] 1997) view, had led to an increase in the number of suicides in industrial societies. Similar misgivings about the rise of individualism have been expressed by modern communitarian thinkers, who have linked the growth of egoism and atomism to a weakening of social duty and moral responsibility. As people are encouraged to take account of their own interests and their own rights, a moral vacuum is created in which society, quite literally, disintegrates. Robert Putnam (2000), for instance, has highlighted the decline of **social capital** in modern societies, reflected in the decline of community activity and political engagement, including voting and party membership. A particular source of communitarian concern has been the 'parenting deficit', the failure of modern parents concerned about their own enjoyment and well-being to adequately control or socialize their children, resulting in a general decline in civility and a rise in levels of delinquency and crime.

On the other hand, liberal theorists in particular have viewed rising individualism as a mark of social progress. In this view, the forward march of individualism has been associated with the spread of progressive, even enlightened, social values, notably toleration and equality of opportunity. If human beings are thought of first and foremost as individuals, they must be entitled to the same rights and the same respect, meaning that all forms of disadvantage or discrimination, based on factors such as gender, race, colour, creed, religion or social background, are viewed as morally questionable, if not indefensible. All modern industrial societies have, to a greater or lesser extent, been affected by the spread of such ideas, not least through changing gender roles and family structures that have resulted from the spread of feminism. The link between individualism and the expansion of choice and opportunity has also been highlighted by the spread in modern societies of **social reflexivity** (Giddens 1994). This has occurred for a variety of reasons, including the development of mass education, much wider access to information through radio, television, the Internet and so on, and intensified cultural flows within and between societies. However, social reflexivity brings both benefits and dangers. On the one hand, it has greatly widened the sphere of personal freedom, the ability of people to define who they are and how they wish to live, a tendency reflected in the increasing domination of politics by so-called 'lifestyle' issues. On the other hand, its growth has coincided with a strengthening of consumerism and materialist ethics.

Nevertheless, it is important not to overstate the advance of individualism or, for that matter, the erosion of community. Individualism has been embraced most eagerly in the Anglophone world, where it has been most culturally palatable given the impact of Protestant religious ideas about personal salvation and the moral benefits of individual self-striving. By contrast, Catholic societies in Europe and elsewhere have been more successful in resisting individualism and maintaining the ethics of social responsibility, reflected in a stronger desire to uphold welfare provision as both an expression of social responsibility and a means of upholding social cohesion. However, the best examples of successful anti-individualist societies can be found in Asia, especially in Japan, China and Asian 'tiger' states such as Taiwan, South Korea and Singapore. This has led to a debate about the viability of a set of so-called 'Asian values', and especially those associated with Confucianism (see p. 202), as an alternative to the individualism of western liberal societies. In addition, the image of modern societies being

Individualism

Individualism is the belief in the supreme importance of the individual over any social group or collective body. As such, individualism has two key implications. First, each individual has a separate, indeed unique, identity, reflecting his or her 'inner' or personal qualities. This is reflected in the idea of **individuality**, and is linked to the notion of people as self-interested and largely self-reliant creatures. Second, all individuals share the same moral status as 'persons', irrespective of factors such as race, religion, nationality, sex and social position. The notion that individuals are of equal moral worth is reflected in the idea of rights, and especially in the doctrine of human rights (see p. 311).

● **Individuality**: Self-fulfilment achieved though the realization of one's own distinctive or unique identity or qualities; that which distinguishes one person from all other people.

● **Countervailing power**: The theory that concentrations of power tend to be temporary because they stimulate oppositional forces and the emergence of rival centres of power; often used to explain challenges to corporate power.

increasingly dominated by 'thin' forms of social connectedness is undermined by evidence of the resurgence of 'thick' social connectedness in many societies, especially in the form of identity politics (see p. 190) and linked to the growing importance of culture, ethnicity and religion in world affairs. The notion of an emerging global monoculture may therefore be a myth, as globalization may be associated as much with the rise of ethnic nationalism and religious fundamentalism (see p. 199) as it is with the spread of consumerism and self-seeking individualism. Barber (2003), indeed, argued that the rise of McWorld is symbiotically linked to the emergence of militant Islam, or 'Jihad', the latter being, in part, a reaction against the imposition of foreign and threatening western cultural and economic practices. The growing importance of culture and religion in global politics is examined in more detail in Chapter 8.

GLOBAL CIVIL SOCIETY

Explaining global civil society

The advance of globalization, and the progressive 'de-territorialization' of economic, cultural and political life, has gradually weakened the idea that society should be understood merely in domestic or national terms. If societies are fashioned out of a usually stable set of relationships between and among their members, involving mutual awareness and at least a measure of cooperation, it has sometimes been suggested that one of the consequences of globalization has been the emergence of 'transnational' or 'world' society (Burton 1973; Buzan 2004). However, the extent to which societal identities have been, or are in the process of being, established across the global population as a whole should not be over-stated. A perhaps fruitful way of thinking about the transnational dimension of society is in terms of what is called 'global civil society' (see p. 156). Interest in the idea of global civil society grew during the 1990s, as a mosaic of new groups, organizations and movements started to appear, which both sought to challenge or resist what was seen as 'corporate' globalization and articulate alternative models of social, economic and political development. This happened against a backdrop of the spread of demands for democratization around the world, in the aftermath of the Cold War, and in the light of the intensifying process of global interconnectedness. In some cases, these groups and organizations rejected globalization altogether, styling themselves as part of an 'anti-globalization' movement, but in other cases they supported a reformed model of globalization, sometimes seen as 'social democratic' or 'cosmopolitan' globalization.

The development of emergent global civil society can best be explained through the theory of **countervailing power**, as developed by J.K. Galbraith (1963). In this view, emergent global civil society is a direct reaction to the perceived domination of corporate interests within the globalization process. The rise of global civil society is therefore part of a backlash against the triumph of neoliberalism (see p. 93). This helps to explain the ideological orientation of most of these new groups and movements, which broadly favour a global social justice or world ethics agenda, reflected in a desire to extend the impact and efficacy of human rights, deepen international law (see p. 339) and develop citizen networks to monitor and put pressure on states and international organ-

Debating...
Is globalization producing a global monoculture?

The dominant image of globalization is that it tends to 'flatten out' cultural differences, advancing sameness and diminishing difference worldwide. However, modern societies have also exemplified a strong tendency towards diversity and pluralization.

FOR

Globalization as homogenization. One aspect of globalization is universalization: the dispersal of objects, images, ideas and experiences to people in all inhabited parts of the world. For example, economic globalization and the rise of TNCs have led to the emergence of 'global goods' (Starbucks coffee, Barbie dolls, and so on). The spread of communications technologies, such as television, film, radio and, of course, the Internet, has homogenized global cultural flows and led to the creation of 'global celebrities' (such as Britney Spears and David Beckham). And English is well on its way to becoming the dominant global language – about 35 per cent of the world's mail, telexes, and cables are in English, approximately 40 per cent of the world's radio programmes are in English, and about 50 per cent of all Internet traffic uses English.

'Americanization of the world'. For many, the globalization-as-homogenization thesis conceals a deeper process: the advance of westernization and, more especially, Americanization. Global sameness reflects the imposition of a dominant economic, social and cultural model on all parts of the world. The rise of an increasingly homogenized popular culture is underwritten by a western 'culture industry', based in New York, Hollywood, London and Milan. Western, and more specifically US, norms and lifestyles therefore overwhelm more vulnerable cultures, leading, for instance, to Palestinian youths wearing Chicago Bulls sweatshirts. The economic and cultural impact of the USA is also reflected in the 'McDonaldization' of the world, reflecting the seemingly unstoppable rise of American-style consumer capitalism.

Global liberalization. A third version of the homogenization thesis highlights a growing worldwide ascendancy of liberal ideas and structures. In economic terms, this is reflected in the global trend in favour of free markets and free trade. In political terms, it is evident in the spread of liberal democracy, based on a combination of electoral democracy and party competition. In cultural and ideological terms, it is reflected in the rise of individualism, an emphasis on technocratic rationalism, and the development of the doctrine of human rights into a cosmopolitan political creed.

AGAINST

Globalization as hybridization. Cultural exchange is by no means a top-down or one-way process; instead, all societies, including economically and politically powerful ones, have become more varied and diverse as a result of the emergence of a globalized cultural market place. So-called 'reverse cultural flows' reflect the growth of 'hybridity' or creolization (the cross-fertilization that takes place when different cultures interact). In return for Coca-Cola, McDonald's and MTV, developed states have increasingly been influenced by non-western religions, food (soy sauce, Indian curry spices, tortillas), medicines and therapeutic practices (acupuncture, yoga, Buddhist meditation), sports (judo, karate, kick-boxing), and so on.

Return of the local. The globalization-as-homogenization thesis is undermined by the extent to which globalization either adapts to local circumstances or strengthens local influences. In developing states, for instance, western consumer goods and images have been absorbed into more traditional cultural practices through a process of indigenization (through which alien goods and practices are adapted to local conditions and needs). Examples include the Bollywood film industry and the Al-Jazeera television network. The process of cultural borrowing by which local actors select and modify elements from an array of global possibilities has been described by Robertson (1992) as 'glocalization'.

Cultural polarization. Where economic and cultural globalization have imposed alien and threatening values and practices, a backlash has sometimes been provoked, resulting not in homogenization but in polarization. This can be seen in Barber's (2003) image of a world culture shaped by symbiotic links between 'McWorld' and 'Jihad'. Similarly, Samuel Huntington (see p. 540) dismissed the idea of a global monoculture in proclaiming, instead, the emergence of a 'clash of civilizations'. This suggested that with the end of the Cold War, global politics had moved out of its western phase, its centrepiece increasingly becoming interaction between the West and non-western civilizations as well as among non-western civilizations. Key civilizational conflict would thus occur between the USA and China and between the West and Islam.

CONCEPT

Global civil society

The term 'civil society' refers to a realm of autonomous groups and associations that operate independently of government. Global civil society thus highlights a realm in which transnational non-governmental groups and associations interact. These groups are typically voluntary and non-profitmaking, setting them apart from TNCs. However, the term 'global civil society' is complex and contested. In its 'activist' version, transnational social movements are the key agents of global civil society, giving it an 'outsider' orientation and a strong focus on humanitarian goals and cosmopolitan ideals. In its 'policy' version, NGOs are the key agents of global civil society, giving it an 'insider' orientation and meaning that it overlaps significantly with global governance (see p. 462).

● **New Left**: A current in leftist thought that rejected both orthodox communism and social democracy in favour of a new politics of liberation based on decentralization and participatory democracy.

izations (Kaldor 2003). The growth of such groups has also been facilitated by the emergence of a framework of global governance, which has both provided civil society groups with sources of funding and given them the opportunity to engage in policy formulation and, sometimes, policy implementation. Other factors include the wider availability of advanced ICT to facilitate transnational communication and organization; and the development of a pool of educated professionals in both developed and developing countries who, albeit in different ways and for different reasons, feel alienated by the globalized capitalist system.

The 'Earth Summit' held in Rio de Janeiro in 1992 is often cited as the earliest evidence of a functioning global civil society. The formation of the World Social Forum in 2001 gave the global civil society sector a greater sense of focus and organizational direction, enabling it to challenge its great capitalist rival, the World Economic Forum. In this sense, global civil society has emerged as a third force between TNCs and international organizations, representing neither the market nor the state. However, the concept of global civil society remains controversial. A neologism of the 1990s, the idea of global civil society quickly became fashionable, being used by world leaders and policy-makers as well as by political activists. But is it a reality, or merely an aspiration? Participation in global civil society, for instance, is restricted to a relatively small number of people. None of its groups yet constitutes a genuine mass movement, comparable, say, to the trade union movement or the mass membership of political parties of the late nineteenth and early twentieth centuries. Moreover, there are doubts about the degree of interconnectedness within global civil society: is it one thing or a number of things? In particular, there are differences between the two main actors within global civil society: transnational social movements and NGOs.

Transnational social movements and NGOs

Transnational social movements, sometimes called 'new' social movements, developed during the 1960s and 1970s against the backdrop of growing student radicalism, anti-Vietnam war protest and the rise of 'counter-cultural' attitudes and sensibilities. Key examples included the women's movement, the environmental or green movement and the peace movement. These movements attracted the young, the better-educated and the relatively affluent, and typically embraced a 'postmaterialist' ethic (see p. 157). They tended to be more concerned with quality of life issues and cultural change than with social advancement in the traditional sense. Although they articulated the views of different groups, they nevertheless subscribed to a common (if not always clearly defined) ideology, linked broadly to the ideas of the **New Left**. From the outset, these movements had a transnational, even global, orientation. This reflected the fact that, in many cases, support for them spills naturally across borders (for example, the women's movement) and also that, given the nature of their concerns, national divisions are seen as part of the problem rather than as part of the solution (for instance, the peace movement and the green movement).

Such tendencies were accentuated by the development, from the 1990s onwards, of a new wave of social movement activism, with the emergence of what has variously been called the 'anti-globalization', 'anti-capitalist', 'anti-

CONCEPT

Postmaterialism

Postmaterialism is a theory that explains the nature of political concerns and attitudes in terms of levels of economic development. It is loosely based on Abraham Maslow's (1908–70) 'hierarchy of needs' (see p. 361), which places esteem and **self-actualization** above material or economic needs. Postmaterialism assumes that conditions of material scarcity breed egoistical and acquisitive values, meaning that politics is dominated by economic issues. However, in conditions of widespread prosperity, individuals express more interest in postmaterial or quality of life issues. These are typically concerned with morality, political justice and personal fulfilment, and include feminism, world peace, poverty reduction, racial harmony, environmental protection and animal rights.

● **Self-actualization**: Personal fulfilment brought about by the refinement of sensibilities; self-actualization is usually linked to the transcendence of egoism and materialism.

● **New politics**: A style of politics that distrusts representative mechanisms and bureaucratic processes in favour of strategies of popular mobilization and direct action.

corporate' or 'global justice' movement. This loose and ideologically diverse 'movement of movements' has been in the forefront of the so-called '**new politics**', stressing decentralization and participatory decision-making and embracing a more innovative and theatrical form of protest politics. Examples of this have included the 'Battle of Seattle' in 1999, in which mass demonstrations against the World Trade Organization (WTO) (see p. 537) degenerated into violent clashes between the police and groups of protesters, and other similar anti-capitalism protests that now regularly accompany meetings of groups such as the WTO, the OECD and the G-20 (see p. 121).

As such, transnational social movements represent the 'outsider' face of global civil society. Their 'outsider' status is largely a result of the nature of their ideological and political goals, which are radical rather than mainstream, and so are generally incompatible with those of conventional policy-makers at both national and global levels. Their use of 'outsider' strategies, such as marches, demonstrations and protests, is a way of attracting media attention and of turning potential supporters into activists. However, 'outsider' status also places massive limitations on the policy impact of global social movements. Insofar as they have influence, it is more in terms of bringing about a wider and more nebulous shift in values and cultural awareness. This can clearly be seen in relation to the environment movement and the women's movement. The anti-globalization movement, though much younger, has already contributed to a politico-cultural shift in terms of attitudes, particularly amongst young people, towards free trade practices and consumerist values.

Many, nevertheless, view NGOs as the key actors within global civil society, their advantage being that they are institutionalized and professionalized 'insiders'. There can be little doubt that major international NGOs and the NGO sector as a whole now constitute a significant group of political actors on the global stage. Advocacy NGOs have had a variety of high-profile successes, often constraining the influence of TNCs and altering the policy direction of national governments and international organizations. NGO pressure during the UN's Earth Summit in Rio in 1992, exerted by some 2,400 respresentatives of NGOs and a parallel NGO 'Global Forum' that attracted about 17,000 people, initiated the process for controlling the emissions of greenhouse gases. The International Campaign to Ban Land Mines, a network of more than 14,000 NGOs working in 90 countries, was effective in 1997 in getting the agreement of some 120 states to ban the production, use and stockpiling of anti-personnel landmines. Without concerted pressure from NGOs, the International Criminal Court may never have been established, an influence that continues to be vital for the effective working of the Court (see p. 158).

As NGOs have been accepted as key policy-makers, policy-influencers and even policy-implementers, they have developed into 'tamed' social movements. The price for their participation in the process of global governance has been the adoption of more mainstream or 'responsible' policy positions. This trend is reflected in the fact that distinctions between NGOs and governments and international organizations, and between NGOs and TNCs, have become increasingly blurred. Not only do NGOs have formal rights of consultation within international organizations, being accepted as a source of specialist advice and information, but NGOs and international organizations will often work together in formulating and carrying out a range of humanitarian projects. Many NGOs are

NGOs and the International Criminal Court

Events: The International Criminal Court (ICC) came into operation in 2002, when the minimum required 60 states ratified the 1998 Rome Statute. NGOs played an unprecedented role in helping to bring the ICC into existence, doing much to set the international political agenda over the prosecution of genocide, crimes against humanity and war crimes, and participating in drafting the Rome Statute. This was accomplished largely through the Coalition for an International Criminal Court (CICC), formed in 1995, which has come to have a membership of over 2,500 NGOs worldwide. Some 235 NGOs attended the Rome Conference, larger ones such as Amnesty International and Human Rights Watch sending more delegates than most countries, and with the World Federalist Movement's delegation of 60 experts exceeding even the largest government delegation. Once the Rome Statute was approved, the CICC mounted a huge lobbying campaign designed to pressure UN member states into signing and ratifying the treaty. By May 2013, 139 countries had signed the treaty, 122 having also ratified it. NGOs also play a significant and ongoing role in supporting the workings of the Court. Amongst other things, they provide support for victims and witnesses in giving evidence and submit legal analyses and policy arguments through so-called *Amicus Curiae* ('Friend of the Court') briefs.

Significance: The uniquely influential role played by NGOs in the establishment of the ICC can be explained in at least three ways. First, the CICC was highly effective in bringing together and coordinating diverse NGOs with different goals and focus areas (such as gender justice, victims, children), enabling them to act in a cohesive manner to achieve set ends. Second, NGO influence was closely linked to their expertise and, sometimes, political skills. Governments were keen to utilize reports and documents prepared by NGOs, benefiting both from their legal expertise and their ability to supply services, including translating and interpreting services. During the Rome Conference's five weeks of negotiations, the CICC not only ensured that government delegates were adequately informed, but also helped to broker compromises when difficulties emerged. Third, NGOs took full advantage of the UN's willingness, dating back to the early 1990s, to encourage non-governmental as well as governmental participation in global policy-making. Over this issue, policy was therefore made through a process of international cooperation, structured

around diverse global networks of NGOs in collaboration with governments and the UN.

Some commentators have viewed the establishment of the ICC as a crucial stage in the emergence of global civil society, marking the point in which NGOs, acting as the 'conscience of humanity', were first able to place constraints on the state-centric politics of old. Certainly, the CICC had injected an urgency into the campaign for an ICC just as the support of governments started to falter, the creation of *ad hoc* UN-backed tribunals for former Yugoslavia and Rwanda having created a fear that the ICC might come for them one day. Moreover, the ICC moves significantly beyond the principles enshrined in the International Court of Justice, in that the ICC may, potentially, breach state sovereignty by prosecuting citizens of states that have not ratified the Rome Statute. The notion that NGOs are in the process of superseding states is, nevertheless, misleading. Although NGOs undoubtedly provided much-needed encouragement for states to sign and ratify the Rome Statute, they did not, and could not, force reluctant governments to act against their perceived interests. The simple fact is that humanitarian sensibilities have not only underpinned the growth of NGOs, but also, in many cases, led to adjustments in state behaviour. Finally, for all the energies expended in the establishment of the ICC, its impact continues to be restricted, not least by the refusal of many of the world's most powerful states, including the USA, China, India and Russia, to sign the Rome Statute.

also part-funded by government – *Médecins Sans Frontières* (known in English as 'Doctors without Borders'), for example, receives almost half its funding from governmental sources. Indications of the growing links between NGOs and TNCs can be found, for instance, in the fact that the World Economic Forum now embraces representatives of leading NGOs, and that a 'revolving door' has developed through which TNCs demonstrate their commitment to corporate social responsibility by employing former NGO leaders and specialists.

Globalization from below?

Has global civil society contributed to a reconfiguration of global power? Does it represent an alternative to top-down corporate globalization, a kind of bottom-up democratic vision of a civilizing world order, or 'globalization from below'? Optimists about global civil society argue that it has two main advantages. First, it provides a necessary counter-balance to corporate power. Until the 1990s, the advance of TNC interests met little effective resistance, meaning that international organizations in particular fell too easily under the sway of a neoliberal agenda committed to free markets and free trade. Transnational social movements and NGOs help to ensure that such interests and ideas are checked, challenged and scrutinized, not (necessarily) to block corporate interests or inhibit economic globalization, but to strengthen the global policy-making process by bringing more views and voices to the table. Second, emergent civil society is often seen as form of fledgling democratic global politics. This has occurred because civil society bodies have articulated the interests of people and groups who have been disempowered by the globalization process, acting as a kind of counter-hegemonic force. Similarly, by introducing an element of public scrutiny and accountability to the workings of international bodies, conferences, summits and the like, global civil society functions as a channel of communication between the individual and global institutions.

However, emergent global civil society also has its critics. In the first place, the democratic credentials of NGOs and, for that matter, social movements are entirely bogus. For example, how can NGOs be in the forefront of democratization when they are entirely non-elected and self-appointed bodies? Large memberships, committed activists and the ability to mobilize popular protests and demonstrations undoubtedly give social movements and NGOs political influence, but it does not give them democratic authority, when there is no mechanism for testing the weight of their views against those of society at large. Second, the tactics of popular activism and **direct action**, so clearly associated with social movements and certain NGOs, have also attracted criticism. For instance, the violence that has accompanied many major anti-capitalist protests has, arguably, alienated many potential supporters, giving the entire movement an image of recklessness and irresponsibility. A final criticism is that NGOs and social movements distort national and global political agendas through their fixation on gaining media attention, both as the principal means of exerting pressure and in order to attract support and funding. This, nevertheless, may lead them to making exaggerated claims in order to 'hype' political issues, and to indulge in knee-jerk protest politics, aided and abetted by a mass media desperate for 'impact' stories in an age of 24/7 news and current affairs.

● **Direct action**: Political action taken outside the constitutional and legal framework; direct action may range from passive resistance to terrorism.

SUMMARY

● Societies are fashioned out of a usually stable set of relationships between and among their members. However, the 'thick' social connectedness of close bonds and fixed allegiances is giving way to the 'thin' connectedness of more fluid, individualized social arrangements. This reflects the impact of post-industrialism and the wider use of communication technology.

● The thinning and widening of social connectedness has been associated with a general increase in risk, uncertainty and instability. The risks and instabilities of modern society include growing environmental threats, economic crises due to an increase in economic interconnectedness and the emergence of new security threats.

● Cultural globalization is the process whereby information, commodities and images that have been produced in one part of the world enter into a global flow that tends to 'flatten out' cultural differences between nations, regions and individuals. It is often associated with the worldwide spread of consumerism and the rise of individualism.

● The image of an emerging global monoculture has nevertheless been challenged. Diversity and pluralization have increased in modern societies due to factors such as the adaptation of cultural products to local traditions and understandings to facilitate their spread and because of the backlash against the perceived domination of foreign ideas, values and lifestyles.

● The rise, during the 1990s, of a mosaic of new groups, organizations and movements which sought to challenge 'corporate' globalization has been interpreted as the emergence of global civil society. However, global civil society has been interpreted differently depending on whether transnational social movements or NGOs have been viewed as its key agents.

● Supporters of global civil society argue that it has effectively reconfigured global power, providing a kind of 'bottom-up' democratic vision of a civilizing world order. Critics, on the other hand, have questioned the democratic credentials of social movements and NGOs, condemned their use of direct action, and accused them of distorting national and global political agendas.

Questions for discussion

● What makes a society a society?
● Why has social connectedness become 'thinner'?
● Is cultural globalization really just a form of cultural imperialism?
● Is individualism the enemy of social solidarity and cohesion?
● Do Asian values offer a viable alternative to western individualism?
● Has the network society substituted 'virtual' communities for real communities?
● Have new forms of communication altered the global distribution of power?
● Does consumerism liberate people or enslave them?
● Are NGOs little more than self-serving and unaccountable bodies?
● To what extent can global civil society be viewed as a democratizing force?

Further reading

Bauman, Z., *Liquid Times: Living in an Age of Uncertainty* (2007). An examination of the changing human condition in the light of the emergence of 'liquid' or 'light' modernity.

Beck, U., *World at Risk* (2009). A discussion of the nature of modern society that considers the multiple manifestations of 'world risk'.

Cohen, R. and P. Kennedy, *Global Sociology* (2013). A rich and diverse analysis of contemporary issues and the dynamics of social change.

Keane, J., *Global Civil Society?* (2003). An exploration of the contradictory forces currently nurturing or threatening the growth of global civil society.

 ONLINE RESOURCES AVAILABLE

Links to relevant web resources can be found on the *Global Politics* website

CHAPTER 7

The Nation in a Global Age

'Nations are the irreplaceable cells of the human community.'

FRANJO TUDJMAN, *Nationalism in Contemporary Europe* (1981)

PREVIEW

Nationalism has, arguably, been the most powerful force in world politics for over 200 years. It has contributed to the outbreak of wars and revolutions. It has been closely linked to the birth of new states, the disintegration of empires and the redrawing of borders; and it has been used to reshape existing regimes as well as to bolster them. The greatest achievement of nationalism has been the establishment of the nation as the key unit for political rule, meaning that the so-called 'nation-state' has come to be accepted as the most basic – and, nationalists argue, the only legitimate – form of political organization. However, the character of nationalism and its implications for world politics are deeply contested. Has nationalism advanced the cause of political freedom, or has it simply legitimized aggression and expansion? Nevertheless, modern nations are under pressure perhaps as never before. Globalization is widely seen to have weakened nationalism as territorial nation-states have been enmeshed in global political, economic and cultural networks, and significantly increased international migration has led to the development of transnational communities, giving a growing number of societies a multicultural character and creating other strains. Is nationalism a political force in retreat? Can nationalism survive in a world on the move? Finally, despite frequent predictions to the contrary, there is evidence of the resurgence of nationalism. Since the end of the Cold War, new and often highly potent forms of nationalism have emerged, often linked to cultural, ethnic or religious self-assertion. Nationalism has also re-emerged as a reaction against the homogenizing impact of globalization and as a means of resisting immigration and multiculturalism. How can the revival of nationalism best be explained, and what forms has it taken?

KEY ISSUES

- What is a nation? How is nationalism best understood?
- How, and to what extent, has nationalism shaped world politics?
- Why has international migration increased in recent decades?
- How has population movement affected world politics?
- Why has nationalism resurfaced since the end of the Cold War?
- Does contemporary nationalism differ from earlier forms of nationalism?

CONCEPT

The Nation

Nations (from the Latin *nasci*, meaning 'to be born') are complex phenomena that are shaped by a collection of cultural, political and psychological factors. *Culturally*, a nation is a group of people bound together by a common language, religion, history and traditions, although all nations exhibit some degree of cultural heterogeneity. *Politically*, a nation is a group of people who regard themselves as a 'natural' political community, usually expressed through the desire to establish or maintain sovereignty. *Psychologically*, a nation is a group of people who are distinguished by a shared loyalty or affection, in the form of patriotism, although people who lack national pride may still, nevertheless, recognize that they 'belong' to the nation.

● **Patriotism**: Literally, love of one's fatherland; a psychological attachment of loyalty to one's nation or country.

● **Race**: A group of people who (supposedly) share the same physical or biological characteristics, based on common descent.

NATIONALISM AND WORLD POLITICS

Modern nations and the idea of nationalism were born in the late eighteenth century; some commentators see them as a product of the 1789 French Revolution (Kedourie 1966). Previously, countries had been thought of as 'realms', 'principalities' or 'kingdoms'. The inhabitants of a country were 'subjects', their political identity being formed by allegiance to a ruler or ruling dynasty, rather than any sense of national identity or **patriotism**. However, the revolutionaries in France who rose up against Louis XVI did so in the name of the people, and understood the people to be the 'French nation'. Nationalism was therefore a revolutionary and democratic creed, reflecting the idea that 'subjects of the crown' should become 'citizens of France'. Such ideas, nevertheless, were not the exclusive property of the French. In the early nineteenth century, a rising tide of nationalism spread throughout Europe, exploding in 1848 in a series of revolutions that affected the mainland of Europe from the Iberian peninsula to the borders of Russia. During the twentieth century, the doctrine of nationalism, which had been born in Europe, spread throughout the globe as the peoples of Asia and Africa rose in opposition to colonial rule.

Making sense of nationalism

However, nationalism is a complex and deeply contested political phenomenon. In the most simple sense, nationalism is the belief that the nation is, or should be, the most basic principle of political organization. But what is a nation? In everyday language, words such as 'nation', 'state', 'country' and even '**race**' are often confused or used as if they are interchangeable. The United Nations, for instance, is clearly misnamed, as it is an organization of states, not one of national populations. It is common in international politics to hear references to 'the Americans', 'the Chinese', 'the Russians' and so on, when in fact it is the actions of these people's governments that are being discussed. In the case of the UK, there is confusion about whether it should be regarded as a nation or as a state that comprises four separate nations: the English, the Scots, the Welsh and the Northern Irish (who may, indeed, constitute two nations, Unionists viewing themselves as British, while Republicans define themselves as Irish). The Arab peoples of North Africa and the Middle East pose very similar problems. For instance, should Egypt, Libya, Iraq and Syria be treated as nations in their own right, or as part of a single and united Arab nation, based on a common language (Arabic), a common religion (Islam), and descent from a common Bedouin tribal past?

Such difficulties spring from the fact that all nations comprise a mixture of objective and subjective factors, a blend of cultural and political characteristics. On the most basic level, nations are cultural entities, collections of people bound together by shared values and traditions, in particular a common language, religion and history, and usually occupying the same geographical area. From this point of view, the nation can be defined by objective factors: people who satisfy a requisite set of cultural criteria can be said to belong to a nation; those who do not can be classified as non-nationals or members of foreign nations. Such factors certainly shape the politics of nationalism. The nationalism of the Québécois in Canada, for instance, is based largely on language differences between French-speaking Quebec and the predominantly English-speaking rest of Canada. Nationalist tensions in India invariably arise from religious divisions, examples being the struggle of Sikhs in the Punjab for a separate homeland (Khalistan), and the campaign by Muslims in Kashmir for the incorporation of Kashmir into Pakistan. Nevertheless, it is impossible to define the nation using objective factors alone. All nations, to a greater or lesser extent, are characterized by cultural heterogeneity, and some to a high degree. The Swiss nation has proved to be enduring and viable despite the use of three major languages (French, German and Italian), as well as a variety of local dialects. Divisions between Catholics and Protestants that has given rise to rival nationalisms in Northern Ireland have been largely irrelevant in mainland UK, and have only marginal significance in countries such as Germany.

The cultural unity that supposedly expresses itself in nationhood is therefore difficult to pin down. It reflects, at best, a varying combination of cultural factors, rather than any precise formula. This emphasizes the fact that, ultimately, nations can only be defined subjectively, by their members. In the final analysis, the nation is a psycho-political entity, a group of people who regard themselves as a natural political community and are distinguished by shared loyalty and affection in the form of patriotism. The political dimension of nationhood is evident in the difference between a nation and an **ethnic group**. An ethnic group undoubtedly possesses a communal identity and a sense of cultural pride, but, unlike a nation, it lacks collective political aspirations: it does not seek to establish or maintain sovereign independence or political autonomy. The psychological dimension of nationhood is evident in the survival of nationalist aspirations despite the existence of profound objective difficulties, such as the absence of land, a small population or lack of economic resources. Latvia, for example, became an independent nation in 1991 despite having a population of only 2.6 million (barely half of whom are Lats), no source of fuel and very few natural resources. Likewise, the Kurdish peoples of the Middle East retain nationalist aspirations, even though the Kurds have never enjoyed formal political unity and are presently spread over parts of Turkey, Iraq, Iran and Syria.

Confusions over the factors that define the nation are nevertheless compounded by controversy over the phenomenon of nationalism. Is nationalism a feeling, an identity, a political doctrine, an ideology or a social movement? Or is it all these things at once? Moreover, how can the emergence of nationalism best be explained: is it a natural phenomenon, or has it somehow been invented? Since the 1970s, students of nationalism have increasingly fallen into two great camps: primordialists versus modernists (Hearn 2006). **Primordialism** portrays national identity as historically embedded: nations are rooted in a common cultural heritage and language that may long predate statehood or the quest for independence. All nationalists, in this sense, are primordialists. The dominant themes of primordialism are:

- People are inherently group-orientated and nations are a manifestation of this.
- National identity is forged by three key factors: common descent, a sense of territorial belonging, and a shared language.

● **Ethnic group**: A group of people who share a common cultural and historical identity, typically linked to a belief in common descent.

● **Primordialism**: The theory that nations are ancient and deep-rooted, fashioned variously out of psychology, culture and biology.

● To describe a collection of people as a nation is to imply that they share a common cultural heritage. In that sense, all nations are myths or illusions, as no nation is culturally homogeneous (the Japanese being perhaps the closest thing to an exception in this respect). Nations, in that sense, are 'invented' or 'imagined'.

Deconstructing . . .

'NATION'

● Nations appear to be cohesive entities, which act as organically unified wholes. This gives rise to what is called 'methodological nationalism', an approach to understanding in which discrete nations are taken to be the primary global actors. In practice, this apparent cohesiveness is achieved only by the fact that the leading actors on the world stage are states or governments, which legitimize their actions by claiming to act on behalf of 'the nation'. To refer to, say, 'the Chinese', 'the Russian' or 'the Americans' as global actors is therefore deeply misleading.

● The assumption that people are members of a nation suggests that national identity is the principal form of collective identity. Other sources of collective identity – based, for instance, on social class, gender, ethnicity or religion – are thus of secondary importance, especially as each of these has transnational or subnational implications.

● Nations are historical entities: they evolve organically out of more simple ethnic communities.
● Nationalism is characterized by deep emotional attachments that resemble kinship ties.

Such views can be traced back to the writings of the German philosopher Johann Herder (1744–1803), who argued that each nation possesses a **Volksgeist**, which reveals itself in songs, myths and legends, and provides a nation with its source of creativity. The implications of Herder's culturalism is that nations are natural or organic identities that can be traced back to ancient times and will, by the same token, continue to exist as long as human society survives. Modern commentators have advanced similar ideas. Anthony Smith (see p. 169), for instance, highlighted the continuity between modern nations and pre-modern ethnic communities, which he called 'ethnies'. This implies that nationalism is a variant of ethnicity (see p. 193), modern nations essentially being updated versions of immemorial ethnic communities.

● **Volksgeist**: (German) Literally, the spirit of the people; the organic identity of a people revealed in their culture and particularly their language.

By contrast, modernist approaches to nationalism suggest that national identity is forged in response to changing social and historical circumstances. In many cases, modernism links the origins of nationalism to the process of modernization and, in particular to the emergence of industrialization. Although different modernist theorists place an emphasis on different factors, modernism can be associated with three broad themes:

- The emergence of industrial and capitalist economies weakened traditional social bonds and generated new social tensions, so creating a need for a unifying national identity.
- States often play a key role in forging a sense of national identity, implying that the state predates and, in a sense, 'constructs' the nation.
- The spread of mass literacy and mass education contributed significantly to the construction of national identity.

Ernest Gellner (see p. 169) thus stressed that while premodern or 'agro-literate' societies were structured by a network of feudal bonds and loyalties, emerging industrial societies promoted social mobility, self-striving and competition, and so required a new source of cultural cohesion (as discussed in Chapter 6). This new source of cultural cohesion was provided by nationalism, which, in effect, means that nationalism invented the nation, not the other way round. Although Gellner's theory suggests that nations coalesced in response to particular social conditions and circumstances, it also implies that the national community is deep-rooted and will be enduring, as a return to premodern loyalties and identities is unthinkable. Benedict Anderson (see p. 169) also portrayed modern nations as a product of socio-economic change, in his case stressing the combined impact of the emergence of capitalism and the advent of modern mass communications, which he dubbed 'print-capitalism'. In his view, the nation is an 'imagined community', in that, within nations, individuals only ever meet a tiny proportion of those with whom they supposedly share a national identity (Anderson 1983). If nations exist, they exist as imagined artifices, constructed for us through education, the mass media, and the process of political socialization. Marxists, such as Eric Hobsbawm (1992), tend to view nationalism as a device through which the ruling class counters the threat of social revolution by ensuring that national loyalty is stronger than class solidarity, thereby binding the working class to the existing power structure.

A world of nation-states

Nationalism has helped to shape and reshape world politics for over 200 years. However, the nature of its impact has been the subject of considerable debate. Nationalism is a chameleon-like ideology, capable of assuming a bewildering variety of political forms. At different times, it has been progressive and reactionary, democratic and authoritarian, liberating and oppressive, aggressive and peaceful, and so on. Some, as a result, distinguish between good and bad nationalism, dispensing altogether with the idea of nationalism as a single, coherent political force. The liberating or progressive face of nationalism is evident in what is often seen as classical political nationalism. Classical nationalism dates back to the French Revolution, and embodies many of its values. Its ideas spread

APPROACHES TO . . .

NATIONALISM

Realist view

Realists do not generally place an emphasis on nationalism as such. In their view, the crucial stage in the development of the modern international system was the emergence of sovereign states in the 1500–1750 period (particularly through the 1648 Peace of Westphalia), rather than the transformation of these states, from the early nineteenth century onwards, into nation-states through the advent of nationalism. The international system is thus, more accurately, viewed as an inter-state system. Despite this, realists have tended to view nationalism in broadly positive terms. From the realist perspective, nationalism is a key auxiliary component of state power, a source of internal cohesion that consolidates the external effectiveness of a nation-state. By interpreting state interests (generally) as 'national interests', realists recognize nationalism as a force that sustains international anarchy, limits the scope for cooperation between and among states, and implies that universal values, such as human rights (see p. 311), are defective.

Liberal view

Liberals have long endorsed nationalism. Indeed, in nineteenth-century Europe in particular, to be a liberal meant to be a nationalist. Liberal nationalism is a principled form of nationalism, based above all on the notion of national self-determination, which portrays the nation as a sovereign entity and implies both national independence and democratic rule. Although liberal nationalists, like all nationalists, view the nation as a 'natural' community, they regard nations as essentially civic entities, based on the existence of common values and political loyalties. This makes their form of nationalism tolerant and inclusive. From the liberal perspective, the nation-state (see p. 168) is a political ideal, representing the goal of freedom and the right of each nation to fashion its own destiny. Self-determination, moreover, is a universal right, reflecting the equality of nations (at least in a moral sense) and implying that liberals aim not merely to achieve sovereign statehood for their particular nation but to construct a world of independent nation-states. Liberals argue that such a world would be characterized by peace and harmony, both because nation-states are likely to respect each other's rights and freedoms, and because no nation-state would wish to endanger its own civic and cultural unity. Liberals nevertheless view nationalism and internationalism (see p. 67) as complementary, not conflicting, principles. The most prominent forms of liberal internationalism are support for free trade to promote economic interdependence, making war so costly it becomes almost unthinkable, and the construction of intergovernmental or supranational bodies to ensure an international rule of law.

Critical views

Critical views of nationalism have been developed within the Marxist, social constructivist, poststructuralist and feminist traditions. For Marxists, nationality is an example of 'false consciousness', an illusion that serves to mystify and confuse the working classes, preventing them from recognizing their genuine interests. In particular, in emphasizing the bonds of nationhood over those of social class, nationalism serves to distort, and conceal, the realities of unequal class power and prevent social revolution. Social constructivists have been particularly critical of the primordialist image of 'fixed' ethnic and national identities, emphasizing instead that the sense of national belonging is 'constructed' though social, political and other processes. They therefore tend to argue that nations are fashioned by nationalism itself, sympathizing with Eric Hobsbawm's (1983) image of nations as 'invented traditions'.

Poststructuralist and postmodernist approaches to nationalism tend to suggest that at the heart of the nationalist project is a narrative, or collection of narratives. The story of the nation is told by history books, works of fiction, symbols, myths and so on, with particular importance being given to a foundational myth that locates the origins of the nation in a time long ago and imbues the nation with special qualities. Feminist theories of nationalism build to these ideas by emphasizing the gender dimension of national identity. The nation is often depicted as female – as the 'motherland' rather than the 'fatherland' – a tendency that draws from an emphasis on women as the (biological) reproducers of the nation and as symbols of the nation's values and culture (usually emphasizing the home, purity and selflessness). On the other hand, when the nation is constructed as masculine, this often links national identity to heroism, self-assertion and aggression, tending to conflate nationalism with militarism.

Focus on . . .
The two nationalisms: good and bad?

Does nationalism embrace two, quite distinct traditions? Does nationalism have a 'good' face and a 'bad' face? The idea that there are, in effect, 'two nationalisms' is usually based on the belief that nationalism has contrasting civic and ethnic forms. What is often called **civic nationalism** is fashioned primarily out of shared political allegiances and political values. The nation is thus an 'association of citizens'. Civic nationalism has been defended on the grounds that it is open and voluntaristic: membership of the nation is based on choice and self-definition, not on any pre-determined ethnic or historical identity. It is a form of nationalism that is consistent with toleration and liberal values generally, being forward-looking and compatible with a substantial degree of cultural and ethnic diversity. Critics, however, have questioned whether civic nationalism is meaningful (Kymlicka 1999). Most citizens, even in a 'civic' or 'political' nation, derive their nationality from birth, not choice. Moreover, divorced from the bonds of ethnicity, language and history, political allegiances and civic values may simply be incapable of generating the sense of belonging and rootedness that gives nationalism its power.

By contrast, **ethnic nationalism** is squarely rooted in ethnic unity and a deep sense of cultural belonging. This form of nationalism is often criticized for having a closed or fixed character: it is difficult, and perhaps impossible, for non-citizens to become members of the nation. Nationalism therefore acquires a homogenizing character, breeding a fear or suspicion of foreigners and strengthening the idea of cultural distinctiveness, often interwoven with a belief in national greatness. Ethnic nationalism is thus irrational and tends to be tribalistic, even bloodthirsty. On the other hand, its capacity to generate a closed and fixed sense of political belonging may also be a virtue of ethnic nationalism. 'Ethnic' or 'cultural' nations tend to be characterized by high levels of social solidarity and a strong sense of collective purpose.

● **Civic nationalism**: A form of nationalism that emphasizes political allegiance based on a vision of a community of equal citizens, allowing respect for ethnic and cultural diversity that does not challenge core civic values.

● **Ethnic nationalism**: A form of nationalism that emphasizes the organic and usually ethnic unity of the nation and aims to protect or strengthen its national 'spirit' and cultural sameness.

quickly through much of Europe and were expressed, for example, in the emergence of unification movements in the Italian states and the Germanic states in particular, and through the growth of independence movements in the Austro-Hungarian empire and later in the Russian empire and the Ottoman empire. The ideas and aspirations of classical European nationalism were most clearly expressed by the prophet of Italian unification, Giuseppe Mazzini (1805–72). Perhaps the clearest expression of classical nationalism is found in US President Woodrow Wilson's (see p. 445) 'Fourteen Points'. Drawn up in 1918, these were proposed as the basis for the reconstruction of Europe after WWI, and provided a blueprint for the sweeping territorial changes that were implemented by the Treaty of Versailles (1919).

Classical nationalism has been strongly associated with liberal ideas and values. Indeed, in nineteenth-century Europe, to be a nationalist meant to be a liberal, and *vice versa*. In common with all forms of nationalism, classical nationalism is based on the fundamental assumption that humankind is naturally divided into a collection of nations, each possessed of a separate identity. Nations are therefore genuine or organic communities, not the artificial creation of political leaders or ruling classes. The characteristic theme of classical nationalism, however, is that it links the idea of the nation with a belief in popular sovereignty (see p. 4), ultimately derived from Jean-Jacques Rousseau's

CONCEPT

Nation-state

A nation-state is an autonomous political community bound together by the overlapping bonds of citizenship and nationality, meaning that political and cultural identity coincide. Nation-states thus reflect Mazzini's goal: 'Every nation a state, only one state for the entire nation'. Most modern states are nation-states, in that, thanks to classical nationalism, the nation has come to be accepted as the basic unit of political rule. However, the nation-state is more a political ideal than a reality, as all states are, to some degree, culturally and ethnically heterogeneous. However, the term 'nation-state' has (often incorrectly) become a synonym for the 'state' in much public, and some academic, discourse.

● **National self-determination**: The principle that the nation is a sovereign entity; self-determination implies both national independence and democratic rule.

(1712–78) idea of the 'general will'. This fusion was brought about because the multinational empires against which nineteenth-century European nationalists fought were also autocratic and oppressive. Mazzini, for example, wished not only to unite the Italian states, but also to throw off the influence of autocratic Austria. Woodrow Wilson, for his part, wished not only that the constituent nations of Europe should achieve statehood but also that they should be reconstructed on the basis of US-style liberal republicanism. The central theme of this form of nationalism is therefore a commitment to the principle of **national self-determination**. Its goal is therefore the construction of a nation-state.

This form of nationalism has had profound implications for world politics. From the early nineteenth century onwards, the seemingly irresistible process of nation-state formation transformed the state-system, reconfiguring political power, ultimately across the globe, and giving states an internal cohesion and sense of purpose and identity they had previously lacked. This was, nevertheless, a complex process. Although primordialists, such as Anthony Smith (1986, 1991), tend to view pre-modern ethnic communities as a kind of template for modern states, nation-state formation changed nationalism every bit as much as nationalism changed the state-system. Nationalism was an important component of the 1848 revolutions that spread across Europe, from the Iberian peninsula to the borders of Russia (see p. 181). However, nationalist movements were nowhere strong enough to accomplish the process of nation-building alone. Where nationalist goals were realized, as in Italy and Germany (both were finally unified in 1871), it was because nationalism coincided with the ambitions of powerful states, in this case Piedmont and Prussia. The character of nationalism also changed. Nationalism had previously been associated with liberal and progressive movements, but was increasingly taken up by conservative and reactionary politicians and used to promote social cohesion, order and stability, or, as discussed in the next section, projects of imperial expansion.

During the twentieth century, the process whereby multinational empires were replaced by territorial nation-states was extended into Africa and Asia. Indeed, in a sense, nineteenth-century European imperialism (see p. 28) turned nationalism into a genuinely global creed by generating anti-colonial or 'national liberation' movements across much of the developing world. The independence movements that sprang up in the inter-war period gained new impetus from the conclusion of WWII. The over-stretched empires of the UK, France, the Netherlands and Portugal crumbled in the face of rising nationalism. India was granted independence in 1947. China (see p. 238) achieved genuine unity and independence only after the 1949 communist revolution. During the 1950s and early 1960s, the political map of Africa was entirely redrawn through the process of decolonization. Africa's last remaining colony, Southwest Africa, finally became independent Namibia in 1990. The last stage in this process was the collapse of the world's final major empire, the Russian empire, which was brought about by the fall of communism and the disintegration of the Soviet Union in 1991.

The image of a world of sovereign nation-states nevertheless remains misleading. In the first place, despite the collapse of major empires, significant unresolved nationalist tensions persist. These range from those in Tibet and the predominantly Muslim province of Xinjiang in China to Chechnya and elsewhere in the Russian Caucasus, the Kurds in the Middle East and the Basques in Spain. Second,

KEY THEORISTS IN NATIONALISM

Ernest Gellner (1925–95)

A UK social philosopher and anthropologist, Gellner made major contributions to a variety of academic fields, including social anthropology, sociology and political philosophy. The most prominent figure in the modernist camp in the study of nationalism, Gellner explained the rise of nationalism in terms of the need of industrial societies, unlike agrarian ones, for homogeneous languages and cultures in order to work efficiently. Gellner's major writings include *Legitimation of Belief* (1974), *Nations and Nationalism* (1983), *Culture, Identity and Politics* (1987) and *Reason and Culture* (1992).

Anthony D. Smith (born 1933)

A UK academic and one of the founders of the interdisciplinary field of nationalism studies, Smith has been particularly concerned to transcend the debate between crude primordialism and modernism. Although his work does not contain a comprehensive explanation for the emergence and character of nationalism, it explores the ethnic origins of nations as well as the historical forces that help to fashion nationalism's various forms. Smith's key works include *Theories of Nationalism* (1972), *The Ethnic Origin of Nations* (1986) and *Nations and Nationalism in a Global Era* (1995).

Benedict Anderson (born 1936)

An Irish academic who was brought up mainly in California, Anderson's main publication on nationalism is the celebrated *Imagined Communities* (1983). He views nationalities and nationalism as cultural artefacts of a particular kind, defining the nation as an 'imagined community', in the sense that it generates a deep, horizontal comradeship regardless of actual inequalities within the nation and despite the fact that it is not a face-to-face community. Anderson's other publications in the field include *The Spectres of Comparison* (1998) and *Under Three Flags* (2005).

nation-states are inherently imperfect, as none is ethnically and culturally 'pure' and all rely, to some degree, on political circumstances to maintain themselves in existence. This can be illustrated by the rise and fall of Yugoslavia. Finally, given that nation-states are, and are destined to remain, unequal in terms of their economic and political power, genuine national self-determination remains elusive for many. This is a tendency that has been further compounded by the advance of globalization (see p. 8) and the erosion of state sovereignty.

Nationalism, war and conflict

However, nationalism has not merely supported liberating causes, related to the achievement of national unity and independence. Nationalism has also been

Debating...
Is nationalism inherently aggressive and oppressive?

Is nationalism as a whole, in principle, defensible? While some argue that its association with expansionism and oppression exposes deep and dark forces that are intrinsic to nationalism itself, others suggest that nationalism, in the right circumstances, can be peaceful and socially enlightened.

YES

Nationalism as narcissism. All forms of nationalism are based on partisanship, a preference for one's own nation over other nations, underpinned by the belief that it has special or unique qualities. Nationalism is thus the enemy of universal values and global justice. In promoting self-love within the nations of the world, it encourages each nation to restrict its moral concerns to its own people, and to believe that their interests somehow outrank those of any other people. Nationalism is thus inherently chauvinistic and embodies, at minimum, a *potential* for aggression. The only question is whether national chauvinism is explicit or implicit, and therefore whether aggression is overt or latent.

Negative integration. National identity is forged not only through the belief that one's own nation is unique or 'special', but also through negative integration, the portrayal of another nation or race as a threat or an enemy. Nationalism therefore breeds off a clear distinction between 'them' and 'us'. There has to be a 'them' to deride or hate in order to forge a sense of 'us'. This tendency to divide the world into an 'in group' and an 'out group' means that nationalism is always susceptible to dark and pathological forces. As a necessarily homogenizing force, all forms of nationalism harbour intolerance, hostility and racist tendencies. 'True' nationalism is therefore ethnic nationalism.

Nationalism and power. Nationalism is invariably associated with the quest for power and therefore leads to rivalry and conflict rather than cooperation. The nationalism of the weak draws from a sense of powerlessness and subjugation, a desire to assert national rights and identities in the context of perceived injustice and oppression. However, it is a delusion to believe that the quest for power is assuaged once a nation achieves sovereign statehood. In established states and even great powers, nationalism is strongly linked to self-assertion, as national identity is remodelled around aggrandizement and the quest for 'greatness'.

NO

Nationalism and freedom. Nationalism is a chameleon ideology. Its character is determined by the circumstances in which nationalist aspirations arise and the (highly diverse) political causes that it articulates. When nationalism is a reaction against the experience of foreign domination or colonial rule, it tends to have a liberating character and is linked to the goals of liberty, justice and democracy. Committed to the principle of self-determination, nationalism has been an anti-expansionist and anti-imperialist force that has expanded freedom worldwide. Moreover, self-determination has powerful implications for the domestic organization of political power, implying equal citizenship and democratic accountability.

Civic nationalism. Nationalism only becomes intolerant and oppressive when the nation is defined in narrowly ethnic or racial terms. Some nations, however, are very clearly 'political' nations, constructed out of allegiances to particular values and civic ideals rather than on the basis of cultural homogeneity. The forms of nationalism that develop in such cases are typically tolerant and democratic, managing to sustain a remarkable degree of social harmony and political unity against a background of sometimes profound religious, linguistic, cultural and racial diversity. National identity can therefore be inclusive, flexible and always evolving, adapting itself to changing political and social circumstances.

Cultural belonging. The central benefit of nationalism is that it gives people a sense of cultural inheritance, a sense of who or what they are, binding them together and promoting sociability. Nationalism's success in this respect helps to explain why citizenship and nationality are invariably overlapping ideas. The 'inner' benefits of nationalism, which help to promote political stability and social cohesion, are not always, or necessarily, associated with projects of expansionism, conquest and war. The link between nationalism and militarism is therefore strictly conditional, and tends to occur in particular when nationalist sentiments are generated by international rivalry and conflict.

expressed through the politics of aggression, **militarism** and war. In many ways, expansionist nationalism is the antithesis of the principled belief in equal rights and self-determination that is the core of classical nationalism. National rights, in this context, imply, not respect for the rights of all nations, but the rights of a particular nation *over* other nations. The recurrent, and, many would argue, defining, theme of expansionist nationalism is therefore the idea of national **chauvinism**. Derived from the name of Nicholas Chauvin, a (possibly apocryphal) French soldier noted for his fanatical devotion to Napoleon and the cause of France, chauvinism is underpinned by the belief that nations have particular characteristics and qualities, and so have very different destinies. Some nations are suited to rule; others are suited to be ruled. Typically, this form of nationalism is articulated through doctrines of ethnic or racial superiority, thereby fusing nationalism and racialism (see p. 172). The chauvinist's own people are seen as unique and special, in some way a 'chosen people', while other peoples are viewed either as weak and inferior, or as hostile and threatening. An extreme example of this can be found in the case of the German Nazis, whose 'Aryanism' portrayed the German people (the Aryan race) as a 'master race' destined for world domination, backed up by virulent **anti-Semitism**.

From this perspective, the advance of nationalism is associated not so much with balance or harmony amongst independent nation-states as with deepening rivalry and ongoing struggle. Some, indeed, argue that nationalism from its inception was infected with chauvinism and has always harboured at least implicit racist beliefs, based on the assumption that it is 'natural' to prefer one's own people to others. In this light, nationalism may appear to be inherently oppressive and expansionist. All forms of nationalism may thus exhibit some form of **xenophobia**. The aggressive face of nationalism became increasingly prominent from the late nineteenth century onwards, as European powers indulged in the 'scramble for Africa' in the name of national glory and their 'place in the sun'. Aggression and expansion were also evident in the forms of **pan-nationalism** that developed in Russia and Germany in the years leading up to WWI. The build up to WWII was similarly shaped by nationalist-inspired programmes of imperial expansion pursued by Germany, Japan and Italy. Nationalism can therefore be seen as a major contributory factor explaining the outbreak of both world wars of the twentieth century. Neither was this form of nationalism extinguished in 1945. The break-up of Yugoslavia in the early 1990s, for example, led to a quest by Bosnian Serbs to construct a 'Greater Serbia' which was characterized by militarism and an aggressive programme of '**ethnic cleansing**'.

NATIONS IN AN AGE OF MIGRATION

One of the ironies of nationalism is that just as it was completing its greatest accomplishment – the destruction of the world's final remaining empires – the nation-state was being undermined by forces within and without. This has led some to talk of a 'crisis of the nation-state', or even the 'twilight of the nation-state'. These forces are many and various. They include the tendency for economic globalization (see p. 98) to diminish the state's capacity to function as an

● **Militarism**: The achievement of ends by military means; or the spread of military ideas and values throughout civilian society.

● **Chauvinism**: An irrational belief in the superiority or dominance of one's own group or people; it can be applied to a nation, an ethnic group, a gender and so on.

● **Anti-Semitism**: Prejudice or hatred towards Jewish people; Semites are by tradition the descendants of Shem, son of Noah.

● **Xenophobia**: A fear or hatred of foreigners; pathological ethnocentrism.

● **Pan-nationalism**: A style of nationalism dedicated to unifying a disparate people through either expansionism or political solidarity ('pan' means all or every).

● **Ethnic cleansing**: A euphemism that refers to the forcible expulsion of an ethnic group or groups in the cause of racial purity, often involving genocidal violence.

CONCEPT

Racialism

Racialism is, broadly, the belief that political or social conclusions can be drawn from the idea that humankind is divided into biologically distinct races. Racialist theories are thus based on two assumptions. The first is that there are fundamental genetic, or species-type, differences amongst the peoples of the world (a highly unlikely claim in the light of modern scientific knowledge). The second is that these genetic or racial differences are reflected in cultural, intellectual and/or moral differences, making them politically and socially significant. In political terms, racialism is manifest in calls for racial segregation (such as apartheid, or 'apartness', in South Africa), and in doctrines of 'blood' superiority or inferiority (for example, Aryanism and anti-Semitism).

● **Hybridity**: A condition of social and cultural mixing; the term derives from cross-breeding between genetically unalike plants or animals.

● **Migration**: The movement of a person or group of persons, either across an international border, or within a state.

autonomous economic unit (examined in Chapter 4) and the trend for cultural globalization (see p. 151) to weaken the cultural distinctiveness of the nation-state (discussed in Chapter 6). However, some argue that the most potent threat to the nation stems from the upsurge in international migration and the growth, as a result, of transnational communities and **hybridity** generally. Population movement has thus had major implications for modern world politics.

A world on the move

Migration has been part of human experience throughout history. Indeed, settlement (which was brought about by the emergence of agriculture, some 8,000 years ago) is of relatively recent origin, human societies having been fluid communities of hunters and gatherers that can now be traced back for over three million years. The development of substantial villages, and subsequently towns and cities, did not put an end to migration, however. The early empires of the Hittites, the Phoenicians and the Greeks, for example, reshaped the culture of much of Europe, parts of North Africa, the Near East and Central Asia between the third and the first millennia BCE. This process is reflected most strikingly in the distribution of the closely related languages of the Indo-European group, which embraces both Sanskrit and Persian at one end, and such European languages as Greek, Latin, French, German and English at the other. The Vikings, Magyars and Saracens invaded much of northern and central Europe in the ninth and tenth centuries, the Vikings also establishing settlements in Iceland, Greenland and Newfoundland. European expansion overseas started in the sixteenth century with the Spanish invasion of Mexico and Peru, followed by the colonization of North America, mainly by the British. Hardly any nation in the world, in short, can claim always to have lived where it does now.

Migration has occurred for a variety of reasons. Until early modern times, as the examples above demonstrate, migration was usually a consequence of conquest and invasion, followed by settlement and colonization. In cases such as the USA (see p. 46), Canada, Australia and throughout Latin America, conquest and settlement led to the emergence of nations of immigrants, as native peoples were reduced to the status of marginalized minorities through the combined impact of disease, repression and discrimination. Mass migration has also been a forcible process, the best examples of which were the slave trade and the system of indentured labour. An estimated 40 million people in the Americas and the Caribbean are descended from slaves, who, between the mid-sixteenth and mid-eighteenth centuries, were captured in Africa and transported, via Europe, to work in the expanding sugar and tobacco plantations of the 'New World'. Indentured workers, derogatorily known as 'Coolies' and living in conditions little different from slavery, were taken from China and India in the nineteenth century to work in the various British, French, German and Dutch colonies around the world. Some 37 million people were sent abroad under such circumstances, and, although many of those who had left India returned once slavery was abolished, modern-day Indian communities in the Caribbean, East Africa and the Pacific are mainly composed of descendants of indentured labourers.

Other migrants, however, have travelled by choice for economic reasons, albeit ones that have sometimes involved considerable privation and hardship. This applies to the voluntary mass migration from Europe to the Americas from

Focus on ...
International migration: are people pulled or pushed?

Theories of migration can be divided into those that emphasize the role of the individual and those that highlight the importance of structural factors. In practice, it is highly likely that these factors interact, as individual decision-making cannot be understood separately from the structural context in which it takes place.

Individual theories stress the role of individual calculation in making migration decisions, influenced by the pursuit of rational self-interest. This is an economic model of migration, which relies on a kind of cost–benefit analysis. It implies that migration occurs because people are 'pulled' by an awareness on the part of potential migrants that its likely benefits will outweigh its possible costs. In this view, migration can be contained by increasing the cost of migration (for

example, through the imposition of immigration quotas and controls) or by reducing its benefits (for example, by restricting immigrants' access to social security and imposing work restrictions).

Structural theories stress the degree to which social, economic or political factors influence, or determine, individuals' actions. Migrants are therefore either 'pushed' from their country of origin (by factors such as chronic and acute poverty, political unrest and civil strife), or they are 'pulled' to their country of settlement (by the need of expanding economies for additional labour, particularly in relation to jobs the domestic population is unwilling, or, through lack of skills, unable to fill). From this perspective, migration can best be contained by strategies such as a reduction in global inequality and the spread of stable governance.

● **Diaspora**: (from the Hebrew) literally, dispersion; implies displacement or dispersal by force, but is also used to refer to the transnational community that arose as a result of such dispersal.

● **Emigration**: A process whereby people leave their native country, to settle in another.

● **Internally displaced person**: A person forced to flee from his or her habitual residence by the effects of armed conflict, generalized violence or natural or man-made disaster.

● **Refugee**: A person compelled to leave his or her country because their life, security or freedom have been threatened.

the mid-nineteenth century until the outbreak of WWI, which involved, for example, the migration of about a million Irish people escaping the potato famine of 1845–47 and over 3 million people from the German territories fleeing from rural poverty and periodic crop failures. A final reason for migration has been religious or political persecution. The classic example of this was the Jewish **diaspora**, which was initiated by Roman repression in Judea and involved the expulsion of Jews in the Middle Ages from England, France, Spain, Portugal and many of the German cities. **Emigration** from Europe to North America, both in the colonial period and in the late nineteenth century, also often reflected a desire to escape from religious persecution on the part of groups of Puritans, Nonconformists of various kinds, Catholics and Jews.

The bulk of migration has always been, and continues to be, internal. For instance, the number of **internally displaced persons** (28.8 million in 2012) consistently exceeds the number of **refugees** (15.4 million); and labour migration is more commonly associated with urbanization than with globalization (over 260 million people have moved from the countryside to urban areas since the 1990s in China alone). However, international migration has become an increasingly important feature of the modern world. The number of international migrants (never an easy figure to calculate in view of the proportion of irregular (or 'undocumented' or 'illegal') migrants) rose from 81 million in 1970 to 214 million in 2010, or 3.1 per cent of the world's population. If international migrants lived together, they would constitute the fifth most populous country in the world. The idea that the modern period is an 'age of migration' highlights not only the intensification of cross-border migration in what has come to be a hyper-mobile planet, but also the growing significance of migration in economic, social, cultural and political terms (Castles *et al.* 2013). Above all, the age of migration is characterized by the challenges posed by international migration to the sovereignty of states, seemingly unable to regulate the movements of people across their borders effectively, despite increasing efforts to do so. Transnational and trans-border population flows, just like flows of money, goods and other economic resources, thus underline how far the divide between the domestic and international spheres has been undermined.

Why and how have migratory patterns changed in recent years? In addition to the acceleration of migration, international migration has become increasingly differentiated. One dimension of modern migration is clearly linked to economic globalization. The onset of globalization has intensified pressures for international migration in a variety of ways. These include the development of genuinely global labour markets for a small but growing number of high-paid and high-profile jobs, and the fact that the restructuring that globalization has fostered both creates a range of skills needs that the domestic population cannot meet and, where turbulence has caused insecurity and hardship, enlarges the ranks of those looking for, or needing to find, new economic opportunities. Such trends also serve to explain the 'globalization of migration'; that is, the tendency both for more countries to be affected by migratory movements at the same time, and for **immigration** to come from a larger number of source countries. This contrasts markedly with the pattern of labour migration in the early post-1945 period, when migratory flows predominantly from poorer countries to either their richer neighbours or their former colonial rulers. In the latter case, this was sometimes orchestrated by a deliberate policy of recruiting workers from abroad.

A further dimension of modern migration is linked to refugees, and has been the result of war, ethnic conflict and political upheaval in areas ranging from Algeria, Rwanda and Uganda to Bangladesh, Afghanistan and Syria. The political upheavals associated with the collapse of communism in eastern Europe in 1989–91 created, almost overnight, a new group of migrants, having, later, even greater impact due to the rise of ethnic conflict in former Yugoslavia. Although the number of refugees has declined since reaching a peak of 18 million in 1993, mass and sudden refugee flows continue to provoke humanitarian emergencies. The large-scale displacement of people across borders remains a major issue in many developing countries, which, together, host about 80 per cent of the world's refugees. A final dimension of modern migration is **human trafficking**. Although it is very difficult to assess the real extent of human trafficking, the UN has put the number of victims at any one time at 2.5 million, a disproportionate number of whom are women. The most commonly identified form of human trafficking is sexual exploitation (79 per cent), followed by forced labour (18 per cent). Almost always a form of organized crime, trafficking usually takes place from less-developed countries to more-developed countries, people being rendered vulnerable to trafficking by virtue of poverty, conflict or other conditions.

● **Immigration**: A process whereby non-nationals move into a country for the purpose of settlement.

● **Human trafficking**: The recruitment and harbouring of persons for the purpose of exploitation, brought about by the threat or use of coercion or force.

Transnational communities and diasporas

Modern migration flows have had significant implications for the domestic politics of states. These include the development in many societies of communities bound together by transnational, rather than national, allegiances. There is, of

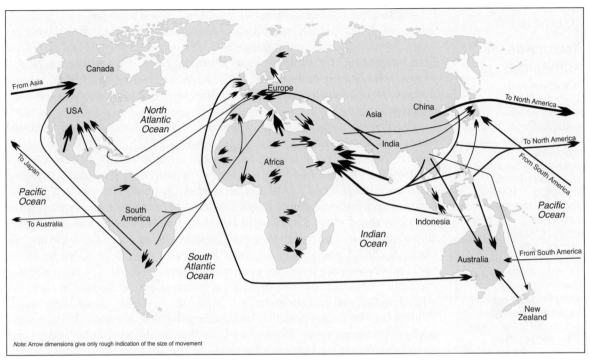

Map 7.1 Global migratory flows since 1973
Source: Castles *et al.* (2013).

course, nothing new about scattered communities that have nevertheless maintained their cultural distinctiveness and resisted pressure for **assimilation**. The Jewish diaspora, which can be traced back to the eighth century BCE, is the classic example of a transnational community. Ironically, the remarkable resilience of Judaism and the Hebrew language in the absence of a Jewish homeland can be significantly explained by a history of discrimination and persecution through various forms of anti-Semitism. Other examples include the Armenians, many of whom have been forced into exile by successive invasions and conquests, dating back to the Byzantine Empire. However, many argue that the emergence of transnational communities is one of the chief features of the modern, globalized world (Basch *et al.* 1994).

An increase in international migration does not in itself create new, transnational social spaces: for transnational communities to be established, immigrant groups must forge and, crucially, sustain relations that link their societies of origin and of settlement. This is made easier in the modern world by a variety of developments. Whereas, say, Irish emigrants to the USA in the nineteenth century had little prospect of returning home and only a postal service to keep them in touch with friends and family, modern communities of Filipinos in the Gulf states, Indonesians in Australia and Bangladeshis in the UK benefit from cheaper transport and improved communications. Air travel enables people to return 'home' on a regular basis, creating fluid communities that are bound neither by their society of origin nor their society of settlement. The near-ubiquitous mobile phone has also become a basic resource for new immigrants,

● **Assimilation**: The process through which immigrant communities lose their cultural distinctiveness by adjusting to the values, allegiances and lifestyles of the host society.

CONCEPT

Transnational community

A transnational community is a community whose cultural identity, political allegiances and psychological orientations cut across or transcend national borders. In that sense, they challenge the nation-state ideal, which clearly links politico-cultural identity to a specific territory or 'homeland'. Transnational communities can therefore be thought of as 'deterritorialized nations' or 'global tribes'. However, not every diasporic community is a transnational community, in the sense that its members retain allegiances to their country of origin. Transnational communities typically have multiple attachments, as allegiances to their country of origin do not preclude the formation of attachments to their country of settlement.

helping to explain, amongst other things, its increasing penetration in the developing world, including the rural parts of Asia and Africa. Transnational communities, moreover, are bound together by a network of family ties and economic flows. Migration, for example, may maintain rather than weaken extended kinship links, as early immigrants provide a base and sometimes working opportunities for other members of their families or village who may subsequently emigrate.

The idea of a transition from territorial nation-states to deterritorialized transnational communities should not be over-stated, however. The impact of modern migration patterns, and of globalization in its various forms, is more complex than is implied by the simple notion of transnationalism. In the first place, the homogeneous nation that has supposedly been put at risk by the emergence of transnational communities is always, to some extent, a myth, a myth created by the ideology of nationalism itself. In other words, there is nothing new about cultural mixing, which long pre-dates the emergence of the hyper-mobile planet. Second, transnational communities are characterized as much by difference and division as they are by commonality and solidarity. The most obvious divisions within diaspora communities are those of gender and social class, but other divisions may run along the lines of ethnicity, religion, age and generation. Third, it is by no means clear that transnational loyalties are as stable and enduring as nationalism. Quite simply, social ties that are not territorially rooted and geographically defined may not be viable in the long term. Doubts about the enduring character of transnational communities are raised by the phenomenon of return migration, often stimulated by improved political or economic circumstances in the country of origin. For example, there has been a general tendency for people to return to Asia, notably China and Taiwan, to take advantage of improving economic prospects since the 1980s. Finally, it is misleading to suggest that transnationalism has somehow displaced nationalism when, in reality, each has influenced the other, creating a more complex web of hybrid identities. Hybridity or 'creolization', has thus become one of the major features of modern society. It is examined in Chapter 8, in relation to multiculturalism (see p. 192).

Economic impact of migration

Assessments of the economic impact of migration are problematic for at least three reasons. First, debates about migration are often highly politically charged, meaning that *perceptions* about the extent and implications of migration commonly differ from 'hard' evidence on the matter. This applies particularly in 'receiving' countries, where the dominant political discourse about immigration tends to focus on issues of management and control. Since the early twentieth century, no country has permitted unchecked immigration, with pressure for tighter immigration controls being exerted from the 1970s onwards. This trend was markedly intensified in the aftermath of September 11. Indeed (as discussed in the final section of the chapter), anti-immigration sentiment is one of the factors that has contributed to the revival of nationalism in the modern period. Second, generalizations about the impact of migration are notoriously misleading. This occurs not only because migration has an uneven impact on host and 'sending' countries, but also because (as we shall see) what may be beneficial in one set of circumstances may be a serious drawback in other circumstances. Third, when it comes to the impact of migration, 'proof' may be very difficult to establish. For instance, although there is often a correlation between increased immigration and economic growth in receiving countries, it is less clear whether immigration is a cause or a consequence of economic growth, and, if it is a cause, how significant a factor it is.

From the point of view of sending countries, the clearest economic benefit of migration comes in the form of **remittances**. The World Bank estimated that, in 2011, global remittance flows stood at $501 billion, $372 billion of which went to developing countries. Not only do remittances dwarf international aid (see p. 383) in their scale, being some three times the size of official development assistance, but, in sharp contrast to aid, remittances are largely unaffected by downturns in the world economy. Remittance levels thus rose during the global financial crisis of 2007–09 while levels of international aid shrank. In this light, remittances may be vital in reducing the extent and severity of poverty, lowering incidences of child labour (and thereby improving levels of literacy and education) and boosting business investment and entrepreneurship. On the other hand, remittances, like international aid, may entrench patterns of global inequality, discouraging initiative and self-reliance within sending countries and strengthening a culture of dependency. A further alleged advantage of migration is that it can act as a pressure valve, especially in countries such as Mexico, the Philippines and Morocco, which have fast-growing and youthful populations but high levels of unemployment. Emigration may therefore help to prevent an explosion in welfare spending and thus tax increases, to say nothing of the political and social benefits of avoiding rampant unemployment, particularly among the young. This helps to explain why emigration has sometimes been orchestrated and encouraged by governments, as has happened in Mexico (see p. 178). Such advantages may nevertheless be offset by the damage caused to sending countries by the loss of workers with technical skills or knowledge, a phenomenon often called a '**brain drain**'. Critical theorists have therefore sometimes argued that the free movement of people within a global capitalist economy has a similar effect to the free movement of goods and capital, in that it serves to benefit wealthy or 'core' countries at the expense of poor or 'peripheral' ones.

However, how accurate is it to treat migration as a greater benefit for (usually wealthier) receiving countries than for sending countries? Certainly, allegations that immigrants 'steal' the jobs of local workers or 'sponge off' the welfare state would suggest otherwise. Such claims are based on the assumption that, because they are escaping from poverty, immigrants are prepared to accept lower wages and less attractive conditions of work than local workers, and that many migrants are 'pulled' by the prospect of accessing better-funded public services and more generous welfare provision. However, the former notion is based on what economists call the **lump of labour fallacy**, which implies that new entrants to the workforce can only find jobs by displacing those who already have them. In practice, this is misleading because immigration may stimulate economic growth, reducing, rather than increasing, unemployment. This applies especially if immigrants take jobs that local workers either cannot take (because they lack the necessary skills or training) or will not take (because they consider the work to be demeaning or too low paid). Immigration controls in wealthier countries invariably, therefore, make exceptions for certain categories of

● **Remittances**: Monies earned or acquired by non-nationals that are transferred back to their country of origin.

● **Brain drain**: The emigration of trained or talented individuals from their country of origin to another country, sometimes called 'human capital flight'.

●**Lump of labour fallacy**: The fallacious belief that there is a fixed amount of work to be done, suggesting that unemployment levels are determined simply by how work is shared out amongst the available labour force.

GLOBAL POLITICS IN ACTION . . .

Mexican immigration into the USA

Events: With more than 10 per cent of its native population living abroad, overwhelmingly in the USA, Mexico is the country with the most emigrants in the world. In 2011, some 10.8 per cent of the US population were Mexican-Americans, over 35.5 million Americans having full or partial Mexican ancestry, not including an estimated 6.1 million 'undocumented' or 'illegal' Mexicans. Until the early twentieth century, Mexicans were free to move across the border with the USA, and even when immigration controls started to be applied, exceptions were often made in the case of Mexican immigrants. Special allowances for Mexican immigrants ended abruptly in the 1930s, as, fuelled by the Great Depression, anti-immigration sentiment spread across the USA. Tighter immigration control in the post-WWII period nevertheless failed to prevent the level of immigration from Mexico exceeding that from any other single country in US history. However, there are signs that this trend may have ceased: between 2005 and 2010, the net flow of Mexicans into the USA dwindled to a trickle and may have gone into reverse.

Significance: The high level of migration across the Mexican-US border – the most crossed border in the world – is easy to explain. The chief underlying factor has been the dramatic imbalance in the economic fortunes of Mexico and the USA. Powerful 'push' factors, including low pay, widespread unemployment, poor medical facilities and limited education prospects, encouraged generation after generation of Mexicans to seek better opportunities in *el Norte*. This was facilitated by relatively easy access from Mexico to the USA. Not only are Mexico and the USA neighbouring countries, but the length of the border between them (3,169 km) means that immigration control is, at best, imperfect, despite the efforts of over 20,000 border patrol agents. The main reason for the altered pattern of migration in recent years is that while the USA has suffered an economic downturn, particularly associated with the 2007–09 global financial crisis, the Mexican economy has been growing steadily. Other factors may include a crackdown on illegal immigrants under Obama since 2009, and increased violence in Northern Mexico associated with drugs cartels and organized crime.

It has widely been assumed that emigration has been a key factor inhibiting economic growth in Mexico. Persistent migratory flows have left the Mexican countryside with a shortage of economically active people, and social problems have emerged due to the fact that most migrants are males and relatively young, leaving fewer people to support the elderly and the very young. And yet, at $22.45 billion in 2012, remittances, overwhelmingly from the USA, constitute Mexico's second largest source of foreign revenue (after petroleum), and make a major contribution to improving domestic living standards. Over time, Mexico's formal policy of discouraging emigration has given way to an emphasis on supporting the integration of the Mexican emigrant community in the USA, largely through the Institute of Mexicans Abroad.

US policy on immigration from Mexico has tended to focus on a combination of efforts to reduce irregular immigration (both by increased border enforcement and strengthened legal sanctions on the employment of undocumented workers) and attempts to stimulate economic growth in Mexico, not least through the 1994 North American Free Trade Agreement (NAFTA). However, a recognition of the vital importance of workers of Mexican ancestry to certain sectors of the US economy, and, above all, the growing political significance of Latino voters in the USA, have dictated a more liberal approach to immigration. Although this has primarily affected the Democratic Party, encouraging, amongst other things, President Obama to support the DREAM Act (which would provide a conditional path to citizenship for a proportion of undocumented immigrants), it is difficult to see how the Republican Party can long remain immune from the same pressures.

workers, namely those whose aquisition would bring about a 'brain gain'. Supporters of immigration also argue that the allegation that immigrants are 'welfare scroungers' is undermined by evidence showing that immigrants are often less likely than the population at large to rely on the benefit system, in part because the act of migration demonstrates a strong commitment to finding work and making social progress. Finally, immigration may bring economic benefit to receiving countries by modifying, or even reversing, demographic trends in developed societies. In particular, an influx of predominantly young migrants, who also tend to have larger families than the local population, may help to solve the problem of an aging population, in which the growing ranks of elderly people are supported by a shrinking workforce.

NATIONALISM REVIVED

As the twentieth century progressed, there were growing predictions of the decline of nationalism, even of the construction of a 'post-national' world. Not only had the barbarism and destruction of WWII created a distaste for nationalism as an ideology seemingly inherently linked to expansionism and conflict, but increasing cross-border cultural, economic and population flows appeared to render the sovereign nation-state redundant. Surely political identity was in the process of being redefined, even though it was unclear whether the successor to nationalism would be multiculturalism, transnational communities, cosmopolitanism or whatever? The reality, however, has been very different. Nationalism has demonstrated remarkable resilience and durability: in the twenty-first century, the overwhelming mass of people across the globe accept that they belong to a nation, and nationality continues to retain an unrivalled position as the basis for political allegiance. Indeed, in a number of ways, there has been a resurgence of nationalism. How and why has this happened? Primordialists, of course, may argue that the survival of nationalism simply bears out the truth of their theories: nationalism cannot be a dying doctrine because ethnic communities have not, and cannot, die out. Modernists, for their part, follow Gellner in explaining the rise of nationalism since the late twentieth century in terms of the simultaneous spread of industrial capitalism around the globe. However, resurgent nationalism has a number of manifestations, and therefore a number of underlying causes. Its main manifestations are an increase in national self-assertion in the post-Cold War period, the rise of cultural and ethnic nationalism, and the emergence of anti-globalization nationalism.

National self-assertion in the post-Cold War period

The Cold War period certainly did not witness the eclipse of nationalism. However, during the Cold War, nationalist conflict took place within a context of East–West rivalry and the ideological antagonism between capitalism and communism. For example, the Vietnamese invasion and occupation of Cambodia in 1978–9 was the only large-scale conventional war waged between one revolutionary Marxist regime and another (Anderson 1983). The end of the Cold War, and the declining significance of ideology as an organizing principle of global politics, nevertheless provided opportunities for the resurgence of nationalism as a modernizing force. This certainly happened in East and South-east Asia, where 'tiger' states such as Singapore, South Korea and Taiwan very deliberately used nation-building as a strategy for economic success in a global context. Although globalization may provide new and challenging circumstances for nationalism, such examples also show how globalization can generate new opportunities for redefining nationhood and national identity. Singapore is a particular example of this. Lacking the ethnic and cultural unity of a conventional nation-state, Singapore has nevertheless become possibly the most globalized state in the world. Basic to this process have been attempts by the ruling People's Action Party (PAP) to inculcate civic nationalism by instilling a sense of pride in the public institutions of the state as well as patriotic pride in the populace itself, in part by generous investment in technologically glossy public amenities. Civic nationalism thus helps to legitimize authoritarian rule and ensure social control, which, in turn, attracts foreign capital, thereby maintaining the growth levels that underpin patriotic pride and state allegiance.

National self-assertion has also become a strategy of growing significance for emerging powers, especially in the light of the fluid nature of world order in the post-Cold War world. Nationalism has thus once again proved its capacity for investing the drive for economic and political development with an ideological impetus that emphasizes strength, unity and pride. For instance, China's remarkable economic revival has been accompanied by clear evidence of rising nationalism. This has been apparent in the greater pressure that has been brought to bear on Taiwan to prevent moves towards the declaration of formal independence, in a firm and sometime forcible response to independence movements in Tibet and Xinjiang, and sometimes in the growth of anti-Japanese sentiment. The 2008 Beijing Olympics, as well as a host of other engineering and technological achievements, have been used to instil patriotic pride at home and to project an image of China abroad as advanced and successful. Rising nationalism in India, particularly Hindu nationalism, led to the establishment of a Bharatiya Janata Party (BJP) government in 1998. The BJP government intensified pressures to develop nuclear weapons, achieved in 1998, which have since remained hugely popular within India as a symbol of great power status. In the case of Russia, nationalism has been significantly more prominent since the rise of Vladimir Putin in 1999. Most clearly demonstrated by the aggressive resurgence of the war in Chechnya, revived nationalism has also been evident in the form of so-called 'fuel nationalism' (the use of price adjustments and restrictions on the flow of Russian gas and oil to exert control over fuel-dependent neighbouring countries) and in a firmer and more combative stance adopted towards the West in general and the USA in particular, not least through the 2008 Georgian War.

Rise of cultural and ethnic nationalism

There is evidence that although globalization may have weakened forms of classical nationalism, based on a nation-state ideal that is increasingly difficult to sustain in an age of 'borderless' economic flows, it has strengthened cultural and ethnic forms of nationalism. If the conventional nation-state is no longer capable of generating meaningful collective identities, particularist nationalisms based on region, religion, ethnicity or race may develop to take its place. Such

GLOBAL ACTORS . . .

RUSSIA

Type: State • **Population:** 143.3 m • **GDP per capita:** $21,246 • **HDI ranking:** 55/187 • **Capital:** Moscow

The Russian federation was formed as a result of the break-up of the Soviet Union on 31 December 1991. This happened in the context of the collapse of communism across the Soviet bloc during 1989–91, strengthening nationalism within the non-Russian Soviet republics and growing opposition to communist rule within Russia itself. Under Yeltsin in the 1990s, drastic economic reforms led to a reduction in living standards, soaring inflation, industrial decline and financial instability. The rise of Vladimir Putin, first as prime minister in 1999, and later as president, prime minister and (since 2012) president, has been associated with strengthened political leadership, economic recovery and the emergence of 'electoral authoritarianism'. Russia is an illiberal democracy with the following major institutions:

● The State Duma, a 450-member lower house of the legislature, and the Federal Council, the upper chamber which contains 2 members from each of the 59 federal units.
● A semi-presidential executive, comprising the prime minister, who heads the Council of Ministers, working alongside a directly elected executive president.

Significance: Russian power stems, in large part, from its vast size. It is the largest country in the world, almost twice the size of the USA. By the eighteenth century, the Russian Empire had been established, the

third largest empire in history, stretching from Poland in Europe to Alaska in North America. Russia's ascendancy to world power dates from the 1917 Russian Revolution and the establishment of the Soviet Union (founded in 1922) as the world's first communist state. The Soviet Union played a decisive role in the allied victory in WWII, emerging in 1945 as a superpower (see p. 38), by virtue of its military might and control over the expanding communist world. The political basis for the revival of Russian power after the chaos and instability of the 1990s was laid by a combination of strong government, resurgent nationalism (linked not least to the Chechen War) and the use of the state as a modernizing tool. These developments have nevertheless been underpinned by economic recovery, based on Russia's abundant supply of natural gas, oil, coal and precious metals. This has been used both to boost industrial and agricultural investment and to exert leverage over neighbouring states (Russia's 'near abroad') and Europe generally. Russia's 2008 invasion of Georgia was widely interpreted as marking Russia's re-emergence as a global power. A further dimension of Russian influence is the fact that its enormous nuclear arsenal means that it is the only state capable of threatening the USA with destruction.

Nevertheless, Russian power should not be overstated. In the first place, Russia's emergence as a 'resource superpower' has been significantly linked to hikes in the price of oil, natural gas and minerals

which have been fuelled by globalization and the expansion of the world economy. This leaves the Russian economy vulnerable to a downturn in world commodity prices, especially as customs duties and taxes from the fuel and energy sector account for nearly half of the federal government's revenues. In some respects, commodity-driven growth has undermined the long-term prospects of the Russian economy, because it has slowed the pace of economic diversification and concealed other structural weaknesses. The 2007–09 global financial crisis hit Russia particularly hard because it led to a drop in oil prices, so reducing capital in-flows and leading to a 16 per cent fall in industrial production in 2008 alone. Further concerns about Russian power stem from the possibility that 'electoral authoritarianism' may ultimately prove to be an unreliable basis for modernization. In this view, if strong government persists it will be ultimately at the expense of economic flexibility and modernization, and if pressure for liberal democratic reform becomes irresistible, the result may be a long period of political and social instability. A final threat to Russia is the changing political and economic complexion of eastern Europe, due to the expansion of the EU (see p. 509) and NATO (see p. 259). Russia's strategic interests may thus remain more regional than global, focusing on attempts to ensure that its 'near abroad' and, in particular, countries such as Ukraine, Georgia and the former Soviet republics of central Asia do not fall outside its sphere of influence.

tendencies can be traced back to the 1960s when secessionist groups and forms of **cultural nationalism** sprang up in many parts of western Europe and North America. This was evident in Quebec in Canada, Scotland and Wales in the UK, Catalonia and the Basque area of Spain, Corsica in France and Flanders in Belgium. It created pressures for political decentralization, and sometimes precipitated major constitutional upheavals. Similar manifestations of ethnic assertiveness were found in the emergence of black nationalism in the USA and amongst the Native Americans in Canada in the USA, the Aboriginal peoples in Australia and the Maoris in New Zealand. In the latter two cases, at least, this has brought about a major reassessment of national identity.

Ethnic nationalism became significantly more prominent after the end of the Cold War. What is sometimes called 'new nationalism' (Kaldor 2007) led in the 1990s to a series of wars in former Yugoslavia, which also featured programmes of 'ethnic cleansing' and the worst massacres in Europe since WWII. A number of new nation-states were created but other states that have emerged from this process have been subject to deep ethnic rivalries and tensions. For example, Bosnia has effectively been divided into 'ethnically pure' Muslim, Serb and Croat areas, while Kosovo's declaration of independence in 2008 precipitated acute tensions between its Serb minority in northern Kosovo and the majority Muslim population. Other examples of ethnic assertiveness include secessionist uprisings in Chechnya and elsewhere in the Caucasus, and the genocidal bloodshed that broke out in Rwanda in 1994, when between 800,000 and 1 million Tutsis and moderate Hutus were slaughtered in an uprising by militant Hutus.

Rising ethnic nationalism in the post-Cold War period has been explained in terms of the tendency of communist rule and East–West rivalry to drive religious, ethnic and national identities underground, only for these to rise dramatically to the surface once the suppressing factors were removed. However, the process is more complex and, in some senses, deep-seated. Smith (1995) highlighted three components that explain why nationalism resurfaced in the late twentieth century. The first is what he called 'the uneven distribution of ethnohistory', meaning that under-privileged or relatively deprived communities have been drawn to emulate more powerful nations who are able to celebrate their identity without fear. The second is the ability of nationalism to call on the 'deep resources' of religious belief to legitimize rule and mobilize populations, helping to explain the parallels that exist between ethnic nationalism and religious fundamentalism. Finally, the idea of an 'ancestral homeland' has remained, and will continue to remain, a potent symbol. This highlights the fact that the quest for self-determination can never be fully achieved in a world of unequally powerful nations. (Ethnic nationalism is examined further in Chapter 8 in connection with the rise of identity politics.)

Anti-globalization nationalism

● **Cultural nationalism**: A form of nationalism that places primary emphasis on the regeneration of the nation as a distinctive civilization rather than on self-determination.

While certain forms of nationalism have developed as a means of allowing states to manage the globalization process, nationalism has more commonly developed as a reaction against globalization, as a form of resistance. Nationalism has often prospered in conditions of fear, insecurity and social dislocation, its strength being its capacity to represent unity and certainty. The forms of nationalism that develop in such circumstances tend not to be orientated around established nation-states but, instead, provide opportunities for generally right-wing parties' movements to mount campaigns against conventional politics. This has been most apparent since the 1970s in the rise of far-right anti-immigration parties, which tend to define national identity in terms of a 'backward-looking' and culturally and perhaps ethnically 'pure' model.

Such parties have become a feature of politics in many European states. The National Front in France, led by Marine Le Pen, has attracted growing electoral support since the 1980s for a platform largely based on resistance to immigration. In 2002, Marine's father, Jean-Marie Le Pen, the founder of the party, gained 5.8 million votes (18 per cent) and got through to the run-off stage in the presidential election. In Austria in 2000, the Freedom Party, then under the leadership of Joerg Haider, won 27 per cent of the vote in the general election and became a member of the coalition government. The Northern League in Italy, which campaigns against immigration and advocates autonomy for that part of northern Italy they call Padania, served in a coalition government under Silvio Berlusconi. Vlaams Blok, which campaigns both against immigration and in favour of Flemish independence, has become a major force in Belgian politics. In the Netherlands, the Freedom Party (PVV), which was founded in 2005 and is headed by Geert Wilders, has called for a ban on immigration from Muslim countries and places a strong emphasis on cultural assimilation. The main anti-immigration parties in Scandinavia are the Progress Party in Norway and the Danish People's Party, which broke away from the Progress Party in 1995.

SUMMARY

● Nationalism is a complex and deeply contested political phenomenon. This stems in part from the fact that all nations comprise a blend of cultural and political, and objective and subjective, characteristics. Nationalism has also been a cross-cutting ideology, associated with a wide range of doctrines, movements and causes.

● From the perspective of primordialism, national identity has been seen to be rooted in a cultural heritage and language that may long predate statehood or the quest for independence. From the contrasting perspective of modernism, national identity is forged in response to changing social and historical circumstances, especially linked to industrialization.

● The liberating 'face' of nationalism is reflected in the reconfiguration of the world into a collection of nation-states, based on the principle of self-determination. However, it oppressive 'face; is evident in a common link to the politics of aggression, militarism and war. While some argue that nationalism is inherently aggressive and oppressive, others suggest that there are 'good' and 'bad' nationalisms.

● Nationalism in the modern world has been weakened by an upsurge in international migration which has led to the growth of hybridity and cultural mixing in most, if not all, societies. Migratory flows have led to the formation of transnational communities and the diasporas that some believe provide an alternative to conventional nations, and stimulated sometimes passionate debate about the economic impact of migration.

● Nations and nationalism have demonstrated remarkable resilience. Indeed, nationalism has revived in that it has been used to underpin state self-assertion in a 'de-ideologized' post-Cold War period. It has also re-emerged in the forms of cultural and ethnic nationalism, and it has provided a vehicle through which the transformations brought about through globalization can be challenged or resisted.

Questions for discussion

● How can nationality and ethnicity be distinguished?

● Are nations simply nothing more than 'invented' or 'imagined' communities?

● Why has the nation-state been such a successful political form?

● To what extent is nationalism a single doctrine?

● Is nationalism inherently oppressive and destructive?

● Is increased international migration an inevitable consequence of economic globalization?

● Do transnational communities constitute a viable alternative to conventional nations?

● Does population movement bring economic benefit, and if so, to whom?

● How and why has nationalism revived in the post-Cold War period?

● Does nationalism have a future in a globalizing world?

Further reading

Castles, S., H. de Haas and M. J. Miller, *The Age of Migration: International Population Movements in the Modern World* (2013). An up-to-date and comprehensive assessment of the nature, extent and dimensions of international population movements.

Pryke, S., *Nationalism in a Global World* (2009). An exploration of the complex relationship between globalization and nationalism.

Spencer, P. and H. Wollman, *Nationalism: A Critical Introduction* (2002). An accessible study of nationalism that surveys both classical and contemporary approaches to the subject.

Sutherland, C., *Nationalism in the Twenty-First Century* (2012). An insightful analysis of the continuing improtance of nationalism in contemporary global politics.

ONLINE RESOURCES AVAILABLE

Links to relevant web resources can be found on the *Global Politics* website

CHAPTER 8

Identity, Culture and Challenges to the West

'Identity is the theft of the self.'

ESTEE MARTIN

PREVIEW The end of the Cold War, and particularly developments such as September 11 and the 'war on terror', has altered thinking about global order and the balance between conflict and cooperation in world affairs in an important way. In addition to – and, some would argue, in place of – a concern with shifting power balances between and among states, global order appears to be increasingly shaped by new forces, especially those related to identity and culture. Some even argue that culture has replaced ideology as the key organizing principle of global politics, reflected in the growing significance in world affairs of factors such as ethnicity, history, values and religion. How can this trend towards so-called 'identity politics' best be explained, and what have been its implications? Most importantly, does the increasing importance of culture mean that conflict, perhaps conflict between different civilizations, is more likely, or even inevitable? The growing salience of culture as a factor affecting world affairs has been particularly evident in relation to religion. Not only has there been, in some cases, a revival in religious belief, but more radical or 'fundamentalist' religious movements have emerged, preaching that politics, in effect, *is* religion. To what extent has religious revivalism, and especially the trend towards religious fundamentalism, affected global politics? Finally, issues of identity, culture and religion have played a particularly prominent role in attempts to challenge and displace the politico-cultural hegemony of the West. The process through which former colonies have tried to establish non-western and sometimes anti-western political identities has affected Asia, but it has been especially crucial in the Muslim world, encouraging some to talk in terms of a civilizational clash between Islam and the West. What is the basis for conflict between Islam and the West, and can this conflict be overcome?

KEY ISSUES
- Why has identity politics become a prominent feature of world affairs?
- Has culture displaced ideology as the organizing principle of global politics?
- Is there an emerging 'clash of civilizations'?
- How important is religion in modern global politics?
- Is conflict between Islam and the West unavoidable?
- How has the West sought to deal with the 'Muslim question'?

CONCEPT

Colonialism

Colonialism is the theory or practice of establishing control over foreign territory and turning it into a colony. Colonialism is thus a particular form of imperialism (see p. 28). Colonialism is usually distinguished by settlement and economic domination. As typically practised in Africa and South-east Asia, colonial government was exercised by a settler community from the mother country who were ethnically distinct from the native population. In French colonialism, colonies were thought of as part of the mother country, meaning that colonial peoples were granted formal rights of citizenship. In contrast, neo-colonialism involves economic domination without direct political control, as, for example, in so-called US 'dollar imperialism' in Latin America.

● **The Enlightenment**: An intellectual movement that reached its height in the eighteenth century and challenged traditional beliefs in religion, politics and learning in general in the name of reason and progress.

● **Individualism**: The belief in the supreme importance of the individual over any social group or collective body (see p. 154).

RISE OF IDENTITY POLITICS

Westernization as modernization

Modernization has traditionally worn a western face. Western societies have conventionally been portrayed as 'developed' or 'advanced' societies, implying that they offer a model that will, over time, be accepted by all other societies. This view was fostered by the economic, political and military ascendancy that European states established from the sixteenth century onwards, underpinned by the expansion of trade, leading to the industrial revolution, and the spread of colonialism. From the nineteenth century onwards, European ascendancy developed into the ascendancy of the West (see p. 26) generally, through the growing importance of former colonies, most notably the USA. By the end of the nineteenth century, some nine-tenths of the entire land surface of the globe was controlled by European, or European-derived, powers.

The philosophical and intellectual roots of western civilization lie in Judeo-Christian religion and the rediscovery in early modern Europe of the learning of classical Greece and Rome, which provided the foundation for the scientific revolution of the seventeenth century and subsequent technological advances. During the eighteenth and nineteenth centuries, political, economic and cultural life in Europe was deeply permeated by liberal ideas, so much so that liberalism has sometimes appeared to be indistinguishable from western civilization in general. Influenced by the **Enlightenment**, liberal thinkers preached the values of **individualism**, reason, freedom and toleration. This form of liberalism was boldly universalist: it implied that human history would be marked by the gradual but inevitable triumph of liberal principles and institutions. Progress, in short, was understood in strictly liberal terms.

What were the features of this western model of modernization? Westernization had significant economic, political and cultural implications. In economic terms, it meant the growth of a market or capitalist society. Capitalism, based as it was on private property and competition, stimulated an unprecedented level of economic dynamism, underpinned by an ethic of individual self-striving. This gave rise to industrialization and urbanization, as well as new patterns of social stratification, based on a rising middle class, brought about through the expansion of business and the professions, and an increasingly factory-based working class. From a western perspective, market capitalism is the only reliable mechanism for generating wealth and widespread prosperity. The political face of westernization took the form of the advance of liberal democracy. The key feature of such a system is that the right to rule is gained through success in regular and competitive elections. In this way, a competitive and market-based economic system was complemented by an open and pluralistic political system. Such economic and political arrangements have very particular implications for the culture (see p. 194) of western societies, however.

As liberal societies tend to espouse universal values and emphasize the importance of personal autonomy and freedom of choice, they are often seen to weaken cultural bonds and identities. This can be seen in the changing nature of social relationships in liberal societies. Ferdinand Tönnies noted the decline of *Gemeinschaft*, or 'community', typically found in traditional societies and characterized by natural affection and a mutual respect, and the rise of *Gesellschaft*, or 'association', the looser, artificial and contractual relationships that are typically found in urban and industrialized societies. *Gesellschaft* relationships tend to liberate people from their cultural inheritance, allowing them to adopt beliefs, values and norms more in line with individual tastes and personal preferences. Liberal societies have therefore tended to 'privatize' culture, in that issues such as religious belief, moral principles and sexual conduct have been increasingly thought of as matters to be decided by the individual rather than the larger society. This has been reflected, particularly since the 1960s, in the spread of so-called '**permissive**' values and social norms. Such a trend has been associated with a general decline in **deference** and the weakening authority of traditional values and traditional hierarchies (not least those linked to gender roles).

The notion that westernization provided the only viable model for modernization gained its greatest impetus during the final decades of the twentieth century. Globalization (see p. 8) appeared to be bringing about the universalization of the western economic model together with the spread of the values and appetites of consumer capitalism. And, as Fukuyama (see p. 539) and other 'end of history' theorists gleefully proclaimed, the collapse of communism and the end of the Cold War appeared to herald the universalization of western-style liberal democracy. However, the same period also witnessed early signs that universalist liberalism was under pressure, both in its western homeland and beyond. In western society itself, there were signs of a backlash against the spread of liberal values and of atomistic individualism. In the USA and elsewhere, this took the form of growing support for **social conservatism**, articulating hostility towards the 'permissive 1960s' and calling for a strengthening of traditional values, often rooted in religion (see p. 197). Liberalism also came under pressure from communitarian theorists who argued that, in conceiving of the individual as logically prior to and 'outside' the community, liberalism had legitimized selfish and egotistical behaviour and downgraded the importance of collective identity. They argued that social fragmentation and breakdown had become a feature of western society largely as a result of individuals' obsession with rights and their refusal to acknowledge reciprocal duties and moral responsibilities. This was demonstrated by the so-called 'parenting deficit'; that is, the abandonment of the burdens of parenthood by fathers and mothers who are more concerned about their own lifestyles and careers. However, powerful forces were also emerging beyond western societies that sought to challenge, and overturn, the hegemony of universalist liberalism, and with it the notion that westernization represented the only legitimate model of modernization. These forces have been associated with the emergence of a new politics of **identity**, in which identity is linked to 'particularisms', such as culture, ethnicity, locality and religion.

Politics of collective identity

Whereas politics during the 'short' twentieth century, and especially during the Cold War era, was dominated by ideological rivalry, politics since appears to have been structured increasingly by issues of cultural difference. The East–West rivalry between communism and capitalism was based on a clash between contrasting models of industrial society, each offering a supposedly universal solution to economic and social ills. They each practised the politics of owner-

● **Permissiveness**: The willingness to allow people to make their own moral choices; permissiveness suggests that there are no authoritative values.

● **Deference**: Willing compliance with the wishes or expectations of others.

● **Social conservatism**: The belief that societies should be based on a bedrock of shared values and a common cultures, providing a necessary social 'cement'.

● **Identity**: A relatively stable and enduring sense of selfhood; identity may be *personal* (unique to an individual), *social* (shared with a group) or *human* (shared with all people).

IDENTITY

Realist view

Realists have given relatively little attention to the issue of identity. Their primary focus is on the interests and behaviour of the state, seen as the dominant global actor, rather than on the make-up of its constituent population. Nevertheless, since states are viewed as unified and cohesive entities, this reflects assumptions about political allegiance and social belonging. Notably, as most states are nation-states (see p. 168), realists tend to assume that identity is forged through the over-lapping ties of nationality and citizenship. National identity, indeed, may be 'natural', in that it reflects an irresistible psychological disposition for people to iden-tify with others who are similar to themselves.

Liberal view

Liberals generally understand identity in strictly personal terms. Human beings are first and foremost individuals, possessed of a unique identity. However, emphasizing the importance of the individual has two contrasting implications. Individuals are defined by 'inner' qualities and attributes that are specific to themselves, but such thinking is also universalist, in that it implies that, as individuals, all human beings share the same status and so are entitled to the same rights and opportunities. This is reflected in liberal support for the doctrine of human rights (see p. 311). For liberals, then, identity is both unique and universal. The liberal commitment to individualism has impor-tant implications for any theory of social or collective identity. In particular, it suggests that factors such as race, religion, culture, gender and social class are at best of secondary importance: they are not 'core' to human identity. Nevertheless, liberals have adopted a wide range of views on such issues, and have also recognized the social dimension of personal identity. This is evident in the ideas of liberal communitarianism (Taylor 1994) and liberal nationalism (Miller 2007).

Critical views

A variety of critical approaches to identity have been developed. Theorists in the Marxist tradition have conventionally understood identity in terms of social class. They believe that people tend to identify with those who have the same economic position, and therefore class interests, as themselves, other forms of

identity (linked to nationality, religion, ethnicity (see p. 193) and so on) being written off simply as 'false consciousness' (deluded and manipulated thinking). Class identities, nevertheless, were provisional, not fundamental. They were essentially a manifestation of the inequalities of the capitalist system, and would be swept away once a classless, communist society had been established. Social constructivists, for their part, have emphasized the extent to which the interests and actions of global actors, be they states or individuals, are fashioned by their sense of identity, which is in turn conditioned by non-material factors. As Wendt (see p. 77) put it, 'identities are the basis of interests'. Such a position rejects any fixed or unchanging notion of identity, as it does the idea that actors encounter each other with pre-determined sets of preferences. Individuals can thus adopt different identities in differ-ent cultural and ideational circumstances, including, potentially, cosmopolitan identities.

Since the 1970s, however, critical theorists from various traditions have increasingly understood iden-tity in terms of 'difference'. This reflects both the decline of the politics of social class and a growing awareness of other sources of social injustice, linked, for example, to gender (see p. 423), race, ethnicity and sexual orientation. Conventional models of identity came to be seen as forms of cultural control and subor-dination, in that they are constructed on the basis of the norms and characteristics of dominant groups. The emphasis on difference, by contrast, allowed marginal-ized and subordinated groups to embrace, even cele-brate, their distinctive, and therefore more 'authentic', identity. Identity formation thus became a vehicle for political self-assertion, as in the ideas of 'black libera-tion', 'women's liberation', 'gay liberation' and so on. Such thinking has been particularly embraced by femi-nist theorists, for whom identity is linked to gender. However, while egalitarian feminists have been concerned to reduce or remove gender differences (on the grounds that gender serves to divide otherwise identical human beings), so-called difference feminists have argued that gender is the very root of identity. The theory of gender identity suggests that women should be 'woman-identified', thinking of themselves in terms of the distinctive capacities, needs and interests of women.

(see p. 190)

CONCEPT

Liberal democracy

A liberal democracy is a political regime in which a 'liberal' commitment to limited government is blended with a 'democratic' belief in popular rule. Its key features are: (1) the right to rule is gained through success in regular and competitive elections, based on universal adult suffrage; (2) constraints on government imposed by a constitution, institutional checks and balances, and protections for individual rights; and (3) a vigorous civil society including a private enterprise economy, independent trade unions and a free press. While some view liberal democracy as the political expression of western values and economic structures, others argue that it is universally applicable, as it allows for the expression of the widest possible range of views and beliefs.

ship, capitalism standing for private property and market competition, while communism stood for collective ownership and central planning. Although the former clearly vanquished the latter, its worldwide victory has been thrown into doubt, particularly since the 1980s, by the growing importance of identity politics (see p. 190). What all forms of identity politics have in common is, first, that they view liberal universalism as a source of oppression, even a form of cultural imperialism, that marginalizes and demoralizes subordinate groups and peoples. It does this because, behind the façade of universalism, the culture of liberal societies is constructed in line with the interests of its dominant groups – men, whites, the wealthy and so forth. Subordinate groups and peoples are either assigned an inferior or demeaning stereotype or they are encouraged to identify with the values and interests of dominant groups, their oppressors.

However, identity politics is also a source of liberation and empowerment. It promises that social and political advancement can be achieved through a process of cultural self-assertion aimed at cultivating a 'pure' or 'authentic' sense of identity. In many ways, the archetypal model for identity politics was the black consciousness movement that first emerged in the early twentieth century, inspired by activists such as Marcus Garvey, who preached a 'back to Africa' message. Black nationalism gained greater prominence in the 1960s with an upsurge in both the reformist and revolutionary wings of the movement. In its reformist guise, the movement took the form of a struggle for civil rights that reached national prominence in the USA under the leadership of Martin Luther King (1929–68) and the National Association for the Advancement of Coloured People (NAACP). The strategy of protest and non-violent civil disobedience was nevertheless rejected by the emerging Black Power movement, which supported black separatism and, under the leadership of the Black Panthers, founded in 1966, promoted the use of physical force and armed confrontation. Of more enduring significance in US politics, however, have been the Black Muslims, founded in 1929, who advocate a separatist creed based on the idea that black Americans are descended from an ancient Muslim tribe. The underlying strategy of black nationalism was, however, to confront a dominant white culture through a process of consciousness-raising that has subsequently been adopted by other forms of identity politics.

Marcus Garvey (1887–1940)

Jamaican political thinker and activist, and an early advocate of black nationalism. Garvey was the founder in 1914 of the Universal Negro Improvement Association (UNIA). In 1916, he left Jamaica for New York, where his message of black pride and economic self-sufficiency gained him a growing following, particularly in ghettos such as Harlem. Although his black business enterprises failed, and his call for a return to Africa was largely ignored, Garvey's emphasis on establishing black pride and his vision of Africa as a 'homeland' provided the basis for the later Black Power movement. Rastafarianism is also based largely on his ideas. Garvey was imprisoned for mail fraud in 1923, and was later deported, eventually dying in obscurity in London.

Focus on ...

Identity politics: who are we?

Identity politics is an orientation towards social theorizing and political practice, rather than a coherent body of ideas with a settled political character. Its central feature is that it seeks to challenge and overthrow oppression by reshaping a group's identity through what amounts to a process of politico-cultural self-assertion. Manifestations of identity politics are varied and diverse, ranging from second-wave feminism and the gay and lesbian movement to ethnic nationalism, multiculturalism (see p. 192) and religious fundamentalism (see p. 199). Identity can be reshaped around many principles – gender, sexuality, culture, ethnicity, religion and so on. All forms of identity politics nevertheless exhibit two characteristic beliefs. First, group marginalization is understood not merely as a legal, political or social phenomenon, but is, rather, a cultural phenomenon. It operates through stereotypes and values developed by dominant groups that structure how marginalized groups see themselves and are seen by others. Conventional notions of identity therefore inculcate a sense of inferiority, even shame, helping to entrench marginalized groups in their subordination.

Second, subordination can be challenged by reshaping identity to give the group concerned a sense of (usually publicly proclaimed) pride and self-respect, for example, 'black is beautiful', 'gay pride' and so on. Embracing and proclaiming a positive social identity thus serves as an act of defiance (liberating people from others' power to determine their identity) and as an assertion of group solidarity (encouraging people to identify with those who share the same identity as themselves). Critics of identity politics have argued that it 'miniaturizes' humanity, by seeing people only in terms of group belonging; that it fosters division, often because it embraces exclusive and quasi-absolutist notions of identity; and that it embodies tensions and contradictions (for example, between the women's liberation movement and patriarchal religious fundamentalists).

Why has there been an upsurge in identity politics since the final decades of the twentieth century? As discussed later in the chapter, the phenomenon is often associated with postcolonialism (see p. 200), and attempts in former European colonies to give political independence a cultural dimension by developing a non-western, and sometimes anti-western, sense of identity. A second factor was the failure of socialism and, ultimately, the collapse of communism. Until the 1970s, there had been a clear tendency for socially disadvantaged groups and peoples to articulate their political aspirations through socialism in one of its various forms. By providing a critique of exploitation and oppression, and by standing for social development and equality, socialism exerted a powerful appeal for oppressed peoples in many parts of the world, often, but not always, linked to the wider influence of the Soviet Union. Anticolonial nationalism in the developing world was typically orientated around socialist values and goals and sometimes embraced Marxist-Leninist doctrines.

However, the failure of developing-world socialist regimes, particularly those with Soviet-style central planning systems, to eradicate poverty and deliver prosperity meant that postcolonial nationalism was increasingly remodelled in line with values and identities that were more deeply rooted in developing-world societies. This was evident in the growing importance of ethnic nationalism and the rise of religious fundamentalism. The collapse of communism in Eastern Europe added powerfully to such tendencies. Communist rule had merely fossilized ethnic and national loyalties by driving them underground, meaning that ethnic and religious nationalism became the most natural vehicles for expressing anti-communism or anti-Sovietism. In addition, the political instability and economic uncertainty precipitated by the collapse of communism were a perfect breeding ground for a form of politics that offered an 'organic' sense of collective identity. This was most clearly demonstrated by the break-up of Yugoslavia in the 1990s through a growing stress on the politics of national and ethnic identity, which resulted in a series of wars and, for example, left the former Yugoslav republic of Bosnia divided into 'ethnically pure' Muslim, Serb and Croat areas.

A third factor explaining the growth of identity politics was globalization. In a sense, identity politics can be seen as a form of resistance against the cultural impact of globalization. As discussed in Chapter 6, globalization has been associated with a process of homogenization, through which a relatively narrow common culture has tended to be adopted the world over. The features of this include growing urbanization, the use of common technology (televisions, computers, mobile phones and so on), so-called 'global goods', the growth of consumerism and materialism, and an increasing cultural mixing through the 'multiculturalization' of national cultural traditions. Globalization has therefore been seen in many parts of the world as a threat to their national culture, and so to traditionally-based forms of identity. However, resistance to what Benjamin Barber (2003) called 'McWorld', a complex of western, and often specifically US, influences, appetites and values, has rarely taken the form of simple **traditionalism**. Whereas traditional conceptions of social belonging were 'given', in the sense that they stemmed largely from unquestioned (and perhaps unquestionable) bonds and loyalties, those generated by identity politics are 'modern' in that they are shaped by a process of individualization and so involve, to a greater or lesser extent, a process of *self*-definition. It is the intersection of individual cognitive processes with broader cultural, political and economic forces that gives identity, in this sense, its political potency and emotional power. This also helps to explain why identity politics tends to take root not in traditional societies but either in modern societies or in societies in which a traditional sense of belonging is being disrupted by modern influences.

Multiculturalism and hybridity

One of the most significant manifestations of identity politics in modern societies is multiculturalism (see p. 192). This emerged as, thanks to increased international migration since the 1970s (examined in Chapter 7), more and more countries came to accept and even (although with different degrees of enthusiasm) embrace their multicultural characters, abandoning the politics of assimilation or strategies of voluntary repatriation. Multiculturalism proclaims the idea of 'togetherness in difference' (Young 1995), taking particular account of cultural differentiation that is based on race, ethnicity or language. Multiculturalism not only recognizes the fact of cultural diversity, but also holds that such differences should be respected and publicly affirmed. Although the USA, an immigrant society, has long been a multicultural society, the cause of multiculturalism in this sense was not taken up until the rise of the black consciousness movement in the 1960s. Australia has been officially committed to multiculturalism since the

● **Traditionalism**: A belief in the value of tradition and continuity, providing society with a historically-rooted sense of identity.

1970s, in recognition of its increasing 'Asianization'. In New Zealand, it is linked to a recognition of the role of Maori culture in forging a distinctive national identity. In Canada, it is associated with attempts to achieve reconciliation between French-speaking Quebec and the English-speaking majority population, and an acknowledgement of the rights of the indigenous Inuit peoples.

Multiculturalism, however, is a broad term that encompasses a range of ambiguities as well as different approaches to the challenge of diversity. The ambiguity that lies at the heart of multiculturalism is reflected in the tension between, on the one hand, the idea of ethnic belonging and the embrace, even celebration, of diversity on the other. Multicultural theorists highlight the importance of ethnicity as a basis for identity. Multiculturalism can be seen as a form of communitarianism, in that it focuses on the group and not the individual, seeing an individual's self-worth as being inextricably linked to respect and recognition for the beliefs, values and practices of his or her ethnic community. The advance of multiculturalism has therefore gone hand in hand with campaigns for minority rights, sometimes called 'special' or 'polyethnic' rights. These are rights that acknowledge and seek to protect a community's ethnic distinctiveness, and affect matters such as dress, language, schooling and public holidays. In states such as Canada, Australia and New Zealand, they extend to special representation or territorial rights for indigenous peoples. However, at the same time, multiculturalism proclaims the supposed benefits of cultural mixing and hybridity, the value each community derives from living within a society characterized by cultural difference. Cultures can thus learn from and enrich each other, widening cultural opportunities and strengthening intercultural understanding. The result is a kind of 'mix-and-match' multiculturalism that operates in tandem with cultural globalization to create deeper levels of social and cultural mixing in modern societies, blurring national distinctiveness in the process.

There are, moreover, competing models of multiculturalism, offering different approaches to how diversity and togetherness can be reconciled, and providing rival views on the complex relationship between multiculturalism and nationalism. Liberal multiculturalists tend to stress the importance of civic unity, arguing that diversity can and should be confined to the private sphere, leaving the public sphere as a realm of integration. Moral, cultural and lifestyle choices can thus largely be left to the individual, while common political or civic allegiance help to bind people together. In this view, multiculturalism and nationalism are compatible, even creating a new, possibly twenty-first century model of national identity in the form of multicultural nationalism, which balances cultural diversity against a common citizenship. Insofar as this destroys the link between nationality and ethnicity, it is very clearly based on a form of civic nationalism. However, conservatives, who argue that stable and successful societies must be based on shared values and a common culture, argue that nationalism and multiculturalism are fundamentally incompatible. In this view, human beings are limited and dependent creatures, who are naturally drawn to others similar to themselves but, by the same token, fear or distrust people who are in some way different. Multicultural societies are therefore inherently fractured and conflict-ridden: suspicion, hostility and even violence between different ethnic communities are not products of intolerance, ignorance or social inequality, but are a simple fact of social psychology. Ethnic

CONCEPT

Ethnicity

Ethnicity is the sentiment of loyalty towards a distinctive population, cultural group or territorial area. The term is complex because it has both racial and cultural overtones. The members of ethnic groups are often seen, correctly or incorrectly, to have descended from common ancestors, meaning that they tend to be thought of as extended kinship groups, united by blood. More commonly, however, ethnicity is understood as a form of cultural identity, albeit one that operates at a deep and emotional level. An 'ethnic' culture encompasses values, traditions and practices but, crucially, it also gives people a common identity and sense of distinctiveness, usually by focusing on their origins and descent.

and cultural diversity are therefore the implacable enemy of national unity and political stability.

The record of multicultural societies nevertheless suggests that there is nothing natural or inevitable about inter-ethnic conflict or hostility. This can be seen in relation to the revival of ethnic nationalism in the late twentieth century (discussed later in the chapter), but it is also evident in the close relationship between ethnic conflict and socio-economic divisions. In a sense, communal tensions have always been as much about social class as they have been about ethnicity: different ethnic groups tend to occupy differing positions within the economy and enjoy different levels of economic and social security. In some respects, these economically based ethnic tensions have become more acute in an age of globalization. This has happened in at least two ways. First, as Amy Chua (2003) argued, in many developing countries, the increased concentration of wealth in the hands of those in a position to exploit the benefit of global markets has often allowed small ethnic minorities to acquire hugely disproportional economic power. Examples of such 'market dominant' economic minorities include the Chinese in much of southeast Asia, Indians in East Africa and, though in a less extreme form, the Ipos in West Africa. In such circumstances, widening economic divisions have provoked growing hostility and racial prejudice on the part of ethnic majorities, which are increasingly expressed in violence, creating what Chua called a 'world on fire'. The second way in which economic and ethnic tensions intermingle is in developed countries, where ethnic minorities are usually confined to marginal, low-status and low-income occupations. Such circumstances are usually linked to discrimination and other forms of structural disadvantage, and have led to civil unrest and even rioting amongst ethnic minority youths. Examples of this occurred in various parts of the UK in 1981, in Los Angeles in 1992, in Queensland, Australia in 2004 and across much of France in 2005.

Is cultural conflict inevitable?

The rise of identity politics is often seen as part and parcel of a broader phenomenon: the growing salience of culture as a factor affecting international relations and world affairs. Some, indeed, believe that since the end of the Cold War culture has effectively displaced ideology as the organizing principle of global politics. One of the most widely discussed and controversial attempts to highlight the importance of culture in contemporary global politics has been Samuel Huntington's (see p. 540) **'clash of civilizations' thesis**. Although the thesis was very much born in the context of the end of the Cold War (Huntington 1993, 1996), the notion of a 'clash of civilizations' attracted growing attention during the 1990s as early, optimistic expectations of the establishment of a liberal 'new world order' were shaken by an upsurge in ethnic conflict in the former Yugoslavia, Rwanda and elsewhere. However, the thesis had its greatest impact after September 11 (see p. 20), when it was widely used as an explanation of the changing nature of world order as global terrorism was seen as a symptom of an emerging clash between Islam and the West. Nevertheless, the extent to which it informed the Bush administration's approach to the 'war on terror' (see p. 230) should not be exaggerated, as it certainly would not have encouraged the adoption of strategies of democratization in Iraq and Afghanistan.

● **Clash of civilizations thesis**: The theory that, in the post-Cold War world, conflict would not primarily be ideological or economic but, rather, cultural in character.

CONCEPT

Culture

Culture, in its broadest sense, is the way of life of a people; their beliefs, values and practices. Sociologists and anthropologists tend to distinguish between 'culture' and 'nature', the former encompassing that which is passed on from one generation to the next by learning, rather than through biological inheritance. Culture therefore embodies language, religion, traditions, social norms and moral principles. A distinction is sometimes drawn between 'high' culture, represented especially by the arts and literature, which is supposedly the source of intellectual and personal development, and 'low' or 'popular' culture, which is orientated around mass consumption and populist instincts, and may even have a debasing impact on society.

Huntington's basic assertion was that a new era in global politics was emerging in which civilization would be the primary force, a civilization being 'culture writ large'. As such, the 'clash of civilizations' thesis contrasted sharply with the neoliberal image of world affairs, which stresses the growth of interdependence (see p. 7), particularly in the light of globalization. Huntington's relationship to realism is more complex, however. Insofar as he accepted that traditional, power-driven states remain the key actors on the world stage, he was a realist, but his realism was modified by the insistence that the struggle for power now took place within a larger framework of civilizational, rather than ideological, conflict. In Huntington's view, cultural conflict is likely to occur at a 'micro' level and a 'macro' level. 'Micro-level' conflict will occur at the 'fault-lines' between civilizations, where one 'human tribe' clashes with another, possibly resulting in communal wars. In that sense, civilizations operate rather like tectonic plates that rub up against one another at vulnerable points. At the 'macro-level', conflict may break out between the civilizations themselves, in all likelihood precipitated by clashes between their 'core' states. Huntington particularly warned about the likelihood of conflict between China (wedded to distinctive Sinic cultural values despite rapid economic growth) and the West, and between the West and Islam. He also identified the potential for conflict between the West and 'the Rest', possibly spearheaded by an anti-western alliance of Confucian and Islamic states.

This account of emerging and seemingly irresistible cultural conflict has been severely criticized, however. For example, Huntington's 'tectonic' notion of civilizations presents them as being much more homogeneous, and therefore distinct from one another, than is in fact the case. In practice, civilizations have always interpenetrated one another, giving rise to blurred or hybrid cultural identities. Furthermore, just as orthodox Marxists made the mistake of 'economism', by overstating the importance of economic and class factors in determining identity, Huntington made the mistake of **culturalism**, in that he failed to recognize the extent to which cultural identities are shaped by political and social circumstances. This, indeed, may be a defect of all forms of identity politics. What appears to be a cultural conflict may therefore have a quite different, and more complex, explanation. For instance, the ethnic conflicts that broke out in the former Yugoslavia in the 1990s were not so much a product of natural hatreds and tensions rising to the surface but were, rather, a consequence of the growth of nationalist and racialist doctrines in the power vacuum that had been created by the collapse of communism. Similarly, conflict between civilizations may be more an expression of perceived economic and political injustice than of cultural rivalry. The rise of militant Islam (discussed later in the chapter) may thus be better explained by tensions and crises in the Middle East in general and in the Arab world in particular, linked to the inheritance of colonialism, the Arab–Israeli conflict, the survival of unpopular but often oil-rich autocratic regimes, and urban poverty and unemployment, rather than by cultural incompatibility between western and Islamic value systems.

However, though partial in its account of the emerging twenty-first century global order, the idea of a 'clash of civilizations' has been effective in drawing attention to important tendencies in global politics. These include the growing political importance of culture in an apparently de-ideologized world and the power of the backlash against globalization in particular and against western global hegemony in general. As such, it provides a context that helps to explain

● **Culturalism**: The belief that human beings are culturally-defined creatures, culture being the universal basis for personal and social identity.

the rising importance of religious movements in the post-Cold War world. In addition, Huntington helpfully underlines the *capacity* of cultural difference to generate political conflict, even though this may too often be portrayed as a natural, rather than political, process. Nevertheless, Huntington's theories are often more flexible and sophisticated than his critics allow. He recognized, for example, that a global war involving the 'core' states of the world's major civilizations is highly improbable (but not impossible), and he acknowledged that the prospects of a global inter-civilizational conflict are linked to the shifting balance of power amongst civilizations and their 'core' states, especially the rise of China as the 'biggest player in the history of man'. He also recognized that civilizational conflict can be managed by political intervention. For example, he warned against the West pursuing democracy promotion (see p. 212) on the grounds that this would merely inflame non-western cultures and encourage them to form anti-western alliances.

RELIGIOUS REVIVALISM

Religion and politics

The most prominent aspect of the growing political importance of culture has undoubtedly been religious revivalism and the rise of religious movements. In Huntington's (1996) view, religion is the 'central defining characteristic' of civilizations, in which case the 'clash of civilizations' effectively implies a clash of religions. Such a view is difficult to sustain, however. Not only are there considerable parallels and overlaps amongst the world's religions: for example, Buddhism developed out of Hinduism, and Christianity, Islam and Judaism, the 'religions of the book', are rooted in a common belief in the Old Testament of the Bible – but the role of religion in different societies and cultures varies considerably. For instance, although Judeo-Christian beliefs are clearly a component of western civilization (one that is, nevertheless, shared with Orthodox and Latin American civilizations), it is not necessarily its *defining* feature, Greco-Roman influences and the related tradition of Enlightenment rationalism being at least equally important. Ideas such as social equality, toleration, critical rationality and democracy are thus key elements in western culture, but none of these can be traced directly to Christianity. Indeed, one of the features of western, and particularly European societies is their **secularism**, the USA, where about one-quarter of voters define themselves as 'born-again Christians', being an exception. Such developments are based on the so-called '**secularization thesis**'. The advance of secularism, nevertheless, does not necessarily imply the decline of religion. Rather, it is concerned to establish a 'proper' sphere and role for religion, in line with the liberal belief in a so-called 'public/private divide'. Its aim is to fence religion into a private arena, in which people are free to do as they like, leaving public life to be organized on a strictly secular basis. Freedom of religious belief therefore developed into a key liberal-democratic principle. However, other forces, such as the advance of rationalism and scientific doctrines and the growth of materialistic and consumerist values, have strengthened 'this-worldly' concerns in many societies.

However, advocates of the secularization thesis have been confounded by developments from the late twentieth century onwards. Religion has become

● **Secularism**: The belief that religion should not intrude into secular (worldly) affairs, usually reflected in the desire to separate church from state.

● **Secularization thesis**: The theory that modernization is invariably accompanied by the victory of reason over religion and the displacement of spiritual values by secular ones.

Debating ...
Is there an emerging 'clash of civilizations'?

The 'clash of civilizations' thesis suggests that twenty-first century global order will be characterized by growing tension and conflict, but that this conflict will be cultural in character, rather than ideological, political or economic. But how compelling is the thesis?

YES

The rise of culture. Culture is destined to be the primary force in twenty-first century global politics because, as Huntington put it, 'If not civilization, what?' Since the end of the Cold War, ideology has faded in significance and globalization has weakened the state's ability to generate a sense of civic belonging, while there is little evidence of global or cosmopolitan identities becoming a reality. In such a context, peoples and nations are confronted by the most basic of human questions: who are we? This forces them to define themselves increasingly in terms of ancestry, religion, language, history, values and customs; in short, in terms of culture. States and groups from the same civilization will therefore rally to the support of their 'kin countries', and political creeds such as socialism and nationalism will give way to 'Islamization', 'Hinduization', 'Russianization' and so on.

Cultural conflict. A stronger sense of cultural belonging cannot but lead to tension and conflict. This is, first, because different cultures and civilizations are incommensurate: they establish quite different sets of values and meanings; in effect, different understandings of the world. However desirable cross-cultural understanding may be, it is impossible to bring about. Second, there is an irresistible tendency for people's sense of who they are to be sharpened by an awareness of the 'other': the people they are not; those they are *against*. This divides people into 'us' and 'them', or 'our civilization' versus 'those barbarians'.

Civilizational tensions. Certain trends to which Huntington drew attention have undoubtedly generated tension, giving the world an increasingly problematical multipolar and 'multicivilizational' character. These include the long-term decline of the West, and, more specifically, the fading of US hegemony; the so-called 'Asian affirmation', the economic rise of Asia and especially the rise of China; and the resurgence of Islam, driven by a population explosion in a still unstable Muslim world. Tensions between China and the USA and between Islam and the West thus have an inescapable civilizational dimension.

NO

Complex and fragmented civilizations. Huntington's notion of culture and civilization can be dismissed as simplistic at best. In the 'clash of civilizations' thesis, cultures are portrayed as rigid and 'hermetically sealed', giving rise to a narrow association between civilizations and seemingly unchanging sets of traditions, values and understandings. The idea of 'fault-line' conflict between civilizations is based on a homogeneous or 'tectonic' model of civilizations. In practice, civilizations are not homogeneous and unified blocs, but are, rather, complex, fragmented and often open to external influence. For instance, the notions of an 'Islamic civilization' or a 'western civilization' fail to take account of either the extent of political, cultural and social division within each 'civilization', or the extent to which Islam and the West have influenced, and continue to influence, one another.

Cultural harmony and peaceful coexistence. The idea that cultural difference is always and inevitably linked to political antagonism is highly questionable. Cultural similarity is, for example, no guarantee of peace and stability: most wars take place between states from the same, not different, civilizations. Moreover, there is considerable evidence that people from different cultures, religions or ethnic origins have been able to live together in relative peace and harmony as, for instance, applied in the Balkans during the Ottoman era. Finally, when cultures or cultural groups clash this is less a reflection of 'natural' antipathies or rivalries, and more a manifestation of deeper political and social factors, linked to the distribution of power or wealth.

Trends towards cultural homogenization. The 'clash of civilizations' thesis offers, at best, a one-sided account of contemporary cultural trends. In particular, it ignores the extent to which globalization and other forces have already blurred cultural differences in many parts of the world. Although the 'one world' image advanced by so-called 'hyperglobalizers' and liberal internationalists may be naive, there are nevertheless strong tendencies towards economic interdependence and integration which at least counter-balance, and perhaps contain, any centrifugal tendencies that civilizational rivalry may generate.

CONCEPT

Religion

Religion, in its most general sense, is an organized community of people bound together by a shared body of beliefs concerning some kind of transcendent reality. However, 'transcendent' in this context may refer to anything from a belief in a distinctly 'other-worldly' supreme being or creator God, to a more 'this-worldly' experience of personal liberation, as in the Buddhist concept of nirvana. There are major differences between monotheistic religions (Christianity, Islam and Judaism), which have a single, or limited number of, sacred texts and a clear authority system, and pantheistic, non-theistic and nature religions (Hinduism, Buddhism, Jainism, Taoism and so on), which tend to have looser, more decentralized and more pluralized structures.

● **Moral relativism**: The belief that there are no absolute values, or a condition in which there is deep and widespread disagreement over moral issues.

more important, not less important. This has been evident in the emergence of new, and often more assertive forms of religiosity, in the increasing impact of religious movements and, most importantly, in a closer relationship between religion and politics, through both the religionization of politics and politicization of religion. This became evident in the 1970s within Islam, and was most dramatically demonstrated by the 1979 'Islamic Revolution' in Iran, which brought the Ayatollah Khomeini (see p. 198) to power as the leader of the world's first Islamic state. Nevertheless, it soon became clear that this was not an exclusively Islamic development, as so-called 'fundamentalist' movements emerged within Christianity, particularly in the form of the 'new Christian Right' in the USA, and within Hinduism and Sikhism in India. Other manifestations of this include the spread of US-style Pentecostalism in Latin America, Africa and East Asia; the growth in China of Falun Gong, a spiritual movement that has been taken by the authorities to express anti-communism and is reportedly supported by 70 million people; the regeneration of Orthodox Christianity in post-communist Russia; the emergence of the Aum Shinrikyo doomsday cult in Japan; and growing interest across western societies in myriad forms of Eastern mysticism and spiritual and therapeutic systems (yoga, meditation, Pilates, Shiatsu and so forth).

Although religious revivalism can be seen as a consequence of the larger upsurge in identity politics, religion has proved to be a particularly potent means of regenerating personal and social identity in modern circumstances. As modern societies are increasingly atomistic, diffuse and pluralized, there is, arguably, a greater thirst for the sense of meaning, purpose and certainty that religious consciousness appears to offer. This applies because religion provides believers with a world-view and moral vision that has higher, or indeed supreme, authority, because it stems from a supposedly divine source. Religion thus defines the very grounds of people's being; it gives them an ultimate frame of reference as well as a moral orientation in a world increasingly marked by **moral relativism**. In addition, religion generates a powerful sense of social solidarity, connecting people to one another at a 'thick' or deep level, as opposed to the 'thin' connectedness that is conventional in modern societies.

Religious revivalism has nevertheless served a variety of political purposes. Three of these have been particularly prominent. The first is that religion has been an increasingly important component of social conservatism, offering to strengthen the moral fabric of society through a return to religious values and practices. Such a religiously-orientated moral conservatism has been particularly evident in the USA since the 1970s, as the new Christian Right sought to fuse religion and politics in attempting to 'turn America back to Christ'. Through its influence on the Republican Party, and particularly on presidents such as Ronald Reagan and George W. Bush, the new Christian Right has made moral and cultural issues, such as anti-abortion, 'creationism' and opposition to gun control, gay rights and stem cell research, as prominent in US politics as traditional ones such as the economy and foreign policy. Second, religion has been an increasingly significant component, even the defining feature, of forms of ethnic nationalism. The attraction of religion rather than the nation as the principal source of political identity is that it provides a supposedly primordial and seemingly unchangeable basis for the establishment of group membership. India has witnessed an upsurge in both Hindu nationalism and Sikh nationalism. Hindu

Ayatollah Khomeini (1900–89)

Iranian cleric and political leader. The son and grandson of Shi'a clergy, Khomeini was one of the foremost scholars in the major theological centre in Qom until being expelled from Iran in 1964. His return from exile in 1979 sparked the 'Islamic Revolution', leaving the Ayatollah (literally, 'gift of Allah') as the supreme leader of the world's first Islamic state until his death. Breaking decisively with the Shi'a tradition that the clergy remain outside politics, Khomeini's world-view was rooted in a clear division between the oppressed, understood largely as the poor and excluded of the developing world, and the oppressors, seen as the twin Satans: the USA and the Soviet Union, capitalism and communism. Islam thus became a theo-political project aimed at regenerating the Islamic world by ridding it of occupation and corruption from outside.

nationalists in the Bharatiya Janata Party (BJP), the more radical World Hindu Council and its parent body, the RSS, have sought to make Hinduism the basis of national identity and called for the 'Hinduization' of Muslim, Sikh, Jain and other communities. Sikh nationalists have looked to establish 'Khalistan', located in present-day Punjab, with Sikhism as the state religion and its government obliged to ensure its unhindered flourishing. In Israel, a collection of small ultra-orthodox Jewish parties and groups have become more prominent in transforming Zionism into a defence of the 'Greater Land of Israel'. This has often been expressed in a campaign to build Jewish settlements in territory occupied in the Six-Day War of 1967 and then formally incorporated into Israel. Third, religion has gained its greatest political influence through providing the basis for militant politico-cultural regeneration, based on the belief that, in Khomeini's words, 'Politics is religion'. This notion of religion as a theo-political project is usually referred to as 'religious fundamentalism'.

The fundamentalist upsurge

The term '**fundamentalism**' was first used in debates within American Protestantism in the early twentieth century. Between 1910 and 1915, evangelical Protestants published a series of pamphlets entitled *The Fundamentals*, upholding the inerrancy, or literal truth, of the Bible in the face of modern interpretations of Christianity. However, the term is highly controversial, being commonly associated with inflexibility, dogmatism and authoritarianism. As a result, many of those who are classified as fundamentalists reject the term as simplistic or demeaning, preferring instead to describe themselves as 'traditionalists', 'conservatives', 'evangelicals', 'revivalists' and so forth. However, unlike alternative terms, fundamentalism has the advantage of conveying the idea of a religio-political movement or project, rather than simply the assertion of **scriptural literalism** (although this remains a feature of certain forms of fundamentalism). Religious fundamentalism is thus characterized by a rejection of the distinction between religion and politics. Politics, in effect, *is* religion. This implies that religious principles are not restricted to personal or private life, but are seen as the organizing principles of public existence, including law, social conduct and the economy as well as politics. Although

● **Fundamentalism**: A style of thought in which certain principles are recognized as essential truths that have unchallengeable and overriding authority, often associated with fierce, and sometimes fanatical, commitment.

● **Scriptural literalism**: A belief in the literal truth of sacred texts, which as the revealed word of God have unquestionable authority.

Religious fundamentalism

The word 'fundamentalism' derives from the Latin *fundamentum*, meaning 'base'. The core idea of religious fundamentalism is that religion cannot and should not be confined to the private sphere, but finds its highest and proper expression in the politics of popular mobilization and social regeneration. Although often related, religious fundamentalism should not be equated with scriptural literalism, as the 'fundamentals' are often extracted through a process of 'dynamic' interpretation by a charismatic leader. Religious fundamentalism also differs from ultra-orthodoxy, in that it advances a programme for the moral and political regeneration of society in line with religious principles, as opposed to a retreat from corrupt secular society into the purity of faith-based communal living.

some claim that fundamentalist tendencies can be identified in all the world's major religions – Christianity, Islam, Hinduism, Judaism, Buddhism and Sikhism – others argue that they tend to be confined to Islam and Protestant Christianity, as only these religious traditions have the capacity to throw up comprehensive programmes of political renewal, albeit with very different characters and ambitions.

It is difficult to generalize about the causes of the fundamentalist upsurge that has occurred since the late twentieth century because, in different parts of the world, it has taken different doctrinal forms and displayed contrasting ideological features. What is clear, nevertheless, is that fundamentalism arises in deeply troubled societies, particularly societies afflicted by an actual or perceived crisis of identity. Ruthven (2005) thus emphasized that fundamentalism is driven by a 'search for meaning' in a world of growing doubt and uncertainty. A variety of developments have helped to generate such doubt and uncertainty. Three factors in particular have strengthened the fundamentalist impulse in religion by contributing to such crises: secularization, globalization and postcolonialism. Secularization has contributed to a decline of traditional religion and a weakening of established morality. In that sense, fundamentalism represents a moral protest against decadence and hypocrisy; it aims to restore 'rightful' order and re-establish the link between the human world and the divine. Fundamentalism can therefore be seen as the antidote to moral relativism.

Religious fundamentalism may also be intrinsically linked to the advance of globalization. As traditional societies are disrupted by increased global flows of people, goods, ideas and images, religious fundamentalism may emerge as a counter-revolutionary force, a source of resistance to the advance of amorality and corruption. This helps to explain why fundamentalists generally possess a Manichaean world-view, one that emphasizes conflict between 'light' and 'darkness', or good and evil. If 'we' are a chosen people acting according to the will of God, 'they' are not merely people with whom we disagree, but a body actively subverting God's purpose on Earth; they represent nothing less than the 'forces of darkness'. Political conflict, for fundamentalists, is therefore a battle or war, and ultimately either the believers or the infidels must prevail. Finally, the impact of postcolonialism helps to explain why, although fundamentalism can be found across the globe, its most potent and influential manifestations have been found in the developing world in general and the Muslim world in particular. Postcolonial societies inherited a weakened sense of identity, compounded by a debilitating attachment to western values and institutions, particularly among elite groups. In such circumstances, religious fundamentalism has been attractive both because it offers the prospect of a non-western, and often specifically anti-western, political identity, and because, particularly since the decline of revolutionary socialism in the 1970s, it articulates the aspirations of the urban poor and the lower middle classes.

CHALLENGES TO THE WEST

The issues of identity, culture and religion have acquired particular prominence through their association with attempts to challenge and displace the politico-cultural hegemony of the West. This marks a recognition of two things. The first is that the material and political domination of the West had an important

● **Non-Aligned Movement**: An organization of countries, founded in 1961, that avoided formal political and economic affiliation to either of the Cold War power blocs and committed itself to values such as peaceful coexistence and mutual non-interference.

cultural dimension, reflected in the advance of so-called 'western' values, such as individualism, formal equality, secularism and materialism. The second was that, if this culture bore the imprint of western domination, a non-western, or perhaps anti-western, culture had to be established in its place. This can be seen in the development of the broad phenomenon of postcolonialism, as well as in attempts in Asia to develop a distinctive system of values. However, it has been expressed most significantly in the rise of political Islam, and in the idea that Islam represents a morally superior alternative to western liberalism.

Postcolonialism

The structures of western political domination over the rest of the world were challenged many years before its cultural and ideological domination was called into question. Anti-colonialism emerged in the inter-war period, but it reached its high point of influence in the post-1945 period, as the British, French, Dutch and other European empires collapsed in the face of the growing strength of independence movements. In a sense, the colonizing Europeans had taken with them the seeds of their own destruction, the doctrine of nationalism. Anti-colonialism was therefore based on the same principle of national self-determination that had inspired European nation-building in the nineteenth century, and which had provided the basis for the reconstruction of Europe after WWI. Although liberal ideas about self-government and constitutionalism were sometimes influential, most anti-colonial movements in Africa, Asia and Latin America were attracted to some form of socialism, and most commonly, revolutionary Marxism. Drawing inspiration from the same Enlightenment principles as liberalism, Marxism's strength was both that its theory of class struggle provided an explanation for imperialism in terms of capitalism's quest for profit, and that its commitment to revolution provided colonized peoples with a means of emancipation in the form of the armed struggle. However, as discussed earlier, the influence of socialism and particularly Marxism in the developing world steadily declined from the 1970s onwards, as the emergence of postcolonialism was reflected in the quest for non-western and sometimes anti-western political philosophies. A major contributory factor to this was growing resentment against ex-imperial powers that, in many cases, continued to exercise economic and cultural domination over those countries that they had formerly ruled as colonies. Postcolonialism and neo-colonialism were therefore often linked processes.

The characteristic feature of postcolonialism is that it sought to give the developing world a distinctive political voice separate from the universalist pretensions of liberalism and socialism. An early but highly influential attempt to do this was undertaken at the Bandung Conference of 1955, when 29 mostly newly-independent African and Asian countries, including Egypt, Ghana, India and Indonesia, initiated what later became known as the **Non-Aligned Movement**. They saw themselves as an independent power bloc, offering a 'Third World' (see p. 36) perspective on global political, economic and cultural priorities. This 'third-worldism' defined itself in contradistinction to both western and Soviet models of development. A more militant form of third world politics nevertheless emerged from the Tricontinental Conference held in Havana in 1966. For the first time, this brought Latin America (including the Caribbean) together with Africa and Asia – hence the name 'tricontinental'.

Frantz Fanon (1925–61)

A Martinique-born French revolutionary theorist, Fanon is best known for his views on the anti-colonial struggle. In *Black Skin, White Masks* (1952), he mixed personal reflection with social analysis to explore the psychological damage done to black people in a 'whitened' world. In his classic work, *The Wretched of the Earth* (1961), he drew on psychiatry, politics, sociology and the existentialism of Jean-Paul Sartre in arguing that only total revolution and absolute violence can help black or colonized people liberate themselves from the social and psychological scars of imperialism. Fanon died after contracting leukaemia, and, at his request, his body was returned to Algeria and buried with honours by the Algerian National Army of Liberation. His other works include *Towards the African Revolution* (1964).

However, as it is a form of identity politics that draws inspiration from indigenous religions, cultures and traditions, postcolonial theory tends to be highly disparate. It has been reflected in Gandhi's political philosophy, which was based on a religious ethic of non-violence and self-sacrifice that was ultimately rooted in Hinduism. In this view, violence, 'the doctrine of the sword', is a western imposition upon India. By contrast, Frantz Fanon emphasized the link between anti-colonialism and violence. He argued that decolonization requires, in effect, a new species of man to be created, and that this is largely achieved as the psychological burden of colonial subjugation is rejected through the cathartic experience of violence. Edward Said (see p. 204), perhaps the most influential postcolonial theorist, examined how Eurocentric values and theories served to establish western cultural and political hegemony over the rest of the world, especially through the device of **Orientalism**. However, critics of postcolonialism have argued that, in turning its back on the western intellectual tradition, it has abandoned progressive politics and been used, too often, as a justification for traditional values and authority structures. This issue has been particularly controversial in relation to the tension between cultural rights and women's rights (see p. 203).

Asian values

● **Orientalism**: Stereotypical depictions of 'the Orient' or Eastern culture generally which are based on distorted and invariably demeaning western assumptions.

● **Asian values**: Values that supposedly reflect the history, culture and religious backgrounds of Asian societies; examples include social harmony, respect for authority and a belief in the family.

The idea that Asian culture and beliefs may constitute an alternative to western ones gained momentum during the 1980s and 1990s, fuelled by the emergence of Japan as an economic superpower and the success of the so-called Asian 'tiger' economies – Hong Kong, South Korea, Thailand and Singapore. This position was outlined most clearly by the Bangkok Declaration of 1993, when Asian state representatives from Iran to Mongolia, meeting in preparation for the World Conference on Human Rights in Vienna, issued a bold statement in favour of what they called '**Asian values**'. While not rejecting the idea of universal human rights, Asian values drew attention to supposed differences between western and Asian value systems as part of an argument in favour of taking culture difference into account in formulating human rights. Particularly keen advocates of this view included Mahathir Mohamad and Lee Kuan Yew, at that

CONCEPT

Confucianism

Confucianism is a system of ethics formulated by Confucius (551–479 BCE) and his disciples that was primarily outlined in *The Analects*. Confucian thought has concerned itself with the twin themes of human relations and the cultivation of the self. The emphasis on *ren* ('humanity' or 'love') has usually been interpreted as implying support for traditional ideas and values, notably filial piety, respect, loyalty and benevolence. The stress on *junzi* (the virtuous person) suggests a capacity for human development and potential for perfection realized, in particular, through education. Confucianism has been seen, with Taoism and Buddhism, as one of the three major Chinese systems of thought, although many take Confucian ideas to be coextensive with Chinese civilization itself.

time the prime ministers, respectively, of Malaysia and Singapore. From this perspective, human rights had traditionally been constructed on the basis of culturally-biased western assumptions. Individualism had been emphasized over the interests of the community; rights had been given preference over duties; and civic and political freedoms had been extolled above socio-economic well-being. The recognition of Asian values sought to rectify this. At their heart, was a vision of social harmony and cooperation grounded in loyalty and respect for all forms of authority – towards parents within the family, teachers at school and the government within society as a whole. Allied to a keen work ethic and thrift, these values were seen as a recipe for social stability and economic success.

The idea of Asian values was dealt a damaging blow by the Asian financial crisis of 1997–8. This occurred not only because it cast doubt over the image of 'rising Asia', but also, and more seriously, because Asian values were sometimes held to be responsible for the crisis in the first place. In this view, Asian economies had faltered because of a failure fully to embrace market principles such as entrepreneurialism, competition and 'rugged' individualism, and this failure had stemmed from aspects of Asian culture, particularly an emphasis on deference, authority, duty and loyalty. Nevertheless, the rise of China and, to a lesser extent, India has revived interest in the idea of Asian values, although in its modern form it tends to be orientated more specifically around the alleged strengths of Chinese civilization and particularly of Confucianism. However, the general notion of Asian values has also attracted criticism. For some, it simply serves as an excuse for the survival of authoritarian rule and absence of liberal-democratic reform in many parts of Asia. The key Asian value, from this perspective, is political passivity, an unwillingness to question authority based on a trade-off between economic well-being and political freedom. The notion of an 'Asian civilization' from which a distinctive set of values can be seen to derive has also been criticized, in line with wider concerns about the 'tectonic' model of civilizations. Not only does Asian culture encompass a wide range of national traditions and a mixture of religions (Islam, Hinduism, Buddhism, Christianity and so on), but its national traditions are often highly diverse as well. For example, so-called 'Chinese civilization' is not defined by Confucianism but, rather, by the competing influences of Confucianism, Buddhism and Daoism overlaid, in the modern period, by a Maoist version of Marxism-Leninism.

Islam and the West

The rise of political Islam, and particularly 9/11 and the advent of the 'war on terror', created the image of a deep, and perhaps civilizational, clash between Islam and the West. 'Clash of civilizations' theorists were quick to proclaim that this was to be one of the major fault-lines in twenty-first-century global politics. However, the image of deeply-rooted tension between Islam and the West has two quite distinct faces. The first portrays political Islam, and possibly Islam itself, as implacably anti-western, committed to the expulsion of western influences from the Muslim world and maybe to the wider overthrow of western secularism. In this view, the West is subject to an 'Islamic threat' that must be combatted, not simply through the defeat of terrorism and *jihadist* insurrection,

● **Jihad**: (Arabic) An Islamic term literally meaning 'strive' or 'struggle'; although the term is sometimes equated with 'holy war' (lesser *jihad*), it is more properly understood as an inner struggle for faith (greater *jihad*).

Focus on ...

Cultural rights or women's rights?

Are women's rights essentially a western concept? Which identity is more important: culture or gender? Feminists and others often argue that cultural rights in general (linked also, for example, to multiculturalism) and opposition to the West in particular are often invoked to defend or justify violations of a whole range of women's rights, thereby strengthening patriarchal power. This has been particularly evident when attempts have been made to reconfigure culture and politics on the basis of religion. Ruthven (2005), for instance, identified one of the key features of religious fundamentalism as the tendency to control, and limit, the social role of women, and to act as a 'patriarchal protest movement'. The values and norms of Muslim societies have drawn special criticism is this respect, based on practices ranging from female dress code and polygamy through to so-called 'honour killings'. Not only do such cultural beliefs and practices block the advance of universal human rights, but, by oppressing women, they may hold back social and economic development, increase birth rates and distort gender relations, making such societies poorer and, arguably, more prone to violence.

However, some postcolonial feminists have argued that women's rights should be understood within a cultural context, recognizing that issues of gender cannot be separated from matters of race, religion and ethnicity. In this view, the western idea of gender equality, based on supposedly universalist liberalism, often fails women because it is based on a model of female identity that abstracts women from the family, social and cultural context that gives their lives meaning and purpose. Gender equality both devalues women's traditional roles as home-makers and mothers and exposes them to the rigours and pressures of life in the public sphere. In Muslim countries, such as Iran, Pakistan, Sudan and, to some extent, Turkey, forms of 'Islamic feminism' have thus emerged, in which the imposition of *Shari'a* law and a return to traditional moral and religious principles have been portrayed as a means of enhancing the status of women, threatened by the spread of western attitudes and values. From this perspective, the veil and other dress codes, and the exclusion of women from public life, have been viewed by some Muslim women as symbols of liberation.

but also through the destruction of the fundamentalist ideas and doctrines that have nourished and inspired them. The second image of this clash suggests that Islam, and especially the Arab world, has consistently been a victim of western intervention and manipulation, supported by demeaning and insulting forms of 'Islamophobia'. In other words, the problem is the West, not Islam. Is conflict between the Muslim world and the Christian West inevitable? And what role has religion played in inspiring this antagonism?

Nature of political Islam

Islam is the world's second largest religion and its fastest growing. There are between 1.5 and 1.7 billion Muslims in the world today, more than one fifth of the world's population, with at least 49 countries having a Muslim majority. The strength of Islam is concentrated geographically in Asia and Africa; it is estimated, for example, that over half the population of Africa will soon be Muslim. However, it has also spread into Europe and elsewhere. Islam is certainly not, and has never been, just a religion. Rather, it is a complete way of life, with instructions on moral, political and economic behaviour for individuals and nations

Edward Said (1935–2003)

Jerusalem-born US academic and literary critic. Said was a prominent advocate of the Palestinian cause and a founding figure of postcolonial theory. He developed, from the 1970s onwards, a humanist critique of the western Enlightenment that uncovered its links to colonialism and highlighted 'narratives of oppression', cultural and ideological biases that disempower colonized peoples by representing them as the non-western 'other', particularly applying this to the Middle East. He is best known for the notion of 'Orientalism', which operates through a 'subtle but persistent Eurocentric prejudice against Arabo-Islamic peoples and culture'. Said's key works include *Orientalism* ([1978] 2003) and *Culture and Imperialism* (1993).

alike. The 'way of Islam' is based on the teachings of the Prophet Mohammed (*circa* 570–632), as revealed in the Koran, which is regarded by all Muslims as the revealed word of Allah, and the *Sunnah*, or 'beaten path', the traditional customs observed by devout Muslims and said to be based on the Prophet's own life. There are two principal sects within Islam, which developed within fifty years of Mohammed's death. The Sunni sect represents the majority of Muslims, while the Shi'a or Shi'ite sect (sometimes called Shi'ism) contains just over one tenth of Muslims, mainly concentrated in Iran and Iraq.

Fundamentalism in Islam does not mean a belief in the literal truth of the Koran, for this is accepted by all Muslims, and in that sense all Muslims are fundamentalists. Instead, it means an intense and militant faith in Islamic beliefs as the overriding principles of social life and politics, as well as of personal morality. Islamic fundamentalists wish to establish the primacy of religion over politics. In practice, this means the founding of an 'Islamic state', a **theocracy** ruled by spiritual rather than temporal authority, and applying the **Shari'a**. The *Shari'a* lays down a code for legal and righteous behaviour, including a system of punishment for most crimes as well as rules of personal conduct for both men and women. In that sense, Islam should be distinguished from 'Islamism' (see p. 205). Islamism refers either to a political creed based on Islamic ideas and principles, or to the political movement that has been inspired by that creed. It has a number of core aims. First, it promotes pan-Islamic unity, distinguishing Islamism from traditional political nationalism. Second, it seeks the purification of the Islamic world through the overthrow of 'apostate' leaders of Muslim states (secularized or pro-western leaders). Third, it calls for the removal of western, and especially US, influence from the Muslim world, and possibly a wider politico-cultural struggle against the West itself. However, the relationship between Islam and Islamism is complex and contested. While Islamists have claimed that their ideas articulate the deepest insights of Islam shorn of western and colonial influence, critics argue that Islamism is a political distortion of Islam, based on a selective and perverted interpretation of religious texts.

Although the revival of Islamic fundamentalism can be traced back to the 1920s, and particularly the founding of the Muslim Brotherhood (see p. 206), its most significant developments came in 1979 with the popular revolution that brought Ayatollah Khomeini to power and led to Iran declaring itself an Islamic

● **Theocracy**: Literally, rule by God; the principle that religious authority should prevail over political authority, usually through the domination of church over state.

● **Shari'a**: (Arabic) Literally the 'way' or 'path'; divine Islamic law, based on principles expressed in the Koran.

Focus on . . .

Islamism: religion as politics?

Islamism (also called 'political Islam', 'radical Islam' or 'activist Islam') is a controversial term with a variety of definitions. It is usually used to describe a politico-religious ideology, as opposed to simply a belief in Islam (although Islamists themselves reject this distinction, on the grounds that Islam is a holistic moral system that applies to public as well as private affairs). Some link Islamism to Salafism or Wahhabism, a Sunni Islamic movement that surfaced in what later became Saudi Arabia during the nineteenth century and was committed to rooting out modern and particularly western influences and/or to imposing a strictly literal interpretation of the scriptures. However, Shi'a versions of Islamism have also developed, usually linked to Iran's 'Islamic Revolution', that are based on an 'activist' interpretation of the scriptures. Although Islamist ideology has no single creed or political manifestation, certain common beliefs can be identified. These include the following:

- Society should be reconstructed in line with the religious principles and ideals of Islam; Islamism is thus often portrayed as 'political Islam'.
- The modern secular state is rejected in favour of an 'Islamic state', meaning that religious principles (usually embodied in *Shari'a* law) and authority have primacy over political principles and authority.
- The West and western values are viewed as corrupt and corrupting, justifying, for some, the notion of a *jihad* against them.

Two broad tendencies can nevertheless be identified within Islamism. In one, it operates primarily as a form of identity politics, based on the search for a distinctively Muslim political identity and emphasizing religious revivalism. In the other, it is an explicitly theocratic and anti-democratic political project that aims for the rebirth of Islam through the restoration of the *Caliphate* (an Islamic republic ruled by the *Caliph*, literally the 'successor' or 'representative').

Republic. The Soviet war in Afghanistan, 1979–89, led to the growth of the Mujahideen, a loose collection of religiously-inspired resistance groups that received financial or military support from the USA, Iran and Pakistan. The Taliban, who ruled Afghanistan, 1996–2001, developed out of these Mujahideen groups. Islamists have also seized power, usually temporarily, in states such as Sudan, Pakistan, Somalia and Lebanon (through the influence of the pro-Iranian Hezbollah movement). A range of new *jihadi* groups have also emerged since the 1990s – the most important of which is al-Qaeda (see p. 301), led by Osama bin Laden – which have given expression to a particularly militant form of Islamism. For these groups, a commitment to Islam takes the form of a *jihad*, carried out especially against the USA and Israel (the 'Jewish-Christian crusaders'), which seeks to remove western influence from the Arab world in general and from Saudi Arabia in particular. What is the significance of militant Islamism, and how is it best understood? Three broad interpretations have been advanced.

First, the source of Islamist militancy has been seen to lie within Islam itself. Such a view is in line with the 'clash of civilizations' thesis, in that it implies that there is a basic incompatibility between Islamic values and those of the liberal-democratic West. From this perspective, Islam is inherently totalitarian: the goal of constructing an Islamic state based on *Shari'a* law is starkly anti-pluralist and irreconcilable with the notion of a public/private divide. In other words, what neoconservative US theorists called 'Islamo-fascism' is not a perversion of Islam,

THE MUSLIM BROTHERHOOD

Type: Religious movement • **Established:** 1928 • **Location:** Egypt, West Asia and North Africa

The Muslim Brotherhood was founded in 1928 at Ismailia, Egypt, by Hassan al-Banna (1906–49). Initially focused on building up a network of schools, hospitals and social services, the Brotherhood turned to politics during the 1930s and, briefly, to violence, operating in and out of the shadows until it was banned by President Nasser in 1954. By this time, it had spread into Jordan, Syria, Palestine, Libya, Sudan and elsewhere. Although it remained outlawed in Egypt under Hosni Mubarak, the Brotherhood fielded 'independent ' candidates in the 2005 parliamentary election, winning 88 seats and becoming, in effect, the first legitimate opposition force in modern Egypt. Following the 2011 uprising that overthrew Mubarak, the Brotherhood formally entered politics, under the banner of the Freedom and Justice Party. When parliamentary elections were held in Tunisia, Egypt and Morocco in late 2011 and early 2012, in each case they brought parties set up, or inspired, by the Brotherhood to power, Mohamed Morsi, the Brotherhood-backed candidate, becoming Egypt's president in June 2012. However, Morsi was removed by the military in July 2013 after mass protests, the Egyptian courts later outlawing the Brotherhood and any organization or activity associated with it.

Significance: The Muslim Brotherhood is the world's oldest and most influential Islamist movement. It pioneered a model of political activism combined with Islamic charitable works that has subsequently been widely embraced across the Muslim world. By the end of WWII, the Brotherhood had an estimated membership of two million, about 500,000 in Egypt alone. However, although it kept alive the flame of political Islam, legal proscription and political repression consigned the Brotherhood to the political margins for most of the post-1945 period. Although the rise of Islamism from the 1970s onwards generated renewed interest in the Brotherhood, it was the Arab Spring of 2011 (see p. 211) that transformed its fortunes, allowing it to spearhead a form of pan-Islamism that promised to alter the politics of the Middle East and North Africa fundamentally. As well as winning power in Egypt, Tunisia and Morocco, and forming the main opposition Jordan, the Brotherhood's influence extended to the Gaza Strip (though Hamas, founded by members of the Brotherhood in 1987) and Iraq (through the Iraqi Islamic Party, the largest Sunni party in the country). Brotherhood-linked parties have had the advantage that were better organized and usually better funded than their political rivals; that they were untainted by association with ousted regimes; and that a religiously-based appeal continues to be strong in societies that remain, despite revolutionary upheavals, socially conservative. Nevertheless, the dramatic reversal that the Brotherhood's suffered in Egypt in 2013 highlights the movement's vulnerability if it fails to maintain popular support and/or comes into direct conflict with the military.

However, debate surrounds the ideological character of the Muslim Brotherhood. Since its inception, the Brotherhood has been committed to the establishment of an Islamic state based on the *Shari'a*, but the shift towards pragmatic politics that began after the 1970s has seen Brotherhood-linked parties enter the political mainstream by attempting to reconcile Islamism with democratic and, sometimes, liberal beliefs. As such, it was perhaps reconstructing itself around the goal of a Turkish-style secular state run by an Islamist party, rather than an Iranian-style explicitly Islamic state. The attempt to construct a form of democratic or constitutional Islamism may, nevertheless, weaken the Muslim Brotherhood by exposing it to attack from both the secular and liberal-democratic forces that initiated the Arab Spring, and from Salafi groups pushing for bolder and more radical Islamization. Critics of the Muslim Brotherhood allege either that it has not fully broken with its violent past, or that, behind a liberal-democratic façade, it remains committed to militant Islamism, meaning that commitments on women's rights, tolerance towards religious minorities and genuine political pluralism may be only paper thin. Developments in Egypt under Morsi, such as seizure of 'temporary' unlimited powers by the presidency, have been used to support the latter view.

but a realization of certain of its core beliefs. However, such a view of Islam seriously misrepresents Islam's central tenets. According to the Prophet Mohammed, for instance, the 'greater *jihad*' is not a political struggle against the infidel, but an inner struggle: the struggle to become a better person through moral and spiritual discipline. Moreover, such thinking ignores the extent to which Islam has not only drawn on western ideas, including the philosophy of Aristotle, but has also had a significant impact on western, and particularly European, art and culture.

Second, resurgent Islamism has been portrayed as a specific response to particular historical circumstances. Bernard Lewis (2004), for example, argued that the Muslim world is in crisis largely because of the decline and stagnation of the Middle East and the sense of humiliation that has therefore gripped the Islamic, and more specifically Arab, world. This decline stems from the collapse of the once powerful Ottoman empire and its carve-up by the UK and France after WWI, as well as the sense of powerlessness that has been engendered by the protracted Arab–Israeli conflict (see p. 208). Furthermore, the end of colonialism in the post-1945 period brought little benefit to the Arab world, both because Middle Eastern regimes tended to be inefficient and corrupt, and because formal colonialism was succeeded by neo-colonialism, particularly as US influence in the region expanded. In the final decades of the twentieth century, population growth across the Arab world, combined with economic stagnation, growing foreign interference and the failure of Arab socialism, meant that Islamist ideas and creeds attracted growing support from amongst the young and the politically committed.

Third, Islamism has been interpreted as a manifestation of a much broader and, arguably, deeper ideological tendency: anti-westernism. Paul Berman (2003) thus placed militant Islamism within the context of the totalitarian movements that emerged from the apparent failure of liberal society in the aftermath of WWI. The significance of WWI was that it exploded the optimistic belief in progress and the advance of reason, fuelling support for darker, anti-liberal movements. In this light, political Islam shares much in common with fascism and communism, in that each of them promises to rid society of corruption and immorality and to make society anew as a 'single blocklike structure, solid and eternal'. Buruma and Margalit (2004) portrayed Islamism as a form of **Occidentalism**. From this perspective, western society is characterized by individualism, secularism and relativism; it is a mechanical civilization organized around greed and materialism. Occidentalism, in contrast, offers the prospect of organic unity, moral certainty and politico-spiritual renewal. Such ideas were first developed in the writings of counter-Enlightenment thinkers in Germany in the early nineteenth century, and they helped to fuel European fascism and Japanese imperialism in the inter-war period. However, in the modern world they are most clearly articulated through the ideas of political Islam.

However, Islamism does not have a single doctrinal or political character. The two most influential forms of political Islam have stemmed from **Salafism** and Shi'a Islam. Salafism (or **Wahhabism**) is the official version of Islam in Saudi Arabia, the world's first fundamentalist Islamic state. Its origins date back to the eighteenth century and an alliance between the supporters of a particularly strict and austere form of Islam and early figures in the Saudi dynasty. Salafis seek to restore Islam by purging it of heresies and modern inventions; amongst other things, they ban pictures, photographs, musical instruments, singing, videos and

● **Occidentalism**: A rejection of the cultural and political inheritance of the West, particularly as shaped by the Reformation and the Enlightenment; another term for 'anti-westernism'.

● **Salafism**: A Sunni school of thought that is associated with a literalist, strict and puritanical approach to Islam.

● **Wahhabism**: An ultra-conservative movement within Sunni Islam, sometimes portrayed as an orientation within Salafism.

The Arab–Israeli conflict

1880s	Jewish immigration into Palestine begins and Zionist ideology emerges.
1917	The Balfour Declaration, at the beginning of the British mandate (1917–47), establishes UK support for the creation of a 'Jewish national home' in Palestine.
1947	The UN partition plan proposes the creation of Arab and Jewish states in Palestine, rejected by the Arabs.
1948	Declaration of the State of Israel precipitates the 1948 Arab–Israeli war which leads to many Palestinians becoming refugees in surrounding Arab countries.
1956	The Suez crisis leads to an Israeli invasion of the Sinai peninsula, although it later withdraws under US and international pressure.
1967	Israel defeats Egypt and Syria in the Six-Day War, leading to the occupation of the Gaza Strip (from Egypt), the West Bank (from Jordan) and the Golan Heights (from Syria).
1973	Israel defeats Egypt and Syria in the Yom Kippur War, after a surprise joint attack on the Jewish day of fasting.
1978–9	The Camp David Accords, negotiated by the USA, lead to the 1979 Israel–Egypt Peace Treaty.
1982	Israel attacks Lebanon in response to Palestinian terrorist attacks, retreating from most Lebanese territory by 1985.
1987–93	The First *Intifada* (rebellion) witnesses a Palestinian uprising against the occupation of the West Bank and Gaza Strip, and the Palestinian Declaration of Independence in 1988.
1990-1	The Gulf War involves Iraqi missile attacks on Israeli cities and Israel's nuclear facilities.
1993–2000	Oslo Accords negotiated between Israel and the Palestine Liberation Organization (PLO), preparing the way for the establishment of a self-governing Palestinian authority.
2000–5	The Second *Intifada* marks a resurgence of Palestinian protest and militancy.
2006	Clashes between Israel and Hezbollah lead to Israeli attacks on Beirut and much of southern Lebanon and a Hezbollah bombardment of northern Israeli cities.
2007–8	Israel launches full-scale invasion of Gaza Strip after a ceasefire negotiated with Hamas breaks down.

Sayyid Qutb (1906–66)

Egyptian writer and religious leader, sometimes seen as the father of modern political Islam. The son of a well-to-do farmer, Qutb was radicalized during a two-year study visit to the USA, which instilled in him a profound distaste for the materialism, immorality and sexual licentiousness he claimed to have encountered. Qutb's world-view, or 'Qutbism', highlighted the barbarism and corruption that westernization had inflicted on the world, with a return to strict Islamic practice in all aspects of life offering the only possibility of salvation. Qutb's primary targets were the westernized rulers of Egypt and other Muslim states. Imprisoned under Nasser in 1954–64, he was eventually tried for treason and executed.

television, and celebrations of Mohammad's birthday. Salafi ideas and beliefs had a particular impact on the Muslim Brotherhood, being most uncompromisingly expressed by its leading theorist, Sayyid Qutb. The Egyptian writer Mohammad Abd al-Salam Faraj, who was implicated in the assassination of President Anwar Sadat and executed in 1982, developed a revolutionary model of 'Qutbism', in which *jihad*, as the 'neglected obligation' or 'forgotten duty', was understood literally as the struggle for Islam against God's enemies. Such militant ideas influenced Osama bin Laden and al-Qaeda, as well as the Taliban regime in Afghanistan and the subsequent Taliban insurgencies in Afghanistan and Pakistan.

Shi'a fundamentalism stems from the quite different temper and doctrinal character of the Shi'a sect as opposed to the Sunni sect. Shi'as believe that divine guidance is about to re-emerge into the world with the return of the 'hidden imam', or the arrival of the Mahdi, a leader directly guided by God. Such ideas of revival or imminent salvation have given the Shi'a sect a messianic and emotional quality that is not enjoyed by the traditionally more sober Sunnis. This was evident in the mass demonstrations that accompanied Iran's 'Islamic Revolution', and it has also been apparent in popular agitation in Iran against the USA and western influence, as well as the campaigns against Israel by Hezbollah and Hamas. Iran's political system is nevertheless a complex mix of democratic and theocratic elements, the former represented by an elected president and parliament, and the latter by the highly powerful Supreme Leader (currently Ayatollah Ali Khamenei). Although hardliners gained control of the presidency in 2005, the 2013 presidential elections brought the pragmatic conservative, Hassan Rouhani, to power.

It would be a mistake, however, to suggest that all forms of Islamism are militant and revolutionary. By comparison with Christianity, Islam has generally been tolerant of other religions and rival belief systems, a fact that may provide the basis for reconciliation between Islamism and political pluralism. This can most clearly be seen in relation to the political developments in Turkey, where tensions have existed between the military, committed to the strict secularist principles on which the state of Turkey was established, and a growing Islamist movement. The Justice and Development Party (AK) has been in power since 2003, advancing a constitutional form of Islamism. AK has attempted to balance moderate conservative politics based on Islamic values with an acceptance of Turkey's secular democratic framework. Rather than choosing between East and West, it has tried to establish a Turkish identity that is confident in being part of both. A key aspect of this compromise is continuing attempts by Turkey to gain membership of the EU.

The political complexion of the Muslim and, more specifically, Arab world has been radically reshaped by the Arab Spring (also known as the 'Arab revolutions' or the 'Arab rebellions') of 2011 and its aftermath (see p. 211). The Arab Spring was a revolutionary wave of demonstrations and protests that swept through North Africa and parts of the Middle East, toppling four dictators. In January 2011, President Ben Ali fled Tunisia, bringing an end to his 23-year rule. The following month, Egypt's President Hosni Mubarak resigned after 18 days of mounting protests. In Libya, the 42-year rule of President Muammar Gaddafi was brought to an end by an eight-month civil war, in which rebel forces were supported by NATO aerial attacks, by means of a no-fly zone authorized by the UN Security Council. Other significant popular uprisings in the Arab world occurred in Yemen, where President Saleh was forced from power in February 2012, and in Syria, where protests against President Assad that began in March 2011 developed into a prolonged and bloody civil war.

In its initial phase, the Arab Spring appeared to herald a transition to democratic rule, giving the lie to the view that, being mired in a 'backward' culture and religious beliefs, the Arab world was not ready for democracy. The key demands of protestors were for the introduction of western-style democratic reforms, notably free and competitive elections, the rule of law and protections for civil liberties. Moreover, where regimes collapsed, this was invariably accompanied by the promise to hold free elections, as duly occurred in Tunisia and Egypt. However, the shift to electoral democracy created opportunities for Islamist radicals, who initially appeared to play only a marginal role in the protests. Not only were Islamist groups, often linked to the Muslim Brotherhood or its offshoots, generally better organized than their rivals, but post-revolutionary chaos and uncertainty offered fertile grounds for advancing the politics of religious regeneration. Some claimed that this development threatened to bring about a resurgence of political Islam, citing attempts in Egypt during Mohammed Morsi's one year as president, 2012–13, to skew the constitution and impose a moralizing agenda as evidence that 'liberal' or pluralist Islamism is a contradiction in terms. However, Morsi's overthrow by the Egyptian military in July 2013, and the subsequent banning of the Muslim Brotherhood and the seizure of its asserts, highlighted the continuing strength of forces associated with the old regime and created the possibility of an on-going struggle between the army and the Brotherhood, which may have repercussions far beyond Egypt. Such developments, together with the civil war in Syria and political instability in Libya, nevertheless underline the uncertainty that continues to surround the ideological significance of the Arab Spring.

The West and the 'Muslim question'

Not only has the Muslim world been troubled and challenged by its encounters with the 'modernized' West, but the West has also, at times, struggled to come to terms with Islam. This is what is sometimes called the 'Muslim question'. There are two versions of the idea of an 'Islamic threat', one internal and the other external. The idea of Islam as the 'enemy within' emerged not so much through

GLOBAL POLITICS IN ACTION . . .

The Arab Spring and its legacy

Events: On 17 December 2010, Mohamed Bouazizi, a Tunisian market trader who lived in Sidi Bouzid, some 300 km south of the capital Tunis, set fire to himself in protest against the confiscation of his cart and produce and his treatment by the police. Bouaziz died on 4 January 2011. This incident is often credited with having sparked the wave of protests in Tunisia which, on 14 January, led to the removal of President Ben Ali, after 24 years in power. Inspired by events in Tunisia, Egyptian demonstrators took to the streets on 25 January, calling for the removal of President Hosni Mubarak. Under growing pressure from the Egyptian military, and as protests escalated, Mubarak resigned

on 11 February. In Libya, demonstrations quickly led to an armed uprising and a civil war, in which rebel forces were supported by NATO aerial attacks, the capture and killing of Muammar Gaddafi on 22 October effectively signalling the collapse of his regime. The following month, Ali Abdullah Saleh agreed to step down as Yemeni president, formerly ceding power in February 2012. In Syria, protests that started in March 2011 against President Basher Assad developed, over succeeding months, into a highly complex and intractable civil war.

Significance: The protest movements that swept through much of North Africa and parts of the Middle East in 2011 were quickly dubbed the 'Arab Spring'. These rebellions have nevertheless unleashed a complex range of forces, meaning that debate about the significance of the Arab Spring may continue for many years. At least four interpretations have been advanced, although none is likely to be persuasive on its own. In the first, the Arab Spring is seen as the 'Arab world's 1989', the beginning of its transition from authoritarianism to sustainable democracy. The overthrow of at least four dictators and the holding of the Arab world's first free and fair elections, in Tunisia, Egypt and Morocco in late 2011 and early 2012, help to support this view. However, democratization requires a process of consolidation through which key groups and interests (including those linked to the old regime) are reconciled to the new, democratic 'rules of the game'. In the case of the Arab Spring, this applies particularly to the military and the Muslim Brotherhood (in whatever form), and, as

Mohamed Morsi's short and controversial presidency in Egypt demonstrated, the reconciliation of neither group can be taken for granted.

In the second interpretation, the Arab Spring has sparked a resurgence of political Islam. Despite their initial marginalization, Brotherhood-linked groups were bolstered by the Arab Spring, both because it led to the lifting of restrictions on their political activities and because the introduction of elections provided them, by virtue of their level of organization and the appeal of religion, with a sure route to power. However, as once again shown by developments in Morsi's Egypt, attempts by Brotherhood-linked parties to advance an Islamist agenda may weaken their public support and leave them politically vulnerable.

In the third interpretation, the Arab Spring has been seen as a brief interlude before the (inevitable) return of dictatorship to the Arab world. In this view, the divisions and instability provoked by the Arab Spring have merely underlined the importance of the military as the only reliable source of political order, and created opportunities for it to re-enter politics sooner or later, claiming to be the 'nation's saviour'. In the fourth interpretation, the Arab Spring has significantly strengthened divisions in the Arab and wider Muslim world between Sunni and Shi'a forms of Islam. Although the flames of this conflict were lit in Iraq, they have burned most fiercely during the Syrian civil war, which can be seen as a 'proxy war' between Sunni Muslims and Shi'a Muslims, ultimately for control of the Middle East.

Focus on ...

Promoting democracy: for or against?

Do democratic states have a right, even a duty, to interfere in the affairs of other states in order to promote democracy? If 'democracy promotion' is a legitimate foreign policy goal, how should it be pursued? Democracy promotion can be justified in at least four ways. First, as democracy is founded on values such as human dignity, individual rights and political equality, democratic rule is a universal good, applicable to all societies regardless of their history, culture and values. All those who have the ability to promote democracy therefore have a duty to do so. This assumes that there is, in effect, a thirst everywhere for democratic governance. Second, as authoritarian regimes repress opposition and deny citizens the right of political participation, democracy cannot be built through internal pressures alone and therefore needs external support. This support is likely to involve the use of force, as authoritarian regimes will rarely give up power willingly. Third, as suggested by the 'democratic peace' thesis, democracy increases the likelihood of peace and cooperation, at least in terms of relations amongst democratic states themselves. Fourth, democracy may have the practical advantage that, in widening access to political power, it reduces levels of discontent and disaffection and so helps to counter political extremism and even terrorism. In this view, authoritarian or despotic rule is one of the chief causes of instability and political violence.

The policy of democracy promotion has been widely criticized, however. For some, it is based on specious and self-serving reasoning, providing a high-sounding justification for what in practice amounts to an imperialist project designed to expand western hegemony and ensure access to vital energy resources. A second concern arises from doubts about the supposed universality of western-style democracy. While some argue, crudely, that Arab and wider Muslim populations are simply 'not ready for democracy', others suggest that democracy will legitimately take different forms in different parts of the world. In this case, a narrow focus on liberal-democratic reform is an example of Eurocentrism, and is likely to fail. A third concern is that the link between democracy and political moderation is by no means assured. For example, the introduction of multi-party elections in Algeria in 1991 looked likely to result in a sweeping victory for the militant Islamic Salvation Front, before the Algerian army intervened to repress a popularly backed tide of religious fundamentalism. Finally, the idea of intervention to promote democracy has been criticized as both morally and politically confused. Violating national self-determination in order to promote political freedom appears to be, at best, a contradictory position. Aside from moral qualms about this approach, it also risks arousing widespread resentment and hostility, which, in turn, makes the process of state-building (or democracy-building) intensely difficult.

the growth of Muslim immigration but through the emergence, from the late 1980s onwards, of a Muslim identity that gradually took on political overtones. This applied particularly amongst second-generation Muslim immigrants in Europe and the USA, who felt less attached than their parents to the culture of a 'country of origin' while feeling socially and culturally marginalized within their host society. Such circumstances can favour the emergence of religious consciousness, investing Islamic identity with a renewed fervour and pride. The so-called 'Rushdie affair' in 1989, when Islamic groups protested against the publication of Salman Rushdie's *Satanic Verses* on the grounds that it was anti-Islamic, provided both evidence of and a stimulus to cultural tensions that were growing within western societies, as did the publication in 2005 of twelve Danish cartoons, criticized for being insulting to the Prophet Mohammed. International developments also played a part in reinforcing a consciousness of Islamic identity. Whereas the Iranian Revolution and Afghan resistance to Soviet occupation provided evidence of Muslim self-assertion, the failure to resolve the Arab–Israeli conflict, western inaction over genocidal attacks on Bosnian Muslims in the 1990s, and the 'war on terror' generally and the wars in Afghanistan and Iraq in particular fuelled a sense of outrage and injustice, sometimes seen to reflect the wider 'Islamophobia' of western society. In cases such as the London bombings of 2005 (also known as '7/7'), such pressures have contributed to the growth of so-called 'home-grown' terrorism. It is also notable that, while not second-generation Muslim immigrants, many of those who established al-Qaeda and almost all of the men involved in the 9/11 attacks knew the West and in some cases had received a western education.

Western societies have reacted to the growth of Islamic consciousness in a variety of ways. In some cases, it has led to a backlash against multiculturalism, based on the belief that, as Islam is essentially anti-pluralist and anti-liberal, Muslim communities can never be properly integrated into western societies. This is an approach that has received particular support in France where the wearing of religious symbols and dress in state schools has been prohibited, largely in an attempt to prevent the adoption of Islamic headgear by Muslim girls. In other cases, it has led to attempts to support the emergence of moderate Muslim groups and ideas, while radical Islamic organizations, such as Hizb al-Tahrir (the Party of Liberation), have been banned or subject to restrictions. However, such attempts to defend liberal society, sometimes in the name of counter-terrorism, may also be counter-productive, in that they contribute to the idea that Islam is being demonized and that Muslim communities are under attack (as discussed in Chapter 12). Moreover, the size and nature of this internal 'Islamic threat' may be seriously exaggerated, as opinion polls consistently show that a large majority of Muslims in western societies support what are seen as liberal and pluralistic values. It is also evident that 'home-grown' terrorism appears to be least in evidence in the USA (despite being the 'Great Satan' for many Islamists) perhaps because, of all western societies, the USA, through its Constitution and the Bill of Rights, is the most clear about the values and principles on which its society is founded.

Nevertheless, Islam is also sometimes portrayed as an 'enemy without', confronting the West from beyond its own shores. This idea has certainly been strengthened by the development of the 'war on terror' into counter-insurgency wars in Afghanistan and Iraq, aimed at the eradication of Islamic terrorist organizations and the radical ideologies to which they adhere. In some senses, the thinking behind the 'war on terror' may reflect anti-Islamic, or anti-Arab, assumptions. For example, the notion that democracy has to be 'imposed' on the Middle East through US military intervention may reflect the belief that Muslim, and particularly Arab, societies are so entrenched in their backwardness and wedded to authoritarian values that they are incapable of bringing about democratization through their own efforts. This reflects the emphasis that has been placed by US policy-makers since the 1990s on 'democracy promotion' as a strategy for bringing peace to the Middle East and, in particular, for countering the spread of militant Islam and the associated threat of terrorism. Such thinking has, in part, been informed by the 'democratic peace' thesis (see p. 69), and can be traced back to Woodrow Wilson (see p. 445) or even, some argue, to Kant (see p. 15). A greater emphasis on promoting democracy was evident under the

● **Wilsonianism**: An approach to foreign policy that emphasizes the promotion of democracy as a means of ensuring peace, in line with the ideas of Woodrow Wilson.

Clinton administration, partly in an attempt to counter the criticism that the USA routinely propped up unpopular, authoritarian regimes in the Middle East in return for secure oil supplies. This departed from President Bush Sr's conception of the post-Cold War 'new world order', in which the norms of non-intervention and non-aggression were applied regardless of a state's constitutional structure (the 1991 Gulf War was, for instance, waged to defend autocratic Kuwait). However, Clinton's 'soft' **Wilsonianism** turned into 'hard' Wilsonianism under George W. Bush after September 11, as a policy of militarily-imposed 'regime change' was justified in terms of the promotion of democracy across the troubled Middle East. In an attempt to move beyond such thinking, and to distance himself from rhetoric associated with the 'war on terror', President Obama, in a speech in Cairo in June 2009, called for a 'new beginning' in relations between the Islamic world and the West. Although the fruits of this revised approach have been limited, especially on the issue of Palestine, it helped to set expectations for how the USA, and the wider West, would respond to the Arab Spring and subsequent developments. The significant rise in drone strikes against targets in Pakistan and elsewhere that has occurred under Obama nevertheless casts a shadow over the idea of a peaceful 'new beginning'.

SUMMARY

● Western societies have conventionally been portrayed as 'developed' or 'advanced' societies, implying that they offer a model that will, over time, be accepted by all other societies. Westernization is linked to the growth of a market or capitalist economy, the advance of liberal democracy, and the spread of values such as individualism, secularism and materialism.

● Politics since the end of the Cold War has been structured less by ideological rivalry and more by issues of cultural difference, especially those related to identity. Identity politics, in its various forms, including multiculturalism, seeks to reshape a group's identity through a process of politico-cultural self-assertion.

● 'Clash of civilizations' theorists argue that twenty-first century global politics will increasingly be characterized by conflict between nations and groups from 'different civilizations'. However, such a view ignores, amongst other things, the complex and fragmented nature of civilizations, and the extent to which different cultures have coexisted peacefully and harmoniously.

● The most prominent aspect of the growing political importance of culture has been the rise of religious movements. This has been most evident in the fundamentalist upsurge, in which fundamentalism is expressed through a religio-political movement sometimes, but not necessarily, linked to a belief in the literal truth of sacred texts.

● The issues of identity, culture and religion have acquired particular prominence through their association with attempts to challenge and displace the politico-cultural hegemony of the West. This has been reflected in the general phenomenon of postcolonialism, but it has also been expressed through the idea that there are distinctive Asian values and cultural beliefs.

● The most significant challenge to the West has come from the rise of political Islam. The image of a clash between Islam and the West may nevertheless be based either on the implacably anti-western ideas of Islamism or on the extent to which Islam, and especially the Arab world, have consistently been a victim of western intervention and manipulation.

Questions for discussion

● What is 'the West'?
● What are the main factors explaining the growth of identity politics?
● To what extent is multiculturalism compatible with civic unity?
● How persuasive is the 'tectonic' model of civilizations?
● In what ways is religious fundamentalism linked to globalization?
● Are women's rights essentially a western concept?
● Do Asian values merely serve as an excuse for authoritarian rule?
● Does the tension between Islam and the West have a civilizational character?
● What have been the implications of the Arab Spring for Islamist militancy?
● What is the 'Muslim question', and does it have an answer?

Further reading

Huntington, S. P., *The Clash of Civilizations and the Remaking of World Order* (2002). A bold, imaginative and deeply controversial elaboration of the clash of civilizations thesis by its originator.

Kepel, G., *Jihad: The Trial of Political Islam* (2006). A challenging and illuminating overview of the phenomenon of Islamism.

Parekh, B., *A New Politics of Identity: Political Principles for an Interdependent World* (2008). A wide-ranging analysis of the impact of globalization on ethnic, religious, national and other identities.

Young, R., *Postcolonialism: A Very Short Introduction* (2003). An accessible account of the nature and implications of postcolonialism.

ONLINE RESOURCES AVAILABLE

Links to relevant web resources can be found on the *Global Politics* website

CHAPTER **9** **Power and Twenty-First-Century World Order**

'A new world order is taking shape so fast that governments and private citizens find it difficult to absorb the gallop of events.'

MIKHAIL GORBACHEV, quoted in *The Washington Post*, February 1990

PREVIEW

The issue of world order is vitally important because it reflects the distribution of power amongst states and other actors, affecting the level of stability within the global system and the balance within it between conflict and cooperation. However, this raises questions about the nature of power itself. Is power an attribute, something that states and other actors *possess*, or is it implicit in the various structures of global politics? Does power always involve domination and control, or can it also operate through cooperation and attraction? During the Cold War period, it was widely accepted that global power had a bipolar character: two superpowers confronted one another, the USA and the Soviet Union, although there was disagreement about whether this had led to peace and stability, or to rising tension and insecurity. Since the end of the Cold War, nevertheless, there has been deep debate about the nature of world order. An early view was that the end of the superpower era had given rise to a 'new world order', characterized by peace and international cooperation. But what was the 'new world order', and what was its fate? A second view emphasized that the emergence of the USA as the world's sole superpower has created, in effect, a unipolar world order, based on US 'hegemony'. Is the USA a 'global hegemon', and what are the implications of unipolarity? A third view highlights the trend towards multipolarity and the fragmentation of global power, influenced by developments such as the rise of emerging powers (China, Russia, India, Brazil and so on), the advance of globalization, the increased influence of non-state actors and the growth of international organizations. Will a multipolar world order bring peace, cooperation and integration, or will it herald the emergence of new conflicts and heightened instability?

KEY ISSUES
- What is power?
- How, and to what extent, has the nature of power changed?
- What were the implications for world order of the end of the Cold War?
- Is the USA a hegemonic power, or a power in decline?
- To what extent is the world now multipolar, and are these trends set to continue?
- How is growing multipolarity likely to affect global politics?

216

CONCEPT

Power

Power, in its broadest sense, is the ability to influence the outcome of events, in the sense of having the 'power *to*' do something. In global politics, this includes the ability of a country to conduct its own affairs without the interference of other countries, bringing power very close to autonomy. However, power is usually thought of as a relationship: that is, as the ability to influence the behaviour of others in a manner not of their choosing, or 'power *over*' others. Power can therefore be said to be exercised whenever A gets B to do something that B would not otherwise have done. Distinctions have nevertheless been drawn between potential/actual power, relational/ structural power and 'hard/soft' power.

POWER AND GLOBAL POLITICS

Politics is, in essence, power: the ability to achieve a desired outcome, through whatever means. This notion was neatly summed up in the title of Harold Lasswell's book *Politics: Who Gets What, When, How?* (1936). But this merely raises another question: what, exactly, is power? How can power, particularly in global politics, best be understood? Power is a complex and multidimensional phenomenon. Joseph Nye (see p. 222) likened power to love – 'easier to experience than to define or measure, but no less real for that'. The problem with power is that it is an essentially contested concept: there is no settled or agreed concept of power, only a series of rival concepts. Power can be understood in terms of *capability*; that is, as an attribute, something that states or other actors 'possess'. Power can be understood as a *relationship*; that is, as the exercise of influence over other actors. And power can be understood as a property of a *structure*; that is, as the ability to control the political agenda and shape how things are done. To add to the confusion, there are also debates about the changing nature of power, and in particular about the key factors through which one actor may influence another.

Power as capability

The traditional approach to power in international politics is to treat it in terms of capabilities. Power is therefore an attribute or possession. Such an approach has, for instance, been reflected in attempts to list the 'elements' or 'components' of national power (see p. 219). The most significant of these usually include the size and quality of a state's armed forces, its per capita wealth and natural resources, the size of its population, its land mass and geographical position, the size and skills of its population and so on. The advantage of this approach is that it enables power to be analyzed on the basis of observable, tangible factors, such as military and economic strength, rather than intangibles, suggesting that power is quantifiable. Over time, nevertheless, greater attention has been paid to less tangible factors, such as morale and leadership skills. One of the most significant implications of the capabilities approach to power has been that it enables states to be classified on the basis of the power or resources they possess, allowing the international system to be analyzed on a hierarchical basis. States were thus classified as 'great powers' (see p. 6), 'superpowers' (see p. 38), 'middling powers', 'regional powers' and so forth.

However, the idea that power can be measured in terms of capabilities has a number of drawbacks, making it an unreliable means of determining the outcome of events. The often quoted example of the Vietnam War (1959–75) helps to illustrate this. The USA (see p. 46) failed to prevail in Vietnam despite enjoying massive economic, technological and military advantages over North Vietnam and its communist ally, the Vietcong. At best, capabilities define *potential* or *latent* power rather than *actual* power, and translating a capability into a genuine political asset may be difficult and perhaps impossible. This applies for a number of reasons:

● The relative importance of the attributes of power is a matter of uncertainty and debate. Is a large population more significant than geographical size? Is economic power now more important than military power?

- Some elements of national power may be less beneficial than they at first appear. For example, a highly-educated population may limit a state's ability to wage or sustain warfare, and natural resources may impair economic growth, as in the so-called 'paradox of plenty' (see p. 416).
- Subjective factors may be as significant as quantifiable, objective factors. These include the will and resolve of the armed forces and what can be called 'national morale'. Strategy and leadership may also be decisive, allowing, for instance, weaker actors to prevail over stronger ones in so-called 'asymmetrical' wars. Terrorism (see p. 291) and insurrection can thus be examples of 'the strength of the weak' (Ignatieff 2004).
- It may only be possible to translate resources or capacities into genuine political efficacy in particular circumstances. For example, the possession of nuclear weapons may be irrelevant when a state is confronting a terrorist threat or fighting a guerrilla war, and such weapons are 'unusable' in most political circumstances.
- Power is dynamic and ever-changing, meaning that power relations are never fixed or 'given'. Power may shift, for example, due to economic booms or slumps, financial crises, the discovery of new energy resources, the acquisition of new weapons, natural disaster, an upsurge in ethnic conflict and so on.

Relational power and structural power

Most accounts of power portray it as a relationship. In its classic formulation, power can be said to be exercised whenever A gets B to get something that B would not otherwise have done. If a concern with capabilities equates power with 'strength', a concern with relationships equates power with 'influence'. Capabilities and relationships are clearly not distinct, however. Power relations between states or other actors may be taken to reflect the balance of their respective capabilities. In this case, the relationship model of power suffers from many of the drawbacks outlined above. For this reason, **relational power** is often understood in terms of actions and outcomes – that is, the effect one actor has on another – rather than in terms of contrasting assessments of capabilities. This is particularly the case because power is about perception. States and other actors deal with one another on the basis of their *calculations* of relative power. This may mean, for example, that reputation can sustain national power despite its decline in 'objective' terms. Foreign policy decisions may thus be based on under-estimates and over-estimates of the power of other actors, as well as various kinds of misinterpretation and misperception (see Perception or misperception? p. 137). Furthermore, especially in military matters, A may exert influence on B in one of two ways: either by getting B to do what B would not otherwise have done (**compellance**), or by preventing B from doing what B would otherwise have done (**deterrence**). Generally, the former will be riskier and require the use of greater resources than the latter. This can be seen in the contrast between the 2003 invasion of Iraq to bring about 'regime change' (an example of compellance) and the previous policy of preventing attacks on the Kurds and Shia Muslims by maintaining 'no-fly zones' (an example of deterrence).

- **Relational power**: The ability of one actor to influence another actor or actors in a manner not of their choosing.

- **Compellance**: A tactic or strategy designed to force an adversary to make concessions against its will through war or the threat of aggression.

- **Deterrence**: A tactic or strategy designed to prevent aggression by emphasizing the scale of the likely military response (the cost of an attack would be greater than any benefit it may bring).

Focus on . . .

Elements of national power

A common (if now less fashionable) approach to power, particularly associated with the ranking of states within a hierarchy, has been to identify the capacities that states or other actors use to exert influence. In this view, the key elements of national power include the following:

- *Military strength*. For many commentators, especially in the realist school, power in international politics boils down to military capacity. Realists, for example, have traditionally favoured a 'basic force' model of power, on the grounds that military capacity both enables a country to protect its territory and people from external aggression and to pursue its interests abroad through conquest and expansion. Key factors are therefore the size of the armed forces, their effectiveness in terms of morale, training, discipline and leadership, and, crucially, their access to the most advanced weaponry and equipment.

- *Economic development:* States' 'weight' in international affairs is closely linked to their wealth and economic resources. This applies, in part, because economic development underpins military capacity, as wealth enables states to develop large armies, acquire modern weapons and wage costly or sustained wars. Modern technology and an advanced industrial base also gives states political leverage in relation to trading partners, especially if the national currency is so strong and stable that it is widely used as a means of international exchange.

- *Population*. A large population benefits a state both economically and materially, giving it a sizeable workforce and the potential to develop an extensive army. Level of literacy, education and skills may be just as important, however. Economic development, and particularly industrialization, require mass literacy and at least basic levels of work-related skills. As production, distribution and exchange are increasingly dependent on modern technology, higher-level scientific and ICT skills have become a requirement for economic success.

- *Geography*. The primary significance of geographical variables, such as land area, location, climate, topography and natural resources, has traditionally been stressed by geopolitics (see p. 414). Beneficial geographical features include access to the sea (for trading and military purposes); a temperate climate away from earthquake zones and areas where violent tropical storms are frequent; navigable rivers for transport, trade and energy production (hydroelectric power); arable land for farming; and access to mineral and energy resources (coal, oil and gas).

Whereas the capabilities and relationship models of power clearly assume the existence of an actor or agent, usually the state, **structural power** links the distribution of power to biases within the social structures through which actors relate to one another and make decisions. A most influential account of structural power was provided by Susan Strange (see p. 220), who defined it as 'the power to decide how things shall be done, the power to shape frameworks within which states relate to one another, relate to people or relate to corporate enterprises'. Strange further distinguished between four primary power structures:

- **Structural power**: The ability to shape the frameworks within which global actors relate to one another, thus affecting 'how things shall be done'

- The *knowledge* structure, which influences actor's beliefs, ideas or perceptions
- The *financial* structure, which controls access to credit or investment
- The *security* structure, which shapes defence and strategic issues

Susan Strange (1923–98)

UK academic and leading exponent of international political economy. A self-described 'new realist', Strange made contributions in a number of areas. Her idea of structural power challenged the prevalent realist theory of power and reframed the debate, fashionable in the 1980s, about US decline and its implications. In *States and Markets* (1988), Strange analyzed the growing ascendancy of the market over political authority since the 1970s, an idea further developed in *The Retreat of the State* (1996), in which she declared that 'state authority has leaked away, upwards, sideways and downwards'. In *Casino Capitalism* (1997) and *Mad Money* (1998), Strange examined the instability and volatility of market-based economies, particularly in the light of innovations in the way in which financial markets work.

- The *production* structure, which affects economic development and prosperity.

Strange insisted that the same state or states need not dominate each of these structures but, rather, that their structural power may vary across the structures. This analysis of power provides an alternative to state-centrism and highlights the important and growing role played by regimes (see p. 71) and international organizations (see p. 440). Nevertheless, structural power operates alongside relational power, providing an alternative way of explaining how outcomes are determined. The issue of structural power also clearly demonstrates how questions about the nature of power are closely linked to debates about the shape of world order. During the 1980s, Strange used the theory of structural power to reframe the debate about hegemonic stability theory (see p. 236) and to challenge the then fashionable notion of US decline (discussed later in the chapter), which had largely been based on the USA's economic decline relative, in particular, to Japan and Germany.

Changing nature of power

Recent debates about the changing nature of power reflect less on the emergence of conceptually new forms of power, and more on the changing mechanisms through which relational power is exercised. Two alleged shifts in this respect have attracted attention. The first is a general shift from military power to economic power. Military power is the traditional currency of world politics. Realist theorists place a particular emphasis on military power because, in their view, the international system is structured above all by security and survival. In a self-help world, states face national disaster unless they have the capacity for self-defence. However, this image of militarily-based power politics has been challenged by neoliberals who argue that growing trade links and increasing interdependence (see p. 7) make inter-state war more costly and so less likely. Military force has thus become a less reliable and less important policy option. In the modern world, states therefore compete through trade rather than through the use of force. (The debate about the declining significance of military power is examined on p. 253.)

The second shift is the alleged wider decline of **'hard' power**, which encompasses both military power and economic power. Hard power is 'command power', the ability to change what others do through the use of inducements (carrots) or threats (sticks). By contrast, there has been a growth in **'soft' power**. Soft power is 'co-optive power'; it rests on the ability to shape the preferences of others by *attraction* rather than *coercion* (Nye 2004). Whereas hard power draws on resources such as force, sanctions, payments and bribes, soft power operates largely through culture, political ideals and foreign policies (especially when these are seen to be attractive, legitimate or to possess moral authority). The differences between hard and soft power are illustrated in Figure 9.1. For some feminists, the hard/soft power distinction highlights deeper factors, linked to the relationship between power and gender. In this view, the idea of 'power over', particularly when it is associated with 'hard' strategies such as coercion and the use of threats and rewards, reflects 'masculinist' biases that generally underpin the realist theory of power politics (see p. 222). Feminists, on the other hand, have emphasized the extent to which, in domestic and transnational social relations especially, power is exercised through nurturing, cooperation and sharing. Instead of conflictual and capacity conceptions of power, this suggests the alternative notion of power as collaboration, or 'power *with*'.

How has this alleged shift from hard to soft power come about? The key explanation is that the growth of interdependence and interconnectedness means that people see more, hear more and know more about what happens around the globe. Increasing cross-border flows of images, information and ideas make it easier for people to form judgements about the culture and values of other states as well as about the foreign and domestic policies of their governments. This trend is also aided by generally improving literacy levels and educational standards worldwide, and by the spread of democracy, particularly as democratic systems operate largely through soft-power mechanisms (the personalities of leaders, the image and values of political parties and so on). In such circumstances, a state's use of hard-power strategies may risk the loss of 'hearts and minds'. For example, the Bush administration's approach to the 'war on terror' (see p. 230), and particularly the 2003 invasion of Iraq, may have been

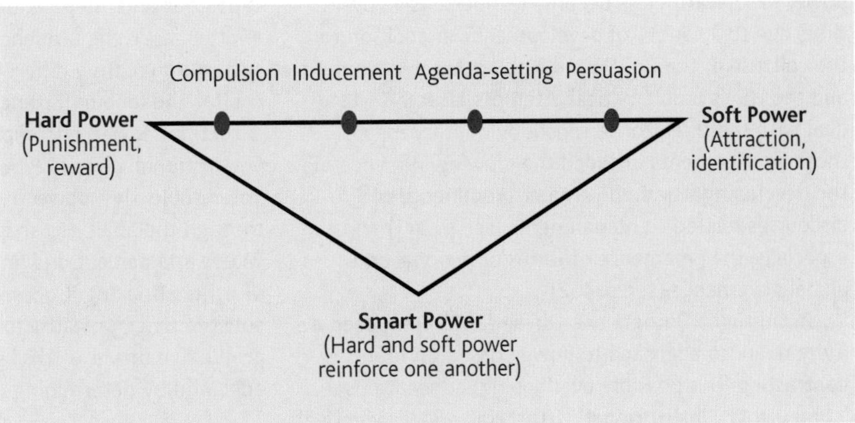

● **Hard power**: The ability of one actor (usually but not necessarily a state) to influence another through the use of threats or rewards, typically involving military 'sticks' or economic 'carrots'.

● **Soft power**: The ability to influence other actors by persuading them to follow or agree to norms and aspirations that produce the desired behaviour.

Figure 9.1 **Hard, soft and smart power**

Joseph S. Nye (born 1937)

US academic and foreign policy analyst. Nye was, with Robert Keohane (see p. 442), one of the leading theorists of 'complex interdependence', which offered an alternative to the realist belief in international anarchy (Keohane and Nye 1977). In *Bound to Lead* (1990) and *The Paradox of American Power* (2002) he has emphasized the need for the USA to redefine the national interest in the light of developments such as globalization and the information revolution, recognizing that the new conditions of global interdependence placed a greater stress on multilateral cooperation. As he put it, the USA 'can't go it alone'. Nye has been particularly associated with the idea of 'soft power' (the ability to attract and persuade), a term he coined, and later with the notion of 'smart power', a blend of 'soft' and 'hard' power. Nye's other major works include *Soft Power* (2005), *Understanding International Conflict* (2008a) and *The Powers to Lead* (2008b).

Focus on . . .
Beyond 'power over'?

Is the conventional notion of power as domination and control – that is, material 'power over' others – still sustainable? Does power have a single expression or form, or a variety of expressions and forms? Until the 1980s, the prevalent understanding of power was based on realist assumptions about the primacy of states and the importance of military might and economic strength in world affairs. This was consistent with the billiard ball image of world politics (see p. 4), in which power is demonstrated when billiard balls (representing states) collide with one another. This conception of power has nevertheless become less persuasive over time, due to a variety of developments. In addition to the collapse of the Cold War's bipolar threat system and the USA's problematical attempts after 9/11 to deal with the threat of terrorism by military means, these developments included the growing influence of the developing world, the greater prominence of discourses related to human rights (see p. 311) and, especially, the emergence of forms of regional and global governance (see p. 462).

In this light, Barnett and Duvall (2005) proposed a more nuanced approach to power, based on four contrasting (but possibly overlapping) conceptions – 'compulsory', 'institutional', 'structural' and 'productive' power. The first two of these are familiar from conventional realist and liberal thinking on the subject. *Compulsory* power allows one actor to have direct control over another, usually through the exercise of military or economic means. *Institutional* power occurs when actors exercise indirect control over others, as, for instance, when states establish international institutions that work to their own long-term advantage and to the disadvantage of others. The other two are more commonly used by critical theorists. *Structural* power operates through structures that shape the capacities and interests of actors in relation to one another, as in the tendency of the global capitalist system to create a differential relationship between capital and labour. (Strange's (1996) conception of 'structural power' encompasses both this notion and 'institutional' power.) *Productive* power is, in a sense, 'inter-subjective' power: it is power that operates through the ability to shape either one's own beliefs, values and perceptions (making it liberating) or those of others (making it oppressive). Influenced by social constructivist, poststructuralist and feminist thinking, productive power works by defining 'legitimate' knowledge and by determining whose knowledge matters.

CONCEPT

Bipolarity

Bipolarity refers to an international system which revolves around two poles (major power blocs). The term is most commonly associated with the Cold War, restricting its use to the dynamics of East–West rivalry during the 'superpower era'. For a system to be genuinely bipolar, a rough equality must occur between the two pre-eminent powers or power blocs, certainly in terms of their military capacity. Neorealists have argued that this equilibrium implies that bipolar systems are stable and relatively peaceful, being biased in favour of a balance of power (see p. 262). Liberals, however, have associated bipolarity with tension and insecurity, resulting from their tendency to breed hegemonic ambition and prioritize military power.

counter-productive in that it provoked increased anti-Americanism across the Arab and wider Muslim world, possibly even fuelling support for terrorism. It is noticeable that, since 2009, the Obama administration has placed much greater emphasis on the use of soft-power strategies. In most circumstances, however, hard and soft power operate in tandem. Figures within the Obama administration, for instance, have thus championed the idea of '**smart power**'. There are, nevertheless, some examples of soft power that operate in the absence of hard power, such as the Vatican, the Dalai Lama, Canada and Norway.

POST-COLD WAR GLOBAL ORDER

End of Cold War bipolarity

Although there is considerable debate about the nature of twenty-first-century **world order**, there is considerable agreement about the shape of world order during the Cold War period. Its most prominent feature was that two major power blocs confronted one another, a US-dominated West and a Soviet-dominated East. In the aftermath of the defeat of Germany, Japan and Italy in WWII and with the UK weakened by war and suffering from long-term relative economic decline, the USA and the Soviet Union emerged as 'superpowers', powers greater than traditional 'great powers'. Their status was characterized by their preponderant military power (particularly in terms of their nuclear arsenals) and their span of ideological leadership. Cold War bipolarity was consolidated by the formation of rival military alliances, NATO in 1949 and the Warsaw Pact in 1955, and it was reflected in the division of Europe, symbolized by the Berlin Wall erected in 1961. The bipolar model of the Cold War, however, became increasingly less accurate from the 1960s onwards. This was due, first, to the growing fragmentation of the communist world (notably deepening enmity between Moscow and Beijing, the Chinese Revolution having occurred in 1949) and, secondly, to the resurgence of Japan and Germany as economic superpowers. One of the consequences of this emerging multipolarity (see p. 237) was *détente* between East and West. This was reflected in President Nixon's historic visit to China (see p. 238) in 1972 and the Strategic Arms Limitation talks between 1967 and 1979 that produced the SALT I and SALT II Agreements.

What were the implications for the international system of Cold War bipolarity? For neorealists in particular, bipolarity is biased in favour of stability and order. This occurs for a number of reasons. First, and most importantly, bipolar systems tend towards a balance of power (see p. 262). During the Cold War, the approximate, if dynamic, military equality between the USA and the Soviet Union inclined both of them towards a strategy of deterrence. Once a condition of Mutually Assured Destruction (MAD) was achieved, the two superpowers effectively cancelled each other out, albeit through a 'balance of terror'. Second, stability of this period was guaranteed by the fact that there were but two key actors. Fewer great powers reduced the possibilities of great-power war, but also, crucially, reduced the chances of miscalculation, making it easier to operate an effective system of deterrence. Third, power relationships in the Cold War system were more stable because each bloc was forced to rely on inner (economic and military) resources, external (alliances with other states or blocs) means of

● **Smart power**: The use of soft power backed up by the possible use of hard power.

● **World order**: The distribution of power between and amongst states and other key actors giving rise to a relatively stable pattern of relationships and behaviours.

expanding power not being available. Once the division of Europe was developed, in effect, into the division of the world, shifting alliances that may have destabilized the balance of power were largely ruled out. Bipolarity therefore led to the 'long peace' between 1945 and 1990, in particular bringing peace to a Europe that had been the crucible of world war twice before in the twentieth century.

However, not all theorists had such a positive view of Cold War bipolarity. One criticism of the bipolar system was that it strengthened imperialist tendencies in both the USA and the USSR as, discouraged from direct confrontation with each other, each sought to extend or consolidate its control over its sphere of influence. In the capitalist West, this led to neocolonialism, US political interference in Latin America and the Vietnam War, whereas in the communist East it resulted in the Warsaw Pact invasion of Hungary (1956) and the Soviet invasions of Czechoslovakia (1968) and Afghanistan (1979). A further criticism of bipolarity was that superpower rivalry and a strategy of nuclear deterrents produced conditions of ongoing tension that always threatened to make the Cold War 'hot'. In other words, the Cold War may have remained 'cold' more because of good fortune or the good sense of individual leaders, rather than through the structural dynamics of the system itself.

Even though neorealism may be effective in highlighting some of the benefits of Cold War bipolarity, it struggles to explain its collapse (see p. 225). The programme of accelerating reform, initiated by Mikhail Gorbachev from 1985 onwards, ended up with the Soviet Union relinquishing many of its core strategic achievements, notably its military and political domination over Eastern Europe, as well as, ultimately, over the non-Russian republics of the Soviet Union. On the other hand, the image of equilibrium within the Cold War bipolar system may always have been misleading. As will be discussed later, in many ways the USA became the hegemonic power in 1945, with the Soviet Union always as a challenger but never as an equal. This was reflected in the fact that while the Soviet Union was undoubtedly a military superpower it, arguably, never achieved the status of an economic superpower. Moreover, the imbalance between its military capacity and its level of economic development always made it vulnerable. This vulnerability was exploited by Ronald Reagan's 'Second Cold War' in the 1980s, when increased US military spending put massive pressure on the fragile and inefficient Soviet economy, providing the context for the Gorbachev reform process.

The 'new world order' and its fate

The end of the Cold War produced a burst of enthusiasm for the ideas of liberal internationalism (see p. 67), reminiscent of Woodrow Wilson's designs for the post-WWI peace and the post-WWII process that saw the creation of the United Nations and the Bretton Woods system. The idea that the post-Cold War era would be characterized by a 'new world order' was first mooted by Gorbachev in a speech to the UN General Assembly in December 1988. In addition to calling for a strengthening of the UN and a reinvigoration of its peacekeeping role, Gorbachev called for the de-ideologization of relations amongst states to achieve greater cooperation and proposed that the use or threat of force should no longer be considered legitimate in international affairs. At the Malta Conference

THE END OF THE COLD WAR

Realist view

The end of the Cold War came as a shock to the overwhelming majority of realist theorists, creating something of a crisis within realist theory. The problem was that the events of 1989–91 simply do not fit in with realist assumptions about how states behave. States are meant to pursue their national interests, particularly though the maintenance of military and territorial security. However, under Gorbachev, the Soviet Union was prepared to relinquish its military and political domination over Eastern Europe and accepted the break-away of its non-Russian republics. This was, moreover, accomplished without the Soviet Union being subject to irresistible strategic pressure from outside. Nevertheless, realism may shed some light on these developments. From a realist perspective, the Cold War could only end either in the military defeat of one superpower by another, or through the decline in the relative power of one or both of the superpowers, either bringing about the collapse of bipolarity. The contours of the bipolar system were certainly affected in the 1970s and 1980s by the relative decline of the Soviet Union. However, it is difficult to argue that bipolarity had disappeared altogether, certainly as far as military matters were concerned.

Liberal view

Although the end of the Cold War led to a burst of optimism amongst liberal theorists who anticipated that morality, rather than power politics, could be placed at the heart of international diplomacy, liberals fared little better than realists in predicting the end of the Cold War. Nevertheless, since the 1970s, liberals had been highlighting a general trend in favour of cooperation and away from the use of military power. This was based on the tendency of economic modernization to create patterns of 'complex interdependence' that both favoured integration and encouraged states to compete through trade rather than war. Cold War-style antagonism and military confrontation in the form of the nuclear arms race were therefore seen to be increasingly outmoded, as the tendency towards *détente* demonstrated. In this view, the Soviet Union's reluctance to use military force to maintain its control over Eastern Europe as well as its own territorial integrity stemmed, in part, from the recognition that ending East–West rivalry would be likely to bring economic benefits.

Critical views

The end of the Cold War struck many critical theorists with disquiet. While disillusionment with the Soviet Union had steadily grown in critical and radical circles, many theorists, especially those linked to the Marxist tradition, continued to regard the actually existing socialism of the Eastern bloc as a viable, if imperfect, alternative to western capitalism. Communist regimes were therefore usually viewed as stable and cohesive, especially in view of their ability to deliver economic and social security. The levels of public disaffection with the communist system that were demonstrated across Eastern Europe in 1989 therefore caught most critical theorists by surprise, particularly as these revolutions sought to reverse history, by ditching socialism in favour of capitalism. The one way in which critical thinkers can claim to help to explain the end of the Cold War is through the extent to which the Gorbachev reform process was inspired by a model of 'market socialism', which some had seen as the best hope for a non-authoritarian or 'reform' communism. However, the failure of the Gorbachev reforms merely demonstrated the limitations of market socialism.

The end of the Cold War nevertheless gave significant impetus to social constructivism. The failure of conventional theories adequately to explain why the Cold War ended highlighted, in a sense, a missing dimension: the role played by ideas and perceptions. What was changing during the 1990s was the identity of the Soviet Union, which informed its interests and, in turn, its actions. The social identity of the Soviet Union was reshaped by the 'new thinking' that Gorbachev and a younger generation of Soviet leaders brought to the conduct of domestic and foreign policy. Believing that Soviet interests would best be served by international engagement across the capitalist–communist divide and no longer perceiving the USA and the capitalist West as a security threat, they calculated that political and military domination over Eastern Europe had ceased to be a key strategic interest for the Soviet Union, and may indeed have become an impediment.

of 1989 Bush Sr and Gorbachev committed themselves to a shift from an era of containment and superpower antagonism to one of superpower cooperation based on new security arrangements. In his 'Towards a New World Order' speech to Congress in September 1990, Bush outlined his vision for the post-Cold War world in more detail. Its features included US leadership to ensure the international rule of law, a partnership between the USA and the Soviet Union including the integration of the latter into the world economic bodies, and a check on the use of force by the promotion of collective security. One way in which Bush's version of the 'new world order' differed from that of Woodrow Wilson was the assertion, as shown by the 1991 Gulf War, that the 'international community' should protect the sovereign independence of all regimes, regardless of their complexion, and not give priority to liberal-democratic states on the grounds that they are likely to be more peaceful.

However, the wave of optimism and idealism that greeted the birth of the post-Cold War world did not last long. Many were quick to dismiss the 'new world order' as little more than a convenient catchphrase and one that was certainly not grounded in a developed strategic vision. Much of how this 'new world' would work remained vague. For example, how and how far should the UN be strengthened? What institutional arrangements were required to ensure that the US–Soviet partnership would be enduring? How could the renunciation of the use of force be squared with the USA's emerging role as the 'world's police officer'? For that matter, the advent of superpower cooperation was only a manifestation of Soviet weakness and, anyway, owed much to the personal relationship between Bush Sr and Gorbachev.

Moreover, alternative interpretations of the post-Cold War world order were not slow in emerging. Some heralded the rise not of a new world order, but of a new world *dis*order. One reason for this was the release of stresses and tensions that the Cold War had helped to keep under control. By maintaining the image of an external threat (be it international communism or capitalist encirclement), the Cold War had served to promote internal cohesion and given societies a sense of purpose and identity. However, the collapse of the external threat helped to unleash centrifugal pressures, which usually took the form of ethnic, racial and regional conflicts. This occurred in many parts of the world, but particularly in eastern Europe as demonstrated by the prolonged bloodshed in the 1990s amongst Serbs, Croats and Muslims in the former Yugoslavia, and by the war between Russia (see p. 181) and the secessionist republic of Chechnya that broke out in 1994. Far from establishing a world order based on respect for justice and human rights, the international community stood by in former Yugoslavia and, until the Kosovo crisis of 1999, allowed Serbia to wage a war of expansion and perpetrate genocidal policies reminiscent of those used in WWII. Nevertheless, the greatest weakness of the idea of an emerging liberal world order was a failure to take account of the shifting role and status of the USA. The main significance of the end of the Cold War was the collapse of the Soviet Union as a meaningful challenger to the USA, leaving the USA as the world's sole superpower. Indeed, talk of a 'new world order' may have been nothing more than an ideological tool to legitimize the global exercise of power by the USA. In other words, the 'liberal moment' in world affairs turned out to be the 'unipolar moment'. But what was to be the shape of emerging unipolarity (see p. 229), and how was the USA to respond to its new status?

US HEGEMONY AND GLOBAL ORDER

Rise to hegemony

Since the end of the Cold War, the USA has commonly been referred to as an 'American empire', a 'global hegemon' or a '**hyperpower**'. Comparisons have regularly been made between the USA and the British Empire of the nineteenth century and, though less convincingly, with sixteenth-century Spain and seventeenth-century Holland. However, the USA is a hegemon of a very different, and perhaps unique, kind, with some suggesting that the only helpful historical parallel is Imperial Rome. In particular, if the USA has developed into an 'empire', it has done so (usually) by eschewing traditional imperialism in the form of war, conquest and the formation of colonies. This happened for two main reasons. The first is that, as the child of revolution, the USA is a 'political' nation defined more by ideology than by history or culture. The American Revolution of 1776, being a revolt against British colonialism, not only imbued the fledgling USA with an anti-imperialist self-image but also highlighted a range of 'American values', such as political freedom, individual self-sufficiency and constitutional government. Not only did this ideological heritage incline the USA to oppose traditional European imperialism, but it has also given US foreign policy a recurrent moral dimension. The second factor is that, in contrast to a medium-sized country such as the UK, the territorial size of the USA enabled it to develop economically through internal expansion rather than external expansion. Thus, the USA was able to surpass the UK on most industrial measures by the 1880s by relying on its seemingly unlimited mass home market and despite relatively low levels of international trade. In sharp contrast to settler colonies, the USA was and remains a receiver, not a sender, of populations. Such factors meant that while the European great powers (with the possible exception of territorially massive Russia) became increasingly outward-looking in the nineteenth and early twentieth centuries, linking national power to imperial expansion, the USA remained firmly inward-looking, and often isolationist.

The twentieth century has often been portrayed as the 'American century'. However, despite being the world's largest economy (in the 1920s and in the early post-WWII period the USA accounted for about 40 per cent of global manufacturing output), such a description is in some ways misleading. The USA only became a truly global actor through its involvement in WWII and its aftermath. Indeed, the 'American century' may only have lasted from Pearl Harbor in 1941 (when the USA's entry into the war probably determined its outcome) to the explosion of the first Soviet atom bomb in 1949 (when the USA ceased to be the world's sole nuclear power). Nevertheless, the Cold War ensured that there would be no return to pre-war isolationism, with the USA increasingly assuming a position of economic, political and military leadership within the capitalist West. The USA was the chief architect of the institutions of the 'multilateralist' post-1945 world (the United Nations (see p. 456), the International Monetary Fund (IMF) (see p. 475), the World Bank (see p. 380) and so on), it underpinned the economic recovery of war-exhausted Western Europe and Japan, and US corporations quickly achieved international dominance in most economic sectors. Theorists such as Robert Cox (see p. 124) interpreted such developments in terms of the USA's rise to hegemony (see p. 228). In this view, the USA

● **Hyperpower**: A state that is vastly stronger than its potential rivals, and so dominates world affairs.

CONCEPT

Hegemony

Hegemony (from the Greek *hegemonia*, meaning 'leader') is, in its simplest sense, the leadership or domination of one element of a system over others. Gramsci (see p. 73) used the term to refer to the ideological leadership of the bourgeoisie over subordinate classes. In global or international politics, a hegemon is the leading state within a collection of states. Hegemonic status is based on the possession of structural power, particularly the control of economic and military resources, enabling the hegemon to shape the preferences and actions of other states, typically by promoting willing consent rather than through the use of force. Following Gramsci, the term implies that international or global leadership operates, in part, through ideational or ideological means.

● **Imperial over-reach**: The tendency for imperial expansion to be unsustainable as wider military responsibilities outstrip the growth of the domestic economy.

provided the political framework for the growing world economy, exercising the 'military-territorial power of an enforcer' (Cox 1994).

However, during the 1970s and 1980s it became fashionable to proclaim the decline of US hegemony. This occurred through the emergence of both internal and external challenges. Internally, politico-cultural tensions arose as a result of the growth, from the 1960s onwards, of the civil rights movement, an anti-establishment youth 'counter-culture' and the women's movement, challenging traditional views on matters such as race, consumerism, abortion and gender roles. These were compounded by the shock to the national psyche of the Watergate scandal of 1974, which led to the resignation of President Nixon. External challenges included the USA's effective defeat in the Vietnam War, the Iran hostage crisis (in which the US embassy in Tehran was seized and 66 US citizens were held hostage for 444 days, between November 1979 and January 1981), and, most importantly, the rise of economic competitors such as Germany, Japan and the 'Asian tigers'. Indeed, it became increasingly common during this period to assert that the USA was succumbing to a tendency common amongst earlier great powers to **imperial over-reach**. This implies, as Paul Kennedy (1989) put it, that 'military conflict must always be understood in the context of economic change'. The rise and fall of great powers is therefore not only determined by their ability to engage in lengthy armed conflict, but also by the impact such conflicts have on their economic strength relative to other major states.

Nevertheless, the USA proved to be remarkably resilient, both politically and economically. The Reagan administration (1981–89) helped to strengthen American nationalism, both by preaching a 'frontier ideology' based on entre-preneurialism, tax cuts and 'rolled back' welfare and by adopting a more assertive and explicitly anti-communist foreign policy. This involved a military build-up against the Soviet Union, sparking what is called the 'Second Cold War'. Moreover, while some of its erstwhile economic rivals, notably Japan and Germany, started to falter during the 1980s and 1990s, the USA's high level of spending in research, development and training helped to improve US produc-tivity levels and gave the country an unchallengeable lead in high-tech sectors of the global economy. The most significant event, however, was the collapse of communism and the fall of the Soviet Union in the revolutions of 1989–91. These provided the USA with a unique opportunity to establish global hege-mony in what appeared to be a unipolar world.

The end of the Cold War gave economic globalization (see p. 98) a consider-able boost as new markets and new opportunities opened up for western, and often US, capitalist enterprises. Encouraged by the IMF, many post-communist countries embarked on a 'shock therapy' transition from central planning to *laissez-faire* capitalism. Moreover, the US model of liberal-democratic gover-nance was quickly and eagerly adopted by many post-communist states and else-where. The Gulf War and the growing trend in the 1990s towards humanitarian intervention (see p. 326) also seemed to reflect the USA's willingness to adopt the role of the 'world's police officer'. Nevertheless, the tendencies and dynamics of the unipolar system were different from those of the bipolar system it had replaced. Not only does the existence of a single dominant state breed resent-ment and hostility amongst other states, but the global hegemon can also, poten-tially, disregard the multilateral constraints that restrict a state's freedom of

CONCEPT

Unipolarity

Unipolarity refers to an international system in which there is one pre-eminent state, or 'pole'. In a unipolar system there is but a single great power, implying an absence of constraints or potential rivals. However, as this implies some form of world government, unipolarity is always relative and not absolute. Unipolarity has been defended on the grounds that the dominant actor is able to act as the 'world's police officer' settling disputes and preventing war ('Pax Britannicus' and 'Pax Americana') and guaranteeing economic and financial stability by setting and maintaining ground rules for economic behaviour. Critics argue that unipolarity promotes megalomania on the part of the dominant actor, as well as fear, resentment and hostility among other actors.

manoeuvre. This was seen in the **unilateralist** tendency of US foreign policy following the election of George W. Bush in 2000, evidenced by the decision to withdraw from the International Criminal Court and a continued refusal to sign the Kyoto Protocol on global climate change. However, the events of September 11 (see p. 20) significantly altered the direction of US foreign policy and with it the balance of world order.

The 'war on terror' and beyond

September 11, 2001 is often treated as a decisive point in the formation of world order, equivalent to 1945 or 1990. Indeed, some commentators have argued that 9/11 was the point at which the true nature of the post-Cold War era was revealed and the beginning of a period of unprecedented global strife and instability. In that sense, the advent of the 'war on terror', rather than the collapse of communism, marked the birth of the 'real' twenty-first century. On the other hand, it is possible to exaggerate the impact of 9/11. As Robert Kagan (2004) put it, 'America did not change on September 11. It only became more itself'.

A variety of theories have been advanced to explain the advent of global or transnational terrorism (see p. 291) and the nature of the 'war on terror'. One of the most influential of these is Samuel Huntington's (see p. 540) theory of a 'clash of civilizations' (discussed in Chapter 8), which suggests that it is part of a larger trend for cultural, and more specifically religious, conflict to assume greater prominence in twenty-first-century global politics. Alternative explanations highlight the significance of changes in world order. According to Robert Cooper (2004), the East–West confrontation of the old world order had given way to a world divided into three parts:

- In the 'premodern' world, by which he meant those post-colonial states that had benefited neither from political stability nor from economic development, chaos reigns. Examples of such states include Somalia, Afghanistan and Liberia, sometimes seen as 'weak states', 'failed states' (see p. 126) or 'rogue states' (see p. 231).
- In the 'modern' world, states continue to be effective and are fiercely protective of their own sovereignty (see p. 4). Such a world operates on the basis of a balance of power, as the interests and ambitions of one state are only constrained by the capabilities of other states.
- In the 'postmodern' world, which Cooper associated primarily with Europe and the European Union (EU) (see p. 509), states have evolved 'beyond' power politics and have abandoned war as a means of maintaining security in favour of multilateral agreements, international law (see p. 339) and global governance (see p. 462).

This view of the new world order, however, embodies a range of challenges and new security threats. Not the least of these arises from the proliferation of weapons of mass destruction which in the premodern world can easily get into the hands of 'rogue' states or non-state actors such as terrorist organizations. Particular concern has been expressed about nuclear proliferation, with the so-called 'nuclear club' having expanded from five (the USA, Russia, China, France and the UK) to nine, with the acquisition of nuclear weapons by India, Pakistan,

● **Unilateralism**: One-sidedness; a policy determined by the interests and objectives of a single state, unconstrained by other states and bodies.

Focus on ...
The 'war on terror'

The 'war on terror' (or the 'war on terrorism'), known in US policy circles as the Global War on Terror or GWOT, refers to the efforts by the USA and its key allies to root out and destroy the groups and forces deemed to be responsible for global terrorism. Launched in the aftermath of 9/11, it supposedly mapped out a strategy for a 'long war' that addresses the principal security threats to twenty-first-century world order. It aims, in particular, to counter the historically new combination of threats posed by non-state actors and especially terrorist groups, so-called 'rogue' states, weapons of mass destruction and the militant theories of radicalized Islam. Critics of the idea of a 'war on terror' have argued both that its inherent vagueness legitimizes an almost unlimited range of foreign and domestic policy interventions, and that, in building up a climate of fear and apprehension, it allows the USA and other governments to manipulate public opinion and manufacture consent for (possibly) imperialist and illiberal actions. Others have questioned whether it is possible to have a 'war' against an abstract noun. (See Deconstructing the 'war on terror', p. 303.)

Israel and North Korea, and with other countries, such as Iran, being thought to be close to developing them. Although Europe may be a 'zone of safety', outside Europe there is a 'zone of danger and chaos', in which the instabilities of the premodern world threaten to spill over into the modern and even the postmodern worlds. Cooper (2004) acknowledged that a kind of 'new' imperialism may be the only way of bringing order to chaos.

Such an analysis overlaps at significant points with the neoconservative – or 'neo-con' – ideas that had a particular impact on the Bush administration in the USA in the years following 9/11, and which were reflected in what came to be known as the 'Bush doctrine' . According to this, the USA had a right to treat states that harbour or give aid to terrorists as terrorists themselves. Neoconservatism (see p. 233) sought to preserve and reinforce what was seen as the USA's 'benevolent global hegemony' (Kristol and Kagan 2004). Its key features included a build-up of the USA's military strength to achieve a position of 'strength beyond challenge' and a policy of worldwide 'democracy promotion', focused primarily on the Middle East, seen as a region of particular conflict and instability.

After 9/11, the USA's approach to the 'war on terror' quickly started to take shape. Its opening act was the US-led military assault on Afghanistan in October 2001 that toppled the Taliban regime within a matter of weeks. In January 2002, President Bush identified Iraq, Iran and North Korea as part of an 'axis of evil', later expanded to include Cuba, Syria and (though subsequently removed from the list) Libya. The 'war on terror', however, moved in a more radical and controversial direction as it became clear that 'regime change' in Saddam Hussein's Iraq was the Bush administration's next objective. This led to the 2003 Iraq War, fought by the USA and a 'coalition of the willing'. What made the Iraq War controversial was that whereas the attack on Afghanistan was widely seen as a form of self-defence (Afghanistan had provided al-Qaeda (see p. 301) with the closest thing to a home base, and there were strong politico-ideological links between al-Qaeda and the Taliban regime), the war against Iraq was justified

Rogue state

A rogue state is a state whose foreign policy poses a threat to neighbouring or other states, through its aggressive intent, build-up of weapons (particularly WMD), or association with terrorism. However, the term is controversial. It was used by US policy-makers in the early post-Cold War period to draw attention to new threats to regional and possibly global security (examples included Afghanistan, Iraq, Iran, Libya and North Korea). Critics have argued that the term has been used in a selective and self-serving fashion to justify US intervention in other countries' affairs, that it is simplistic in disregarding the complex causes of 'rogueness', and that it may entrench 'rogue' behaviour by strengthening a state's sense of alienation from the international community.

using the doctrine of pre-emptive attack. Although the Bush administration alleged (with little substantiation) that there were links between the Saddam regime and al-Qaeda, and asserted (contrary to subsequent evidence) that Iraq was in possession of WMD, the central justification was that a 'rogue' regime such as Saddam's that actively sought, and may have acquired, WMD could not be tolerated in the twenty-first century.

In both Afghanistan and Iraq, despite early dramatic successes (the overthrow of the Taliban and Saddam's Ba'athist regime), the USA and its allies found themselves fighting wars that proved to be more problematical and protracted than anticipated. Both developed into complex counter-insurgency wars against enemies whose use of the tactics of guerrilla warfare, terrorism and suicide bombings highlighted the limitations of preponderant US military power, as discussed in Chapter 10. The conduct of the 'war on terror' was undermined both by tactical failings and strategic difficulties. Among the tactical flaws were the deployment initially of an insufficient number of troops in Iraq, the absence of an exit strategy if the USA's objectives proved to be more difficult to achieve than anticipated, and the failure to develop clear plans for a post-Saddam Iraq before the invasion took place. The invasion of Iraq also, crucially, drew attention and resources away from Afghanistan, allowing Taliban insurgency to gain renewed strength.

However, the deeper, strategic approach to the 'war on terror' may also have been flawed. Three problems have received particular attention. First, the USA, arguably, overestimated the efficacy of military power. Not only, as in the Vietnam War, have guerrilla warfare tactics proved to be highly effective against a much more powerful and better resourced enemy, but the use of military means has weakened the USA's 'soft' power and damaged its reputation across the Middle East, and, if anything, alienated moderate Muslim opinion. In that sense, the USA has threatened to create the very 'arc of extremism' that it set out to destroy. Second, the strategy of imposing 'democracy from above' has proved to be naive at best, failing in particular to recognize the difficulties involved in 'nation-building' and that stable democratic institutions usually rest upon the existence of a democratic culture and require a certain level of socio-economic development. Third, lack of progress with the 'Palestinian question' continues to poison the politics of the Middle East. The neo-cons were inclined to support Israel as an article of faith, but this tended to embitter public opinion against the USA and the West across the Arab world and, in the process, strengthened support for militant Islam.

Growing difficulties in making progress with the 'war on terror' as deeper insurgencies arose first in Iraq and then increasingly in Afghanistan inclined the Bush administration to edge towards **multilateralism** during Bush's second term in office, 2005–9. However, more significant shifts occurred once President Obama was inaugurated in January 2009. In line with the advice of soft-power theorists for the USA to 'learn to cooperate, and to listen' (Nye 2004), Obama certainly altered the *tone* of the USA's engagement with world affairs generally, and with the Muslim world in particular. In a keynote speech in Cairo in June 2009, he called for a 'new beginning' between the USA and Muslims around the world, acknowledging that 'no system of government can or should be imposed upon one nation by another'. In March, he had released a video with Farsi subtitles to coincide with the Iranian new year, in which he declared that the USA

● **Multilateralism**: A policy of acting in concert with other states or international organizations, or a system of coordinated relations amongst three or more actors (see p. 467).

Focus on . . .
Pre-emptive attack

A pre-emptive attack (sometimes called 'preventive war') is military action that is designed to forestall or prevent likely future aggression. It is therefore a form of self-defence in anticipation; it involves 'getting your retaliation in first'. As such, it is an alternative to strategies such as deterrents, containment and 'constructive engagement' as a means of dealing with potential aggressors. It has attracted particular attention since the 1990s in relation to threats from 'rogue' states and terrorism, especially in the case of the 2003 invasion of Iraq.

The attraction of a pre-emptive attack is that military action can take place before a potential aggressor gets too strong (for example, before they acquire weapons of mass destruction), meaning that the overall cost of military conflict is reduced. Moreover, alternative strategies may constitute appeasement, and help to embolden an unchallenged potential aggressor. However, its drawbacks include the possibility that the calculations of future actions or threats, on which pre-emptive attacks are based, may be flawed. In addition, being based on anticipated rather than actual aggression, it may be difficult to establish or maintain domestic or international support for such attacks. Finally, it is almost certainly illegal under the UN Charter, which authorizes war only in cases of individual or collective self-defence.

wanted to end decades-old strains in its relationship with Iran (a particular object of neo-con hostility, especially in the light of alleged attempts to acquire nuclear weapons), calling on Tehran to tone down its bellicose anti-American rhetoric. Such attempts to reach out to the Muslim world and establish greater cross-cultural understanding were linked to other initiatives designed to alter how the USA was fighting the 'war on terror'. Notably, an order banning the use of torture was signed and a commitment was made to close the Guantánamo detention camp (although the promise to do this within Obama's first year of office was soon abandoned). A greater emphasis was also placed on making progress with the Palestinian problem. This issue, nevertheless, has proved to be no less complex and difficult than had previously been the case.

However, even though the rhetoric of the 'war on terror' was quickly toned down and the strategic approach to it revised, military engagement has continued to play an important role under Obama. This was reflected in a significant shift of emphasis from Iraq to Afghanistan and Pakistan, in the form of what became known as the 'Af-Pak' policy. Thanks to the success of the 'surge' in US troops, which started in 2007, in reducing levels of civil strife and civilian deaths in Iraq, responsibility for maintaining security in Iraqi towns and cities was passed from US and allied troops to Iraqi forces in 2009, and the USA's combat mission in Iraq ended in 2010. Under Obama's redrawn battle strategy for Afghanistan, a similar 'surge' was initiated in early 2010, which saw some 30,000 additional US troops deployed in the country, in an attempt to refocus and re-energize NATO's deeply problematical mission there. A phased withdrawal of US and other coalition troops from Afghanistan nevertheless began in 2011, with Obama giving a commitment that this will be completed by December 2014. At the same time, efforts were intensified to prepare the Afghan police and military to take control of their own national security. However, there is disagreement

CONCEPT

Neoconservatism

Neoconservatism was an approach to foreign policy-making that sought to enable the USA to take advantage of its unprecedented position of power and influence in a unipolar world. It consisted of a fusion between neo-Reaganism and 'hard' Wilsonianism. Neo-Reaganism took the form of a Manichean worldview, in which 'good' (represented by the USA) confronted 'evil' (represented by 'rogue' states and terrorist groups that possess, or seek to possess, WMD). This implied that the USA should deter rivals and extend its global reach by achieving a position of 'strength beyond challenge' in military terms. 'Hard' Wilsonianism involved the desire to spread US-style democracy throughout the world by a process of 'regime change', achieved by military means if necessary ('democracy from above').

about the significance of the shifts that have occurred under Obama. Some have seen them as a reassertion of US power, in the form of 'smart power', involving the use of soft and hard power in tandem to create a more sophisticated approach to tackling the challenges of religious-based militancy and global terrorism. Others, however, have seen them as evidence of the limitations within which the USA now operates, reflecting, perhaps, the end of the period of US hegemony. Certainly, after the experience of Afghanistan and Iraq, there has been a marked reluctance in the USA to intervene abroad in any way that may lead to US boots being 'on the ground' (although a similar reluctance had been in evidence after the Vietnam War).

Benevolent or malign hegemony?

After the end of the Cold War, and especially after September 11, attitudes towards the USA became a major fault-line in global politics, to some extent displacing the older left–right battle between capitalism and socialism. Was the USA the 'indispensable nation', a benevolent hegemon whose widening influence brought peace and prosperity? Or was it a malign hegemon, the source of much of the chaos and injustice in the modern world? The popularity of the 'malign' interpretation of US hegemony was evident in the sometimes very different reaction to September 11 in the developing South compared with the widely sympathetic reaction in the developed North. Anti-Americanism grew in reaction to the increasingly unilateralist turn in US foreign policy, and peaked when the USA pressed ahead with the invasion of Iraq despite failing to gain clear UN approval for military action. From a realist perspective, all global hegemons are destined to be malign, regardless of their political, economic and ideological characters. As all states pursue their national interest by seeking to accumulate power, hegemons will simply be able to do this in a more ruthless and determined fashion because they are unconstrained by serious rivals. The idea of 'benevolent global hegemony', once favoured by neoconservative analysts, was therefore an illusion.

Nevertheless, the most trenchant critics of the USA have been radical theorists, amongst whom Noam Chomsky (see p. 235) has been the most prominent. Chomsky's analysis of international affairs is influenced by anarchism and the belief that violence, deceit and lawlessness are natural functions of the state. In Chomsky's 'radical' realism, the more powerful the state, the greater will be its tendency towards tyranny and oppression. His analysis of the USA emphasizes its abiding and, in many ways, intensifying inclination towards imperialism. US expansionism, through the growth of corporate power and the spread of neo-colonialism, as well as through large- and small-scale military intervention in places such as Vietnam, Panama, Somalia, Afghanistan and Iraq was motivated by a desire to ensure economic advantage and to secure control of vital resources. US policy in the Middle East and the wider 'war on terror' were therefore largely driven by the desire for secure oil supplies. In this view, the USA, as a 'rogue superpower', was the principal source of terrorism and violence across the globe.

However, such views were also subject to criticism, and quite different images of the USA have been offered. For example, even some of those who welcomed Chomsky's 'new anti-imperialism', on the grounds that it shed light on forms of tyranny, injustice and hypocrisy that might otherwise not have been exposed, accept that his analysis was often simplistic and one-sided. US power has done

Debating . . .
Does the USA remain a global hegemon?

Debates about the decline of the USA's global hegemony are nothing new. They date back to the late 1950s and the launch by the Soviet Union of the Sputnik satellite, and to the 1970s and 1980s when the eclipse of the USA by resurgent Japan and Germany was widely predicted. However, renewed interest in the issue has been generated by the 'war on terror' and other developments.

YES	NO
Global military dominance. The USA's military lead over the rest of the world is huge. In 2011, the USA accounted for 42 per cent of the world's military spending, and had a five-fold lead over China, the second largest military spender. The USA has some 700 military bases in over 100 countries, as well as an unchallengeable lead in high-tech weaponry and in air power. The USA is the sole power that can intervene militarily in any part of the world and sustain multiple operations.	*Redundant military power.* Preponderant military power may no longer be a secure basis for hegemony. There is a huge gap between the destructive capacity of the US military machine and what it can achieve politically. The forced withdrawals of the USA from Lebanon in 1984 and Somalia in 1993, and the difficulty of winning asymmetrical wars in Iraq and Afghanistan, demonstrate how the use of terrorist, guerrilla and insurrectionary tactics can thwart even the most advanced power.
Economic resilience. The USA accounts for about 32 per cent of world spending on research and development, giving it an almost unassailable technological lead over other countries and ensuring high productivity levels. China is generations away from rivalling the USA in the technologically advanced economic sectors. Moreover, just as the British Empire remained a global hegemon until the mid-twentieth century despite having been overtaken by the USA and Germany, the USA may continue to retain global leadership in a world in which it is no longer the economic number one.	*Relative economic decline.* Although the USA remains the world's largest economy, its competitors, notably China and India, have been growing much more quickly in recent decades, with the Chinese economy predicted to outstrip the US economy, perhaps by 2020. The 2007–09 global financial crisis may have further weakened the USA, exposing the flaws of the US economic model and bringing the dollar's position as the world's leading currency into question. Related issues include the USA's pressing fiscal problems, which affect its standing in the world and the stability of US politics (Mabee 2013).
The US population. The US population is expected to reach 439 million by 2050, with big increases in the number of Hispanics and Asians, helping to underpin economic performance and to keep the US age profile low relative to fast-ageing Europe, Japan and China. Allied to this is the highly educated and skilled nature of the US population, particularly in areas such as science and technology. It is commonly accepted that up to seven US universities feature in the world's top 10, while no Asian university has yet entered the top 20.	*Damaged soft power.* The USA's 'soft' power has declined in a number of respects. Its reputation has been damaged by its association with corporate power and widening global inequality, resentment developing against 'globalization-as-Americanization'. Serious damage has also been done to the USA's moral authority by the 'war on terror' generally and the Iraq War in particular, made worse by the treatment of prisoners at Abu Ghraib and in the Guantánamo detention camp.
Unrivalled structural power. The USA exercises disproportional influence over the institutions of global economic governance and over NATO. Despite the growing influence of the developing world and of emerging economies, no country is close to challenging the USA's influence over global economic decision-making. This was reflected in the leading role that the USA played in formulating a global response to the 2007–09 global financial crisis.	*Declining diplomatic influence.* The USA has lost influence in Latin America (formerly seen as 'America's backyard'); it has to rely on Chinese diplomacy to exert influence over North Korea; EU diplomacy is needed to influence Iran; and even its capacity to exert pressure on Israel is limited. Moreover, China (for instance, over Tibet) and Russia (for instance, over Georgia) are largely immune from US diplomatic pressure. The decline of the USA's structural power is also evident in the rise of the G-20 (see p. 121) as the key forum for global economic policy-making.

Noam Chomsky (born 1928)

US linguistic theorist and radical intellectual, Chomsky was born in Philadelphia, the son of eastern European immigrant parents. His *Syntactic Structures* (1957) revolutionized the discipline of linguistics with the theory of 'transformational grammar', which proposed that humans have an innate capacity to acquire language. Radicalized during the Vietnam War, Chomsky subsequently became the leading radical critic of US foreign policy, developing his views in an extensive range of works including *American Power and the New Mandarins* (1969), *New Military Humanism* (1999) and *Hegemony and Survival* (2004). In works such as (with Edward Herman) *Manufacturing Consent* (1988), he developed a radical critique of the mass media and examined how popular support for imperialist aggression is mobilized.

much to foster and not just frustrate democracy (as, for instance, in the post-WWII reconstruction of Germany and Japan), and the assumption that 'the USA is the problem' tends to ignore, and perhaps legitimize, other – and perhaps more serious – sources of oppression and threats to security. An essentially positive view of US hegemony can also be constructed on the basis of hegemonic stability theory, which highlights the benefits that a global hegemon can bring to other states and the international system as a whole. The USA has demonstrated its willingness and ability to be such a hegemon, mainly through its leadership of the institutions of global economic governance since 1945 and the role of the dollar as an international currency (even though both of these have come under threat in the twenty-first century). The final basis for upholding the image of the USA as a 'benevolent' hegemon is based on its (perhaps uniquely) moral approach to world affairs. While not ignoring the pursuit of national self-interest – after all, the USA is a state like any other state – the USA's 'liberal' self-image as a land of freedom and opportunity usually inclines it towards self-restraint and multilateralism in world affairs. This was most clearly evident in the USA's contribution to post-war reconstruction after WWI and WWII, and there is no reason, as the impact of the 'war on terror' fades, why the balance between self-interest and self-restraint should not be restored in the twenty-first century.

A MULTIPOLAR GLOBAL ORDER?

Debate about the decline, or even end, of US hegemony is invariably linked to an assessment of rising multipolarity. This involves two main issues. First, to what extent, and in what ways, is world order acquiring a multipolar character? Second, what are the likely implications of multipolarity?

Rise of multipolarity

World order, in the modern period, is being shaped by a number of multipolar trends. The most significant of these is the rise of so-called 'emerging powers'. These are the new, or the would-be, great powers of the twenty-first century. Some states already have a significant measure of regional influence – Brazil and, possibly, Argentina, Chile, Mexico and Venezuela in Latin America; South Africa

Focus on . . .
Hegemonic stability theory

Hegemonic stability theory is the theory, accepted by realists and many neoliberals, that a dominant military and economic power is necessary to ensure the stability and prosperity in a liberal world economy (Kindleberger 1973; Gilpin 1987). The two key examples of such liberal hegemons are the UK during the late nineteenth and early twentieth centuries, and the USA since 1945.

The theory has two main components. First, it recognizes that a liberal world economy is in constant danger of being subverted by rising nationalism and the spread of protectionism. This was clearly demonstrated by the so-called 'beggar-thy-neighbour' policies that helped to create the Great Depression of the 1930s. A set of ground rules for economic competition are therefore needed, particularly focused on upholding free trade, in order for such an economy to be success-ful. Second, a dominant or hegemonic power is likely to be both willing and able to establish and enforce such

rules. Its *willingness* derives from the fact that, being a hegemon, its interests coincide significantly with those of the system itself. It has a crucial stake in the system: in ensuring the stability of the world economy, the hegemon is attending to its own long-term interests (it does not act altruistically). Its *ability* to do this stems from the fact that it alone has the capacity to deliver **public goods**; that is, goods that bring collective benefit rather than benefit merely to the state respon-sible. The hegemon, in other words, is powerful enough to act in line with 'absolute gains' rather than 'relative gains' (see p. 443). By contrast, smaller, less powerful states are forced to act more narrowly in line with national self-interest. To be a hegemon, a state must therefore (1) have sufficient power to enforce the rules of the system, (2) possess the will to use this power, and (3) be committed to a system that brings benefit to the mass of states.

and Nigeria in Africa; Israel, Egypt, Saudi Arabia and Iran in the Middle East; and South Korea, Indonesia, Pakistan and Australia in Asia and Oceania. However, a range of other powers have acquired, or are acquiring, wider, and possibly global, significance. These include, most obviously, China, Russia and India, but also Japan and the European Union (see Chapter 20). Between them, and together with the USA, these powers account for over half the world's population, about 75 per cent of global GDP and around 80 per cent of global defence spending.

Of all the powers that may rival, and even eclipse, the USA, the most signifi-cant is undoubtedly China. Indeed, many predict that the twenty-first century will become the 'Chinese century', just as the twentieth century had supposedly been the 'American century'. The basis for China's great power status is its rapid economic progress since the introduction of market reforms in the mid-1970s under Deng Xiaoping (1904–97), the most dramatic phase of which began only in the 1990s. Annual growth rates of between 8 and 10 per cent for almost thirty years (over twice the levels achieved by the USA and other western states) have meant that China became the world's largest exporter in 2009, and in 2010 it overtook Japan to become the world's second largest economy. By 2010, the Chinese economy was 90 times larger than it had been in 1978. With the world's largest population (1.35 billion), China has a seemingly inexhaustible supply of cheap labour, making it, increasingly, the manufacturing heart of the global economy. The resilience of the Chinese economic model (see p. 92) was further demonstrated by the ease with which it weathered the 2007–9 global financial

● **Public good**: A good or service that, by its nature, benefits everyone, meaning that no party can be denied access to it.

CONCEPT

Multipolarity

Multipolarity refers to an international system in which there are three or more power centres. However, this may encompass arrangements ranging from tripolar systems (the USA, Japan and the EU in the latter decades of the twentieth century) to effectively non-polar systems (Haass, 2008), in which power is so diffuse that no actor can any longer be portrayed as a 'pole'. Neorealists argue that multipolarity creates a bias in favour of fluidity and uncertainty, which can lead only to instability and an increased likelihood of war ('anarchical' multipolarity). Liberals nevertheless argue that multipolar systems are characterized by a tendency towards multilateralism, as a more even division of global power promotes peace, cooperation and integration ('interdependent' multipolarity).

crisis. China also has a growing military capacity, being second only to the USA in terms of arms expenditure. China's emerging global role is evident in the influence it now exerts within the WTO and G-20 and over issues such as climate change, as well as in its much strengthened resource links with Africa, Australia and parts of the Middle East and Latin America. An often neglected aspect of China's growing influence is the extraordinary rise of its 'soft' power. This reflects both the significance of Confucianism (see p. 202) in providing a cultural basis for cooperation in Asia, and the attraction of its anti-imperialist heritage in Africa and across much of the developing South. By contrast, the reputations of the USA and western powers are usually tainted by colonialism in one form or another. The prospect of the twenty-first century becoming the 'Chinese century' is discussed at greater length in Chapter 21.

Nevertheless, the rise of China is often seen as part of a larger shift in the balance of global power from West to East, and specifically to Asia, and maybe from the USA to the BRICs countries (see p. 463), sometimes dubbed 'the Rest'. Some argue that the twenty-first century will not so much be the 'Chinese century' as the 'Asian century', with India and Japan in particular also being viewed as key actors. The transformation of India into an emerging power has been based on economic growth rates only marginally less impressive than China's. It is estimated that if current trends persist, by 2020 China and India will jointly account for half of the world's GDP. However, the Indian economic model differs markedly from China's 'market Stalinism'. As the world's largest liberal democracy, India's increased growth rates stem from the introduction of liberal economic reforms in the early 1990s, more than a decade after China began its market reforms. India has become a world leader in industries such as computer software and biotechnology, while Bollywood films have become a global entertainment phenomenon. Japan, on the other hand, emerged as a major power though its post-1945 'economic miracle', becoming the second largest economy in the world during the 1970s. Indeed, until the 1990s, Japan, together with Germany, was widely seen as an economic superpower and perhaps as a model for the 'de-militarized' great powers of the twenty-first century.

However, the continued forward march of a Chinese-led Asia cannot be taken for granted. The Japanese economy stalled badly in the 1990s (Japan's 'lost decade'), and its economic and political significance in the twenty-first century may largely depend on its developing relationship with the other emerging powers of Asia, notably China and India. Japan's record of 10 per cent growth rates in the 1950s, progressively declining in each subsequent decade, may also contain lessons for China and India about the long-term sustainability of their high growth rates. India's emergence as a great power is constrained by a number of factors. India still suffers from acute problems of poverty and illiteracy, which are being fuelled by a population growth crisis that is fast getting out of hand. India has also been less interested than China in projecting itself militarily, despite having joined the 'nuclear club' in 2001. In part, this is because significant regional tensions, mainly with Pakistan but also with China, tend to divert India's attention away from a larger world role. As far as China is concerned, there are reasons for questioning whether it can yet be viewed as a serious rival of the USA. The Chinese economy remains heavily dependent on supplies of cheap labour, and a transition to a more highly-technologized economy based

GLOBAL ACTORS . . .

CHINA

Type: State • **Population:** 1,353.8 m • **GDP per capita:** $9,146 • **HDI ranking:** 101/187 • **Capital:** Beijing

The People's Republic of China was founded on 1 October 1949, by Mao Zedong. During the 1950s, the Chinese Communist Party (CCP) sought to establish control over the entire country. This involved not just political control but also the establishment of a collectivist economy and the ideological coordination of Chinese society and culture. In 1966, Mao launched the 'Great Proletarian Cultural Revolution', which resulted in a dramatic purge of the CCP, as well as of economic and cultural elites. Following the deaths in 1976 of Mao and his loyal deputy, Zhou Enlai, dramatic changes took place that saw the introduction of market-based economic reforms, linked to the rapid re-emergence of the pragmatic Deng Xiaoping. China is a one-party communist state, based on:

● The National People's Congress, an almost 3,000-member legislature that meets for only brief periods.
● The State Council, headed by the prime minister (China has a president, who serves as a ceremonial head of state.)

Political change in modern China has been much slower than economic change, meaning that the most important aspect of the Chinese political system remains the leading role of the CCP. Party members occupy the key positions in all major political institutions, and the media, including the Internet, are tightly controlled.

Significance: China's re-emergence as a world power dates back to the 1949 Chinese Revolution. The modern rise of China nevertheless stems from the market-based economic reforms that have been introduced since 1977. Growth rates of consistently around 10 per cent a year for over 30 years have made the Chinese economy the second largest in the world, after the USA. China is the second largest trading state in the world, the largest exporter and the second largest importer of goods. If current trends persist, China will become the largest economy in the world during the 2020s. Although China's world power is very closely related to its economic resurgence, its influence is also growing in other respects. China has by far the largest army in the world and is second only to the USA in terms of military spending. Its influence over Africa in particular has expanded considerably due to massive investment, linked to securing supplies of energy and raw materials. China's structural power has also grown, as is reflected in the growing influence of the G-20 (see p. 121), its role within the WTO (see p. 537) and the fate of the 2009 Copenhagen climate change conference. China's 'soft' power is linked to its association with anti-colonialism and its capacity to portray itself as the representative of the global South.

China's global power should not be over-stated, however. In the first place, China is still some way from challenging the USA as the world's number one power. Indeed, the Chinese leadership appears to recognize that continued US hegemony has a variety of advantages as far as China is concerned, not least insofar as it means that China can have global power without global responsibility. Thus, for example, it was the USA rather than China that was instrumental in orchestrating the international response to the 2007–09 global financial crisis. Similarly, China has been reluctant to mark out a clear global role for itself, being more concerned to act in conjunction with other states, as in the case of the so-called BRICs (see p. 463). In this sense, Chinese foreign policy is structured less around global power projection and more around establishing conditions that are favourable for continued economic success. Many, nevertheless, argue that internal contradictions may ultimately establish limits to China's external influence. The most important of these relate to the political pressures that are likely to be generated by economic liberalization, which may, in time, render one-party authoritarian rule unsustainable. This may either mean that the CCP's monopoly of political power will, sooner or later, become a constraint on continued economic growth, or that economic reform will inevitably build up pressure for political reform, leading to greater instability and perhaps the downfall of the CCP.

on advanced skills and production techniques has yet to be achieved. China's one child policy, introduced in 1979, also means that China has the most rapidly ageing population in the world, putting its future economic prospects seriously at risk. The most serious challenge facing China, however, may be how it reconciles tensions between its political and economic structures. While the Chinese political system remains firmly Stalinist, based on single-party rule by the Chinese Communist Party (CCP), its economic system is increasingly market-orientated and firmly embedded in the global capitalist system. Although authoritarianism may have advantages in terms of managing large-scale economic change and, for instance, pushing through audacious infrastructure programmes, it may be unable to cope with the pluralizing and liberalizing pressures generated by a market capitalist system.

Russia's re-emergence as a great power has been evident in two major respects. First, since the sharp economic decline witnessed in the 1990s, associated with the 'shock therapy' transition to a market economy, a notable revival has taken place. This has largely been driven by the substantial expansion of oil and gas production, itself made possible by the fact that, at 7 million square kilometres, the Russian land mass is significantly greater than any other country and is still largely unexplored, and by steadily rising commodity prices. Although its economy is in serious need of diversification and remains heavily dependent on world commodity markets, Russia has emerged as an energy superpower. This allows it, for instance, to exert influence over the states of Eastern Europe and beyond by controlling the flow and price of oil and gas resources. Second, fuelled by growing economic confidence and strengthened nationalism, Russia has demonstrated a renewed appetite for military assertiveness, especially in relation to the so-called 'near abroad'. This was particularly demonstrated by the 2008 war with Georgia. Nevertheless, Russia's military spending lags a long way behind NATO's, with much of its equipment still stemming from the Cold War era, and extensive and exposed borders make Russia strategically vulnerable at a number of points.

Not all multipolar trends in twenty-first-century world order are associated with the rise of emerging powers, however. Three broader developments have supported the fragmentation and pluralization of global power, and perhaps suggest that all state-centric models of world order (bipolar, unipolar or multipolar) and the distribution of global power are outmoded. The first of these developments is unfolding globalization. As all great powers are embedded to a greater or lesser extent in global economic arrangements and participate within an interlocking capitalist system, the pursuit of national self-interest can only mean, globalists argue, increased integration and cooperation. This implies that great power rivalry in terms of major geopolitical conflicts, and certainly world war, may be a thing of the past. In a context of increased interdependence and interconnectedness, economic rivalry may have displaced military conflict (at least amongst great powers). The second development is the growing trend towards global and sometimes regional governance. This stems from the fact that the principal challenges confronting states – climate change, crime, migration, disease and so on – are increasingly transnational in character and so can only be tackled through transnational cooperation, emphasizing that power is as much about collaboration as it is about conflict. (Such developments are discussed in detail in Chapters 18, 19 and 20.)

Focus on . . .
Offensive or defensive realism?

Does uncertainty and instability in the international system encourage states to prioritize survival or to seek domination? Are states content with maintaining national security, or do they seek 'power after power'? Such questions have been at the heart of an important debate which has been conducted within neorealist theory about the primary motivation of states within an anarchic international order. So-called 'offensive realists', such as Mearsheimer (2001), argue that the combination of anarchy and endemic uncertainty about the actions of others forces states continually to seek to accumulate power, meaning that the primary motivation of states is to improve their position within the power hierarchy. In this view, all states are would-be 'hyperpowers' or 'global hegemons', meaning that perpetual great-power competition is inevitable.

On the other hand, 'defensive realists', such as Mastanduno (1991), argue that while states can be expected to act to prevent other states from making gains at their expense, thereby achieving relative gains, they do not necessarily seek to maximize their own gains. In other words, the primary motivation of states is to guarantee their own security, in which case power is only a means to an end. This may, for example, have been evident in the USA's benign and essentially supportive response to the industrial advance of Japan in the post-1945 period. However, neither offensive realism nor defensive realism offers, on its own, a persuasive model of global politics. The former suggests endless war and violence, while the latter suggests that international affairs are characterized by peace and stability. It is almost the cornerstone of realist analysis that neither of these images is realistic.

Thirdly, the trends towards globalization and in favour of regional and global governance have had the effect of strengthening the role of non-state actors in world affairs. These non-state actors are many and various, ranging from transnational corporations (TNCs) (see p. 94) and non-governmental organizations (NGOs) (see p. 10) to terrorist networks and international criminal groups. For some, the emergence of global civil society (see p. 156) is in the process of bringing a form of cosmopolitan democracy into existence, thereby empowering previously weak or marginalized groups and movements (Archibugi and Held 1995), as discussed in Chapter 22. If global power is dispersed amongst a growing collection of great powers, as well as an expanding range of international organizations and non-state actors, the very idea of polarity is brought into question, meaning that world order may be acquiring a nonpolar character (Haass 2008).

Multipolar order or disorder?

If twenty-first-century world order has a multipolar character, what does this imply about the prospects for war, peace and global stability? Will the twenty-first century be marked by bloodshed and chaos, or by the advance of cooperation and prosperity? There are two quite different models of a multipolar world order. The first highlights the pessimistic implications of a wider diffusion of power amongst global actors. Neorealists have been particularly prominent in warning against the dangers of multipolarity, seeing a tendency towards insta-

John Mearsheimer (born 1947)

US political scientist and international relations theorist. Mearsheimer is one of the leading exponents of offensive realism and a key architect of neorealist stability theory. In 'Back to the Future' (1990) he argued that the Cold War had been largely responsible for maintaining peace in Europe, warning that the end of Cold War bipolarity created the prospect of increased international conflict. In *The Tragedy of Great Power Politics* (2001), Mearsheimer argued that, as it is impossible to determine how much power is sufficient to ensure survival, great powers will always seek to achieve hegemony, behaving aggressively when they believe they enjoy a power advantage over their rivals. Mearsheimer has been a vocal critic of US policy towards China, believing that this is strengthening China, ultimately at the expense of the USA. He was also an outspoken opponent of the Iraq War (see p. 521). His other major works include (with Stephen Walt) *The Israel Lobby and US Foreign Policy* (2007).

bility and chaos as the key feature of its structural dynamic. Mearsheimer (1990) thus lamented the end of Cold War bipolarity, warning that Europe's future in particular would be characterized by a 'back to the future' scenario. By this, he was referring to the multipolar world orders that, arguably, gave rise to WWI and WWII by allowing ambitious powers to pursue expansionist goals precisely because power balances within the international system remained fluid. In this view, multipolarity is inherently unstable, certainly by comparison with bipolarity. This applies because more actors increases the number of possible conflicts and creates higher levels of uncertainty, intensifying the security dilemma (see p. 19 for all states. In addition, shifting alliances amongst multiple actors mean that changes in power balances are likely to be more frequent and possibly more dramatic. Such circumstances, 'offensive' realists in particular point out, encourage restlessness and ambition, making great powers more prone to indiscipline and risk-taking with inevitable consequences for global peace (see p. 240).

In addition to concerns about the structural implications of multipolarity, a number of emerging fault-lines and tensions have been identified. The most common of these has been the possibility of growing enmity, and possibly war, between the USA, the old hegemon, and China, the new hegemon (see p. 243). Will China's rise continue to be peaceful? Those who are most pessimistic about the changing power relationship between the USA and China argue that hegemonic powers rarely adjust easily or peacefully to declining status, while rising hegemons will, sooner or later, seek a level of politico-military power that reflects their economic dominance. Moreover, there are a number of sources of potential Sino–US conflict. For example, cultural and ideological differences between 'liberal-democratic' USA and 'Confucian' China may provide the basis for growing enmity and misunderstanding, in line with the 'clash of civilizations' thesis. In this light, the peaceful transition from British hegemony in the nineteenth century to US global hegemony in the twentieth century was only possible because of historical, cultural and political similarities that allowed the UK to view the rise of the USA as essentially unthreatening. Conflict could also arise from divisions that already exist over issues such

Focus on . . .
To balance or to bandwagon?

Neorealist theorists tend to see the balance of power as a consequence of structural pressures generated by the distribution of power (or capacities) between and amongst states. But how does the international system produce such a fortuitous balance of power? Confronted by the uncertainties and instabilities of international anarchy, states have to choose between 'balancing' (opposing a rising or major power by aligning themselves with other weaker states) or what can be called 'bandwagoning' (siding with a rising or major power). Neorealists argue that balancing behaviour tends, in most circumstances, to prevail over bandwagoning. This happens because, in a context of anarchy, rising or major powers are an object of particular fear, as there is no constraint on how they may treat weaker states. Quite simply, powerful states cannot be trusted. Structural dynamics within the international system therefore tend to favour the balance of power. This helps also to explain the formation of alliances between states that are political and ideological enemies, as in the case of the US–Soviet alliance during World War II.

as Taiwan, Tibet and human rights generally, as well as over growing resource rivalry in Africa, the Middle East and elsewhere. However, others have portrayed the rise of China in a far less threatening light. Not only are China and the USA bound together by the bonds of economic interdependence (the USA is China's main export market, and China is the USA's most important creditor), but, as the twenty-first century progresses, these two powers may create a new form of bipolarity, which, as neorealists argue, would usher in a higher level of security and stability. The USA, furthermore, has an interest in China assuming greater global responsibilities, both to share the burden of such responsibilities and to encourage China to **bandwagon** rather than **balance**.

Another possible source of global tension arises from the renewed power and assertiveness of Russia, leading some to proclaim the emergence of a new Cold War. Although Russia's GDP is less than one-twenty-fifth of that of the combined NATO members, it is, because of its nuclear stockpiles, the only power in the world that could destroy the USA. US policy towards Russia has therefore attempted both to integrate it into the institutions of global governance (for example, through membership of the G-8) and to prevent the possible return of Russian expansionism and territorial influence. This latter goal has been pursued through backing for EU and NATO expansion into the states of the former Soviet bloc and by the agreement, later abandoned, to site US anti-ballistic missiles in Poland and the Czech Republic. These developments are, however, unlikely to generate a new Cold War, as the dynamics of US–Russia relations have changed significantly since the superpower era, as has the global context in which this relationship takes place. An alternative scenario has nevertheless been suggested by Kagan (2008), who proclaimed the 'return of history', in the form of deepening tensions between democracy and authoritarianism, the latter led by the rising power of China and Russia. The difficulty with such a view, however, is that tensions between democratic states (for example,

● **Bandwagon**: To side with a stronger power in the hope of increasing security and influence; 'jumping on the bandwagon'.

● **Balance**: To oppose or challenge a stronger or rising power for fear of leaving oneself exposed.

Sino-US relations in the twenty-first century

Events: In a remarkable coincidence, during November 2012 the world's two major powers, the USA and China, made important decisions about the shape of their senior political leadership within days of one another. On 6 November, the US presidential election was held. This resulted in victory for the Democratic incumbent, President Barack Obama, over his Republican challenger, Mitt Romney. On the day after the US elections, the 18th Congress of the Chinese Communist Party (CCP) began, charged with carrying out China's once-in-a-decade renewal of its political leadership. By the end of the Party Congress, Xi Jinping had been appointed General Secretary of the CCP. In March 2013, the National People's Congress confirmed him as president of China.

Significance: The significance of individual political leaders, or, for that matter, of the nature of a political regime, for foreign policy remains a key issue of debate. While liberals argue that the internal organization of political power may have profound implications for a state's external behaviour, realists and critical theorists are much more likely to explain foreign policy in terms of structural factors, such as the balance of power, global capitalism or patriarchy. However, whether they shape their own, and thus their state's, destinies, or their destinies are shaped for them by broader forces, what will the world of Obama and Xi look like? In particular, how will Sino–US relations develop as the twenty-first century unfolds? Neorealists have issued dark warnings about the implications of a power transition, when an 'old' hegemon is challenged by a rising or 'new' hegemon (Mearsheimer 2001, 2006). This is because, confronted by a rising or major power, other states tend to 'balance' (oppose or challenge that power for fear of leaving themselves exposed), rather than 'bandwagon' (side with that power by 'jumping on the bandwagon'). China will therefore adopt an increasingly assertive, if not aggressive, foreign-policy stance, as its growing economic strength creates an appetite for political and strategic power. This has, for example, been reflected in increased conflict with Japan and other states over disputed islands in the East and South China Seas. The USA, for its part, has acted to constrain rising China, and, in the process, to consolidate its own hegemonic position, through its 'pivot' to Asia, announced by the Obama administration in 2010. Under this, the USA has bolstered its defence ties across Asia and expanded its naval presence in the Pacific.

However, this pessimistic image of intensifying great-power rivalry, as a stubborn USA confronts an ever-more ambitious China, can be questioned for a number of reasons. First, and most importantly, Sino–US relations are unfolding within a context of historically unprecedented levels of interdependence, brought about, in large part, by globalization. The USA and China both benefit enormously from transnational production patterns and the existence of an open trading system, developments that would be put at risk by worsening Sino–US relations, and especially by the prospect of war. Apart from anything else, the two countries are bound together by the fact that China holds much of the USA's sovereign debt. Second, the stark military imbalance between the USA and China (US military spending continues to dwarf China's) means that any inclination China may have to 'balance' against the USA will be confined to the adoption of 'soft' (non-military) balancing strategies rather than 'hard' (military) ones. China will therefore continue its 'peaceful rise', emphasizing trade rather than war. Third, rather than having an appetite for challenging and displacing the USA, policy-makers in China appear to recognize the benefits that China derives from continued US hegemony. This allows China to concentrate on its primary goal of economic development while the USA shoulders the structural and institutional burdens of maintaining the existing global system.

tensions between the USA and Europe) and between authoritarian states (notably between China and Russia) may be just as significant as those across the democracy–authoritarian divide.

However, there is an alternative, and more optimistic, model of multipolarity. In the first place, this suggests that the emergence of new powers and the relative decline of the USA may be managed in a way that preserves peace and keeps rivalry under control. The USA's established approach to likely rivals has been to accommodate them in line with enlightened self-interest and in order to discourage them from aspiring to a greater role. This was evident in US support for the post-1945 Japanese reconstruction and in consistent encouragement given to the process of integration in Europe. A similar approach has been adopted to China, India and, in the main, Russia. Such an approach tends to encourage emerging powers to 'bandwagon' rather than 'balance', becoming part of the usually US-led global trading and financial system rather than putting up barriers against the USA. It also makes the prospects of a 'USA versus the Rest' conflict significantly less likely, as potential rivals are at least as concerned about each other as they are about the USA. The USA's drift back to multilateralism, following its early unilateralist reaction to the emergence of a unipolar world order, not only reflects its recognition of the importance and efficacy of legitimate power, but also enhances its ability to manage shifting balances of power while maintaining peace and cooperation.

SUMMARY

- Power, in its broadest sense, is the ability to influence the outcome of events. Distinctions are nevertheless drawn between actual/potential power, relational/structural power and 'hard/soft' power. The notion of power as material 'power over' others has been subject to increased criticism, leading to more nuanced and multi-dimensional conceptions of power.

- The Cold War was marked by bipolar tension between a US-dominated West and a Soviet-dominated East. The end of the Cold War led to proclamations about the advent of a 'new world order'. However, this new world order was always imprecisely defined, and the idea quickly became unfashionable.

- As the sole remaining superpower, the USA has commonly been referred to as a 'global hegemon'. The implications of US hegemony became particularly apparent following September 11, as the USA embarked on a so-called 'war on terror', based on a neoconservative approach to foreign policy-making. This, nevertheless, drew the USA into deeply problematical military interventions.

- Although neo-con analysts argued that the USA had established a 'benevolent global hegemony', critics, who included realists, radicals and many in the global South, particularly in Muslim countries, argued that the USA was motivated by a desire to ensure economic advantage and to secure control of vital resources, even acting as a 'rogue superpower'.

- Twenty-first-century world order increasingly has a multipolar character. This is evident in the rise of so-called 'emerging powers', notably China, but it is also a consequence of wider developments, including the advance of globalization and global governance, and the growing importance of non-state actors.

- For neo-realists, a multipolar diffusion of power amongst global actors is likely to create a tendency towards instability and even war. On the other hand, multipolarity may strengthen the trend towards multilateralism, leading to stability, order and a tendency towards collaboration.

Questions for discussion

- Why has the notion of power-as-capabilities been criticized?

- To what extent are global outcomes determined by 'structural' power?

- Has 'hard' power become redundant in world affairs?

- Did Cold War bipolarity tend towards stability and peace, or tension and insecurity?

- Was the idea of a 'new world order' merely a tool to legitimize US hegemony?

- What are the implications of hegemony for world order?

- How has the 'war on terror' affected the global status of the USA?

- Is China in the process of becoming the next global hegemon?

- Is tension between the USA and 'the rest' a growing fault-line in global politics?

- Should emerging multipolarity be welcomed or feared?

Further reading

Cooper, R., *The Breaking of Nations: Order and Chaos in the Twenty-first Century* (2004). A stimulating interpretation of the implications of the end of the Cold War, based on the division between the pre-modern, modern and so-called 'postmodern' worlds.

Emmott, B., *Rivals: How the Power Struggle between China, India and Japan will Shape our Next Decade* (2009). A thought-provoking analysis of Asian rivalry and its implications for world affairs.

Parmar, I. and M. Cox (eds), *Soft Power and US Foreign Policy* (2010). A wide-ranging and insightful collection of essays on the role of soft power in affecting the balance of world order.

Young, A., J. Duckett and P. Graham (eds), *Perspectives on the Global Distribution of Power* (2010). A collection of essays that reviews the shifting global distribution of power and examines the changing power resources of key protagonists.

ONLINE RESOURCES AVAILABLE

Links to relevant web resources can be found on the *Global Politics* website

CHAPTER **10** # War and Peace

'War is the continuation of politics by other means.'

KARL VON CLAUSEWITZ, *On War* (1833)

PREVIEW   Military power has been the traditional currency of international politics. States and other actors have exercised influence over each other largely through the threat or use of force, making war a ubiquitous feature of human history, found in all ages, all cultures and all societies. However, even though war appears to be as old as humankind, there are questions about its nature. What distinguishes war from other forms of violence? What are the main causes of war and peace? And does the declining incidence of war in some parts of the world mean that war has become obsolete and military power is a redundant feature of global politics? Nevertheless, the nature of warfare has changed enormously over time, particularly through advances in the technology of fighting and military strategy. The longbow was replaced by the musket, which in turn was replaced by rifles and machine-guns, and so on. Major shifts were brought about in the twentieth century by the advent of 'total' war, as industrial technology was put to the service of fighting. The end of the Cold War was also believed to have ushered in quite different forms of warfare. So-called 'new' wars tended to be civil wars (typically involving small-scale, low-intensity combat), which blurred the distinction between civilians and the military and were often asymmetrical. In the case of so-called 'postmodern' warfare, a heavy reliance was placed on 'high-tech' weaponry. How new were these new forms of warfare, and what were their implications? Finally, there are long-standing debates about whether, and in what circumstances, war can be justified. While some believe that matters of war and peace should be determined by hard-headed judgements about the national self-interest, others insist that war must conform to principles of justice, and others still reject war out of hand and in all circumstances. How can war be justified? Can and should moral principles be applied to war and its conduct?

KEY ISSUES
- What is war? What types of war are there?
- Why do wars occur?
- How, and to what extent, has the face of war changed in the post-Cold War era?
- Why has it become more difficult to determine the outcome of war?
- When, if ever, is it justifiable to resort to war?
- Can war be replaced by 'perpetual peace'?

NATURE OF WAR

Types of war

What is war (see p. 248)? What distinguishes war from other forms of violence: murder, crime, gang attacks or genocide? First, war is a conflict between or among political groups. Traditionally, these groups have been states (see p. 118), with inter-state war, often over territory or resources – wars of plunder – being thought of as the archetypal form of war. However, inter-state war has become less common in recent years, seemingly being displaced by **civil wars** and the growing involvement of non-state actors such as guerrilla groups, resistance movements and terrorist organizations. Second, war is organized, in that it is carried out by armed forces or trained fighters who operate in accordance with some kind of strategy, as opposed to carrying out random and sporadic attacks. **Conventional warfare**, in fact, is a highly organized and disciplined affair, involving military personnel subject to uniforms, drills, saluting and ranks, and even acknowledging that war should be a rule-governed activity as set out by the 'laws of war' (as discussed in Chapter 14). Modern warfare has, nevertheless, become less organized in nature. It involves more irregular fighters who are loosely organized and may refuse to fight by the rules, developments that tend to blur the distinction between military and civilian life, as discussed later in the chapter.

Third, war is usually distinguished by its scale or magnitude. A series of small-scale attacks that involve only a handful of deaths is seldom referred to as a war. The United Nations defines a 'major conflict' as one in which at least 1,000 deaths occur annually. However, this is an arbitrary figure, which would, for example, exclude the Falklands War of 1982, which is almost universally regarded as a war. Finally, as they involve a series of battles or attacks, wars usually take place over a significant period of time. That said, some wars are very short, such as the Six-Day War of 1967 between Israel and the neighbouring states of Egypt, Syria and Jordan. Other wars are nevertheless so protracted, and may involve sometimes substantial periods of peace, that there may be confusion about exactly when a war starts and ends. For example, the Hundred Years' War was in fact a series of wars between England and France, dated by convention 1337–1453, which form part of a longer conflict that began when England was linked to Normandy (1066). Similarly, although WWI and WWII are usually portrayed as separate conflicts, some historians prefer to view them as part of a single conflict interrupted by a twenty-year truce.

However, the nature of war and warfare has changed enormously over time, as they have been refashioned by developments in military technology and strategy. Wars, indeed, reflect the technological and economic levels of developments of their eras. From the days of smoothbore muskets, with soldiers fighting in lines and columns, war gradually became more flexible, first through the advent of rifles, barbed wire, the machine gun and indirect fire, and then through the development of tanks and extended movement, especially in the form of the **Blitzkrieg** as used by the Germans in WWII. Industrialization and the greater capacity of states to mobilize whole populations gave rise in the twentieth century to the phenomenon of **total war**, exemplified by the two world wars of the twentieth century. Other differences between wars are based on the scale of the conflict and the nature of the outcomes at stake. At one

● **Civil war**: An armed conflict between politically organized groups within a state, usually fought either for control of the state or to establish a new state.

● **Conventional warfare**: A form of warfare that is conducted by regular, uniformed and national military units and uses conventional (not nuclear) military weapons and battlefield tactics.

● **Blitzkrieg**: (German) Literally, lightning war; penetration in depth by armoured columns, usually preceded by aerial bombardment to reduce enemy resistance.

● **Total war**: A war involving all aspects of society, including large-scale conscription, the gearing of the economy to military ends, and the aim of achieving unconditional surrender through the mass destruction of enemy targets.

● **Hegemonic war**: War that is fought to establish dominance of the entire world order by restructuring the global balance of power.

● **Guerrilla war**: (Spanish) Literally, 'little war'; an insurgency or 'people's' war, fought by irregular troops using tactics that are suited to the terrain and emphasize mobility and surprise rather than superior firepower.

extreme there are **hegemonic wars**, sometimes called 'global', 'general', 'systemic' or 'world' wars, which usually involve a range of states, each mobilizing its full economic and social resources behind a struggle to defend or reshape the global balance of power. On the other hand, there are 'limited' or 'regional' wars that are fought in line with more limited objectives, such as the redrawing of boundaries or the expulsion of enemy occupiers, as in the 1991 Gulf War (expelling Iraq from Kuwait) and the 1999 US-led NATO bombing of Kosovo (expelling Serb forces). Finally, a range of conflicts are often considered to be examples of 'unconventional warfare', either because of the use of nuclear, chemical or biological weapons (as discussed in Chapter 11) or because they fall into the classification of 'new' wars (discussed later in the chapter), sometimes seen as **guerrilla wars**.

Why do wars occur?

Each war is unique in that it stems from a particular set of historical circumstances. Chapter 2, for instance, examines the origins of WWI, WWII and the Cold War. However, the fact that war appears to be a historical constant has inclined some theorists to argue that there are deeper or underlying explanations of war that apply to all ages and all societies (Suganami 1996). In line with what remains the standard work on the subject of war, Kenneth Waltz's *Man, the State and War* (1959), these theories can be categorized in terms of three levels of analysis, depending on whether they focus on human nature, the internal characteristics of states, or structural or systemic pressures. The most common explanation for war is that it stems from instincts and appetites that are innate to the human individual. Thucydides (see p. 249) thus argued that war is caused by 'the lust for power arising from greed and ambition'. War is therefore endless because human desires and appetites are infinite, while the resources to satisfy them are always finite; the struggle and competition that this gives rise to will inevitably express itself in bloodshed and violence. Scientific support for human self-interestedness has usually been based on the evolutionary theories of the British biologist Charles Darwin (1809–82) and the idea of a struggle for survival, developed by social Darwinians such as Herbert Spencer (1820–1903) into the doctrine of the 'survival of the fittest'. Evolutionary psychologists, such as the Austrian zoologist Konrad Lorenz (1966), have argued that aggression is biologically programmed, particularly in men, as a result of territorial and sexual instincts that are found in all species. Whether war is fought to protect the homeland, acquire wealth and resources, achieve national glory, advance political or religious principles or establish racial or ethnic dominance, it provides a necessary and inevitable outlet for aggressive urges that are hard-wired in human nature.

Such assumptions underpin classical realist theories about power politics, which portray contention amongst states or other political groups as a manifestation, on a collective level, of individual selfishness and competitiveness. However, biological theories of war also have their drawbacks. They offer an unbalanced view of human nature that places too much emphasis on 'nature', which implies that human nature is fixed or given, and too little emphasis on 'nurture', the complex range of social, cultural, economic and political factors that shape human behaviour and may modify instinctual drives or channel them in particular directions. Furthermore, even if the idea of innate aggression is

Thucydides (ca. 460–406 BCE)

Greek historian with philosophical interests. Thucydides' great work *The History of the Peloponnesian War* recounts the struggle between Athens and Sparta for control of the Hellenic world, 431–404 BCE, which culminated in the destruction of Athens, the birthplace of democracy. He explained this conflict in terms of the dynamics of power politics and the relative power of the rival city-states. As such, he developed the first sustained realist explanation of international conflict and, arguably, propounded the earliest theory of international relations. His dark view of human nature influenced Hobbes (see p. 14). In the **Melian dialogue**, Thucydides showed how power politics is indifferent to moral argument, a lesson sometimes taken to be a universal truth.

accepted, it by no means proves that large-scale, organized warfare is inevitable.

The second range of theories suggest that war is best explained in terms of the inner characteristics of political actors. Liberals, for example, have long argued that states' constitutional and governmental arrangements incline some towards aggression while others favour peace. This is most clearly reflected in the idea that democratic states do not go to war against one another, as is implied by the 'democratic peace' thesis (see p. 69). By contrast, authoritarian and imperialist states are inclined towards **militarism** and war. This happens because such regimes rely heavily on the armed forces to maintain domestic order in the absence of representative processes and through the need to subdue subordinate national and ethnic groups, meaning that political and military elites often become fused. This typically leads to a glorification of the armed forces, a political culture shaped by an atavistic belief in heroism and self-sacrifice, and the recognition of war as not only a legitimate instrument of policy, but also as an expression of national patriotism.

Social constructivists place particular stress on cultural and ideological factors that make war more likely, either by portraying the international environment as threatening and unstable, or by giving a state or political group a militaristic or expansionist self-image. The spread of social Darwinian thinking in late nineteenth-century Europe has thus been linked to the growing international tensions that led to WWI, while the Cold War was, in part, sustained by US fears about the expansionist character of international communism and Soviet fears about the dangers of capitalist encirclement. Similarly, doctrines of Aryan racial superiority and the idea of German world domination contributed to Nazi aggression in the lead-up to WWII, and *jihadist* theories about a fundamental clash between the Muslim world and the West have inspired Islamist insurgency and terrorist movements. Alternative 'internal' explanations for aggression include that war may be used to prop up an unpopular regime by diverting attention away from domestic failure (as in the Argentine attack on the Falkland Islands in 1982), or that it is a consequence of demographic pressures, notably a bulge in the numbers of fighting age males at a time of economic stagnation and social dislocation (a theory used by Huntington (1996) to explain the growing political assertiveness of the 'Islamic civilization').

● **Melian dialogue**: A dialogue between the Melians and the Athenians, quoted in Thucydides' *Peloponnesian War*, in which the latter refused to accept the Melian wish to remain neutral in the conflict with Sparta, eventually besieging and massacring them.

● **Militarism**: A cultural or ideological phenomenon in which military priorities, ideas and values come to pervade the larger society.

A variety of structural or systemic theories of war have been advanced. The most influential of these has been the neorealist assertion that war is an inevitable consequence of an anarchic international system that forces states to rely on self-help. In its gloomiest form, as advanced by offensive realists, who believe that states, regardless of their constitutional or governmental structures, seek to maximize power and not merely security, this suggests that international relations are destined always to be characterized by a restless struggle for advantage, with military conflict being an unavoidable fact of life. This tendency is accentuated by the security dilemma (see p. 19) that arises from fear and uncertainty amongst states, which are inclined to interpret defensive actions by other states as potentially or actually offensive. For realists, the only way that war can be banished permanently from the international system is through the establishment of world government (see p. 464) and thus the abolition of anarchy (a development they nevertheless regard as highly improbable as well as dangerous).

Other structural theories of war place a heavier emphasis on economic factors. Marxists, for instance, view war as a consequence of the international dynamics of the capitalist system. Capitalist states will inevitably come into conflict with one another as each is forced to expand in the hope of maintaining profit levels by gaining control over new markets, raw materials or supplies of cheap labour. All wars are thus wars of plunder carried out in the interests of the capitalist class. In its liberal version, the economic impulse to war is often seen to stem from the practice of economic nationalism, through which states seek to become self-sufficient economic units. The pursuit of **autarky** inclines states towards protectionist policies and ultimately towards colonialism, deepening economic rivalry and making war more likely. However, economic theories of war have become less influential since 1945 as trade has been accepted as a more reliable road to prosperity than expansionism and conquest. Insofar as economic pressures have encouraged interdependence (see p. 7) and integration, they are now seen to weaken the impulse to war, not fuel it.

War as a continuation of politics

The most influential theory of war was developed by Clausewitz (see p. 252) in his master work, *On War* ([1833] 1976). In Clausewitz's view, all wars have the same 'objective' character: 'War is merely a continuation of politics (or policy) by other means'. War is therefore a means to an end, a way of forcing an opponent to submit to one's will. Such a stance emphasizes the continuity between war and peace. Both war and peace are characterized by the rational pursuit of self-interest, and therefore by conflict; the only difference between them is the means selected to achieve one's goals, and that is decided on an instrumental basis (Howard 1983). States thus go to war when they calculate that it is in their interest to do so. This implied use of a form of cost–benefit analysis is entirely in line with the realist view of war as a policy instrument. The Clausewitzian, or 'political', conception of war is often seen as a product of the Westphalian state-system, in which international affairs were shaped by relations between and amongst states (although, strictly speaking, any political actor, including non-state ones, could use war as a policy instrument). The image of war as the 'rational' pursuit of state interest was particularly attractive in the nineteenth century when wars were overwhelmingly fought between opposing states and roughly four-fifths of all

● **Autarky**: Literally, self-rule; usually associated with economic self-sufficiency brought about by either colonial expansion or a withdrawal from international trade.

WAR AND PEACE

Realist view

For realists, war is an enduring feature of international relations and world affairs. The possibility of war stems from the inescapable dynamics of power politics: as states pursue the national interest (see p. 135) they will inevitably come into conflict with one another, and this conflict will sometimes (but not always) be played out in military terms. Realists explain violent power politics in two ways. First, classical realists emphasize state egoism, arguing that rivalry between and among political communities reflects the inherent tendency within human nature towards self-seeking, competition and aggression. Second, neorealists argue that, as the international system is anarchic, states are forced to rely on self-help in order to achieve survival and security, and this can only be ensured through the acquisition of military power. For offensive realists in particular, this leads to a strong likelihood of war (see Offensive or defensive realism? p. 240). All realists, however, agree that the principal factor that helps to prevent a descent into war is the balance of power (see p. 262). States will avoid war if they calculate that their chances of victory are slim. Decisions about war and peace are therefore made through a kind of cost–benefit analysis, in which rational self-interest may dictate either the use of war or its avoidance. States that wish to preserve peace must therefore prepare for war, hoping to deter potential aggressors and to prevent any other state or coalition of states from achieving a position of predominance.

Liberal view

Liberals believe that peace is a natural, but by no means an inevitable, condition for international relations. From the liberal perspective, war arises from three sets of circumstances, each of which is avoidable. First, echoing realist analysis, liberals accept that state egoism in a context of anarchy may lead to conflict and a possibility of war. However, liberals believe that an international anarchy can and should be replaced by an international rule of law, achieved through the construction of supranational bodies. Second, liberals argue that war is often linked to economic nationalism and autarky, the quest for economic self-sufficiency tending to bring states into violent conflict with one another. Peace can nevertheless be achieved through free trade and other forms of economic interdependence, especially as these may make war so economically costly that it becomes unthinkable. Third, the disposition of a state towards war or peace is crucially determined by its constitutional character. Authoritarian states tend to be militaristic and expansionist, accustomed to the use of force to achieve both domestic and foreign goals, while democratic states are more peaceful, at least in their relations with other democratic states (for a discussion of the 'democratic peace' thesis, see p. 69).

Critical views

Critical theorists in the Marxist tradition have tended to explain war primarily in economic terms. WWI, for instance, was an imperialist war fought in pursuit of colonial gains in Africa and elsewhere (Lenin 1970). The origins of war can thus be traced back to the capitalist economic system, war, in effect, being the pursuit of economic advantage by other means. Such an analysis implies that socialism is the best guarantee of peace, socialist movements often having a marked anti-war or even pacifist orientation, shaped by a commitment to internationalism (see p. 67). Critical theorists in the anarchist tradition, such as Chomsky (see p. 235), have shown a particular interest in the phenomenon of hegemonic war, believing that the world's most powerful states use war, directly or indirectly, to defend or expand their global economic and political interests. War is therefore closely associated with hegemony (see p. 228), while peace can be built only through a radical redistribution of global power. Feminists, for their part, have adopted a gender perspective on war and peace. Not only are wars fought essentially between males, but the realist image of international politics as conflict-ridden and prone to violence reflects 'masculinist' assumptions about self-interest, competition and the quest for domination. For difference feminists in particular, the origins of war stem either from the warlike nature of the male sex or from the institution of patriarchy (see p. 424). By contrast, feminists draw attention to what they see as the close association between women and peace, based either on the 'natural' peacefulness of women, or on the fact that women's experience of the world encourages an emphasis on human connectedness and cooperation.

Karl von Clausewitz (1780–1831)

Prussian general and military theorist. The son of a Lutheran Pastor, Clausewitz entered the Prussian military service at the age of 12, and achieved the rank of Major-General by the age of 38. Having studied the philosophy of Kant (see p. 15) and been involved in the reform of the Prussian army, Clausewitz set out his ideas on military strategy in *On War* ([1833] 1976). Widely interpreted as advancing the idea that war is essentially a political act, an instrument of policy, the book sets out a 'trinitarian' theory of warfare which involves (1) the masses, who are motivated by a sense of national animosity; (2) the army, which devises strategies to take account of the contingencies of war; and (3) political leaders, who establish the aims and objectives of military action. Clausewitz is usually regarded as the greatest writer on military theory and war.

wars were won by the state that started them. Moreover, although the hostility of the people was needed to fight a war, wars were fought by armies and therefore affected formal combatants rather than the larger civilian population. This made the costs of warfare more limited and easier to calculate.

The Clausewitzian conception of war has nevertheless attracted growing criticism. Some of these criticisms are moral in character. Clausewitz has been condemned for presenting war as a normal and inevitable condition, one, furthermore, that can be justified by reference to narrow state interest rather than wider principles such as justice. This therefore suggests that if war serves legitimate political purposes its moral implications can be ignored, a position that is discussed in the final section of this chapter. On the other hand, had Clausewitz's suggestion that the recourse to war should be based on rational analysis and careful calculation been followed more consistently, many modern wars may not have taken place. Other criticisms of the Clausewitzian conception of war emphasize that it is outdated, relevant to the Napoleonic era but certainly not to modern wars and warfare. First, modern economic and political circumstances may dictate that war is a less effective, and perhaps even an obsolete, policy instrument. If modern states are rationally disinclined to resort to war, military power may have become irrelevant in world affairs (van Creveld 1991; Gray 1997) (see p. 253). Second, the advent of industrialized warfare, and particularly the phenomenon of total war, has made calculations about the likely costs and benefits of war much less reliable. If this is the case, war may have ceased to be an appropriate means of achieving political ends. Finally, most of the criticisms of Clausewitz highlight changes in the nature of war that make the Clausewitzian paradigm of war no longer applicable. To what extent are modern wars post-Clausewitzian wars?

CHANGING FACE OF WAR

From 'old' wars to 'new' wars?

One of the most widely debated features of the post-Cold War era is how it has affected war and warfare. Modern wars are often considered to be 'new', 'postmodern', 'post-Clausewitzian' or 'post-Westphalian' wars (Kaldor 2012). In the

Debating ...
Has military power become redundant in global politics?

Military power has traditionally been viewed as the chief currency of international politics. However, some argue that in recent decades the threat and use of force have become increasingly obsolete as a means of determining global outcomes.

YES

Obsolescence of war. Military power is redundant because war, certainly in the form of large-scale, high-intensity conflict, is now obsolete in many parts of the world. The spread of democratic governance has lead to widening 'democratic zones of peace', democratic states being reluctant to go to war with one another. The emergence, since 1945, of a system of international law (see p. 339) centred around the UN has also changed moral attitudes towards the use of force, making wars of plunder non-legitimate. The advent of total war, and especially the development of nuclear weapons, means that the impact of war is so devastating that it has ceased to be a viable instrument of state policy. Finally, states increasingly have other, more pressing, claims on their resources, notably public services and welfare provision.

Trade not war. One of the key reasons for the obsolescence of war is globalization (see p. 8). Globalization has reduced the incidence of war in at least three ways. First, states no longer need to make economic gains by conquest because globalization offers a cheaper and easier route to national prosperity in the form of trade. Second, by significantly increasing levels of economic interdependence, globalization makes war almost unthinkable because of the high economic costs involved (trade partnerships destroyed, external investment lost, and so on). Third, trade and other forms of economic interaction build international understanding and so counter insular (and possibly aggressive) forms of nationalism.

Unwinnable wars. Changes in the nature of warfare have made it increasingly difficult to predict the outcome of war on the basis of the respective capabilities of the parties concerned. This is reflected in the difficulty that developed states have had in winning so-called 'asymmetrical' wars, such as the Vietnam War and in the counter-insurgency wars in Iraq and Afghanistan. If the USA as the world's only military superpower is unable to wage war with a guaranteed likelihood of success, alternative, non-military means of exerting influence over world affairs are likely to become increasingly attractive.

NO

War is endless. Realists dismiss the idea that war has, or could, come to an end, on the grounds that the international system continues to be biased in favour of conflict. Military power remains the only sure guarantee of a state's survival and security, and the irresolvable security dilemma (see p. 19) means that fear and uncertainty persist. Moreover, 'zones of peace' may contract due to the 'rolling back' of globalization and a shift towards economic nationalism and intensifying great-power rivalry (as occurred before WWI). Further, the USA's massive global military predominance, a major reason for the decline of inter-state wars, is destined to change as world order becomes increasingly multipolar and therefore unstable.

New security challenges. The decline of inter-state war does not mean that the world has become a safer place. Rather, new and, in some ways, more challenging, security threats have emerged. This particularly applies in the case of terrorism (see p. 291), as demonstrated by 9/11 and other attacks. Terrorism, indeed, shows how globalization has made the world more dangerous, as terrorists gain easier access to devastating weaponry, and can operate on a transnational or even global basis. Such threats underline the need for states to develop more sophisticated military strategies, both to ensure tighter domestic security and, possibly, to attack foreign terrorist camps and maybe states that harbour terrorists.

Humanitarian wars. Since the end of the Cold War, the purpose of war and the uses to which military power is put have changed in important ways. In particular, armed force has been used more frequently to achieve humanitarian ends, often linked to protecting citizens from civil strife or from the oppressive policies of their own governments, examples including Northern Iraq, Sierra Leone, Kosovo and East Timor. In such cases, humanitarian considerations go hand in hand with considerations of national self-interest. Without military intervention from outside, civil wars, ethnic conflict and humanitarian disasters often threaten regional stability and result in migration crises, and so have much wider ramifications.

conventional view, war is an armed conflict between opposing states, an image that sprang out of the acceptance of the Westphalian state-system. During this period, war appeared to conform to a Clausewitzian paradigm. War as an instrument of state policy meant that wars were fought by uniformed, organized bodies of men – national armies, navies and air forces. A body of norms or rules also developed to regulate armed conflict, including formal declarations of war and declarations of neutrality, peace treaties and the 'laws of war'. However, war appears to have changed. Starting with the tactics employed in the 1950s and 1960s by national liberation movements in places such as Algeria, Vietnam and Palestine, and then extending to conflicts in countries such as Somalia, Liberia, Sudan and the Congo, a new style of warfare has developed, possibly even redefining war itself (Gilbert 2003). Following the break-up of the Soviet Union and Yugoslavia in the 1990s, such 'new' wars occurred in Bosnia and in the Caucasus, particularly Chechnya, as well as in Iraq and Afghanistan, often seen as part of the larger 'war on terror' (see p. 230). In what sense are these wars 'new', and how clear is the distinction between 'new' wars and 'old' wars?

Although not all 'new' wars are the same, they tend to exhibit some, if not all, of the following features:

- They tend to be civil wars rather than inter-state wars.
- Issues of identity are usually prominent.
- Wars are asymmetrical, often fought between unequal parties.
- The civilian/military distinction has broken down.
- They are more barbaric than 'old' wars.

The decline of traditional inter-state war and the rise of civil war has been a marked feature of the post-Cold War era. About 95 per cent of armed conflicts since the mid-1980s have occurred within states, not between states. Recent exceptions to this trend have included the Iran–Iraq War (1980–8) and the 2008 Russian war with Georgia. The decline of inter-state war, and even the obsolescence of war in some parts of the world (so-called 'zones of peace'), can be explained by a variety of factors. These include the spread of democracy, the advance of globalization, changing moral attitudes to war often linked to the role of the UN, and developments in weapons technology, especially nuclear weapons, that would massively increase the devastation wreaked by large-scale war. On the other hand, civil wars have become more common in the postcolonial world, where colonialism often left a heritage of ethnic or tribal rivalry, economic underdevelopment and weak state power, hence the emergence of 'quasi states' or 'failed states' (see p. 126). Most of the weakest states in the world have been concentrated in sub-Saharan Africa, classic examples including Somalia, Sierra Leone, Liberia and the Congo. These states have been weak in that they failed the most basic test of state power: they were unable to maintain domestic order and personal security, meaning that civil strife and even civil war became routine. As the borders of such states were invariably determined by former colonial rulers, they typically contained a range of ethnic, religious and tribal differences, meaning that this postcolonial world often appeared to be a 'zone of turmoil'.

Modern wars are often portrayed as **identity wars**. Whereas earlier wars were motivated by geopolitical or ideological goals, modern wars often arise

● **Identity war**: A war in which the quest for cultural regeneration, expressed though the demand that a people's collective identity is publicly and politically recognized, is a primary motivation for conflict.

from cultural discord expressed in terms of rival identities. Identity politics (see p. 190), in its various forms, has arisen from the pressures generated by economic and cultural globalization, especially as these have affected postcolonial societies, and the declining effectiveness of solidarities based on social class and ideology. Not all forms of identity politics give rise to hatred, communal conflict and bloodshed, however. This is more likely to occur when groups embrace exclusive models of identity that define 'us' in terms of a hostile and threatening 'them'. According to Sen (2006), identity politics is most likely to lead to violence when it is based on a 'solitaristic' form of identity, which defines human identity in terms of membership of a *single* social group. This encourages people to identify exclusively with their own monoculture, thereby failing to recognize the rights and integrity of people from other cultural groups, and is evident in the rise of militant ethnic, religious and nationalist movements. The wars that broke out in former Yugoslavia in the 1990s (see p. 256), conflicts between Muslims and Hindus in the Indian subcontinent, the *intifadas* in the occupied territories of Israel and the 'war on terror' in general and especially the Iraq and Afghanistan wars, could thus be viewed as examples of identity wars. Because identity wars are ultimately based on how people see themselves, they are often fought with unusual passion and ferocity. They also tend to be long-standing and may appear to be intractable, rendering the traditional notion of victory redundant.

Whereas inter-state war usually took place between opponents at a relatively similar level of economic development, modern wars have frequently been asymmetrical, in that they pit industrially advanced and militarily sophisticated states against enemies that appear to be 'third-rate'. This applied in the case of US, or US-led, wars in Vietnam, Kosovo, Iraq and Afghanistan, and in the case of the Russian war against Chechnya. **Asymmetrical wars** are characterized by the adoption of military strategies and tactics designed to create a more level playing field between opponents with very different military and economic capabilities, meaning that asymmetrical wars do not have assured and inevitable outcomes. Guerrilla warfare, which places a premium on manoeuvre and surprise, through the use of small-scale raids, ambushes and attacks, has been effective in defeating much better-resourced enemies with greater fire power. This is also often supplemented by the use of terrorist tactics, ranging from roadside bombs to suicide attacks. A particular effort is usually made to strengthen links with the civilian population, so that war becomes a form of popular resistance, or **insurgency**. Such tactics aim less to defeat the enemy in strict military terms (something that may be impossible), but rather to demoralize the enemy and break its political will, as in Vietnam, Israel, Iraq and Afghanistan. However, having tried to adapt to small-scale, low-intensity counter-insurgency warfare, there are clear indications that developed states are trying to find alternatives to 'boots-on-the-ground' wars (see p. 260).

The civilian/military divide has been blurred in a variety of ways. Since the Thirty Years' War (1618–48), a clear distinction has been recognized between combatants and civilians, which was relatively easy to respect while warfare was largely confined to the battlefield and strictly military personnel. However, by their nature, modern wars have a greater impact on civilian populations. This has occurred partly because of the diffuse nature of modern warfare, which tends to involve a succession of small-scale engagements rather than set-piece,

● **Asymmetrical war**: War fought between opponents with clearly unequal levels of military, economic and technological power, in which warfare strategies tend to be adapted to the needs of the weak.

● **Insurgency**: An armed uprising, involving irregular soldiers, which aims to overthrow the established regime.

KEY EVENTS . . .

Conflicts in the former Yugoslavia

1919	State of Yugoslavia recognized by the Treaty of Versailles, following the collapse of the Austro-Hungarian empire.
1945	Yugoslavia becomes a communist state, including six republics (Serbia, Croatia, Bosnia Herzegovina, Slovenia, Macedonia and Montenegro) and two autonomous provinces within Serbia (Kosovo and Vojvodina).
1986–9	Rise of nationalism in Serbia (the largest and most influential republic), associated with the leadership of Slobodan Milosević after 1987.
1990	Following the fall of communism across the rest of eastern Europe, each republic holds multiparty elections, strengthening support for independence in Slovenia and Croatia.
1991	The break-up of Yugoslavia starts with declarations of independence by Slovenia and Croatia (June), Macedonia (September) and Bosnia Herzegovina (January 1992). By April 1992, all that remains within Yugoslavia is Serbia and Montenegro.
1991	The secession of Slovenia precipitates the Ten-Day War in which the Slovenians successfully resist the Serb-led Yugoslav army.
1991–5	The Croatian War of Independence occurs, a bitter civil war fought against the Croatian Serb minority, who are helped by the Yugoslav army.
1992–5	The Bosnian Civil War occurs, becoming the longest and most violent European war in the second half of the twentieth century. Caused by opposition by ethnic Serbs to Bosnia's secession from Yugoslavia, the war witnesses the massacre of thousands of Bosnian Muslims and a brutal programme of 'ethnic cleansing', whereby Muslims and Croats are expelled from areas under Serb control. Despite the 1995 Dayton Agreement to re-establish a united country, Bosnia remains effectively divided into two autonomous halves, one Muslim-Croat and the other Serb controlled.
1996–9	The Kosovo War occurs, in which the Kosovo Liberation Army takes up armed resistance against the Serbs, with accusations of massacres and 'ethnic cleansing' on both sides. In 1999, a US-led NATO (see p. 259) campaign of aerial bombing forces Serb troops to withdraw from Kosovo, leading to the removal of the Milosević government in Belgrade in 2000. Kosovo declares its independence from Serbia in 2008.

major battles, meaning that the conventional idea of a battlefield has to be discarded as redundant. War has developed into 'war amongst the people' (Smith 2006). The blurring has also occurred because civilian populations have increasingly been the target of military action (through the use of land mines, suicide bombs, vehicle bombs and terrorism generally), its objective being to create economic and social dislocation, and to destroy the enemy's resolve and appetite for war. Modern warfare is therefore often accompanied by refugee crises in

KEY CONTEMPORARY THEORISTS OF WAR

Mary Kaldor (born 1946)

UK academic and international relations theorist. In *New Wars and Old Wars* (2012), Kaldor linked new wars to the crisis in state authority that has occurred through the impact of privatization and globalization. Violent struggles to gain access to or control the state lead to massive violations of human rights, with violence usually being carried out in the name of identity and mainly being directed against civilians. Kaldor's other works include *Global Civil Society* (2003) and *Human Security* (2007).

Martin van Creveld (born 1946)

Israeli military historian and theorist of war. Van Creveld's *The Transformation of War* (1991) attempts to explain the apparent military impotence of the developed world due to the predominance, since 1945, of low-intensity conflicts and non-conventional warfare. In this context, Clausewitzian ideas about political war no longer apply, as war often becomes an end in itself, rather than an instrument of national power. Van Creveld's other key works include *Supplying War* (1977) and *The Art of War* (2000).

David Kilkullen (born 1967)

Australian former army officer and adviser on counter-terrorism and counter-insurgency. He argues that as the contemporary conflict environment is often complex, diverse, diffuse and highly lethal, counter-insurgency must seek to control the overall environment, paying particular attention to its 'cultural ethnography'. Kilkullen's ideas have influenced the USA's altered approach to the 'war on terror'. His works include 'Countering Global Insurgency' (2005), *The Accidental Guerrilla* (2009) and *Counter Insurgency* (2010).

which thousands and sometimes millions of displaced people seek shelter and security, on a temporary and sometimes permanent basis (as discussed in Chapter 7). The civilian/military divide has also been blurred by the changing nature of armies and security forces. Guerrilla armies, for instance, consist of irregular soldiers or armed bands of volunteers, and insurgency often comes close to assuming the character of a popular uprising. The use of **mercenaries** continues to be an important feature of armed conflict in parts of Africa, as in the failed 2004 coup in Equatorial Guinea. Such trends are, nevertheless, also apparent in developed states and especially the USA. The Iraq War was the most 'privatized' in history, with, by mid-2007, more private military contractors operating in Iraq, working for companies such as Blackwater (now renamed Xe Services) and Halliburton, than regular soldiers. At times, Blackwater even assumed control over US marines, as when it was given lead responsibility for quelling the April 2004 uprising in Najav.

● **Mercenaries**: Hired soldiers in the service of a foreign power.

Focus on . . .
The Iraq War as a 'new' war?

The Iraq War can be viewed as an 'old' war in a number of respects. First, the war was, in origin, an inter-state war between the US-led 'coalition of the willing' and Saddam Hussein's Iraq. Second, the USA justified its invasion of Iraq in March 2003 in the conventional terms of self-defence. Its purpose was 'regime change' in Iraq, based on the (subsequently disproved) assertion that Iraq possessed weapons of mass destruction (WMD) and the (questionable) assertion that the Saddam regime had links to and had sponsored terrorist groups including al-Qaeda, suggesting that Iraq was a threat to the USA. Third, critics of the war have often portrayed it more as a conventional imperialist war, fought primarily to strengthen US control over oil supplies in the Gulf region.

Nevertheless, the Iraq War exhibits many of the characteristics of a 'new' war. Once the initial phase of the war, which led, within three weeks, to the fall of Baghdad and the overthrow of Saddam's 24-year rule, was completed, the conflict gradually developed into a complex insurgency war. Becoming increasingly fero-cious from 2004 onwards, the insurgency had two dimensions. One was a conflict between US troops and Sunni guerrilla fighters, many of whom were initially Saddam loyalists, and a growing number of Iraqi religious radicals and foreign al-Qaeda fighters. The other was between Iraq's Sunni and Shia communities and led to an escalating orgy of sectarian violence. Identity-related issues were therefore clearly entangled with more conventional political ones. The USA also, over time, adapted its strategies to the challenges of a 'new' war. From early 2007 onwards, US military tactics were geared around counter-insurgency goals, particularly through the so-called 'surge'. In addition to increasing the USA's military deployment in Iraq, this involved putting more US troops onto Iraqi streets in an attempt to improve relations with the domestic population, and cultivating an alliance between US forces and Sunni insurgents (based in part on payments made by the USA and later the Shia-dominated Iraqi government to the Sunni 'Sons of Iraq'), helping to marginalize religious radicals and al-Qaeda fighters.

Finally, new wars have often been more barbaric and horrific than old ones, as the rules that have constrained conventional inter-state warfare have commonly been set aside. Practices such as kidnapping, torture, systematic rape and the indiscriminate killings that result from landmines, car bombs and suicide attacks have become routine features of modern warfare. This is sometimes explained in terms of the implications of identity politics, through which the enemy is defined in terms of their membership of a particular group, rather than in terms of their role or actions. An entire people, race or culture may therefore be defined as 'the enemy', meaning that they are seen as worthless or fundamentally evil and that military and civilian targets are equally legitimate. Exclusive religious, ethnic or nationalist movements are therefore often characterized by their **militancy**, often expressed in terrorism or violence. This also explains why inter-communal strife is often associated with programmes of '**ethnic cleansing**'.

● **Militancy**: Heightened or extreme commitment; a level of zeal and passion typically associated with struggle or war.

● **Ethnic cleansing**: The forcible expulsion or extermination of 'alien' peoples; often used as a euphemism for genocide.

'Postmodern' warfare

War and warfare have always been affected by changes in the technology of fighting. Two historical examples of such radical changes were the use of the longbow at the Battle of Agincourt (1415), which enabled heavily outnumbered English

GLOBAL ACTORS . . .

NORTH ATLANTIC TREATY ORGANIZATION

Type: Intergovernmental military alliance • **Founded:** 1948 • **Headquarters:** Brussels, Belgium
Membership: 28 states

The North Atlantic Treaty Organization (NATO) was formed in 1948, when Belgium, the UK, the Netherlands, France and Luxembourg signed the North Atlantic Treaty (sometimes called the Brussels Treaty). The following year, seven further countries – the USA, Canada, Denmark, Norway, Iceland, Italy and Portugal – joined the alliance. By 2010, NATO membership stood at 28, most of its newer members being former communist states. The central aim of NATO is to safeguard the freedom and security of its member countries by political or military means. Its key principle as a military alliance is that an attack against one or several members would be considered an attack against all (Article 5 of the NATO Charter). All NATO decisions are taken jointly on the basis of consensus.

Significance: NATO is the world's premier military alliance. The combined military spending of all NATO members constitutes about 70 per cent of the world's military spending, mainly thanks to the USA. NATO was in origin, and remained for almost 40 years, a child of the Cold War. Its primary purpose was to act as a deterrent against the threat posed by the Soviet Union and its Eastern bloc satellite states, whose collective military alliance was the Warsaw Pact (1955). As its first Secretary General, Lord Ismay,

put it, its role was 'to keep the Russians out, the Americans in, and the Germans down'. As such, NATO cemented the post-1945 bond between the USA and Western Europe, and contributed, with its communist bloc equivalent the Warsaw Pact, to the military stand-off that characterized the Cold War period.

However, with the ending of the Cold War in 1990, NATO effectively had to find a new role. It did so by establishing itself as a force for European and global peacemaking and crisis management. It performed a valuable role as the UN's peacekeeping force in Bosnia in 1996, and extended its authority by setting up a Partnership for Peace (PFP) which provides former Warsaw Pact and other states with an opportunity to associate with NATO on a bilateral basis. PFP membership is often seen as the first step towards full NATO membership. NATO's new role was evident in its peacekeeping and enforcement operations in the former Yugoslavia, 1993–6. In 1999, it carried out its first broad-scale military operation through the 11-week bombing campaign (Operation Allied Force) that expelled Serb forces from Kosovo. Although NATO has usually acted under UN mandates, most NATO countries opposed efforts to require the UN Security Council to approve NATO military strikes.

September 11 caused NATO to

invoke, for the first time in its history, Article 5. This was to have significant ramifications for NATO, eventually giving it a potentially global role. In 2003, NATO took over command of the International Security Assistance Force in Afghanistan, marking the alliance's first mission outside the north Atlantic area. It also drew NATO more closely into the 'war on terror' and gave it responsibility for a complex counter-insurgency struggle. An additional shift in focus arose during the 2000s as a result of NATO's expansion into the former communist states and republics of eastern Europe, paralleling the eastward expansion of the European Union. However, whereas EU expansion was relatively uncontroversial, NATO expansion became a growing source of tension between NATO, and particularly the USA, and Russia, encouraging some to talk of the revival of NATO's traditional Cold War role. The issue of Ukrainian and Georgian accession to NATO has been particularly controversial, the prospect of the latter having been one of the factors that contributed to Russia's war with Georgia in 2008. Tensions with Russia also surfaced over calls for a NATO missile defence system that would complement the USA's missile defence system, due to be sited in Poland and the Czech Republic, although these plans were abandoned in 2009.

Focus on . . .
The rise and fall of counter-insurgency?

Have the counter-insurgency wars in Iraq and Afghanistan (the 'wars of 9/11') established a model for twenty-first century? Or will they come to be seen as an aberration? In both wars, after an initial phase of highly promising progress, the USA and its allies found themselves confronting an escalating and bloody insurgency, which, seemingly, they had little capacity to understand or contain. This eventually precipitated a change in military strategy, with the adoption in Iraq of a counter-insurgency (COIN) approach that sought, in a sense, to take on the enemy at its own game. Associated with the 2007 'surge' in troop numbers (more than 20,000 additional US troops were deployed to Iraq), this was widely credited with having brought about a de-escalation in violence, preparing the way for the Iraqi government to assume responsibility for domestic security, and allowing for the withdrawal of US and other foreign troops. A similar switch in strategy took place in Afghanistan linked to President Obama's decision in 2009 to initiate an Afghan 'surge' (which saw the dispatch of a further 30,000 US troops to the country).

However, over time, counter-insurgency has fallen out of favour, as the USA and other states have placed greater stress on alternative forms of warfare, including special-forces missions, drone operations, and the use of private-security contractors and foreign-trained local proxies. The special forces raid which killed Osama bin Laden in 2011 (see p. 305) may therefore offer a more convincing model of twenty-first century warfare (Kennedy and Waldman 2013). Counter-insurgency warfare has a number of drawbacks. These include that counter-insurgency is not a strategy as such, but, rather, a collection of tactics that depend on the nature of the insurgency it confronts, and it is always likely that insurgents will be more flexible, tactically astute and sensitive to the needs of the local population than a foreign counter-insurgency army. Counter-insurgency may also be flawed because it is, first and last, a political strategy, which only succeeds when it weakens popular support for the insurgency; but it is overseen by military commanders whose political skills are limited. The greatest drawback of counter-insurgency warfare is, nevertheless, that it is highly costly in both economic and human terms. Winning a 'hearts and minds' struggle for the loyalties of the domestic population cannot happen overnight, nor can it occur without the deployment of large numbers of counter-insurgency forces, whose work within local communities makes them vulnerable to attack. The chief lesson of the wars in Iraq and Afghanistan may therefore be that 'boots-on-the-ground' warfare should in future be avoided.

---

men-at-arms and archers to defeat the French cavalry, and the emergence of ballistic missiles and long-range nuclear weapons in the post-1945 period. It is widely argued that advances in weapons technology and military strategy from the 1990s onwards, particularly undertaken by the USA, have had a similar significance, amounting to a **revolution in military affairs** (RMA). Modern war has therefore been replaced by 'postmodern' war, sometimes called 'virtual war', 'computer war' or 'cyberwar' (Der Derian 2001). Although the term means different things to different people, the key feature of postmodern war is usually taken to be a reliance on technology rather than mass conflict. Postmodern wars keep weapons development to a maximum and actual conflict between major powers to a minimum (Gray 1997). The nature of postmodern war was revealed by the 1991 Gulf War, which witnessed the first widespread used of a range of new technologies. These included computing and satellite technology to facilitate 'surgical' strikes, stealth technology that eludes radar detection, anti-missile missiles,

● **Revolution in military affairs**: The development in the USA in particular of new military strategies, based on 'high-tech' technology and 'smart' weapons, aimed at achieving swift and decisive outcomes.

Thomas Aquinas (1225–74)

Italian Dominican monk, theologian and philosopher. Born near Naples, the son of a noble family, Aquinas joined the Dominican order against his family's wishes. Aquinas' vast but unfinished *Summa Theologica*, begun in 1265, deals with the nature of God, morality and law – eternal, divine, natural and human. Influenced by Aristotle and Augustine, he identified three conditions for a war to be just: (1) war should be declared by a person with the authority to do so, (2) the war should have a just cause, and (3) the belligerents should have a right intention (that is, the desire for peace and the avoidance of evil). Aquinas was canonized in 1324, and in the nineteenth century Pope Leo III recognized Aquinas' writings as the basis of Catholic theology.

widespread electronic surveillance and sophisticated networked communications across all parts of the armed forces. In many ways, the Tomahawk cruise missile, essentially a precision-guided flying bomb that has a range of hundreds of kilometres, has become the leading symbol of this new form of warfare. Postmodern war aims not only massively to increase the accuracy and scale of devastation that a military assault can inflict, so achieving objectives speedily and with assurance, but also, and crucially, to do this while suffering very few casualties. In that sense, it is a form of war that takes account of the unwillingness of democratic electorates to put up with large-scale casualties over a prolonged period of time, as demonstrated by Vietnam. This explains the importance accorded to aerial bombardment in postmodern war. The US-led NATO (see p. 259) bombardment that expelled Serb forces from Kosovo in 1999 was thus an example of 'no casualty' warfare (albeit, of course, on one side only).

How effective has postmodern war proved to be? The examples of the Gulf War and Kosovo seem to suggest that it can be highly effective, at least in achieving limited goals (the expulsion of Iraqi and Serb forces, respectively). Furthermore, the USA's huge lead in 'high-tech' weaponry has been vital in consolidating its global military predominance and thus its hegemonic role in the world, especially as this encourages other states to bandwagon rather than to balance (see To balance or to bandwagon? p. 242). On the other hand, as in the past, advances in the technology of warfare and military strategy have not always or easily been translated into increased strategic effectiveness. One reason for this is that air power can seldom win wars on its own. As examples dating back to the 1940–1 **Blitz** in London, the 1945 Allied bombing of the German city of Dresden and modern examples, such Israel's air attacks on Hezbollah in July 2006 and Hamas in December 2008, demonstrate, aerial assaults rarely dispense altogether with the need for a land attack and therefore higher casualties, and, indeed, they may strengthen the resolve of the enemy. Even in the case of Kosovo, a planned three-day air onslaught went on for 78 days, and then only led to the withdrawal of Serb forces once Russia indicated that it would not support Serbia in the event of an all-out war. The other reason is that 'high-tech' warfare is of only limited value in the context of small-scale, low-intensity wars, especially when the enemy is highly mobile and difficult to distinguish from the civilian

● **Blitz**: An intensive and sustained aerial bombardment.

Balance of power

The term 'balance of power' has been used in a variety of ways. As a *policy*, it refers to a deliberate attempt to promote a power equilibrium, using diplomacy, or possibly war, to prevent any state achieving a predominant position. As a *system*, the balance of power refers to a condition in which no one state predominates over others, tending to create general equilibrium and curb the hegemonic ambitions of all states. Although such a balance of power may simply be fortuitous, neorealists argue that the international system tends naturally towards equilibrium because states are particularly fearful of a would-be hegemon (see Approaches to the balance of power, p. 274).

● **Drone**: An unmanned aerial vehicle that may be used for surveillance or attack purposes.

● *Realpolitik*: (German) Literally, realistic or practical politics; a form of politics or diplomacy that is guided by practical considerations, rather than by ideals, morals or principles.

● **Negative peace**: Peace defined as a period when war is neither imminent nor actually being fought, although the forces that give rise to war remain in place.

population. For example, the USA's 'shock and awe' assault on Baghdad in the early days of the Iraq War may have led to the speedy fall of Saddam Hussein and the collapse of the Ba'athist regime, but it did not prevent the development of a protracted and highly complex counter-insurgency war. As the limitations of counter-insurgency became increasingly apparent, pressure has grown to develop new styles of warfare, not least the much wider use of **drones** and other unmanned devices (see p. 260).

JUSTIFYING WAR

While the nature of war and warfare have changed enormously over time, debates about whether, and in what circumstances, war can be justified have a much more enduring character, dating back to Ancient Rome and including medieval European philosophers such as Augustine of Hippo (354–430) and Thomas Aquinas (see p. 261). Three broad positions have been adopted on this issue. These are as follows:

● *Realpolitik* – suggesting that war, as a political act, needs no moral justification.
● Just war theory – suggesting that war can be justified only if it conforms to moral principles.
● Pacifism – suggesting that war, as an unnecessary evil, can never be justified.

Realpolitik

The defining feature of political realism, sometimes referred to as *realpolitik*, is that matters of war and peace are beyond morality, in that they are – and should be – determined by the pursuit of national self-interest. In this view, war is accepted as a universal norm of human history; although war may be punctuated by possibly long periods of peace, peace is always temporary. For practitioners of *realpolitik*, the bias in favour of fighting and armed conflict derives usually either from innate human aggression or the aggressiveness that arises from the mismatch between unlimited human appetites and the scarce resources available to satisfy them. Either way, this implies, at best, a belief in **negative peace**, defined by the absence of its opposite, namely war or (more generally) active violence (Dower 2003).

Nevertheless, it would be a mistake to portray political realists as warmongers, who are unconcerned about the death and devastation that war can wreak. Carl Schmitt (1996), for example, argued against just wars, on the grounds that wars fought for political gain tend to be limited by the fact that their protagonists operate within clear strategic objectives, whereas just wars, and especially humanitarian war, lead to total war because of their expansive goals and the moral fervour behind them. Indeed, one of the reasons why realists have criticized utopian liberal dreams about 'perpetual peace' is that they are based on fundamental misunderstandings about the nature of international politics that would, ironically, make war more likely, not less likely. For example, during the interwar period, UK and French policy-makers, deluded by the theories of liberal internationalism, failed to act to prevent the re-emergence of Germany as an expansionist power, thereby contributing to the outbreak of WWII. The essence of *realpolitik*, then, is that it is better to be 'hard-headed' than 'wrong-headed'. The sole reliable way of maintaining peace from this point of view is through the balance of power (see p. 262), and the recognition that only power can be a check on power. Moreover, it may also be misleading to portray *realpolitik* as amoral. Rather, it is an example of moral relativism, in that it is informed by a kind of ethical nationalism that places considerations of the national self-interest above all other moral considerations. In other words, its enemy is the notion of universal moral principles, not morality as such.

However, *realpolitik* has been subject to severe criticism. In the first place, it draws on assumptions about power politics, conflict, greed and violence that serve to legitimize war and the use of force by making them appear to be part of the 'natural order of things'. Feminist theorists, for their part, have argued that the emphasis on the national interest and military might reflect an essentially masculinist view of international politics, rooted, for example, in myths about 'man the warrior' (Elshtain 1987; Tickner 1992). Second, in view of the scope of devastation and suffering that war wreaks, the assertion that matters of war and peace are beyond morality (universal or otherwise) reflects a remarkable stunting of ethical sensibilities. Most thinking about why and when war can be justified therefore focuses on how the resort to war and its conduct can be reconciled with morality, usually through the notion of a 'just war'.

Just war theory

The idea of a '**just war**' is based on the assumption that war can be justified and should be judged on the basis of ethical criteria. As such, it stands between realism or *realpolitik*, which interprets war primarily in terms of the pursuit of power or self-interest, and **pacifism**, which denies that there ever can be a moral justification for war and violence. However, just war theory is more a field of philosophical or ethical reflection, rather than a settled doctrine. Its origins can be traced back to the Roman thinker, Cicero, but it was first developed systematically by philosophers such as Augustine of Hippo, Thomas Aquinas, Francisco de Vitoria (1492–1546) and Hugo Grotius (see p. 341). Modern contributors to the tradition include Michael Walzer (see p. 265), Jean Bethke Elshtain (see p. 435) and David Rodin (2002).

Can standards of justice be applied to war, and what are the implications of doing so? Those who subscribe to the just war tradition base their thinking on two assumptions. First, human nature is composed of an unchangeable mixture of good and evil components. People may strive to be good, but they are always capable of immoral acts, and these acts include killing other human beings. War, in other words, is inevitable. Second, the suffering that war leads to can be ameliorated by subjecting warfare to moral constraints. As politicians, the armed forces and civilian populations become sensitized to the principles of a just war and the laws of war, fewer wars will occur and the harm done by warfare will be reduced. Just war theorists therefore argue that the purpose of war must be to re-establish peace and justice. But has a war ever fulfilled these high ideals? WWII is often identified as the classic example of a just war. The Nazis' record of growing aggression in the 1930s leaves little doubt about Hitler's determination to pursue bold and far-reaching expansionist goals, and possibly even world domination. The murder of 6 million Jewish people and others during the war itself demonstrates clearly the brutality and terror that Nazi domination would

• **Just war**: A war that, in its purpose and conduct, meets certain ethical standards, and so is (allegedly) morally justified.

• **Pacifism**: A commitment to peace and a rejection of war or violence in any circumstances ('pacific' derives from the Latin and means 'peace-making').

Focus on . . .
Principles of a just war

Principles of *jus ad bellum* (just recourse to war)

- *Last resort.* All non-violent options must have been exhausted before force can be justified. This is sometimes seen as the principle of necessity.
- *Just cause.* The purpose of war is to redress a wrong that has been suffered. This is usually associated with self-defence in response to military attack, viewed as the classic justification for war.
- *Legitimate authority.* This is usually interpreted to imply the lawfully constituted government of a sovereign state, rather than a private individual or group.
- *Right intention.* War must be prosecuted on the basis of aims that are morally acceptable (which may or may not be the same as the just cause), rather than revenge or the desire to inflict harm.
- *Reasonable prospect of success.* War should not be fought in a hopeless cause, in which life is expended for no purpose or benefit.
- *Proportionality.* War should result in more good than evil, in that any response to an attack should be measured and proportionate (sometimes seen as 'macro-proportionality' to distinguish it from the

jus in bello principle). For example, a wholesale invasion is not a justifiable response to a border incursion.

Principles of *jus in bello* (just conduct in war)

- *Discrimination.* Force must be directed at military targets only, on the grounds that civilians or non-combatants are innocent. Death or injury to civilians is therefore only acceptable if they are the accidental and unavoidable victims of deliberate attacks on legitimate targets, sometimes seen as **collateral damage**.
- *Proportionality.* Overlapping with *jus ad bellum*, this holds that the force used must not be greater than that needed to achieve an acceptable military outcome, and must not be greater than the provoking cause.
- *Humanity.* Force must not be directed ever against enemy personnel if they are captured, wounded or under control (prisoners of war). Together with the other *jus in bello* principles, this has been formalized over time, in the so-called 'laws of war'.

● **Collateral damage:**
Unintended or incidental injury or damage caused during a military operation (usually used as a euphemism).

● ***Jus ad bellum***: A just recourse to war, reflected in principles that restrict the legitimate use of force.

● ***Jus in bello***: The just conduct of war, reflected in principles that stipulate how wars should be fought.

have entailed. Humanitarian intervention (see p. 326) has also been widely justified in terms of just war theory, as discussed in Chapter 14.

Just war theory addresses two separate but related issues. The first of these deals with the right to go to war in the first place, or what in Latin is called ***jus ad bellum***. The second deals with the right conduct of warfare, or what in Latin is called ***jus in bello***. Although these branches of just war thinking complement one another, they may have quite different implications. For example, a state fighting for a just cause may use unjust methods. Nevertheless, it is unclear whether, for a war to be just, it must fulfil all the conditions of *jus ad bellum* and *jus in bello*, or just a substantial number. There is also debate amongst just war theorists about the priority that should be accorded the various conditions. For instance, some have argued that greatest emphasis should be placed on ensuring that war is waged for a just cause, while others have suggested that it is more important that war is always a last resort. In the same vein, some just war theorists have argued that the conditions for *jus ad bellum* have greater moral purchase that the principles of *jus in bello*, on the grounds that the ends justify

Michael Walzer (born 1935)

A Jewish US political philosopher, Walzer has made major contributions to thinking about the ethics of war. In *Just and Unjust Wars* ([1977] 2006), he developed a just war theory based on the 'legalist paradigm', which draws parallels between the rights and responsibilities of the individual and those of political communities (understood as states). This implies that states may defend themselves against aggression, possibly through pre-emptive attack (just wars), but that aggression in pursuit of self-interest is ruled out (unjust wars). Walzer also acknowledged that a 'supreme emergency' (stemming from an imminent and overriding threat to a nation) may require that 'the rules are set aside', and defended humanitarian intervention. Walzer's other key texts include *Spheres of Justice* (1983) and *Arguing about War* (2004).

the means. Finally, although the requirements of a just war may appear to be straightforward, they often raise difficult political, moral and philosophical problems when they are applied in practice.

For example, the principle that war should only be fought as a last resort fails to take account of the possibility that, by delaying the use of force, an enemy may become stronger, thereby leading to substantially greater bloodshed when confrontation eventually occurs. This, arguably, happened in the case of Nazi Germany in the 1930s. The 'just cause' principle is complicated by debate about whether it implies only retaliation against a wrong that has already been committed, or whether it can be extended to include the *anticipated* need for self-defence, as in the case of a pre-emptive attack (see p. 232). Difficulties, similarly, arise over the principle of legitimate authority, in that some argue that only governments that are constitutionally and democratically constituted can be regarded as legitimate. The requirement that there should be a reasonable prospect of success has been criticized on the grounds that it may sometimes be necessary to stand up to bullying and intimidation, whatever the cost (as in Finland's resistance to Russian aggression in 1940). The application of this principle has, anyway, become more difficult due to the advent of 'new' wars, in which calculations of success based on the relative power of the parties concerned are notoriously unreliable.

Nevertheless, a range of deeper criticisms have been levelled at just war theory. In the first place, however desirable they may be, the elements that make up a just war may set states standards with which it is impossible to comply. It is questionable whether there has ever been a war in which one side at least has followed fully the rules of a just war. Even in a 'good war' such as WWII, the British used saturation bombing tactics against German cities such as Dresden, which were of no military importance, in order to terrorize the civilian population. The war against Japan was ended by the dropping of atomic bombs on Hiroshima and Nagasaki, killing, overwhelmingly, civilians. Indeed, the idea of a just war has, arguably, been made irrelevant by modern methods of conducting war, which make it impossible to avoid harming civilians. Second, attempts to apply just war principles may result in the 'wrong' outcome. This could happen as the requirements of *jus in bello* may contradict those of *jus ad bellum*, in the

GLOBAL POLITICS IN ACTION . . .

The war in Afghanistan as a 'just war'

Events: In October 2001, the USA and its NATO allies attacked Afghanistan with the specific intention of over-throwing the Taliban regime on the grounds that it provided a base and support for al-Qaeda terrorists. With the support of Afghan warlords and tribal leaders, notably the Northern Alliance, the Taliban regime was toppled by December 2001 with the bulk of al-Qaeda terrorists being killed or forced to flee to the border regions of Pakistan. However, a protracted counter-insurgency war then ensued against remnants of the Taliban regime, other religious militants and forces opposed to the newly-established pro-western government in Kabul, whose strongholds were in Helmand province and neighbouring provinces in the south of Afghanistan.

Significance: In a number of respects, the Afghan War can be viewed as a 'just war'. In the first place, the war can be justified on the basis of self-defence, as a way of protecting the USA in particular and the West in general from the threat of terrorism, as demonstrated by the 9/11 attacks on New York and Washington. Commentators such as Elshtain (2003) argued that the 'war on terror', of which the Afghan War was a crucial part, was just in that it was fought against the genocidal threat of 'apocalyptic terrorism', a form of warfare that posed a potential threat to all Americans and Jews and made no distinction between combatants and non-combatants. The 2001 attack on Afghanistan also had a clear, and clearly stated, goal: the removal of a Taliban regime whose links to al-Qaeda were clearly established and undisputed. Furthermore, the USA and its allies acted as a legitimate authority, in that they were backed by NATO and enjoyed wide international support, including from Russia and China. Finally, the perpetrators of the 9/11 attacks could not have been reliably neutralized by diplomacy or non-violent pressure. The UN, for example, lacked the capability, authority and will to respond to the threat posed to global security by Islamist terrorism.

However, critics have portrayed the war as unjust and unjustifiable. Their arguments have included the following. First, the purpose of the war and the intentions with which it has been fought, may be unjust to the extent that the USA was motivated by a desire to consolidate its global hegemony, or by a wish to strengthen control of oil resources in the Middle East. In this respect, the attack on Afghanistan amounted to unwarranted aggression. Second, the USA and its allies could not be considered as legitimate authorities in that, unlike the 1991 Gulf War, the Afghan War had not been authorized by a specific UN resolution. Third, although the chances of success in toppling the Taliban regime were high, the likelihood of defeating Islamist terrorists through the Afghan War was much more questionable. This was because of the probability that an invasion would inflame and radicalize Muslim opinion and also because of the dubious benefits of technological superiority in fighting a counter-insurgency war against an enemy using guerrilla tactics. Fourth, the USA violated accepted conventions of warfare through its treatment of prisoners of war (who were despatched to Guantánamo Bay and subjected to forms of torture) and in launching strikes against al-Qaeda and Taliban bases that often resulted in civilian deaths. Fifth, Islamists would argue that justice was on the side of the Taliban and al-Qaeda, not the invading forces, as they were engaged in a *jihad* – in this case, literally a 'holy war' – to purify Islam and expel foreign influence from the Muslim world.

sense that a party with a just cause risks defeat because it is fighting with its hands tied behind its back. Surely, once a war has started, military tactics should be determined by practical considerations, aimed at ensuring a swift and certain victory, rather than moral considerations? This issue has become particularly topical in relation to the issue of combating terrorism, sometimes linked to the so-called problem of '**dirty hands**'. Walzer (2007), for example, drew attention to the 'ticking bomb scenario', in which a politician orders the torture of a terrorist suspect to extract information about the location of a bomb, thus saving the lives of hundreds of people. Third, just war thinking may be applicable only in circumstances in which the parties to a dispute share the same or similar cultural and moral beliefs. Only then can one party be deemed to be just, while the other is unjust. As many modern wars, such as those that have been fought under the banner of the 'war on terror', are cross-cultural wars, if not civilizational struggles, this requirement is no longer achievable. Military rivals may thus both legitimately claim to have justice on their side, reflecting the incompatibility of their value systems and ethical beliefs.

Pacifism

While just war theory attempts to reconcile war with morality by placing war within a framework of justice, pacifism views war and morality as irreconcilable. Pacifism, in short, is the belief that all war is morally wrong. Such a stance is based on two lines of thought, often combined as part of pacifist argument (Holmes 1990). The first is that war is wrong because killing is wrong. This principled rejection of war and killing in all circumstances is based on underpinning assumptions about the sanctity or oneness of life, often (but not always) rooted in religious conviction. Strains of pacifism have been found within Christianity, particularly associated with the Quakers and the Plymouth Brethren, within Hinduism and especially with Gandhi's ethic of non-violence, and also within Buddhism and Jainism. Strongly-held pacifist convictions have thus provided the moral basis for **conscientious objection** to military service. The second line of argument, sometimes called 'contingent pacifism', places greatest stress on the wider and often longer-term benefits of non-violence for human well-being. From this perspective, violence is never a solution because it breeds more violence through developing a psychology of hatred, bitterness and revenge. This has been reflected in the use of pacifism or non-violence as a political tactic that derives its force from the fact that it is morally uncontaminated, as demonstrated by Martin Luther King and the civil rights movement in the USA in the 1960s.

Pacifism has served as an important force in international politics in two main ways. First, in the form of so-called 'legal pacifism', it has provided support for the establishment of supranational bodies, such as the League of Nations and the United Nations (see p. 456), which aim to ensure the peaceful resolution of international disputes through upholding a system of international law (see p. 339). For this reason, pacifists have been amongst the keenest advocates of a world federation, or even world government. In that pacifists have often sought to transcend a world of sovereign states, they have embraced the notion of **positive peace**, linking peace to the advance of political and social justice. Second, pacifism has helped to fuel the emergence of a growing, if disparate, 'peace move-

● **Dirty hands, problem of** : The problem that it may (arguably) be necessary for politicians to transgress accepted moral codes for the sake of the political community, making it right to do wrong.

● **Conscientious objection**: Objection to conscription into the armed forces on the grounds of conscience, usually based on the belief that it is morally wrong to act as an agent of war.

● **Positive peace**: Peace defined in terms of harmony and wholeness; the absence not just of war but of the *causes* of war.

Mohandas Karamchand Gandhi (1869–1948)

Indian spiritual and political leader (called *Mahatma*, 'Great Soul'). A lawyer trained in the UK, Gandhi worked in South Africa, where he organized protests against discrimination. After returning to India in 1915, he became the leader of the nationalist movement, campaigning tirelessly for independence, finally achieved in 1947. Gandhi's ethic of non-violent resistance, *satyagraha*, reinforced by his ascetic lifestyle, gave the movement for Indian independence enormous moral authority. Derived from Hinduism, Gandhi's political philosophy was based on the assumption that the universe is regulated by the primacy of truth, or *satya*, and that humankind is 'ultimately one'. Gandhi was assassinated in 1948 by a fanatical Hindu, becoming a victim of the ferocious Hindu–Muslim violence which followed independence.

ment'. Peace activism first emerged as a response to the advent of the nuclear era, with the formation of groups such as European Nuclear Disarmament (END) and the UK-based Campaign for Nuclear Disarmament (CND) reflecting an awareness of the fact that the invention of nuclear weapons had fundamentally altered calculations about the human cost, and therefore the moral implications, of warfare. Support for such groups grew particularly strongly during the 1960s, especially after the Cuban Missile Crisis of 1962. Pacifism has also helped to strengthen anti-war movements, with demonstrations against the Vietnam War establishing a model followed by later protests, for example over Iraq. Although anti-war protests are by no means entirely motivated by pacifist sentiments, they have established domestic constraints on the ability of governments to undertake or, perhaps more significantly, sustain military action.

Pacifism has nevertheless been criticized on a number of grounds. For instance, pacifists have been criticized for being cowards, for being 'free riders' who remain morally uncontaminated whilst at the same time benefiting from the security that the existence of a military and the willingness of others to fight affords them. They thus subscribe to the deluded belief that it is possible to have 'clean hands' in politics. However, pacifism has also been associated with deeper moral and philosophical difficulties. First, pacifism has been regarded as incoherent in that it is based on the right to life, but this can only be defended, in certain circumstances, through a willingness to use force to protect oneself or others (Narveson 1970). In this view, the right not to be attacked must include the right to defend oneself with, if necessary, killing force when attacked. The second difficulty concerns the implications of according overriding importance to the avoidance of killing, a position that treats other considerations, for example about matters such as liberty, justice, recognition and respect, as of secondary importance. However, the value of life is closely, and inevitably, linked to the conditions in which people live, which implies a necessary trade-off between the avoidance of killing and the protection of other values. It is precisely such a trade-off that has been used to justify humanitarian wars, in which the moral costs of forcible intervention are balanced against the alleviation of suffering and the protection of human rights as far as the domestic population is concerned. This issue is discussed further in Chapter 13.

SUMMARY

● War is a condition of armed conflict between two or more parties, traditionally states. However, the nature of war and warfare has changed enormously over time, as they have been refashioned by developments in military technology and strategy. There is nevertheless considerable debate about why wars occur, with explanations focusing on human nature, the internal characteristics of states, or structural or systemic pressures.

● The classic account of war, developed by Clausewitz, views it as a continuation of politics by other means. However, the Clausewitzian conception of war has been criticized for ignoring the moral implications of war, and on the grounds that it is outdated, either because war has become a less effective policy instrument or because modern wars are less easy to interpret in instrumental terms.

● Many argue that the nature of war has changed in the post-Cold War period. So-called 'new' wars tend to be civil wars rather than inter-state wars, often fought over issues of identity. They are also commonly asymmetrical wars, fought between unequal parties, tend to blur the civilian/military distinction, and, arguably, involve higher levels of indiscriminate violence.

● War and warfare have also been affected by the development of 'hi-tech' technology and 'smart' weapons, giving rise to so-called 'postmodern' warfare. Although such warfare was effective in the Gulf War and in Kosovo, its strategic effectiveness has been called into question, especially in the context of small-scale, low-intensity wars, when the enemy is highly mobile and difficult to distinguish from the civilian population.

● Three broad positions have been adopted on the issue of the relationship between war and morality. *Realpolitik* suggests that war, as a political act, needs no moral justification. Just war theory seeks to justify war but only if it conforms to moral principles about both the just recourse to war and the just conduct of war. Pacifism suggests that war, as an unnecessary evil, can never be justified.

Questions for discussion

● What is the difference between war and other forms of violence?

● Is there a meaningful difference between conventional and unconventional warfare?

● Is war inevitable, and if so, why?

● How persuasive is the idea that war is a political act?

● Why is it so difficult to win asymmetrical wars?

● Are 'new' wars really more barbaric and horrific than 'old' wars?

● In what sense has counter-insurgency 'failed'?

● Does realism reject the link between ethics and war?

● How valid are the traditional just war principles of *jus ad bellum*?

● Do the principles of *jus in bello* constitute an obstacle to the effective conduct of war?

● Why do pacifists reject war?

Further reading

Burke, J. *The 9/11 Wars* (2012). A close examination of the development of warfare in Afghanistan and Iraq in particular in the aftermath of 9/11, exploring both their military and political consequences.

Frowe, H. *The Ethics of War and Peace: An Introduction* (2011). A fresh and accessible introduction to ethical debates about war and warfare, which discusses self-defence, just war theory and matters related to the laws of war.

Howard, M., *The Invention of Peace and the Reinvention of War* (2002). A short but deeply insightful overview of the issues of war and peace from a historical perspective.

Kaldor, M., *New and Old Wars: Organized Violence in a Global Era* (2012). A highly influential account of the phenomenon of 'new wars' which examines both their nature and the conditions in which they emerge.

ONLINE RESOURCES AVAILABLE

Links to relevant web resources can be found on the *Global Politics* website

CHAPTER 11

Nuclear Proliferation and Disarmament

'The human race cannot co-exist with nuclear weapons.'

ICCHO ITOH, Mayor of Nagasaki, 1995–2007

PREVIEW   The development and use of nuclear weapons in 1945 marked a major turning point in the history of warfare and, indeed, in the history of humanity. Very quickly, enough nuclear warheads had been created and stockpiled to destroy civilization many times over, giving humanity, for the first time, the capacity to end its own existence. As the Cold War developed, the world thus fell under the shadow of 'the bomb'. However, while some saw nuclear weapons as the lynchpin of a deterrence system that effectively ruled out war between major powers, others viewed the nuclear arms race as a source of unending tension and insecurity. Does the theory of nuclear deterrence work? Do nuclear weapons promote responsible statesman-ship, or do they fuel expansionist ambition? Nevertheless, anxieties about nuclear proliferation have, if anything, intensified during the post-Cold War period. Not only has the 'nuclear club' grown from five to at least nine, but many argue that the constraints that had previously prevented nuclear weapons from being used have been dangerously weakened. In what ways have the incentives for states to acquire nuclear weapons intensified? Is it now more likely that nuclear weapons will get into the 'wrong' hands? Finally, greater anxiety about nuclear proliferation has been reflected in an increasing emphasis on the issues of arms control and disar-mament. Although non-proliferation strategies have ranged from diplomatic pres-sure and the imposition of economic sanctions to direct military intervention, nuclear arms control has been notoriously difficult to bring about. In this context, non-proliferation has increasingly been linked to a commitment to nuclear disarmament. Why is it so difficult to prevent states from acquiring nuclear weapons? Why has greater emphasis been placed on the goal of creating a world free of nuclear weapons?

KEY ISSUES
- How do nuclear weapons differ from other kinds of weapons?
- How can nuclear proliferation best be explained?
- Do nuclear weapons promote, or threaten, international peace and stability?
- How can the spread of nuclear weapons best be controlled, or even reversed?
- Is a post-nuclear age possible or desirable?

NUCLEAR PROLIFERATION

Nature of nuclear weapons

The first and only **nuclear weapons** that have been used in warfare were the atomic bombs, developed by the Manhattan Project, which were exploded over Hiroshima and Nagasaki on 6 and 9 August 1945, respectively. Developed under the scientific direction of the US physicist J. Robert Oppenheimer, and first tested in the New Mexico desert on 16 July 1945, these bombs represented an entirely new kind of weapon. Atomic bombs work through nuclear fission (the splitting of nuclei of highly-enriched uranium (usually U-235) or plutonium). Fission weapons operate through a chain reaction, as each fission gives out excess neutrons, which in turn go on to cause more fissions. An even more powerful nuclear weapon was developed in the hydrogen bomb. This is based on nuclear fusion (the combining of nuclei), but it can only take place if they are subject to enormously high temperatures and pressures. Fusion weapons are therefore sometimes called 'thermonuclear' weapons. Nuclear bombs cause devastation in three ways. Immediate devastation is wreaked by a *blast effect* of awesome explosive force, which is combined with *thermal radiation*, that can create a firestorm travelling at several hundred miles per hour with temperatures rising to 1000°C. However, longer-lasting and more widespread effects come from *nuclear radiation*. Detonation of the weapon creates an immediate pulse of nuclear radiation and by-products of the detonation form radioactive fall-out. Exposure to either of these sources of radiation can cause radiation sickness and long-term diseases including a range of cancers. In the form of the hydrogen bomb, nuclear weapons have colossal destructive power. The Hiroshima and Nagasaki bombs were relatively small by comparison with the thermonuclear weapons later tested, some of which released destructive forces over 2000 times greater than those used against Japan.

The massive destructive capacity of nuclear weapons means that they have affected international and domestic politics in a way that no other weapons ever have. They are the archetypal example of a new category of weapons, recognized by the United Nations since 1948: '**weapons of mass destruction**', or WMD. The category of WMD now also covers chemical and biological weapons (CBW) sometimes grouped together as atomic, biological and chemical weapons (ABC). They are distinguished from conventional weapons in three main ways:

- As the name suggests, they are weapons that have the potential to inflict massive collateral damage, having devastating implications for civilian populations.
- Their mass impact has raised important moral questions, notably through the suggestion that these weapons are 'non-legitimate, inhuman' forms of warfare.
- They have a particularly powerful deterrent effect, making attacks on states which possess WMD almost unthinkable.

However, the classification of all these weapons as WMD is questionable. This is partly because each of these weapon types has different effects: CBW, for instance, may be small-scale and more 'usable' than nuclear weapons, in which

● **Nuclear weapons**: Weapons that use nuclear fission (atom bombs) or nuclear fusion (hydrogen bombs) to destroy their targets, through the effect of blast, heat and radiation.

● **Weapons of mass destruction**: A category of weapons that covers nuclear, radiological, chemical and biological weapons, which have a massive and indiscriminate destructive capacity.

CONCEPT

Arms race

An arms race is a concerted military build-up that occurs as two or more states acquire weapons or increase their military capability in response to each other. Classic examples include the UK–German naval arms race that preceded WWI, and the US–Soviet nuclear arms race during the Cold War. Arms races may be fuelled by defensive calculations or miscalculations (the security dilemma), or they may occur as one or more states seek military advantage in order to pursue offensive policies. While arms races may increase the likelihood of war, by heightening fear and paranoia and strengthening militarism and aggressive nationalism, they may also help to maintain an overall balance of power (see p. 262) and so ensure deterrence.

● **Nuclear proliferation**: The spread of nuclear weapons, either by their acquisition by more states or other actors (*horizontal* proliferation), or their accumulation by established nuclear states (*vertical* proliferation).

case nuclear weapons may be the only true WMD. Similarly, trends in recent years away from nuclear weapons with large explosive potential have created a distinction between 'unusable' strategic nuclear weapons and possibly 'usable' tactical or 'battlefield' nuclear weapons. The distinction between conventional weapons and WMD is also, in some ways, unreliable. Not only may the use of WMD be dependent on conventional weapons systems (as in the use of inter-continental ballistic missiles (ICBM) to deliver nuclear weapons), but a sustained conventional aerial bombardment is capable of inflicting massive collateral damage with devastating implications for civilian populations.

Proliferation during the Cold War

The unprecedented destructive potential of nuclear weapons explains why the issue of **nuclear proliferation** has been at the forefront of the international security agenda since 1945. How can nuclear proliferation best be explained? A general logic lies behind the tendency for any weapons to proliferate. This is based on the security dilemma (see p. 19), which recognizes the symbolic significance of weapons as well as their military purpose. In short, weapons acquired for defensive purposes may be *perceived* by other states as having, potentially or actually, offensive significance. This, then, encourages them to strengthen their own defensive military capacity, an action which, in turn, may be viewed by other states as offensive. A classic arms race therefore develops out of the simple fact that international politics is inevitably characterized, at some level, by fear and uncertainty. In addition, the potential costs of inaction (when an offensive military build-up is interpreted as merely defensive) greatly outweigh the cost of action (when unnecessary steps are taken in response to an essentially defensive military build-up).

However, in the case of nuclear weapons, a range of other factors has been relevant. These include the particular importance of their deterrent effect. In view of the devastating potential of nuclear weapons, an attack on a nuclear power is almost unthinkable. The USA's atomic attack on Japan in 1945 therefore encouraged the Soviet Union to intensify its efforts to develop nuclear weapons, leading to the first Soviet nuclear test in 1949. Another factor is that nuclear weapons quickly acquired huge symbolic significance, particularly in terms of the political prestige associated with their possession. Members of the so-called 'nuclear club' are thus usually considered to rank amongst states of the first order. It was therefore no coincidence that during the Cold War the 'club' expanded to include all five of the permanent members of the UN Security Council (the P-5), with nuclear tests also being carried out by the UK (1952), France (1960) and China (1962).

During the Cold War, sometimes seen as the 'first nuclear age', nuclear proliferation was primarily vertical rather than horizontal. Greatest attention was given to restricting the spread of nuclear arms beyond the 'big five', particularly through the Nuclear Non-Proliferation Treaty (NPT), which was introduced in 1968 and extended indefinitely in 1995. Almost all states have signed the NPT, with the notable exceptions of India, Pakistan and Israel. By contrast, during this period, the USA and the Soviet Union built up the capacity to destroy the world many times over. By 2002, the joint US and Russian nuclear capacity accounted for 98 per cent of all the nuclear warheads that had been built (see Figure 11.1).

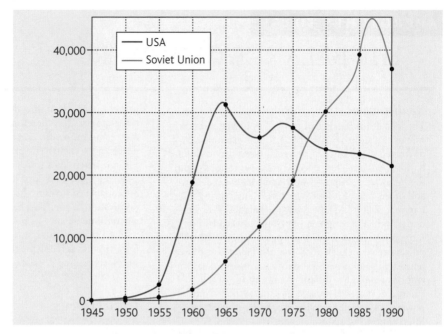

Figure 11.1 Accumulation of nuclear warheads by the USA and the Soviet Union, 1945–90

Source: Data from Norris and Kristensen (2010).

Both sides quickly developed massive **first-strike** capability, but also acquired **second-strike** capabilities that would enable them to withstand an enemy's attack and still destroy major strategic targets and population centres. By the early 1960s, both superpowers had an invulnerable second-strike capability which ensured that nuclear war would result in Mutually Assured Destruction (MAD), thus completing what Jervis (1990) called the 'nuclear revolution'. This system of nuclear deterrence led to a 'balance of terror' that some have viewed as the most powerful evidence of the capacity of the balance of power (see p. 274) to maintain peace and security. Nuclear war, indeed, threatened such environmental devastation that it created the possibility of the extinction of life itself, not least through a **nuclear winter**.

Proliferation in the post-Cold War era

The end of the Cold War produced early, optimistic expectations that the issue of nuclear proliferation would be of declining relevance. If East–West rivalry had fuelled the nuclear arms race and created a balance of terror, its end surely opened up the possibility that nuclear proliferation could also be ended, if not reversed. Such expectations were fuelled by the 1991 Strategic Arms Reduction Treaty (START), and by START II in 1993, through which the USA and Russia agreed, for the first time, to reduce the number of their nuclear warheads and to eliminate certain categories of weapons, such as land-based intercontinental ballistic missiles with multiple warheads. Such early optimism quickly faded, however. The post-Cold War era, sometimes seen as the 'second nuclear age', has

● **First strike**: A pre-emptive or surprise attack on an adversary; 'getting one's retaliation in first'.

● **Second strike**: A retaliatory attack on an adversary in response to a first-strike attack.

● **Nuclear winter**: The theory that the smoke and dust created by nuclear explosions would extinguish the sun's rays and dramatically lower temperatures on the earth.

THE BALANCE OF POWER

Realist view

The idea of the balance of power has played a central role in realist theory. Waltz (1979), for example, portrayed the balance of power as *the* theory of international politics This reflects core assumptions about the importance of power in shaping state behaviour and of the role of power relations in structuring international politics. Realists view the balance of power, understood as a rough equilibrium between two or more power blocs, in strongly positive terms. As only power can be a check on power, the balance of power tends to lead to peace and stability. However, realism embraces two quite different conceptions of the balance of power. For classical realists, the balance of power is essentially a policy, a product of political intervention and statesmanship. This example of *voluntarism* (implying faith in free will and personal commitment) assumes that key decision-makers in foreign policy enjoy great (though not unlimited) freedom of manoeuvre. For neorealists, on the other hand, the balance of power is treated more as a system, as a set of arrangements that tend to arise automatically, rather than through the self-willed actions of decision-makers. This example of *determinism* (implying that human actions are entirely conditioned by external factors) suggests that the balance of power is essentially 'imposed by events' on statesman who are constrained by the dynamics of the international system. This happens because states in a self-help system are likely to act to prevent the emergence of hegemonic domination by a single state. A balance of power, nevertheless, is more likely to develop in a bipolar system than it is in either a multipolar or unipolar system (see Neorealist stability theory, p. 57).

Liberal view

Liberals have generally been critical of the idea of balance of power. In their view, the balance of power legitimizes and entrenches power politics and international rivalry, creating inherent instability and deepening distrust. This is because the basic premise of the balance of power is that other states, or coalitions of states, pose a threat to security, and this can only be contained through a rival build-up of power or the formation of a rival alliance. A balance-of-power mindset is therefore more likely to cause war than

prevent it. Much of liberal thinking about international politics has therefore focused on finding alternative and more effective mechanisms for ensuring peace and security. The principal liberal solution is the construction of international organizations such as the League of Nations or the United Nations, which are capable of turning the jungle of international politics into a zoo. This happens, in part, because whereas the balance of power fosters private agreements amongst states, international organizations foster public agreements that cover most if not all states, so making possible a system of collective security (see p. 447).

Critical views

A variety of critical approaches to the balance of power have emerged. Social constructivists, for instance, have emphasized the extent to which any assessment of the balance of power is dependent on perception, ideas and beliefs. Any assessment of the balance of power is therefore shaped by the identities that states have of themselves and of other states. In short, paraphrasing Wendt's (1999) oft-quoted assertion about anarchy, the balance of power is what states make of it. International society theorists have, similarly, argued that the balance of power is an artefact: it emerges out of the existence of common norms and values and a mutual desire of states to avoid war. The balance of power, then, works because states *want* it to work (Bull [1977] 2002). Feminist theorists have shared with liberals the belief that balance-of-power thinking tends to intensify international conflict and make war more likely, not less likely. For feminists, this reflects a gendered conception of the balance of power, in which power is almost always conceived as 'power over', the ability to control or dominate others. The balance of power therefore invariably becomes a struggle for power. Finally, postcolonial theorists have viewed the balance of power as an essentially European, or western, game, which excludes consideration of the rest of the world. The European balance-of-power system in the late nineteenth century thus coincided with the 'scramble for Africa', and a deepening of global inequalities and imbalances.

been characterized by heightened anxiety about nuclear proliferation. This has happened for at least four reasons:

● Established nuclear powers continued to use nuclear strategies.
● The incentives for states to acquire nuclear weapons have increased.
● Proliferation is easier, as nuclear weapons and nuclear technology are more readily available.
● Fears have heightened that nuclear weapons may get into the 'wrong' hands.

First, after early progress, attempts to reduce nuclear stockpiles, or encourage nuclear states to abandon nuclear weapons, petered out. START III talks began in Moscow in 1999 but broke down over disagreements about a possible renegotiation of the ABM Treaty. The 2002 Strategic Offensive Reduction Treaty (SORT) amounted to little more than a 'gentleman's agreement'. It contained no verification measures, allowed the USA and Russia to deploy between 1,700 and 2,200 warheads with the rest being put in storage rather than being destroyed, and enabled either side to withdraw from the Treaty at three months' notice. If established nuclear powers had substantially maintained their nuclear arsenals in the absence of a Cold War 'justification', this both demonstrated the wider strategic significance of nuclear weapons and weakened the moral and diplomatic pressure that nuclear powers could exercise on non-nuclear states. (Attempts to revive disarmament through the 2010 deal between the USA and Russia to cut nuclear weapons are discussed in the final section of the chapter.) Furthermore, there is evidence that established nuclear powers were keen to develop a new generation of weapons. These included low-yield battlefield nuclear weapons, or 'mini-nukes', that may potentially be usable, and missile shields, such as the USA had planned to site in Poland and the Czech Republic to protect itself from Iran and possibly Russia. The UK also decided in 2007 to update and replace its Trident nuclear weapon system.

Second, non-nuclear states came, in many cases, under growing pressure to acquire nuclear weapons. This occurred in a variety of ways. For example, the superpower era operated, in part, through a system of 'extended' deterrents, based on the capacity of the USA and the Soviet Union to offer allied states a **'nuclear umbrella'**. Concern about the withdrawal of the US or Russian nuclear umbrella was likely to encourage states to stand on their own two feet in nuclear terms. This was particularly the case where regional tensions were deepening, as in South Asia in the 1990s. In 1998, both India and Pakistan tested nuclear devices and joined the 'nuclear club', responding to increasingly bitter rivalry over Kashmir and other issues as well as the scaling back of US support for Pakistan and India's loss of the backing of the Soviet Union. Regional tensions in the Middle East have also played a major role in encouraging Israel's acquisition of nuclear weapons, as well as Iran's quest for a nuclear capacity. Nevertheless, the greatest incentive to acquire nuclear weapons arises from their evident benefit in terms of discouraging intervention by much more powerful states, as the comparison between Iraq and North Korea demonstrates. The USA invaded Iraq in 2003, in significant part because of evidence uncovered by the 1991 Gulf War and subsequently that the Saddam regime had a nuclear weapons programme and was intent on acquiring WMD (although the failure of the invasion to find evidence of WMD suggests that such programmes had been aban-

● **Nuclear umbrella**: Protection afforded non-nuclear states or minor nuclear powers by guarantees made to them by major nuclear powers; a form of extended deterrent.

doned sometime during the 1990s). Although the USA had similar concerns about North Korea, its capacity to intervene was drastically reduced in 2006 when North Korea carried out its first nuclear test, even though it was not until 2009 that it achieved a proper reaction when it exploded a Hiroshima-sized weapon. The desire to prevent a possible US invasion has undoubtedly intensified Iran's desire to acquire nuclear weapons. Figure 11.2 shows the number of warheads that are held by nuclear powers.

Third, acquiring or developing nuclear weapons is much easier than it was during the Cold War. During the 'first nuclear age', the fact that the production of nuclear weapons required a broad-based and sophisticated technological structure, and a workforce containing people with key scientific skills, helped enormously to contain the horizontal proliferation of nuclear weapons. Only a small number of states had achieved the technological threshold that made the development of nuclear weapons possible. However, such technology had become much more diffuse by the 1990s, as demonstrated by the apparent ease with which India and Pakistan moved from a 'threshold' position to achieving full nuclear capability. Particular concern was raised about the implications of the collapse of the Soviet Union and the political and economic instability in Russia in the 1990s. This created fears that Russian nuclear technologies and fissile (radioactive) materials may flood onto the open market. Whereas the scientific know-how to create nuclear weapons as well as the components of the weapons themselves were once controlled by tightly-disciplined military-industrial complexes, these, it seemed, had become available to the highest bidders, with very few questions asked.

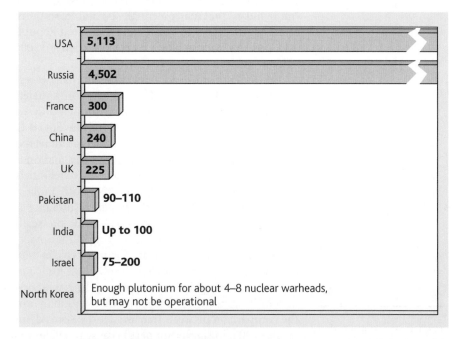

Figure 11.2 Number of warheads held by nuclear powers, 2012 (estimates of deployed and non-deployed weapons)

Source: Data from Arms Control Association, April 2013.

Finally, concerns about nuclear proliferation have intensified due to anxieties about the nature of the states and other actors that may acquire nuclear capabilities. While the 'nuclear club' consisted only of the P-5, the permanent members of the UN Security Council, it was possible to argue that they were in the hands of responsible states, whose calculations about military strategy in general, and the use of nuclear weapons in particular, were based on careful cost–benefit analysis. In these circumstances, caution would always win out over recklessness and there was a strong tendency for nuclear weapons to form part of a deterrent system in which their significance would always be symbolic rather than practical. However, as the obstacles to horizontal proliferation have diminished, the chances of nuclear weapons getting into the hands of states or other actors that may use them have significantly increased. This particularly applies in the case of 'rogue' states (see p. 231), in which military-based dictatorial government combines with factors such as ethnic and social conflict and economic underdevelopment to dictate an aggressive foreign policy, particularly in the context of regional instability. In the post-Cold War era, US foreign policy has increasingly focused on attempts to prevent such states from acquiring nuclear weapons, with particular concern focusing in 2002 on the states dubbed 'axis of evil' by President Bush: Iraq, Iran, Syria, Libya and North Korea. More serious, though, is the prospect of nuclear weapons getting into the hands of non-state actors such as terrorist groups, especially ones motivated by radical politico-religious ideologies, for whom the traditional constraints on the use of WMD, arising in part from the fear of retaliation, simply do not apply. Concerns about 'nuclear terrorism' are discussed in Chapter 12.

However, the image of a world in which all states, to say nothing of a collection of non-state actors, seek to acquire nuclear weapons is misleading. Indeed, the extent of proliferation is much less than we might otherwise have expected in an anarchic, self-help system (Smith 2010). A number of states with clear economic and technological potential to develop nuclear weapons have demonstrated a consistent determination not to do so. These include Australia, Canada, Germany, Japan and South Korea. A further collection of states have voluntarily abandoned nuclear programmes and renounced nuclear weapons. Brazil, Argentina and South Africa are all former 'opaque' nuclear states. The Ukraine, Belarus and Kazakhstan each inherited nuclear weapons after the break-up of the Soviet Union, but returned them to Russia in exchange for US economic aid. The US invasion of Iraq revealed that the Saddam regime, under pressure from the International Atomic Energy Agency (IAEA) (the UN agency that monitors states' compliance with their commitments under the NPT and other non-proliferation agreements), had abandoned its nuclear programme, along with its chemical and biological weapons, some time after the Gulf War; while Libya voluntarily gave up all its WMD programmes in 2003, in return for new trade agreements with the USA and the UK, and an end to diplomatic isolation. The reasons for this level of unilateral self-policing or self-restraint are many and various. They include that states recognize that the costs of acquiring nuclear weapons may outweigh the benefits they bring, that the possession of nuclear weapons is widely viewed by the international community as illegitimate, and that non-proliferation is clearly favoured by established nuclear powers, particularly the P-5.

Debating...
Do nuclear weapons promote peace and stability?

Views about the implications of nuclear proliferation vary significantly. Whereas realists have interpreted nuclear weapons as a major component of the 'long peace' of the Cold War, others have warned that they pose an ever-present, and indeed deepening, threat to peace and security.

YES

Absence of nuclear war. The most remarkable thing about nuclear weapons is how rarely they have been used. Nuclear weapons have only been used as an instrument of war in 1945, to hasten the end of war in the Pacific by bringing about the surrender of Japan (even if the USA was also concerned to send a message to the Soviet Union). The fact that they have not been used subsequently, and that conventional war has never broken out between two nuclear powers, suggests that nuclear weapons are weapons of a very particular kind. They are almost entirely of symbolic, not practical, importance.

Effective deterrence. The primary motive for acquiring nuclear weapons is deterrence, the prevention of war through the massive devastation that would befall an aggressor. Nuclear weapons are particularly well-suited to this role, both because of their enormous destructive capability and because they are relatively ineffective as defensive weapons. This means that there is a low possibility of a state achieving a first-strike nuclear knockout, since nuclear powers invariably seek to develop a second-strike capability. This makes a nuclear war, fought between two nuclear powers, virtually unthinkable.

International stability. The vertical proliferation of nuclear arms has not destabilized international politics because it has tended to preserve the balance of power, albeit through a 'balance of terror'. Horizontal proliferation has been gradual (with the 'nuclear club' growing from five in 1964 to eight by 2005, although Israel and possibly Iran are widely seen as 'opaque' nuclear states). Arguably, the gradual spread of nuclear weapons preserves international stability better than either no spread or a rapid spread would.

Nuclear statesmanship. The possession of nuclear weapons may engender a sense of responsibility and a strong bias in favour of caution, even in states that had previously been inclined towards adventurism or aggression. For, example, regional tensions between India and Pakistan are much less likely to lead to war now that both powers possess nuclear weapons.

NO

Fallibility of deterrent systems. The theory of nuclear deterrence is naive and dangerous. A world in which there are nuclear weapons will always carry the threat of nuclear war. Deterrence may always fail due to miscalculations and accidents. For instance, states may make miscalculations about whether other states possess an invulnerable second-strike capability or, for that matter, whether they possess nuclear weapons at all. Conventional wars may also escalate into nuclear wars, through mistakes made in the frenetic atmosphere that often surrounds decision-makers in war-time situations.

Danger of nuclear imbalances. There is no guarantee that vertical or horizontal nuclear proliferation will preserve the balance of power. Indeed, proliferation inevitably creates temporary imbalances which may then be exploited by aggressive states. After all, the Hiroshima and Nagasaki bombs were dropped to take advantage of precisely such a military imbalance.

Useable nuclear weapons. Developments in recent years have focused increasingly on the production of nuclear weapons that have a more precise and contained impact, making them 'useable'. These 'tactical' or 'battlefield' nuclear weapons are no longer of symbolic importance alone. This has led to the theory of nuclear utilization target selection (NUTS), which rejects the logic of MAD in suggesting that it is possible for a limited nuclear exchange to occur.

Irresponsible nuclear powers. Although the deterrent effect of nuclear weapons worked during the bipolar 'first nuclear age', it is far less reliable in the less stable, multipolar circumstances of the 'second nuclear age'. The possibility of a nuclear first strike relies on the existence of a political or military leadership that is not averse to risk-taking, or a leadership that, because of its values and beliefs, pursues symbolic violence as a method of 'total war' in isolation from strategic considerations. The greatest concern is therefore that nuclear weapons may fall into the hands of military-based dictatorial regimes, or even terrorist organizations, which may have fewer scruples about using them.

NUCLEAR ARMS CONTROL AND DISARMAMENT

Arms control and anti-proliferation strategies

Nuclear **arms control** has been seen as a central means of containing conflict and ensuring global security. Arms control is, nevertheless, a less ambitious goal than nuclear **disarmament**, which aims to decrease the size and capability of a state's armed forces, possibly depriving it of weapons. The objective of arms control is therefore to regulate arms levels either by limiting their growth or by restricting how they can be used. There is nothing new about arms agreements: for example, in 600 BCE a disarmament league was formed amongst Chinese states. However, formal bilateral agreements and multilateral agreements to control or reduce arms were rare before the twentieth century. What changed this was the advent of industrialized warfare through the development of technologically advanced weapons. It is therefore no surprise that, since 1945, the arms control agenda has been dominated by attempts to limit the spread of WMD and particularly nuclear weapons (see p. 280). The principal means through which this has been attempted are treaties and conventions of various kinds, which attempt to establish security regimes to counter the uncertainty, fear and paranoia that are generated by the security dilemma.

How effective has nuclear arms control been? On the credit side, there are some undoubted, if partial, successes. For example, the Partial Test Ban Treaty went a long way to ensuring the elimination of atmospheric nuclear testing. Similarly, the NPT, the single most important nuclear arms control treaty, has made a major contribution to slowing the pace of horizontal proliferation, especially amongst developed states that clearly possess the economic and technological capacity to acquire nuclear weapons. Moreover, even when their specific provisions were effectively ignored, bilateral treaties between the USA and the Soviet Union at least went some way to reduce tension and promote caution, arguably helping to prepare the way ultimately for the end of the Cold War. On the debit side, however, nuclear treaties and conventions singularly failed to prevent the vertical proliferation of nuclear weapons during the Cold War, as the USA and the Soviet Union each built up nuclear arsenals of staggering proportions. START I and START II were, for example, simply 'dead letters', even though they set out only to reduce the increase in nuclear weapons, not to reduce them.

Why has arms control been so difficult to bring about? The first answer is, as realists would point out, that the security dilemma is an intractable problem, meaning that security regimes are always likely to break down and arms races are unavoidable. Second, there is a difference between national security, calculated on the basis of the interests of particular states, and the sense of collective or international security on which bilateral or multilateral agreements are based. In other words, states are always liable to view their build-up of arms as legitimate in terms of providing defence and ensuring deterrence, regardless of the international agreements that they are encouraged to join or have signed up to. India, Pakistan and Israel have thus never signed the NTP, while North Korea withdrew from the treaty in 1985. Third, the greatest difficulty in ensuring effective and enforceable arms control is that it seeks to control the most heavily

● **Arms control**: Mechanisms through which the proliferation of arms is constrained by agreements limiting their production, distribution and use.

● **Disarmament**: The reduction of fighting capacity, either through scaling-down or eliminating arms or, more likely, categories of weapons.

Major nuclear arms control agreements

1959	Antarctic Treaty – prohibits weapons testing and deployment in Antarctica (multilateral)
1963	Limited Test Ban Treaty – bans atmospheric, underwater and outer-space nuclear tests (multilateral)
1967	Outer Space Treaty – bans the deployment of nuclear weapons in space
1968	Nuclear Non-Proliferation Treaty (NPT) – (a) prohibits the acquisition of nuclear weapons by non-nuclear states, and (b) commits the five recognized nuclear powers to the reduction and removal of their weapons over time (multilateral)
1972	Strategic Arms Limitation Treaty 1 (SALT 1) – limits strategic nuclear weapons and freezes ICBMs at 1972 levels (USA/USSR)
1972	Anti-Ballistic Missile (ABM) Treaty – limits the number of anti-ballistic missiles (USA/USSR)
1987	Intermediate Nuclear Forces (INF) Treaty – eliminates all intermediate range nuclear weapons in Europe (USA/USSR)
1991	Strategic Arms Reduction Treaty 1 (START I) – limits the number of nuclear warheads and delivery systems (USA/USSR)
1993	Strategic Arms Reduction Treaty 2 (START II) – further limits the number of nuclear warheads and eliminates certain categories of warhead (USA/Russia)
1996	Comprehensive Test Ban Treaty (CTBT) – bans the testing of weapons, but not ratified by the USA, China, India, Pakistan and North Korea (multilateral)
2002	Strategic Offensive Reduction Treaty (SORT or Moscow Treaty) – limits the number of deployed nuclear warheads (USA/Russia)
2010	New START Treaty (or Prague Treaty) – limits both sides' nuclear warheads to 1,550, a 30 per cent reduction on SORT and a 74 per cent reduction on START 1 (USA/Russia).

● **Peace dividend**: The opportunity afforded by the end of superpower rivalry to reduce military spending and increase economic and social expenditure, often described as turning 'guns' into 'butter'.

armed, and therefore the most powerful, of the world's states. Great powers, and especially superpowers, will only be prepared to be bound by security regimes if they calculate that it is in their national interests to do so. Until 2010, genuine progress towards nuclear disarmament between the USA and Russia was confined to the relatively brief period after the end of the Cold War, forming part of the so-called '**peace dividend**'. However, the security priorities of both states soon changed. By the late 1990s, the USA, undoubtedly the most significant actor over the issue of arms control in the post-Cold War era, was revising its calculations about the dangers of nuclear proliferation, as well as about the means of countering it.

Concerns about nuclear proliferation, especially in the USA, have increasingly come to focus on the threat posed by 'rogue' states. By their nature, such states are not susceptible to the pressures that are constructed by security regimes. This was highlighted in particular in the aftermath of the Gulf War, when weapons inspectors revealed that Iraq, a signatory of the NPT since 1968, had been covertly developing nuclear weapons. Inspectors from the IAEA, supplemented by the UN Special Commissioners (UNSCOM), were then authorized to disarm Iraq of all nuclear, biological and chemical weapons and materials. However, the failure of the Saddam regime to cooperate consistently with UNSCOM and the weapons inspectors convinced many in the USA and in allied states that Iraq was hiding a significant weapons programme and that the inspection process was ultimately flawed. This resulted in 1998 in Operation Desert Fox, a short bombing campaign launched by the USA and the UK, which targeted installations that were believed to be housing Iraq's biological, chemical and nuclear weapons. Following September 11 (see p. 20), the US approach to 'rogue' states in general and Iraq in particular was significantly revised. Abandoning altogether the idea of containment and a reliance on diplomacy, the USA adopted the **Bush doctrine**, through which the combined threat from 'rogue' states and WMD would in future be addressed through pre-emptive war (see p. 232) and regime change. This resulted in Operation Iraqi Freedom in 2003 and the outbreak of the Iraq War. The invasion of Iraq nevertheless failed to uncover stockpiles of WMD or evidence of an ongoing weapons programme, suggesting that, behind its stance of non-compliance, the Saddam regime had destroyed its weapons and abandoned its weapons programmes, even though this may have been only a temporary adjustment.

The USA's more assertive stance towards 'rogue' states that may possess, or be seeking to acquire, WMD became evident in its relations with Iran and North Korea. In 2003, IAEA inspectors found that Iran, an NPT member, had constructed a uranium enrichment plant at Natanz and a heavy water production plant at Arak, fuelling fears that it had an illicit nuclear weapons programme, supported by technology from Pakistan. This occurred in the context of growing Iranian anxieties about possible US intervention (maybe using Israel as a proxy), following the outbreak of the Iraq War. The Iranian authorities have nevertheless insisted that their facilities are for peaceful purposes only, highlighting the problem of 'dual use' nuclear technology that may generate both civil nuclear energy and weapons materials. However, resisting diplomatic pressure from the USA and the EU3 (France, Germany and the UK), and despite the possibility of Iraq-style, US-imposed pre-emptive regime change, Iran announced in 2006, first, that it would restart small-scale uranium enrichment and later confirmed that it had restarted its nuclear programme. Iran's progress towards achieving nuclear-capable status was underlined in 2009 by the launch of its first home-built satellite into orbit, provoking intense debate about the implications of a nuclear Iran for regional stability and world affairs generally (see p. 282). The election in 2013 of Hassan Rouhani as Iranian president nevertheless raised hopes of a diplomatic thaw with the West over the issue of nuclear weapons.

Concerns about North Korea acquiring nuclear weapons stem, in large part, from the threat that this would pose to South Korea, which would then be under pressure itself to follow suit, possibly leading to a nuclear arms race in the Korean peninsular. A further worry arises from the possibility of a North Korean nuclear attack on the US mainland. However, despite pressure to isolate North

● **Bush doctrine**: The doctrine that pre-emptive military action, possibly aimed at achieving regime change, would be taken against states thought to be threatening the USA through the development of WMD and/or by harbouring terrorists.

Iran and the Bomb

Events: Iran's pursuit of civil nuclear power dates back to the 1950s, when it took place with the support of the USA and under the UN's 'Atoms for Peace' programme. After Iran's 1979 'Islamic Revolution', a clandestine nuclear programme was disbanded, although small-scale research into nuclear weapons may have been restarted during the Iran-Iraq War. The 'exposure' in 2002 of Iranian nuclear facilities in Natanz and Arak convinced many in the USA, Israel and else-where that Iran's civil nuclear programme was being used as a cover for the development of nuclear weapons. Less than full cooperation with the International Atomic Energy Authority (IAEA) inspection regime also led to escalating economic sanctions being imposed on Iran. The launching in 2009 of Iran's first domestically-made

satellite into orbit not only gave Iran an official presence in space but also provoked concerns about the possible development of long-range ballistic missiles. In 2010, Iran announced that it had become a 'nuclear state', based on the ability to produce uranium enriched up to 20 per cent, intended for medical usages.

Significance: The possibility of Iran building nuclear weapons continues to be at the forefront of debates about global security, despite assurances on the issue given by Hassan Rouhani since his election as Iranian president in 2013. But what would be the consequences of Iran getting the Bomb? Does the prospect of Iran becoming the world's tenth nuclear power pose profound and unacceptable risks to regional and global security? At least three major concerns have been raised about Iran 'going nuclear'. In the first place, a nuclear Iran would constitute a threat to the very existence of Israel. It is claimed that this is because the politico-religious nature of the Iranian regime makes it both an implacable enemy of Israel and immune to the conventional logic of nuclear deterrence. A first-strike nuclear attack by Iran on Israel, almost regard-less of its consequences, can therefore not be ruled out. Short of a full-scale attack, Iran may pass on nuclear weapons to groups such as Hamas and Hezbollah, which could be used against Israel. Second, the advent of a nuclear Iran would deeply upset regional stability, trans-forming the balance of power in the Middle East and encouraging states such as Turkey, Egypt and Saudi Arabia

to acquire nuclear weapons in order to prevent Iran becoming the regional hegemon. Third, a nuclear Iran would pose a threat to the USA, either through the possi-bility of an intercontinental ballistic strike, or through the support an emboldened Iran may give to anti-American terrorism around the world.

On the other hand, it can be argued that such fears are either greatly exaggerated or based on fundamental misunderstandings. Instead of seeking nuclear weapons for offensive purposes, Iran may be motivated more by a fear of both Israel (which has enjoyed a nuclear monopoly in the Middle East, probably since the 1960s) and the USA, underpinned by a history of adverse treatment by western powers (especially the UK) dating back to the nineteenth century. Moreover, Iran's acquisition of nuclear weapons may improve, rather than inflame, relations with Israel, as a nuclear balance of power tends to engender more responsible and risk-averse behaviour by all parties. Similarly, it is by no means clear that a nuclear Iran would spark a nuclear arms race across the Middle East, since states such as Turkey, Egypt and Saudi Arabia did not initi-ate nuclear weapons programmes while Israel stood as the region's sole nuclear power; and, anyway, if regional nuclear proliferation did occur, it may generate greater stability rather than instability (Waltz 2012). Finally, if the logic of nuclear deterrence effectively rules out an Iranian attack (whether conventional or nuclear) on Israel, such an attack on the enormously more powerful USA is surely unthinkable.

Korea, which intensified after September 11, US diplomatic leverage over North Korea has been weak and may have been counterproductive, especially as North Korea's geographical proximity to China makes pre-emptive regime change much less likely. North Korea rejected calls for it to open its nuclear facilities to IAEA inspection, before withdrawing from the NPT in 2003. In 2006, North Korea detonated a nuclear device, making it the world's ninth nuclear state. However, following six-party talks, spearheaded by China and involving the USA, South Korea, North Korea, Russia and Japan, North Korea announced in 2007 that it had frozen its nuclear weapons programme, even though it resumed plutonium reprocessing (a precursor to producing atomic weapons) the following year. The, albeit failed, launch of a long-range missile in 2009, and the decision to expel nuclear weapons inspectors and pull out of six-party talks for good appear to indicate the continuing determination of North Korea to become a fully-fledged nuclear weapon state (see p. 284). From the perspective of post-colonialism (see p. 200), however, the concentration of non-proliferation energies on countries such as Iran and North Korea, and the wider link between non-proliferation and the 'problem' of 'rogue' states, is largely driven by Eurocentric perceptions and assumptions.

An alternative approach to security in a world of nuclear proliferation is to erect missile shields. The idea behind missile defence systems is that, as arms control and security regimes can never ultimately be relied on to prevent nuclear attacks, particularly from ICBM, the surest form of protection is provided by a network of anti-ballistic missiles. The USA is currently the only state with the economic and technological resources seriously to contemplate this approach to nuclear defence. Its first attempt to do so was through the Strategic Defense Initiative (SDI), popularly known as 'Star Wars', which was proposed by President Reagan in 1983. Intended as an alternative to MAD, the SDI was never fully developed or deployed, although, in stepping up the arms race with the Soviet Union, it placed the Soviet economy under greater pressure and thus contributed to the end of the Cold War. The idea of a national missile defence (NMD) was nevertheless revived by George W. Bush, who committed the USA to the construction of a missile shield to be sited in Poland, the Czech Republic and possibly other eastern European states, particularly to take account of the threat posed by Iran.

However, missile shields also have their drawbacks. First, they are enormously expensive to develop, as they have to be sufficiently comprehensive, sophisticated and reliable to be able to guarantee that no missiles will be able to penetrate the shield, in view of the devastating potential of a single nuclear warhead. Second, many doubt whether, regardless of the resources devoted to their construction, missile shields can ever provide protection that is absolutely guaranteed, particularly as they are based, in effect, on the assumption that one bullet will *always* hit another bullet. Third, just as with the acquisition of any other weapons, the construction of missile shields may be perceived by other states as an aggressive or offensive act. The USA's NMD, and especially the proposal to site it in eastern Europe, thus provoked strong criticism from Russia and strengthened its assertiveness, possibly contributing to its 2008 war with Georgia. Recognizing that the NMD had become an obstacle to gaining Russian support for more pressing issues, such as Iran, President Obama announced the shelving of the missile shield in 2009. However, this was only part of a much more wide-ranging reappraisal of the USA's nuclear non-proliferation strategy

Focus on ...
North Korea: a rogue nuclear state?

What are the implications for international security of North Korea becoming in 2006 the world's ninth nuclear state? North Korea is often seen as the archetypal example of what happens when a 'rogue' state is able to acquire WMD, and especially nuclear weapons. Instead of the acquisition of such weapons fostering caution, even statesmanship, in the case of North Korea it creates the prospect of a nuclear adventurism that threatens not only South Korea but also Japan and even the USA. The belief that a nuclear first strike by North Korea is a real and present danger is based on at least three factors. First, North Korea is almost unique in being a hermetically sealed state, contemptuous of international opinion and heedless of multinational agreements, as demonstrated by its withdrawal from the NPT and its resistance to diplomatic pressure, even from China. Second, its leadership is erratic and autocratic (its leader, Kim Jong-un is the grandson of the founder of North Korea, Kim Il-sung (The 'Great Leader')), is closely linked to the military (North Korea has the fourth largest standing army in the world) and is imbued by a Marxist-Leninist ideology that has effectively been abandoned everywhere else in the world. Third, the regime's record of brutal internal repression suggests a clear willingness to use violence to achieve political ends.

However, such an image may demonstrate a crude and limited understanding of the North Korean regime and serve to overstate the threat that a nuclear-capable North Korea poses to international security. The uncooperative and often belligerent stance that North Korea adopts towards the rest of the world needs to be understood in the light of Korea's position as a small but strategically positioned country, which has been battered by invasion and exploitation for centuries. Harsh Japanese colonial rule was overthrown in 1945 only for civil war to break out between the Russian-backed North and the US-sponsored South, which left millions dead in the early 1950s. As the Korean War ground to stalemate and resulted in temporary armistice rather than a permanent peace, the North Korean regime and its military have, in a sense, never stopped fighting it. What is more, the fall of the Soviet Union and gradual liberalization of China left North Korea economically and politically isolated, facing a highly-trained South Korean army backed by US marines and dealing with economic collapse and widespread famine. Such a view suggests that diplomatic engagement with North Korea should recognize that, being motivated more by fear than aggression, its overriding priority is regime preservation, especially as (perhaps unlike Iran) it lacks serious regional ambitions.

by the Obama administration, which countenanced the possibility of a post-nuclear world.

A world free of nuclear weapons?

The idea of a post-nuclear world has long been advanced by the peace movement, for whom anti-nuclear activism has often been its most prominent cause. In a sense, the campaign against nuclear weapons was born at the moment that the world's first atomic bomb was tested. When it was detonated in July 1945, J. Robert Oppenheimer, often called the 'father of the atomic bomb', recalled the words of the *Bhagavad Gita*: 'Now I am become Death, the destroyer of worlds'. Oppenheimer later would oppose, unsuccessfully, the development of the still more fearsome hydrogen bomb. For many, the historically unprecedented scale of death and destruction that nuclear weapons made possible fundamentally altered thinking about the ethics of war, perhaps making the notion of a just war entirely redundant. As the nuclear arms race accelerated during the Cold War period, large-scale peace movements were mobilized focusing on anti-nuclear protest. The UK-based Campaign for Nuclear Disarmament (CND) was founded in 1958, with the aim of ridding the world of nuclear weapons and other WMD, and European Nuclear Disarmament (END) emerged in the early 1980s as an attempt to extend anti-nuclear activism across Europe, even (though with limited success) into the Soviet bloc. The largest demonstrations took place in 1983, in protest against NATO's decision to site US cruise and Pershing intermediate-range missiles in western Europe. An estimated 1 million people protested in London, while some 600,000 also took to the streets in West Germany. The International Campaign to Abolish Nuclear Weapons (ICAN) was launched in 2007 and represents over 200 organizations in some 50 countries. Its chief goal is the establishment of a legally binding and verifiable Nuclear Weapons Convention, under which the use, for whatever reason, of a nuclear weapon would constitute a violation of international law (see p. 339).

The campaign against nuclear weapons has also been advanced through the establishment of nuclear-free zones in many parts of the world. The earliest of these were in the Antarctic (1959), Latin America and the Caribbean (1967) and the South Pacific (1985). The Treaty of Pelindaba (1996) declared Africa to be a nuclear-free zone, as did the Bangkok Treaty (1997) in relation to South-east Asia. Taken collectively, these treaties mean that most of the Southern hemisphere is now a nuclear-free zone. Such trends and movements have been motivated by a variety of considerations. Most prominently, nuclear weapons have been seen as morally indefensible, if not quintessentially evil. In this view, the development, use or threatened use of a weapon that would lead to the indiscriminate deaths of tens of thousands or, more likely, millions of people can never be justified, in any circumstances. The economic and political case in favour of nuclear disarmament is based on considerations such as the huge cost of their development, the belief that the strategy of nuclear deterrence simply leads to an escalating, and unstable, arms race (making nuclear war more likely not less likely), and that nuclear weapons deepen inequality amongst states as the elite 'nuclear club' try to dictate to the rest of the world. Psychological arguments against nuclear weapons have also been advanced, not least linked to their capacity to generate unending anxiety and dread, as post-1945 generations have lived under the shadow of the bomb (Lifton and Falk 1982).

Liberals and social constructivists have nevertheless always emphasized the scope for state policy on nuclear weapons to evolve beyond narrow national security concerns. This was briefly evident in the re-energizing of US and Soviet disarmament efforts as the Cold War crumbled, but it has re-surfaced in the stress the Obama administration has placed on the idea of a nuclear-free world. In a speech beneath the walls of Prague Castle in April 2009, in advance of the signing of the new START Treaty with Russia, Obama set out his vision of a world free from nuclear weapons (although he acknowledged that the goal of complete nuclear disarmament may not be achieved in his own lifetime). In September 2009, Obama became the first US President to chair a meeting of the UN Security Council, the chief purpose of which was to call for an end to the proliferation of nuclear weapons, in the hope of strengthening the non-proliferation regime ahead of the five-yearly review of the NPT due to take place in May 2010. Obama's

Focus on . . .
Nuclear ethics: indefensible weapons?

Should nuclear weapons be treated as 'normal' weapons? Is the use, for whatever reasons, of a nuclear weapon ever justifiable? Realists have often viewed nuclear weapons as simply one rung, albeit a major one, on the ladder of arms escalation. To view nuclear weapons as normal, in this sense, is to countenance their acquisition and possible use if circumstances allow. This was certainly evident during the Cold War period, when a large proportion of realists took nuclear weapons to be legitimate, on the grounds of deterrence theory and especially the doctrine of MAD, as outlined by games theorists such as Kahn (1960). In this view, thinking 'the unthinkable' – that is, about nuclear warfare – is a defensible, and perhaps necessary, aspect of a national security strategy. However, realist support for nuclear weapons is not principled but strictly conditional. It is noticeable, for example, that realist support for nuclear weapons has declined in the post-Cold War period, as emerging multipolarity and new security challenges from non-state actors render traditional, bipolar deterrence theory redundant (Shultz et al. 2007).

However, nuclear weapons are widely viewed as incompatible with any sense of morality. For pacifists, nuclear weapons are simply an example of the insanity of war: to contemplate the use of nuclear weapons is to countenance the destruction of the human species. It is, furthermore, difficult to see how nuclear warfare can be reconciled with the principles of a just war (see p. 264), whatever the circumstances. In particular, by their nature, nuclear weapons violate each of the principles of *jus in bello* – discrimination, proportionality and humanity. Nye (1988) nevertheless attempted to reconcile the policy of nuclear deterrence with the broad just war tradition by advancing five 'maxims of nuclear ethics'. These are (1) the only acceptable reason for possessing a nuclear deterrent is self-defence; (2) nuclear weapons should never be treated as 'normal' weapons; (3) the purpose of any nuclear strategy must be to minimize harm to innocents (that is, non-combatants); (4) we should work to reduce the risks of war in the near term; and (5) we should work to reduce the reliance on nuclear weapons in the longer term.

strategy, supported by then-President Medvedev of Russia, aimed to move beyond outdated Cold War thinking about nuclear deterrence. The key motivation behind it was to gain the moral authority to place greater pressure on non-nuclear states to abandon their quest for nuclear weapons. As such, this strategy acknowledges the link between nuclear disarmament and non-proliferation. If established nuclear powers are not seen to be serious about abandoning their weapons, their capacity to influence non-nuclear states is crucially undermined; indeed, their calls for non-proliferation are dismissed as simple hypocrisy. In this respect, the USA is particularly vulnerable, as it remains the world's pre-eminent nuclear power, has consistently failed to carry out its obligation under the NPT to divest itself of nuclear weapons over time, and has not signed the CTBT.

However, this strategy faces at least three problems. In the first place, it is unclear whether such pressures, even based on bolstered moral authority, will have any impact on states such as Iran and North Korea, which have already demonstrated a willingness to endure condemnation from the international community in pursuit of what they see as key national security goals. Second, great power unanimity on this issue may be fragile. China, for instance, has made it clear that it has no plans to scrap its nuclear weapons, and, in a context of the shifting location of global power, it perhaps has little incentive to follow the

USA's lead. In any event, creating conditions and levels of confidence among established nuclear powers in which the abolition of nuclear weapons is generally viewed as a safer option than retention is going to be challenging. Third, significant technical problems will have to be surmounted if abolition is to become a reality. Not the least of these are about how the elimination of nuclear warheads can be verified and whether nuclear material can be monitored with high confidence. It is difficult, therefore, to pretend that the task of abolishing nuclear weapons will be easy or that it will be accomplished in the near future (Perkovich and Acton 2008).

There are some, nevertheless, who argue that even if the elimination of nuclear weapons is possible, it may not be desirable. Concerns, for example, have been expressed about the impact the strategy of nuclear disarmament may have, if successfully implemented, on the likelihood of war. To the extent that the decline in inter-state war since 1945, especially between major powers, has been a consequence of the fear that conventional wars may escalate into nuclear wars, a reduction in (or, worse, the elimination of) nuclear arsenals may only create conditions that allow such wars to break out again. This suggests that the deterrent effect of nuclear weapons did not end with the end of the Cold War. A further concern is that, ironically, nuclear disarmament may damage the cause of non-proliferation as well as strengthen it. A major factor helping to prevent nuclear proliferation in recent decades has been the existence of the USA's nuclear umbrella. If making a credible commitment to nuclear disarmament means reducing the range and effectiveness of the US umbrella, states ranging from Japan, South Korea and Taiwan in Asia to ones across the Middle East and the Gulf may be forced to reconsider their non-nuclear status. Efforts to create a world free of nuclear weapons may therefore prove to be counter-productive.

SUMMARY

- The massive destructive capacity of nuclear weapons means that they have affected international and domestic politics in a way that no other weapons ever have. Vertical nuclear proliferation during the Cold War period witnessed the build-up of massive nuclear arsenals in the USA and the Soviet Union.

- While some believe that the Cold War nuclear arms race effectively underpinned the 'long peace' of the post-1945 period, especially once the condition of Mutually Assured Destruction was achieved, others have associated the 'balance of terror' with instability and the ever-present danger that deterrence would fail.

- The post-Cold War era has been characterized by heightened anxiety about nuclear proliferation. This occurred for reasons such as a growth in the number of states that have shown an interest in acquiring nuclear weapons, the easier availability of nuclear materials and technology, and the increased danger that nuclear weapons get into the hands of actors who may use them.

- Despite the development of an extensive non-proliferation regime, effective arms control has been difficult to bring about because states tend to place concerns about national security above their obligations under bilateral or multilateral agreements. Particular anxiety has been expressed about nuclear proliferation in relation to North Korea and Iran, based on the supposedly unstable and risk-prone natures of their regimes and the existence of significant regional tensions.

- The idea of a nuclear-free world has been advanced both by peace activists and, more recently, by senior politicians in the USA and Russia. The Obama administration's defence strategy links a commitment to nuclear disarmament to the ability to exert strong moral and diplomatic pressure to ensure non-proliferation.

- Non-proliferation strategies may nevertheless have little impact on nuclear and would-be nuclear 'rogue' states. They may also fail to enjoy unanimous backing from major powers, possibly make inter-state war more likely, and may intensify defence anxieties in states that once benefited from the USA's nuclear umbrella.

Questions for discussion

- Are WMD a distinct category of weapons, and are nuclear weapons the only genuine example of WMD?
- Why do states seek to acquire nuclear weapons?
- Why do some states not seek to acquire nuclear weapons?
- How convincing is the theory of nuclear deterrence?
- Is the idea of nuclear weapons getting into the 'wrong hands' simply an example of Eurocentrism?
- Why has effective nuclear arms control been so difficult to bring about?
- Is a nuclear Iran a significant threat to international peace and security?
- Are efforts to achieve nuclear non-proliferation largely based on hypocrisy and Eurocentric biases?
- Are missile shields a solution to the threat of nuclear attack?
- Are nuclear weapons morally indefensible?
- Is a nuclear-free world possible or desirable?

Further reading

Herring, E. (ed.), *Preventing the Use of Weapons of Mass Destruction* (2000). A collection of essays that consider the various strategies that have been used to prevent the use of WMD.

Hymans, J., *The Psychology of Nuclear Proliferation: Identity, Emotions and Foreign Policy* (2006). A fascinating analysis, using the examples of France, Australia, Argentina and India, of the dynamics of nuclear decision-making.

Nye, J. S., *Nuclear Ethics* (1988). A balanced, rigorous and comprehensive discussion of the ethical dilemmas raised by nuclear weapons.

Solingen, E., *Nuclear Logics: Contrasting Paths in East Asia and the Middle East* (2007). An examination of the contrasting logics of nuclearization and denuclearization in different parts of the world.

ONLINE RESOURCES AVAILABLE

Links to relevant web resources can be found on the *Global Politics* website

CHAPTER 12

Terrorism

'Fervour is the weapon of choice of the impotent.'

FRANZ FANON, *Black Skin, White Masks* (1952)

PREVIEW

Until the 1990s, terrorism was widely considered to be a security concern of the second order, often being ignored by standard text books on international politics. However, the events of 11 September 2001 changed this dramatically, encouraging a major reappraisal of the nature and significance of terrorism. For some, what was variously dubbed 'new' terrorism, 'global' terrorism or 'catastrophic' terrorism had become the principal security threat in the early twenty-first century, reflecting the fact that, in conditions of globalization, non-state actors (in this case, terrorist groups) had gained important advantages over states. Beyond this, the inauguration of the 'war on terror' suggested that resurgent terrorism had opened up new fault lines that would define global politics for the foreseeable future. However, terrorism is both a highly contested phenomenon and a deeply controversial concept. Critical theorists, for example, argue that much commonly accepted thinking about terrorism amounts to stereotypes and misconceptions, with the significance of terrorism often being grossly overstated, usually for ideological reasons. How should terrorism be defined? Why and how have scholars disagreed over the nature of terrorism? Does modern terrorism have a truly global reach and a genuinely catastrophic potential? Disagreements over the nature and significance of terrorism are nevertheless matched by debates about how terrorism should be countered. Not only are there divisions about the effectiveness of different counter-terrorism strategies, but there has also been intense debate about the price that may have to be paid for protecting society from terrorism in terms of the erosion of basic rights and freedoms. Should terrorism be countered through strengthening state security, through military repression or through political deals, and what are the implications of such strategies?

KEY ISSUES

- What is terrorism?
- What are the key perspectives on terrorism?
- Has the nature of terrorism changed in recent years?
- Has terrorism 'gone global'?
- How significant is modern terrorism?
- How can, and should, the threat of terrorism be countered?

UNDERSTANDING TERRORISM

Terrorism (see p. 291) is by no means a modern phenomenon. Early examples include the Sicarri ('dagger men'), usually seen as an extreme splinter wing of the Jewish Zealots, who, in the first century, used killings and kidnappings in their campaign against the Romans in Judea and against Jews who collaborated with the Romans. Similarly, the Thugee (or Thugs) in India, a cult which carried out ritual killings supposedly in honour of the goddess Kali, and which came to particular prominence in the nineteenth century, may have emerged as early as the thirteenth century. The term 'terrorist', nevertheless, derives from the French Revolution and the Reign of Terror, 1793–94. This witnessed a wave of mass executions, carried out by the Jacobins under the leadership of Robespierre, in which up to 40,000 alleged 'enemies of the revolution' lost their lives.

The first widespread association of western societies with terrorism occurred with the upsurge in clandestine violence by anarchist groups in the late nineteenth century, which reached its peak in the 1890s. Amongst its victims were Tsar Alexander II (1881), Empress Elizabeth of Austria (1898), King Umberto of Italy (1900) and Presidents Carnot (1894) of France and McKinley (1901) of the USA. Anarchist terrorism was a form of 'propaganda by the deed': it used violence as a way of raising political consciousness and stimulating the masses to revolt, sometimes by attacking what were seen as symbols of oppression and exploitation. This was evident in the attack on the Café Terminus in Paris in 1894, which was justified as an assault on 'bourgeois society', and the mysterious incident in the same year in which a man, later identified as a French anarchist, blew himself up in the vicinity of the Royal Observatory at Greenwich, London (the incident that inspired Joseph Conrad's novel *The Secret Agent*). A further wave of anarchist violence broke out in the 1960s and 1970s, undertaken by groups such as the Baader-Meinhof Group in West Germany, the Italian Red Brigades, the Japanese Red Army and the Angry Brigade in the UK.

However, in the post-1945 period, terrorism generally had a nationalist orientation. During the 1940s and 1950s, it was associated with Third World anticolonial struggles in Africa, Asia and the Middle East, later being taken up by national liberation movements such as the Palestine Liberation Organization (PLO) and groups such as Black September. Terrorism was also used by disaffected national or ethnic minorities in developed western societies, notably by the IRA in Northern Ireland and on the UK mainland, by ETA in the Basque region of Spain, and by the FLQ in Quebec. Nevertheless, the September 11 attacks on New York and Washington (see p. 20) convinced many people that terrorism had been reborn in a new and more dangerous form, leading some to conclude that it had become the principal threat to international peace and security. However, before this assertion is addressed, it is necessary to consider the nature of terrorism, the different ways in which terrorism has been understood, and whether terrorism has changed in recent years.

Defining terrorism

The central feature of terrorism is that it is a form of political violence that aims to achieve its objectives through creating a climate of fear and apprehension (Goodin 2006). As such, it uses violence in a very particular way: not primarily

CONCEPT

Terrorism

Terrorism, in its broadest sense, refers to attempts to further political ends by using violence to create a climate of fear, apprehension and uncertainty. The most common forms of terrorist action include assassinations, bombings, hostage seizures and plane hijacks, although the advent of terrorism with a global reach, as demonstrated by September 11, has threatened to redefine the phenomenon. The term is highly pejorative and it tends to be used selectively (one person's terrorist can be another's freedom fighter). While terrorism is often portrayed as an anti-government activity, governments may also employ terror against their own or other populations, as in the case of 'state terrorism'. Terrorism is nevertheless a deeply controversial term (see Deconstructing terrorism, p. 293).

● **State terrorism**: Terrorism carried out by government bodies such as the police, military or intelligence agencies.

to bring about death and destruction, but to create unease and anxiety about possible future acts of death and destruction. Terrorist violence is therefore clandestine and involves an element of surprise, if not arbitrariness, designed to create uncertainty and widening apprehension. Terrorism, therefore, often takes the form of seemingly indiscriminate attacks on civilian targets, although attacks on symbols of power and prestige and the kidnapping or murder of prominent businessmen, senior government officials and political leaders are usually also viewed as acts of terrorism. Nevertheless, the concept of terrorism remains deeply problematical. This applies, in part, because of confusion about the basis on which terrorism should be defined. It can be defined by the nature of:

● The *act* itself: clandestine violence that has a seemingly indiscriminate character. However, the nature of terrorism is not inherent in the violent act itself, because it rests, crucially, on intentions, specifically the desire to intimidate or terrify (Schmid and Jongman 1988). Not only does this mean that terrorism is always a social fact rather than a brutal fact, but also that the intentions behind acts of terrorism may be complex or uncertain (Jackson 2009).
● Its *victims*: innocent civilians. However, does this mean that attacks on military targets and personnel or the assassination of political leaders cannot be described as terrorism? Some terrorists, moreover, have viewed civilians as 'guilty', on the grounds that they are implicated in, and benefit from, structural oppression that takes place on a national or even global level.
● Its *perpetrators*: non-state bodies that are intent on influencing the actions of governments or international organizations. However, such a focus on what Laqueur (1977) called 'terrorism from below' risks ignoring the much more extensive killing of unarmed civilians through 'terrorism from above', sometimes classified as **state terrorism** or 'state-sponsored' terrorism.

Terrorism, however, is only a meaningful term if it can reliably be distinguished from other forms of political violence. Terrorism differs from conventional warfare in that, as a 'weapon of the weak', it is most often embraced by those who have no realistic possibility of prevailing against their opponents in a conventional armed contest (Crenshaw 1983). Lacking the organizational strength or destructive capacity to engage in open conflict, terrorists rely on strategies of provocation and polarization. Indeed, terrorism can even be thought of as the negation of combat, as its targets are attacked in such a way as to make self-defence difficult or perhaps impossible. Terrorism, nevertheless, shares more in common with guerrilla warfare. Both are examples of asymmetrical warfare, in which tactics and strategies are adopted specifically to compensate for an enemy's greater technological, economic and (conventional) military strength. In addition, both terrorism and guerrilla warfare place an emphasis on corroding an enemy's will to resist by drawing it into a protracted armed struggle. The similarities, indeed, may go further, in that terrorism is often used as part of a guerrilla or insurrectionary war, as demonstrated, for instance, by the Taliban in Afghanistan. In this light, terrorism can perhaps be thought of as either a special kind of 'new' war (as discussed in Chapter 10), or a strategy characteristically employed in 'new' wars.

Nevertheless, terrorism can also be distinguished from guerrilla warfare. In the first place, terrorism is characterized by the disproportionate weight it places on highly-publicized atrocities as a mechanism for shaping the consciousness and behaviour of target audiences (Phillips 2010). This reflects the extent to which terrorists rely on 'propaganda by the deed', high visibility and conscience-shocking acts of violence that are designed to dramatize the impotence of government, to intimidate rival ethnic or religious communities or the public in general, or, in its classic form, to mobilize popular support and stimulate political activism. Second, the essentially covert nature of terrorist activity usually restricts the extent to which terrorists are able to engage in popular activism, by contrast with guerrilla armies which typically rely heavily on a mass base of popular support.

This, however, by no means exhausts the controversies that have emerged over the concept of terrorism. The term 'terrorism' is ideologically contested and emotionally charged; some even refuse to use it on the grounds that it is either hopelessly vague or carries unhelpful pejorative implications. Its negative associations mean that the word is almost always applied to the acts of one's opponents, and almost never to similar acts carried out by one's own group or a group one supports. Terrorism thus tends to be used as a political tool, a means of determining the legitimacy, or illegitimacy, of a group or political movement under consideration. This also raises questions about whether terrorism is evil in itself and beyond moral justification. Whereas mainstream approaches to terrorism usually view it as an attack on civilized or humanitarian values, even as an example of **nihilism**, radical scholars sometimes argue that terrorism and other forms of political violence may advance the cause of political justice and counter other, more widespread forms of violence or abuse, suggesting that they are justifiable (Honderich 1989). Finally, critical theorists have warned against the dangers of 'essentializing' terrorism, treating it as the defining feature of a person's or group's nature. This implies that being a terrorist is an identity, akin to nationality, religion (see p. 197) or ethnicity (see p. 193). Using the same label to describe groups such as al-Qaeda (see p. 301), Hezbollah, the IRA and ETA obscures or ignores the very different historical, political, social and cultural contexts in which they operate, and the different causes with which they have been associated.

Rise of 'new' terrorism?

Further debates about terrorism have been stimulated by the idea that terrorism comes in various forms and that it can be, or has been, transformed. This tendency was significantly intensified by September 11, which some claimed marked the emergence of an entirely new brand of terrorism. Ignatieff (2004), for instance, distinguished between four types of terrorism, as follows:

● *Insurrectionary* terrorism – this is aimed at the revolutionary overthrow of a state (examples include anarchist and revolutionary communist terrorism).
● *Loner* or *issue* terrorism – this is aimed at the promotion of a single cause (examples include the bombing of abortion clinics in the USA and the 1995 sarin nerve gas attack on the Tokyo subway by the religious cult Aum Shrinrikyo).

● **Nihilism**: Literally a belief in nothing; the rejection of all conventional moral and political principles.

● The use of the term 'terrorism' assumes that certain forms of political violence can be reliably distinguished from other forms by the fact that they aim to provoke 'terror' rather than simply lead to destruction. However, all forms of political violence or warfare aim, at some level, to strike fear into the wider population. This introduces an arbitrary element into the use of the term, and implies that no conception of terrorism can ever be objective or impartial. Terrorism can thus be thought of as a political or social construct.

Deconstructing . . .

'TERRORISM'

● 'Terrorism' carries deeply pejorative implications, meaning that the term tends to be used as a political weapon, implying that the group or action to which it is attached is immoral and illegitimate. To described a person or group as a 'terrorist' implies that they are the enemy of civilized society, that they are intent on causing death, destruction and fear for their own sake, not for a larger purpose (unlike 'freedom fighters' or 'revolutionaries'), and that they are clandestine, shadowy and sinister.

● In conventional usage, the term is associated only with non-state actors. This can have politically conservative implications. Not only does the fact that states cannot be accused of terrorism imply that state violence is legitimate violence, but it also suggests that attempts to challenge government or overthrow the status quo that involve violence are politically and morally suspect. This may also apply to attempts to challenge the hegemonic or dominant state within the modern international system, specifically the USA.

● *Nationalist* terrorism – this aims to overthrow colonial rule or occupation, often with the goal of gaining independence for an ethnic, religious or national group (examples include the FLN in Algeria, the Liberation Tigers of Tamil Eelam (commonly know as the Tamil Tigers) in Sri Lanka and Hamas and Hezbollah in Israel and the occupied territories).
● *Global* terrorism – this is aimed at inflicting damage and humiliation on a global power or at transforming global civilizational relations (examples include al-Qaeda and other forms of Islamist terrorism).

● **New terrorism**: A form of terrorism that is supposedly more radical and devastating than 'traditional' terrorism because of the nature of its organization, political character, motivations and strategies.

However, the concept of **'new' terrorism**, suggesting that there has been a revolutionary change in the nature of terrorism, predates the September 11 attacks, interest in it being stimulated by events such as the 1995 Aum Shinrikyo attack on the Tokyo subway system and the 1997 massacre in Luxor, Egypt, which left 62 tourists dead (Laqueur 1996, 1999). But what is new terrorism, and how new is it? Although new terrorism supposedly has a number of features

APPROACHES TO . . .

TERRORISM

Realist view

Realist thinking about terrorism tends to place a strong emphasis on the state/non-state dichotomy. Terrorism is usually viewed as a violent challenge to the established order by a non-state group or movement, often as part of a bid for power. The realist emphasis on politics as a realm of power-seeking and competition can thus be seen to apply to the behaviour of non-state actors as well as to that of states. From this perspective, the motivations behind terrorism are largely strategic in character. Groups use clandestine violence and focus on civilian targets mainly because they are too weak to challenge the state openly through conventional armed conflict. They attempt to exhaust or weaken the resolve of a government or regime that they cannot destroy. The crucial feature of the realist approach to terrorism is nevertheless that, being an attempt to subvert civil order and overthrow the political system, the state's response to terrorism should be uncompromising. In a political tradition that can be traced back to Machiavelli (see p. 58), this reflects the belief that political leaders should be prepared to contravene conventional morality in order to protect a political community that is under threat. This is often called the problem of 'dirty hands' – because they have wider public responsibilities, political leaders should be prepared to get their hands dirty, and set aside private scruples. Realists therefore tend to be relatively unconcerned about whether counter-terrorist strategies infringe civil liberties; the important matter is whether counter-terrorism works.

Liberal view

Liberals, like realists, tend to view terrorism as an activity primarily engaged in by non-state actors. Insofar as they have different views about the motivations behind terrorism, liberals are more inclined to emphasize the role of ideology rather than simple power-seeking. A key factor in explaining terrorism is therefore the influence of a political or religious ideology that creates an exaggerated sense of injustice and hostility, and so blinds the perpetrators of violence to the moral and human costs of their actions. However, liberal thinking about terrorism has tended to be dominated by the ethical dilemmas that are posed by the task of counter-terrorism. On the one hand, liberals typically view terrorism as an attack on the very principles of a liberal-democratic society – openness, choice, debate, toleration and so on. On the other hand, liberals have been anxious to ensure that attempts to counter terrorism are consistent with these same values, and, in particular, that they should not infringe human rights and civil liberties. (For an account of the relationship between counter-terrorism and individual rights and freedoms, see p. 307).

Critical views

There are two main critical perspectives on terrorism. The first reflects the views of radical theorists such as Chomsky (see p. 235) and Falk (1991). In their view, terrorism amounts to the killing of unarmed civilians, and it is something that is engaged in both by states and by non-state actors. State terrorism ('wholesale terrorism'), indeed, is much more significant than non-state terrorism ('retail terrorism'), because states have a far greater coercive capacity than any non-state actors. Terrorism is thus largely a mechanism through which states use violence against civilians either to maintain themselves in power, or to extend political or economic influence over other states. In this respect, particular attention has focused on its role in promoting US hegemony, the USA being viewed as the world's 'leading terrorist state' (Chomsky 2003).

The alternative critical perspective on terrorism is shaped by constructivist and poststructuralist thinking. It is characterized by the belief that much, and possibly all, commonly accepted knowledge about terrorism amounts to stereotypes and misconceptions. In this view, terrorism is a social or political construct. It is typically used to define certain groups and political causes as non-legitimate, by associating them with the image of immorality and wanton violence. This, in turn, tends to imply that the institutions and political structures against which terrorism is used are rightful and legitimate. Such thinking has been applied in particular to the discourses that have emerged in connection with the 'war on terror' (see p. 230), in which the term 'terrorism' is allegedly used to de-legitimize the enemies of the dominant actors in the modern global system (Dedeoglu 2003).

(Field 2009), its most important, and perhaps defining, feature is that religious motivations for terrorism have replaced secular motivations. The secular character of 'traditional' terrorism derived from the idea that, for much of the post-1945 period, terrorism was associated with nationalist and particularly separatist movements. The goal of terrorism, in these cases, was narrow and political: the overthrow of foreign rule and the establishment of national self-determination. Insofar as nationalist terrorism was inspired by wider ideological beliefs, these were often rooted in revolutionary Marxism, or Marxism-Leninism. By the 1980s, however, religion had started to become an important motivation for political violence. According to Hoffman (2006), by 1995 almost half of the 56 terrorist groups then believed to be in operation could be classified as religious in character and/or motivation. Al-Qaeda was certainly an example of this trend, being motivated by a broad and radical politico-religious ideology, in the form of Islamism (see p. 205), but it was by no means an isolated example.

Proponents of the idea of new terrorism suggest that because terrorism had become a religious imperative, even a sacred duty, rather than a pragmatically selected political strategy, the nature of terrorist groups and the function of political violence had changed crucially. While traditional terrorists could be satisfied by limited political change or the partial accommodation of their demands, new terrorists could not so easily be bought off, their often amorphous but substantially broader objectives making them inflexible and uncompromising. Similarly, religious belief supposedly altered the moral context in which groups resorted to, and used, violence. Instead of terrorist violence having an essentially strategic character, being a means to an end, violence became increasingly symbolic and was embraced as a manifestation of 'total war'. Insofar as violence had become a cathartic experience, psychological, ethical and political constraints on the use of violence supposedly fell away, making new terrorists more likely to embrace indiscriminate and lethal forms of violence. Such thinking has been used to explain the growing association of terrorism with weapons of mass destruction (WMD), and possibly even nuclear weapons, as well as the increased use of **suicide terrorism**. Furthermore, changes in the moral parameters within which terrorist violence was undertaken have, allegedly, also been matched by changes in the organizational character of terrorism. Whereas traditional terrorists tended to employ military-style command and control structures, new terrorists tend to operate within more diffuse and amorphous international networks of loosely connected cells and support networks (Wilkinson 2003). Al-Qaeda, for instance, is often portrayed more as an idea than as an organization, its network of cells being so loosely organized that it has been seen as a form of 'leaderless Jihad' (Sageman 2008).

Nevertheless, the notion of new terrorism has also been subject to criticism, many arguing that distinction between new terrorism and traditional terrorism is largely artificial or, at least, much exaggerated (Copeland 2001). For example, religiously inspired terrorism is certainly not an entirely new phenomenon. Apart from more ancient examples, elements within the Muslim Brotherhood, which was formed in 1928, have often been linked to assassinations and other attacks, while nationalist groups, such as the Moro National Liberation Movement (MNLF), Egyptian Islamic Jihad and Hezbollah, have fused religious and political objectives. Similarly, it is possible to find examples of traditional terrorist groups that have been every bit as fanatical and uncompromising in

● **Suicide terrorism**: A form of terrorism in which the perpetrator (or perpetrators) intends to kill himself or herself in the process of carrying out the attack (see p. 299).

their strategies, and as unrestrained in their use of political violence, as groups classified as new terrorists. This applies, for instance in the case of secular groups such as the Tamil Tigers, the Popular Front for the Liberation of Palestine (PFLP) and the Kurdistan Workers' Party (PKK). Finally, the notion of clear organizational differences between new and traditional terrorist groups may also be misleading. Apparently traditional terrorist groups, such as the Provisional IRA and Fatah, the largest faction in the Palestine Liberation Organization (PLO), often delegated significant autonomy to individual terrorist cells, frequently allowing them to conduct operations independently of any command and control structure.

SIGNIFICANCE OF TERRORISM

Regardless of whether September 11 reflected a change in the *nature* of terrorism, it is widely assumed that it brought about a profound shift in its significance. The threat posed by terrorism was suddenly accorded a historically unprecedented level of importance, based on the belief that terrorism was a manifestation of new fault lines that would define global politics in the twenty-first century. This was reflected, most obviously, in the launch of the 'war on terror' and in the changing shape of world order that occurred in its wake (as discussed in Chapter 9). But how well-founded are these assumptions? Has the potency and significance of terrorism dramatically increased, and, if so, how and why has this happened? There are, allegedly, two aspects of this process. The first is that terrorism has acquired a truly global reach, and the second is that its destructive potential has greatly increased.

Terrorism goes global

There is nothing new about the idea that terrorism has an international, transnational or even global dimension. Late nineteenth-century anarchists, for example, saw themselves as part of an international movement and operated, in Western Europe at least, across national borders. The extreme Leftist groups of the 1960s and 1970s, such as the Baader-Meinhof Group, the Japanese Red Army and the Italian Red Brigades, believed that they were engaged in a global struggle, both to overthrow the capitalist system and to expel the US military presence from Western Europe and elsewhere. The birth of what is sometimes classified as 'international' terrorism is often traced back to the advent of aeroplane hijackings in the late 1960s, carried out by groups such as the PLO. However, the development of terrorism into a genuinely transnational, if not global, phenomenon is generally associated with the advance of globalization (see p. 8). Modern terrorism is sometimes, therefore, portrayed as a child of globalization. This has happened for a number of reasons. First, increased cross-border flows of people, goods, money, technology and ideas have generally benefited non-state actors at the expense of states, and terrorist groups have proved to be particularly adept at exploiting this hyper-mobility. Second, increased international migration flows have often helped to sustain terrorist campaigns, as diaspora communities can become an important source of funding, as occurred, for instance, with the Tamil Tigers. Third, globalization has generated pressures that have contributed to a growth in political militancy generally. This has either occurred as a backlash against cultural globalization (see p. 151) and the spread of western goods, ideas and values, or it has been a consequence of imbalances within the global capitalist system that have impoverished and destabilized parts of the global South.

Globalization may have provided a backdrop against which terrorism acquired an increasingly transnational character, but it does not in itself explain the emergence of transnational or global terrorism. This is evident in the case of the form of terrorism that appears to be most clearly transnational: Islamist, or *jihadist*, terrorism. Although Islamist terrorism has been portrayed as a nihilistic movement or as a manifestation of religious revivalism, it is better understood as a violent response to political conditions and crises that have found expression in a politico-religious ideology (Azzam 2008). It emerged from the late 1970s onwards, and was shaped by three major developments. In the first place, a growing number of Muslim states experienced crises of governmental legitimacy, as popular frustrations mounted against corrupt and autocratic regimes that were thought to have failed to meet their citizens' economic and political aspirations. In the light of the defeat of Arab nationalism, this led to a growing religiously-based movement to overthrow what were dubbed 'apostate' (a person who forsakes his or her religion) Muslim leaders in countries such as Egypt, Saudi Arabia, Sudan and Pakistan. These leaders and their regimes came to be seen as Islamism's 'near enemy'. Second, coinciding with this, US influence in the Middle East expanded, filling the power vacuum that had been created by the UK's post-1968 withdrawal from military bases to the east of the Suez Canal. The USA thus came to be seen as the 'far enemy', as policies such as implacable support for Israel, the siting of US troops in the Muslim 'holy ground' of Saudi Arabia, and support for 'apostate' Muslim leaders across the region made the USA appear to be a threat to Islam. Third, there was a growth in politically engaged forms of religious fundamentalism (see p. 199) in many parts of the Islamic world, a trend that was radically accelerated by the 1979 Iranian 'Islamic Revolution'. (The origins and development of political Islam are discussed in Chapter 8.)

As far as Islamist terrorism is concerned, however, domestic *jihad* predominated over global *jihad* during the 1970s and 1980s, as hostility to the USA and the idea of a larger struggle against the West provided merely a backdrop for attempts to achieve power on a national level. This only changed from the mid-1990s onwards, and it did so largely through the failure of political Islam to achieve its domestic goals (Kepel 2006). 'Apostate' regimes often proved to be more stable and enduring that had been anticipated, and, in cases such as Egypt and Algeria, military repression was used successfully to quell Islamist insurgents. In this context, *jihad* went global, as growing elements within the Islamist movement realigned their strategies around the 'far enemy': western, and particularly US, policy in the Middle East and across the Islamic world. In that sense, the rise of global *jihad* was a mark of Islamism's decline, not of its resurgence (Roy 1994). The war in Afghanistan to expel Soviet troops, 1979–89, nevertheless played an important role in facilitating the shift to globalism. The emergence of a transnational Mujahadeen resistance against the Russians helped to forge a 'corporate' sense of belonging among Islamist groups that often had different backgrounds and sometimes different doctrinal beliefs, strengthening also the belief that domestic struggles are part of a wider global struggle.

These were the circumstances in which al-Qaeda emerged, usually viewed as the clearest example of global terrorism. In what sense does al-Qaeda represent the global face of Islamist terrorism? Al-Qaeda's goals are transnational, if not civilizational: it seeks to purify and regenerate Muslim society at large, both by overthrowing 'apostate' Muslim leaders and by expelling western, and particularly US, influence, and by engaging in a larger struggle against the moral corruption of what it sees as western 'crusaders'. Moreover, it has been associated with terrorist attacks in states as disparate as Yemen, Saudi Arabia, Kenya, the USA, Spain and the UK, and has cells or affiliate organizations across the world. The emergence of transnational or global terrorism therefore appears to be a particularly alarming development. Not only does it seem to be a form of terrorism that may strike anywhere, any time, but, by defining its goals in civilizational terms (the overthrow of secular, liberal society), it appears massively to increase its potential targets.

However, the global character of modern terrorism may be over-stated in at least three respects. First, the Islamist or *jihadist* movement is by no means a single, cohesive entity but encompasses groups with often very different beliefs and goals. Many of them, indeed, are better thought of as religious nationalists, or perhaps pan-Islamic nationalists, rather than as global revolutionaries. To treat attacks such as September 11, the 2002 and 2005 Bali bombings, the 2004 Madrid bombing, the 2005 London bombing and the 2008 Mumbai bombings as linked events, especially as events with a common inspiration and unified purpose, may therefore be seriously to misunderstand them. Second, although terrorism has affected a broad range of countries, the vast majority of terrorist attacks take place in a relatively small number of the countries that are beset by intense political conflict – such as Israel and the occupied territories, Afghanistan, Iraq, Russia and particularly Chechnya, Pakistan, Kashmir, Algeria and Colombia – leaving much of the world relatively unaffected by terrorism. Third, the image of Islamist terrorism as global terrorism may stem less from its own intrinsic character and more from how others have responded to it. In this view, the establishment of a global 'war on terror' may have done much to create and sustain the idea that there is such a thing as global terrorism.

Catastrophic terrorism

Apart from the idea that it has acquired a global reach, terrorism is often thought to have become a more significant security threat because its impact has greatly increased. September 11 is usually cited in defence of this view. There is no doubt that the terrorist attacks on the USA in September 2001 were events of profound significance. The assaults on the World Trade Centre, the Pentagon and the crash of United Airlines flight 93, believed to be heading for the White House, resulted in the deaths of around 3,000 people, making this the most costly terrorist attack in history. Its impact was all the greater because its targets were, respectively, symbols of global financial power, global military power and global political power. The psycho-emotional impact of September 11 on the USA has only been matched by Pearl Harbor in 1941, both incidents destroying the myth of US invulnerability. However, September 11 does not in itself demonstrate the global significance of terrorism. The scale of death, for example, was relatively small compared with other forms of warfare. For example, about 1.5 million soldiers were killed during the Battle of the Somme in July and August 1916, and 200,000 died as a result of the Hiroshima atomic

Focus on . . .
Suicide terrorism: religious martyrdom or political strategy?

How can the rise in suicide terrorism best be explained? In particular, are suicide bombings best understood as the fulfilment of a religious quest? Although suicide attacks are nothing new (between 2,800 and 3,900 Japanese pilots died in *kamikaze* ('divine wind') attacks during WWII), there has been a marked increase in suicide attacks in recent years. From an average of three attacks a year in the mid-1980s, these rose to ten attacks a year in the 1990s and over 100 attacks a year since 2000. This trend has commonly been explained in terms of the rise of religiously-inspired martyrdom, as exemplified in particular by Islamist groups such as al-Qaeda and Hezbollah. In this view, the heightened fervour and absolute dedication that is required to persuade people to kill themselves in the process of carrying out political violence is most likely to arise in a context of fundamentalist religious belief, especially when this is associated with faith in an afterlife. In this respect, particular attention has been given to the impact on Islamist terrorism of the prospect of entering an Islamic paradise in which (according to the Hadith, not the Koran) 70 virgin maidens await each young man who has sacrificed himself for his religion.

However, based on an analysis of all key incidents of suicide terrorism from 1980 to 2003, Pape (2005) concluded there is little evidence of a link between terrorism and Islamic fundamentalism or, for that matter, religion of any kind. Most suicide terrorism has taken place in a context of nationalist or separatist struggles, with the leading exponents of suicide attacks being the Sri Lankan Tamil Tigers, a nationalist movement subscribing to a secular ideology. In this light, suicide terrorism may be best explained in terms of strategic considerations. The strategic basis for suicide attacks is that, being difficult to protect against, they are an unusually effective form of terrorism. Thus, although in 2007 suicide attacks accounted for just 3 per cent of terrorist attacks worldwide, they led to 18 per cent of deaths in terrorist incidents. This is backed up by the fact that suicide attacks carry enormous moral force, demonstrating the strength of the convictions that inspire them and highlighting the depth of the injustice they seek to protest against.

attack in August 1945. The significance of September 11 is, rather, that it highlighted the emergence of a particularly intractable security threat, one that has the *potential* to wreak almost untold devastation and death and is profoundly difficult to protect against.

Modern terrorism has sometimes been dubbed 'catastrophic terrorism' (Carter *at al.* 1998) or 'hyper-terrorism' (Sprinzak 2001). Why is this form of terrorism so radical and devastating, as well as so difficult to counter? This, arguably, applies for at least three reasons. First, by its nature, terrorism is particularly difficult, and maybe impossible, to defend against. Terrorism is a clandestine activity, often carried out by small groups or even lone individuals who, unlike regular armies, go to considerable lengths to be indistinguishable from the civilian population. Such difficulties have nevertheless been greatly exaggerated by the advent of new terrorist tactics, notably the growth of suicide terrorism. How can protection be provided against attackers who are willing to sacrifice their own lives in order to kill others? This contributes to the idea that, although it may be possible to reduce the likelihood of terrorist attacks, the threat can never be eradicated.

Second, the potential scope and scale of terrorism has greatly increased as a result of modern technology and particularly the prospect of WMD falling into the hands of terrorists. Since September 11, governments have been trying to plan for the possibility of terrorist groups using chemical or biological weapons, with the prospect of nuclear terrorism no longer being dismissed as a fanciful idea. Allison (2004) argued that, unless a global alliance could be built that effectively locked down all nuclear materials in the world, a nuclear terrorist attack on the USA during the following decade was likely, and, over a longer time scale, inevitable. This reflects both the greater availability of nuclear materials and technology, in large part due to the collapse of the Soviet Union, and the fact that the doctrine of mutually assured destruction (MAD), which helped to prevent nuclear war during the superpower era, does not apply to terrorist networks whose identities and locations may be shrouded in mystery. Third, in line with debates over the rise of new terrorism, it is sometimes argued that modern terrorists not only have easier access to WMD, but also have a greater willingness to use them. This, allegedly, is because they may be less constrained by moral or humanitarian principles than previous generations of terrorists. In the case of Islamist terrorism, this is supposedly explained by the radical politico-religious ideology which inspires it, in which western society and its associated values are viewed as evil and intrinsically corrupt, the implacable enemy of Islam.

However, there are those who argue that the threat of terrorism, even of new or global terrorism, has been greatly overstated. In the first place, there are doubts about the military effectiveness of terrorism. Although particular terrorist attacks may have a devastating impact, by its nature terrorism consists of a series of sporadic attacks on a variety of targets, which is very different from the concerted, sustained and systematic destruction that is wreaked by mass warfare conducted between states. In fact, the number of casualties caused by terrorist attacks is usually small, with only around twenty attacks since 1968 having resulted in more than 100 fatalities. Terrorism, moreover, cannot overthrow a government (although, through assassination, it can remove political leaders), or destroy a society. Indeed, insofar as terrorism works it is not through its military impact, but through how governments and populations react to the fear and anxiety that it generates. Second, where terrorist campaigns have been successful, they have usually been linked to attempts to advance or defend the interests of a national or ethnic group, in which case its goals have enjoyed a significant measure of popular support. This applied to Jewish terrorism before the creation of the state of Israel in 1948 and the terrorism employed by the African National Congress (ANC) against the apartheid regime in South Africa. Where terrorist campaigns enjoy limited popular support they may well be counter-productive, provoking popular hostility and outrage (instead of fear and apprehension amongst the civilian population), as well as military retaliation from the government. This certainly applied to the anarchist terrorism of the late nineteenth century and the 1960s and 1970s, and it may also explain why, although Islamist terrorism has played a significant role as part of insurrectionary wars in Iraq, Afghanistan and elsewhere, it does not, and cannot, pose a serious threat to western societies.

Third, fears about terrorism may be exaggerated because they are based on questionable assumptions about a civilizational conflict between Islam and the West, sustained particularly by the rhetoric that surfaced around the 'war on

GLOBAL ACTORS . . .

AL-QAEDA

Type: Transnational terrorist network • **Formed:** 1988 • **Size:** 500–1000 members (estimated)

Al-Qaeda (Arabic for 'The Base') was founded in 1988. It emerged in the context of the struggle in Afghanistan after the Soviet intervention of 1979, but it drew on an ideological heritage that can be traced back to Sayyid Qutb (see p. 209) and the Muslim Brotherhood (see p. 206). Like other groups of anti-Soviet fighters, it was supported during this period by US funds and arms supplies. Its founder, Osama bin Laden was killed in 2011 (see p. 305), although he was better portrayed as a figurehead of a loosely organized transnational network, rather than as an operational leader. Bin Laden's hostility to 'Un-Islamic' Muslim rulers and to western, and particularly US, influence in the Muslim world had deepened as a result of the 1991 Gulf War and the siting of US troops in Saudi Arabia, and the rejection, by Saudi Arabia, of his offer of support. The leadership of al-Qaeda was located in the Sudan from 1992 to 1996, before taking refuge in Taliban-controlled Afghanistan. After the overthrow of the Taliban regime in 2001, it operated from the tribal lands on the Pakistan–Afghan border. In addition to September 11, al-Qaeda has been associated with the 1993 attack on the World Trade Centre, the 1996 Khobar Towers bombing (Saudi Arabia), the 1998 bombings of the US embassies in Tanzania and Kenya, the 2000 attack on the *USS Cole*, the 2004 Madrid train bombings and the 2005 London bombings.

Significance: Al-Qaeda is often credited with having redefined the nature of terrorism and, in the process, contributed to a reconfiguration of global power. This has occurred, it has been argued, in at least three respects. In the first place, al-Qaeda has adapted itself to the new conditions of global interconnectedness, operating, for example, as a loose network rather than a command-and-control organization, and making extensive use of modern information and communication technology (mobile phones, satellite television, the Internet and so on). Second, al-Qaeda has developed a series of new and particularly devastating terrorist techniques. These include suicide attacks and the simultaneous bombing of a range of targets. In addition, flexibility in the use of 'weapons' (including passenger airliners) has significantly expanded the level of devastation that terrorism can wreak. Third, al-Qaeda is the chief inspiration behind the sprawling network of bodies that, taken together, constitutes the military wing of the modern Islamist movement, with an influence that spreads across the Middle East and into North and East Africa, Asia, North America, Europe and beyond. As such, al-Qaeda contributes to what has been viewed as a global civilizational struggle between the West and Islam, typified by the September 11 and other attacks and by the USA's response in launching the 'war on terror'.

The continuing significance of al-Qaeda is a matter of debate, however. Some have argued that al-Qaeda's role in generating a civilizational struggle between Islam and the West has been greatly overstated. For example, the USA's motives in launching the 'war on terror' were mixed and complex, some suggesting that al-Qaeda terrorism was used as a pretext for consolidating the USA's geopolitical hold over the oil-rich Middle East. Certainly the idea that al-Qaeda has mobilized the Islamic world in the cause of global *jihad* is open to question, particularly as revulsion against terrorist tactics has encouraged political Islam to become more moderate. Moreover, in a quest for high-profile exposure, al-Qaeda may have made a serious strategic mistake in launching the September 11 attacks, in that the full military and political weight of the USA was deployed in the attempt to destroy the organization. The 'war on terror' not only deprived al-Qaeda of a secure base and training grounds in Afghanistan, but it also resulted in the deaths of many al-Qaeda leaders and fighters, seriously undermining its operational effectiveness. Finally, critical theorists have emphasized the extent to which the 'catastrophic terrorism' that al-Qaeda represents has been constructed less on the basis of the nature and scope of the threat that it represents and more on the basis of how the USA chose to respond to September 11 by demonizing al-Qaeda and transforming it into a global brand.

terror'. Not only are there doubts about the broad idea of an emerging 'clash of civilizations' (see p. 196), but the civilizational interpretation of Islamist terrorism may also not stand up to examination. Rather than being the vanguard of a resurgent Muslim world, Islamism, particularly in its *jihadist* form, is a perverted offshoot of orthodox Islam, which is not firmly rooted in traditional Islamic values and culture. There is little evidence, moreover, that Muslim populations generally are hostile towards 'western' values such as human rights, the rule of law and democracy, albeit not in the form of militarily-imposed 'democracy promotion' (see p. 212). Critical theorists, indeed, have gone further and argued that the 'war on terror', and the exaggerated fears of terrorism on which it is based, serve both to legitimize US attempts to maintain its global hegemony (in particular, helping to justify the USA's presence in the oil-rich Middle East) and to promote a wider 'politics of fear' (Altheide 2006). This latter idea suggests that the 'war on terror' was essentially an ideological construct, which has been created by the USA and other western states in order to generate internal cohesion and a sense of purpose in societies that are no longer afraid of the 'communist threat'. In this view, ruling elites, in democratic as well as authoritarian societies, consolidate their position by creating myths about a threatening or hostile 'other'. In modern circumstances this role may be filled by terrorism, especially when fears about terrorism can be bolstered by linking terrorism to WMD and the spectre of nuclear terrorism.

COUNTERING TERRORISM

Terrorism poses particularly difficult challenges to established societies. Unlike other military threats, terrorists often do not have a conventional base or location and they may be particularly difficult to distinguish from the civilian population at large. Furthermore, it is notoriously difficult to protect against, still less to prevent, kidnappings, armed attacks (which may lead to hostage-taking), vehicle bombs and suicide attacks.

How can terrorism best be countered? What are the possible benefits and the likely costs of different approaches to counter-terrorism? The main counter-terrorism strategies include the following:

● Strengthening state security
● Military repression
● Political deals.

Strengthening state security

In states such as Israel, Sri Lanka, Spain and the UK, which have experienced long campaigns of nationalist-based terrorism, tighter state security, often based on emergency legislation, has long been enforced. Nevertheless, September 11 and subsequent terrorist attacks in places such as Bali, Madrid and London have encouraged a much broader range of countries to revise, and strengthen, their arrangements for state security. In many ways, this reflects an attempt to deprive terrorists of the advantages they gain from operating in a context of democracy and globalization. Liberal-democratic societies may be uniquely vulnerable to the threat of terrorism because they protect individual rights and freedoms, and

- The notion of a 'war on terror' created confusion about the nature of the enemy ('terror' is an abstract noun, and terrorism is a military tactic, not a group, an ideology or an institution). This introduced an arbitrary element into the choice of the enemy, while, at the same time, associating them with evil, immorality and wanton violence by representing them as 'terror'.

- The 'war on terror' portrayed terrorism as a single phenomenon – 'terror'. As such, the slogan blurred the differences between different types of terrorism and ignored the range of political, ideological or other goals that terrorists may fight for.

Deconstructing . . .

'WAR ON TERROR'

- By describing the campaign against terror as a 'war', it implied that terrorism should be, and perhaps can only be, addressed through military means. Such an approach focused essentially on the manifestations of terrorism and, arguably, ignored its causes. As such, it predetermined the choice of counter-terrorism strategies.

- The idea of a 'war on terror' may have been counter-productive. From the viewpoint of the general public, it risked exaggerating the threat of terrorism, maybe promoting the very fear and anxiety that terrorists set out to produce. From the viewpoint of decision-makers, it encouraged overreaction and may, thereby, have risked perpetuating terrorism by strengthening disaffection amongst marginalized groups or peoples.

contain checks on government power, while the 'borderless world' that globalization creates affords non-state actors such as terrorist groups considerable scope to organize and exert influence. In the main, state security has been strengthened by extending the legal powers of government. For example, states have reasserted control over global financial flows; immigration arrangements have been made more rigorous, especially during high-alert periods; the surveillance and control of domestic populations, but particularly of members of 'extremist' groups or terrorist sympathizers, has been significantly tightened; and, in many cases, the power to detain terrorist suspects has been strengthened. For instance, UK anti-terrorist measures allowed suspected terrorists to be held for up to 28 days without charge (although this returned to 14 days when the powers lapsed in 2011), while in the USA the Patriot Act (2001) permits the indefinite detention of immigrants.

In other cases, however, state security measures have had an extra-legal or, at best, quasi-legal character. In the post-9/11 period, the Bush administration in the USA took this approach furthest, notably by establishing the Guantánamo Bay detention camp in Cuba, and by practices such as '**extraordinary rendition**'. Terrorist suspects held at Guantánamo Bay were subject to the authority of military courts, which were, until 2008, beyond the jurisdiction of the US Supreme Court, and by refusing to classify them as 'enemy combatants' the Bush administration denied the detainees the protections afforded by the Geneva Conventions. Moreover, interrogation methods were used at Guantánamo Bay, such as 'waterboarding' (a form of suffocation in which water is poured over the face of an immobilized person), which have widely been seen as forms of **torture**.

However, state security responses to terrorism have at least two key drawbacks. First, they endanger the very liberal-democratic freedoms that counter-terrorism is, ultimately, meant to safeguard. This results in difficult trade-offs between liberty and security which have provoked impassioned debate in many democratic countries. Second, such measures may be counter-productive insofar as they appear to target particular groups (often young, male Muslims), who thereby become more disaffected and therefore more likely to support, or possibly engage in, terrorist activity. English (2009) thus argued that the most serious danger posed by terrorists is their capacity to provoke ill-judged and sometimes extravagant state responses that, by creating an atmosphere of panic, serve the interests of terrorists themselves. It is notable that, under Obama, distinctive changes have taken place to at least the tone of US counter-terrorism policy, reflecting particularly the need to redress the imbalance between liberty and security. This was symbolized by the commitment in January 2009 to close the Guantánamo Bay detention camp within one year (even though the commitment was not carried out) and to cease using the harsh interrogation techniques that had been employed during the Bush era.

Military repression

Force-based or repressive counter-terrorism has, in recent years, been particularly associated with the 'war on terror'. Military responses to terrorism have been based on two complementary strategies. In the first, attempts have been made to deny terrorists the support or 'sponsorship' of regimes that had formerly given them succour. This was done most clearly through the overthrow of the Taliban regime in Afghanistan in 2001, although alleged links to terrorism was also one of the pretexts for the toppling of Saddam Hussein in 2003. The second approach is to launch direct attacks on terrorist training camps and terrorist leaders. Thus, US air strikes were launched against terrorist targets in Afghanistan and Sudan in 1998, in retaliation for the bombing of US embassies in Kenya and Tanzania; the al-Qaeda leadership were attacked in Afghanistan in late 2001 in their Tora Bora cave complex; Israel carried out military strikes against Hezbollah targets in southern Lebanon in 2006; and Osama bin Laden was killed in a special forces operation in Abbottabad, Pakistan in 2011 (see p. 305). Amongst others, the most concerted attempts to destroy terrorist groups through military might occurred in Chechnya and Sri Lanka. In response to continued separatist agitation and an escalating series of terrorist attacks, Russia launched the Second Chechen War, 1999–2000, which left between 25,000 and 50,000 people dead and devastated the Chechen capital, Grozny. During 2008–

● **Extraordinary rendition**: The extra-legal transport of foreign terrorist suspects to third countries for interrogation.

● **Torture**: The infliction of intense physical or mental pain or suffering as a means of punishment, or in order to gain information or a confession.

The killing of Osama bin Laden

Events: On 2 May 2011, Osama bin Laden was killed in a US special forces operation in Abbottabad in north-western Pakistan. This brought to an end a more than fifteen-year campaign by the USA to capture or kill bin Laden, dating back to the establishment in 1996 of a CIA unit to plan operations against the Saudi Islamist leader. These efforts were radically intensified after 9/11, with President George W. Bush declaring that bin Laden was 'wanted dead or alive'. Bin Laden survived the massive bombing campaign against al-Qaeda bases in Afghanistan in October 2001, retreating to the Tora Bora mountains in eastern Afghanistan, and then over the border into Pakistan. Bin Laden is believed to have lived mainly in the north-western region of Waziristan, moving frequently and accompanied by a small group of bodyguards. He had possibly lived in the large, custom-built walled compound in Abbottabad from as early as 2005.

Significance: The USA justified the attack squarely on the basis of the right to national self-defence, a position that assumed that, almost ten years after 9/11, bin Laden continued to pose a threat to the USA (either through his leadership of al-Qaeda or his symbolic capacity to inspire *jihadhi* militancy). The notion that bin Laden was a 'lawful military target' was based both on Article 51 of the UN Charter, which establishes the 'inherent right of individual or collective self-defence', and Resolutions 1368 and 1373, adopted by the UN Security Council in the aftermath of 9/11. These recognized the attack as a threat to international peace and security. Critics have, nevertheless, portrayed the death of bin Laden as an extra-judicial killing, part of a global assassination policy that the USA was using to remove those perceived to be causing it trouble. The fact that bin Laden was shot dead (rather than captured) and his body allegedly thrown into the sea contributed to this perception. The raid was, without doubt, a violation of Pakistan's national sovereignty (Pakistan had not been given prior warning of the attack), and, arguably, an opportunity was missed to arrest bin Laden and hand him over to an international court.

How did the killing of bin Laden affect al-Qaeda and the wider campaign against Islamist militancy? The belief that bin Laden's death would deal a major blow to al-Qaeda is based on the assumption that, aside from his continuing operational significance, bin Laden was a uniquely charismatic leader and the chief symbol of Islamist resistance to the USA and the West in general. Such an analysis may, however, misunderstand the nature of the al-Qaeda movement. If al-Qaeda consists, as many argue, of an essentially leaderless network, then bin Laden's importance was always largely symbolic, and there is no reason why his mythic influence should end with his death. It has therefore been argued that the killing was primarily of significance in helping to restore a sense of national honour in the USA and boosting President Obama's chances of winning re-election. However, bin Laden's death also raised questions about the value of 'decapitation' (the removal by capture or killing of senior figures) as a counter-terrorism strategy. The aim of 'decapitation' is both to undermine the cohesion and operational effectiveness of an organization and to deliver a moral blow to its members and supporters. The fact that it can be achieved at a relatively low human and economic cost (relying, as it does, on intelligence operations and the use of drones or special forces, rather than large-scale armies) also adds to its appeal. On the other hand, in line with other force-based counter-terrorism strategies, the record of 'decapitations' is that they are generally ineffective at best and counterproductive at worst. This is because they may either precipitate a violent backlash or generate deep local resentment, especially when they also result in civilian casualties.

09, the Sri Lankan army carried out a major offensive against the Tamil Tigers, which effectively destroyed the separatist movement as a fighting force and brought an end to the 26-year armed conflict in Sri Lanka. Estimates of the number of civilian deaths that occurred in this final phase of the conflict range from 7,000 to 20,000.

Nevertheless, it is difficult to see how terrorism can, in usual cases, be defeated by military approaches alone. For one thing, to wage war on terrorist organizations and groups is, arguably, to attack the *manifestation* of the problem rather than its underlying cause. The record of force-based counter-terrorism has thus been very poor. In cases such as Israel, Northern Ireland, Algeria and Chechnya, the application of massive counter-terrorist violence by the state only resulted in ever greater levels of terrorist violence. Military repression is especially likely to be counter-productive when the conduct of military action against terrorism is seen to be insensitive to human rights and the interests of civilian populations. The exposure, in 2004, of widespread torture and prisoner abuse at the Abu Ghraib prison in Iraq therefore seriously damaged the image of the USA as a defender of the 'free world' and helped to strengthen anti-Americanism across the Muslim world. Moreover, as terrorism in cases such as Iraq and Afghanistan has been used as part of wider insurgency wars, it is difficult to see how anti-terrorist warfare can be 'winnable' in the conventional sense. Many military commanders therefore argue that terrorism and insurgencies can only ever be reduced to manageable levels, rather than eradicated altogether.

Political deals

Finally, political solutions can be found to terrorist problems. In a sense, most terrorist campaigns have political endings, in that their general ineffectiveness means that, over time, leading figures in terrorist movements tend to gravitate towards respectability and constitutional politics. Nevertheless, governments have also pursued strategies designed specifically to encourage terrorists to abandon political violence by drawing them into a process of negotiation and diplomacy. For example, a willingness to engage politically with the Provisional IRA provided the basis for an end to Republican terrorism in Northern Ireland, a process that led eventually to the 1998 Belfast Agreement (sometimes called the Good Friday Agreement) through which agreement was reached on the status and future of Northern Ireland. Similarly, negotiations conducted during 1990–3 by the South African government under President de Klerk and the African National Congress prepared the way for the end of apartheid and establishment, in 1994, of South Africa as a multi-racial democracy, with the ANC leader, Nelson Mandela, as its president. Political approaches to counter-terrorism involve a 'hearts and minds' strategy that seeks to address the political causes of terrorism and not just its manifestations. They also attempt to convince terrorists that they have more to gain by working within the political process than by working against it. In the case of Islamist terrorism, a political solution would certainly involve progress being made on the 'Palestinian question'. Indeed, the stuttering progress that has been made with the Arab–Israeli conflict (see Key events: the Arab–Israeli conflict, p. 208) is a consequence of a tendency on both sides to favour military solutions over political ones.

Debating ...
Does the need to counter terrorism justify restricting human rights and basic freedoms?

Terrorism is an unusual security threat in that it appears to exploit the vulnerabilities of liberal-democratic societies. While some claim that this implies that rights and freedoms must be curtailed if the public is to be protected from terrorism, others argue that such an approach is morally indefensible as well as counter-productive.

YES

The weakness of the strong. Liberal-democratic societies are weak in the sense that rights such as freedom of movement and freedom of association, and legal or constitutional checks on government power, can be exploited by terrorist groups that are covert and often operate in small, loosely-organized cells. In other words, openness, toleration and legality can become their own worst enemy, providing advantages for groups that oppose all these things. Effective counter-terrorism must deprive terrorists of these advantages, and this can only mean selective and appropriate restrictions on individual rights and freedoms.

The lesser evil. Curtailing rights and freedoms may be morally justifiable when the 'rightness' or 'wrongness' of an action is judged on the basis of whether it produces the 'greatest good for the greatest number'. Such restrictions may therefore be the 'lesser evil' (Ignatieff 2004) when set against the wider benefits that are derived from protecting society at large. For example, infringing terrorist suspects' rights, even subjecting them to detention without trial, is a lesser moral abuse than violating the most important human freedom, the right to life. Similarly, the greater good may be served if violations on individual and minority rights help to preserve the rights of the majority.

The necessity of 'dirty hands'. The doctrine of 'dirty hands' is based on the belief that public morality is separate from private morality. It may thus be 'right' for political leaders to do 'wrong', if this serves public morality. The classic circumstance in which this applies is when, confronted by a supreme danger, politicians must set aside accepted moral rules in order to ensure the survival of the political community (Walzer 2007). This doctrine may even justify the torture in a 'ticking bomb scenario', when saving the lives of possibly hundreds of people may require that information is extracted from a terrorist suspect, by almost whatever means, about the location of a bomb.

NO

Counter-productive anti-terrorism. In a sense, all terrorism seeks to provoke an over-reaction on the part of government. Terrorism achieves its ends not through violent attacks but through a government's response to violent attacks. By adopting draconian measures, governments are invariably playing into the hands of terrorist groups, which are able to gain support and sympathy, and even increase recruitment, if the groups they claim to support feel stigmatized and resentful. Matters, indeed, get worse if governments are drawn into a cycle of over-reaction, as when repressive measures that fail to eradicate a terrorist threat lead only to the adoption of still more repressive policies.

Freedom as a fundamental value. For supporters of human rights, morality is not a question of trade-offs and calculations about the greater good; it is about the intrinsic rightness or wrongness of certain actions. As human rights are universal, fundamental, absolute and indivisible, actions such as restricting civil liberties or any violation of them is simply wrong, however politically inconvenient this may be. The danger, moreover is greater: once governments start to treat morality in terms of trade-offs, they start to descend a slippery slide towards authoritarianism. Governments become increasingly accustomed to the use of force and de-sensitized to concerns over human rights, and security agencies become more powerful and less accountable.

Moral authority and 'soft' power. Terrorism cannot be combated through robust state security measures alone; in important ways, terrorism is a 'hearts and minds' issue. If a clear ethical line cannot be drawn between terrorism and counter-terrorism, governments lose moral authority, and this undermines their public support at home and abroad. For example, controversial practices associated with the Guantánamo Bay detention camp damaged the USA's 'soft' power and weakened international support for the 'war on terror', particularly, but not only, in Muslim countries. Securing and maintaining the moral high ground, by combating terrorism whilst scrupulously upholding human rights and basic freedoms, therefore makes ethical and political sense.

Nevertheless, the idea of tackling terrorism by making political deals with terrorists, or by acceding to their demands, has also attracted criticism. In the first place, it is sometimes seen as an example of appeasement, a moral retreat in the face of intimidation and violence, even an unwillingness to stand up for one's beliefs. Whereas military approaches to containing terrorism promise to weaken and possibly destroy terrorist groups, political approaches may strengthen or embolden them, by treating the group and the cause it pursues as legitimate. Moreover, political approaches are most likely to be effective in the case of nationalist terrorism, where deals can be done over matters such as power-sharing, political autonomy and even sovereignty. Islamist terrorism, on the other hand, may simply be beyond the reach of political 'solutions'. What, for instance, would constitute a political solution to forms of terrorism that aim to establish theocratic rule in western societies and overthrow liberal-democratic institutions and principles? Finally, the capacity of political deals to provide a comprehensive solution to large-scale political violence may have been undermined by links that have become more pronounced since the end of the Cold War between terrorism and insurgency generally and forms of criminality (Cockayne et al. 2010). The path of peace and negotiation may seem distinctly unattractive to terrorist groups in places such as Afghanistan, the Balkans, the Democratic Republic of the Congo, Guatemala and Somalia, which are able to raise enormous amounts of money from drug-running, targeted violence and other illicit activities.

SUMMARY

- Terrorism, broadly, refers to attempts to further political ends by using violence to create a climate of fear, apprehension and uncertainty. Terrorism is nevertheless a deeply controversial term, not least because it is highly pejorative and tends to be used as a political tool. Mainstream, radical and critical perspectives offer quite different views on the nature of terrorism and the value of the concept.

- Proponents of the idea of 'new' terrorism suggest that since the 1990s a more radical and devastating form of terrorism has emerged whose political character, motivations, strategies and organization differs from 'traditional' terrorism, particularly in the growing importance of religious motivation. But serious doubts have been cast on the value of this distinction.

- It is widely assumed that September 11 marked the emergence of a profoundly more significant form of terrorism, which can strike anywhere, any time. However, although many accept that there are important links between modern terrorism and the processes of globalization, many have questioned whether terrorism has genuinely gone global.

- The impact of terrorism has increased supposedly because of the advent of new terrorist tactics and because of easier access to, and a greater willingness to use, WMD. However, critical theorists argue that the threat of terrorism has been greatly overstated, usually through discourses linked to the 'war on terror' and often to promote the 'politics of fear'.

- Key counter-terrorism strategies include the strengthening of state security, the use of military repression and political deals. State security and military approaches have often been counter-productive and have provoked deep controversy about the proper balance between freedom and security.

- Effective solutions to terrorism have usually involved encouraging terrorists to abandon violence by drawing them into a process of negotiation and diplomacy. Although such an approach has sometimes worked in the case of nationalist terrorism, it has been seen as an example of appeasement and as inappropriate to dealing with Islamist terrorism.

Questions for discussion

- How can terrorism be distinguished from other forms of political violence?
- Is there such a thing as 'state terrorism'?
- Are there any circumstances in which terrorism can be justified?
- Has the growing importance of religious motivation transformed the nature of terrorism?
- Did September 11 mark the emergence of a truly global form of terrorism?
- Is nuclear terrorism an 'invented' fear?
- Why is terrorism so rarely effective, and in what circumstances does it work?
- Are restrictions on liberty merely the lesser evil compared with the threat of terrorism?
- Why are military approaches to dealing with terrorism so often counter-productive?
- Should political deals ever be done with terrorists?

Further reading

Bloom, M., *Dying to Kill: The Allure of Suicide Terror* (2007). A balanced and informative analysis of suicide terrorism and the motivations behind it.

Hoffman, B., *Inside Terrorism* (2006). An excellent general introduction to the nature and development of terrorism, which also considers the challenges facing counter-terrorism.

Jackson, R., M. Smyth, J. Gunning and L. Jarvis, *Terrorism: A Critical Introduction* (2011). An accessible assessment of terrorism and its study which rethinks mainstream assumptions and thinking.

Sageman, M., *Leaderless Jihad: Terror Networks in the Twenty-First Century* (2008). A thought-provoking study of Islamist terrorism, and particularly al-Qaeda, which emphasizes the need to understand the networks that allow modern terrorism to proliferate.

ONLINE RESOURCES AVAILABLE

Links to relevant web resources can be found on the *Global Politics* website

CHAPTER 13

Human Rights and Humanitarian Intervention

'All human beings are born free and equal in dignity and rights.'

UN Declaration of Human Rights, 1948, Article 1

PREVIEW   Moral and ethical questions have always been important in international politics. However, since the end of the Cold War they have attracted intensified interest, as issues of global justice have come to vie with more traditional concerns, such as power, order and security. Moreover, when matters of justice and morality are raised, this is increasingly done through a doctrine of human rights that emphasizes that people everywhere enjoy the same moral status and entitlements. Human rights have come to compete with state sovereignty as the dominant normative language of international affairs and human development. This has created tension between human rights and states' rights, as the former implies that justice should extend *beyond*, as well as *within*, national borders. Difficult questions have nevertheless been raised about human rights. Not the least of these are about the nature of, and justifications for, human rights. In what sense are these rights 'human' rights, and which rights do they cover? Other debates concern the extent to which human rights are protected in practice, and whether they are genuinely universal, applying to all peoples and all societies. How far are human rights applied in practice, and how far should they be applied? Tensions between states' rights and human rights have become particularly acute since the 1990s through the growth of so-called 'humanitarian intervention'. Major states have assumed the right to intervene militarily in the affairs of other states to protect their citizens from abuse and possibly death, often at the hands of their own government. How, and to what extent, is such intervention linked to human rights? Can intervention ever be genuinely 'humanitarian'? And, regardless of its motives, does humanitarian intervention actually work?

KEY ISSUES
- What are human rights, and on what basis can they be claimed?
- How, and how effectively, have international human rights been protected?
- On what grounds has the doctrine of human rights been criticized?
- What explains the growth of humanitarian intervention, and its subsequent decline?
- Under what circumstances is it right to intervene in the affairs of another state?
- Why has humanitarian intervention been criticized?

CONCEPT

Human rights

Human rights are rights to which people are entitled by virtue of being human; they are a modern and secular version of 'natural rights'. Human rights are *universal* (in the sense that they belong to human beings everywhere, regardless of race, religion, gender and other differences), *fundamental* (in that a human being's entitlement to them cannot be removed), *indivisible* (in that civic and political rights, and economic, social and cultural rights are interrelated and co-equal in importance) and *absolute* (in that, as the basic grounds for living a genuinely human life, they cannot be qualified). 'International' human rights are set out in a collection of UN and other treaties and conventions (see p. 318).

HUMAN RIGHTS

Defining human rights

The individual in global politics

International politics has traditionally been thought of in terms of collective groups, especially states. Individual needs and interests have therefore generally been subsumed within the larger notion of the 'national interest'. As a result, international politics largely amounted to a struggle for power between and amongst states with little consideration being given to the implications of this for the individuals concerned. People, and therefore morality (in terms of the happiness, suffering and general well-being of individuals), were factored out of the picture. However, this divorce between state policy and the individual, and thus between power and morality, has gradually become more difficult to sustain.

Many cultures and civilizations have developed ideas about the intrinsic worth and dignity of individual human beings. However, these theories were traditionally rooted in religious belief, meaning that the moral worth of the individual was grounded in divine authority, human beings usually being seen as creatures of God. The prototype for the modern idea of human rights was developed in early modern Europe in the form of '**natural rights**'. Advanced by political philosophers such as Hugo Grotius (see p. 341), Thomas Hobbes (see p. 14) and John Locke (1632–1704), such rights were described as 'natural', in that they were thought to be God-given and therefore to be part of the very core of human nature. Natural rights did not exist simply as moral claims but were, rather, considered to reflect the most fundamental inner human drives; they were the basic conditions for leading a truly human existence. By the late eighteenth century, such ideas were expressed in the notion of the 'rights of man' (later extended by feminists to include the rights of women), which was used as a means of constraining government power by defining a sphere of autonomy that belongs to the citizen. The US Declaration of Independence (1776), which declared life, liberty and the pursuit of happiness to be inalienable rights, gave expression to such ideas, as did the French Declaration of the Rights of Man and of the Citizen (1789).

Such thinking gradually acquired an international dimension during the nineteenth and twentieth centuries through attempts to set standards for international conduct, usually based on **humanitarianism**. For example, the growth of humanitarian ethics helped to inspire attempts to abolish the slave trade, a cause endorsed by the Congress of Vienna (1815) and was eventually achieved by the Brussels Convention (1890), with slavery itself being formally outlawed by the Slavery Convention (1926) (even though forms of slavery continue to exist in practices such as bonded labour, forced marriage, child labour and the trafficking of women). The Anti-Slavery Society, formed in 1837, can perhaps be seen as the world's first human rights NGO (see p. 10). Other humanitarian causes that were translated into a form of international standard setting included the regulation of the conduct of war, through the Hague Conventions (1907) and the Geneva Conventions (1926), and attempts to improve working conditions, spearheaded by the International Labour Office, formed in 1901, and its

● **Natural rights**: God-given rights that are fundamental to human beings and are therefore inalienable (they cannot be taken away)

● **Humanitarianism**: A concern about the well-being of humanity as a whole, typically expressed through acts of compassion, charity or philanthropy.

successor, the International Labour Organization, which was established in 1919 as part of the Treaty of Versailles and became, in 1946, the first specialized agency of the United Nations.

Such developments nevertheless remained piecemeal and largely marginal to the general thrust of international politics until the end of WWII. The adoption by the UN General Assembly of the Universal Declaration of Human Rights (1948), later supplemented by the International Covenant on Civil and Political Rights and the International Covenant on Economic, Social and Cultural Rights (both in 1966), established the modern human rights agenda by outlining a comprehensive code for the internal government of its member states, which has arguably acquired the status of customary international law (see p. 339). Reflecting a major change in the general climate of thought, deeply influenced by the horrors of WWII (especially the so-called 'Final Solution', the murder of some six million Jews, Gypsies and Slavs in the extermination camps of Nazi Germany), the Declaration led to a burst of law-making and standard-setting that sought to establish international protection for the full range of human rights. The year 1948 thus brought to an end a period of exactly 300 years since the Treaty of Westphalia (1648), during which state sovereignty (see p. 4) had stood unchallenged as the dominant norm of international politics. However, although the Declaration established the rival norm of human rights, tensions between states' rights and human rights were by no means resolved in 1948, as will be discussed later. In the meantime, it is necessary to examine the nature and implications of human rights. What are human rights, and why should they be respected?

Nature and types of human rights

A right is an entitlement to act or be treated in a particular way. As such, rights entail duties: the claim to have a right imposes obligations on others to act, or, perhaps, to refrain from acting in a particular way. Human rights are essentially moral claims or philosophical assertions, but they have gained, since 1948, a measure of legal substance. Human rights, most basically, are rights to which people are entitled by virtue of being human. They are therefore 'universal' rights, in the sense that they belong to all human beings rather than to members of any particular nation, race, religion, gender, social class or whatever. This **universalism** was clearly expressed in the words of the American Declaration of Independence, written by Thomas Jefferson (1743–1826), which proclaimed: 'We hold these truths to be self-evident, that all men are created equal; that they are endowed by their Creator with certain unalienable rights'. However, there have been very deep divisions about what rights human beings should enjoy. Indeed, thinking about the content of human rights has developed significantly over time, enabling three different types, or 'generations' of human rights to be identified (Vasak 1977) (see Table 13.1). These are:

● **Universalism**: The belief that it is possible to uncover certain values and principles that are applicable to all people and all societies, regardless of historical, cultural and other differences.

● Civil and political rights
● Economic, social and cultural rights
● Solidarity rights.

Civil and political rights were the earliest form of natural or human rights. They were advanced through the English Revolution of the seventeenth century and the French and American Revolutions of the eighteenth century. The core civil and political rights are the rights to life, liberty and property, although they have been expanded to include, for example, freedom from discrimination, freedom from slavery, freedom from torture or other inhuman forms of punishment, freedom from arbitrary arrest and so on. Civil and political rights are often typically seen as **negative rights**, or 'forbearance' rights: they can be enjoyed only if constraints are placed on others. Negative rights therefore define a private sphere within which the individual can enjoy independence from the encroachments of other individuals and, more particularly, from the interference of the state. Negative human rights thus correspond closely to classic **civil liberties**, such as the rights to freedom of speech, freedom of the press, freedom of religion and conscience, freedom of movement, and freedom of association. However, it would be misleading to suggest that all civil and political rights are 'negative' in this respect. The right to non-discrimination, for instance, can only be upheld through legislation and a framework of enforcement on the part of government, while the right to a free and fair trial requires the existence of a police force and a court system. Civil liberties are therefore often distinguished from **civil rights**, the latter involving positive action on the part of government rather than simply forbearance. The dual character of civil and political rights is evident in the complex relationship between human rights and democracy.

The struggle for *economic, social and cultural rights* gained greater prominence during the twentieth century, especially in the post-1945 period. By contrast with traditional 'liberal' rights, these so-called 'second-generation' rights often drew on socialist assumptions about the tendencies of capitalist development towards social injustice and unequal class power. Socio-economic rights – including the right to social security, the right to work, the right to paid holidays, the right to healthcare, the right to education and so on – were designed to counter-balance inequalities of market capitalism, protecting the working classes and colonial peoples from exploitation. These rights are **positive rights**, in that they imply a significant level of state intervention, usually in the form of welfare provision (welfare rights), the regulation of the labour market (workers' rights) and economic management generally.

However, deep controversy has surrounded economic and social rights. Supporters have argued that economic and social rights are, in a sense, the most basic of human rights, as their maintenance constitutes a precondition for the enjoyment of all other rights. In this view, human dignity is more severely threatened by poverty, disease, ignorance and other forms of social disadvantage than it is by the denial of 'liberal' rights. Nevertheless, especially in the USA and other western states, economic and social rights have often been thought of as, at best, second-class human rights, if not as entirely bogus moral claims. Critics have alleged, first, that the maintenance of such rights requires material resources and political capabilities that many states simply do not possess. Economic and social rights can therefore only be viewed as aspirations rather than entitlements. Second, it is unclear who or what is responsible for upholding economic and social rights. If, through a lack of resources or capabilities, a national government cannot deliver economic and social rights, do these obligations then fall on other states (if so, which ones?), international organizations or, somehow, on the

● **Negative rights**: Rights that are enjoyed by virtue of the inactivity of others, particularly government; often seen (somewhat misleadingly) as 'freedoms from'.

● **Civil liberties**: Rights and freedoms that define a 'private' sphere of existence that belongs to the citizen, not the state; freedoms from government.

● **Civil rights**: Rights of participation and access to power, typically voting and political rights and the right to non-discrimination.

● **Positive rights**: Rights that can only be enjoyed through positive intervention on the part of government, often linked to the idea of 'freedom to'.

Focus on . . .
Democracy as a human right?

In their earliest formulation, natural or human rights were profoundly anti-democratic. This is because their purpose was to empower individuals, and this implied limiting the authority of government, regardless of whether government was democratic or authoritarian. Democracy, indeed, threatened to transfer sovereignty from the individual to the people, creating a particular concern that democratic rule would lead to a 'tyranny of the majority', which may threaten minority rights and individual freedoms. 'Liberal democracies' uphold human rights to the extent that they are 'liberal' (that is, they practise limited government), rather than to the extent that they are 'democratic' (that is, they ensure a system of government by the people). This implies that in liberal democracies human rights, sometimes seen as civil liberties, are given priority over democracy.

However, tensions between human rights and democracy have, over time, reduced, even to the point that many have come to view 'democracy promotion' (see p. 212) as a key element in the modern human rights agenda. This has happened for both practical and theoretical reasons. In practical terms, democratization has generally led to greater, if still imperfect, respect for human rights in post-communist or former authoritarian regimes, helping to establish a link between the two. In theoretical terms, the defence of traditional civil liberties has increasingly been seen as providing the preconditions for free and informed political participation. Similarly, there has been a greater stress on civil rights and an equal access to power as a means of upholding all other rights.

peoples of the world? Third, from the perspective of economic liberalism, economic and social rights may be counter-productive, in that higher levels of (albeit well-intentioned) state intervention may simply undermine the vigour and efficiency of capitalist economies.

Since 1945, a further set of rights have emerged in the form of *solidarity rights*, or so-called 'third-generation' rights. These encompass a broad spectrum of rights whose main characteristic is that they are attached to social groups or whole societies, as opposed to separate individuals. They are sometimes, therefore, seen as collective rights or people's rights. Whereas 'first-generation' rights were shaped by liberalism and 'second-generation' rights were shaped by socialism, 'third-generation' rights have been formed by the concerns of the global South. The right to self-determination was thus linked to the post-1945 process of decolonization and the rise of national liberation movements. Other such rights include the right to development, the right to peace, the right to environmental protection and multicultural rights. Solidarity rights have therefore been used to give issues such as development, environmental sustainability and cultural preservation a moral dimension. Nevertheless, critics of 'third-generation' rights have highlighted their inherent vagueness and, more seriously, questioned whether human rights can actually belong to peoples or groups as opposed to individuals. From this perspective, the very idea of human rights is based on a model of individual self-worth, which is in danger of being weakened whenever people are thought of in terms of group membership.

Table 13.1 Three generations of human rights

Generation	Type	Key theme	Rights	Key documents
First generation (eighteenth and nineteenth centuries)	Civic and political rights	Liberty	• Life, liberty and property • Non-discrimination • Freedom from arbitrary arrest • Freedom of thought	• UN Declaration, Articles 3 to 21 • International Covenant on Civil and Political Rights
Second generation (twentieth century)	Economic, social and cultural rights	Equality	• Work • Social security • Healthcare • Education • Paid holidays	• UN Declaration Articles 22 to 27 • International Covenant on Economic, Social and Cultural Rights
Third generation (post-1945)	Solidarity rights	Fraternity	• Self-determination • Peace • Development • Environmental protection	• Stockholm Convention on the Human Environment, 1972 • Rio 'Earth Summit', 1992

Implications of human rights for global politics

Human rights, by their nature, have profound implications for global politics. Why is this? The first answer to this question is that, being universal and fundamental, human rights invest governments with powerful obligations, affecting their foreign as well as domestic policies. The protection and realization of human rights is thus a key role of government, and perhaps, according to liberals, its core purpose. Interactions between states should therefore have, at least, a human rights dimension. This, in theory at least, imposes major constraints on the behaviour of national governments, both in terms of how they treat their domestic population and in their dealings with other peoples and countries. This affects matters ranging from the recourse to, and conduct of, war (where a concern for human rights has generally been seen to be compatible with the requirements of a 'just war' (see p. 264)), to foreign aid and trade policies. More radically and controversially, these obligations may extend to taking action, perhaps military action, to prevent or discourage other countries from violating human rights within their own borders, what has come to be called 'humanitarian intervention' (see p. 326), discussed later in this chapter.

The second way in which human rights have implications for global politics is that they imply that the boundaries of moral concern extend beyond national borders; indeed, in principle, they disregard national borders. Human rights are nothing less than a demand *of* all humanity *on* all of humanity (Luban 1985). Growing acceptance of the doctrine of human rights therefore goes hand in hand with the growth of cosmopolitan sensibilities. For Pogge (2008), human rights fulfil each of the three elements of cosmopolitanism (see p. 21): individualism (an ultimate concern with human beings or persons, not groups), universality (a recognition of the equal moral worth of all individuals) and generality (the belief that persons are objects of concern for everyone, regardless of nationality and so on). The cosmopolitan implications of human rights are evident not only in attempts to use international law, albeit usually 'soft' law, to set standards for the behaviour of states, but also in attempts to strengthen regional and global governance (see p. 462) and thereby constrain, or perhaps redefine the nature of, state sovereignty. However, despite the strengthening of human rights law and increased interest in cosmopolitan thinking in general and human rights thinking in particular, the theoretical implications of human rights are counter-balanced by powerful practical and sometimes moral considerations. This makes the protection of human rights a complex and often difficult process.

Protecting human rights

The human rights regime

Since 1948, an elaborate international regime (see p. 71) has developed to promote and protect human rights globally. At the heart of this regime continues to stand the UN Universal Declaration of Human Rights. Although the 1945 UN Charter urged the promotion of 'universal respect for, and observation of, human rights and fundamental freedoms for all', it failed to specify the human rights that states had to guarantee and respect. This defect was rectified by the UN Declaration. Although the UN Declaration is not a legally binding treaty, it is commonly seen as a form of customary international law that is used as a tool to apply diplomatic and moral pressure to governments that violate any of its articles. By establishing that states could no longer violate human rights without the risk that their actions would come onto the agenda of the principal organs of the UN, the Declaration challenged states' exclusive jurisdiction over their own citizens and weakened the principle of non-interference in domestic affairs. The incorporation of the Declaration into a legally-binding codification of human rights – in effect, human rights law – was achieved through the adoption in 1966 of the international covenants on Civil and Political Rights and Economic, Social and Cultural Rights. Collectively, the 1948 Declaration and the two covenants are commonly referred to as the 'International Bill of Human Rights'.

Until the mid-1960s, the UN concentrated almost exclusively on the generation of human rights norms and standards. Subsequently, it placed greater emphasis on their implementation. A major step in this direction was taken by the establishment of the Office of the UN High Commissioner for Human Rights, which had been one of the key proposals of the 1993 World Conference on Human Rights in Vienna. The role of the High Commissioner is to promote worldwide respect for the human rights enshrined in international laws by supporting the bodies created by human rights treaties. However, the Office of the High Commissioner has proved to be more effective in highlighting human rights violations than it has been in enforcing human rights law. As its main sanction remains the publication and denunciation of violations by individual states – that is, naming and shaming – the Office relies very largely on persuasion and observation to improve governments' human rights policies. The UN's 47-member Human Rights Council, which replaced the much criticized UN Human Rights Commission in 2006, also addresses situations of human rights violations. However, it has no authority other than to make recommendations to the General Assembly which, in turn, can only advise the Security Council. It has

HUMAN RIGHTS

Realist view

Realists have tended to view a concern with human rights as, at best, a 'soft' issue in international affairs, by contrast with 'hard', or 'core', concerns such as the pursuit of security and prosperity. Other realists go further and believe that human rights thinking in relation to international and global issues is entirely wrong-headed. This is because realists hold that it is impossible, and undesirable, to view international politics in moral terms. Morality and the national interest are two distinct things, and states fail adequately to serve their own citizens (and often those of other states) when they allow ethical considerations – particularly ones as inherently vague and confused as human rights – to affect their behaviour. Realist objections to the culture of human rights have at least three bases. In the first place, they take issue with the essentially optimistic model of human nature that underpins human rights, which emphasizes dignity, respect and rationality. Second, realists are primarily concerned about collective behaviour, and especially the capacity of the state to ensure order and stability for their citizens. The national interest should therefore take precedence over any individually-based conception of morality. Third, being based on positivism, realism is keen to uphold its scientific credentials. This implies a concern with what *is*, rather than with what *should be*.

Liberal view

The modern doctrine of human rights is very largely a product of liberal political philosophy. Indeed, so entangled with liberal assumptions are they that some doubt whether human rights can ever properly be described as 'above' ideological differences, bearing the cultural imprint of western liberalism. At a philosophical level, the image of humans as 'rights bearers' derives from liberal individualism. On a political level, liberals have long used the notion of natural or human rights to establish the basis of legitimacy. Social contract theorists thus argued that the central purpose of government is to protect a set of inalienable rights, variously described as 'life, liberty and property' (Locke), or as 'life, liberty and the pursuit of happiness' (Jefferson). If governments become tyrannical, by abusing or failing to protect such rights, they break an implicit contract between the people and government, entitling citizens to rebel. The English, American and French revolutions were all justified using such ideas. During the twentieth century, liberals increasingly used such thinking to outline the basis for international legitimacy, arguing that states should be bound, preferably legally, to uphold human rights in their dealings with their domestic population as well as with other states. The 1948 UN Declaration therefore has, for liberals, a near-religious significance. Nevertheless, liberals tend to regard only civil and political rights as fundamental rights, and sometimes view economic rights and any conception of group rights with grave suspicion.

Critical views

Critical approaches to human rights have either tended to revise or recast the traditional, liberal view of human rights, or they have been openly hostile to the idea itself. The global justice movement has used economic and social rights as the basis of calls for a radical redistribution of power and resources, both within countries and between them (Shue 1996; Pogge 2008). Human rights have thus been turned into a doctrine of global social justice, grounded in moral cosmopolitanism. Feminists, for their part, have demonstrated a growing interest in the cause of human rights. In particular, they have sought to transform the concept and practice of human rights to take better account of women's lives, highlighting the issues of 'women's human rights' (Friedman 1995). This marks a recognition by feminist activists of the power of the international human rights framework, and especially its capacity to place women's issues on mainstream agendas. Human rights have thus been redefined to include the degradation and violation of women. At the same time, however, feminists have taken a critical view of rights that men have designed to protect their entitlement to private commerce, free speech and cultural integrity, which have been used to legitimize practices such as child marriages, the trafficking of women and child pornography (see Cultural rights or women's rights? p. 203). The postcolonial critique of human rights is examined in the main body of the text; see pp. 323–5.

KEY EVENTS . . .

Major international human rights documents

1948	Universal Declaration of Human Rights
1949	Geneva Conventions on the Treatment of Prisoners of War and Protection of Civilian Persons in Time of War
1950	European Convention on Human Rights (Convention for the Protection of Human Rights and Fundamental Freedoms)
1951	Genocide Convention (Convention on the Prevention and Punishment of the Crime of Genocide)
1954	Convention Relating to the Status of Refugees
1966	International Covenant on Civil and Political Rights (came into force in 1976)
1966	International Covenant on Economic, Social and Cultural Rights (came into force in 1976)
1969	Convention on the Elimination of All Forms of Racial Discrimination
1975	Declaration on Torture
1981	Convention on the Elimination of All Forms of Discrimination Against Women
1984	Convention against Torture and Other Cruel, Inhuman and Degrading Treatment or Punishment
1990	Convention on the Rights of the Child
1993	Vienna Convention on Human Rights (Vienna Convention on the Law of Treaties)
2000	Charter of Fundamental Rights of the European Union

also, like its predecessor, been criticized for being biased and inconsistent in the exposure of human rights abuses. Not only does it include states that have themselves a dubious human rights record, but member states also tend to protect each other (and developing states generally) from criticism and they have, allegedly, been over-willing to highlight violations carried out by Israel.

One of the main features of the human rights regime is the prominent role played within it by a wide range of NGOs. For example, over 1,500 NGOs participated in the World Conference on Human Rights in Vienna, while the number of registered international NGOs reached 37,000 by 2000, most of them claiming to have some kind of human rights or humanitarian purpose. In the case of groups such as the International Committee of the Red Cross, *Médecins Sans Frontières* and Oxfam, operational NGOs work directly in the field to relieve suffering but also campaign on behalf of those they treat to promote the observance of human rights treaties and humanitarian law. The most prominent advocacy NGOs are Human Rights Watch (initially named Helsinki Watch, and set up to respond to the activities of East European dissidents' groups) and Amnesty International (see p. 320). They exert pressure by gaining media coverage, based, in part, on the high moral purpose that people customarily attach to their activities. In this way, NGOs have made a substantial contribution to the growth worldwide of a human rights culture, influencing not only governments but also transnational corporations (see p. 94), over matters such as pay and working conditions in overseas factories. The impact of NGOs within the human rights regime nevertheless goes far, particularly through behind-the-scenes lobbying of government delegations and experts, and the drafting of resolutions. A campaign by Amnesty International and the International Commission of Jurists during 1972–3 thus initiated the process that led to the 1975 Declaration on Torture. NGOs played a particularly prominent role in drafting the 1990 Convention on the Rights of the Child, and were highly influential in the establishment of the Land Mine Treaty of 1997. Nevertheless, NGOs also suffer from limitations. These include that human rights NGOs cannot *force* governments to change their ways, and that their impact within the UN is weakest in relation to the Security Council, the only body with the power to enforce UN decisions. Finally, NGOs have sometimes been criticized for adopting a 'bandwagon' approach, joining in on popular, or media-led, issues in the hope of enhancing their status or attracting funding.

The protection of human rights is generally seen to be most advanced in Europe. This largely reflects the widespread acceptance, and status, of the European Convention on Human Rights (ECHR) (1950), which was developed under the auspices of the Council of Europe and is based on the UN Declaration. All 47 member states of the Council of Europe have signed the Convention. The ECHR is enforced by the European Court of Human Rights in Strasbourg, France. Complaints can be made to the Strasbourg court by signatory states or, much more commonly, by individual citizens. About 45,000 applications are submitted annually to the European Court of Human Rights. This often creates a substantial backlog, meaning that cases commonly take three to five years before they are considered, added to the fact that they are also highly costly. Nevertheless, the almost total compliance with the Court's verdicts attests to the effectiveness of this mechanism for the protection of human rights. The rate of compliance within the time allowed for the Court is about 90 per cent. This makes the ECHR the nearest thing to human rights 'hard' law.

Human rights in a world of states

The key dilemma of human rights protection is that states are the only actors powerful enough to advance human rights, while also being the greatest human rights abusers. This reflects the inherent tension between human rights and foreign policy (see p. 134) to which Vincent (1986) drew attention (although he may well have included domestic policy as well). Nevertheless, the image of unavoidable antagonism between human rights and states' rights is misleading. In the first place, the trend for states to establish civil liberties and human rights in domestic law long pre-dates the advent of the international human rights regime. Second, international human rights standards have not been foisted on

GLOBAL ACTORS . . .

AMNESTY INTERNATIONAL

Type: NGO • **Established:** 1961 • **Headquarters:** London • **Staff:** About 500
Membership: 3 million

Amnesty International (commonly called Amnesty or AI) is an international NGO that draws attention to human rights abuses and campaigns for compliance with international standards, placing a special emphasis on the rights of political prisoners (the 'forgotten prisoners' or 'prisoners of conscience', in the words of Amnesty's founder and general secretary, 1961–6, Peter Benenson). From being a small group of writers, academics, lawyers and sympathetic journalists, AI has developed into a global organization with over 50 sections worldwide and a presence in about 100 more countries. An International Council represents Amnesty's various sections, international networks and affiliated groups. It elects the International Executive Committee, which lays out the broad strategy of the organization. The International Secretariat, headed by a General Secretary, is responsible for the conduct and day-to-day affairs of the organization.

Significance: Amnesty primarily targets governments, seeking to free political and religious prisoners, ensure fair trials for those arrested, eliminate torture, the death penalty and other harsh punishments, and bring those who abuse human rights to justice. Its main weapons are publicity, education and political pressure. These are typically exerted by highlighting individual cases, in which Amnesty staff interview

victims, encourage their 'adoption' by Amnesty members and supporters who engage in a letter-writing campaign, and publish detailed reports. Such activities are supported by wider campaigns, current ones including those on terrorism and security, human rights in China, refugees and asylum, arms control, stopping violence against women, poverty and human rights, and stopping Internet repression. Since the 1970s, Amnesty has been increasingly involved in proposing and drafting human rights legislation, such as the UN's 1975 Declaration on Torture.

Amnesty is widely considered to be the single dominant force in the field of human rights advocacy, being more influential than most of the other groups put together (Alston 1990). In 1974, Sean MacBride, chair of the International Executive Committee, was awarded a Nobel Peace Prize, with Amnesty itself being awarded a Nobel Peace Prize in 1977 for 'having contributed to securing the ground for freedom, for justice, and thereby also for peace in the world'. The organization was awarded the UN Prize in the Field of Human Rights in 1978. Amnesty's strengths include its global public profile as the organization with the longest history and the broadest name recognition in the field of human rights. Its reputation is bolstered by an emphasis on painstaking investigations and impartial report writing. The self-

imposed limited mandate of Amnesty also has advantages. By focusing mainly on political prisoners, the organization has been able to build up a remarkable consensus about the justice of its cause as well as providing assistance to many victims. Amnesty therefore has a clear sense of purpose and, through success in individual cases, can bring a not infrequent sense of achievement to its members.

Amnesty has nevertheless been criticized on two main grounds. First, its self-acknowledged tendency to focus disproportionately on human rights abuses in relatively more democratic and open countries means that it has sometimes been condemned for giving too little attention to some of the world's worst human rights violations. Amnesty's justification for this bias is both that it is inclined to focus public pressure where it is most likely to make a difference and that it is concerned to build up credibility, and therefore influence, in the global South by ensuring that abuses in the North clearly receive attention. Second, Amnesty has been accused of ideological bias, sometimes linked to wider criticisms of the doctrine of human rights, by China, the Democratic Republic of the Congo, Russia, South Korea, the USA (over Amnesty's campaigns against the death penalty and the Guantánamo Bay prison camp) and the Catholic Church (over its stance on abortion).

reluctant states – by, for instance, pressure from NGOs, citizens' campaigns or international bodies – rather, they have been the creation of states themselves, or, more precisely, of particular states. The USA and other western states took a leading role in the establishment of the post-1945 human rights regime, supported from the 1990s onwards by many post-communist states and a growing number of developing world states. The main reason why human rights protection is more effective in Europe than elsewhere is simply because of the high degree of consensus among European states about the importance of human rights.

Why, then, have states accepted, and sometimes championed, the cause of human rights? Virtually all states, for example, have signed the UN Declaration, with a large majority of them also having signed the two optional international covenants. From a liberal perspective, support for international human rights is merely an external expression of values and commitments that are basic to liberal-democratic states. In this view, foreign affairs can, and should, have a moral purpose; the pursuit of national interests should operate in tandem with the global promotion of freedom and democracy. A further reason for states to sign human rights conventions and at least support the rhetoric of human rights is that, since 1948, this has been seen as one of the preconditions for membership of the international community, bringing diplomatic and possibly trade and security benefits. Support for human rights is therefore one of the common norms that has transformed the international system into an international society (see p. 9). This, nevertheless, allows for, at times, a significant gulf between the international standards that a state supposedly supports and how it actually behaves towards its own citizens and towards other states. In other circumstances, states may make cynical use of the human rights agenda. Realists, for instance, argue that, behind the cloak of humanitarianism and moral purpose, human rights are often entangled with considerations about the national interest (see p. 135). This is reflected in the selective application of human rights, in which human rights failings on the part of one's enemies receive prominent attention but are conveniently ignored in the case of one's friends. The USA was therefore criticized in the 1970s for condemning human rights violations in Soviet bloc countries, while at the same time maintaining close diplomatic, economic and political ties with repressive regimes in Latin America and elsewhere. For radical theorists, such as Chomsky (see p. 235), the USA has used human rights as a moral cloak for its hegemonic ambitions.

If the success of international human rights is judged in terms of whether they have served to improve the behaviour of states and other bodies and, in particular, helped to prevent acts of barbarism and systematic repression, the record is often unimpressive. When they conflict, as they often do, state sovereignty usually trumps human rights. This is particularly true in the case of powerful states, which may either simply be immune to human rights criticism, whether expressed internally or externally, or their transgressions are not forcefully exposed by other governments, for fear of damaging diplomatic relations and economic interests. There is little evidence that the Soviet Union was affected by condemnation of its human rights record, and a fear of criticism on such grounds certainly did not prevent the Warsaw Pact invasion of Hungary in 1956, the Soviet invasions of Czechoslovakia in 1968 and Afghanistan in 1979, or

Russia's brutal suppression of the Chechen uprising in the 1990s. On the other hand, human rights activism both inside and outside the Soviet bloc may have contributed more subtly to the eventual collapse of the East European communist regimes. It did this by fostering a growing appetite for political freedom, thereby helping to undermine the legitimacy of these regimes, and contributing to the wave of popular protest that spread across eastern Europe in 1989. It is also notable that Mikhail Gorbachev, the General Secretary of the Soviet Communist Party, 1985–91, used human rights rhetoric to justify his economic and political reforms as well as the realignment of the Soviet Union's relations with the rest of the world, arguing that human rights are principles that transcended the divide between capitalism and communism.

Since the Tiananmen Square protests of 1989, China has been a frequent target of human rights criticism, from the USA and from groups such as Amnesty International and Human Rights Watch. Human rights controversies in China have focused on its suppression of political dissent, its widespread use of capital punishment, its treatment of religious minorities such as supporters of Falun Gong, political repression in the predominantly Muslim provinces of north-western China, such as Xinjiang, and, most particularly, its occupation of Tibet and the systematic subjugation of Tibetan culture, religion and national identity. It is notable that China's emergence as an economic superpower has not been matched by an appetite for political reform. If anything, China has become more uncompromising on human rights issues, both as an expression of growing national assertiveness and in order to contain the pressures that have been unleashed by economic reform. Condemnation by other governments has also become increasingly muted as China's economic resurgence has become more evident.

As far as the USA is concerned, its commitment to human rights and humanitarian law was called seriously into question by its conduct of the 'war on terror' (see Does the need to counter terrorism justify restricting human rights and basic freedoms?, p. 307). For many, September 11 marked the culmination of the period initiated by the end of the Cold War in which the growing acceptance of human rights norms appeared to be irresistible. If the state that had been largely responsible for constructing the post-1948 international human rights regime appeared to violate human rights so clearly, what hope was there that other states would be recruited to the cause?

Human rights have been particularly difficult to uphold in conflict situations. In part, this reflects the fact that power politics amongst the permanent members of the Security Council usually prevents the UN from taking a clear line on such matters. The world has therefore often appeared to stand by as gross violations of human rights have taken place. This happened particularly tragically in the 1994 Rwandan genocide, in which about 800,000 mainly ethnic Tutsis and some moderate Hutus were killed, and in the 1995 Srebrenica massacre, in which an estimated 8,000 Bosnian men and boys were killed. However, from the 1990s onwards, greater emphasis has been placed on extending international law to ensure that those responsible for the gross breaches of rights involving genocide (see p. 333), crimes against humanity and war crimes are brought to account. The role and effectiveness of international criminal tribunals and, since 2002, of the International Criminal Court (ICC) in dealing with human rights violations is discussed in Chapter 14.

Challenging human rights

Despite its growing prominence, the doctrine of human rights has come under growing pressure, particularly since the 1970s, from a variety of sources. The chief thrust of more recent attacks on human rights has been to challenge the universalist assumptions that underpin them, creating a battle between universalism and **relativism**. However, there are two grounds on which universalism has been condemned. The first of these views the universalist approach as philosophically unsound, while the second portrays it as politically damaging.

Philosophical backlash

The authority of universalist liberalism, which underpins the doctrine of human rights, has been challenged by two main philosophical developments in the West. From the perspective of communitarianism, liberalism is defective because its view of the individual as an asocial, atomized, 'unencumbered self' makes little sense (Sandel 1982, Taylor 1994). Communitarians emphasize, by contrast, that the self is embedded in the community, in the sense that each individual is an embodiment of the society that has shaped his or her desires, values and purposes. An individual's experiences and beliefs cannot therefore be separated from the social context that assigns them meaning. This implies that universalist theories of rights and justice must give way to ones that are strictly local and particular. Similar conclusions have been reached by postmodern theorists, albeit on a different basis. Postmodernism has advanced a critique of the 'Enlightenment project', which was expressed politically in ideological traditions such as liberalism and Marxism that were based on the assumption that it is possible to establish objective truths and universal values, usually associated with a faith in reason and progress. Instead, postmodernists have emphasized the fragmented and pluralistic nature of reality, meaning that foundationalist thinking of any kind is unsound. In the words of Jean-François Lyotard (1984), postmodernism can be defined as 'an incredulity towards metanarratives'. Human rights and other theories of universal justice must therefore either be abandoned altogether or be used only in a strictly qualified way that takes account of the political and cultural context within which the ideas emerged.

Postcolonial critiques

Whereas western concerns about human rights have been largely philosophical in orientation, postcolonial concerns have been more clearly political. Relativism has been defended by postcolonial thinkers on two grounds. First, in line with communitarian and postmodern thinking, postcolonial theorists have argued that circumstances vary so widely from society to society, and from culture to culture, as to require differing moral values and, at least, differing conceptions of human rights. What is right for one society may not be right for other societies, a position that suggests that the outside world should respect the choices made by individual nation-states. Second, and more radically, postcolonial theorists have portrayed universal values in general, and human rights in particular, as a form of cultural imperialism. Such thinking was evident in Edward Said's *Orientalism* ([1978] 2003), sometimes seen as the most influential text of post-

● **Relativism**: The belief that ideas and values are valid only in relation to particular social, cultural and historical conditions, implying that there are no universal truths (epistemological relativism) or no universal values (moral or cultural relativism).

● The idea of human rights advances the notion that the similarities between and amongst human beings are greater than the differences. This implies that there is such a thing as a common humanity, of which each individual is an expression. Such a view treats national, cultural, social and other differences amongst human beings as, at best, secondary considerations.

Deconstructing . . .

'HUMAN RIGHTS'

● Human rights are merely philosophical and moral constructs. No surgical operation is capable of exposing our human rights and of proving those to which we are entitled. As there is no objective model of human nature, any conception of human rights is bound to be based on particular ideological and moral assumptions. Conceptions of human rights thus constantly evolve as they are deployed strategically in a global context, examples including 'women's human rights'.

● The idea of human rights suggests that people are essentially 'rights bearers', defined by the claims that they may make on others, rather than by their duties or obligations towards them. The notion of human rights is therefore not merely atomistic, implying that each individual is largely self-reliant, but it also legitimizes egoism and self-interest by implying that these are 'human' traits.

colonialism. Said (see p. 204) developed a critique of Eurocentrism in which Orientalism ensures the cultural and political hegemony of Europe in particular, and of the West in general, through establishing belittling or demeaning stereotypes of the peoples or culture of the Middle East, although this is sometimes extended to include all non-western peoples.

Attempts to highlight the cultural biases that operate through the doctrine of 'universal' human rights have been particularly prominent in Asia and in the Muslim world. As discussed in Chapter 8, the Asian critique of human rights emphasizes the existence of rival 'Asian values', which supposedly reflect the distinctive history, culture and religious backgrounds of Asian societies. Key Asian values include social harmony, respect for authority and a belief in the family, each of which is meant to sustain social cohesion. As such, they challenge, and seek to counter-balance, the bias within traditional conceptions of human rights in favour of rights over duties, and in favour of the individual over community. A further difference is that, from an Asian values perspective, political legitimacy is more closely tied up with economic and social development than it is with democracy and civil liberty. Although those who have championed the idea of Asian values rarely reject the idea of human rights in principle, greater emphasis is usually placed on economic and social rights rather than on 'western' civic and political rights. The Bangkok Declaration of 1993, adopted by Asian ministers in the run-up to the Vienna World Conference on Human Rights, thus attempted a delicate balancing act by recognizing both the distinctiveness of Asian cultures and the interdependence and indivisibility of human rights. It is also notable that the Chinese government often responds to criticism of its human rights record by arguing that collective socio-economic rights are more important than civic and political rights, highlighting its success in relieving an estimated 300 million people from poverty.

Islamic reservations about human rights have been evident since Saudi Arabia refused to adopt the UN Declaration in 1948, on the grounds that it violated important Islamic principles, notably its rejection of apostasy (the abandonment or renunciation of one's religion). The basis of the Islamic critique of human rights, as outlined by the Cairo Declaration on Human Rights in Islam (1990), is that rights, and all moral principles, derive from divine, rather than human, authority. As such, the UN Declaration and, for that matter, any other human principles and laws are invalid if they conflict with the values and principles outlined in divine *Shari'a* law. Indeed, in principle, the former should derive from the latter. From this perspective, the doctrine of universal human rights is merely a cultural expression of the political and economic domination that the West has customarily exerted over the Middle East in particular, and the Muslim world in general. Indeed, many of the concerns raised by the Asian values debate have been echoed within Islamic political thought. These include concern about the secular nature of western societies, implying a lack of sympathy with, if not outright hostility towards, religion, and an excessive individualism that threatens traditional values and social cohesion. The West, in short, is morally decadent, and through the idea of human rights is in danger of foisting its moral decadence on the rest of the world. Nevertheless, the Islamic critique is not so much a form of cultural relativism as a form of alternative universalism, as Islam, like liberalism, contains supposedly universal codes that are applicable to all cultures and all societies.

HUMANITARIAN INTERVENTION

Rise of humanitarian intervention

The state-system has traditionally been based on a rejection of **intervention**. This is reflected in the fact that international law has largely been constructed around respect for state sovereignty, implying that state borders are, or should be, inviolable. Nevertheless, it has long been recognized that intervention may be justifiable on **humanitarian** grounds. Francisco de Vitoria (*c.* 1492–1546) and Hugo Grotius (see p. 341), for example, each acknowledged a right of intervention to prevent the maltreatment by a state of its own subjects, making them, effectively, early theorists of humanitarian intervention. Examples of such intervention, though traditionally rare, can also be found. In the Battle of Navarino Bay in 1827, the British and French destroyed the Turkish and Egyptian fleets off south-west Greece in order to support the cause of Greek independence. In the post-1945 period, interventions that had a significant humanitarian dimension included

● **Intervention**: Forcible action taken by one state against another state, without the latter's consent.

● **Humanitarian**: Being concerned with the interests of humanity, specifically through a desire to promote the welfare or reduce the suffering of others; altruistic.

CONCEPT

Humanitarian intervention

Humanitarian intervention is military intervention that is carried out in pursuit of humanitarian rather than strategic objectives. However, the term is contested and deeply controversial (see p. 332). The term is necessarily evaluative and subjective. Nevertheless, some define humanitarian intervention in terms of intentions: an intervention is 'humanitarian' if it is motivated *primarily* by the desire to prevent harm to other people, accepting that there will always be mixed motives for intervention. Others define humanitarian intervention in terms of outcomes: an intervention is 'humanitarian' only if it results in a net improvement in conditions and a reduction in human suffering.

those that occurred in Bangladesh and Cambodia. In 1971, the Indian army intervened in a brief but brutal civil war between East and West Pakistan, helping East Pakistan to gain its independence as Bangladesh. In 1978, Vietnamese forces invaded Cambodia to overthrow Pol Pot's Khmer Rouge regime, which had, during 1975–79, caused the deaths of between 1 and 3 million people due to famine, civil war and executions. However, none of these military actions were portrayed as forms of 'humanitarian intervention'. India and Vietnam, for instance, justified their interventions squarely in terms of the national interest and the need to restore regional stability. The modern idea of humanitarian intervention was a creation of the post-Cold War period, and it was closely linked to optimistic expectations of the establishment of a 'new world order'.

Humanitarian intervention and the 'new world order'

The 1990s are sometimes seen as the golden age of humanitarian intervention. The end of the Cold War appeared to have brought to an end an age of power politics, characterized as it was by superpower rivalry and a 'balance of terror'. Instead, a 'liberal peace' would reign, founded on a common recognition of international norms and standards of morality. Key to this was the belief that in a global age states could no longer restrict their moral responsibilities to their own peoples (Wheeler 2000). In order to explain the upsurge in humanitarian intervention in the early post-Cold War period, two questions must be answered. First, why did so many humanitarian emergencies arise? Second, why did other states intervene?

Optimistic expectations of the establishment of a world of peace and prosperity in the post-Cold War era were soon punctured by the growth of disorder and chaos in what were sometimes called the 'zones of turmoil' (Singer and Wildavasky 1993), or the 'pre-modern world' (Cooper 2004). However, such turmoil and disorder can be explained in two quite different ways. They can be explained in terms of *internal* factors, faults and failings within the society itself. These include dictatorial government, rampant corruption, entrenched economic and social backwardness, and festering tribal or ethnic rivalries. On the other hand, they can be explained in terms of *external* factors, structural imbalances and inequalities within the global system. These include the inheritance of colonialism, strains generated by economic globalization and, sometimes, the impact of structural adjustment programmes (see p. 378) imposed by the International Monetary Fund (IMF) (see p. 475), the World Bank (see p. 380) and other bodies. To the extent to which humanitarian crises arise as a result of internal factors, intervention appears to be warranted as a way of saving the 'pre-modern world' from itself. However, if external factors have made a significant contribution to precipitating humanitarian emergencies, it is less easy to see how further interference, in the form of military intervention, would provide an appropriate solution.

Four factors help to explain a growing willingness by governments in the 1990s to intervene in situations in which humanitarian interests are at stake. In the first place, as realists and neorealists tend to argue, humanitarian considerations often overlapped with concerns about the national interest. The motives for humanitarian intervention are invariably mixed and complex. For example, US intervention in Haiti was partly motivated by the desire to stem the flow of Haitian refugees to the USA. Similarly, NATO's (see p. 259) actions in Kosovo were

Key examples of humanitarian intervention

1991	*Northern Iraq.* In the aftermath of the Gulf War, the USA launched Operation Provide Comfort to establish 'safe havens' for the Kurdish people in Northern Iraq by establishing a no-fly zone policed by US, UK and French aircraft.
1992	*Somalia.* On the brink of a humanitarian catastrophe, a UN-authorized and US-led intervention (Operation Restore Hope) sought to create a protected environment for conducting humanitarian operations in southern Somalia.
1994	*Haiti.* Following a military coup and in the context of growing lawlessness and accelerating Haitian emigration to the USA, 15,000 US troops were despatched to Haiti to restore order and help in the establishment of civil authority.
1994	*Rwanda.* Following the Rwandan genocide and once the Tutsi RPF had gained control of most of the country, the French established a 'safe zone' for Hutu refugees to flee to (Operation Turquoise).
1999	*Kosovo.* In a context of fears about the 'ethnic cleansing' of the Albanian population, a campaign of air strikes, conducted by US-led NATO forces, forced the Serbs to agree to withdraw their forces from Kosovo
1999	*East Timor.* As Indonesia stepped up a campaign of intimidation and suppression, a UN-authorized peacekeeping force, led by Australia, took control of the island from Indonesia.
2000	*Sierra Leone.* After a prolonged civil war in Sierra Leone, the UK government sent a small force, initially to protect UK citizens, but ultimately to support the elected government against rebel forces that were accused of carrying out atrocities.
2011	*Libya.* In the context of a popular uprising against President Gaddafi, a US-led coalition launched air and missile strikes against Libyan forces, NATO quickly taking over responsibility for policing the no-fly zone (see p. 331).

significantly affected by a wish to avoid a refugee crisis and also prevent regional instability that may, in time, have required more politically risky levels of intervention. The simple reality is that, aside from moral justifications, states remain reluctant to commit their troops in circumstances in which important national interests are not at stake. Second, in a world of 24/7 news and current affairs and global television coverage and communications, governments often came under considerable public pressure to act in the event of humanitarian crises and emergencies. This was particularly demonstrated by the impact of 'non-interventions', especially the failure to prevent the Rwandan genocide and the Srebrenica massacre. What is sometimes called the 'CNN effect', shows how global information and communication flows make it increasingly difficult for governments to restrict their sense of moral responsibility to their own people alone.

Third, the end of Cold War rivalry, and the emergence of the USA as the world's sole superpower, created circumstances in which it was much easier to build consensus amongst major powers favouring intervention. In particular, neither Russia, then suffering from the political and economic turmoil of the collapse of the Soviet Union, nor China, in the early phase of its economic emergence, were strongly minded to block or challenge the USA, the major driving force behind most interventions. Fourth, in view of high expectations about the possibility of building 'new world order', politicians and other policy-makers were more willing to accept that the doctrine of human rights lays down accepted standards for ethical conduct. For Kofi Annan, UN Secretary-General (1997–2007), and national politicians such as President Clinton in the USA, (1993–2001), and UK Prime Minister Blair (1997–2007), the idea of human rights provided the basis for attempts to establish when and where states had a 'right to intervene' in the affairs of other states. In her constructivist account of changes in states' behaviour with respect to military intervention, Martha Finnemore (2003) thus emphasized 'social influence plus internalization, in drawing attention to the impact of new norms about who is human and our obligations to save such people'.

Humanitarian intervention and the 'war on terror'

The 'war on terror' cast the issue of humanitarian intervention into a very different light. Whereas, before 2001, there was a growing belief that there had been too few humanitarian interventions – the failure to prevent massacres and barbarity in Rwanda and Bosnia served as a stain on the conscience of many in the international community – since then there has been the perception that there have been too many humanitarian interventions. This is because the controversial wars in Afghanistan and Iraq were both justified, in part, on humanitarian grounds. Strictly speaking, neither the Afghan War nor the Iraq War were examples of humanitarian intervention. In both cases, self-defence was the primary justification for military action, their purpose being to prevent 'future 9/11s' rather than 'future Rwandas'. However, supporters of the wars also, to a greater or lesser extent, portrayed them as humanitarian ventures. In the case of Afghanistan, the Taliban was seen to have established a brutal and repressive regime that, in particular, violated the rights of women, who were entirely excluded from education, careers and public life. In the case of Iraq, the Saddam regime was viewed as an ongoing threat to the Kurds in the north and the majority Shia population, both of whom had been subject to political exclusion and physical attack. 'Regime change' through the overthrow of the Taliban and Saddam Hussein therefore promised to bring about respect for human rights, greater toleration and the establishment of democratic government. In the process, supporters of the 'war on terror' further extended the doctrine of humanitarian intervention, but, arguably, contaminated the idea to such an extent that it has become more difficult to apply in other circumstances.

During the 1990s, humanitarian intervention was seen to have strictly limited objectives. Military action was taken in emergency conditions with the intention of restoring peace and order and of allowing humanitarian relief to be deployed. Intervention was generally not linked to the wider restructuring of society, even though in cases such as East Timor, Sierra Leone and Kosovo (by contributing to the fall of Slobodan Miloševic in 2000) one of the outcomes was the establishment of a multi-party democratic process. As used in Afghanistan and Iraq, however, the idea of humanitarian intervention was drawn into a larger project of **liberal interventionism**. Liberal interventionism is based on two assumptions. First, liberal values and institutions, notably market-based economies and liberal democracy (see p. 189), are universally applicable and superior to alternative values and institutions. Second, in circumstances where the advance of liberalism is being blocked by obstacles that the domestic population finds impossible to remove, notably a dictatorial and repressive government, established liberal states have a right, and maybe even a duty, to provide support. This support may take the form of diplomatic pressure, economic sanctions or, when basic human rights are being flagrantly violated, possibly military intervention. However, such intervention aims not merely to provide humanitarian relief but, further, to address the source of the problem: the government or regime that has become a threat to its own citizens. Liberal interventionists therefore link humanitarian intervention to the wider and more long-term goals of regime change and democracy promotion. Such ideas overlapped with and helped to inform the neoconservatism (see p. 233) that shaped the USA's strategic approach to the 'war on terror'.

However, its association with the 'war on terror' has created problems for the idea that intervention can and should be used to promote humanitarian or wider liberal goals. In the first place, many have argued that the human rights rationale for intervention in Afghanistan and Iraq was mere window-dressing. Despite the records of both the Taliban and the Saddam regimes, in neither case were there humanitarian emergencies or an imminent threat of genocidal massacres. Radical critics of the 'war on terror', indeed, argued that goals such as regime change and democracy promotion were only elements in a larger strategy of consolidating the USA's global hegemony and securing oil supplies from the Middle East. Second, the interventions in Afghanistan and Iraq proved to be considerably more problematical than initially anticipated, as both wars turned into protracted counter-insurgency struggles. This highlighted the danger of getting bogged down in an intervention, especially as domestic support for intervention tends, sooner or later, to weaken due to the 'body bag effect', regardless of the motives behind it. Third, the 'war on terror' raised serious questions about the universalist assumptions that underpin liberal interventionism. Not only have doubts surfaced about the viability of imposing western-style democracy 'from above', but the wars in Afghanistan and Iraq also in many ways deepened tensions between the Islamic world and the West. If liberal values such as human rights and multi-party democracy are not universally applicable, it is difficult to see how consistent standards can be established for interventions that have a humanitarian or moral basis.

Such problems help to explain why it has been more difficult to mobilize support for humanitarian intervention since 2001. This is demonstrated by 'non-interventions' in places such as Darfur, Zimbabwe, Burma and Syria. Since 2004, the conflict in the Darfur region of western Sudan has led to the deaths of at least 200,000 people and forced more than 2.5 million to flee their homes in the face of atrocities and the destruction of villages. Nevertheless, the UN has left the task of peacemaking to a relatively small African Union Force. More systematic and concerted intervention has been prevented by the opposition of China and Russia, a lack of public support for intervention in the USA while the wars

● **Liberal interventionism**: The theory that liberal values and institutions are universally applicable and (in appropriate circumstances) should be promoted by intervention in the affairs of other states.

in Iraq and Afghanistan persisted, and the UN's lack of resources and political will. In Zimbabwe during the 2000s, the regime of President Robert Mugabe presided over a country whose economy was in tatters, where poverty and unemployment were endemic and political strife and repression were commonplace. However, it has proved difficult to mobilize support for western intervention, not least because such action would have been perceived as a return to colonialism in many parts of Africa, and because of the opposition of South Africa, the major power in the area. In Burma, also known as Myanmar, a military junta has been in power since 1988, which has been accused of gross human rights abuses, including the forcible relocation of civilians, the widespread use of forced labour, including children, and the brutal suppression of political opposition. Nevertheless, despite widely being regarded as a **pariah state** until the initiation of political reform in 2011–12, pressure for intervention in Burma had been restricted by the fact that it is not a threat to regional stability and by China's outright rejection of any form of western action. In the case of Syria, the world seemed to stand on the sidelines and watch as what started off as a wave of peaceful protests in the spring of 2011 developed into one of the bloodiest armed conflicts of the twenty-first century to date (see p. 450). In this light, the 2011 NATO intervention in Libya came as a surprise to many, but it was unclear whether it was an aberration, or whether it marked the beginning of a new trend in favour of intervention (see p. 331).

Conditions for humanitarian intervention

Considerable attention has focused on the attempt to establish when, if ever, humanitarian intervention is justifiable. This reflects the fact that the case for humanitarian intervention requires that just war theory (see p. 257) is extended in bold and challenging ways. The moral challenges posed by humanitarian intervention include the following:

- It violates the established international norm of non-intervention, based on the idea of the 'inviolability of borders'. It is therefore difficult to reconcile humanitarian intervention with the conventional notion of state sovereignty, under which states are treated as equal and self-governing entities, exclusively responsible for what goes on within their borders. Any weakening of state sovereignty may threaten the established rules of world order.
- It goes beyond the just war idea that self-defence is the key justification for the use of force. Instead, in the case of humanitarian intervention, the use of force is justified by the desire to defend or safeguard others, people from different societies. Humanitarian intervention is therefore rooted in cosmopolitan ethical theories that allow states to risk the lives of their own military personnel in order to 'save strangers'.
- It is based on the idea that the doctrine of human rights provides standards of conduct that can be applied to all governments and all peoples. This may, nevertheless, take insufficient account of ethical pluralism and the extent to which religious and cultural differences across the world establish contrasting moral frameworks.
- It may allow the 'last resort' principle, basic to most versions of a just war, to be downgraded. Faced with the imminent danger of genocide or an

● **Pariah state**: A state whose behavioural norms place it outside the international community, leading to diplomatic isolation and attracting widespread condemnation.

Humanitarian intervention in Libya

Events: On 19 March 2011, a US-led coalition began a campaign of air and missile strikes against Libyan forces loyal to President Gaddafi. This took place in a context of an emerging civil war, and particularly as pro-Gaddafi troops moved on the rebel stronghold of Benghazi, threatening to cause 'violence on a horrific scale', as President Obama put it. In accordance with UN Security Council Resolutions 1970 and 1973, the strikes were intended to enforce an arms embargo on Libya, establish a no-fly zone and use 'all necessary measures' to protect Libyan civilians and civilian populated areas. Within days, and as planned, command and control responsibility for the military operation passed from the USA to NATO. NATO intervention effectively neutralized Libya's air force and severely

reduced the effectiveness of its heavy weapons, helping, possibly decisively, to tip the balance of the conflict in favour of the Libyan opposition. By early October, the Libyan National Transitional Council had secured control over the entire country and rebels had captured and killed Gaddafi. The NATO operation ended on 31 October, 222 days after it had begun (Daalder and Stavridis 2012).

Significance: Did Libya mark revived support for humanitarian intervention, or was it an aberration? As no major humanitarian interventions had occurred since those in Kosovo and East Timor in 1999, and in Sierra Leone in 2000, some had concluded that the era of humanitarian intervention was over, and that it had essentially been a reflection of the unusual circumstances that prevailed during the early post-Cold War period – notably, a strengthened belief that world politics should be guided by moral principles and the emergence of the USA as the world's sole superpower. Humanitarian interventions appeared to have ended both because of the USA's declining appetite for military involvement abroad (in the light of the wars in Afghanistan and Iraq) and because the rise of Russia and China meant that the USA was less likely to have a free hand in such matters. And yet, Libya proved that humanitarian interventions can still take place, and so cannot be ruled out in the future.

Aside from issues of motivation, ranging from self-interest (oil) to genuine humanitarianism, a diverse range of factors conspired to favour intervention in Libya. In the first place, the strong likelihood of impending slaughter in

Benghazi, a city of some 750,000 people, galvanized President Obama, French President Sarkozy and the UK Prime Minister Cameron, the key supporters of intervention. To have stood passively by while mass bloodshed took place in Libya, particularly having given such clear support to earlier Arab Spring uprisings, may have been highly politically damaging. Second, significant international and regional support appeared to give intervention a sound legal basis. Authorization by the UN Security Council and backing for intervention from key regional bodies, notably the Arab League and the Gulf Corporation Council, was made possible by the fact that Gaddafi's Libya was a pariah state with few reliable friends and no close ties to Russia or China. NATO forces also gained greater legitimacy through the participation of partners such as Sweden, the United Arab Emirates, Jordan and Morocco. Third, the operation was deemed to be militarily feasible. Libya's relatively weak air and missile defences and an emphasis on aerial and military strikes promised to keep NATO casualties to a minimum (in the event, there were no NATO casualties) and meant that a 'boots-on-the-ground' war could be avoided. Finally, military and political assessments at the time were optimistic about the likely outcomes of intervention. These suggested (accurately, as it turned out) that, with NATO assistance, the Libyan opposition would be able to overthrow the Gaddafi regime without a protracted, bloody civil war, and (but more questionably) that the Libyan National Transitional Council constituted the basis for a stable and effective post-Gaddafi government.

- Describing such interventions as 'humanitarian' cloaks them in moral rightfulness and legitimacy. The term 'humanitarian intervention' thus contains its own justification: the interventions in question serve the interests of humanity, presumably by reducing suffering and death. At the very least the term is specious, in that it fails to acknowledge the invariable mixed and complex motives for intervention.

Deconstructing . . .
'HUMANITARIAN INTERVENTION'

- 'Intervention' refers to various forms of interference in the affairs of others. It therefore conceals the fact that the interventions in question are, by their nature, military actions that involve the use of force and some level of violence. 'Humanitarian military intervention' or just 'military intervention' are thus preferred by some. 'Humanitarian intervention' could, in this light, be viewed as a contradiction in terms.

- The notion of 'humanitarian intervention' may reproduce important power asymmetries. Intervening powers (invariably developed western states) possess both power and moral benevolence while the people needing to be 'saved' (invariably in the developing world) are portrayed as victims living in conditions of chaos and barbarity (Orford 2003). The term thus reinforces the notion of modernization as westernization, even Americanization.

ongoing humanitarian emergency, it may be morally indefensible to waste precious time exhausting all non-violent options before force can be justified. Instead, force may become a 'first resort' response.

In view of such considerations, military intervention for humanitarian purposes must always be an exceptional and extraordinary measure. Without clear guidelines about when, where and how humanitarian intervention can and should take place, states will always be able to cloak their expansionist ambitions in moral justifications, allowing humanitarian intervention to become a new form of imperialism. Two key issues have attracted particular attention: the 'just cause' that warrants military intervention, and the 'right authority' that legitimizes the intervention in practice.

Although it is widely accepted that the doctrine of human rights provides a moral framework for humanitarian intervention, human rights do not in themselves provide adequate guidance about justifications for intervention. This is because human rights are many and various – the UN Universal Declaration of

CONCEPT

Genocide

Genocide is the attempt to destroy, in whole or in part, a national, ethnic, racial or religious group. The UN's Genocide Convention (1948) identifies five genocidal acts: (1) killing members of a group; (2) causing serious bodily or mental harm to members of a group; (3) deliberately inflicting on a group conditions of life calculated to bring about its physical destruction in whole or in part; (4) imposing measures intended to prevent births within a group; and (5) forcibly transferring children from a group to another group. Genocide must involve a definite decision, plan or programme to wipe out a particular group of people. It may overlap with 'ethnic cleansing', although the latter also includes forcibly relocating an ethnic group.

Human Rights (1948), for instance, contains 29 Articles – meaning that the 'violation of human rights' would legitimize intervention in a bewildering range of circumstances. A better guide is provided by the idea of 'crimes against humanity', a notion that emerged through the Nuremberg Trials at the end of WWII. However, the most widely used justification for humanitarian intervention is to stop or prevent genocide, viewed as the worst possible crime against humanity, the 'crime of crimes'. Nevertheless, it is difficult to see how genocide could provide a consistent and reliable 'just cause' threshold for humanitarian intervention. This is because genocide is usually viewed as a deliberate act, if not as a planned programme of slaughter and destruction, while many large-scale killings arise through random acts of violence or the total breakdown of political order without any party having 'genocidal intent'. The most thorough and considered attempt to establish principles for military intervention can be found in the report *The Responsibility to Protect* (R2P), produced by the International Commission on Intervention and State Sovereignty (ICISS), set up by the Canadian government in 2000. R2P outlines just two criteria for justifiable military action:

- *Large-scale loss of life*, actual or apprehended, with genocidal intent or not, which is the product either of deliberate state action, or state neglect or inability to act, or a failed state situation; or
- *Large-scale ethnic cleansing*, actual or apprehended, whether carried out by killing, forcible expulsion, acts of terrorism or rape.

When these criteria are met, the ICISS asserts that there is not merely a right to intervene, but an international responsibility to protect those who are, or are in imminent danger of becoming, victims of these acts. Their advantage is that they are more specific than the more generalized idea of a 'crime against humanity', while also allowing for intervention to be triggered by 'large-scale loss of life' that is not the result of deliberate human action. Intervention can therefore be justified, for instance, in order to prevent people from starving to death, if their state is unable or unwilling to provide assistance.

However, once criteria for humanitarian intervention have been established, we are left with the question: who should decide when the criteria have been satisfied? Who has the 'right authority' to authorize military intervention for humanitarian purposes? The generally accepted answer to this question is that the most appropriate body is the UN Security Council. This reflects the UN's role as the principal source of international law and the Security Council's responsibility for maintaining international peace and security (as discussed in Chapter 18). Two difficulties arise from this, however. The first is that, as discussed further in Chapter 14, international law on humanitarian intervention hovers somewhere between its clear prohibition in the UN Charter, and its broad but ill-defined acceptance in customary international law. As these difficulties stem from the legal and moral implications of state sovereignty, supporters of humanitarian intervention have often sought to reshape the concept of sovereignty itself. While he was UN Secretary-General, Kofi Annan tried to reconcile the tension between sovereignty and human rights by arguing that, in a context of globalization and international cooperation, the state should be viewed as 'the servant of its people, and not vice versa' (Annan 1999). Such thinking has led to a growing acceptance of the idea of '**responsible sovereignty**'. The R2P, for

● **Responsible sovereignty**: The idea that state sovereignty is conditional upon how a state treats its citizens, based on the belief that the state's authority arises ultimately from sovereign individuals.

instance, was fashioned in line with the ICISS recommendation that greater moral content be put into sovereignty, in that a state's right to sovereignty is conditional on fulfilling its duty to protect its citizens. In this view, the state is merely the custodian of a sovereignty that is ultimately located in the people.

The second problem is that it may be difficult to gain Security Council authorization for intervention because its five 'veto powers' may be more concerned about issues of global power than they are with humanitarian concerns. The R2P principles acknowledge this problem by requiring that Security Council authorization should be *sought* prior to any military intervention being carried out, but accept that alternative options must be available if the Security Council rejects a proposal or fails to deal with it in a reasonable time. Under the R2P, these alternatives are that a proposed humanitarian intervention should be considered by the UN General Assembly in Emergency Special Session or by a regional or sub-regional organization. In practice, NATO has often been used in such matters, helping to legitimize humanitarian interventions, and serving as the military machine that carries out interventions, as in Kosovo, Afghanistan and Libya.

Does humanitarian intervention work?

Do the benefits of humanitarian intervention outweigh the costs? In simple terms, does humanitarian intervention actually save lives? This is to judge intervention not in terms of its motives or intentions, or in terms of international law, but in terms of its outcomes. It is, nevertheless, a question that can never be finally settled, as this would require that *actual* outcomes can be compared with those that would have occurred in *hypothetical* circumstances (in which either an intervention had not taken place, or a possible intervention had occurred). The widespread assumption that earlier and more concerted intervention in Rwanda in 1994 would have saved, possibly, hundreds of thousands of lives, can thus never be proved. However, there are certain examples of interventions that produced beneficial outcomes that would have been unlikely in other circumstances. The establishment of a 'no-fly zone' in northern Iraq in 1991 not only prevented possible reprisal attacks and even massacres after the Kurdish uprising, but also allowed Kurdish areas to develop a significant degree of autonomy. The intervention in Kosovo in 1999 succeeded in its goal of expelling Serbian police and military from the area, helping to end a massive displacement of the population and prevent possible further attacks. The 2011 intervention in Libya is widely credited with having prevented the Libyan revolution from turning into a protracted, bloody civil war. As these three operations were carried out by NATO air strikes, they involved minimal casualties but only amongst intervening military personnel. Estimates of the civilians and combatants killed in Kosovo, for instance, ranged from 1,500 (NATO) to 5,700 (Serbia). Intervention in Sierra Leone was effective in bringing to an end a ten-year-long civil war that had killed about 50,000 people, and also in providing the basis for parliamentary and presidential elections, held in 2007.

However, other interventions have been far less effective. UN peacekeepers have sometimes been sidelined as humanitarian catastrophes have occurred (the Democratic Republic of the Congo), while other interventions have been quickly abandoned as unsuccessful (Somalia), or have resulted in protracted counter-

Debating...
Is humanitarian intervention justified?

Humanitarian intervention is one of the most hotly disputed issues in global politics. While some see it as evidence that world affairs are being guided by new and more enlightened cosmopolitan sensibilities, others view humanitarian intervention as deeply misguided and morally confused.

YES

Indivisible humanity. Humanitarian intervention is based on the belief that there is a common humanity. This implies that moral responsibilities cannot be confined merely to one's 'own' people or state, but extend, potentially, to the whole of humanity (see p. 81). There is therefore an obligation to 'save strangers', if the resources exist to do so and the cost is not disproportionate.

Global interdependence. The responsibility to act in relation to events on the other side of the world is increased by a recognition of growing global interconnectedness and interdependence. States can no longer act as if they are islands. Humanitarian intervention can therefore be justified on grounds of enlightened self-interest; for example, to prevent a refugee crisis that may create deep political and social strains in other countries.

Regional stability. Humanitarian emergencies, especially in the context of state failure, tend to have radical implications for the regional balance of power, creating instability and wider unrest. This provides an incentive for neighbouring states to support intervention, with major powers opting to intervene in order to prevent a possible regional war.

Promoting democracy. Intervention is justified in circumstances in which endangered or suffering people do not possess the democratic means to alleviate their own hardship. Humanitarian interventions therefore invariably take place in a context of dictatorship or authoritarianism. 'Democracy promotion' is a legitimate long-term goal of intervention, as it will strengthen respect for human rights and reduce the likelihood of future humanitarian crises.

International community. Humanitarian intervention provides not only demonstrable evidence of the international community's commitment to shared values (peace, prosperity, democracy and human rights), but also strengthens these by establishing clearer guidelines for the way in which governments should treat their people, reflected in the principle of 'responsible sovereignty'. Humanitarian intervention thus contributes to the development of a rule-bound global order.

NO

Against international law. International law only clearly authorizes intervention in the case of self-defence. This is based on the assumption that respect for state sovereignty is the surest, if still an imperfect, means of upholding international order. To the extent that intervention for humanitarian purposes is permitted, international law becomes, at best, confused and the established rules of world order are weakened.

National interests rule. As realists argue, since states are always motivated by concerns of national self-interest, their claim that military action is motivated by humanitarian considerations is invariably an example of political mendacity. On the other hand, if an intervention were genuinely humanitarian, the state in question would be putting its own citizens at risk in order to 'save strangers', violating its national interests.

Double standards. There are many examples of pressing humanitarian emergencies in which intervention is either ruled out or never considered. This can happen because no national interest is at stake, because of an absence of media coverage or because intervention is politically impossible (for example, Chechnya and Tibet). This makes the doctrine of humanitarian intervention hopelessly confused in political and moral terms.

Simplistic politics. The case for intervention is invariably based on a simplistic 'good *v* evil' image of political conflict. This has sometimes been a consequence of distortion (the exaggeration of atrocities, for example), but it also ignores the moral complexities that attend all international conflicts. Indeed, the tendency to simplify humanitarian crises helps to explain the tendency towards 'mission drift' and for interventions to go wrong.

Moral pluralism. Humanitarian intervention can be seen as a form of cultural imperialism, in that it is based on an essentially western notion of human rights that may not be applicable in other parts of the world. Historical, cultural and religious differences may therefore make it impossible to establish universal guidelines for the behaviour of governments, making the task of establishing a 'just cause' threshold for intervention unachievable.

insurgency struggles (Afghanistan and Iraq). The deepest problem here is that interventions may do more harm than good. To replace old dictators with foreign occupying forces may only increase tensions and create a greater risk of civil war, which then subjects civilians to a state of almost constant warfare. If civil strife results from an effective breakdown in government authority, foreign intervention may make things worse not better. Thus, while political stability, democratic governance and respect for human rights may all be desirable goals, it may not be possible for outsiders to impose or enforce them. There may, in other words, be little that could be done to alleviate the horrors of Darfur, Burma, Zimbabwe or Syria. From this perspective, humanitarian intervention should be looked at, at the very least, from a long-term perspective and not become a knee-jerk reaction to a humanitarian emergency and growing public pressure for 'something to be done'. Many humanitarian interventions have failed because of inadequate planning for reconstruction and an insufficient provision of resources for rebuilding. The R2P principles therefore place an emphasis not merely on the 'responsibility to protect', but also on the 'responsibility to prevent' and the 'responsibility to rebuild'. Long-term progress in such matters has therefore been increasingly linked to efforts to achieve peace-building (see p. 452) or nation-building, as discussed in Chapter 18.

SUMMARY

● Human rights are supposedly universal, fundamental, indivisible and absolute. Distinctions are nevertheless drawn between civil and political rights; economic, social and cultural rights; and solidarity rights. Human rights imply that national governments have significant foreign domestic obligations, and that justice has acquired a cosmopolitan character.

● Human rights are protected by an elaborate regime that involves an expanding array of international human rights documents, with supporting UN bodies, a wide range of human rights NGOs and states committed to advancing human rights. Nevertheless, states are also the greatest human rights abusers, reflecting an inherent tension between human rights and states' rights.

● Since the 1970s, the universalist assumptions that underpin human rights have come under growing pressure. Communitarians and postmodernists argue that human rights are philosophically unsound because morality is always relative. Postcolonial theorists often view the doctrine of human rights as an example of western cultural imperialism, even though they may accept the broad notion.

● Humanitarian intervention is military intervention carried out in pursuit of humanitarian rather than strategic objectives. It flourished in the 1990s due to the liberal expectations linked to the prospect of a 'new world order' and the (temporary) hegemony of the USA. However, deep concerns have been thrown up about humanitarian intervention by US military involvement in Afghanistan and Iraq.

● The R2P has laid down conditions for humanitarian intervention, based on a large-scale loss of life, possibly due to ethnic cleansing, where the state in question is unwilling or unable to act itself. Such thinking has often involved attempts to reconceptualize sovereignty, particularly through the idea of 'responsible sovereignty'.

● Humanitarian intervention works when its benefits exceed its costs, in terms of lives lost and human suffering. Although this calculation is difficult to make in objective terms, there have clearly been examples of successful intervention. Other interventions, however, have possibly done more harm than good, sometimes because of the intractable nature of underlying economic and political problems.

Questions for discussion

● How do human rights differ from other kinds of rights?

● Are economic and social rights genuine human rights?

● To what extent have NGOs been effective in ensuring the protection of human rights?

● Is the tension between states' rights and human rights irresolvable?

● Are human rights simply a form of western cultural imperialism?

● Why did humanitarian interventions increase so markedly in the 1990s?

● Is military intervention ever truly 'humanitarian'?

● Can humanitarian intervention ever be reconciled with the norm of state sovereignty?

● Does humanitarian intervention merely reinforce global power asymmetries?

Further reading

Donnelly, J., *Universal Human Rights in Theory and Practice* (2013). A wide-ranging examination of human rights which considers their significance in the light of key post-Cold War issues.

Dunne, T. and N. J. Wheeler (eds), *Human Rights in Global Politics* (1999). An excellent collection of essays that explore the philosophical basis for, and the political implications of, the doctrine of universal human rights.

Hehir, A., *Humanitarian Intervention: An Introduction* (2013). An accessible and comprehensive overview of the history, theory and practice of humanitarian intervention.

Weiss, T. G., *Humanitarian Intervention: Ideas in Action* (2007). A wide-ranging account of the issue of humanitarian intervention that defends the 'restrictive' criteria established by the R2P.

ONLINE RESOURCES AVAILABLE

Links to relevant web resources can be found on the *Global Politics* website

CHAPTER 14

International Law

'*Whenever law ends, tyranny begins.*'

JOHN LOCKE, *Second Treatise on Government* (1690)

PREVIEW   International law is an unusual phenomenon. As traditionally understood, law
consists of a set of compulsory and enforceable rules; it reflects the will of a sovereign power. And yet, no central authority exists in international politics that is
capable of enforcing rules, legal or otherwise. Some, therefore, dismiss the very idea
of international law as meaningless. Nevertheless, international law has greater
substance and significance than first appearances suggest. In particular, more often
than not, international law is obeyed and respected, meaning that it provides an
important – and, indeed, an increasingly important – framework within which
states and other international actors interact. However, what is the nature of international law, and where does it come from? Also, if international law is rarely
enforceable in a conventional sense, why do states comply with it? The growing
significance of international law is reflected in changes in its scope, purpose and
operation since the early twentieth century. These include a shift from 'international' law, which merely determines relations between and among states, to
'world' or 'supranational' law, which treats individuals, groups and private organizations also as subjects of international law. This has drawn international law into the
controversial area of humanitarian standard-setting, especially in relation to the
'laws of war'. It has also, particularly since the end of the Cold War, led to attempts
to make political and military leaders at all levels personally responsible for human
rights violations through a framework of international criminal tribunals and courts.
To what extent has 'international' law been transformed into 'world' law? How have
the laws of war been developed into international humanitarian law? And have
international criminal tribunals and courts proved to be an effective way of upholding order and global justice?

KEY ISSUES   ● How does international law differ from domestic law?

● What are the sources of international law?

● Why is international law obeyed?

● How and why has international law changed in recent years?

● What are the implications of holding individuals responsible for violating international humanitarian law?

NATURE OF INTERNATIONAL LAW

What is law?

Law is found in all modern societies, and is usually regarded as the bedrock of civilized existence. But what distinguishes law from other social rules, and in what sense does law operate at an international or even global level? Is there such a thing as 'international law'? In the case of domestic law, it is relatively easy to identify a series of distinguishing characteristics. First, law is made by the government and so applies throughout society. Not only does this mean that law reflects the will of the state and therefore takes precedence over all other norms and social rules, but it also gives domestic law universal jurisdiction within a particular political society. Second, law is compulsory; citizens are not allowed to choose which laws to obey and which to ignore, because law is backed up by a system of coercion and punishment. Law thus requires the existence of a legal system, a set of norms and institutions through which legal rules are created, interpreted and enforced. Third, law has a 'public' quality in that it consists of codified, published and recognized rules. This is, in part, achieved by enacting law through a formal, and usually public, legislative process. Moreover, punishments handed down for law-breaking are predictable and can be anticipated, whereas arbitrary arrest or imprisonment has a random and dictatorial character. Fourth, law is usually recognized as binding on those to whom it applies, even if particular laws may be regarded as unjust or unfair. Law is therefore more than simply a set of enforceable commands; it also embodies moral claims, implying that legal rules *should* be obeyed.

Although the term 'international law' came into common use only in the nineteenth century, the idea of international law is much older and can be traced back at least as far as to ancient Rome. Nevertheless, the origins of international law as an **institution** are usually located in sixteenth- and seventeenth-century Europe and the passage of a series of treaties that, in establishing the rules of the emerging state-system, laid down the foundations of international public law. These treaties included the following:

- The Peace of Augsburg, 1555 – this consisted of a series of treaties that, amongst other things, reaffirmed the independence of German principalities from the Holy Roman Empire, and allowed them to choose their own religion.
- The Peace of Westphalia, 1648 – consisting of the Treaties of Osnabrück and Münster, this initiated a new political order in central Europe based on the principle of state sovereignty (see p. 4) and the right of monarchs to maintain standing armies, build fortifications and levy taxes.
- The Treaties of Utrecht, 1713 – these established the Peace of Utrecht, which consolidated the principle of sovereignty by linking sovereign authority to a fixed territorial boundary.

Ideas and theories of international law also emerged against this backdrop, not least through the writings of Hugo Grotius (see p. 341), an important early figure in the emergence of international law. Much of this early theorizing focused on the conditions of the just war (see p. 264). Nevertheless, it was

---

CONCEPT

International law

International law is the law that governs states and other international actors. There are two branches of international law: private and public. Private international law refers to the regulation of international activities carried out by individuals, companies and other non-state actors. As such, private international law relates to the overlapping jurisdictions of domestic legal systems, and so is sometimes called 'conflict of laws'. Public international law applies to states, which are viewed as legal 'persons'. As such, it deals with government-to-government relations as well as those between states and international organizations or other actors. International law nevertheless differs from domestic law, in that it operates in the absence of an international legislative body and a system of enforcement.

● **Institution**: A body of norms, rules and practices that shape behaviour and expectations, without necessarily having the physical character of an international organization (see p. 440).

evident from the outset that international law differs from domestic law in a number of important respects. Most importantly, international law cannot be enforced in the same way as domestic law. There is, for example, no supreme legislative authority to enact international law and no world government or international police force to compel states to uphold their legal obligations. The closest we have come to this is through the establishment in 1945 of the United Nations (see p. 456), which is endowed, at least in theory, with certain supranational powers, and through its principal judicial organ, the International Court of Justice (ICJ) (see p. 348). However, the ICJ has no enforcement powers, and even the UN Security Council, which has the ability to impose military and economic sanctions, possesses no independent mechanism for ensuring compliance with its resolutions, even though its decisions are technically binding on all UN members. International law is thus **'soft' law** rather than **'hard' law**. On the other hand, levels of compliance with international law, particularly, but not only, international private law, are surprisingly high, even by domestic standards. This is sometimes referred to as the paradox of international law, as it reflects the extent to which a system of international law can operate effectively despite the absence of conventional compliance mechanisms. To some extent this was acknowledged by Grotius, for whom the enforcement of international law was largely based on a sense of solidarity, or potential solidarity, amongst states.

However, as law has developed, two quite different accounts of its nature, and especially its relationship to morality, have emerged. Those thinkers who insist that law is, or should be, rooted in a moral system subscribe to some kind of theory of **natural law**. The central theme of all conceptions of natural law is the idea that law should conform to a set of prior ethical standards, implying that the purpose of law is to enforce morality. Medieval thinkers such as Thomas Aquinas (see p. 261) thus took it for granted that human laws have a moral basis. Natural law, he argued, could be penetrated through God-given natural reason and guides us towards the attainment of the good life on Earth. However, this notion came under attack from the nineteenth century onwards through the rise of the 'science of **positive law**'.

The idea of positive law sought to free the understanding of law from moral, religious and mystical assumptions. Many have seen its roots in Thomas Hobbes' (see p. 14) command theory of law: 'law is the word of him that by right hath command over others'. By the nineteenth century, such thinking had been developed into the theory of 'legal positivism', in which the defining feature of the law is not its conformity to higher moral or religious principles, but the fact that it is established and enforced by a political superior, a 'sovereign person or body'. This boils down to the belief that law is law because it is obeyed. One of the implications of this is that the notion of international law is highly questionable. If, for example, treaties and UN resolutions cannot be enforced, they should be regarded as a collection of moral principles and ideals, and not as law. Although the rise of legal positivism made natural law theories distinctly unfashionable in the nineteenth century, interest in them revived significantly during the twentieth century. This occurred, in part, through unease about the cloak of legality behind which Nazi and Stalinist terror had taken place. The desire to establish a higher set of moral values against which national law could be judged was, for example, one of the problems which the Nuremberg Trials (1945–6) and Tokyo

● **Soft law**: Law that is not binding and cannot be enforced; quasi-legal instruments that impose only moral obligations.

● **Hard law**: Law that is enforceable and so establishes legally binding obligations.

● **Natural law**: A moral system to which human laws do, or should, conform; natural law lays down universal standards of conduct derived from nature, reason or God.

● **Positive law**: A system of enforceable commands that operates irrespective of their moral content.

Hugo Grotius (1583–1645)

Dutch jurist, philosopher and writer. Born in Delft into a family of professional lawyers, Grotius became a diplomat and political adviser and held a number of political offices. In *On the Law of War and Peace* (1625), he developed a secular basis for international law, arguing that it is grounded not in theology but in reason. This was largely accomplished by constructing a theory of the just war, based on natural rights. For Grotius there were four causes of a just war: (1) self-defence, (2) to enforce rights, (3) to seek reparations for injury and (4) to punish a wrong-doer. By restricting the right of states to go to war for political purposes, Grotius emphasized the common purposes of the international community and helped to found the idea of international society (see p. 9), as developed by the 'neo-Grotian' English School.

Trials (1946–48), sought to address. This was made possible by reference to the notion of natural law, albeit dressed up in the modern language of human rights (see p. 311). Indeed, it is now widely accepted that both domestic and international law should conform to the higher moral principles set out in the doctrine of human rights. As far as international law is concerned, this has been reflected in a substantial expansion of **international humanitarian law**, as discussed later in the chapter.

Sources of international law

Where does international law come from? In the absence of world government and an international legislative body, the sources of international law are various. As defined by the Statute of the International Court of Justice, there are four sources of international law:

- International conventions, whether general or particular, establishing rules expressly recognized by the contesting states
- International custom, as evidence of a general practice accepted as law
- The general principles of law recognized by civilized nations
- Judicial decisions and teachings of the most highly-qualified legal scholars of the various nations.

● **International humanitarian law**: A body of international law, often identified as the laws of war, that seeks to protect combatants and non-combatants in conflict situations.

● **Treaty**: A formal agreement between two or more states that is considered binding in international law.

The most common form of international convention, and the most important source of international law, consists of **treaties**, formal, written documents through which states agree to engage in, or refrain from, specified behaviours. Treaties may be either bilateral or multilateral. Bilateral treaties are concluded between two states, such as the START treaties through which the USA (see p. 46) and Russia (see p. 181) have agreed to reduce their stockpiles of nuclear weapons. Most treaties are nevertheless multilateral treaties, in that they are concluded by three or more states. Some multilateral treaties have specific provisions, such as the 1968 Nuclear Non-Proliferation Treaty (NPT), while others are broad and far-reaching, such as the Charter of the United Nations. Treaties, nevertheless, are a distinctive form of international law in two key respects. First, with the possible exception of the UN Charter, they violate one of the usual characteristics of law, which is that law applies automatically and unconditionally to all members of a political community. Treaties, by contrast, only apply to states that are party to the agreement in question, although it is sometimes argued that certain treaties, such as the NPT, are so widely respected that they impose customary obligations even on states that have not signed them. Second, the legal obligations that arise from treaties are very clearly rooted in **consent**, in that states enter into treaties freely and voluntarily. Once treaties are signed and ratified, they must be obeyed, as expressed in the principle of ***pacta sunt servanda***. This consent is nevertheless conditional, in that states can contract out of treaties on the grounds that significant changes have occurred in the conditions existing at the time the agreement was originally entered into. In these cases, the notion of ***rebus sic stantibus*** can be invoked. The contractual nature of treaties and conventions places them clearly within the tradition of positive law, as international law in these cases is a product for negotiations between sovereign states, not the command of God or the dictates of higher morality. International law has therefore come to assume the character of reciprocal accord.

International **custom**, or what is often called 'customary international law', is the second most important source of international law, although until the rapid expansion of treaties during the twentieth century, it was the most important. Customary international law derives from the actual practice of states, in that practices among states that are common and well-established come, over time, to be viewed as legally binding. Customary obligations thus arise from the expectation that states should carry out their affairs consistently with past accepted conduct. Unlike treaties, customary law does not require explicit consent; rather, consent is inferred from the behaviour of states themselves. On the other hand, unlike treaties, customary international law is often assumed to have universal jurisdiction, particularly when it is grounded in deeply-held norms and moral principles, in which case it is closely associated with the natural law tradition. Examples of customary law include many of the laws regarding how diplomacy is carried out, which developed over time as rules of conduct shaped by the mutual convenience of the states concerned. These, for instance, include the practice of granting **diplomatic immunity** to foreign diplomats.

The weakness of customary law is that, being based on practice rather than formal, written agreements, it may be difficult to define, and it may be difficult to decide when and how common practices have acquired the force of law. For this reason, there has been a growing tendency to translate customs into treaties and conventions. The Vienna Conventions on Diplomatic and Consular Relations (1961, 1963) thus gave many of the norms related to the conduct of diplomacy the status of written law, while the 1926 Slavery Convention gave formal recognition to long-established customs prohibiting slavery and the slave trade. However, in circumstances in which customary law reflects deeply-embedded moral understandings, it may appear to be more powerful than treaty-based law. For example, it is usually accepted that the custom-based prohibition on genocide (see p. 333) would apply regardless of whether a state had signed up to the 1948 Genocide Convention, making it a universal moral imperative.

The final two sources of international law are of less significance than treaties or customs. The rather vague notion of the 'general principles of law' and the idea of 'legal scholarship' tend to be invoked when no clear rights or obligations

● **Consent**: Assent or permission; a voluntary agreement to be subject to binding obligations or a higher authority.

● ***Pacta sunt servanda***: (Latin) The principle that treaties are binding on the parties to them and must be executed in good faith.

● ***Rebus sic stantibus***: (Latin) The doctrine that states can terminate their obligations under a treaty if a fundamental change of circumstances has occurred.

● **Custom**: A practice that is so long-established and widely accepted that it has come to have the force of law.

● **Diplomatic immunity**: A collection of rights and dispensations that accredited diplomats enjoy in foreign countries, usually including freedom from arrest and trial on criminal charges, and privileged travel and communication arrangements.

can be identified through formal agreements between and amongst states or through custom and practice. The former is usually used to imply that actions that are recognized as crimes in most domestic legal systems should be treated as crimes if they occur in an international context. Thus, although the invasion of another country's territory and the attempt to annex it by force may breach treaty obligations and ignore the customary expectation that sovereign states should live in peace, it can also be seen as a violation of international law on the grounds that it offends what could be viewed as the general principles of civilized conduct. In the case of legal scholarship, the ICJ recognizes that the sum of written arguments of the most highly-qualified and respected judges and lawyers can be used to resolve points of international law when these are not resolved by reference to the first three sources.

Why is international law obeyed?

Those who dismiss the very idea of international law tend to view law strictly in terms of command. This implies that enforcement is the only reliable means of bringing about compliance. However, if compliance were seen as the core feature of an effective legal system, few, if any, domestic legal arrangements would qualify as such. Rape, theft and murder continue to occur in all countries of the world despite being legally prohibited. Indeed, if laws were never violated, there would be little need for them in the first place. Nevertheless, it is difficult to view widespread non-compliance, reflected in a wholesale breakdown of social order and the routine use of intimidation and violence, as compatible with a functioning system of law. In all legal systems, then, there is a balance between compliance and violation, and international law is no exception. However, the remarkable thing about international law is just how high levels of compliance with it tend to be, even though violations have often been grotesque and highly publicized (Franck 1990). Even a noted realist such as Hans Morgenthau (1948) acknowledged that, 'during the 400 years of its existence international law has in most instances been scrupulously observed'. But how can this level of compliance be explained if enforcement, in the conventional sense of the punishment of transgressors, is the exception rather than the rule? Countries tend to obey international law for a variety of reasons, including the following:

- Self-interest and reciprocity
- Fear of disorder
- Fear of isolation
- Fear of punishment
- Identification with international norms.

The main reason why states comply with international law is that it is in their interests to do so. States do not need to be forced to comply with the rules that they have, in the main, either made themselves or to which they have explicitly consented. This is sometimes called 'utilitarian compliance', because states abide by laws because they calculate that, in the long run, doing so will bring benefit or reduce harm. The key to this benefit is reciprocity (see p. 344), a relationship of mutual exchange between or amongst states that ensures that favours are returned for favours or that punishment is returned for punishment (Keohane

CONCEPT

Reciprocity

Reciprocity refers to exchanges between two or more parties in which the actions of each party are contingent on the actions of the others. Good is thus returned for good, and bad for bad, with a rough equivalence applying in terms of reciprocal benefits and rewards. Positive reciprocity ('you scratch my back and I'll scratch yours') explains how and why states are able to cooperate in the absence of an enforcing central authority, as occurs through compliance with international law, the establishment of international regimes or multilateralism (see p. 467). Negative reciprocity ('an eye for an eye, a tooth for a tooth') helps to explain tit-for-tat escalations of conflict and arms races (see p. 272).

● **Reprisal**: An act of retaliation designed either to punish a wrongdoer or redress an injury; reprisal suggests proportionality and usually stops short of war.

1986). For example, although diplomatic immunity may, at times, mean that immoral or even flagrantly criminal actions by foreign diplomats in one's own country go unpunished, states around the world recognize that this is a price worth paying to ensure that their own diplomats in foreign lands can live and work in safety and security. Similarly, the World Trade Organization's (see p. 537) rules about free trade and the abandonment of tariff and non-tariff barriers are usually upheld by states on the grounds that they will benefit from reciprocal action taken by other states.

A second, and related, reason why states tend to comply with international law is out of a general preference for order over disorder. On one level, this is reflected in the ability of international law to create a set of common understandings, through which states become aware of the 'rules of the game'. The framework of rules that international law helps to establish and publicize thus reduces uncertainty and confusion in the relations among states, each of them benefiting from shared expectations and enhanced predictability thus established. States, in other words, have a better sense of how other states will behave. At a deeper level, however, there is a fear of chaos and disorder. This may occur through negative reciprocity, as initial, and perhaps relatively minor, violations of international law lead to an escalating series of **reprisals** that threaten to unravel the entire system of international order and stability. Such considerations may be particularly emphasized by defensive realists, who, like all realists, believe that international order is inherently fragile, but who argue that the primary motivation of states is to maintain security rather than to maximize power (see Offensive or defensive realism? p. 240).

Third, a state's level of conformity to international law is a key determinant of its membership of international society (see p. 9). International law is therefore one of the chief institutions through which cultural cohesion and social integration among states are achieved, facilitating cooperation and mutual support. A record of compliance with international law can therefore enhance the standing and reputation of a state, giving it greater 'soft' power and encouraging other members of the international community to work with it rather than against it. Such considerations can influence even the most powerful of states. For example, after the 2003 invasion of Iraq by the USA and a 'coalition of the willing', which was criticized as a breach of international law by, amongst others, the then-UN Secretary-General, Kofi Annan, the USA came under considerable pressure to demonstrate conformity with international law. In order to build wider support for its 'war on terror' (see p. 230), the USA was increasingly forced to work within a framework of UN resolutions. States that routinely defy international law run the risk of isolation and may even be treated as international pariahs, sometimes paying a high price for this in diplomatic and economic terms. This applied, for instance, to Libya, which suffered decades of isolation from the international community due to its links with terrorism (see p. 291) and attempts to develop weapons of mass destruction. This isolation forced Libya, in 2003, to make a clean break with its past and acknowledge its obligations under international law.

Fourth, although international law is not routinely enforceable, there are circumstances in which obedience to international law is brought about through a fear of punishment. Punishment in these cases is not dispensed by a world police force but by states themselves, acting individually or collectively. International law, indeed, recognizes a right of reprisal or retaliation; this means that actions that would otherwise be impermissible are seen as acceptable if they occur in response to a state's violation of established norms and principles. Article 51 of the UN Charter thus stipulates that states have a right to self-defence in the event of an armed attack by another state. Israel therefore justified its June 1967 destruction of the Egyptian airforce, at the beginning of the Six-Day War, on the grounds that it was a reprisal for an attack launched by Egypt and Syria. Similarly, the 1991 Gulf War could be seen as a form of legally ordained punishment carried out against Iraq for its attempt forcibly to annex Kuwait. Indeed, one of the features of the supposed 'new world order' was the idea that in the post-Cold War world, collective security (see p. 447) would be used to punish military adventurism.

Finally, it would be a mistake to assume that international law is only respected because of considerations that, in their various ways, boil down to concerns about short- or long-term self-interest. In a large proportion of cases, international law is upheld not because of calculations related to the consequences of violating it, but because international law is considered to be rightful and morally binding (Buchanan 2007). This, after all, applies in relation to domestic law, where most citizens, most of the time, refrain from theft, physical attacks and murder not because of the existence of a criminal justice system, but because they view these acts as distasteful or immoral. The same applies to international law, especially when international law embodies norms of behaviour that enjoy widespread popular support, such as prohibitions on slavery, unprovoked attack or genocide. Liberals, who believe that human beings are rational and moral creatures, are likely to place a greater emphasis on moral motivation for state compliance with international law than do realists. However, many would agree that state behaviour in such matters is shaped by mixed motives, as practical considerations, linked to self-interest and possibly a fear of punishment, are entangled with ethical considerations of various kinds. Constructivists, for their part, highlight the extent to which both state interests and a sense of what is morally right in the international sphere are socially constructed, which means that they are shaped, in part, by international law itself.

INTERNATIONAL LAW IN FLUX

Since the early twentieth century, international law has become not only increasingly prominent, but also more politically controversial. The scope, purpose and, indeed, nature of international law has changed in a variety of ways. These include the following:

- A shift from 'international' law to 'world' or 'supranational' law
- The development of the laws of war into international humanitarian law
- The wider use of international criminal tribunals and courts.

From international law to world law?

In its classical tradition, international law has been firmly state-centric. This is the sense in which it is properly called 'international' law: it is a form of law that governs states and determines the relations amongst states, its primary purpose

INTERNATIONAL LAW

Realist view

Realists are generally sceptical about international law and its value, usually drawing a sharp distinction between domestic law and international law. While domestic law derives from the existence of a sovereign authority responsible for enacting and enforcing law, the absence of a central political authority in the international realm means that what is called 'international law' is perhaps nothing more than a collection of moral principles and ideals. As Thomas Hobbes (see p. 14), put it, 'where there is no common power, there is no law'. For Morgenthau (see p. 61), international law amounted to a form of 'primitive law', similar to the behavioural codes established in pre-modern societies. However, only ultra-realists go as far as dismissing international law altogether. Most realists accept that international law plays a key role in the international system, albeit one that is, and should be, limited. International law is limited by the fact that states, and particularly powerful states, are the primary actors on the world stage, meaning that international law largely reflects, and is circumscribed by, state interests. Realists also believe that the proper, and perhaps only legitimate, purpose of international law is to uphold the principle of state sovereignty. This makes them deeply suspicious of the trend towards 'supranational' or 'world' law, in which international law becomes entangled with the idea of global justice and is used to protect individual rights rather than states' rights.

Liberal view

Liberals have a clearly positive assessment of the role and importance of international law. This stems from the belief that human beings are imbued with rights and guided by reason. As the international sphere is a moral sphere, core ethical principles should be codified within a framework of international law. For idealists, such thinking implied that in international politics, as in domestic politics, the only solution to the disorder and chaos of anarchy is the establishment of a supreme legal authority, creating an international rule of law. This doctrine of 'peace through law' was expressed, for example, in the establishment of the League of Nations and in the 1928 Kellogg–Briand Pact which, in effect, banned war. Although modern liberals and particularly neoliberals have long since abandoned such idealism, they nevertheless continue to believe that international law plays an important and constructive role in world affairs. For them, regimes of international law reflect the common interests and common rationality that bind statesmen together. By translating agreements among states into authoritative principles and by strengthening levels of trust and mutual confidence, international law deepens interdependence (see p. 7) and promotes cooperation. The idea that there is a tendency for interdependence to be consolidated through formal rules of international behaviour is reflected in the functionalist theory of integration, as discussed in Chapter 20.

Critical views

The three main critical perspectives on international law have emerged from social constructivism, critical legal studies and postcolonialism. Although there is no developed or coherent constructivist account of the nature of international law, the assertion that political practice is crucially shaped by norms and perceptions emphasizes the extent to which norms embodied in international law structure the identities of states as well as the interests they pursue. This helps to explain why and how state behaviour changes over time, as, for instance, once-accepted practices such as slavery, the use of foreign mercenaries and the ill-treatment of prisoners of war become less common. Influenced by poststructuralist analysis, critical legal studies highlight the inherently indeterminate nature of international law, based on the fact that legal language is capable of multiple and competing meanings. Such insights have, for instance, been used by feminists to suggest that international law embodies patriarchal biases, either because the legal 'person' (whether the individual or the state) is constructed on the basis of masculine norms, or because international law perpetuates the image of women as victims. Postcolonialists, for their part, have viewed international law as an expression, in various ways, of western global dominance (Grovogui 1996; Antony 2005). From this perspective, international law developed out of Christian and Eurocentric thinking about the nature of legal and political order, is tainted by the inheritance of colonialism and possibly racism, and operates through institutions, such as the International Court of Justice, that are wedded to the interests of the industrialized West.

being to facilitate international order. In this view, state sovereignty is the foundational principle of international law. States thus relate to one another legally in a purely *horizontal* sense, recognizing the principle of **sovereign equality**. Not only is there no world government, international community or public interest that can impose its higher authority on the state-system, but legal obligations, determined by treaties and conventions, are entirely an expression of the will of states.

This classical view can be broken down into four features. First, states are the primary *subjects* of international law. Indeed, in this view, the state is a meta-juridical fact: international law merely recognizes the consequence of the establishment of states; it is not able to constitute states in the first place. The 1933 Montevideo Convention on the Rights and Duties of States therefore acknowledged that a state should be admitted into the international legal community so long as it fulfils three criteria: it possesses a stable government, controls a definite territory and enjoys the acquiescence of the population. Second, states are the primary *agents* of international law. In other words, they are the only actors empowered to formulate, enact and enforce international law. Third, the *purpose* of international law is to regulate inter-state relations, which means, in practice, upholding the cardinal principle of sovereignty. Sovereignty not only defines the terms of legitimate statehood, but it also implies the norms of **self-determination** and **non-intervention**. Finally, the *scope* of international law should be strictly confined to issues of order, rather than issues of justice. International law therefore exists to maintain peace and stability, and it should not be used for wider purposes. If humanitarian issues or questions of distributive, environmental or gender justice are to be incorporated into the framework of law, this should happen only at the domestic level, where states, as sovereign entities, are able to address moral concerns in the light of the distinctive values, culture and traditions of their own society. This classical view of international law is exemplified by the role and powers of the International Court of Justice.

However, the classical conception of international law has increasingly been challenged by attempts to use international law to found a world constitutional order, a process described by Habermas (2006) as the 'constitutionalization of international law'. This 'constitutionalist' conception of international law has become, over time, the dominant mainstream approach to international **jurisprudence**. It is constitutional, in the sense that it aims to enmesh states within a framework of rules and norms that have a higher and binding authority, in the manner of a **constitution**. This establishes a *horizontal* relationship between states and international law, transforming international law into what is sometimes called 'supranational' law or 'world' law (Corbett 1956). Stemming probably from the impact of WWI on western consciousness, this trend has been closely related to the emergence of a system of global governance (see p. 462) and is evident in four main developments.

First, individuals, groups and private organizations have increasingly been recognized as *subjects* of international law. States, in other words, are no longer the only legal 'persons'. This has been particularly evident in the focus within modern international law on individual rights, giving rise to an ever-expanding body of international human rights law and a substantial broadening of the 'laws of war', as considered in the next section. Second, non-state actors have become important *agents* of international law, in the sense that civil society organizations,

● **Sovereign equality**: The principle that, regardless of other differences, states are equal in the rights, entitlements and protections they enjoy under international law.

● **Self-determination**: The principle that the state should be a self-governing entity, enjoying sovereign independence and autonomy within the international system.

● **Non-intervention**: The principle that states should not interfere in the internal affairs of other states.

● **Jurisprudence**: The science or philosophy of law, or a system or body of law.

● **Constitution**: A set of rules, written or unwritten, that define the duties, powers and functions of the various institutions of government, define the relations between them and also the relations between the state and the individual.

INTERNATIONAL COURT OF JUSTICE

Type: International court • **Established:** 1945 • **Location:** The Hague, Netherlands

The International Court of Justice (commonly referred to as the World Court or the ICJ) is the principal judicial organ of the United Nations. It was established in June 1945 by the Charter of the UN and began work in April 1946. The role of the ICJ is to settle, in accordance with international law, legal disputes submitted to it by states and to give advisory opinions on legal questions referred to it by authorized UN organs and specialized agencies. The ICJ is composed of 15 judges elected to nine-year terms of office by the UN General Assembly and the Security Council voting separately. One-third of the Court is elected every three years. Permanent members of the Security Council always have a sitting judge, but if a state appearing before the Court does not have a judge of its own on the Court, it may appoint an *ad hoc* judge. A President (since 2009, Hisashi Owada (Japan)) and a Vice-President are elected by the members of the Court every three years by secret ballot. The President presides at all meetings of the Court, directs its work and the work of its various committees, and has a casting vote in the event of votes being equally divided.

Significance: The ICJ is the most far-reaching attempt to date to apply the rule of law to international disputes. The Court, indeed, has had many successes in laying down principles by which disputes may be judged. It has, for example, drawn

baselines concerning issues such as territorial waters, fishing rights and methods of calculating the continental shelf beneath the sea. The Court has also had a number of notable successes in settling international disputes, including the border dispute between El Salvador and Honduras, which led to the 'soccer war' of 1969, and the violent dispute between Cameroon and Nigeria over the ownership of an oil-rich peninsula, which was settled in 2002. In addition, the Court has handed down a number of 'advisory opinions', which have helped set the tone for post-conflict international affairs. These include the decision in 1971 to declare that South Africa's presence in Namibia was illegal, which helped to prepare the ground for South Africa's eventual acceptance of Namibian independence in 1989.

However, the ICJ has a number of significant weaknesses. In the first place, the jurisdiction of the Court is strictly limited to states. Individuals, corporations, NGOs and other non-state bodies are excluded from direct participation in cases. This prevents the Court from taking action over a wide range of human rights and humanitarian issues, meaning that other tribunals and courts (such as the international criminal tribunals for Rwanda and former Yugoslavia, and the International Criminal Court) have had to be established, with the ICJ not being able to establish umbrella responsibility for these

thematic courts. Second, the greatest weakness of the ICJ is that it lacks compulsory jurisdiction and has no mechanism for enforcing its judgements. States that have signed the treaty creating the ICJ are allowed to choose whether they want to be subject to the compulsory jurisdiction of the Court by signing the optional clause (the clause that gives countries the option of agreeing or not agreeing in advance to be bound by the decisions of the Court), and only about one-third of states have agreed to do so. Moreover, states are able to revoke their commitments under the optional clause, as the USA did in 1984 when Nicaragua asked the ICJ to determine whether the mining of Nicaraguan harbours by the CIA constituted a violation of international law. In theory, the Court can appeal to the Security Council to enforce its judgements; however, this has never happened. Finally, the Court, especially in its early days, was widely criticized by developing countries for operating in the interests of western states and interests, in part because of their preponderant representation on the Security Council, and therefore on the Court itself. Nevertheless, this criticism has been advanced less frequently since the end of the Cold War, as the number of cases brought before the ICJ annually has more than doubled, with the parties appearing before the Court also becoming more diverse.

and particularly NGOs (see p. 10), have increasingly helped to shape, and even to draft, international treaties and conventions. The Rome Statute, which led to the establishment of the International Criminal Court (ICC) in 2002, was thus largely drafted by a collection of NGOs (see p. 158). Third, the *purpose* of international law has widened substantially beyond attempts to manage inter-state relations, particularly as it has been drawn into regulating the behaviour of states with their own territories. For instance, the World Trade Organization, the foremost legal body in the area of international trade, has substantial powers to order states to dismantle tariff and non-tariff barriers in the process of resolving trade disputes. Finally, the *scope* of international law has come to extend well beyond the maintenance of international order and now includes the maintenance of at least minimum standards of global justice. This is evident not only in attempts to establish international standards in areas such as women's rights, environmental protection and the treatment of refugees, but also moves to enforce international criminal law through the use of *ad hoc* international tribunals and the International Criminal Court.

The existence of rival conceptions of international law has nevertheless thrown up disagreements, tensions and confusions. These disagreements are largely between realists, on the one hand, and liberals and cosmopolitans, on the other. For realists, any attempt to construct a world constitutional order, based on 'world' law, threatens to weaken sovereignty and put international order at risk (Rabkin 2005). In this view, once international law ceases to be rooted in a commitment to state sovereignty, it ceases to be legitimate. Liberals and cosmopolitans, for their part, have always had concerns about untrammelled state sovereignty, and have often been eager to use international law to give global politics an ethical dimension (Brown 2008). The tensions and confusion have resulted from the fact that 'world' law, if it exists at all, incorporates and extends 'international' law; it has not replaced it. International law thus continues to acknowledge the cornerstone importance of state sovereignty, while, at the same time, embracing the doctrine of human rights and the need for humanitarian standard-setting. In that sense, the 'international' conception continues to enjoy political ascendancy over the 'world' conception. The future development of international law is nevertheless bound to be shaped by how, and how successfully, the tensions between these opposing norms and principles can be managed.

This can be illustrated by the contentious issue of the legality of humanitarian intervention (see p. 326). The international law dealing with humanitarian intervention has evolved significantly since the early 1990s, but a consensus has yet to emerge on what these laws mean. On the face of it, intervention, for whatever purpose, is usually judged to be a violation of international law. For example, Article 2 of the UN Charter states that, 'All Members shall refrain in their international relations from the threat or use of force against the territorial integrity or political independence of any state, or any other manner inconsistent with the Purposes of the United Nations'. Article 7 states that, 'Nothing contained in the present Charter shall authorize the United Nations to intervene in matters which are essentially within the domestic jurisdiction of any state'. The General Assembly Resolution 2131, adopted in 1965, expresses this even more clearly: 'no State has the right to intervene, directly or indirectly, for any reason whatsoever, in the internal or external affairs of another State.' However, at the same time, a variety of legal instruments have also come into existence that affirm the protection of civil, political, social and economic rights, which, at minimum, call the principle of sovereignty, and therefore the norm of non-intervention, into question. These include the Genocide Convention and the two UN Covenants on Human Rights, drafted in 1966. Although there exists no clearly defined and legally binding treaty justifying humanitarian intervention, it may nevertheless be understood as a form of customary international law.

Such confusions were evident in relation to the 1999 Kosovo intervention. In this case, once it became apparent that the UN Security Council would not authorize military action against Serb forces, the USA and its allies turned to NATO (see p. 259) as a regional organization through which they could undertake such action. The then-UN Secretary-General, Kofi Annan, recognized that the intervention was clearly not legal, but nevertheless suggested that it was morally justified. This led him to suggest that the principle of state sovereignty should be revised to mean 'responsible sovereignty', in which a state's entitlement to sovereign jurisdiction is conditional on carrying out its responsibility to protect its own citizens. As discussed in Chapter 13, the idea of a 'responsibility to protect', or R2P, has been widely used by those who wish to provide a legal basis for humanitarian intervention. However, such thinking is by no means universally accepted, humanitarian intervention seeming destined to continue to have an uncertain status in international law, hovering somewhere between its broad but perhaps ill-defined acceptance in customary international law and its clear prohibition in treaty-based law.

Developments in the laws of war

One of the clearest examples of the shift from 'international' law to 'world' law has been the evolution of the laws of war into a body of international humanitarian law. The advent of industrialized warfare, and the experience of the two world wars of the twentieth century, altered thinking about both aspects of just war theory: the idea of *jus ad bellum*, or a just recourse to war, and the idea of *jus in bello*, or the just conduct of war. In the case of the former, there was a backlash against the belief that had become established during the nineteenth century that a state's right to wage war is a fundamental sovereign right. In this view, sovereignty stemmed primarily from the *ability* of a state to establish control over a territory and its people, meaning that claims to rightful authority could result from conquest and expansion. The consequences of such thinking were evident in the European imperialism of the late nineteenth century that provided the backdrop for WWI, and in German, Italian and Japanese expansionism in the run-up to WWII. In effect, might was right. However, the 1945 UN Charter significantly narrowed the scope of legally justified warfare. It laid down only two circumstances in which force could be legitimately used: self-defence, in which states have an unqualified sovereign right to use force if subjected to a physical attack by another state (Article 51), and when the use of force has been sanctioned by the Security Council as part of a peace enforcement action (Article 42). The Nuremberg Principles extended such thinking into international criminal law by establishing the idea of 'crimes against peace', allowing individuals to be prosecuted for 'planning, preparing, initiating or waging a war of aggression, or conspiring to do so'.

In the case of just war thinking related to the conduct of war, rather than the justifications for war, the principal development has been the idea of **war crimes**. There is nothing new about war crimes prosecutions, however. Examples of legal proceedings that stem from misconduct or abuses that occur during war can be traced back to Ancient Greece. The trial of Peter von Hagenbach in 1474 is sometimes thought of as the first war crimes trial. Hagenbach was convicted and beheaded on the authority of an *ad hoc* tribunal of the Holy Roman Empire, having been accused of carrying out wartime atrocities committed in Austria. Modern thinking about war crimes nevertheless stems from the Hague Peace Conferences of 1899 and 1907, which established a permanent court of arbitration for states in dispute wishing to use its services, and also formulated a series of conventions designed to limit the horrors of war. Creating the basis for the modern laws of war, the Hague Conventions prohibited, among other things, the launching of projectiles and explosives from balloons and the use of 'dum dum', or explosive, bullets, and set out rules related to the treatment of prisoners of war and the rights of neutral powers. The war crimes that were recognized by the Nuremberg Principles included the murder or ill-treatment of civilian populations, hostages and prisoners of war. The four Geneva Conventions, adopted in 1949, with two additional protocols in 1977 and a third in 2005, marked the widest and most detailed attempt to codify war crimes, providing one of the foundations for international humanitarian law. Amongst the war crimes they identified are the following:

- Wilful killing
- Torture or inhuman treatment, including biological experiments
- Wilfully causing great suffering or serious injury to body or health
- Compelling civilians or prisoners of war to serve a hostile power
- Wilfully depriving civilians or prisoners of war of a fair trial
- The taking of hostages
- Unlawful deportation, transfer of confinement
- Wanton destruction and appropriation of property not justified by military necessity.

One of the most significant, if controversial, developments in the laws of war is the development of the idea of **'crimes against humanity'**. The earliest notion of a crime against humanity (even though the terminology was not used) surfaced during the campaign to abolish the slave trade. The 1815 Declaration on the Abolition of the Slave Trade, for instance, condemned the slave trade for offending against the 'principles of humanity and universal morality'. The idea that such actions might be considered crimes first emerged in response to what later became known as the 'Armenian genocide', a series of massacres carried out against Armenians, Greeks and Assyrians living in the Ottoman Empire, which peaked between 1915 and 1917. The Triple Entente, an alliance of Russia, France and the UK, declared that the massacres amounted to 'crimes against humanity and civilization'. The 1945 Nuremberg Charter nevertheless took the matter further by drawing a formal distinction between war crimes and crimes against humanity, which has guided international jurisprudence ever since. Whereas war crimes are 'violations of the laws and customs of war', crimes against humanity have the following three characteristics:

● **War crime**: A violation of the laws or customs of war, for which individuals can be held to be criminally responsible.

● **Crimes against humanity**: Intentionally committed acts that form part of a widespread, systematic and repeated attack against a civilian population.

- The crimes must target civilians
- They must be widespread or systematic, and repeated
- They must be intentionally committed.

The most detailed and ambitious attempt to codify the crimes that can be categorized as crimes against humanity is found in the 1998 Rome Statute, which established the International Criminal Court. This highlights crimes including murder, extermination, enslavement, deportation, torture, rape or sexual slavery, racial and other forms of persecution, and the crime of apartheid. Although genocide is clearly a crime against humanity in a general sense, it is treated as a separate category of crime, indeed as the 'crime of crimes', by the Genocide Convention and in the Rome Statute. The virtue of incorporating the concepts of crimes against humanity and genocide into international law is that they attempt to deal with the issue of widespread atrocities by establishing individual responsibility for actions that may not conform to the conventional notion of a war crime. The concept of crimes against humanity in particular is underpinned by a form of moral cosmopolitanism (see p. 21) that holds that the proper stance towards humanity is one of respect, protection and succour, humanity being morally indivisible. Critics of the concept have nevertheless questioned whether such a broad category of crime can ever be meaningful, and have also raised doubts about the supposedly universal moral principles on which it is based. These and other concerns about international humanitarian law have become more acute as a result of steps to anchor individual responsibility for war crimes, crimes against humanity and genocide through the establishment of international criminal tribunals and the International Criminal Court.

International tribunals and the International Criminal Court

After the Nuremberg and Tokyo trials, superpower disagreement precluded the use of international criminal tribunals for the remainder of the Cold War. Such prosecutions as took place occurred in national courts. For instance, in 1971 Lieutenant William Calley was convicted and sentenced to life imprisonment by a US court for ordering the My Lai massacre in 1968, during the Vietnam War. Calley served less than four years before his release in 1974 on the orders of President Nixon. However, the end of the Cold War and the breaking of the logjam in the UN Security Council created circumstances in which international tribunals could once again be established. Reports of massacres and ethnic cleansing in the former Yugoslavia led, in 1993, to the creation of the International Criminal Tribunal for the former Yugoslavia (ICTY), located in The Hague, the Netherlands, the first genuinely international tribunal convened since Nuremberg and Tokyo. The ICTY was also the first tribunal to invoke the Genocide Convention. The Tribunal was mandated to prosecute crimes against humanity, violations of the laws of war, and genocide committed in the various Yugoslav wars. The most prominent figure indicted by the ICTY was Slobodan Miloševic, the former head of state of the Federal Republic of Yugoslavia and the first head of state to be prosecuted under international humanitarian law. He was arrested in 2001, and his trial on 66 counts of genocide, crimes against humanity and war crimes began the following year. However, the proceedings were cut short by Milošević's death in 2006. By November 2012, 161 people had been tried and convicted by the ICTY, receiving sentences of up to life imprisonment. The Tribunal aimed to complete all trials during 2013, although an exception was made for Radovan Karadžic, the former Bosnian Serb politician, Ratko Mladić and Goran Hadžić, whose arrests occurred much later than the other accused.

The UN authorized a second international tribunal following the 1994 genocide in Rwanda, which had led to the murder of about 800,000 Rwandan Tutsis and moderate Hutus. The new tribunal, the International Criminal Tribunal for Rwanda (ICTR), was located in Arusha, Tanzania, and held its first trial in 1997. By November 2012, 54 trial judgements had been delivered against 74 accused. In the most significant of these trials, Jean Kambanda, the former prime minister of Rwanda, became the first, and so far the only, head of government to plead guilty to genocide, when he was convicted in 1998 and sentenced to life imprisonment. In 2002, the Special Court for Sierra Leone was set up jointly by the UN and the government of Sierra Leone, to consider serious violations of international humanitarian law that had occurred during Sierra Leone's ten-year civil war. This involved the prosecution and conviction of the former president of Liberia, Charles Taylor, for war crimes (see p. 354). In 2003, the UN reached an agreement with the Cambodian government to bring to trial the surviving leaders of the Khmer Rouge, who had presided over the deaths of over 1 million people in Cambodia during a four-year rule of terror in the late 1970s.

In other cases, criminal tribunals have been set up at a national level. These have included the East Timor Tribunal, established in 2002 to investigate human rights violations carried out during the period of Indonesian occupation and control, and the war crimes tribunal in Iraq, which in 2006 found Saddam Hussein guilty of the 1982 massacre that took place in Dujail, north of Baghdad, and sentenced him to death. In the case of General Augusto Pinochet, he was indicted in 1998 by a court in Spain for human rights violations committed while he was the dictator of Chile, 1973–90. However, although he was arrested in London on an international arrest warrant, he was released in 2000 on the grounds that he was too ill to face trial and was allowed to return to Chile, where he enjoyed immunity from prosecution as part of the agreement under which he had left office.

These various tribunals and courts, and especially those set up to examine atrocities committed in former Yugoslavia and Rwanda, influenced the development of international criminal law in a number of important ways. In the first place, they re-focused attention on large-scale human rights violations, particularly through high-profile trials of senior political figures. Apart from anything else, this strengthened the idea that establishing personal culpability for war crimes, crimes against humanity or genocide may reduce the incidence of mass atrocities, as leaders recognize they are no longer able to act as if they are above international law. Second, whereas previous war crimes trials had been concerned with acts that took place in the context of inter-state war, the ICTY and the ICTR recognized that crimes against humanity may take place during an internal armed conflict or even during periods of peace, thereby expanding the remit of international humanitarian law. Third, the tribunals nevertheless

Charles Taylor's conviction for war crimes

Events: In April 2012, Charles Taylor, the former president of Liberia, was convicted on 11 charges of war crimes and crimes against humanity by the Special Court for Sierra Leone. The following month, he was sentenced to fifty years in jail. Taylor had been president of Liberia from 1997 until 2003, when he went into exile in Nigeria. However, his crimes relate to the part he played in the bloody civil war in neighbouring Sierra Leone, 1991–2002. Although the Court rejected the claim that Taylor had ordered atrocities, it found that he had given 'sustained and significant support' to the rebel Revolutionary United Front (RUF), which had committed serious violations of international humanitarian law. These included the crimes against humanity of murder, rape, sexual slavery, enslavement and other inhumane acts, as well as the war crimes of murdering civilians, hacking off civilians' limbs with machetes, and conscripting (and drugging) child soldiers. In return for assisting the RUF, Taylor had received a steady stream of what became known as 'blood diamonds'.

Significance: As he was the first head of state to be convicted of war crimes since the Nuremberg trials after WWII, the verdict against Charles Taylor was historic. However, it was also part of a larger trend favouring the prosecution of political leaders for crimes committed while they were in power. Between 1990 and 2009, some 65 former heads of state or government were prosecuted for serious human rights or financial crimes, high-profile examples including Augusto Pinochet (Chile), Alberto Fujimori (Peru), Slobodan Milošević (former Yugoslavia) and Saddam Hussein (Iraq). The conviction of Taylor thereby highlighted a major development in the enforcement of international humanitarian law. The key justification for Taylor's prosecution, as well as the larger trend, is that they serve as a warning to despots and dictators across the globe. By demonstrating that political leaders

are not above the law, such examples are intended to deter those currently in office from engaging in war crimes and crimes against humanity. Enforcing the rule of humanitarian law in such a public way should therefore reduce the number and severity of atrocities carried out worldwide. International courts and tribunals may thus prevent tyranny and abuse in circumstances where institutional checks and balances and forms of public accountability do not operate.

Such developments have, nevertheless, also been criticized. For one thing, there is the danger that if the rationale for such prosecutions is to 'make an example' of prominent figures, less prominent, but, perhaps, equally culpable figures may receive less attention. In the case of the civil war in Sierra Leone, some have suggested that Foday Sankoh, the RUF leader (who died in 2003, while awaiting trial), was significantly more culpable for the atrocities than was Charles Taylor. Furthermore, Taylor's prosecution has been seen as an form of neo-colonialism, an accusation that has also been levelled at international criminal tribunals and courts generally, and especially the International Criminal Court (ICC). Not only has international humanitarian law been viewed as culturally biased because it is founded on western, liberal values (notably about human rights), but international criminal tribunals and courts may also perpetuate the belief that the western world still needs to intervene to 'save' the developing world from chaos and barbarity (up to 2013, all those prosecuted by the ICC had been Africans). Finally, prosecuting heads of government or state for human rights violations may place an undue emphasis on individual culpability and the role of political leadership, ignoring other, maybe deeper, explanations. For example, the origins of the Sierra Leone civil war include widespread corruption and mismanagement, the spread of routine violence and the collapse of the educational system, which date back at least to the 1960s and may have their roots in the colonial period, to say nothing of the 'resource curse' of diamonds (see p. 416).

highlighted the enormous cost, and often inefficiency, of dealing with crimes against international humanitarian law through the mechanism of *ad hoc* UN-backed tribunals. For instance, it took over two years to begin trying cases in the ICTY and the ICTR, and many trials lasted for months and, in some cases, years. During 2000, these tribunals accounted for over 10 per cent of the UN's regular budget, with their total cost by 2009 being estimated at $1.6 billion. Such concerns led to pressure for the replacement of *ad hoc* tribunals by a permanent institution with global jurisdiction, in the form of the International Criminal Court (ICC).

In 1998, delegates from 160 countries, 33 international organizations and a coalition of NGOs met in Rome to draft the Statute of the ICC. The Rome Statute established the ICC as a 'court of last resort', exercising jurisdiction only when national courts are unwilling or unable to investigate or prosecute. The ICC, which came into being in 2002, has broad-ranging powers to prosecute acts of genocide, crimes against humanity, war crimes and, potentially, aggression (a decision on crimes of aggression was reserved to a later date, but its inclusion is now highly unlikely). Although the ICC, like the ICJ, is located in The Hague, the Netherlands, it is an independent international organization and not part of the UN system. However, the ICC's relationship with the UN Security Council has been particularly significant and controversial. The USA, an early and enthusiastic supporter of the idea of an international criminal court, had proposed that the Security Council act as the court's gatekeeper, reflecting the Security Council's primary responsibility for the maintenance of international peace and security. But this proposal was rejected at Rome, on the grounds that it would have given the USA and other permanent members of the Security Council (the P-5) the ability to prevent the ICC from hearing cases in which their citizens were accused of human rights violations by using their veto powers. Instead, under the so-called 'Singapore compromise', the Rome conference allowed the Security Council to delay a prosecution for twelve months if it believed that the ICC would interfere with the Council's efforts to further international peace and security. However, as the Security Council must do this by passing a resolution requesting the Court not to proceed, this effectively prevents any P-5 country from blocking an investigation simply by exercising its veto.

The controversial nature of the ICC was apparent from the outset. Although 120 states voted in favour of the Rome Statute, 21 abstained, including India and a range of Arab and Caribbean states, and 7 voted against. It is widely believed that the states which voted against the Statute were the USA, China (see p. 238), Israel, Libya, Iraq, Qatar and Yemen (although the states were not formally identified). As of February 2013, 122 countries were members of the Court and a further 31 countries have signed but not ratified the Rome Statute. Non-member states include China, India, Russia and the USA, which significantly reduces the scope of the ICC's jurisdiction and threatens its international credibility, perhaps in a way that is reminiscent of the League of Nations. Only two permanent members of the P-5 – the UK and France, its least powerful members – have ratified the Rome Statute. Not one of the nuclear powers outside Europe has ratified the treaty, meaning that the ICC is dominated by European, Latin-American and African states. The opposition of the USA to the ICC has been particularly damaging. President Clinton signed the Rome Statute on his final day in office in 2000, but stated that, as the treaty was fundamentally flawed, it would not be

Debating...
Is the International Criminal Court an effective means of upholding order and justice?

The ICC has proved to be a highly controversial international organization. While it has been hailed by some as an essential guarantee for justice and human rights, others view it as a deeply flawed body, even, sometimes, as a threat to international order and peace.

YES

Strengthening international humanitarian law. The ICC has codified norms and principles of international humanitarian law that have been widely accepted since the Nuremberg and Tokyo trials, in the process providing the most authoritative and detailed definitions of genocide, crimes against humanity and war crimes currently available. By comparison with the system of *ad hoc* tribunals, the ICC brings a much needed coherence to the process of enforcement, and also, by keeping Security Council interference to a minimum, (potentially) prevents the P-5 from exempting themselves from their responsibilities.

Tackling the global justice gap. The global justice gap condemns millions of people to abuse and oppression either because of the repressive policies of their own governments, or because of their government's unwillingness or inability to prevent gross human rights violations. The ICC has been designed specifically to address this problem, providing the basis for external intervention when internal remedies are unavailable. This task is nevertheless being put in jeopardy by a collection of powerful countries that are unwilling fully to sign up to the ICC, either because they want to protect their own military freedom of manoeuvre, or in order to shield allies from criticism. This amounts to a serious failure of global leadership.

Deterring future atrocities. The aim of the ICC is not merely to prosecute crimes that have been committed since its inception in 2002, but also to shape the future behaviour of political and military leaders throughout the world. In this view, atrocities occur, in part, because leaders believe that their actions will go unpunished. The significance of the trials of heads of government is that they demonstrate that this may not be the case in future. No leader is now above international humanitarian law. The fear of possible legal proceedings by the ICC may, indeed, have been instrumental in persuading leaders of the Lord's Resistance Army in Uganda to attend peace talks in 2007.

NO

Threat to sovereignty and national security. The most common criticism of the Court is that it is a recipe for intrusions into the affairs of sovereign states. The ICC threatens state sovereignty because its jurisdiction extends, potentially, to citizens of states that have not ratified the Rome Statute. This happens if their alleged crime was committed in a state that has accepted the jurisdiction of the Court, or when a situation has been referred to the ICC by the UN Security Council. This issue is of particular concern in the USA, because, as the world's sole remaining superpower, the USA deploys its military to 'hot spots' more often than other countries.

Unhelpful obsession with individual culpability. By highlighting the criminal responsibilities of individuals rather than states, the ICC contributes to a worrying trend to use international law to further moral campaigns of various kinds. Not only are questions of personal culpability for humanitarian crimes highly complex but, once international law is used as a vehicle for advancing global justice, its parameters become potentially unlimited. Moreover, by prioritizing individual culpability and criminal prosecution over wider concerns, the ICC may damage the prospects of peace and political settlement, as, arguably, occurred over the indictment of President Bashir of Sudan.

A political tool of the West. The ICC has been criticized for having a western or Eurocentric bias. In the first place, it is based on western values and legal traditions that are grounded in ideas of human rights, which are rejected in parts of Asia and the Muslim world, thus demonstrating the absence of a global moral consensus. Second, the ICC is sometimes seen to be disproportionately influenced by EU member states, all of whom have ratified the Rome Statute. Third, the cases brought before the ICC overwhelmingly relate to events that have occurred in the developing world. The ICC is therefore seen to perpetuate an image of poor countries as chaotic and barbaric.

forwarded to the US Senate for ratification. The Bush administration effectively 'unsigned' the treaty in 2002, and took concerted steps to reduce the USA's exposure to ICC jurisdiction. It did this by negotiating bilateral immunity agreements (BIAs), sometimes called 'Article 98' agreements, with as many countries as possible, under which neither party would transfer citizens of the other country to the jurisdiction of the ICC. Over 100 BIAs have been negotiated, even though their legal status is unclear. The Obama administration's shift towards multilateralism has certainly modified the Bush administration's implacable hostility towards the ICC, but this has yet to produce a clear commitment to 're-sign' the Rome Statute and press ahead with ratification. Nevertheless, opinion is divided on the extent to which the reservations expressed by the USA and other states about the ICC have been based on pragmatism and self-interest, and the extent to which they have been based on principle.

SUMMARY

- International law is law that governs states and other international actors, although it is widely considered to be 'soft' law, because it cannot, in most circumstances, be enforced. The two most important sources of international law are treaties and international custom. In the former, legal obligations are clearly rooted in consent, while in the latter obligations arise from long-established practices and moral norms.

- International law is largely obeyed because states calculate that, in the long run, abiding by laws will bring them benefit or reduce harm. Other reasons for obedience include a fear of disorder, a fear of isolation, a fear, in some cases, of punishment and the wider belief that international law is rightful and morally binding.

- In its classical tradition, international law has been firmly state-centric, being based on the cornerstone principle of state sovereignty However, this conception has increasingly been challenged by a 'constitutionalist' conception of international law, sometimes called 'supranational' law or 'world' law, the scope of which includes the maintenance of at least minimum standards of global justice.

- One of the clearest examples of the shift from 'international' law to 'world' law has been the evolution of the laws of war into a body of international humanitarian law. This has largely happened through the development of the idea of war crimes, which allows individuals to be held to be criminally responsible for violations of the customs of war, and through the notion of crimes against humanity.

- The end of the Cold War allowed international humanitarian law to be implemented more widely through international tribunals and courts. This happened through ad hoc tribunals set up to examine reports of atrocities carried out in former Yugoslavia and Rwanda in particular, but the most significant development was the establishment of the International Criminal Court, which came into operation in 2002. However, the Court has sometimes been seen as a threat to international order and peace.

Questions for discussion

- Is international law really law?
- How and why have treaties become the most important source of international law?
- Why is it in the interest of states to obey international law?
- How strong is the moral motivation for states' compliance with international law?
- What are the implications of the 'constitutionalist' conception of international law for international jurisprudence?
- To what extent are 'international' and 'world' law compatible?
- Is humanitarian intervention justifiable in international law?
- Is a state's right to sovereignty conditional, and if so, on what?
- Is the notion of crimes against humanity too vague and confused to be legally meaningful?
- Should political leaders be held individually culpable for breaching international humanitarian law?

Further reading

Byers, M. (ed.), *The Role of Law in International Politics: Essays in International Relations and International Law* (2000). An excellent collection of essays that explore the political implications of international law in an age of globalization.

Gray, C., *International Law and the Use of Force* (2008). A useful discussion of the implications of the use of force for international law, carried out either by states or by UN or other peacekeepers.

Hehir, A., N. Kuhrt and A. Mumford (eds), *International Law, Security and Ethics* (2013). An examination of how debates about nature and utility of international law have developed since 9/11.

Koskenniemi, M., *From Apology to Utopia: The Structure of International Legal Argument* (2006). A key work outlining a critical approach to international law as argumentative practice aimed at 'depoliticizing' international relations.

ONLINE RESOURCES AVAILABLE

Links to relevant web resources can be found on the *Global Politics* website

CHAPTER 15

Poverty and Development

'Poverty is the worst form of violence.'
MOHANDAS KARAMCHAND GANDHI (1869–1948)

PREVIEW

The issues of development and poverty reduction have become increasingly prominent since the end of WWII. In the early phase, this occurred as decolonization
failed to bring about economic and social progress in what was then portrayed as
the Third World, at the same time that industrially advanced western countries
were experiencing historically unprecedented levels of economic growth. As global
economic disparities widened, some argued that colonialism had given way to 'neo-
colonialism', political domination having been replaced by more subtle but no less
effective economic domination. Others heralded the emergence of a 'North–South
divide'. In this context, bodies as different as the World Bank and the IMF, on the
one hand, and a host of development NGOs and activist groups on the other, came
to view the task of reducing the gap between rich countries and poor countries as a
moral imperative. However, poverty and development are complex and deeply
controversial issues. Is poverty merely an economic phenomenon, a lack of money,
or is it something broader and more profound? Does 'development' imply that poor
societies should be remodelled on the basis of the rich societies of the so-called
'developed West'? A further range of issues address the nature, extent and causes of
global inequality. Is the world becoming a more, or less, equal place, and, in particular, what impact has globalization had on global patterns of poverty and inequality?
Finally, there have been passionate debates about the surest way of bringing about
development. These debates have focused, in particular, on the merits or otherwise
of the market-orientated approaches to development that have dominated especially since the early 1980s. Have bodies such as the World Bank and the IMF failed
the world's poor? Do rich countries have a moral obligation to help poor countries?
If so, how should that obligation be discharged: by providing international aid,
cancelling debt, changing trading practices or whatever?

KEY ISSUES

- What is poverty?
- How should 'development' be understood?
- What are the key trends in global poverty and inequality?
- Has globalization increased, or decreased, global poverty?
- How successful have official development policies been?
- Do international aid and debt relief work?

UNDERSTANDING POVERTY AND DEVELOPMENT

Poverty has been the normal state of affairs for most of world history. Even in well-organized societies with advanced systems of rule (ancient China and Rome, the Incas and so on), economies were technologically simple with modest productivity levels and populations were overwhelmingly poor. Even most of those who were thought of as rich in their day would be poor by modern standards. Poverty, thus, is not the exception; it has been the rule. The exception, from this perspective, is the wealth currently enjoyed in the modern West (see p. 26), and even this has occurred only fairly recently. It was only in the late eighteenth century that European and North American societies started to increase productivity in ways that defied the predictions of Thomas Malthus (see p. 415), who had warned that any improvement in productivity would simply be nullified by demographic growth. How did western societies avoid this Malthusian trap? The answer to this question is '**development**'. Development was certainly associated with a series of innovations in technology and organization that led to the industrial revolution. Nevertheless, there is significant debate about precisely how the affluence of the developed West has been brought about, and, most particularly, about how affluence and development can best be replicated in parts of the non-western world. Before the complex and contested issue of development is considered, however, it is necessary to look more closely at what poverty is and how it can be measured.

Defining and measuring poverty

What is poverty? What distinguishes 'the poor' from 'the rich'? If poverty reduction is a goal of national, regional or global policy, it is necessary to understand what poverty is, and how it can be measured. However, poverty is a complex and contested concept. On the face of it, poverty means being deprived of the necessities of life; that is, lacking sufficient food, fuel, shelter and clothing to maintain 'physical efficiency'. In its original sense, this was seen as an *absolute* standard, below which human existence became difficult to sustain. This means, for instance, that adult males must eat about 2,000–2,500 calories a day simply in order to maintain body weight. According to this view, poverty hardly exists in developing industrialized states like the USA, Canada, the UK and Australia; even the poor in such countries live better than much of the world's population. **Absolute poverty** is founded on the idea of 'basic needs', corresponding to physiological needs in Maslow's (1943) 'hierarchy of needs' (see Figure 15.1).

However, the idea of absolute poverty may miss an important dimension of poverty. People may feel that they are poor not because they suffer from material hardship and their basic needs are not met, but because they lack what others have got. They feel deprived in terms of the standards, conditions and pleasures enjoyed by the majority in their society. In this sense, poverty is a social, and not merely physiological, phenomenon: it is based on people's *relative* position in the social order. **Relative poverty** defines the poor as the 'less well-off' rather than the 'needy'. For instance, the Organisation for Economic Co-operation and Development (OECD) and the European Union (EU) both use a 'poverty line'

● **Development**: Growth, the act of improving, enlarging or refining; development is commonly linked to economic growth, but the term is deeply contested.

● **Absolute poverty**: A standard of poverty that is based on an income level or access to resources, especially food, clothing and shelter, which are insufficient to 'keep body and soul together'.

● **Relative poverty**: A standard of poverty in which people are deprived of the living conditions and amenities which are customary in the society to which they belong.

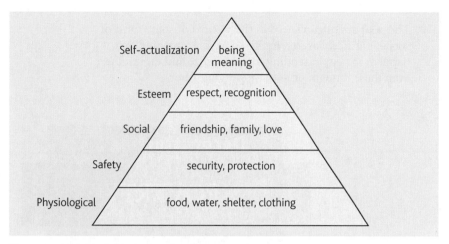

Figure 15.1 Maslow's hierarchy of needs

that is based on a relative poverty threshold, which is set at an income level that is 50 per cent or less than that of the median household. In other words, people are considered to be 'poor' if their available income is substantially lower than that of a typical person in their country of residence. The concept of relative poverty nevertheless raises important political questions because it establishes a link between poverty and inequality, and in so doing suggests that reducing or eradicating poverty can only be achieved through the redistribution of wealth and the promotion of equality, as discussed later in the chapter.

Whereas relative poverty is a subjective calculation, based on feelings of deprivation and disadvantage created by the gap between the poor and the rest of society, absolute poverty can surely be objectively defined. But at what level do people become absolutely poor? The World Bank (see p. 380), which has assumed growing responsibility for global poverty reduction, takes as a standard of extreme poverty an income level of 1 dollar per day, calculated at **purchasing power parity** (PPP). Based on its 2004 recalculation, which now uses $1.25 per day rather than $1 per day, the World Bank estimated in 2012 that 1.29 billion people were living at or below the international poverty line. Nevertheless, this calculation remains somewhat arbitrary, with some commentators preferring to use $2 per day or $2.5 per day. By the former standard, the ranks of the world's poor would almost double to 2.47 billion or 35 per cent of the world's population.

However, there has been growing dissatisfaction with a narrowly income-based definition of poverty. This stems from a recognition that poor people suffer from multiple deprivation involving a failure to meet their non-material needs as well as their material needs. Amartya Sen (see p. 384) contributed to such thinking in pointing out that famines often arise not from a lack of food, but from a complex of social, economic and political factors such as rising food prices, poor food distribution systems and government inefficiency. Poverty is therefore as much about restricted opportunities and the absence of freedom, in particular **positive freedom**, as it is about lack of income or resources. Such thinking has placed greater emphasis on the notion of 'human development', which has become central to the UN's approach to global poverty, as reflected in its annual Human Development Reports. These reports review various issues

● **Purchasing power parity**: A calculation of purchasing power that takes account of the relative cost of living and the inflation rates of different countries, sometimes based on the 'international dollar'.

● **Positive freedom**: Freedom defined in terms of self-realization and the development of human capacities; freedom to be or do something.

- The poor are often viewed as the victims of some form of social injustice. Poverty, in this sense, is something that happens *to* people, tending to demoralize and disempower even those thought of as the 'deserving' poor.

Deconstructing . . .

'POVERTY'

- As poverty is portrayed in terms of deprivation and suffering, it suggests that poverty equals 'bad' while wealth equals 'good'. As such, the concept of poverty endorses a dominant materialist and consumerist ethic. This ignores the idea that *voluntary* poverty may have moral and spiritual benefits, as advocated by some religious traditions, and it disregards the notion of 'sufficiency', as endorsed by some within the environmental and development movements.

- The widely accepted belief that wealth is linked to hard work and ability implies that poverty is associated, at least in part, with laziness and personal failing. This suggests that the poor are 'undeserving' and that attempts to reduce poverty are both misguided and morally wrong.

related to poverty and development and rank states on the basis of the Human Development Index (HDI).

Development: competing visions

Debates about poverty focus not only on the nature of poverty, but also on how it can best be explained and therefore how it should be tackled; that is, how 'development' can be brought about. However, the notion of development is surrounded by political and ideological controversy. What distinguishes a 'developed' society from a 'developing' or 'undeveloped' one? Perspectives on development generally fall into two broad categories, which we will call 'orthodox' and 'alternative'.

Orthodox view of development

The orthodox view of development is rooted in economic liberalism. In this view, poverty is defined squarely in economic terms, as a failure, through a lack of income or resources, to satisfy basic material needs. The reduction or even elimination of poverty is therefore clearly linked to the ability to stimulate economic growth, traditionally calculated on the basis of **gross domestic product** (GDP) per head of population. Development, in effect, is synonymous

● **Gross domestic product**: The total value of all the goods and services produced in an economy, a measure of national income.

Focus on . . .
Human development

Human development is a standard of human well-being that takes account of people's ability to develop their full potential and lead fulfilled and creative lives in accordance with their needs and interests. It is often simply defined in terms of enlarging people's choices. Influenced by Sen's (1999) notion of 'development as freedom', the idea has been most fully elaborated through the Human Development Index, which has been used since 1993 to rank countries in the UN's Human Development Reports. The key Human Development Indicators (HDIs) are:

- Leading a long and healthy life (life expectancy and health profile)
- Acquiring knowledge (education and literacy)
- Access to resources needed for a decent standard of living (fuel, sanitation, shelter and so on)
- Preserving resources for future generations (demographic trends and sustainability)
- Ensuring human security (see p. 430) (food, jobs, crime, personal distress)
- Achieving equality for all women and men (education, careers/jobs, political participation)

with economic growth. But how is economic growth best stimulated? The central mechanism, from this perspective, is the free-market system. The virtues of the free market are that it gives full rein for individuals to pursue self-interest, providing incentives for people to work, engage in trade, set up business and so on, and that it ensures long-term economic equilibrium, helping to bring the forces of demand and supply (market forces) into line with one another. The market is thus the only reliable means of generating wealth, providing, indeed, the possibility of unlimited economic growth. 'Backward' or 'under-developed' societies are therefore destined to be transformed into 'modern' or 'developed' ones. This view of development is reflected in **modernization theory**, which is evident, for example, in Rostow's (1960) theory of the stages of economic growth. Rostow outlined five stages of economic growth, as follows:

- *Traditional societies* – such societies are characterized by rudimentary technology, pre-scientific values and norms, and a subsistence economy.
- *Preconditions for take-off* – at this stage societies exhibit a degree of capital mobilization (banks and currency) and start to develop an entrepreneurial class.
- *Take-off* – this happens when the norms of economic growth are well established and sector-led growth becomes common.
- *Drive to maturity* – this is characterized by growing economic diversification, greatly reduced poverty and rising living standards.
- *High mass consumption* – at this stage, the economy is increasingly orientated around the production of modern consumer goods, with affluence becoming widespread.

● Modernization theory: The theory that there is a single, linear path to development, reflected in the transformation of western countries from traditional, pre-industrial, agrarian societies to modern, industrial and mass consumption ones.

The orthodox view has dominated thinking on matters related to poverty, inequality and development since 1945. Its influence expanded in the 1970s and 1980s through the rise of neoliberalism (see p. 93) and the conversion of the

DEVELOPMENT

Realist view

There is no realist theory of development as such. Nevertheless, in explaining the phenomenon of economic development, realists have generally drawn heavily on the ideas of mercantilism. Mercantilism stresses the interplay between economics and politics, particularly through the extent to which healthy and stable domestic economies rely on a strong dose of state intervention, especially in order to manage external trade relations (implying protectionism). Such a view is highly sceptical of liberal claims about the natural tendency of market economies towards equilibrium and growth, believing, always, that markets need to be managed.

Liberal view

The liberal approach to development is firmly rooted in the ideas of economic liberalism. Classical liberal economics draws heavily on individualist and rationalist assumptions about human nature, placing a strong emphasis on the idea that human beings are primarily motivated by the desire for material consumption. Liberalism therefore provides the basis for the orthodox notion of 'development as growth'. From the liberal perspective, the central mechanism for generating wealth is the market, which operates according to the wishes and decisions of free individuals. The attraction of the market is that it is a self-regulating mechanism, which tends naturally to promote economic prosperity and well-being. However, individual acquisitiveness and market forces are not always, in themselves, powerful enough to deliver economic development. For liberals, 'development failures' stem from factors that are internal to the society itself. These include cultural or religious norms that inhibit individual self-seeking, rigid and authoritarian state institutions, chronic corruption, and ethnic and tribal rivalries that subvert civil order. The best way to overcome these obstacles is through market reform (privatization, financial deregulation, labour flexibility, tax cuts and so on) and the integration of the national economy into the global capitalist economy (free trade and an open economy).

Critical views

Critical approaches to development have been dominated by neo-Marxist theories. These shift attention away from internal obstacles to development, to external ones, particularly those that stem from the structural dynamics of the global capitalist system.

Neo-Marxist thinking about development has been shaped by two main theoretical sub-traditions. Dependency theory highlights the extent to which, in the post-1945 period, traditional imperialism gave way to neo-colonialism, sometimes viewed as 'economic imperialism' or, more specifically, 'dollar imperialism'. Despite enjoying formal independence and sovereignty (see p. 4), developing world states continued to be subject to economic dependency through, for instance, unequal trade relations, the impact of TNCs and biases within bodies such as the IMF and the World Bank that favour the interests of industrially advanced states. The other key neo-Marxist sub-tradition is world-system theory (see p. 374), which portrays the world economy as an interlocking whole, composed of core, peripheral and semi-peripheral areas. In this, economically advanced and politically stable core areas dominate and exploit peripheral areas that are characterized by low wages, rudimentary technology and a dependence on agriculture or primary production.

Amongst other critical approaches to development, green politics has challenged the conventional emphasis on economic growth by championing the notion of 'development as sustainability', usually linked to the concept of sustainable development (see p. 397). In this view, economic growth must be balanced against its ecological costs, a healthy environment being vital for meaningful development. For cosmopolitan theorists, development should be understood in terms of the larger project of advancing global justice. Feminism has been associated with various views about development. Some feminists argue that overturning gender inequality must be seen as a key component of development, thereby highlighting the need to change social structures, institutions and cultural practices in the developing world. However, other feminists stress the extent to which 'development as growth' is constructed on the basis of masculinist assumptions, or the degree to which women already play an important, if usually ignored, role in bringing about development. Postcolonialists, for their part, have sometimes challenged the very idea of development, advancing instead the notion of 'post-development'. While conventional models of development involve the imposition of western institutions and values on non-western societies, 'post-development' allows each society to embrace its own model of economic and social progress, based on aspirations and a cultural heritage that are authentic to the society itself.

institutions of global economic governance and a growing number of states, led by the USA, to pro-market economic philosophy, and again in the 1990s through the widespread introduction of market reforms by former communist states. Nevertheless, the pro-growth and pro-market view of development has attracted growing criticism in recent years. As will later be seen in relation to development strategies, opponents have argued that economic reforms that expose countries to the vagaries of the market and the international trading system may be counter-productive, leading to economic and social dislocation rather than steady growth and the reduction of poverty. In the 1990s, such criticisms focused in particular on the impact of 'structural adjustment programmes' (SAPs) (see p. 378), imposed by the International Monetary Fund (IMF) (see p. 475) and the World Bank. Opponents have, furthermore, questioned whether market-based solutions attend equally to the interests of all states and all regions of the world. Neo-Marxist critics, for instance, argue that the global capitalist system is characterized by deep structural imbalances.

Alternative view of development

The alternative view of poverty and development has become more prominent since the 1980s as disillusionment has grown with technocratic, top-down, pro-growth strategies. They have stemmed from various sources, including resistance movements in the 'global South' (see the North–South divide, p. 367), such as the Zapatista movement in Chiapas in Mexico (see p. 368) and peasant protests in the southern Indian state of Karnataka, UN agencies, development NGOs and their various forums, including the World Social Forum, and the broader anti-capitalist (see p. 74) or anti-globalization movement. However, there is no single or coherent 'alternative' package of ideas about development. While radical elements are strongly anti-western, anti-corporate and place a heavy emphasis on self-management and environmentalism, reformist elements may do little more than modify the application of orthodox liberal principles, seeking merely to rebalance the priorities of major states and the institutions of global economic governance. Nevertheless, certain general themes can be identified, the most important of which are as follows:

- A humanistic view of poverty that emphasizes opportunity, freedom and empowerment (thus meeting material and non-material needs)
- Self-reliance rather than reliance on wealthy states, international bodies or the market
- Ecological balance, sustainability and conservation of the 'global commons' (water, land, air, forest)
- Social and cultural inclusion through respect for cultural diversity and the interests of marginalized groups such as women and indigenous groups
- Local control achieved through community action and democratic participation
- The view that poverty has a structural character, stemming from disparities in the global trading system and elsewhere.

The 'alternative' view rejects the 'one size fits all' implications of orthodox thinking and, in particular, the idea of a linear transition from a 'traditional'

● The term 'development' can be thought of as demeaning because it is based on a contrast between 'underdeveloped' or 'developing' countries or regions and 'developed' ones. The former therefore appear to be immature, basic or in some way deficient, while the latter seem to be fully-formed, sophisticated and advanced.

Deconstructing . . .

'DEVELOPMENT'

● As development also refers to the biological process of growth, in an individual or a species, it implies a single, linear process of change. Development therefore suggests that 'underdeveloped/developing' countries are destined to go through the same stages and phases that developed countries already have. Development thus tends to be linked to a distinctively western form of modernization.

● The primary difference between 'underdeveloped/developing' countries and 'developed' ones is their level of wealth or affluence. This can be seen to prioritize material goods and values over non-material ones. Little attention, for example, is given to the possibility that poor countries may be more morally, spiritually or culturally developed than rich countries.

society to a 'developed' society, in which Latin American, Asian and African states are destined, sooner or later, to go through the same process of modernization as states in the 'global North'. In other words, developing world states are not playing catch up. Indeed, to a significant extent, their plight can be blamed on external factors and the often self-interested impact of western states and transnational corporations (TNCs) (see p. 94), through, for example, aid regimes that are structured around the needs of donor countries and the demand for across-the-board integration into the international economy. On the other hand, few of those who support 'alternative' stances advocate separating developing world economies from the global economy, or seeking to develop a qualitatively different alternative to capitalism. Instead, they seek to combine growth-orientated economic policies with a sensitivity to local and regional needs and interests, placing stress on cultural diversity, ecological balance and self-reliance. What is sometimes called the 'Southern consensus' on development therefore usually allows for a greater role for state intervention than would be acceptable to supporters of economic liberalism. Adopting a

Focus on ...
The North–South divide

The idea of a 'North–South divide' was popularized through the work of the so-called Brandt Reports: *North–South: A Programme for Survival* (1980) and *Common Crisis: North-South Cooperation for World Recovery* (1983). Although the idea that the world is divided into a 'global North' and a 'global South' is based on the tendency for industrial development to be concentrated in the northern hemisphere, and for poverty and disadvantage to be concentrated in the southern hemisphere (apart from Australasia), the terms are essentially conceptual and theoretical rather than geographical.

The concept of the North–South divide draws attention to the way in which aid, developing world debt and the practices of TNCs help to perpetuate structural inequal-ities between the high-wage, high-investment industri-alized North and the low-wage, low-investment, predominantly rural South. The Brandt Reports also highlighted the interdependence of the North and the South, emphasizing that the prosperity of the North is dependent on the development of the South. Some, nevertheless, question the continuing relevance of the idea of a North–South divide. Amongst other things, they draw attention to increasingly uneven develop-ment across the South itself (disparities between China and sub-Saharan Africa, for example), the growing polit-ical influence of the South – the rise of the G-20 (see p. 121) and so on, and the quite different relationships that have emerged between the North and different parts of the South, not all of which are now based on power and dependency.

neo-mercantilist approach to development, the East Asian 'tiger' economies thus relied less on the free market than on the capacity of the state to pursue strategies for international competitiveness, especially through a heavy empha-sis on education and training. The most impressive Southern model of devel-opment has nevertheless been found in China's mixture of market economics and Stalinist political control (see A Chinese economic model?, p. 92). (Feminist thinking on development and the role of women in bringing about development are discussed in Chapter 17.)

A MORE UNEQUAL WORLD?

Making sense of global inequality

Questions about poverty are often linked to the issue of inequality. Indeed, from the perspective of relative poverty, the two concepts are intrinsically linked, in the sense that widening inequality effectively *means* increased poverty. However, the issue of global inequality is an arena of particular contention. On the one hand, there have been assertions, usually linked to criticisms of globalization and biases within the world trading system, that the gap between the richest and poorest countries has been increasing in recent decades, even reaching grotesque proportions. The UN's 1999 *Human Development Report*, for example, noted that the assets of the world's richest three individuals exceeded the combined GDPs of all the countries designated as the world's 'least developed', comprising a total population of some 600 million people. As the rich get richer the poor get

Focus on . . .

The Zapatistas in Mexico: alternative development in action?

The Zapatista Army of National Liberation (EZLN), take their name from Emiliano Zapata (1879–1919), a leading figure in the Mexican Revolution of 1910 and a prominent campaigner for agrarian reform. The main spokesperson of the modern Zapatistas is Subcomandante Marcos, also known as 'Delegate Zero'. The Zapatista uprising started in 1994 when, within hours of the signing of the NAFTA Agreement (see Chapter 20), a seemingly ramshackle group of students, intellectuals, radicals and indigenous peasants emerged from the jungle of the Chiapas region to declare war against the Mexican state. As Mexican federal forces were pushed back from the region, the Zapatistas established what is effectively an autonomous area, leading, since 1994, to something of a stand-off between the EZLN and the Mexican state.

As a result, in many of the mountainous and jungle areas of Chiapas, extending into some of the urban areas, an entirely different set of principles and norms operate, in line with what is sometimes called 'Zapatismo'. Zapatismo draws on anarchist, libertarian, socialist and Marxist ideas. It has been notable for a number of reasons. First, it has implacably rejected globalization, capitalism and neoliberalism, favouring instead the formation of self-managing councils and cooperatives. Zapatismo therefore represents the revolutionary wing of the anti-capitalist movement. Second, the Zapatistas differ from other left-wing revolutionary groups in that they are uninterested in seizing power in order to rule on behalf of the people, and unwilling to support a particular world-view or set of economic arrangements. This 'non-vertical' or 'post-ideological' form of politics means that Zapatistas work in alliance with indigenous peoples and peasant groups rather than rule 'from above'. Third, the Zapatistas have placed particular emphasis on the use of new communication technology to give their ideas a high profile within the anti-capitalist movement in particular and in the wider world.

poorer, in relative and perhaps also in absolute terms. On the other hand, a growing body of commentators have come to the conclusion that in recent years the world has generally become a more equal place (Kay 2004; Wolf 2005; Friedman 2006).

The debate about global inequality is nevertheless beset with difficulties. Not only are there significant difficulties surrounding the task of measuring inequality, but the trends themselves are much more complex than the simple idea of a gap between rich and poor suggests. Ultimately, it may not be possible to identify an overall *trend* in global inequality, meaning that the focus should shift instead onto discussing the *contours* of global inequality. This occurs for a variety of reasons:

- There is a lack of clarity about what is being measured: income, life expectancy, educational opportunities, access to clean water and so on.
- The data to measure inequality may be unreliable or contain biases.
- Different time spans highlight different trends.
- There is confusion about who are 'the rich' and who are 'the poor'.
- Within-country trends may be as significant, or more significant, than between-country trends.

The first problem with any discussion of equality is in determining what is being measured. Equality of what? The World Bank, followed by most other bodies, uses a measure of inequality based on income, especially GDP per capita. This occurs partly because such data are easier to compile and calculate than alternatives, such as access to healthcare or clean water, and partly because income, adjusted for purchasing power parity, provides a broad but reliable indication of people's living standards. However, the principal alternative to this, the UN's notion of human development, is not only multidimensional but also shifts attention away from economic equality to equality of opportunity, the idea of equal life chances. Second, the data that inform judgements about global inequality are not always complete or reliable. The World Bank's annual *World Development Reports* provide the most comprehensive and commonly used data on income distribution in particular. However, some have questioned the neutrality of the World Bank and, until the early 2000s, much data did not take appropriate account of factors such as exchange rates, the cost of living and inflation levels in different countries. Changing approaches to data collection and interpretation have, at different times, forced commentators significantly to revise their views on the nature and extent of global inequality. Moreover, there are important areas in which data on income disparity remains unreliable or is in short supply, notably on within-country inequality in many poor states.

Third, trends in global poverty are crucially affected by the timescales over which they are measured. According to the long view on inequality, which takes account of trends over the nineteenth and twentieth centuries, there has been a profound and steady tendency towards a widening gap between rich and poor countries. It has been estimated, for instance, that in 1800, per capita income in the USA was probably three times greater than in Africa, while by 2000, it was twenty times greater. Compared with the poorest African countries, it may be fifty or sixty times greater. These trends are clearly a consequence of industrialization in the developed North, reflected in steadily rising living standards, particularly from the late nineteenth century onwards. Such a trend towards widening inequality would also be evident from 1945 to the present day, because the benefits of the 'long boom' of the 1950s and 1960s were almost entirely concentrated in the industrially advanced world. However, if global inequality is measured since 1980, a much more complex picture emerges with contending images of widening inequality and diminishing inequality often being advanced. Furthermore, at different points during the post-1980 period different trends can be identified. For instance, during the 1990s there was evidence of widening inequality, due to factors such as the accumulating debt crisis in the developing world and the economic disruption that followed the 'shock treatment' transition to the market economy in Russia and other former communist states. By contrast, the period between the events of 11 September 2001 and the global financial crisis of 2007–9 was characterized by strong growth in the world economy, which sometimes benefited poor and lower-income countries more than wealthy ones.

Fourth, there is no settled or objective definition of who are 'the rich' and who are 'the poor'. Should we, for instance, be comparing the richest and poorest 10 per cent, 20 per cent or even 30 per cent in terms of the average income of the country in which they live? Such questions are not merely of academic interest alone, but may affect the trend uncovered. The 2001 *Human Development Report* thus concluded that the ratio of average income in the countries containing the richest 20 per cent of the world's population to average income in the nations containing the poorest 20 per cent of the world's population had fallen between 1970 and 1997 (from 15:1 to 13:1), while in the case of the richest 10 per cent of countries and the poorest 10 per cent of countries, the ratio had grown (from 19:1 to 27:1). The reason for this is that, in recent decades, the most rapidly growing developing countries have not been among the very poorest.

Finally, the analysis of global inequality is hampered by the fact that it is usually based on comparisons between *countries* rather than *people* or households. GDP per capita is a calculation of the notional average income in a country, not a measure of the actual incomes of people (none of whom may be 'average'). Between-country comparisons would therefore always be limited and misleading unless the within-country distribution of income is also taken into account. Indeed, if there is a strong tendency for within-country income differentials to widen, the gap between rich and poor people may be growing even though the gap between rich and poor countries may be diminishing. This also alerts us to the fact that the problem of poverty is not confined to poor countries: poor people can also be found in rich countries. The most commonly used measure of inequality within a country is the Gini coefficient, which varies between 0 (complete equality) and 1 (complete inequality). Denmark, for instance, has a Gini coefficient of 0.24, while Namibia's is 0.74.

Contours of global inequality

In the light of these considerations, the contours of global inequality in recent decades can be broken down into three key trends:

- Equalizing trends, largely based on economic progress made by China and, to a lesser extent, India.
- Disequalizing trends, largely reflecting deepening poverty in sub-Saharan Africa until the 2000s.
- A general trend for within-country inequality to grow.

The narrowing gap between the richest and poorest countries each containing 25–30 per cent of the world's population is mainly explained by high growth rates in recent decades in China and India. Chinese growth rates since the 1990s have been about 8–10 per cent, while Indian growth rates have been about 7–8 per cent, compared with roughly 2–3 per cent amongst industrially advanced countries. The impact of this is all the greater as China and India jointly account for almost 40 per cent of the world's population. The reduction of poverty in China has been particularly marked. By Chinese calculations of poverty (which are based on the amount of food needed to sustain a human being), absolute poverty fell from 250 million at the start of its reform process in 1978 to 28 million in 2001. The World Bank's figures are marginally lower, but it still accepts that China has brought about the most spectacular reduction in poverty in human history. In its assessment, the success of China in reducing the number of people living on less than $1.25 per day by 663 million between 1981 and 2008 meant that Chines growth, on its own, had ensured that the key Millennium Development Goal (see p. 382) of halving the number of people in extreme poverty by 2015 had been met three years early. China's poverty reduction strategies have included a major expansion in manufacturing production, particularly in export-orientated industries, massive infrastructural projects, population control especially though the 'one child' policy, and improvements to the standard of poverty relief. In this, it has worked with international partners, notably the World Bank. On the other hand, China's remarkable success in poverty reduction has not been without its costs. These have included greatly increased pollution, enormous migration shifts through rapid urbanization, concerns about safety at work and a fracturing of family structures.

While there had been evidence that other parts of the world have made economic progress, sub-Saharan Africa emerged as the principal exception, becoming a kind of 'fourth world'. In the 2009 *Human Development Report*, the 24 lowest countries on the UN's HDI were all in sub-Saharan Africa, including all the countries in the category of 'low human development' (see Table 15.1). Life expectancy in sub-Saharan African in 2010 was 54.17 years (compared with a world average of 69.6 years); 74 per cent of the population was estimated to be undernourished; only 46 per cent of people had reliable access to clean water, and only 30 per cent had access to improved sanitation.

Why had sub-Saharan Africa been left behind? Sub-Saharan Africa had been caught in a **poverty cycle** that made it profoundly difficult to break out of poverty. This was exacerbated by the link between poverty and disease. HIV/AIDS was a particular blight on sub-Saharan Africa, accounting in 2007 for some 68 per cent of HIV/AIDS cases worldwide and 76 per cent of all AIDS deaths. The epidemic was particularly serious in the countries of southern Africa, such as Swaziland (where 26.1 per cent of the population are living with HIV/AIDS), Botswana (23.9 per cent) and Lesotho (23.2 per cent). Africa also accounts for 90 per cent of deaths from malaria, with about 80 per cent of malaria victims worldwide being African children. The association between poverty and civil conflict, crime, corruption and state failure has also seriously disadvantaged sub-Saharan Africa, especially in the light of the legacy of colonialism and entrenched ethnic and tribal tensions. Further factors included the link between poverty and poor educational provision, low investment rates, uncontrolled population growth (27 out of 30 countries with the highest birth rates in the world are in sub-Saharan Africa), as well as the so-called paradox of plenty (see p. 416).

However, there is evidence that the trend of decline in sub-Saharan Africa may have come to an end. According to the World Bank, sub-Saharan Africa reduced the $1.25 poverty rate to 47 per cent in 2008, the first time it had dipped below 50 per cent, and significantly lower than the 1999 peak of 58 per cent. This is largely a reflection of improved rates of economic growth across most of Africa. Despite the global financial crisis of 2007–09, the economies of sub-Saharan Africa grew at an average of 4.7 per cent per year between 2000 and 2011. The explanations that have been put forward for Africa's economic emergence include the impact international aid and particularly debt relief, high commodity prices (driven, in significant part, by the rise of China), the ending of most of Africa's civil wars, and market-based economic reform, as encouraged by the World Bank and the International Monetary Fund. Nevertheless, optimism about Africa's economic boom should be tempered by a recognition that political instability remains widespread and that manufacturing output in sub-

● **Poverty cycle**: A set of circumstances that tend to make poverty self-perpetuating through its wider impact on health, civic order, political and economic performance and so on.

Saharan Africa still accounts for the same proportion of GDP as it did in the 1970s (Devarajan and Fengler, 2013).

Finally, there is growing evidence that while between-country inequality is diminishing, within-country inequality has generally been growing. Cornia (2003) found that two-thirds of the 73 countries he analyzed appeared to have widening within-country inequality rates between 1980 and 2000. This has applied, albeit to different degrees, in a wide variety of states. Amongst OECD countries, it has been most evident in ones, such as the USA and the UK, which embraced neoliberal economics most enthusiastically. Income inequality has widened as a result of financial deregulation, checks on social security spending and cuts in personal and corporate tax levels. The trend has been particularly evident in the former communist states of eastern Europe and in Latin America. In eastern Europe, economic transition involved a wholesale dismantling of the economic and social supports that were customary in communist systems, leading not only to increased relative poverty but also, in cases such as Russia, to growing levels of absolute poverty and falling life expectancy. In Latin America, income inequality rose markedly in the 1980s and 1990s, often associated with external pressures to introduce economic liberalization and deregulation. Chinese experience demonstrates how the tendencies towards falling between-country inequality and widening within-country inequality can be part of the same process. Although Chinese economic reforms since 1978 have substantially boosted average incomes and dramatically reduced absolute poverty, they have also been associated with a fast rise in income inequality, particularly reflected in a widening of the urban–rural divide. The phenomenon of rural poverty is discussed in greater detail in the next section in relation to the impact of globalization.

Globalization, poverty and inequality

The impact of globalization on levels of poverty and inequality has been a source of debate and controversy since the early 1990s. Supporters of globalization have argued that it promises to deliver enhanced opportunities for all (Norberg 2003; Lal 2004;), while critics have linked globalization to polarization and intensified subordination (Held and Kaya 2006). Unfortunately, attempts to resolve this issue through empirical analysis alone have limited value. The most common approach is to identify correlations between the advance of economic globalization (see p. 98) and trends in income disparities. Not only, as already pointed out, are trends in inequality complex and, to some extent, contradictory, but correlations (both up and down) do not necessarily indicate cause or significance, as other factors may be affecting trends in poverty and inequality.

Those who associate globalization with widening inequality draw attention to a number of processes. First, they portray globalization as a game of winners and losers, in the sense that those who benefit do so at the expense of others. This has revived interest in the core/periphery model, advanced by world-systems theory (see p. 374). The North is the core area within the global economy, in that it is the home of sophisticated and high technology production (including most 'global goods') and the world's leading TNCs. The South is the peripheral area within the global economy, still largely restricted to agricultural production and

Table 15.1 Top ten and bottom ten countries on terms of HDI rankings

Top	Bottom
1. Norway	=178. Burundi
2. Australia	=178. Guinea
3. USA	180. Central African Republic
4. Netherlands	181. Eritrea
5. Germany	182. Mali
6. New Zealand	183. Burkina Faso
7. Ireland	184. Chad
8. Sweden	185. Mozambique
9. Switzerland	=186. Niger
10. Japan	=186. Congo (Democratic Republic of)

Source: UN Human Development Report 2013.

supply of raw materials. The East (China, South Asia and so on) operates as a semi-peripheral area in that it has become the manufacturing powerhouse of the global economy without yet rivalling the North in terms of research and development and advanced technology. As such, globalization channels benefits to the rich North at the expense of the poorer South, helping to maintain, if not increase, between-country inequality. TNCs contribute to this process by exploiting raw materials and cheap labour in the South and by expatriating profit to the North. Second, between-country inequalities are exacerbated by the tendencies implicit in the global trading system and particularly the principle of free trade (see p. 480). As discussed in Chapter 19, free trade has been criticised for favouring the interests of rich states by giving them access to the markets of poorer states without exposing themselves to similar vulnerability. This explains both the pressure exerted by industrially advanced states, mainly via the World Trade Organization (WTO) (see p. 537), to encourage other states to embrace economic openness and the persistence of anomalies such as continued agricultural protectionism by the USA and the EU.

Third, the advance of globalization has been associated with growing rural poverty and a widening of rural–urban disparities. Rural areas account for three-quarters of the people living on less than $1 per day. This occurs largely because pressures from the global economy have massively disrupted agricultural practices in the developing world, encouraging peasant farmers to convert to cash crops, produced for export, and abandon subsistence farming geared to local needs and local communities. Fourth, globalization has fostered within-country inequality in at least two ways. The first way is through strengthening social hierarchies. Corporate power has thus become stronger as businesses have been able to exert increased political leverage through their ability to relocate investment and production almost at will, while trade unions have been weakened by the fear that agitation for higher wages or improved conditions will merely threaten job security. The second way is that the emergence of a more open and competitive economy has forced all states, to some extent, to deregulate their economies and restructure their tax systems while also rolling back welfare and redistribu-

Focus on . . .
World-systems theory

World-systems theory offers a neo-Marxist analysis of the nature and workings of the global economy. Its most prominent exponent has been Immanuel Wallerstein (see p. 104). The central idea of world-systems theory is that the expansion of capitalism, from the sixteenth century onwards, has created a global economic system comprising three interlocking parts:

- Core areas that are characterized by relatively high wages, advanced technology and a diversified production mix, including mass market industries and sophisticated agriculture.
- Peripheral areas that are characterized by low wages, more rudimentary technology and a simple production mix geared towards staple goods such as grain, wood, sugar and so on.
- Semi-peripheral areas that are economically mixed, including some core features and some peripheral ones.

The core–periphery model emphasizes how strong states can enforce unequal exchange on weak ones, the transfer of economic surpluses from peripheral to core areas helping to maintain dependency and underdevelopment. Low-wage and low-profit producers in peripheral areas are used to service and support high-wage and high-producers in the core. Semi-peripheral areas act as a buffer or shock absorber within the world-system, helping to ensure that core countries are not faced by a unified opposition. Such relations are further underpinned by political differences between the core and the periphery, the former tending to have democratic governments, effective state machines and developed welfare services, while the latter usually have authoritarian governments, weak or ineffective state machines and very rudimentary welfare provision. An end to global poverty and regional imbalances within the global economy requires the overthrow of the capitalist world-system, or its collapse as a result of inherent instability and recurrent crises.

tive programmes. The wealthy have therefore got wealthier while the poor have got poorer. To make matters worse, the theory of '**trickle down**' has almost everywhere been exposed as a myth.

On the other hand, supporters of globalization have portrayed it as the surest way of reducing poverty and narrowing inequality. This can be seen to apply in two main ways. First, globalization is a positive-sum game: mutual benefits flow from engaging in the global economy. This is what Friedman (2006) meant in proclaiming that the world is becoming 'flatter', meaning that globalization has levelled the competitive playing field between advanced industrial and emerging economies. The period of accelerated globalization, starting in the early 1980s, thus witnessed the rise of newly-industrializing countries (NICs) and significant economic progress in parts of the world that had formerly been characterized by poverty and underdevelopment. NICs, moreover, have based their development on a strategic engagement with the global economy rather than any attempt to opt out of it. Their two main strategies have been **import substitution** industrialization and export-orientated development, in which a range of industries are targeted that it is believed can successfully compete in the world marketplace.

China is the most spectacular example of how an NIC can make globalization work for its benefit, but states such as India, Brazil, Mexico, Malaysia and

● **Trickle down**: The theory that the introduction of free-market policies will, in time, benefit the poor and not only the rich through an increase in economic growth and a general rise in living standards.

● **Import substitution**: An economic strategy through which domestic industries are protected from foreign competition, at least during their infancy.

the East Asian 'tigers' (Hong Kong, Singapore, South Korea and Taiwan) have adopted similar strategies, albeit with national variations. While there is evidence that integration – or at least 'strategic' integration – in the world economy is associated with rising GDP per capita, a failure or refusal to integrate is usually associated with low growth or economic stagnation. This can be borne out by the experience of sub-Saharan Africa. Supporters of globalization also challenge the idea that TNCs are the enemies of the South and a threat to global justice. TNCs, in fact, bring a range of benefits, including employment opportunities, better wages, training and investment in skills, and modern technology. Furthermore, rather than TNCs dictating to developing world governments, alliances are often forged through which governments also use TNCs for their own ends. Finally, even though trickle-down economics appears to have been a failure, pro-globalization theorists tend to argue that if within-country inequality grows as the rich get richer, the important thing is not that the poor keep up but that they become less poor. This raises questions about the general importance of inequality.

Does global inequality matter?

Attitudes to equality have traditionally shaped, if not defined, people's core ideological orientation. While left-wingers have generally supported equality and social justice, right-wingers have typically accepted that inequality is inevitable, and may even be beneficial. These positions also inform debates about globalization and are reflected in the broadly egalitarian stance adopted by most critics of globalization, and the generally inegalitarian stance adopted by its supporters. The case in favour of social equality is based on three considerations: power, conflict and personal well-being. Equality is linked to power in that social inequality affects power relations. The rich control economic and social resources that enable them to control and oppress the poor. In this view, the rich are rich, and may be able to get richer, through their treatment of the poor. An unequal world is therefore unjust and exploitative, meaning that global justice requires not just a reduction in absolute poverty, but also a narrowing of the gap between the rich and the poor.

The link between inequality and conflict is evident in the fact that social disparities breed resentment, hostility and strife. This is of particular concern in relation to within-country inequality in poorer states. The combination of endemic poverty and widening income disparities, perhaps one of the key consequences of globalization in the developing world, creates a breeding ground for ethnic and tribal conflict and the general breakdown of civic order. In this sense, global inequality may have contributed not only to state failure and humanitarian crises, but also to the growth of 'new' wars and the rise in terrorism (see p. 291). The link between inequality and personal well-being arises because human security (see p. 430) and happiness are affected by the fact that people perceive their social position in terms of what others have. If people feel excluded from the benefits and rewards that are customary in their society, they feel marginalized and disempowered (Wilkinson and Pickett 2010). This perhaps has clearer implications for within-country inequality, where the less well-off live in relative proximity to better-off and rich people. However, the growth of global information and communications means that this may also increasingly apply to between-country inequality. For example, a growing awareness of the prosperity enjoyed in other parts of the 'global village' has helped to stimulate massive migratory flows from poor countries to rich ones.

However, others have questioned the importance of inequality, even arguing that efforts to narrow the gap between the rich and the poor are misplaced or doomed to failure. The first such argument places an emphasis on poverty over inequality. From this perspective, absolute poverty is the real issue. Social evils such as hunger, a lack of access to clean water and sanitation, and low life expectancy are much more serious threats to happiness and personal well-being than the gap between the rich and the poor. If this is the case, national, regional and global policy should be structured around the goal of reducing extreme poverty, regardless of its implications for 'relative' poverty. Thus, it may not matter that the rich are getting richer, and perhaps much richer, so long as the poor are becoming less poor.

A second argument is that inequality has certain economic advantages. Economic liberals have long argued that social levelling leads to economic stagnation, as it caps aspirations and removes incentives for enterprise and hard work. From this perspective, one of the reasons for low growth rates, and eventual collapse, of state socialist regimes was their relatively egalitarian social structures. Widening inequality may, indeed, simply be a feature of the 'take-off' phase of industrial development. A third argument is that the distribution of income or wealth, either within or between countries, is morally and politically less important than how that distribution is achieved. In this view, equality is less important than freedom. On an individual level, people should have the opportunity to rise and fall in society, their final position being a reflection of their aspirations, talents and willingness to work. From a global perspective, states should enjoy sovereignty and freedom from foreign interference, allowing them to use their own resources in developing strategies for national advancement within the global economy. So long as states enjoy political independence, how they rank economically against other states may affect their own citizens, but it is not an issue of global justice.

DEVELOPMENT AND THE POLITICS OF AID

Structural adjustment programmes and beyond

The end of empire in the 1950s and 1960s had profound political effects in the developing world, but remarkably few economic consequences. The established division of labour within the world economy between the industrialized North, the home of manufacturing production and the impoverished South, the chief source of primary production, especially raw materials and foodstuffs, remained unchanged. A lack of economic diversification in the South intensified economic vulnerability, as many developing world countries were (and, in some cases, still are) dependent for their export income on a single commodity, or a very narrow range of commodities. In 2005, as many as 43 developing states still depended on a single commodity for more than 20 per cent of their total revenues from exports. A slump in a single economic sector, often brought about by volatility in world export markets, could therefore have devastating consequences. However, from the late 1970s onwards the World Bank and the International Monetary Fund adopted a radically new approach to promoting development, using what became known as structural adjustment programmes, or SAPs. Why did this policy change take place, and what was the nature and purpose of SAPs?

The shift in the approach to development in favour of structural adjustment occurred for two main reasons. The first was a growing **debt crisis** in the developing world. This occurred as poorer countries borrowed heavily from western banks and other private bodies which were themselves flush with 'petro dollars' as a result of dramatic increases in the price of oil introduced in 1973 by the newly-formed Organization of Petroleum Exporting Countries (OPEC). However, a combination of an increase in interest rates and the slowdown in the world economy in the 1970s (in part, because of the world oil crisis) led to economic stagnation across much of the developing world, making it difficult, and sometimes impossible, for their debts to be serviced. In this context, many developing countries looked instead to borrow from the IMF (in order to deal with balance of payments crises) or from the World Bank (in order to fund development projects). Global financial institutions were therefore confronted by growing pressure to increase or restructure loans in a context in which previous loans had done little to promote economic growth. The second factor was the ideological shift that had occurred as a result of the collapse in the early 1970s of the Bretton Woods system (see Chapter 19) and the emergence of the 'Washington consensus' (see p. 96). Based on the belief that the debt crisis and other problems were due to structural inefficiencies in the economies of many developing countries, compounded by bad or misguided government policies, the IMF and the World Bank sought to build **conditionalities** into the provision of any future loans. The purpose of these conditions was to bring about a market-orientated 'structural adjustment' of economic policy in line with the principles of neoliberalism.

The imposition of SAPs proved to be highly controversial. The thinking behind them was clearly rooted in economic liberalism. For officials at the IMF and the World Bank, the key to development was market reform, which would foster the dynamism, innovation and entrepreneurship that they believed are essential for economic growth, employment and poverty reduction. In encouraging the governments of poorer countries to introduce such reforms, IMF and World Bank officials believed that they were acting in the long-term interests of domestic populations. What is more, structural adjustment programmes were not imposed on unwilling or resistant governments, but were, rather, negotiated and agreed between independent states and international bodies based on the former's recognition that alternative sources of loans are not available, and, presumably, through an acceptance of the benefits of market reform. The principal alleged benefit of SAPs was that free trade and market reform would facilitate the integration of national economies into the global economy, thereby offering, it was believed, the best hope for increasing growth rates and ending the poverty cycle. Such thinking, indeed, may be backed by the striking difference between the economic performance of Africa and East Asia. In the 1950s and 1960s, GDP per capita in many African states was little different, and sometimes higher, than in most East Asian states, with countries such as China and India

● **Debt crisis**: A situation in which a country is unable to service its debts because economic surpluses are insufficient to meet interest repayments.

● **Conditionality**: The requirement, usually made by the IMF and the World Bank, that certain conditions about the future direction of economic policy are met before loans are agreed or made.

Focus on ...
Structural adjustment programmes

Structural adjustment programmes (SAPs), and sometimes structural adjustment loans (SALs), are devices that the IMF and the World Bank have used in the attempt to overcome what are viewed as structural inefficiencies that inhibit economic growth in the developing world. Used as the basis for the granting of loans during the 1980s and 1990s in particular, they reflected a strong faith in economic liberalism and a desire to roll back regulation and government intervention in the name of the free markets. SAPs tended to have similar aims and components for all countries to which they applied. The key reforms included:

- Reducing government spending, often through cutbacks to welfare provision, or attempts to balance government budgets through increased government revenues (for example, through higher fees for government services).
- Reducing or removing subsidies to domestic industries, which had often been part of import substitution strategies.
- Reducing or removing tariffs, quotas and other restrictions on the import and export of goods.
- Deregulating the economy generally and particularly removing restrictions on foreign investment to achieve what is called capital market liberalization.
- Privatizing, or selling off, government-owned industries and services.
- Devaluing of the exchange rate in order to encourage exports and reduce imports.

widely being viewed as economic 'basket cases'. However, East Asian countries subsequently made rapid economic progress, first through the success of the export-orientated strategies adopted by the East Asian 'tigers' and subsequently through market reforms that were adopted in China from 1978 onwards and by accelerating market reform in India, particularly after 1991. An example of this widening divide can be seen in the fact that whereas in 1957 Ghana had a larger gross national product (GNP) than South Korea, by 1996 South Korea's GNP was almost seven times larger than Ghana's. Nevertheless, the idea that the improved performance of East Asian economies can be put down to free trade should be treated with caution, particularly in the light of their use of state aid and forms of protectionism (as discussed in Chapter 4).

However, to recognize that the countries that have been most successful in recent years in boosting economic growth and reducing poverty have been ones that have placed emphasis on trade and economic integration, is very far from demonstrating the benefits of SAPs. SAPs, in fact, have been remarkably ineffective in achieving such goals, as the IMF and the World Bank eventually acknowledged (Przeworski and Vernon 2000; Easterly 2001). Top-down programmes of market reform designed by usually US-trained technocrats from the IMF and the World Bank were often harsh and paid little attention to local needs and circumstances. In cases such as Chile (which adopted reforms designed by Chicago School economists, following the ideas of Milton Friedman (see p. 95)), Argentina and Mexico, market-orientated structural adjustment led to years of economic disruption and political instability. Following the Asian financial crisis of 1997, it was notable that Malaysia, which had refused to accept the IMF's offer of a loan and its accompanying conditions, recovered significantly more quickly than Thailand and South Korea, which accepted loans and faithfully carried out IMF prescriptions. The lesson of China and, to a lesser extent, India is that market-orientated and pro-export reforms work most effectively when they are part of national strategies for development, allowing countries to engage with the global economy essentially on their own terms.

What were the drawbacks of SAPs? First, as analysts such as Joseph Stiglitz (see p. 474) have pointed out, they often resulted in greater poverty rather than less. For instance, pressure to reduce government spending frequently led to cuts in welfare, education and health budgets, which had a disproportionate impact on the less well-off and especially on women and girls. Similarly, exposing relatively weak economies to foreign competition often pushed up unemployment while also driving down wages and worsening working conditions, all in the name of greater 'labour flexibility'. Increased foreign investment also tended to focus on the production of consumer goods for world markets rather than the building of schools, roads and hospitals where economic returns are far less impressive. Second, far from creating a rising tide of global economic growth that would 'lift all boats', SAPs, arguably, attended more to the interests of major donor states, especially the USA, which were seeking expanded investment and trading opportunities, than they did to the needs of the developing world. This, indeed, may reflect deep biases that operate within the IMF and the World Bank, based, for instance, on their reliance on largely western, or western-trained, senior officials and analysts, and the fact that, suffering from the pressures of hunger, disease, poverty and spiralling debt, developing countries often have very limited freedom of manoeuvre in dealing with international organizations.

Finally, and perhaps most crucially, many would argue that SAPs were based on a flawed model of development. They had a very weak empirical underpinning, in that it is based on a model of development that no economically developed state had actually followed. In imposing SAPs, industrially advanced countries were, in effect, saying: 'do as we say, not as we did'. The record of countries such as the USA, Germany, Japan and, more recently, China, is that early industrialization is closely linked to a willingness to protect industries from foreign imports until they are strong enough to compete. Such countries only converted to policies of free trade and economic liberalism once they had reached a level of economic maturity that ensured that domestic industries were no longer vulnerable. By contrast, SAPs are based on the myth of free-market development, in that they treat an open economy as a pre-condition for development, rather than as a consequence. As criticism of SAPs intensified during the 1990s, pressure for reform built up. Even the IMF and the World Bank came to accept that SAPs had caused at least short-term economic and social disruption, and were an unreliable means of boosting growth. Since 2002, the 'one size fits all' approach to structural adjustment has largely been abandoned. Conventional SAPs have been replaced by Poverty Reduction Strategy Papers (PRSPs), which are modified SAPs that are more flexible, seek to promote country ownership, place a heavier emphasis on poverty reduction and allow for longer-term loans (up to seven years). Nevertheless, the underlying emphasis on market economics and boosting exports remains unchallenged.

GLOBAL ACTORS . . .

THE WORLD BANK

Type: Intergovernmental organization • **Established:** 1944 • **Headquarters:** Washington, DC
Membership: 188 countries

The World Bank is a bank that provides loans and financial and technical assistance to support reconstruction and development, with a growing emphasis on the task of reducing poverty. The World Bank was created as a result of the Bretton Woods agreement of 1944, with its first loan ($250 million to France for post-war reconstruction) being made in 1947. The Bank comprises two institutions:

● The International Bank for Reconstruction and Development (IBRD)
● The International Development Association (IDA).

The President of the World Bank is responsible for the overall management of the Bank. The Board of Directors oversees the approval of loans and guarantees, new policies, the budget and key strategic decisions. Voting within the World Bank is weighted according to the financial contribution of member states. Although the IBRD obtains funding through the sale of bonds in the world's financial markets, the IDA obtains the majority of its funds from 40 donor countries, most prominently the USA. The President is always a US citizen nominated by the US Treasury Secretary. The capital of the Bank in 1945 was $10 billion; by 2003, it had grown to $189.5 billion. Since 1993, the Bank has made loans annually to the tune of about $20 billion.

Significance: In the early period, the World Bank concentrated on promoting post-war reconstruction. However, over time, promoting development became the principal focus of its work. This, nevertheless, occurred through a number of phases. In the first, sometimes viewed as 'modernization without worry', it mainly supported large infrastructure projects in transport, energy, telecommunications and so on. During the 1970s, under the presidency of Robert McNamara (1968–81), the Bank placed greater emphasis on poverty reduction; for example, by promoting projects in rural development and concentrating on meeting basic needs. From the early 1980s, confronted by the growing debt crisis of many developing countries and under the influence of the ideological shift towards neoliberal economics represented by the 'Washington consensus', the Bank, in conjunction with the IMF, embraced a strategy of 'structural adjustment'. Structural adjustment programmes (SAPs) linked loans and other forms of support to conditions requiring a range of market reforms and, later, even to political conditions. These were designed to re-establish as quickly as possible the credit-worthiness of developing countries in order to focus once again on the fight against poverty. During the 1990s, in the face of growing criticism and a recognition of the failures of many of the SAPs, the Bank started to place less emphasis on macro-economic reform and

greater emphasis on the structural, social and human aspects of development. This was done through the Comprehensive Development Framework (CDF) which, in 1999, in conjunction with the OECD, the IMF and the UN, set six key targets for poverty reduction to be met by 2015. The new strategy has been dubbed the 'post-Washington consensus'.

The World Bank is the world's leading organization concerned with the issues of development and poverty reduction. Its supporters highlight its success in transferring resources, through development projects, from wealthy countries to poorer ones. They also point out that the Bank has learnt from earlier mistakes, recognizing, for instance, the need for more flexible and creative approaches to poverty reduction which place greater emphasis on country ownership. In addition, the Bank is the major collector and disseminator of information about development, its publications including the *World Bank Annual Report*, the *World Development Report* and the review *Global Development Finance*. Critics of the World Bank have argued, variously, that its financing of development is insufficient, that its record of reducing poverty is poor, that its neoliberal bias remains in place despite the abandonment of formulaic SAPs, and that, together with the WTO (see p. 537) and the IMF, it tends to uphold the imbalances and disparities of the global economic order rather than challenge them.

International aid and the development ethic

Since the 1980s, there has been growing political and ethical debate about development and how it can best be achieved. This, in part, reflected mounting disillusionment with 'orthodox', market-based approaches to development, greater attention being paid to more critical and reflective 'alternative' theories of development that, amongst other things, give greater scope for Southern views rather than technocratic intervention by the North. Amartya Sen's (1999) notion of 'development as freedom' and growing interest in the 'human development' approach to poverty are examples of this process. In addition to this, a global anti-poverty movement started to emerge, often acting as the most prominent element within the larger anti-globalization or anti-capitalist movement. The anti-poverty message has been conveyed by a wide range of development NGOs, groups such as Jubilee 2000 (which campaigned for the end of developing world debt by the year 2000) and the Make Poverty History campaign, and by the Live Aid concerts in 1985 (which aimed to raise funds for famine relief in Ethiopia) and the Live 8 concerts and protests that sought to exert influence on the 2005 G8 summit in Gleneagles, Scotland. One consequence of this has been a willingness to make bolder assertions about what Jeffrey Sachs (2005) called the 'end of poverty', and to set ambitious targets for its achievement. The most significant attempt to do this, and to reinvigorate the development agenda took place through the establishment of the Millennium Development Goals (MDGs), although there has been debate about the extent to which they have succeeded (see p. 382).

Underlying these developments has been the emergence of a new development ethic that reflects the declining influence of realist assumptions and a strengthening of cosmopolitan sensibilities. In the realist approach to development, aid and other forms of support for foreign countries are, and should be, motivated for a concern for national self-interest. This is based on the assumption that people's moral obligations are essentially confined by citizenship and culture, and are thus restricted to people who share the same national identity and are part of the same community. This ethical nationalism suggests that concern about the plight of other peoples and other countries should be informed by a kind of enlightened self-interest, in which, for example, rich countries provide international aid (see p. 383) primarily to support the creation of new and more vibrant markets for their own goods. By contrast, cosmopolitanism (see p. 21) globalizes moral sensibilities in that they extend to all peoples and groups, regardless of national differences. As such, it provides a stronger and more positive basis for supporting development and poverty reduction based on the principle of global justice. The extent of moral obligations, and particularly whether our obligations extend to all other people in the world, is therefore a matter of hot dispute (see p. 81).

At least three arguments have been used to support such a development ethic. The first is based on the principle of general benevolence. Peter Singer (1993), for example, used utilitarian arguments, which favour acts that promote overall happiness and reduce overall levels of pain and suffering, to advance the principle that 'if we can prevent something bad without sacrificing anything of comparable significance, we ought to do it'. Thus, if absolute poverty is bad, and at least some absolute poverty can be prevented without significant sacrifices being

GLOBAL POLITICS IN ACTION . . .

The Millennium Development Goals

Events: In September 2000, the largest gathering of world leaders to date took place, as 147 heads of state and government met at the Millennium Summit in New York. The Summit concluded with the adoption of the Millennium Declaration, which, in turn, provided the framework for the Millennium Development Goals (MDGs or MDG-8), a long- and medium-term development agenda approved by UN General Assembly in the December. The eight headline MDGs are: Goal 1: Eradicate extreme poverty and hunger; Goal 2: Achieve universal primary education; Goal 3: Promote gender equality and empower women; Goal 4: Reduce child mortality; Goal 5: Improve maternal health; Goal 6: Combat HIV/AIDS, malaria and other diseases; Goal 7: Ensure environmental sustainability; and Goal 8: Develop a global partnership for development. All 193 UN member states and at least 23 international organizations have agreed to achieve these goals by the year 2015.

Call to Action on the Millennium Development Goals

Poverty Hunger   Education   Gender Equality   Health   Environment   Partner For Deve

Significance: The purpose of the MDGs was to inject renewed urgency into global development efforts by establishing challenging targets in each of the key human development areas. The MDGs are focused not only on transferring wealth, but also on changing the rules of the global economy to remove structural inequalities. This is particularly emphasized by Goal 8 (the only goal that does not have fixed targets), which encompasses the goal of establishing an open trading and financial system that is rule-based, predictable and non-discriminatory. The significance of the MDGs is usually judged by the extent to which key goals have been met, or are on target to be met. On this basis, the record is mixed. In the Millennium Development Goals Report 2012, the UNDP concluded that achieving the MDGs was 'challenging but possible'. Important successes include that the proportion of people living on less than $1.25 a day fell from 47 per cent in 1999 to 24 per cent in 2008 (with, for the first time, poverty rates declining in all developing regions, including sub-Saharan Africa); the target of halving the proportion of people without access to improved sources of water has been met; and, by 2010, the net enrolment rate for children in primary education in the developing regions had reached 90 per cent. However, among the concerns

raised were that maternal mortality rates and the number of people living with HIV/AIDS have remained stubbornly high, and that, in 2011, core development aid fell in real terms for the first time in more than a decade.

The MDGs have, nevertheless, been subject to wider criticism. For instance, the absence of goals related to political and cultural rights, and the lack of strong objectives and indicators for equality, mean that the MDGs paint a partial and possibly misleading picture of development. Similarly, where progress has been made, it may either have been brought about by factors unrelated to the MDGs, or reflect developments in a limited range of countries. Improved growth in sub-Saharan Africa may thus largely be explained by high commodity prices, while the goal of halving the number of people living on less than $1.25 a day was achieved (three years ahead of target) simply by the economic emergence of China. In addition, it has been difficult to gather reliable data to monitor progress, both because of the use of local, and often inflated, data on poverty reduction levels, and because, especially with health-related goals, progress is impossible to measure in practice. Among the deeper structural problems that have been associated with the MDGs are that, being devised by the UN and relying heavily on the global North to provide more generous assistance to the global South, they constitute an essentially 'top-down' approach to promoting development, and are, anyway, guided by a liberal model of development that has brought mixed benefits to the developing world.

CONCEPT

International aid

International aid (sometimes called 'foreign aid' or 'overseas aid') refers to the transfer of goods or services from one country to another country, motivated, at least in part, by the desire to benefit the recipient country or its people. While bilateral aid is direct country-to-country aid, multilateral aid is provided by or through an international organization. Humanitarian aid (or emergency relief) differs from development aid, the former addressing immediate and basic needs, whereas the latter is concerned with longer-term projects. The term is controversial because it assigns an altruistic motive to actions that may be essentially self-serving, as aid often comes with 'strings attached' and is not always clearly humanitarian (loans are often counted as aid, for example).

● **Tobin tax**: A transaction tax on foreign currency dealings, proposed by the US economist James Tobin.

made (charitable giving or protesting, for example), then not to help in these circumstances would be wrong, even, according to Singer, amounting to the moral equivalent of murder. The second argument is based on the doctrine of human rights (see p. 311). The idea of a 'right to development' has emerged out of a combination of economic rights and 'third-generation' solidarity rights (as discussed in Chapter 13). This right imposes important duties on other people. Shue (1996), for instance, argued on this basis that people not only have a duty not to deprive others but, more radically, a duty to relieve their deprivation. The acceptance of this duty would imply a major redistribution of wealth and resources on a global level. The third argument is based on attempts to rectify past injustices. If the wealth of the North has substantially been based on the oppression and exploitation of the South (in particular through colonialism and neo-colonialism), this imposes powerful obligations on rich countries to make amends, compensate or bring about restitution for past actions. Clearly, however, those obliged to support poverty reduction may not themselves be involved in exploitation, but they are the beneficiaries of past and present exploitation, as part of a larger causal chain of exploitation (Dower 1998).

International aid is the principal way in which countries discharge their development responsibilities and help to promote socio-economic development in other countries. Aid may consist of the provision of funds, resources and equipment, or staff and expertise. Nevertheless, despite a series of major international development initiatives, often focused on boosting aid commitments, there are persistent concerns about the levels of aid actually provided. Although rich countries have committed themselves to meeting the UN's target of donating 0.7 per cent of their GNP to aid, donation levels have lagged far behind, with only five OECD states (Norway, Sweden, Luxembourg, Denmark and the Netherlands) achieving the target in 2007. Aid levels have, instead, generally been in the range 0.2–0.4 per cent, and in the case of the USA, also in 2007, 0.16 per cent. Official aid figures, moreover, are notoriously unreliable as they often include money allocated for purposes such as debt relief and administrative costs incurred by donor states that do not take the form of direct economic assistance. On the other hand, official figures take account only of government spending and ignore the fact much more is given by private donations of various kinds. For example, private donations from the USA (from foundations, businesses, NGOs, religious bodies and colleges) are more than twice as large as the US international aid budget, and personal remittances from the USA to developing countries are about three times as large. Nevertheless, there is general agreement that the level of international aid is generally insufficient to support meaningful development, and is putting the achievement of the Millennium Development Goals at risk. Although substantial progress has been made in areas such as primary education, AIDS treatment and access to safe drinking water, poverty in sub-Saharan African countries has been reduced by only about 1 per cent, and these countries appear unlikely to meet their goals by 2015. The quest for equitable development has, furthermore, been damaged by the fact that, in the context of the global financial crisis, developed countries reduced their aid budgets in 2007 and 2008.

Such difficulties have fuelled attempts to generate additional funds that can be used for international aid. These have included the so-called '**Tobin tax**', which also aims to dampen down the volatility of financial markets, an airline ticket levy and the International Finance Facility, which would involve the sale of

KEY THEORISTS IN DEVELOPMENT

Jagdish Bhagwati (born 1934)

An Indian-American economist and adviser to the UN and the GATT/WTO, Bhagwati has been a leader in the fight for freer trade, arguing that globalization has a 'human face', even though this needs to be made more agreeable. His early books helped to encourage the current economic reforms in India. Bhagwati's works include *In Defence of Globalization* (2004) and *Termites in the Trading System* (2008).

Susan George (born 1934)

A Franco-American political scientist and activist, George has been a fierce critic of the 'maldevelopment' policies of the IMF and the World Bank, advancing an uncompromising critique of the impact of capitalism on the world's poor. Her works include *How the Other Half Dies* (1976), *A Fate Worse Than Debt* (1988) and *Another World is Possible If* (2004).

Jeffrey Sachs (born 1954)

A US economist and director of the Earth Institute at Columbia University, Sachs has been a leading exponent of sustainable development, placing an emphasis on ending extreme poverty and hunger and advising the UN on strategies for supporting the Millennium Development Goals. His publications include *The End of Poverty* (2005), *Investing in Development* (2005) and *Common Wealth* (2008).

Amartya Sen (born 1933)

An Indian welfare economist and philosopher, Sen has made a major contribution to shifting thinking about development away from economic models and towards ideas such as capacity, freedom and choice. Sen's thinking had a major impact on the creation of the Human Development Index. His works include *Poverty and Famine* (1981), *Development as Freedom* (1999) and *The Idea of Justice* (2009).

Muhammad Yunus (born 1940)

A Bangladeshi banker, economist and Nobel laureate who founded the pioneering microfinance institution, the Grameen Bank, from which he stood down as managing director in 2011. Yunus' wider influence stems from his ability to turn microcredit into a viable business model as well as an effective poverty-reduction mechanism. His publications include *Banker to the Poor* (2003), *Creating a World Without Poverty* (2008) and *Building Social Business* (2010).

See also **Joseph Stiglitz** (p. 474)

KEY EVENTS . . .

Major development initiatives

1970	Rich countries commit themselves to achieving the UN's target of providing 0.7 per cent of GNP and official assistance to poorer countries.
1974	UN declaration on the New International Economic Order (NIEO), which included a call for the radical redistribution of resources from the North to the South.
1980	The Brandt Report of the Independent Commission on International Development Issues, chaired by Willy Brandt (former German Chancellor), emphasizes the depth of the North–South divide but also stresses the 'mutuality of interests' argument.
1987	The Brundtland Report, *Our Common Future*, prepared by the World Commission on Environment and Development, emphasizes the principle of 'sustainable development', linking economic growth and poverty reduction to stronger environmental protection.
1992	The UN's Conference on Environment and Development, also known as the Earth Summit, attempts to translate sustainable development into a range of policy proposals.
2000	Through the Millennium Development Goals, some 189 states and at least 23 international organizations sign up to a series of bold goals on the reduction of poverty by the year 2015 (see p. 382).
2005	The G8 Summit at Gleneagles, Scotland, agrees to boost aid to Africa and adopt a programme of debt cancellation.

government-backed bonds on the financial market. However, the issue of international aid is not only about numbers. The quality of international aid may be just as important as its quantity. Jeffrey Sachs (2005) identified the standards for successful aid as that it should be targeted, specific, measurable, accountable and scalable (appropriate to the scale of the task for which it is designated). It should, moreover, support a 'triple transformation'. In agriculture, it should boost food production to end cycles of famine, particularly by promoting a '**green revolution**'. In health, it should aim to improve nutrition, the provision of cleaner drinking water and basic health services. In infrastructure, projects should help to tackle economic isolation by improving transport, supply chains and connectivity generally.

The idea that international aid promotes development has not gone unchallenged, however. Economic liberals have even gone as far as to argue that aid is a 'poverty trap' helping to entrench deprivation and perpetuate global disparities. From this perspective, international aid tends to promote dependency, sap initiative and undermine the operation of free markets. Easterly (2006), for example, argued that the $568 billion that had been given by rich countries in international aid to Africa over four decades had resulted in no increase in per capita income. A major factor accounting for this gloomy picture has been the growth

● **Green revolution**: The introduction of pesticides and high-yield crops to boost agricultural productivity.

in **corruption**. The level of corruption in an institutional system is conditioned by factors such as the effectiveness of external checks, the level of administrative discipline, the strength of internal codes and norms, and the general level of economic development. Government-to-government aid to authoritarian or dictatorial regimes has therefore often been siphoned off for the benefit of elite groups and contributed little to the alleviation of poverty or deprivation. This is why aid programmes since the 1990s have increasingly stressed the need to meet conditions for 'good governance'. Moreover, aid is rarely donated disinterestedly. Realists argue that aid, if it is provided at all, invariably reflects donor-state national interests. It comes with 'strings attached'. Much of US official international aid is therefore linked to trade agreements, a practice that the EU now actively discourages. Similarly, food aid that appears to be designed to relieve hunger has commonly taken the form of '**food dumping**', which undercuts local farmers, who cannot compete and may be driven out of jobs and into poverty.

Debt relief and fair trade

The issue of developing world debt has been prominent since the debt crisis of the 1970s and 1980s. This created problems for both the North and the South. As poorer countries (starting with Mexico in 1982) announced that they could no longer service their debts, many Northern banks were faced with the possibility of collapse. More severely, however, Southern countries, due to the size of their debts and their poor economic performance, channelled more and more money into their escalating debt repayments at the expense of building schools and hospitals, investing in the economic infrastructure and helping to alleviate poverty. Even though loans from the World Bank and the IMF were provided on the most favourable terms that developing countries could obtain anywhere in the world, debt escalation was dramatic. For instance, Zimbabwe's foreign debt rose from $814 million in 1970 to nearly $7 billion by 1990. A growing campaign to bring about **debt relief** therefore started to emerge (George 1988).

Powerful voices were, nevertheless, raised against debt relief. Concerns, for example, were raised about its implications for the stability of the world's financial system and about the message it sent poorer countries about the need to uphold financial disciplines. On the other hand, Northern countries were becoming increasingly aware that if the growing debt burden was entrenching poverty in the South, it was merely strengthening the pressure to expand international aid and other forms of assistance. In 1989, the USA launched the 'Brady bonds', through which it underwrote a proportion of Latin America's debt overhang from the 1970s and 1980s. Under the Heavily Indebted Poor Countries (HIPC) Initiative, negotiated in 1996, the World Bank and the IMF agreed to extend the opportunity for debt relief to 40 of the world's poorest countries. Uganda was one of the first to enjoy debt relief under HIPC, and by 2006, 29 countries were enjoying debt relief, at a cost estimated to be about $62 billion. The G8 Gleneagles deal in 2005 significantly accelerated the pace of debt relief, through the agreement to provide 100 per cent cancellation of debts owed to the IMF and the World Bank. By 2013, of the 39 countires eligible or potentially eligible for assistance, 35 were receiving full debt relief from the IMF and other creditors. Greater progress has undoubtedly been made on debt relief than on either increasing aid levels or switching from free trade to fair trade.

● **Corruption**: A failure to carry out 'proper' or public responsibilities because of the pursuit of private gain, usually involving bribery or misappropriation.

● **Food dumping**: The donation of surplus food to poor countries for free or at cheap rates in order to maintain market shares or prop up global prices.

● **Debt relief**: Agreements to write off foreign debt or reduce it to 'sustainable levels', often linked to conditions about good governance.

Debating...
Does international aid work?

Traditionally, international aid has been seen as the main way of fighting poverty and spurring economic growth in poor countries. If we want to promote development, the solution is to give more. The vexing challenge for humanitarians is nevertheless that there has been a lack of evidence that aid is effective.

FOR

A more level playing-field. The idea that self-reliance and global market forces will 'raise all boats' is fundamentally flawed. There are structural biases within the global economy that favour rich countries at the expense of poor ones, not least to do with the impact of free trade and the concentration of corporate power in the North. Poor countries, therefore, cannot compete on equal terms. International aid helps to counter these disparities by ensuring a counter-flow of money and resources from the North to the South. Some, further, argue that there is a moral duty to provide international aid, in that the wealth and prosperity of the North has been, in substantial part, built on its mistreatment of the South.

Building domestic capacity. It is a myth that aid merely provides recipient countries with money that they can put to proper or improper uses, as they wish. International aid is increasingly targeted on long-term development projects and is orientated around capacity-building for the future. Examples include aid provided to improve the economic infrastructure (dams, roads, bridges, airports), to boost food production ('high tech' crops, pesticides, irrigation schemes), and improve health services and education, particularly primary education. The effectiveness of aid is evident in the fact that countries such as China, India, Brazil and Thailand, major recipients of aid in the past, are now developing strategic aid programmes themselves.

Emergency relief. A growing proportion of aid is now so-called 'humanitarian' aid, provided for purposes of emergency relief. The need for emergency relief has grown as 'humanitarian' crises have become more common, through, for example, an increase in civil wars and ethnic conflict, and climate change due to global warming. As emergency relief consists of the provision of food, clean water, shelter, vaccinations and so on, the justification for it is quite simply that it saves lives. The international community increasingly accepts that it has a moral obligation to act in such circumstances.

AGAINST

Ineffective help for the poor. There is little reliable evidence that aid boosts economic growth and contributes to poverty reduction. This is certainly borne out by the experience of Africa and particularly of sub-Saharan Africa, where decades of international assistance have not been associated with meaningful economic progress, and may even, in some cases, have been counterproductive. Aid, indeed, may entrench patterns of global inequality, rather than challenge them, discouraging initiative and self-reliance within recipient countries and strengthening a culture of dependency. The level of aid is, anyway, insufficient to make a difference to poor countries and poor people.

Distorting markets. Any form of aid or external assistance tends to upset the fragile balances of a market economy, which provide poor countries with their best long-term prospect of development. Not only does this reduce incentives and prevent the growth of entrepreneurship, but it also means that resources are not drawn to their most profitable use, leading to economic inefficiency and low productivity. Aid can thus 'hollow out' an economy, effectively displacing local businesses and industries, or at least constraining their growth. This can be seen in the tendency of food aid to weaken domestic agricultural production, thereby contributing to an expansion of rural poverty.

Corruption and oppression. Aid is invariably channeled through recipient-country governments and bureaucracies in which power is often concentrated in the hands of the few and the mechanisms of accountability are, at best, poorly-developed. This tends to benefit corrupt leaders and elites rather than the people, projects and programmes for which it was intended. Indeed, aid may actually foster corruption and deepen oppression, as autocratic rulers may use aid funds not only to support their own affluent lifestyles, but also to widen their own political control by subverting opponents and benefiting favoured ethnic or tribal groups. What is more, aid conditions related to 'good governance' are much easier to establish than to enforce.

● **Fair trade**: Trade that satisfies moral, and not merely economic, criteria, related to alleviating poverty and respecting the interests of sellers and producers in poorer areas.

Nevertheless, some have argued that it has weakened pressure to increase aid, as money allocated for debt relief is usually calculated within international aid budgets.

After international aid and debt relief, the third priority within the anti-poverty agenda is the global trading system. Anti-poverty campaigners have argued that free trade must be replaced by **fair trade**. This stems from the belief that structural disparities that operate within the global trading system systematically benefit the wealthiest and most developed countries at the expense of the poorest and least developed ones. These are often linked to inequalities in the terms of trade, whereby primary goods, often produced in the developing world, are relatively cheap while manufactured goods, usually produced in the developed world, are relatively expensive. 'Free' trade can therefore rob people in developing countries of a proper living, keeping them trapped in poverty. Attempts to promote development through the provision of international aid and debt relief, but which ignore the global trading system, are therefore doomed to failure. Many development NGOs have, as a result, called for fair trade rather than free trade, which would involve setting prices for goods produced in the developing world that protect wage levels and working conditions, thus guaranteeing a better deal for producers in poorer countries. Such campaigns often focus on changing consumer preferences in the developed world in order to alter companies' commercial practices; however, the extent to which they can alleviate poverty is necessarily limited. More significant progress in establishing fair trade requires the reform of the global trading system itself. This issue is discussed in greater depth in Chapter 19.

SUMMARY

- A distinction is commonly drawn between absolute poverty, founded on the idea of 'basic needs', and relative poverty, in which the poor are the 'less well-off' rather than the 'needy'. However, narrowly income-based definitions of poverty have increasingly been viewed as limited or misleading, as greater attention is paid to the broader notion of human development.

- The 'orthodox' view of development takes economic growth to be its goal and understands modernization in terms of western-style industrialization. The 'alternative' view of development rejects such technocratic, top-down and pro-growth strategies, but it encompasses a wide range of views and approaches.

- Trends in global inequality are often highly complex and contradictory. It is widely believed that in recent decades the growing importance of emerging economies has had an equalizing impact, counter-balanced by deepening poverty in sub-Saharan Africa and a general trend towards greater within-country inequality.

- The impact of globalization on levels of poverty and inequality cannot be resolved through empirical trends alone. Some claim that globalization, like a rising tide, will eventually 'raise all boats', but others argue that globalization is based on structural disparities that inevitably benefit some countries and areas at the expense of others.

- Official development policies, particularly during the 1980s and 1990s, were based on structural adjustment programmes that sought to remove blocks to economic growth in the developing world. These proved to be highly controversial, sometimes resulting in deeper, not reduced, poverty, and have, in some respects, been modified in recent years.

- International aid is often viewed as the key mechanism of development. It is justified by a development ethic that suggests that rich countries have an obligation to support poor countries and reduce global inequality. Critics, nevertheless, have argued that aid provides ineffective support for the world's poor because it undermines markets and tends to promote corruption and oppression.

Questions for discussion

- What distinguishes 'the rich' from 'the poor'?
- Why has poverty increasingly been measured in terms of human development?
- What are the advantages and disadvantages of the 'development as growth' model?
- What is the North–South divide, and why has its continuing relevance been called into question?
- Why is there so much disagreement about trends in global inequality?
- To what extent can growing poverty be blamed on the advance of globalization?
- Why have official development policies aimed to adjust the structure of developing economies?
- Have the Millennium Development Goals been mere window dressing?
- Does international aid redress imbalances in the global economy?
- Does writing-off developing world debt make both moral and economic good sense?

Further reading

Brett, E., *Reconstructing Development Theory: International Inequality, Institutional Reform and Social Emancipation* (2009). A systematic assessment of the evolution of development theory and its relationship to other social science disciplines.

Greig, A., D. Hulme and M. Turner, *Challenging Global Inequality: Development Theory and Practice in the 21st Century* (2007). An accessible overview of global inequality and development ideas and practices in the twenty-first century.

Riddell, R., *Does Foreign Aid Really Work?* (2007). A thorough and insightful examination of the benefits as well as the failings of the contemporary world of international aid.

Willis, K., *Theories and Practices of Development* (2011). An accessible introduction to competing theoretical approaches to development and their practical implications.

ONLINE RESOURCES AVAILABLE

Links to relevant web resources can be found on the *Global Politics* website

CHAPTER 16

Global Environmental Issues

'There are no passengers on Spaceship Earth. We are all crew.'

MARSHALL MCLUHAN, *Understanding Media* (1964)

PREVIEW

The environment is often viewed as the archetypal example of a global issue. This is because environmental processes are no respecters of national borders; they have an intrinsically transnational character. As countries are peculiarly environmentally vulnerable to the activities that take place in other countries, meaningful progress on environmental issues can often only be made at the international or even global level. Nevertheless, international cooperation on such matters has sometimes been very difficult to bring about. This has occurred for a number of reasons. In the first place, the environment has been an arena of particular ideological and political debate. Disagreements have emerged about both the seriousness and nature of environmental problems and about how they can best be tackled, not least because environmental priorities tend to conflict with economic ones. Can environmental problems be dealt with within the existing socio-economic system, or is this system the source of those problems? Such debates have been especially passionate over what is clearly the central issue on the global environmental agenda, climate change. Despite sometimes catastrophic predictions about what will happen if the challenge of climate change is not addressed, concerted international action on the issue has been frustratingly slow to emerge. What have been the obstacles to international cooperation over climate change, and what would concerted international action on the issue involve? Finally, climate change is not the only issue on the global environmental agenda. Another issue of major concern is energy security, with some talking in terms of a new international energy order in which a country's ranking in the hierarchy of states is being increasingly determined by the vastness of its oil and natural gas reserves, or its ability to acquire them. To what extent has energy security reshaped global order, and are natural resources always a blessing?

KEY ISSUES

- How and why has the environment developed into a global issue?
- Do modern environmental problems require reformist or radical solutions?
- What are the causes and major consequences of climate change?
- How far has international action over climate change progressed?
- What obstacles stand in the way of international cooperation over climate change?
- How has energy security shaped conflict both between states and within states?

Ecology

The term 'ecology' was coined by the German zoologist Ernst Haeckel in 1866. Derived from the Greek *oikos*, meaning household or habitat, he used it to refer to 'the investigations of the total relations of the animal both to its organic and its inorganic environment'. Ecology developed as a distinct branch of biology through a growing recognition that plants and animals are sustained by self-regulating natural systems – ecosystems – composed of both living and non-living elements. Simple examples of an ecosystem are a field, a forest or, as illustrated in Figure 16.1, a pond. All ecosystems tend towards a state of harmony or equilibrium through a system of self-regulation, referred to by biologists as homeostasis.

● **Ecologism**: A political ideology that is based on the belief that nature is an interconnected whole, embracing humans and non-humans, as well as the inanimate world.

● **Fossil fuels**: Fuels that are formed through the decomposition of buried dead organisms, making them rich in carbon; examples include oil, natural gas and coal.

THE RISE OF GREEN POLITICS

The environment as a global issue

Although forms of environmental politics can be traced back to the industrialization of the nineteenth century, **ecologism** or green politics having always been, in a sense, a backlash against industrial society, the environment did not become a significant national or international issue until the 1960s and 1970s. This occurred through the emergence of an environmental movement that sought to highlight the environmental costs of increased growth and rising affluence, at least in the developed West, drawing attention also to a growing divide between humankind and nature. Influenced in particular by the idea of ecology (see Figure 16.1), the pioneering works of early green politics included Rachel Carson's *The Silent Spring* (1962), a critique of the damage done to wildlife and the human world by the increased use of pesticides and other agricultural chemicals, and Murray Bookchin's *Our Synthetic Environment* ([1962] 1975) which examined how pesticides, food additives and X-rays cause a range of human illnesses, including cancer. This period of the 1960s and 1970s also saw the birth of a new generation of activist NGOs (see p. 10) – ranging from Greenpeace and Friends of the Earth to animal liberation activists and so-called 'eco-warrior' groups – campaigning on issues such as the dangers of pollution, the dwindling reserves of **fossil fuels**, deforestation and animal experiments. From the 1980s onwards, environmental questions were kept high on the political agenda by green parties, which now exist in most industrialized countries, often modelling themselves on the pioneering efforts of the German Greens. The environmental movement addresses three general problems. These are:

● *Resource* problems – attempts to conserve natural materials through reducing the use of non-renewable resources (coal, oil, natural gas and so on), increasing the use of renewable resources (such as wind, wave and tidal power), and reducing population growth, thereby curtailing resource consumption.

● *Sink* problems – attempts to reduce the damage done by the waste products of economic activity, through, for example, reducing pollution levels, increasing recycling, and developing greener (less polluting) technologies.

● *Ethical* problems – attempts to restore the balance between humankind and nature through wildlife and wilderness conservation, respect for other species (animal rights and animal welfare), and changed agricultural practices (organic farming).

During the 1970s, environmental politics focused particularly on resource issues. This reflected a growing awareness that humankind lives in a world of 'global finiteness', an awareness reinforced by the oil crisis of 1973. A particularly influential metaphor for the environmental movement was the idea of 'spaceship Earth', because this emphasized the notion of limited and exhaustible wealth. Kenneth Boulding (1966) argued that human beings had traditionally acted as though they lived in a 'cowboy economy', an economy with unlimited opportunities, like the American West during the frontier period. However, as a spaceship

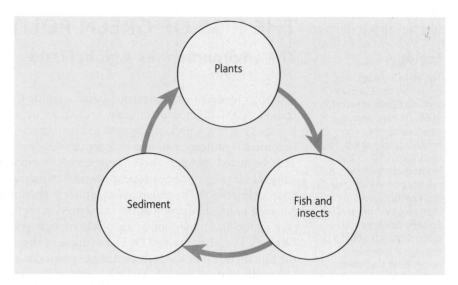

Figure 16.1 A pond as an ecosystem

is a capsule, it is a closed system and all closed systems tend to exhibit evidence of **entropy** in that they decay because they are not sustained by external inputs. Ultimately, however wisely and carefully human beings behave, the Earth, the sun and indeed all planets and stars are destined to be exhausted and die. Similar concerns about global finiteness were also highlighted by the unofficial UN report *Only One Earth* (Ward and Dubois 1972) and the report of the Club of Rome, *The Limits to Growth* (Meadows *et al.* 1972). The latter work had a stunning impact, in that it appeared to predict by extrapolating five variables – world population, industrialization, pollution, food production and resource depletion – that the world's oil supplies would run out by 1992. Although such predictions were subsequently revealed to be gross exaggerations, and despite widespread criticism of the methodology used, the idea of limits to growth dominated thinking about the environment for a decade or more.

Environmental issues also became an increasingly major focus of international concern. This reflected a growing awareness that environmental problems have an intrinsically transnational character: they are no respecters of borders. States are therefore environmentally vulnerable to the economic activities that take place in other states, a lesson that was reinforced during the 1970s by a growing concern about the regional impact of **acid rain** and by the truly global consequences of **ozone depletion** caused by emissions of man-made chemicals such as chlorofluorocarbons (CFCs) and halons. The first major international conference to be held on environmental issues was the 1972 UN Conference on the Human Environment (UNCHE) at Stockholm. The Stockholm conference also led to the establishment of the United Nations Environment Programme (UNEP), which is responsible for coordinating the environmental activities of states and international organizations to promote better regional and global environmental protection. However, the global recession of the 1970s and onset of the 'second Cold War' in the early 1980s subsequently pushed environmental issues down the international agenda. They were

● **Entropy:** A tendency towards decay or disintegration, a characteristic exhibited, sooner or later, by all closed systems.

● **Acid rain:** Rain that is contaminated by sulphuric, nitric and other acids that are released into the atmosphere by the burning of fossil fuels.

● **Ozone depletion:** A decline in the total amount of ozone in the Earth's stratosphere, particularly the development of a so-called 'ozone hole' over the Antarctic.

revived, in part, through the impact of environmental catastrophes such as the 1984 Bhopal chemical plant disaster and the 1986 Chernobyl nuclear disaster, but also by a growing recognition that environmental degradation was closely associated with the advance of globalization (see p. 8), encouraging many, particularly in the South, to link environmental and development issues. The 1987 Brundtland Commission Report, *Our Common Future*, exemplified this through its emphasis on 'sustainable development' (see p. 397), which subsequently provided the dominant mainstream framework for understanding and addressing environmental issues. The Brundtland Report prepared the way for the 1992 Rio 'Earth Summit' (officially, the UN Conference on Environment and Development, or UNCED), which was held twenty years after the landmark Stockholm conference.

From the 1990s onwards, environmental debate increasingly focused on the issue of 'climate change' brought about through **global warming**. Initial concerns about climate change had focused on CFC emissions, but this shifted over time to the impact of so-called '**greenhouse gases**'. One of the consequences of the Earth Summit was the establishment of the UN Framework Convention on Climate Change (FCCC), the first attempt to stabilize greenhouse gas concentrations at a level that would prevent dangerous anthropogenic (human-induced) climate change. Responsibility for reporting on the implementation of the FCCC was invested in the International Panel on Climate Change (IPCC) (see p. 403), established in 1988. Nevertheless, it took until the 1997 Kyoto Protocol to the FCCC to agree measures to control emissions of greenhouse gases. Under the Kyoto Protocol, developed countries agreed to cut their emissions by an average of 5 per cent, usually against 1990 levels, during the 'commitment period', 2008–12. Subsequent conferences were convened in Copenhagen (2009), Durban (2011) and Doha (2012) in an attempt to formulate a successor to Kyoto. However, in their different ways, these conferences demonstrated the difficulty of achieving concerted and effective action on the issue of climate change (see p. 409). These difficulties relate, most basically, to the mismatch between state interests and the collective interests of the international community, as illustrated by the idea of the 'tragedy of the commons' (see p. 395). Potentially, this problem applies to all environmental issues.

Green politics: reformism or radicalism?

The environment is an arena of particular ideological and political debate. Disagreements about the seriousness and nature of environmental problems, and about how they can best be tackled, are rooted in deeper, often philosophical debates about the relationship between humankind and the natural world. Conventional political thought has subscribed to a human-centred approach to understanding, often called **anthropocentrism**. Moral priority has therefore been given to the achievement of human needs and ends, with nature being seen merely as a way of facilitating these needs and ends. In the words of the early liberal English philosopher John Locke (1632–1704), human beings are 'the masters and possessors of nature'. Environmental thought, by contrast, is based on the principle of ecology, which stresses the network of relationships that sustain all forms of life including human life. However, green politics encompasses two broad traditions, which can be called 'reformist' ecology and 'radical' ecology.

● **Global warming**: An increase in the Earth's temperature, widely believed to be due to heat trapped by greenhouse gases, such as carbon dioxide.

● **Greenhouse gases**: Gases (such as carbon dioxide, water vapour, methane, nitrous oxide and ozone) that trap heat in the Earth's lower atmosphere (see The greenhouse effect, p. 404).

● **Anthropocentrism**: A belief that human needs and interests are of overriding moral and philosophical importance.

Major international initiatives on the environment

1946	International Convention for the Regulation of Whaling. This set up the International Whaling Commission (IWC) which attempts to preserve Great Whales by upholding an international moratorium on whaling.
1950	World Meteorological Organization (WMO) established as a specialized agency of the UN for meteorology (weather and climate) and related geophysical sciences.
1959	Antarctic Treaty, which set aside Antarctica, Earth's only continent without a native human population, as a scientific preserve.
1972	United Nations Conference on the Human Environment (UNCHE) in Stockholm, which laid the foundations for environmental action at an international level and prepared the way for the launch of the UN's Environmental Programme (UNEP).
1973	Convention on International Trade in Endangered Species (CITES), which aimed to ensure that international trade in wildlife and plants does not threaten their survival.
1982	UN Convention on the Law of the Sea, which defined the rights and responsibilities of countries in their use of the world's oceans and established guidelines for businesses, the environment and the management of marine natural resources (entered into force in 1994).
1985	Vienna Convention for the Protection of the Ozone Layer, which confirmed the existence of the Arctic 'ozone hole', and attempted to reduce the use of CFC gasses (entered into force in 1987).
1987	Brundtland Commission Report, which highlighted the idea of sustainable development.
1987	Montreal Protocol on Substances that Deplete the Ozone Layer, which provided for the phasing out of CFCs with the goal of the ozone layer having recovered by 2050.
1988	International Panel on Climate Change (IPCC) (see p. 403) established, which reports on the implementation of the UN Framework Convention on Climate Change (FCCC).
1992	UN Conference on Environment and Development (UNCED) held in Rio de Janeiro and commonly called the 'Earth Summit', which included conventions on climate change and biodiversity and established the Commission on Sustainable Development (CSD).
1997	Kyoto Protocol to the FCCC, which established a legally binding commitment by developed states to limit greenhouse gas emissions in a phased process. (Entered into force in 2005 with the first commitment period being 2008–12).
2009–12	The UN Climate Change Conferences held in Copenhagen, Durban and Doha to formulate a successor to the Kyoto Protocol (see p. 409).

Focus on ...
The tragedy of the commons?

Will shared resources always be misused or overused? Does community ownership of land, forests and fisheries lead to inevitable ruin, and what does this imply about modern environmental problems? Garrett Hardin (see p. 411) used the idea of the 'tragedy of the commons' to draw parallels between global environmental degradation and the fate of common land before the introduction of enclosures. He argued that if pasture is open to all, each herder will try to keep as many cattle as possible on the commons. However, sooner or later, the inherent logic of the commons will remorselessly generate tragedy, as the number of cattle exceeds the **carrying capacity** of the land. Each herder calculates that the *positive* benefit of adding one more animal (in terms of the proceeds from its eventual sale) will always exceed the *negative* impact on the pasture, as this is relatively slight and, anyway, shared by all herders. As Hardin put it, 'Freedom in a commons brings ruin to all'. The idea of the 'tragedy of the commons' draws attention to the importance of the **'global commons'**, sometimes seen as 'common pool resources', and of threats posed to these by overpopulation (a particular concern for Hardin), pollution, resource depletion, habitat destruction and over-fishing.

Is the 'tragedy of the commons' an unsolvable problem? Hardin himself argued in favour of strengthened political control, especially to restrict population growth, even showing sympathy for the idea of world government (see p. 464). Liberals, nevertheless, argue that the solution is, in effect, to abolish the commons by extending property rights, allowing the disciplines of the market (the price mechanism) to control resource usage. Although, as capitalism expanded, common land gradually became privately owned, it is more difficult to see how privatization could be applied to the global commons. Ostrom (1990) nevertheless argued that some societies have succeeded in managing common pool resources through developing diverse, and often bottom-up, institutional arrangements. However, others, particularly socialists and anarchists, reject the 'tragedy of the commons' altogether. Not only does historical evidence suggest that common land was usually successfully managed by communities (Cox 1985), as is borne out by examples such as the Aboriginal peoples of Australia, but the argument is also circular: its conclusions are implicit in the assumption that human nature is selfish and unchanging (Angus 2008). Indeed, ecosocialists would argue that selfishness, greed and the wanton use of resources are a consequence of the system of private ownership, not their cause. Community ownership, by contrast, engenders respect for the natural environment.

Reformist ecology

● **Carrying capacity**: The maximum population that an ecosystem can support, given the food, habitat, water and other necessities available.

● **Global commons**: Areas and natural resources that are unowned and so beyond national jurisdiction, examples including the atmosphere, the oceans and, arguably, Antarctica.

Reformist ecology seeks to reconcile the principle of ecology with the central features of capitalist modernity (individual self-seeking, materialism, economic growth and so on), which is why it sometimes called 'modernist' ecology. It is clearly a form of humanist or **'shallow' ecology**. The key feature of reformist ecology is that recognition that there are 'limits to growth', in that environmental degradation (in the form of, for instance, pollution or the use of non-renewable resources) ultimately threatens prosperity and economic performance. The watchword of this form of ecologism is sustainable development, especially what is called 'weak' sustainability. In economic terms, this means 'getting rich more slowly'. From the reformist perspective, damage to the environment is an **externality**, or 'social cost'. By taking account of such costs, modernist ecologists attempted to develop a balance between modernization and **sustainability**.

The chief ideological influence on reformist ecology is **utilitarianism**, which is based on classical liberal thinking. In that sense, reformist ecology practises what can be called 'enlightened' anthropocentrism, encouraging individuals to take account of long-term, not merely short-term, interests. The British utilitarian philosopher and politician John Stuart Mill (1806–73) thus justified a steady-state economy (one without economic growth) on the grounds that the contemplation of nature is a 'higher' pleasure. Peter Singer (1993) justified animal rights on the grounds that all species, and not just humans, have a right to avoid suffering. More generally, utilitarian thinking acknowledges the impact on the quality of human life of environmental degradation by recognizing the interests of future generations (see p. 398). The most straightforward case for conserving resources is therefore that it maximises the welfare or happiness of people, taking account of both the living and of people who have yet to be born. Finally, reformist ecology is defined by the means through which it would deal with environmental problems, as typified by the mainstream environmental movement. It tends to advocate three main solutions to environmental degradation:

- 'Market ecologism' or 'green capitalism'. This involves attempts to adjust markets to take account of the damage done to the environment, making externalities internal to the businesses or organizations that are responsible for them. Examples of this include **green taxes**.
- Human ingenuity and the development of green technologies (such as drought resistant crops, energy-efficient forms of transport and 'clean' coal). The capacity for invention and innovation that created industrial civilization in the first place can also be used to generate an environmentally-friendly version of industrialization.
- International regimes (see p. 71) and systems of transnational regulation. Global governance (see p. 462) offers the prospect that the impact of 'tragedy of the commons' can be reduced, even though it can never be removed.

Radical ecology

Radical ecology, by contrast, encompasses a range of green perspectives that call, in their various ways, for more far-reaching, and in some cases even revolutionary, change. Rather than seeking to reconcile the principle of ecology with the central features of capitalist modernity, these theories view capitalist modernity, and its values, structures and institutions, as the root cause of environmental degradation. A variety of these perspectives can collectively be categorized as forms of **social ecology**, in that they each explain the balance between humankind and nature largely by reference to social structures. The advance of ecological principles therefore requires a process of radical social change. However, this social change is understood in at least three quite different ways:

- *Ecosocialism* advances an environmental critique of capitalism. For ecosocialists, capitalism's anti-ecological bias stems from the institution of private property and its tendency towards **'commodification'**. These reduce nature to mere resources and suggest that the only hope for ecological sustainability is the construction of a socialist society.

- **Shallow ecology**: A green ideological perspective that harnesses the lessons of ecology to human needs and ends, and is associated with values such as sustainability and conservation.

- **Externality**: A cost of an economic activity that has wider impact but does not feature on the balance sheet of a business or form part of the GDP of a country.

- **Sustainability**: The capacity of a system to maintain its health and continuing existence over a period of time.

- **Utilitarianism**: A moral philosophy that equates 'good' with pleasure or happiness, and 'evil' with pain or unhappiness, and aims to achieve 'the greatest happiness for the greatest number' (the principle of general utility).

- **Green taxes**: Taxes that penalize individuals or businesses for, for instance, the waste they generate, the pollution they cause, the emissions they generate or the finite resources they consume.

- **Social ecology**: The idea that ecological principles can and should be applied to social organization, a term originally used mainly by eco-anarchists.

- **Commodification**: Turning something into a commodity that can be bought and sold, having only an economic value.

Focus on...
Sustainable development: reconciling growth with ecology?

Can development be ecologically sustainable? Is there an inevitable tension between economic growth and protecting the environment? The idea of 'sustainable development' has dominated thinking on environmental and development issues since it was highlighted by the 1987 Brundtland Report. The Brundtland Report's highly influential definition of the term is: 'Sustainable development is development that meets the needs of the present without compromising the ability of future generations to meet their own needs. It contains two key concepts: (1) the concept of need, in particular the essential needs of the world's poor, to which overriding priority should be given, and (2) the concept of limitations, imposed by the state of technology and social organization on the environment's ability to meet present and future needs.'

However, there is debate about what sustainable development means in practice, and about how growth and ecology can be reconciled. What is sometimes called

'weak' sustainability accepts that economic growth is desirable but simply recognizes that growth must limited to ensure that ecological costs do not threaten its long-term sustainability. This means, in effect, getting richer slower. Supporters of this view, moreover, argue that human capital can be substituted for natural capital, implying, for example, that better roads or a new airport could compensate for a loss of habitat or agricultural land. In this view, the key requirement of sustainability is that the net sum of natural and human capital available to future generations should not be less than that available to present generations. However, 'strong' sustainability, favoured by radical ecologists, rejects the pro-growth implications of weak sustainability. It focuses just on the need to preserve and sustain natural capital, seeing human capital as little more than a blight on nature. This is sometimes reflected in the belief that natural capital should be evaluated in terms of people's **ecological footprint**, an idea that has radically egalitarian implications.

● **Ecological footprint**: A measure of ecological capacity based on the hectares of biologically productive land that are needed to supply a given person's consumption of natural resources and absorb their waste.

● **Deep ecology**: A green ideological perspective that rejects anthropocentrism and gives priority to the maintenance of nature; it is associated with values such as bioequality, diversity and decentralization.

● **Ecocentrism**: A theoretical orientation that gives priority to the maintenance of ecological balance rather than the achievement of human ends.

● *Eco-anarchism* advances an environmental critique of hierarchy and authority. For eco-anarchists, domination over people leads to domination over nature. This implies that a balance between humankind and nature can only be restored through the abolition of the state and the establishment of decentralized, self-managing communities (Bookchin 1982).

● *Ecofeminism* advances an environmental critique of patriarchy (see p. 424). For ecofeminists, domination over women leads to domination over nature (Merchant 1983, 1992). As men are the enemy of nature because of their reliance on instrumental reason and their inclination to control or subjugate, respect for nature requires the creation of a post-patriarchal society.

While social ecology views radical social change as the key to ecological sustainability, so-called **'deep' ecology** goes further in emphasizing the need for paradigm change, a change in our core thinking and assumptions about the world. This involves rejecting all forms of anthropocentrism, and embracing **ecocentrism** instead. Deep ecology therefore advocates a radical holism that implies that the world should be understood strictly in terms of interconnectedness and interdependence (see p. 7). The human species is merely part of nature,

Focus on . . .
Obligations to future generations?

Do we have obligations towards future generations? In deciding how we should act, should we take account of the interest of people who have not yet been born? These questions are of relevance because it is in the nature of environmental matters that many of the consequences of our actions may not be felt for decades or even centuries. Industrialization, for instance, had advanced for some two hundred years before concerns were raised about the depletion of finite oil, gas or coal resources, or about greenhouse gas emissions. This has forced ecologists to develop ideas about inter-generational justice, suggesting that our obligations extend beyond the present generation to future genera-tions, encompassing the living and the yet to be born.

Such 'futurity' has been justified in different ways. Care for and obligations towards future generations have sometimes been seen as a 'natural duty', an extension of a moral concern for our children and, by extension,

their children, and so on. A concern for future genera-tions has also been linked to the idea of 'ecological stewardship'. This is the notion that the present genera-tion is merely the custodian of the wealth that has been generated by past generations and should conserve it for the benefit of future generations. However, the idea of cross-generational justice has also been criticized. Some argue that all rights depend on reciprocity (see p. 344) (rights are respected because of something that is done, or not done, in return), in which case it is absurd to endow people who have yet to be born with rights that impose duties on people who are currently alive. Moreover, in view of the poten-tially unlimited size of future generations, the burdens imposed by 'futurity' are, in practical terms, incalcula-ble. Present generations may either be making sacri-fices for the benefit of future generations that may prove to be much better off, or their sacrifices may be entirely inadequate to meet future needs.

neither more important, nor more special, than any other part. Such ecocentric thinking has been constructed on a variety of bases, ranging from the new physics (particularly quantum mechanics) and systems theory to Eastern mysti-cism (especially Buddhism and Taoism) (Capra 1975, 1982, 1997) and pre-Christian spiritual ideas, notably ones that stress the notion of 'Mother Earth', as advanced in the so-called Gaia hypothesis (see p. 399). Deep ecologists have radi-cally revised conventional ethical thinking, arguing that morality springs not from human beings, but from nature itself, and supporting the idea of **'biocen-tric equality'**. They are also fiercely critical of consumerism and materialism, believing that these distort the relationship between humankind and nature.

CLIMATE CHANGE

Climate change is not only the most prominent global environmental issue, but it is also, some argue, the most urgent and important challenge currently confronting the international community. However, the issue is bedevilled by controversies and disagreements. The most important of these are over:

● **Biocentric equality**: The principle that all organisms and entities in the ecosphere are of equal moral worth, each being part of an interrelated whole.

● The *cause* of climate change: is climate change happening, and to what extent is it a result of human activity?

Focus on . . .
The Gaia hypothesis: a living planet?

The Gaia hypothesis was developed by James Lovelock (1979, 1989 and 2006). It advances the idea that the Earth is best understood as a living entity that acts to maintain its own existence. At the suggestion of the novelist William Golding, Lovelock named the planet Gaia, after the Greek goddess of the Earth. The basis for the Gaia hypothesis is that the Earth's biosphere, atmosphere, oceans and soil exhibit precisely the same kind of self-regulating behaviour that characterizes other forms of life. Gaia has maintained 'homeostasis', a state of dynamic balance, despite major changes that have taken place in the solar system. The most dramatic evidence of this is the fact that although the sun has warmed up by more than 25 per cent since life began, the temperature on Earth and the composition of its atmosphere have remained virtually unchanged.

The idea of Gaia has developed into an ecological ideology that conveys the powerful message that human beings must respect the health of the planet, and act to conserve its beauty and resources. It also contains a revolutionary vision of the relationship between the animate and inanimate world. However, the Gaia philosophy has also been condemned as a form of 'misanthropic ecology'. This is because Gaia is non-human, and Gaia theory suggests that the health of the planet matters more than that of any individual species presently living on it. Lovelock has suggested that those species that have prospered have been ones that have helped Gaia to regulate its own existence, while any species that poses a threat to the delicate balance of Gaia, as humans currently do, is likely to be extinguished.

- The *significance* of climate change: how serious are the consequences of climate change likely to be?
- The *cures* for climate change: how can climate change best be tackled?

Causes of climate change

What is climate? Climate is different from weather: climate refers to the long-term or prevalent weather conditions of an area. As the US writer Mark Twain noted: 'Climate is what we expect; weather is what we get'. However, this certainly does not imply that the Earth's climate is stable and unchanging. Indeed, it has experienced wild swings throughout it 4.6 billion-year history. There have been numerous ice ages, interspersed with warmer interglacial periods. The last ice age occurred during the Pleistocene epoch, which ended about 10,000 years ago, during which glaciers on the North American continent reached as far south as the Great Lakes and an ice sheet spread over Northern Europe, leaving its remains as far south as Switzerland. By contrast, some 55 million years ago, at the end of the Palaeocene epoch and the beginning of the Eocene epoch, the planet heated up in one of the most extreme and rapid global warming events in geological history. Such changes resulted from a variety of developments: changes in the radiation output of the sun; changes in the Earth's attitude in relation to the sun (as the Earth's orbit alters from elliptical to circular and changes occur in its tilt and how it wobbles on its axis); variations in the composition of the Earth's atmosphere, and so forth. Over the past century, and particularly during the last few decades, a new period of rapid climate change has been initi-

APPROACHES TO . . .

NATURE

Realist view

Realism has traditionally paid little attention to environmental thinking and it would be highly questionable to suggest that realism can be associated with a particular conception of nature. Realism is certainly more concerned with survival than with sustainability. Nevertheless, it has addressed the issue of the relationship between humankind and the natural world in at least two senses. First, classical realists have often explained human behaviour and propensities in terms of those found in other animals and, indeed, in nature itself. Selfishness, greed and aggression have commonly been viewed as innate features of human nature, reflecting tendencies that are found in all species (Lorenz 1966). On a larger scale, the struggle and conflict that realists believe is an ineradicable feature of human existence has sometimes been traced back to the fact that nature itself is 'red in tooth and claw'. Conflict and war have thus been seen as a manifestation of 'the survival of the fittest', a kind of social Darwinism. Second, realists have acknowledged the importance of nature, in recognizing the role that scarcity, and therefore conflict over resources, often plays in generating international tensions. Such thinking has been particularly evident in the ideas of geopolitics (see p. 414), which is itself a form of environmentalism. It is also reflected in the idea that many, and perhaps most, wars are 'resource wars'.

Liberal view

In the liberal view, nature is viewed as a resource to satisfy human needs. This explains why liberals have rarely questioned human dominion over nature. Lacking value in itself, nature is invested with value only when it is transformed by human labour, or when it is harnessed to human ends. This is reflected in Locke's theory that property rights derived from the fact that nature has, in effect, been mixed with labour. Nature is thus 'commodified', assigned an economic value, and it is drawn into the processes of the market economy. Indeed, in emphasizing the virtues of free-market capitalism, classical liberals have endorsed self-interested materialism and economic growth, a position that many ecologists have linked to the rapacious exploitation of nature. The anti-nature or anti-ecological biases of liberalism can be seen to stem from two main sources. First, liberalism is strongly anthropocentric, by virtue of its belief in individualism (see p. 154). Second, liberals have a strong faith in scientific rationality and technology, encouraging them to adopt a problem-solving approach to nature and to place a heavy reliance on human ingenuity. Nevertheless, alternative traditions within liberalism reflect a more positive approach to nature. These include a modern liberal stress on human flourishing, which may be facilitated through the contemplation of nature, and a utilitarian emphasis on maximizing happiness and minimizing suffering, a stance that may be applied to other species or to future generations of humans (Singer 1993).

Critical views

The two critical theories that address the issue of nature most explicitly are feminism and green politics. Feminists generally hold nature to be creative and benign. This is a view that is most closely associated with ecofeminism. For most ecofeminists, there is an essential or natural bond between women and nature. The fact that women bear children and suckle babies means that they cannot live separated from natural rhythms and processes and this, in turn, means that traditional 'female' values (reciprocity, cooperation, nurturing and so on) have a 'soft' or ecological character. While women are creatures of nature, men are creatures of culture: their world is synthetic or man-made, a product of human ingenuity rather than natural creativity. Environmental degradation is therefore an inevitable consequence of patriarchal power. From the perspective of green politics, nature is an interconnected whole which embraces humans and non-humans as well as the inanimate world. Nature thus embodies the principles of harmony and wholeness, implying that human fulfilment comes from a closeness to nature, not from attempts to dominate it. This holistic view is embraced most radically by deep ecologists, for whom nature is the source of all value. Nature is thus an ethical community, meaning that human beings are nothing more than 'plain citizens' who have no more rights and are no more deserving of respect than any other member of the community (Leopold 1968).

ated, with temperatures climbing quickly from normal interglacial levels. This time, however, climate change has been largely, and perhaps entirely, the result of human activity.

During the 1990s, the issue of global warming due to climate change achieved a higher and higher profile on the international environmental agenda. This was due to the fact that environmental groups, such as Greenpeace and Friends of the Earth, increasingly made efforts to stop global warming the primary focus of their activities and because the establishment of the International Panel on Climate Change (IPCC) meant that there was, for the first time, a source of authoritative scientific statements on the issue. This latter development largely put paid to the first and most basic debate about climate change: is it actually happening? Until about 2004–5, a 'denial lobby', sometimes funded by US oil companies, challenged the very idea of global warming, claiming that the data on temperature changes in the Earth's atmosphere was either inconclusive or contradictory. However, in 2005, a series of articles in the journal *Science* highlighted serious flaws in the data that had been used by 'denial lobbyists', helping to establish a new consensus: the world was getting hotter, and this was an incontrovertible fact. According to the IPCC's 2013 Fifth Assessment Report, eleven out of the twelve years between 1995 and 2006 ranked among the twelve warmest years since records began on global surface temperatures in 1850. It also pointed out that the so-called 'pause' in temperature increases since 1998 is too short to reflect a long-term trend. It is more significant that the linear warming trend over the fifty years from 1956 to 2005 was nearly twice that for the 100 years from 1906 to 2005. However, while the fact of global warming was becoming more difficult to deny, the factors accounting for it remained a matter of sometimes passionate dispute.

Climate change 'sceptics' (as opposed to 'deniers') have called into question the link between global warming and human activity, specifically the emission of 'greenhouse gases'. They had done this by emphasizing that the Earth's climate is naturally variable even during an interglacial period. For example, during the so-called 'little ice age', which lasted until the second half of the nineteenth century, Europe and North America suffered from bitterly cold winters and Iceland was frequently ice-locked. Others attempted to establish links between temperatures on Earth and factors such as solar sun spot activity. In the USA, the Bush administration (2001–9), while not denying the fact of global warming or that a proportion of it was anthropogenic, skilfully exploited scientific disagreement over the exact relationship between greenhouse gases and climate change to cast doubt on the value of the larger project of tackling climate change. While climate change sceptics exploited uncertainty and scientific disagreement to justify political inertia, committed environmentalists did precisely the opposite in applying the **precautionary principle**. Nevertheless, over time, the relationship between the emission of greenhouse gases and climate change became more difficult to question. This occurred both as the science of climate change was better understood in terms of the 'greenhouse effect' (see p. 404) and because of an increasingly clear correlation between the rate of global warming and the level of greenhouse gas emissions. Whereas in its Third Assessment Report in 2001, the IPCC stated that it was '*likely*' that temperature increases were due to the observed increase in anthropogenic greenhouse gas concentrations, in its Fourth Assessment Report in 2007, it declared that such a causal link was '*very likely*', meaning that it was more than 90 per cent certain. Needless to say, the debate

● **Precautionary principle**: The presumption in favour of action in relation to major ecological and other issues over which there is scientific uncertainty, based on the fact that the costs of inaction vastly exceed the cost of (possibly unnecessary) action.

- The term 'climate change' has gradually replaced 'global warming' in official discussions about the phenomenon, at national and international levels. For instance, whereas UN reports had previously used both terms, by the establishment of the 1992 FCCC, only one reference was made to the idea of 'warming' and none to 'global warming'.

Deconstructing . . .

'CLIMATE CHANGE'

- Although there may be scientific reasons to prefer the term 'climate change' (for example, it allows for the possibility that temperatures may fall as well as rise), it is also a less frightening term than 'global warming'. The latter is more emotionally charged and has perhaps catastrophic connotations attached to it. The blander and seemingly neutral 'climate change' has thus been preferred by politicians and states reluctant to take urgent action on the issue.

- 'Climate change' has the advantage of being vague, specifically about its origins, in that it seems to cover both natural and human-induced changes to the climate. This vagueness, in turn, has tended to support the idea that there is uncertainty and controversy about the causes and consequences of the phenomenon. By contrast, 'warming' implies that there is an agent doing the warming, thus suggesting that human activity is the likely cause of the problem.

about the causes of climate change was politically vital because this affected not only whether the problem could be addressed, but also how this should be done.

Consequences of climate change

The prominence of the issue of climate change is linked to the idea that, if unaddressed, it will have catastrophic implications for human welfare and, possibly, for the future of humankind. How serious will the consequences of global warming be? What will be the impact of long-term climate change? The consequences of living on a warmer planet have, at times, been as keenly disputed as whether global warming is actually taking place and whether it is linked to human activity. This was particularly true in the early period of climate change research, when the impact of increased greenhouse gas emissions was thought to lie many decades into the future, the case for addressing the issue being linked more to our obligations towards future generations than to a concern about the present generation. However, the impact of climate change has occurred earlier

GLOBAL ACTORS . . .

INTERGOVERNMENTAL PANEL ON CLIMATE CHANGE

Type: Intergovernmental organization • **Founded:** 1988 • **Location:** Geneva, Switzerland

The Intergovernmental Panel on Climate Change (IPCC) is an international panel of scientists and researchers that provide advice on climate change to the international community. The IPCC was established in 1988 by the World Meteorological Organization (WMO) and the United Nations Environment Programme (UNEP) to provide decision-makers and others interested in climate change with an objective source of information about an issue that had become increasingly complex and controversial. The IPCC does not conduct any research, neither does it monitor climate change-related data or parameters. Its role is to assess on a comprehensive, open and transparent basis the latest scientific, technical and socio-economic literature produced worldwide, with a view to better understanding (1) the risks of anthropocentric climate change, (2) its observed and projected impacts, and (3) options for adaptation and mitigation.

Significance: The most significant work of the IPCC is in publishing reports, the most important being Assessment Reports. Hundreds of scientists all over the world contribute to these reports as authors, contributors and reviewers, drawing mainly on reviewed and published scientific literature. Five Assessment Reports have been produced to date:

- *IPCC First Assessment Report* (1990). This played a

decisive role in leading to the FCCC.
- *IPCC Second Assessment Report* (1995). This provided a key input for the negotiations that led to the Kyoto Protocol in 1997.
- *IPCC Third Assessment Report* (2001). This provided further information relevant to the development of the FCCC and the Kyoto Protocol.
- *IPCC Fourth Assessment Report* (2007). This provided more evidence of the link between climate change and anthropogenic greenhouse gas concentrations.
- *IPCC Fifth Assessment Report* (2013). This concluded that it is 95 per cent certain that humans are the 'dominant cause' of global warming.

The wide membership of the IPCC, its reputation for objectivity and its reliance on worldwide scientific expertise gives the IPCC unrivalled influence in shaping how the international community understands, and responds to, the issue of climate change. In this respect, it has played the leading role in building a consensus amongst scientists and national politicians about the existence of climate change and the fact that it is a consequence of anthropogenic greenhouse gas emissions, and is therefore linked to the burning of fossil fuels. Its influence can thus be seen in the growing acceptance that climate change is an issue that demands the attention of the international

community, making it increasingly difficult for countries such as Russia, Australia, the USA, China and India to remain outside the climate change regime. The IPCC was awarded the Nobel Peace Prize in 2006, together with Al Gore, the former US Vice President.

The IPCC has also attracted criticism, however. Some argue that its emphasis on already published scientific data and on exacting reviews (the Fourth Assessment Report took six years to produce) means that its judgements and conclusions are dangerously out of date, and therefore tend to underestimate the seriousness of the climate change challenge. The Summary for Policy Makers, the only bit of an Assessment Report that is read by most politicians and journalists, is a politically negotiated document that sometimes omits controversial judgements found in the larger report. Some scientists also challenge the basis on which IPCC projections and conclusions are developed; for example, IPCC projections about global warming are founded on assumptions about the capacity of the oceans to absorb carbon dioxide that many environmentalists dismiss as unsound. The IPCC has also been criticized for overstating its claims (not least the claim, found in the 2007 Report but retracted in 2010, that the Himalayan glaciers would disappear by 2035) and for sacrificing its reputation for scientific neutrality by being seen to campaign for radical cuts in emissions.

Focus on . . .
The greenhouse effect

The concepts behind the greenhouse effect were first discussed in the nineteenth century by scientists such as the British physicist John Tyndall (1820–93) and the Swedish chemist Svante Arrhenius (1859–1927). The sun is the only source of external heat for the Earth. Sunlight passes through the atmosphere during the day, heating up the surface of the Earth and releasing heat in the form of long-wave, infrared radiation. However, the presence in the atmosphere of greenhouse gases means that this radiation is absorbed and trapped in the lower atmosphere, thereby heating the Earth's surface (see Figure 16.2). In effect, our world is a natural greenhouse. The impact of the greenhouse effect can be demonstrated by comparing temperatures on the Earth to those on the moon, which does not have an atmosphere and on which night-time temperatures fall as low as -173°C. By contrast, on Venus,

which has a thick, carbon dioxide atmosphere, surface temperatures reach a blistering 483°C.

Needless to say, the greenhouse effect is not necessarily a bad thing: were it not for heat-trapping gases such as carbon dioxide, solar radiation would be reflected straight back into space, leaving the world in the iron grip of frost. However, it is widely accepted that the increased emission of anthropogenic greenhouse gases – carbon dioxide, methane and nitrous oxide, the gases recognized in the Kyoto Protocol – is contributing to a significant trend of global warming. These gas emissions are a direct consequence of industrial activity and specifically the burning of fossil fuels. Atmospheric levels of carbon dioxide, the most important greenhouse gas, have risen from 280 parts per million (ppm) in pre-industrial times to 384 ppm in 2007.

and more dramatically than was anticipated, meaning that it can no longer be treated merely as a 'future generations' issue. Nevertheless, anxieties about climate change continue to have a marked future-looking character, as, even if robust action were to be taken shortly, its effects are certain to be felt more severely by today's children and their children.

In its 2013 Assessment Report, the IPCC noted a range of changes to climatic conditions, including following:

- It is *likely* (66–100 per cent certainty) that 1983–2013 was the warmest 30-year period in the Northern Hemisphere for at least 1,400 years.
- It is *virtually certain* (99 to 100 per cent) that the upper 700 m of the Earth's oceans have warmed during the period 1971–2010.
- It can be said with *high confidence* that the Greenland and Antarctic ice sheets have been losing mass in the last two decades, and that glaciers have continued to shrink almost worldwide.
- It is *very likely* (90–100 per cent) that heatwaves will occur with higher frequency and duration, although occasional winter extremes will continue.

The human impact of climate change has been significant and is very likely to increase. Although more warmer days and nights and fewer colder days and nights over most land areas is likely to reduce human mortality from decreased cold exposure, most of the effects of climate change are negative. Increased tropical cyclone activity creates a greater risk of death and injury from flooding and

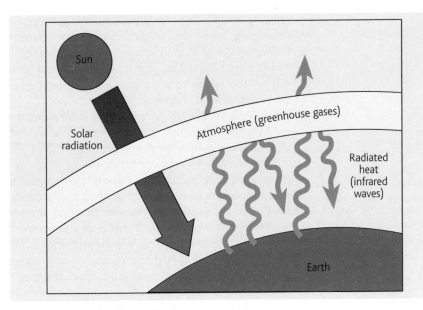

Figure 16.2 The greenhouse effect

from water- and food-borne diseases, and also leads to major displacement of populations. Since the mid-1990s, there has been a 40 per cent increase in Atlantic hurricane activities and, according to some scientists, the most powerful tropical cyclones now occur twice as often as they did thirty years ago. China has been particularly badly affected by flooding on the Yangtze, the Yellow River and on other rivers. The increased incidence of extreme high sea levels also causes a greater risk of death and injury by drowning, especially in the world's great river deltas, such as the Bengal delta in Bangladesh, the Mekong delta in Vietnam, the Nile delta in Egypt and the Yangtze delta in China. If current increases in sea level persist, one-sixth of the land area of Bangladesh could be lost to the sea by the middle of this century, if not earlier, leaving 13 per cent of the country's population with nowhere to live or farm. The prospects for people living in low-lying island groups, such as the Maldives, may be even bleaker, as these may disappear altogether. The greater incidence of drought and the advance of desertification will lead to an increased risk of food and water shortages, malnutrition and, once again, a greater risk of water- and food-borne diseases.

Climate change has affected all parts of the world, but it has not done so evenly. Africa and the Arctic (where sea-ice is shrinking by 2.7 per cent per decade) are likely to bear the brunt of climate impacts, along with low-lying small islands and the Asian river deltas. The IPCC estimates that by 2080, if current trends continue, anything from 1.2 to 3.2 billion people will be experiencing water scarcity, 200–600 million people will be malnourished or hungry and between 2 and 7 million people each year will be subject to coastal flooding. However, the effects of climate change will be truly global, not least through its impact on migration trends and economic development. An estimated 200–850 million people could be forced to move to more temperate zones by 2050 due to water shortages, sea level crises, deteriorating pasture land, conflict and famine, all linked to climate change. Together with widening gaps in birth rates and growing wealth-to-poverty ratios, climate change could therefore also lead to deepening ethnic and social tensions in developed societies. The economic consequences of climate change were highlighted by the Stern Review (2006), which pointed out that global warming could so disrupt economic and social activity that a failure to address it could mean global GDP being up to 20 per cent lower than it otherwise might be.

However, some environmentalists have painted still more dire images of the consequence of climate change, creating a number of 'catastrophe scenarios'. One of these is that the disappearance of the polar icecaps could result in an abrupt increase in temperature levels on Earth as white ice helps to keep the planet cool by reflecting back some 80 per cent of the sunlight that falls on it. Sea water, by contrast, absorbs sunlight and reflects back little. A second is that the melting of the planet's permafrost, the thick level of frozen soil covering much of the ground in the high latitudes of the northern hemisphere, could release trapped greenhouse gases, contributing to a major acceleration in global warming. A third is that the release of cold water through melting Artic ice could, in effect, 'turn off' the Gulf Stream, bringing freezing conditions to much of Northern Europe (the scenario highlighted in the 2004 Hollywood disaster movie *The Day After Tomorrow*). Others, however, have dismissed these catastrophe scenarios as scaremongering. The IPCC, for example, rates the likelihood of the Gulf Stream faltering during the twenty-first century as '*very unlikely*' (a probability of less than 10 per cent).

How should climate change be tackled?

The task of tackling climate change is notoriously difficult; some even fear that it may be impossible. It is instructive, in this respect, to compare efforts to deal with climate change with the response to the problem of ozone depletion. In the case of ozone depletion, there was little scientific disagreement about its cause (the emission of CFC gases from aerosols and other sources); there was general agreement that its consequences were negative and a recognition that they affected developed and developing states alike; and, most importantly, there was a straightforward solution available at an acceptable price – banning CFCs and switching to alternatives that could be developed economically. The Montreal Protocol of 1987 thus demonstrated how effective international cooperation on environmental matters can be. CFC emissions were reduced from the mid-1990s onwards, with a view to being completely phased out by 2030, allowing the ozone layer to recover completely by 2050. Climate change, by contrast, is profoundly difficult because its origins lie not in the use of particular substances or a specific productive process or set of commodities, but, arguably, in the process of industrialization itself. The burning of fossil fuels (coal, oil and natural gas) has not only been the basis for industrialization and thus the key to economic growth for the last 200 years or more, but it has also been the basis for greenhouse gas emissions that have resulted in global warming. Any serious attempt to address the problem of climate change must therefore either recast the nature of industrial society, providing an alternative to 'carbon industrialization', or make significant sacrifices in terms of economic growth and therefore material prosperity. How far has international cooperation on climate change progressed, and what obstacles stand in the way of effective international action?

International cooperation over climate change

The Rio 'Earth Summit' of 1992 was the first international conference to give significant attention to the issue of climate change. It did so by establishing the FCCC as a 'framework convention', calling for greenhouse gases to be stabilized at safe levels on the basis of equity and in accordance with states' 'common but differentiated responsibilities and respective capabilities'. The clear implication was that developed states should take the lead, committing themselves to restoring 1990 levels of emissions by the year 2000. However, although it was accepted by 181 governments, the FCCC was no more than a framework for further action and it contains no legally binding targets. This was just as well for developed states, whose carbon emissions continued to rise during the 1990s. The exclusion of developing states meant, in fact, that the rate of increase got steeper, particularly due to the economic emergence of China and India.

The most significant international agreement on climate change was the Kyoto Protocol to the FCCC, negotiated in 1997. The significance of the Kyoto Protocol was that it set binding targets for developed states to limit or reduce their greenhouse gas emissions by 2012. The targets were designed to reduce total emissions from the developed world to at least 5.2 per cent below their 1990 levels. National targets varied, however, with the EU and the USA being set targets for reductions of 8 per cent and 7 per cent, respectively, while other states, such as Australia, were allowed to exceed their 1990 levels. These targets were accompanied by 'flexibility mechanisms' that introduced a system of carbon trading that was designed to assist countries in meeting their targets. This established a 'cap and trade' approach to climate change, which has since become the dominant strategy for addressing the issue. Kyoto's strengths included that it introduced, for the first time, legally binding targets on greenhouse gas emissions, and by applying these targets to 37 developed states (so-called 'Annex 1' countries) it prepared the way for later participation of developing states, 137 of which ratified the Protocol. Furthermore, in providing a mechanism for **emissions trading**, it helped to promote the idea of carbon as a commodity and introduced a vital element of flexibility that made binding targets appear more acceptable. For example, emissions trading allows developed states to meet their targets in part through technology transfers and investment in the developing world, thereby, at least in theory, contributing to reducing their emissions levels. Critics of carbon trading nevertheless argue that it is a loophole that allows countries to exceed their targets and not take climate change sufficiently seriously, especially as the system is difficult to police and has given rise to many allegations of abuse.

However, the Kyoto Protocol also had significant limitations. In the first place, the targets set at Kyoto were, arguably, inadequate in terms of achieving the Protocol's goals of preventing 'dangerous anthropogenic interference with the climate system'. For example, the EU, which has taken a leading role in the campaign to address climate change, had called for greenhouse gas cuts of 15 per cent by 2010, almost three times greater than the Kyoto cuts and over a shorter time span. Second, the USA's failure to ratify the treaty, first through the Clinton administration's fear that the US Senate would not ratify the treaty and later through the Bush administration's outright opposition, dealt Kyoto a fatal blow and set the process of tackling climate change back for over a decade. This was

● **Emissions trading**: A mechanism that allows parties to the Kyoto Protocol to buy or sell emissions from or to other parties, while keeping within overall emissions targets.

not only because the USA, then the world's largest emitter, accounted for about 25 per cent of all greenhouse gas emissions, but also because US non-participation ensured that developing states, and especially China and India, would remain outside the Kyoto process. Third, the decision to restrict binding targets to developed states alone seriously compromised the Kyoto process from the outset. The USA consistently used the exclusion of China and India as a justi-fication for its non-participation. Moreover, China's carbon emissions continued to rise steeply, and have exceeded those of the USA since 2008, meaning that climate change could no longer be seen merely as a developed world problem.

While the Kyoto Protocol was never going to be the solution to climate change, it provided a perhaps necessary first step along the road. Nevertheless, the faltering progress associated with Kyoto meant that, by 2005, global carbon dioxide emissions were rising four times faster than they were in the 1990s. One consequence of this has been a shift in emphasis away from '**mitigation**' towards 'mitigation and **adaptation**'. Key 'mitigation' technologies and practices identi-fied in the 2007 IPCC Assessment Report include the following:

- Fuel switching from coal to gas
- The wider use of nuclear power
- The greater use of renewable heat and power (hydropower, solar, wind, geothermal and bio-energy)
- Early applications of carbon dioxide capture and storage (e.g. storage of CO_2 removed from natural gas)
- More fuel-efficient vehicles, such as hybrid and cleaner diesel vehicles
- Shifts from road transport to rail, public transport and non-motorized transport (cycling, walking).

The same report nevertheless highlights a range of 'adaptation' strategies, including the following:

- The relocation of settlements, especially coastal zones
- Improved sea walls and storm surge barriers
- Expanded rainwater harvesting and improved water storage and conserva-tion techniques
- Adjustment of planting dates and crop varieties
- Crop relocation and improved land management (e.g. erosion control and soil protection through tree planting)
- Improved climate-sensitive disease surveillance and control.

● **Mitigation**: Moderating or reducing the impact of something; in particular, reducing greenhouse gas emissions in order to limit climate change.

● **Adaptation**: Changing in the light of new circumstances; in particular, learning to live with climate change.

Nevertheless, there were signs that greater scientific agreement on the exis-tence, causes and implications of climate change, together with shifting public attitudes, in part through the work of environmental NGOs, had strengthened international cooperation on the issue. Russia ratified the Kyoto Protocol in 2004, as did Australia in 2007 (although Russia, together with Canada, Japan and New Zealand withdrew from the Kyoto process in 2012). Most significantly, the election of Barack Obama in 2008, together with Democrat control of both houses of Congress (until 2011), appeared to mark a key shift in US policy, creat-ing a willingness to participate in formulating a successor to the Kyoto Protocol, which was due to run out in 2012. What is more, despite China's unapologetic

Climate change after the Kyoto Protocol

Events: The 1997 Kyoto Protocol (to the UNFCCC) marked the first use of binding targets to reduce greenhouse gas emissions. The Protocol entered into force in 2005, and its first commitment period ended in 2012. The principal attempt to construct a post-Kyoto Protocol climate change framework was undertaken at the 2009 UN Climate Change Conference in Copenhagen. However, the Copenhagen conference failed to create any new legally-binding obligations on any country to cut its emissions, even failing to establish any non-legal targets for national or global emissions reductions. The 2011 United Nations Climate Change Conference in Durban, South Africa, nevertheless appeared to get the post-Kyoto process back on track, by supporting a plan for a new treaty to be agreed in Paris in late 2015, and to come into force in 2020, with the Kyoto Protocol continuing to operate until then. Although the 2012 United Nations Climate Change Conference in Doha, Qatar, did not consider the shape of the new treaty, agreement was reached on extending the life of the Kyoto Protocol until 2020.

Significance: Pessimists view this catalogue of failure, delay and obfuscation as a stark abandonment of responsibility on the part of the international community. Extending the life of the Kyoto Protocol achieves little because the treaty is so clearly flawed. Not only did the USA (then the world's largest carbon emitter) never ratify the treaty, and the entire developing world including China (which, in 2008, overtook the USA as the world's largest emitter) remained outside Kyoto's target regime, but, through its 'flexible mechanisms', Kyoto provided a range of loopholes which parties could exploit to fulfil their targets. Thus, although most of the parties to Kyoto met their commitments easily, worldwide emissions have surged by 50 per cent since 1990, driven by economic growth in China and other parts of Asia, South America and Africa. Optimists, nevertheless, questioned this bleak assessment, pointing to a record of slow, but meaningful, progress. For all its limitations, Kyoto was a vital first step, both marking the first use of legally binding emissions targets and introducing the 'cap and trade' systems and carbon taxes that have subsequently been taken up in Europe, Australia, Japan, China, California and parts of Canada. Copenhagen moved beyond Kyoto, in that the USA and China were full participants in the climate change process. Durban formally endorsed the idea of a post-Kyoto treaty, and Doha established the principle that rich countries should compensate poor countries for 'loss and damage' due to climate change, while resisting the idea of legal liability.

Nevertheless, the task of developing a successor to Kyoto remains fraught with problems. These include conflict between the developed world and the developing world over burden sharing. The former emphasizes the need for targets to reflect current emissions levels, as developing countries have, since 2012, been responsible for more than half the world's carbon emissions. The latter argues that targets should reflect the historic responsibility of developed countries for the carbon emitted since the beginning of the industrial revolution. Progress at Copenhagen, Durban, Doha and elsewhere has also been made more difficult by great power rivalries, particularly between the USA and China. Perhaps the most fundamental problem, nevertheless, is that reductions in greenhouse gas emissions that are sufficient to mitigate the effect of climate change are both costly (because of the need to develop alternatives to carbon-based production) and threaten to impede growth and therefore prosperity. Short- and medium-term economic self-interest therefore tend to be given priority over longer-term environmental concerns (despite growing evidence of the economic costs associated with climate change). States thus have an incentive to do as little as possible about climate change, in the hope that others will shoulder the burden, especially in the context of the 2007–09 global financial crisis and its aftermath.

emphasis on largely coal-based industrial growth, the environmental costs of carbon industrialization have become increasingly apparent, through, for instance, heavily polluted cities (eight out of ten of the world's most polluted cities are in China), shrinking glaciers on the Tibet-Qinghai plateau and falling water tables across the country. This created a growing likelihood that China and other developing countries would be more willing to address the issue of climate change and recognize that they have an interest in tackling it. This was the context in which the UN began to consider the shape of the post-Kyoto climate change regime, starting with the 2009 Climate Change Conference in Copenhagen. However, the outcomes of this process have widely been seen as disappointing, highlighting yet again the difficulties of achieving international agreement on the issue of climate change (see p. 409).

Why is international cooperation so difficult to achieve?

Effective international action to tackle climate change will only occur if solutions are found to a series of obstacles to international cooperation. The most significant of these obstacles are the following:

- Conflict between the collective good and national interests
- Tensions between developed and developing states
- Economic obstacles
- Ideological obstacles.

The issue of climate change can be seen as a classic example of the 'tragedy of the commons'. What countries accept would be generally beneficial to all of them may not be the same as what benefits each of them individually. Clean air and a healthy atmosphere are therefore **collective goods**, key elements of the 'global commons'. However, tackling global warming imposes costs on individual states in terms of investment in sometimes expensive mitigation and adaptation strategies, as well as accepting lower levels of economic growth. In such circumstances, states are encouraged to be 'free riders', enjoying the benefits of a healthier atmosphere without having to pay for them. It is entirely rational, therefore, for each actor to try to 'pay' as little as possible to overcome the problem of climate change. This creates a situation in which states are either unwilling to agree to binding targets, or if targets, binding or otherwise, are developed, these are likely to be set below the level needed to deal effectively with the problem. Moreover, the more economically developed a state is, the greater will be the costs incurred in tackling climate change, and the more reluctant such states will be to undertake concerted action. Democracy, in such a context, may create further problems, particularly as party competition tends to be orientated around rival claims about the ability to deliver growth and prosperity.

The second problem is that the issue of climate change exposes significant divisions between the developed world and the developing world. Climate change, in other words, serves to widen the North–South divide (see p. 367). One source of tension is that current emissions levels arguably provide an unfair guide for setting targets because of 'outsourcing'. The transfer of much of manu-

● **Collective good**: A general benefit from which individuals cannot be excluded and, as a result, for which beneficiaries have no incentive to pay.

KEY THEORISTS IN GREEN POLITICS

Ernst Friedrich Schumacher (1911–77)

A German-born UK economist and environmental thinker, Schumacher championed the cause of human-scale production and advanced a 'Buddhist' economic philosophy (economics 'as if people mattered') that stresses the importance of morality and 'right livelihood'. His key work is *Small is Beautiful* (1973).

Arne Naess (1912–2009)

A Norwegian philosopher who was influenced by the teachings of Spinoza, Gandhi and Buddha, Naess was the leading advocate of 'deep ecology', arguing that ecology should be concerned with every part of nature on an equal basis, because natural order has an intrinsic value. His writings include *Ecology, Community and Lifestyle* (1989).

Garrett Hardin (1915–2003)

A US ecologist and microbiologist, Hardin is best known for the idea of the 'tragedy of the commons', which calls attention to 'the damage that innocent actions by individuals can inflict on the environment'. He developed an uncompromising form of ecologism that warned against the dangers of population growth and excessive freedom. Hardin's chief works include *The Tragedy of the Commons* (1968) and *Lifeboat Ethics* (1974).

Murray Bookchin (1921–2006)

A US libertarian socialist, Bookchin highlighted parallels between anarchism and ecology through the idea of 'social ecology', and was also strongly critical of the 'mystical' ideas of deep ecology, which he dubbed 'eco-la-la'. His major works in this field include *The Ecology of Freedom* ([1982]) and *Re-Enchanting Humanity* (1995).

Carolyn Merchant (born 1936)

A US ecofeminist philosopher and historian of science, Merchant portrays female nature as the benevolent mother of all undermined by the 'dominion' model of nature that emerged out of the scientific revolution and the rise of market society. Her main works include *The Death of Nature* (1983) and *Radical Ecology* (1992).

Vandana Shiva (born 1952)

An Indian ecofeminist activist and nuclear physicist, Shiva is a trenchant critic of the biotechnology industry. She argues that the advance of globalization has threatened biodiversity and deepened poverty, particularly among women. Her writings include *Monocultures of the Mind* (1993) and *Stolen Harvest* (1999).

See also **James Lovelock** (p. 79)

facturing industry to the developing world means that over one-third of carbon dioxide emissions associated with the consumption of goods and services in many developed countries are actually emitted outside their borders. Deeper divisions nevertheless stem from rival approaches to the problem of burden-sharing in the area of climate change. From a Southern perspective, the developed world has a historic responsibility for the accumulated stock of carbon emitted since the beginning of the industrial age. In effect, developed countries have used up a large part of the safe carbon-absorbing capacity of the atmosphere, and made substantial gains in terms of economic growth and prosperity as a result. Developing countries, by contrast, are both disproportionately badly affected by climate change and have the fewest capabilities to tackle it, whether through mitigation or adaptation. This implies either that emissions targets should not be imposed on developing countries (as at Kyoto), or that any such targets should take account of historic responsibilities and be structured accordingly, imposing significantly heavier burdens on developed countries than on developing ones.

From a Northern perspective, however, countries cannot be held responsible for actions whose consequences were quite unknown at the time they were carried out, and, anyway, those who were responsible are largely dead and gone. In this view, targets should be set in line with *current* emission levels alone, in which case developed and developing countries would be treated alike. Apart from anything else, the growing importance of emerging economies such as China, India and Brazil means that unless the developing world plays a significant role in cutting emissions global targets will be impossible to meet. Nevertheless, tensions between developed and developing countries are even more acute if population size and per capita income are taken into account. For instance, although China has overtaken the USA as the world's foremost emitter, per capita emissions in the USA remain almost four times higher than in China (19.2 tons against 4.9 tons in 2010). Southern thinking on the matter tends to be rights-based, reflecting both the idea that each human being has an equal right to the world's remaining carbon space and the idea of a right to development (already exercised by the developed North). This suggests that emissions targets should clearly favour the developing world, where most of the world's people live, as well as most of the world's poor. Critics of the rights-based approach to tackling climate change nevertheless argue that it introduces egalitarian assumptions that do not apply to other aspects of life. For example, why should the use of the world's remaining carbon space be allocated equally when there is no agreement on the wider issue that natural resources should be equally shared?

Radical ecologists, including both social ecologists and deep ecologists, tend to argue that inadequate progress in responding to climate change has much deeper, and perhaps structural, roots. The problem is not simply a manifestation of the difficulty of bringing about international cooperation but, rather, is about the underlying economic and ideological forces that have shaped capitalist modernity. As far as economic factors are concerned, criticism usually focuses on the anti-ecological tendencies of the capitalist system, at both national and global levels. In particular, profit-maximizing businesses will always be drawn towards the most easily available and cheapest source of energy: fossil fuels. Short-term profitability will dominate their thinking, rather than issues to do

Debating . . .
Can only radical action tackle the problem of climate change?

The divide in green politics between radicals and reformists is clearly reflected in competing approaches to tackling climate change. While some argue in favour of structural economic and ideological change, others champion less radical, and less painful, options.

YES

Dangerous delays. There is a wide and growing gap between the recognition of the problem of global warming and the introduction of effective international action. The failings of Rio, Kyoto and Copenhagen therefore mean that modest emissions cuts are no longer adequate. The general consensus is that global temperature rises of more than 2°C would mark the 'tipping point' in terms of dangerous human impact, while, according to the IPCC's 2013 prediction, these may increase by up to 4.8°C.

Myth of 'easy' solutions. Sadly, the strategies that are the least economically and politically problematical are also the least effective. Renewable energy sources are likely to make only a minor contribution to reducing the use of fossil fuels. Carbon trading has failed to produce significant emissions reductions. Technological 'fixes' for climate change, such as the use of so-called bio-fuels, carbon storing, 'clean' coal and nuclear power, have often proved to be expensive, ineffective or are associated with other environmental costs.

Economic restructuring. It is difficult to see how global warming can be addressed without changes being introduced to the economic system that has caused it. Market capitalism has proved to be a highly effective way of generating wealth, but it is, arguably, the enemy of ecological sustainability. Although ecosocialists' ideas have been increasingly derided, many environmentalists call for a radical restructuring of capitalism, in particular through the strengthening of state intervention to impose sustainable practices.

Post-material society. Economic restructuring is impossible if the values and appetites that sustain industrial society and 'growthism' go unchallenged. Concerted action on climate change thus has to have a cultural and psychological dimension. Materialism must be overthrown as the demand for 'more and more' is displaced by a steady-state economy based on 'enough'. Only if values and sensibilities alter will policy-makers at national and international levels have the political space to develop meaningful solutions to the problem.

NO

Exaggerated fears. Concern about climate change has been driven by a kind of environmental hysteria. Environmental NGOs try to grab public attention and shift attitudes by highlighting 'doomsday scenarios'. The mass media often conspire in this process to make the coverage of current affairs 'sexy' and attention-grabbing. Policy-makers may therefore adopt radical strategies, not so much to deal with the problem of climate change, but rather to allay public anxieties about the issue.

Adapt to change. Most environmentalists view global warming simply as something that must be stopped, based on the assumption that all of its impacts are negative. However, climate change may bring opportunities (new tourist destinations, improved plant viability and so on), as well as challenges. Moreover, the cost of stopping its negative impact may be unacceptably high. In these circumstances, it may be easier and more cost-effective to understand the implications of global warming and find ways of living with it.

Market solutions. Capitalism is resolutely not anti-green. Capitalism's environmental credentials are reflected in its responsiveness to more eco-sensitive consumer pressures, and the recognition that long-term corporate profitability can only be ensured in the context of sustainable development. Further, carbon usage is best discouraged not through strictures and prohibitions, but by market mechanisms that disincentivize carbon usage and incentivize the development of low-carbon or carbon-neutral technologies.

Human ingenuity. The capacity for innovation and creativity that lay behind carbon industrialization can surely be harnessed to build carbon-neutral businesses, industries and societies. Although investment in renewable energy sources is currently insufficient, its potential is enormous, especially if technology such as superefficient wind turbines is utilized. Solar power plants, using solar cells, are becoming increasingly common in many parts of the world, and zero-carbon 'eco-cities' are being built in China, Abu Dhabi and elsewhere.

● **Resource security:** Security understood in terms of access to energy and other resources sufficient to meet a state's economic and military needs.

● **Resource war:** A war that is fought to gain or retain control of resources which are important to economic development and political power.

with ecological sustainability. In this view, 'green capitalism' is merely a contradiction in terms. At an ideological level, countries' attachment to carbon industrialization may, in the final analysis, be a manifestation of the materialist values that dominate modern society, creating, deep ecologists argue, a profound disjuncture between humankind and nature. Materialism and consumerism mean that the economic and political systems are geared towards economic growth and the quest for rising living standards. From this perspective, the difficulties of tackling climate change stem not only from the problem of persuading people to forego at least a measure of their material prosperity, but, more challengingly, from the task of encouraging people to revise their values.

RESOURCE SECURITY

Although climate change has tended, since the late 1980s, to be the pre-eminent issue on the global environmental agenda, it is by no means the only important issue. Indeed, over very much the same period, non-renewable resources, and particularly energy resources, have come to be seen as having a growing bearing on matters such as security, development and conflict. In fact, in many ways, climate change and **resource security** have become counter-balancing priorities for states. For example, while climate change encourages states to reduce their use of fossil fuels, the quest for resource security encourages them to seek and to exploit new fossil fuel reserves. On the other hand, environmentalists have presented investment in renewable resources and non-carbon technologies as a 'green' road to resource security, although this only applies if such alternatives genuinely have the capacity to generate the same energy levels as fossil fuels. What is clear, though, is that concerns over the adequacy of natural resources to sustain human populations and ensure national power long predate concerns over climate change. They can be traced back to Thomas Malthus' (see p. 415) gloomy prediction that, due to the 'principle of population', living standards in any country would always return to subsistence levels. Although technological innovation and the discovery of new resources have tended to keep Malthusian pessimism at bay, history has been characterized by periods of anxiety, sometimes bordering on panic, over scarce resources. For example, in the nineteenth century the earliest industrial powers scrambled for control over sources of iron and coal, while after WWI the major European powers engaged in a desperate search for foreign sources of petroleum.

Anxieties about resources, nevertheless, subsided during the 1970s and 1980s, due both to the discovery of new, and seemingly abundant, fossil fuel supplies and because accelerated globalization appeared to have created larger and more responsive markets for energy and other resources. However, they have revived with particular force since the 1990s, moving the issue especially of energy security significantly up the international agenda. A growing number of wars, for example, appeared to be **resource wars** (Klare 2001). Geopolitics, once thought dead, had suddenly revived. Why did this happen? At least three developments help to explain it. First, the demand for energy, particularly oil, gas and coal, rose sharply through the arrival of new contenders on the global resources playing-field, notably China and India, but also, to a lesser extent, Brazil and other emerging economies. Second, the world's leading energy consumer, the USA, became increasingly concerned about its dwindling

Thomas Malthus (1766–1834)

A UK political economist and clergyman. Malthus was brought up according to the Enlightenment ideas of thinkers such as Jean-Jacques Rousseau (1712–78) and David Hume (1711–76). He became a Church of England minister in 1788. Malthus is best known for the views set out in his pamphlet, later expanded into a book in many editions, the *Essay on Population* (1798). Its key argument was that (unchecked) population growth will always exceed the growth of the means of subsistence, because population growth is exponential (or geometric) while the growth in the supply of food and other essentials is merely arithmetical. Population growth would therefore always result in famine, disease and war. While some have argued that Malthus' predictions were fundamentally flawed, as they took no account of improvements in agricultural and other technologies, others have suggested that his predictions have merely been postponed.

supplies of cheap domestic oil and its growing reliance on increasingly expensive, and less secure, foreign oil. Third, just as demand pressures intensified, anxieties concerns resurfaced. Fears grew generally that the world's stockpile of essential commodities had started to shrink, and these focused particularly on oil (Deffeyes 2005). Concern was raised not only by the seeming failure of new oil supplies to keep pace with burgeoning demand, but also, more alarmingly, by predictions (debunked by some) that the moment of **peak oil** may soon be reached. The world's oil may be running out, without any alternative energy source, renewable or non-renewable, appearing to be capable of replacing it. Such developments have both contributed to important shifts in global power, as well as created turbulence and often conflict in countries 'blessed' by abundant supplies of oil and other resources.

Resources, power and prosperity

The link between resources and global power can be seen in the emergence of a new international energy order. In this, a state's ranking in the hierarchy of states may no longer be measured by conventional economic and military capabilities (see Elements of national power, p. 219), but by the vastness of its oil and gas reserves and its ability to mobilize other sources of wealth in order to purchase (or otherwise acquire) the resources of energy-rich countries (Klare 2008). This notion divides the world into energy-surplus and energy-deficit states, and further divides them on the basis of the level of their surplus and deficit. The key players in this international energy order are the USA, China and India, all energy-deficit countries, and Russia, an energy-surplus country. As far as the USA is concerned, a context of dwindling domestic reserves of oil and rising international prices has encouraged it to strengthen its geopolitical influence in the area with the most abundant oil supplies, the Gulf region. Many have thus argued that the 1991 Gulf War and the 2003 invasion of Iraq were, in significant ways, motivated by such considerations about oil. One dimension of the 'war on terror' (see p. 230) may therefore have been the USA's concerns about energy security (Heinberg 2006).

● **Peak oil**: The point at which the maximum rate of petroleum extraction is reached.

Focus on . . .
The paradox of plenty: resources as a curse?

Are resources a blessing or a curse? Why are countries and areas that are richly endowed with natural resources often amongst the poorest and most troubled in the world? In the first place, natural resources can be seen to create a number of economic imbalances and difficulties. These include increased volatility in government revenues, which can lead to inflation and boom-and-bust cycles in government spending. Damage can be caused to other economic sectors as revenues from natural resource exports push up wages and the exchange rate (this is sometimes called the 'Dutch disease', from the fact that the discovery of natural gas in the Netherlands the 1960s led to declines in manufacturing industries). There can also be a dangerous lack of economic diversification, as other industries fail to develop because they cannot match the profitability levels of natural resources.

Second, natural resources can also have a damaging impact on the nature and quality of governance. This occurs both because huge flows of money from natural resources tend to fuel political corruption and because, as resource-rich countries have less need to raise revenue from the general public, they often pay little attention to popular pressures. There is therefore a link between abundant natural resources and authoritarianism. Third, natural resources can, and often do, breed conflict and civil strife. Conflict tends to occur over the control and exploitation of resources as well as over the allocation of their revenues, meaning that resource-rich societies are more prone to ethnic conflict, separatist uprisings and general warlordism. While 'diamond wars' have been common, if usually relatively brief, in Africa, oil-related conflicts, ranging from low-level secessionist struggles to full-blown civil wars, have occurred in countries as different as Algeria, Colombia, Sudan, Indonesia, Nigeria and Equatorial Guinea.

The economic emergence of China and India, sometimes collectively referred to in this context as 'Chindia', has transformed the world markets for oil, natural gas, coal, uranium and other primary sources of energy, as well as industrial commodities such as iron ore, copper, aluminium and tin. As far as China is concerned, the search for energy security has had implications for both domestic and foreign policy. Domestically, it has encouraged China to crack down on separatist movements and strengthen political control over western and southwestern provinces such as Xinjiang and Tibet, which may provide access to central Asia and its rich supplies of oil and other resources. China's burgeoning external influence has focused on strengthening diplomatic ties with oil-rich countries such as Iran and, most clearly, undertaking massive investment in Africa, the home of the world's largest untapped energy and mineral supplies. China leads the modern 'scramble for resources' in Africa which, in some respects, resembles the late nineteenth-century 'scramble for colonies'. The new international energy order has particularly favoured Russia as the world's foremost energy-surplus state. Russia thus emerged from the collapse of communism and a decade of post-communist turmoil as an energy superpower. It now operates as a key power broker of Eurasian energy supplies, being able to exert substantial leverage through the growing dependency of EU and other states on Russian oil and natural gas. However, the quest for energy security has also encouraged Russia to strengthen its control over its 'near abroad' and especially

● **Resource curse**: The tendency for countries and regions with an abundance of natural resources to experience low growth, blocked development and, sometimes, civil strife.

over the oil-rich Caucasus region. This, for example, may have been one of the factors contributing to Russia's 2008 invasion of Georgia.

Natural resources, finally, are generally considered to be an unmixed blessing, widely being seen as one of the key components of national power. Energy, mineral and other resources provide a country not only with the basis for long-term economic development, but also with a means of gaining income from, and exercising influence over, other countries. Examples such as Saudi Arabia and other oil-rich Gulf states, Venezuela, Kazakhstan and, of course, Russia appear to bear this out. However, in practice, natural resources often bring as many problems as they bring blessings. This can be seen in the fact that many of the poorest and most troubled parts of the world are also characterized by abundant supplies of energy and minerals, with sub-Saharan Africa and the Middle East being obvious examples. This has lead to the idea of the '**resource curse**', sometimes called the 'paradox of plenty' (see p. 416).

SUMMARY

- The environment is often seen as the archetypal example of a global issue. The intrinsically transnational character of environmental processes means that countries are peculiarly environmentally vulnerable to the environmental activities that take place in other countries. Meaningful progress on environmental issues can therefore often only be made at the international or even global level.

- Disagreements about the seriousness and nature of environmental problems, and about how they can best be tackled, are rooted in deeper, often philosophical debates about the relationship between humankind and the natural world. Reformist and radical strategies are influenced by contrasting views about whether human needs (anthropocentrism) or larger ecological balances (ecocentrism) should take precedence.

- Climate change has dominated the international environmental agenda since the early 1990s. Although some disagreement persists, there has been a growing consensus that climate change is happening, and that it is the product of human activity, notably the emission, since the beginning of the industrial age, of greenhouse gases. However, substantial disagreement persists both about its consequences (and so the seriousness of the problem) and, most particularly, about how it should be tackled.

- Effective international action to tackle climate change is hampered by a variety of obstacles to international cooperation. The most significant of these are: (perhaps fundamental) conflict between national self-interest and the common good; tensions of various kinds between developed and developing states; biases within capitalism in favour of growth; and a deeply-rooted ethic of materialism and consumerism.

- Energy resources have come to be seen as having a growing bearing on matters such as security, development and conflict, particularly as access to oil, gas and coal has become a crucial factor in determining the shape of twenty-first-century world order. However, it is by no means clear that natural resources are always a source of national power, in that resources may be a 'curse' when they, for instance, create economic imbalances and attract unwanted foreign interference.

Questions for discussion

- Why have environmental issues become an increasingly major focus of international concern?
- How does 'shallow' ecology differ from 'deep' ecology?
- What are the implications of the idea of sustainable development?
- Do we have obligations towards future generations and, if so, what does this imply?
- Can it any longer be doubted that climate change stems from human activity?
- Have the negative consequences of climate change been exaggerated?
- Should developed countries take primary responsibility for tackling climate change?
- Should greenhouse gas emissions targets be set on a per capita basis?
- Do concerns about resource security always conflict with those about climate change?
- To what extent are natural resources a 'curse'?

Further reading

Betsill, M., K. Hochstetler and D. Stevis (eds), *International Environmental Politics* (2006). An authoritative collection of essays that review the key debates in international environmental politics.

Dessler, A. and E. Parson, *The Science and Politics of Global Climate Change* (2010). A clear and accessible introduction to the nature of global climate change and the challenges it poses.

Elliott, L., *The Global Politics of the Environment* (2004). A comprehensive and detailed examination of the nature and development of global environmental issues.

Laferrière, E. and P. Stoett, *International Relations Theory and Ecological Thought: Towards a Synthesis* (1999). A stimulating examination of the overlaps between international relations theory and ecophilosophy.

ONLINE RESOURCES AVAILABLE

Links to relevant web resources can be found on the *Global Politics* website

CHAPTER 17

Gender in Global Politics

'Men make wars ... because war makes them men.'
BARBARA EHRENREICH *Blood Rites* (1997)

PREVIEW

The study of international politics has traditionally been 'gender-blind'. In a discipline that focused primarily on states and inter-state relations, sexual politics and gender relations appeared to be of little or no relevance. Since the 1980s, however, feminist perspectives on world affairs have gained growing prominence. To a large degree, this reflected a growing acceptance that people's understanding of the world is shaped by the social and historical context in which they live and work. This implied, amongst other things, that global politics could be understood through a 'gender lens'. But what does it mean to put a 'gender lens' on global politics? How has feminism changed our understanding of international and global processes? One implication of adopting a gender perspective on such matters has been to make women visible, in the sense of compensating for a 'mobilization of bias' within a largely male-dominated discipline that had previously been concerned only with male-dominated institutions and processes. Women, in other words, have always been part of world politics; it is just that their role and contribution had been ignored. At a deeper, and analytically more significant, level, putting a 'gender lens' on global politics means recognizing the extent to which the concepts, theories and assumptions through which the world has conventionally been understood are gendered. Gender analysis is thus the analysis of masculine and feminine identities, symbols and structures and how they shape global politics. Not only does this involve exposing what are seen as 'masculinist' biases that run through the conceptual framework of mainstream theory, but this conceptual framework has also, in some ways, been recast to take account of feminist perceptions. Do women and men understand and act on the world in different ways, and what is the significance of this for the theory and practice of global politics?

KEY ISSUES

- What are the main schools of feminist theory, and over what do they disagree?
- What is gender, and how does it affect political understanding?
- How have feminists understood security, war and armed conflict?
- Are states and nationalism constructed on the basis of masculinist norms?
- How does an awareness of gender relations alter our understanding of issues such as globalization and development?

FEMINISM, GENDER AND GLOBAL POLITICS

Varieties of feminism

Feminism can broadly be defined as a movement for the social advancement of women. As such, feminist theory is based on two central beliefs: that women are disadvantaged because of their sex; and that this disadvantage can and should be overthrown. In this way, feminists have highlighted what they see as a *political* relationship between the sexes, the supremacy of men and the subjugation of women in most, if not all, societies. Although the term 'feminism' may have been a twentieth-century invention, such views have been expressed in many different cultures and can be traced back as far as the ancient civilizations of Greece and China. For example, the *Book of the City of Ladies*, written by the Venetian-born poet Christine de Pisan (1365–1434), foreshadowed many of the ideas of modern feminism in recording the deeds of famous women in the past and advocating women's rights to education and political influence. However, feminism has always been a highly diverse political tradition, encompassing what sometimes appears to be a bewildering range of sub-traditions – 'liberal' feminism, 'socialist' or 'Marxist' feminism, 'radical' feminism, 'postmodern' feminism, 'psychoanalytical' feminism, 'postcolonial' feminism, 'lesbian' feminism and so on. Two broad distinctions are nevertheless helpful. The first of these is between feminism's first wave and its second wave.

'**First-wave feminism**' emerged in the nineteenth century and was shaped, above all, by the campaign for female suffrage, the right to vote. Its core belief was that women should enjoy the same legal and political rights as men, with a particular emphasis being placed on female suffrage on the grounds that if women could vote, all other forms of other forms of sexual discrimination or prejudice would quickly disappear. '**Second-wave feminism**' was born out of a recognition that the achievement of political and legal rights had not solved the 'woman problem'. The goal of second-wave feminism was not merely political emancipation but women's liberation, reflected in the ideas of the growing women's liberation movement, one of the leading 'new' social movements that emerged in the 1960s and 1970s. A key theme of this movement was that women's liberation could not be achieved by political reforms or legal changes alone, but demanded a more far-reaching and perhaps revolutionary process of social change. Whereas first-wave feminism had been primarily concerned with reform in the 'public' sphere of education, politics and work, second-wave feminism sought to re-structure the 'private' sphere of family and domestic life, reflecting the belief that 'the personal is the political'. Second-wave feminism thus practised the 'politics of everyday life', raising questions about power structures in the family, and personal and sexual relationships between women and men. This shift reflected the growing importance within feminist theory of what was called **radical feminism**, which presents female subordination as pervasive and systematic, stemming from the institution of 'patriarchy' (see p. 424) (Millett 1970; Elshtain 1981).

Since the 1970s, however, feminism has undergone a process of deradicalization, defying (repeated) attempts to define a clear feminist 'third wave', but it has

● **First-wave feminism**: The early form of feminism from the mid-nineteenth century to the 1960s, which was based on the liberal goal of sexual equality in the areas of legal and political rights, particularly suffrage rights.

● **Second-wave feminism**: The form of feminism that emerged in the 1960s and 1970s, and was characterized by a more radical concern with 'women's liberation', including, and perhaps especially, in the private sphere.

● **Radical feminism**: A form of feminism that holds gender divisions to be the most politically significant of social cleavages, and believes that these are rooted in the structures of family or domestic life.

also become increasingly diverse. A second broad distinction within feminism has nevertheless become increasingly significant: whether feminism is defined by the quest for 'equality' or by the recognition of 'difference'. Feminism has traditionally been closely associated with, some would say defined by, the quest for gender equality, whether this means the achievement of equal rights (liberal feminism), social equality (socialist feminism) or equal personal power (radical feminism). In what can broadly be called equality feminism, 'difference' implies oppression or subordination; it highlights legal, political, social or other advantages that men enjoy but which are denied to women. Women, in that sense, must be liberated *from* difference. Although socialist feminists and most radical feminists embrace egalitarian ideas, the most influential form of equality feminism is **liberal feminism**. Liberal feminism dominated first-wave feminism and helped to shape reformist tendencies within second-wave feminism, particularly in the USA. The goal of liberal feminism is to ensure that women and men enjoy equal access to the 'public' sphere, underpinned by the right to education, to vote and participate in political life, to pursue a career and so forth.

Such thinking is based on the belief that human nature is basically **androgynous**. All human beings, regardless of their sex, possess the genetic inheritance of a mother and a father, and therefore embody a blend of both female and male attributes and traits. Women and men should therefore not be judged by their sex, but as individuals, as 'persons'. In this view, a very clear distinction is drawn between sex and gender (see p. 423). 'Sex', in this sense, refers to biological differences between females and males, usually linked to reproduction; these differences are natural and therefore are unalterable. 'Gender', on the other hand, is a social construct, a product of culture, not nature. Gender differences are typically imposed through contrasting stereotypes of 'masculinity' and 'femininity'. As the French philosopher and feminist Simone de Beauvoir (1908–86) put it, 'Women are made, they are not born'.

The idea that gender is a social construct was originally conceived as a means of refuting biological determinism, the notion, favoured by many anti-feminists, that 'biology is destiny', implying that women's domestic or 'private' role is an inevitable consequence of their physical and biological make-up. However, it can also imply that gender differences are more deep-rooted, grounded in the quite different material and psycho-sexual experiences of women and men (Squires 1999). This has led to what has been called 'standpoint feminism', in which the world is understood from the unique perspective – or standpoint – of women's experience (Tinkner 1992). Standpoint feminists hold, in particular, that women's experience at the margins of political life has given them a perspective on social issues that provides insights into world affairs. Although not necessarily superior to those of men, women's views nevertheless constitute valid insights into the complex world of global politics. In other cases, forms of **difference feminism** have attempted to link social and cultural differences between women and men to deeper biological differences. They thus offer an **essentialist** account of gender that rests on the assumption that there is an 'essence' of man/woman which determines their gendered behaviours regardless of socialization. However, regardless of whether they have biological, politico-cultural or psycho-sexual origins, a belief in deeply-rooted and possibly ineradicable differences between women and men has significant implications for feminist theory (Held 2005). In particular, it suggests that the traditional goal of gender equality

● **Liberal feminism**: A form of feminism that is grounded in the belief that sexual differences are irrelevant to personal worth and calls for equal rights for women and men in the public realm.

● **Androgyny**: The possession of both male and female characteristics; used to imply that human beings are sexless 'persons' in the sense that sex is irrelevant to their social role or political status.

● **Difference feminism**: A form of feminism that holds that there are ineradicable differences between women and men, whether these are rooted in biology, culture or material experience.

● **Essentialism**: The belief that biological factors are crucial in determining psychological and behavioural traits.

THE WOMEN'S MOVEMENT

Type: Social movement

An organized women's movement first emerged in the mid-nineteenth century, focused on the campaign for female suffrage, the defining goal of feminism's 'first wave'. By the end of the nineteenth century, women's suffrage groups were active in most western countries. Although the goal of female suffrage was largely achieved in developed states in the early decades of the twentieth century (it was introduced first in New Zealand in 1893), gaining votes for women, ironically, weakened the women's movement by depriving it of a unifying goal and sense of purpose. It was not until the 1960s that the women's movement was regenerated with the birth of the 'women's liberation movement'. Often viewed as feminism's 'second wave', this reflected the belief that redressing the status of women required not just political reform, but a process of radical, and particularly cultural, change, brought about by 'consciousness raising' and the transformation of family, domestic and personal life. This radical phase of feminist activism subsided from the early 1970s onwards, but the women's movement nevertheless continued to grow and acquired an increasingly prominent international dimension.

Significance: The impact of social movements is difficult to assess because of the broad nature of their goals, and because, to some extent, they exert influence through less tangible cultural strategies. However, it is clear that in the case of the

women's movement, profound political and social changes have been achieved through shifts in cultural values and moral attitudes brought about over a number of years. Beyond the earlier achievement of female suffrage, feminist activism from the 1960s onwards contributed to profound and far-reaching changes in the structure of western societies. Female access to education, careers and public life generally expanded considerably; free contraception and abortion on demand became more available; women enjoyed considerably greater legal and financial independence; the issues of rape and violence against women received greater prominence and so forth. Such changes brought about major shifts in family and social structures, as traditional gender roles were re-examined and sometimes recast, not least through a major increase in the number of women in the workplace. Similar developments can be identified on the international level, as the advancement and empowerment of women came to be prioritized across a range of international agendas. This happened, for example, through an explicit emphasis on women's empowerment in development initiatives, via ideas such as human development (see p. 363), human security (see p. 430) and women's human rights, and as a result of the adoption of 'gender mainstreaming' by the UN and bodies such as the World Bank.

However, the significance and impact of the women's movement

has been called into question in a number of ways. In the first place, advances in gender equality, where they have occurred, may have been brought about less by the women's movement and more by the pressures generated by capitalist modernity, and especially its tendency to value individuals in terms of their contribution to the productive process, rather than their traditional status. Second, the sexual revolution brought about by the women's movement is, at best, incomplete. The expansion of educational, career and political opportunities for women has been largely confined to the developed world, and even there major disparities persist, not least though the continued under-representation of women in senior positions in the professions, business and political life, and in the fact that everywhere household and childcare responsibilities are still unequally distributed. Third, the women's movement has become increasingly disparate and divided over time. The core traditions of western feminism (liberal, socialist/Marxist and radical feminism) have thus increasingly been challenged by black feminism, postcolonial feminism, poststructuralist feminism, psychoanalytic feminism, lesbian feminism and so on. Finally, social conservatives have accused the women's movement of contributing to social breakdown by encouraging women to place career advancement and personal satisfaction before family and social responsibility.

CONCEPT

Gender

Gender refers, most basically, to the social construction of sexual difference. As such, 'gender' is clearly distinct from 'sex'. For most feminists, 'sex' highlights biological, and therefore ineradicable, differences between females and males, while 'gender' denotes a set of culturally defined distinctions between women and men. Gender either operates through stereotyping (usually based on contrasting models of femininity and masculinity), or it is a manifestation of structural power relations. This constructivist account of gender has nevertheless been challenged by essentialist feminists, who reject the sex/gender distinction altogether, by poststructuralist feminists, who highlight the ambiguity of gender, and by postcolonial feminists, who insist that gender identities are multiple, not singular.

is misguided or simply undesirable. To want to be equal to a man implies that women are 'male-identified', in that they define their goals in terms of what men are or what men have. The demand for equality therefore embodies the desire to be 'like men', adopting, for instance, the competitive and aggressive behaviour that characterizes male society. Difference feminists, by contrast, argue that women should be 'female-identified': women should seek liberation not as supposedly sexless 'persons' but as developed and fulfilled women, celebrating female values and characteristics. In that sense, women gain liberation *through* difference.

An emphasis on difference rather than equality can also be seen, albeit in contrasting ways, in the case of postcolonial feminism and poststructural feminism. Postcolonial feminists take issue with any universalist analysis of the plight of women and how it should be addressed, viewing it as an attempt to impose a political agenda developed out of the experiences of middle-class women in liberal capitalist societies onto women generally (Chowdhry and Nair 2002). Postcolonial feminists have therefore resisted attempts to deal with gender injustice through a 'top-down' international policy process which treats the recipients of its intervention merely as 'victims'. Poststructural or postmodern feminists, for their part, question the idea that there is such a thing as a fixed female identity, rejecting the notion also that insights can be drawn from a distinctive set of women's experiences (Sylvester 1994). From this perspective, even the idea of 'woman' may be nothing more that a fiction, as supposedly indisputable biological differences between women and men are, in significant ways, shaped by gendered discourses (not all women are capable of bearing children, for example).

'Gender lenses' on global politics

Feminist theories have only been widely applied to the study of international and global issues since the late 1980s, some twenty years after feminism had influenced other areas of the social sciences. Since then, however, gender perspectives have gained growing prominence, alongside other critical theories that have, in their various ways, challenged mainstream realist and liberal approaches. Feminism has made a particular contribution to the so-called 'fourth debate' in international relations (see p. 516), which has opened up questions about the nature of theory and the politics of knowledge generally. These newer perspectives have generally accepted that all theory is conditioned by the social and historical context in which the activity of theorizing takes place (Steans 1998). But what does it mean to put a 'feminist lens' or 'gender lens' (or, more accurately, 'lenses', in view of the heterodox nature of feminist theory) on global politics? How can issues such as nationalism, security, war and so on be 'gendered'? There are two main ways which take account of how prevailing gender relations alter analytical and theoretical approaches to global politics. These are sometimes called 'empirical' feminism and 'analytical' feminism (True 2009).

Empirical feminism is primarily concerned to add women to existing analytical frameworks (it is sometimes disparaged as 'add women and stir'). This perspective, influenced in particular by liberal feminism, has an essentially empirical orientation because it addresses the under-representation or misrepresentation of women in a discipline that has conventionally focused only on male-dominated institutions and processes. Its critique of conventional

Patriarchy

Patriarchy literally means rule by the father (*pater* meaning 'father' in Latin). Although some feminists use 'patriarchy' in this specific and limited sense, to describe the structure of the family and the dominance of the husband-father over both his wife and his children, radical feminists in particular use the term to refer to the system of male power in society at large. Patriarchy thus means 'rule by men'. The term implies that the subordination of women both reflects and derives from the dominance of the husband-father within the family. Millett (1970) thus suggested that patriarchy contains two principles: 'male shall dominate female, elder male shall dominate younger male'. A patriarchal society is therefore characterized by both gender and generational oppression.

● **Gender mainstreaming**: The attempt to 'mainstream' gender into decision-making processes by requiring that, before decisions are made, an analysis is carried out of their likely effects on women and men, respectively.

● **Masculinism**: Gender bias that derives from the portrayal of male or masculine views as either superior or as objective and rational.

approaches to international politics is thus encapsulated in the question: 'where are the women?' Making feminist sense of international politics therefore means recognizing the previously invisible contributions that women make to shaping world politics, as, for example, domestic workers of various kinds, migrant labourers, diplomats' wives, sex workers on military bases and so forth (Enloe 1989, 1993, 2000). The influence of such thinking can be seen in the adoption, particularly since the UN Decade for Women (1976–85), of **gender main-streaming** by the United Nations (see p. 456) itself and other bodies such as the World Bank (see p. 380). However, although 'adding women' demonstrates that women are, and have always been, relevant to international political activities and global processes, such a gender lens has its limitations. In the first place, it only recognizes gender as an empirical, not an analytical, category, meaning that it widens our awareness of the range of global processes rather than changes our *understanding* of them. Second, by highlighting the under-representation of women in conventional leadership roles at national, international and global levels, it can be said to be unduly concerned with the interests of elite women, while giving insufficient attention to how rectifying such gender imbalances might affect the behaviour of global actors.

Analytical feminism, by contrast, is concerned to highlight the gender biases that pervade the theoretical framework and key concepts of mainstream international theory, and particularly realism. It is analytical in that it addresses the issue of how the world is seen and understood, drawing on the ideas of difference feminism. Whereas mainstream theories have traditionally been presented as gender-neutral, analytical feminism uncovers hidden assumptions that stem from the fact that such theories derive from a social and political context in which male domination is taken for granted. Key concepts and ideas of mainstream theories therefore reflect a **masculinist** bias. Standpoint feminism has been particularly influential in demonstrating just how male-dominated conventional theories of international politics are. In a pioneering analysis, J. Ann Tickner (1988) thus reformulated Hans Morgenthau's six principles of political realism (see p. 60) to show how seemingly objective laws in fact reflect male values, rather than female ones. Morgenthau's account of power politics portrays states as autonomous actors intent on pursuing self-interest by acquiring power over other states, a model that reflects the traditional dominance of the husband-father within the family and of male citizens within society at large. At the same time, this gendered conception of power as 'power over', or domination, takes no account of forms of human relationship that may be more akin to female experience, such as caring, interdependence and collaborative behaviour. Tickner's reformulated six principles can be summarized as follows:

● Objectivity is culturally defined and it is associated with masculinity – so objectivity is always partial.
● The national interest is multi-dimensional – so it cannot (and should not) be defined by one set of interests.
● Power as domination and control privileges masculinity.
● There are possibilities for using power as collective empowerment in the international arena.
● All political action has moral significance – it is not possible to separate politics and morality.

- A narrowly defined, and 'autonomous', political realm defines the political in a way that excludes the concerns and contributions of women.

GENDERING GLOBAL POLITICS

Gendered states and gendered nations

Issues of identity in global politics are generally dominated by an emphasis on identification with the nation-state (see p. 168). Such an identification is particularly strong because the overlapping allegiances of citizenship (membership of a state) and nationality (membership of a nation) are focused on a territorially defined community. Moreover, the supposedly homogeneous character of the nation-state helps to explain why alternative forms of identity, such as those based on social class, gender, religion and ethnicity, have traditionally been politically marginalized. The rise of the modern women's movement has, to some extent, countered nation-state loyalties by trying to foster a rival sense of 'international sisterhood', based on transnational gender allegiances, although, as with attempts by the twentieth-century socialist movement to inculcate a sense of 'proletarian internationalism', this has had little serious impact. Of greater significance, however, have been feminists' attempts to demonstrate the extent to which both the state and the nation are entangled with gender assumptions and biases.

Feminism does not contain a theory of the state as such (MacKinnon 1989). Furthermore, feminists have usually not regarded the nature of state power as a central political issue, preferring instead to concentrate on the 'deeper structure' of male power centred on institutions such as the family. Nevertheless, radical feminists in particular have argued that patriarchy operates in, and through, the state, meaning that the state is in fact a patriarchal state. However, there are contrasting instrumentalist and structuralist versions of this argument. The *instrumentalist* approach views the state as little more than an 'agent' or 'tool' used by men to defend their interests and uphold the structures of patriarchy. This line of argument draws on the core feminist belief that patriarchy is upheld by the division of society into distinct public and private spheres of life. The subordination of women has traditionally been accomplished through their confinement to a private sphere of family and domestic responsibilities, turning them into housewives and mothers, and through their exclusion from a public realm centred on politics and the economy. Quite simply, in this view, the state is run *by* men *for* men. Whereas instrumentalist arguments focus on the personnel of the state, and particularly the state elite, *structuralist* arguments tend to emphasize the degree to which state institutions are embedded in a wider patriarchal system. Modern radical feminists have paid particular attention to the emergence of the welfare state, seeing it as the expression of a new kind of patriarchal power. Welfare may uphold patriarchy by bringing about a transition from private dependence (in which women as homemakers are dependent on male breadwinners) to a system of public dependence in which women are increasingly controlled by the institutions of the extended state. For instance, women have become increasingly dependent on the state as clients or customers of state services (such as childcare institutions, nurseries, schools and social services) and as employees, particularly in the so-called 'caring' professions (such as nursing, social work and education).

APPROACHES TO . . .

GENDER RELATIONS

Realist view

There is no realist theory of gender as such. Realists, indeed, would usually view gender relations as irrelevant to international and global affairs. This is because the principal actors on the world stage are states, whose behaviour is shaped by an overriding concern about the national interest (see p. 135) and the fact that, within an anarchic international system, they are forced to prioritize security (especially military security) over other considerations. States are therefore 'black boxes': their internal political and constitutional structures and their social make-up, in terms of gender, class, ethnic, racial or other divisions, have no bearing on their external behaviour. However, in arguing that state egoism derives from human egoism, classical realists such as Morgenthau have suggested that the tendency to dominate is an element in all human associations including the family. The patriarchal family and the sexual division of labour between 'public' men and 'private' women (Elshtain 1981) therefore tend to be thought of as natural and unchangeable.

Liberal view

Liberals have long been concerned about the issue of gender equality, so much so that liberal feminism was the earliest, and in countries such as the USA continues to be the most influential, school of feminist thought. The philosophical basis of liberal feminism lies in the principle of individualism (see p. 154). Individuals are entitled to equal treatment, regardless of their gender, race, colour, creed or religion. If individuals are to be judged, it should be on rational grounds, on the content of their character, their talents, or their personal worth. Any form of sexual discrimination should clearly be prohibited. Liberal feminists therefore aim to break down the remaining legal and social pressures that restrict women from pursuing careers and being politically active, and, in particular, to increase the representation of women in senior positions in public and political life. They believe that this would both serve the interests of justice (in promoting equal opportunities for women and men) and, probably, make a difference to how politics is conducted. This is because liberals have usually assumed that women and men have different natures and inclinations, women's leaning towards family and domestic life being shaped,

at least in part, by a natural impulse towards caring and nurturing. Feminist thinking has had a significant impact on liberal international relations scholars such as Keohane (1989, 1998), who accepted that standpoint feminism in particular had given ideas such as complex interdependence and institutional change a richer and more gender-conscious formulation. As a liberal rationalist, however, he criticized the attachment of some feminist scholars to postmodern or poststructural methodologies, insisting that knowledge can only be advanced by developing testable hypotheses.

Critical views

Critical theories of global politics have engaged with feminist thinking and gender perspectives in a number of different ways. Social constructivism had a significant impact on early radical feminist conceptions of gender, which placed a particular emphasis on the process of socialization that takes place within the family as boys and girls are encouraged to conform to contrasting masculine and feminine stereotypes. Gender is therefore a social construct, quite distinct from the notion of biological sex. Frankfurt critical theory, as with any tradition that derives from Marxism, has tended to ignore or marginalize gender, preferring instead to concentrate on social class. However, a form of feminist critical theory has emerged that tends to fuse elements of standpoint feminism with a broadly Marxist emphasis on the links between capitalism and patriarchy, seen as interlocking hegemonic structures. In this view, women's groups have considerable emancipatory potential, operating as a force of resistance against the advance of global capitalism and TNCs (see p. 94). Postmodern or poststructuralist feminists have taken issue in particular with forms of feminism that proclaim that there are essential differences between women and men. Finally, postcolonial feminists have been critical of Eurocentric, universalist models of female emancipation that fail to recognize that gender identities are enmeshed with considerations of race, ethnicity and culture. For instance, forms of Islamic feminism have developed in which the return to traditional moral and religious principles has been seen to enhance the status of women (see Cultural rights or women's rights?, p. 203).

The gendered character of the state is not only significant in consolidating, and possibly extending, the internal structures of male power, but also in shaping the external behaviour of states and thus the structure of the international system. Here, patriarchy dictates that states will be competitive and at least potentially aggressive, reflecting the forms of social interaction that are characteristic of male society generally. A patriarchal state-system is thus one that is prone to conflict and war. Moreover, such tendencies and behaviour are legitimized by the conceptual framework through which the international system has conventionally been interpreted. This can be seen, for instance, in the case of sovereignty (see p. 4). State sovereignty, the central principle of the Westphalian state-system, presents states as separate and independent entities, autonomous actors operating in an anarchic environment. Such an image can be seen to reflect an essentially masculinist view of the world insofar as male upbringing stresses the cultivation of independence, self-reliance and robustness generally. Just as boys and men are accustomed to think of themselves as separate, self-contained creatures, it is natural to think that states have similar characteristics. Very much the same can be said about the stress in mainstream international theory on the national interest (see p. 135) as the primary motivation of states. This may be seen to derive from an emphasis in male upbringing on self-assertion and competitiveness. Indeed, in this light, the classical realist belief that state egoism reflects human egoism, should perhaps be recast as: state egoism reflects male egoism.

Gendered perspectives on nations and nationalism have also been developed (Yuval-Davis and Anthias 1989; Yuval-Davis 1997). These have adopted a number of approaches, but one important aspect of gendering nationalism has focused on the extent to which women have been used to symbolize the cultural heritage of an ethnic, religious or national group. As such, gender becomes entangled with issues of national or cultural difference. This can be seen in the common tendency to depict the nation in explicitly gendered terms, usually as a 'motherland' but sometimes as a 'fatherland'. In a sense, such images merely reflect parallels between the nation and the family, both being viewed, in some sense, as 'home' and both being fashioned out of kinship, or at least kinship-like ties. The rhetoric of nationalism is also often heavily sexualized and gendered, as, for instance, in the idea of patriotism as a love of one's country. Gender images are nevertheless particularly prominent in the case of regressive forms of ethnic, religious or national identity. As these tend to stress the role of women as 'mothers of the nation', reproducers of the ethnic or national group itself as well as transmitters of its distinctive culture, they place a special emphasis on female 'purity'. This can be seen in the tendency for religious fundamentalism (see p. 199) to be closely linked to attempts to re-establish traditional gender roles, religious revivalism being symbolized by 'idealized womanhood'. However, such tendencies can also have wider implications, not least in linking nationalist conflict to the possibility of violence against women. The notion that women embody the symbolic values of chastity and motherhood can mean that aggressive forms of nationalism target women through rape and other forms of sexual violence. The honour of men (as protectors of women) and the moral integrity of the nation is best destroyed through physical attacks on the honour of women. Incidents of gendered violence have occurred, for example, in Croatia and Bosnia in the 1990s as well as in the anti-Muslim riots in Gujarat, India in 2002 (see p. 428).

Gendered violence in anti-Muslim riots in Gujarat

Events: On 28 February 2002, communal rioting broke out in the Indian province of Gujarat. The pretext for these riots was the horrific killing, the previous day, of 58 mainly militant Hindu volunteers who had been burnt alive on a train returning from Ayodhya. The communal riots in Gujarat continued until 3 March, after which there was a hiatus followed by a new round of violence from 15 March. Estimates of the numbers killed in the riots range from below 1,000 to over 2,000, with Muslim deaths outnumbering Hindu deaths by a ratio of 15:1. Over 500 mosques and *dargahs* (shrines) were destroyed and enormous numbers of Muslims in Gujarat were displaced: by mid-April, nearly 150,000 people were living in some 104 relief camps.

There was, furthermore, evidence of the complicity of the authorities in the Gujarat violence as well as of precision and planning, linked to the family of organizations associated with the RSS (Rashtriya Swayamsevak Sangh), which preaches a creed of 'India for the Hindus'. One of the most notable features of the anti-Muslim riots was the use of the sexual subjugation of women as an instrument of violence. At least 250 young girls and women were brutally gang-raped and burnt alive. Other atrocities included the stripping naked of groups of women who were then made to run for miles, the insertion of objects into women's bodies and the carving of religious symbols onto their bodies. What is more, women who were raped by Hindu zealots saw no action taken against their aggressors, as the police were generally unwilling to take their complaints seriously.

Significance: Hindu–Muslim violence has been a recurring feature of politics in India for three-quarters of a century or more. Although they are often portrayed as a manifestation of spontaneous hostility between the Hindus and Muslims, the deep involvement of the organizations of militant Hindu nationalism have given rise to 'institutionalized riot systems' (Brass 2003). However, why was gendered violence so prominent in the Gujarat riots of 2002, as, indeed, it has been in much of the communal rioting that has spasmodically gripped India?

The answer appears to be that a crisis of identity, linked to the desire to reassert or purify the Hindutva identity in the face of a perceived threat from Islam, has become entangled with a crisis of masculinity. Young males, organized on paramilitary lines, have conflated Hindu nationalism with masculinity and violence. This is evident not only in the emphasis within Hindu nationalist literature on the image of 'the man as warrior', but also in the fact that the political goals of Hindu nationalism are commonly expressed in sexual terms. Stress, for instance, is often placed on the 'threat' posed to Hindu identity by the generally higher fertility rates of Muslim communities. Hostility towards Muslims therefore tends to be expressed in the desire to dehumanize Muslim women, who are then viewed, and treated, primarily as sexual objects. Hindu nationalists thus rape and otherwise attack minority women to destroy not only their bodies, but also the integrity and identity of Muslim society, viewed as the 'enemy other' (Chenoy 2002). In that sense, the sexual violence against Muslim women that marked the 2002 Gujarat riots was very much a public act. Attacking Muslim women sexually served two purposes: it brutalized Muslim women and denigrated Muslim men for failing to protect their women. It was therefore an attempt to terrorize Muslims and drive them out of 'Hindu India' by violating their communal honour (Anand 2007).

Gendering security, war and armed conflict

Feminist analysis has placed particular emphasis on developing a gendered conception of security and war (Tickner 1992, 2001). Conventional approaches to security present it as 'the highest end' of international politics (Waltz 1979). In this view, states have prime responsibility for maintaining security, as reflected in the notion of 'national security'. The major threats to security are therefore external, coming in particular from other states. In this way, the threat of violence and other forms of physical coercion are intrinsically linked to the prospect of inter-state war. National security is thus closely linked to the prevention of such wars, usually through a build-up of military capacity to deter potential aggressors. Feminists, for their part, have criticized this view of security on two grounds. First, it is premised on masculinist assumptions about rivalry, competition and inevitable conflict, arising from a tendency to see the world in terms of interactions among a series of power-seeking, autonomous actors. Second, the conventional idea of national security tends to be self-defeating as a result of the **security paradox**. This creates what has been called the 'insecurity of security'.

Feminist theorists, by contrast, have embraced alternative conceptions of security, most commonly the notion of 'human security'. Nevertheless, the parameters of human security are sometimes unclear. While some argue that it should be confined to 'freedom from fear' (in which case the key threats to security would be armed conflict and human-made physical violence), others extend it to include 'freedom from want' (in which case poverty, inequality and **structural violence** become key threats). Further controversies have arisen from attempts to make the concept of human security measurable, in order to make it easier for researchers and policy-makers to apply it in practice. For example, the Human Security Gateway, an online database of human security-related resources, classifies a human security crisis as a situation where at least 1,000 civilian deaths have occurred. For some feminists, such tendencies implicitly privilege physical security and military threats over threats such as rape, loss of property, inadequate food and environmental degradation, which may not result in death, but which nevertheless lead to profound insecurity and, sometimes, vulnerability to further violence (Truong *et al.* 2007).

Feminists have been drawn to a broader and multidimensional notion of security both through long-standing concerns about violence against women in family and domestic life, and though an awareness of growing threats to women arising, for example, from sex slavery and armed conflict. From a gender perspective, therefore, the apparently clear distinction between 'war' and 'peace', which arises from a primary concern with the threat of inter-state war, is quite bogus and merely serves to conceal the wide range of other threats from which women suffer. The absence of war, in the conventional sense, certainly does not guarantee that people, and especially women, live without fear or safe from want. However, feminists have gone further than simply gendering security. They have also sought to apply a gender lens to the understanding of war.

For difference feminists in particular, war is closely associated with masculinity. Such an association may operate on several levels. In the first place, the dominance of men in senior positions in political and military life may mean that decisions about war and peace are made by people whose world-view acknowledges that armed conflict is an inevitable, and perhaps even a desirable, feature

● **Security paradox**: The paradox that a build-up of military capacity designed to strengthen national security may be counter-productive, as it can encourage other states to adopt more threatening and hostile postures.

● **Structural violence**: A form of violence that stems from social structures that perpetuate domination, oppression or exploitation, as opposed to 'direct violence' which stems (supposedly) from individual or group motivations.

Focus on . . .
Human security: individuals at risk?

In its broadest sense, human security refers to the security of individuals rather than of states. As such, it contrasts with 'national security', which is invariably linked to states and military power, the main threats to security deriving from the aggressive behaviour of other states. The notion of human security was an attempt to broaden and deepen the concept of threat, influenced by ideas such as human development (see p. 363) (the idea can be traced back to the 1994 *UN Human Development Report*) and to the doctrine of human rights (see p. 311). Human security is often seen as having a variety of dimensions:

- Economic security – an assured basic income
- Food security – physical and economic access to basic food
- Health security – protection from disease and unhealthy lifestyles

- Environmental security – protection from human-induced environmental degradation
- Personal security – protection from all forms of physical violence
- Community security – protection for traditional identities and values
- Political security – the existence of rights and free-doms to protect people from tyranny or govern-ment abuse.

Critics of human security tend to argue either that it has so deepened and widened the concept of security that it is virtually meaningless (particularly as it extends beyond 'freedom from fear' and includes 'freedom from want'), or that it creates false expecta-tions about the international community's capacity to banish violence and insecurity.

of world politics. This stems from a tendency amongst men to see the world in terms of conflict, rivalry and competition, whether this arises from the influence of masculine gender stereotypes or from deeper, biologically-based drives. As women, in this analysis, are less warlike than men, having a greater inclination towards cooperation, consensus-building and the use of non-confrontational strategies, the increased representation for women in positions of political or military leadership can be expected to lead to a reduced use of force in world affairs. This, indeed, may lead to a feminist alternative to the 'democratic peace' thesis (see p. 69), favoured by liberals, which would assert that societies become more peaceful not to the extent that they embrace democracy but to the extent that they practise gender equality at all levels. A **matriarchal** society would, from this perspective, certainly be more peaceful than a patriarchal one. The empirical evidence to support such thinking is nevertheless mixed, with some evidence suggesting that, while empowering women at the domestic level often translates into peaceful international politics, the presence of a female leader may at times increase the severity of violence used in a crisis (Caprioli and Boyer 2001). This tends to occur because female leaders operate in a 'man's world' and so are encouraged to adopt 'hyper-masculine' behavioural patterns.

The second link between war and masculinity operates through the role that militarized masculinity plays as a national ideal in times of international tension and conflict. This is evident in the image of the (invariably male) 'heroic warrior' and in the emphasis in military training on the cultivation of supposedly 'manly'

● **Matriarchy**: Literally, rule by the mother (*mater* being Latin for 'mother'); a society, whether historical or hypothesized, that is governed by women.

virtues, such as discipline, obedience, ruthlessness and, above all, the ability to divorce action from emotion. Military training can even be seen as a systematic attempt to suppress feminine or 'womanly' impulses or responses. Goldstein (2001) thus observed that the most warlike cultures are also the most sexist, arguing that the link between war and gender is forged both by the ways in which masculinity is constructed so as to motivate soldiers to fight, and by the impact that war-making has on masculinity. Third, war is often justified in terms of the 'protection myth': the idea that it is the role of the warrior male to protect the weak and the vulnerable, namely women and children (Enloe 1993). In that sense, war both exaggerates the masculine/feminine dichotomy in gender relations and also serves to legitimize it. The masculinity of war was most easily perpetuated when fighting, at least in conventional armies, was an exclusively male activity.

However, gendering war is concerned not only with exploring links between the causes of war and masculinity, but also with recognizing the differing implications of war and armed conflict for women and men. Armed conflict has traditionally been thought of as a 'man's world', the traditional exclusion of women from military life meaning that fighting, killing and dying has been carried out by male combatants. Insofar as women played a significant role in warfare, it was in maintaining the 'home front', as was evident in the large-scale recruitment of women into the workforce in developed countries during WWI and WWII. The distinction between male combatants and female non-combatants nevertheless conceals the extent to which women affect, and are affected by, armed conflict in a wide variety of ways. This certainly applies in the sense that women and girls have increasingly become the victims of war and armed conflict. The advent of 'total' war in the twentieth century meant that women were as likely to be casualties of war as men. For instance, 42 million civilians died in WWII, most of them women, compared with 25 million military deaths. Nevertheless, the development of 'new' wars, as discussed in Chapter 10, has had particularly serious implications for women and girls. As these wars commonly spring from racial, religious and/or ethnic divisions, and involve the use of guerrilla and insurrectionary tactics, they lead to the victimization of civilian populations on a massive scale. It is estimated that as many as 75 per cent of the casualties in such conflicts are civilians, compared with a mere 5 per cent at the beginning of the twentieth century. Women and children are disproportionately targeted and constitute the majority of all victims in contemporary armed conflicts (Moser and Clark 2001).

A particular concern has been the use of rape and other forms of sexual violence as a systematic, organized tactic of war. **War rape** is by no means simply a modern phenomenon. The Old Testament of the Bible, for instance, refers to the rape of the women of conquered tribes as a routine act, in effect a reward to the victors. Indeed, random rape by soldiers has probably been a feature of all wars and armed conflicts, particularly prevalent when there has been a lack of military discipline. However, rape has also been used as a military strategy, designed to demoralize, punish or shame the enemy, with examples including the German advance through Belgium in WWI, the Rape of Nanking by the invading Japanese army in 1937–38, and the Russian Red Army's march to Berlin towards the end of WWII. Nevertheless, modern armed conflict appears to be particularly characterized by the systematic and widespread use of rape. For instance, by 1993, the Zenica Centre for the Registration of War and Genocide Crimes in Bosnia-Herzegovina had documented over 40,000 cases of war-related

● **War rape**: Rape committed by soldiers, other combatants or civilians during armed conflict or war.

Debating...
Would a matriarchal society be more peaceful?

The feminist analysis of war has emphasized its linkage to men and masculinity. In some cases, this has been based on the distinction between 'peaceful' women and 'aggressive' men. But would a larger proportion of women in leadership positions reduce the likelihood of war?

YES

Biology is destiny. In their different ways, conservative anti-feminists, essentialist feminists and evolutionary psychologists have argued that there are biologically-based differences between women and men, which are reflected in contrasting behavioural tendencies. Fukuyama (1998) thus used the idea that aggression is 'hard-wired' in men to argue that a world dominated completely by female leaders would be more peaceful than one where female leaders are in the minority. He did this by using evidence of the murderous behaviour of chimpanzees, humankind's closest relatives.

Militarized masculinity. In this view, men are more warlike than women because of social conditioning, not biology. Self-assertion, competition and fighting are seen to be 'natural' for boys, helping to prepare them for the 'public' sphere in general and also, if necessary, for military life. Girls, by contrast, are encouraged to be cooperative and submissive, preparing them for a 'private' sphere of domestic responsibilities. Masculinity and war are therefore mutually reinforcing social constructs.

Aggressive young males. An alternative theory of gendered war gives less attention to gender imbalances amongst political and military leaders and more attention to wider demographic trends, particularly the predominance of young men for whom there are insufficient peaceful occupations. Many war-ravaged areas, such as El Salvador, former Yugoslavia and the Muslim world generally have high proportions of unmarried and unemployed young men, who are more inclined to accept risk in order to increase their access to resources.

Women as peacemakers. Women's inclination towards peace rather than war may not only stem from biological or sociological factors, but also from the fact that the changing nature of armed conflict makes women peculiarly vulnerable. As women and children now account for the vast majority of the casualties of armed conflict, suffering not just death but also rape, sexual attack, mutilation, humiliation and displacement, women have a particular interest in the avoidance of war and thus tend to play a prominent role in movements for peace and reconciliation.

NO

The myth of 'natural' aggression. Biologically-based explanations for behavioural traits such as aggression are badly flawed. Such theories ignore inconvenient examples (Bonobo monkeys, as closely related to humans as chimpanzees, display no tendency towards collective violence) and disregard anthropological evidence about the diversity of human cultures and societies, making it very difficult, and perhaps impossible, to develop generalizations about behavioural propensities. The idea of 'aggressive' men and 'peaceful' women is, at best, highly simplistic.

Misleading gender stereotypes. The idea that culture and social conditioning disposes men to favour war while women favour peace breaks down as soon as the behaviour of real women and men is examined. For example, women also fight, as demonstrated by female terrorists and guerrilla fighters. Women leaders (Margaret Thatcher, Golda Meir and Indira Gandhi) have also adopted distinctively 'manly' approaches to foreign policy, while male leaders (Gandhi, Martin Luther King and Willy Brandt) have embraced strategies of non-violence and conciliation.

Power trumps gender. The social factors that condition political and military leaders into competitive and aggressive behaviour may have more to do with authority than gender. Leaders, both women and men, are liable to be corrupted by their ruling positions, acquiring an exaggerated sense of their own importance and a desire to expand their own power, possibly by military means. Male leaders may appear to have a greater propensity for militarism and expansionism, but this only reflects the fact that most political leaders have been male.

States make war. Wars are complex, orchestrated and highly-organized activities that cannot be explained by individual behavioural traits of any kind. Realists, for instance, dismiss the influence of gender on the grounds that war stems from the inherent fear and uncertainty of an anarchic state-system. Liberals, for their part, link militarism to factors such as empire, authoritarianism and economic nationalism. Foreign policy is thus shaped by wider considerations, and has nothing to do with gender relations.

rape, and between 23,000 and 45,000 Kosovo Albanian women are believed to have been raped during 1998–9, at the height of the conflict with Serbia. These incidents have probably been a consequence of a nexus of factors – the social dislocation that typically accompanies civil strife and internal conflict, the irregular and at best semi-trained nature of fighting forces, and, not least, the potent mixture of resentment, masculinity and violence that tends to characterize extremist identity politics (see p. 190).

A final link between women and armed conflict is the relationship between military bases and prostitution. In one sense, history is so filled with examples of women as 'war booty' or 'camp followers' that the phenomenon of **military prostitution** is seldom analyzed or even recognized. However, since the 1980s there has been a growing recognition of the systematic character of military prostitution and of its implications for national and personal security. In the early 1990s, the Japanese government apologized for the sexual enslavement of so-called 'comfort women' in Korea during WWII. The extent of military prostitution around US bases in Okinawa, the Philippines, South Korea and Thailand has increasingly been understood to have been facilitated by local and national government, as well as by the connivance of military authorities. US military deployments in the Gulf War, the Afghan War and the Iraq War have reinvigorated prostitution and the trafficking of women in the Middle East. Nevertheless, the significance of military prostitution perhaps goes beyond the physical, sexual and economic exploitation of women and has implications for international politics as well. For example, the exploitative sexual alliances between Korean prostitutes and US soldiers defined and helped to support the similarly unequal military alliance between the USA and South Korea in the post-war era (Moon 1997). By undertaking to police the sexual health and work conduct of prostitutes, the South Korean government sought to create a more hospitable environment for US troops, sacrificing the human security of the women concerned for the benefit of national security.

Gender, globalization and development

There has been a long tradition of feminist theorizing about economic issues, particularly undertaken by socialist feminists. The central idea of socialist feminism is that patriarchy and capitalism are overlapping and interlocking systems of oppression. The sexual division of labour, through which men dominate the public sphere while women are customarily confined to the private sphere, has served the economic interests of capitalism in a number of ways. For some socialist feminists, women constitute a 'reserve army of labour', which can be recruited into the workforce when there is a need for increased production, but easily shed and returned to domestic life during a depression, without imposing a burden on employers or the state. At the same time, women's domestic labour is vital to the health and efficiency of the economy. In bearing and rearing children, women are producing the next generation of capitalist workers. Similarly, in their role as housewives, women relieve men of the burden of housework and child-rearing, allowing them to concentrate their time and energy on paid and productive employment. The traditional family also provides male workers with the necessary cushion against the alienation and frustrations of life as a 'wage slave'. However, such gendered processes are largely ignored by conventional

● **Military prostitution**: Prostitution that caters to, and is sometimes organized by, the military.

theories of political economy which concentrate only on commercial exchange and paid labour, thus rendering much of women's contribution to productive activity invisible. This is further accentuated by gender biases that operate within the conceptual framework of conventional political economy, and especially economic liberalism. This can be seen, in particular, in the feminist critique of the notion of 'economic man' (Tickner 1992a). The idea that human beings are rationally self-seeking creatures who pursue pleasure primarily in the form of material consumption, a foundational idea of market capitalism, has been constructed in line with masculinist assumptions about egoism and competition. Feminists, in other words, suggest that 'economic woman' would behave otherwise.

The restructuring of the economy as a result of globalization has had a number of further implications for gender relations. In the first place, it has brought about the global 'feminization of work'. In the developing world, this has been evident in the expansion of employment opportunities for women, both as agricultural workers in, for instance, Latin America's export-orientated fruit industry and through a process of global industrial restructuring that has seen the export of manufacturing jobs from the developed to the developing world. Examples of this include the growth of the Asian electronics industry and of clothing assembly plants in Mexico. The developed world has also witnessed the growth of new 'feminized', or 'pink-collar', jobs through the expansion of the service sectors of the economy, such as retailing, cleaning and data processing. Although the number of women in paid work has grown, such trends have also been associated with vulnerability and exploitation. Not only are women workers usually cheap (in part, because of an abundant supply of labour), but they also tend to be employed in economic sectors where there are few workers' rights and weak labour organizations. Women workers therefore suffer from the double burden of low-paid work and continued pressure to undertake domestic labour, often, thanks to the advance of neo-liberal globalization, in the context of a reduction of state support for health, education and basic food subsidies.

Economic globalization has also unleashed dynamics that have led to the 'feminization of migration'. Pressures both in developed and the developing countries have contributed to this trend. For instance, female immigrants have been pulled by a 'care deficit' that has emerged in wealthier countries, as more women have entered paid employment but with revised aspirations in terms of education and careers. Not only has this created an increased demand for nannies and maids to replace the domestic roles traditionally carried out by mothers, but it has also made it more difficult to fill jobs traditionally taken by women, such as cleaners, care workers and nurses. Major female migratory flows have therefore developed, notably from South-east Asia to the oil-rich Middle East or the 'tiger' economies of East Asia, from the former Soviet bloc to western Europe, from Mexico and Central America to the USA, and from Africa to various parts of Europe. At the same time, poverty in the developing world pushes women to seek employment overseas. Migrant women, indeed, have come to play a particularly significant role in supporting their families through the remittances they send home, women workers, because of their family ties and obligations, usually being a more reliable source of remittances than male workers. The pressures of globalization have therefore combined to redefine the sexual division of labour in both global and ethnic terms, creating a dependency

KEY THEORISTS IN FEMINIST INTERNATIONAL RELATIONS

Jean Bethke Elshtain (1941–2013)

A US political philosopher, Elshtain's *Public Man, Private Woman* (1981) made a major contribution to feminist scholarship in examining the role of gender in informing the division between the public and private spheres in political theory. In *Women and War* (1987), she discussed the perceptual lenses that determine the roles of men and women in war, interweaving personal narrative and historical analysis to highlight the myths that men are 'just warriors' and women are 'beautiful souls' to be saved. In *Just War against Terror* (2003), Elshtain mounted an impassioned defence of the 'war on terror' based on just war theory.

Cynthia Enloe (born 1938)

A US feminist academic, Enloe's writings aim to expose the multiplicity of roles women play in sustaining global economic forces and inter-state relations. Often associated with feminist empiricism, she has been concerned to counter the tendency within conventional paradigms to limit, usually in a gendered fashion, our perceptual and conceptual fields, effectively excluding women from analysis. In works such as *Bananas, Beaches and Bases* (1989), *The Morning After* (1993) and *Manoeuvres* (2000) Enloe has examined international politics as if the experiences of women are a matter of central concern.

See also **J. Ann Tickner** (p. 78)

of a particularly intimate kind, as affluent and middle-class families in the developed world come to rely on migrant women to provide childcare and homemaking services (Ehrenreich and Hochschild 2003).

The global transfer of the services associated with a wife's traditional role are nevertheless most intimate when it comes to sex. The era of globalization has substantially boosted the sex industry on both a national and global level, with alarming numbers of women and girls being trafficked by smugglers and sold into bondage. Thailand, for example, has an estimated half a million to one million women working as prostitutes, and one out of every twenty of these is enslaved. Prostitution expanded rapidly in Thailand during the economic boom of 1970s, a consequence of both rising demand due to increased living standards amongst male workers and of growing supply through a flood of children being sold into slavery in the traditionally impoverished mountainous north of the country (Bales 2003). On a global level, sexual exchange has a variety of faces. These include the growth of sex tourism, particularly affecting countries such as the Dominican Republic and Thailand, and the phenomenon of overseas, or 'mail order', brides, through which men in affluent regions such as North America and western Europe acquire wives mainly from South-east Asia and the former Soviet bloc. In its most brutal and exploitative form, sexual exchange manifests itself in human smuggling and **people-trafficking**. Estimates of the number of people involved in some kind of trafficking range from 4 million to 200 million persons worldwide, with women and young girls constituting about 80 per cent of all victims. According to the UN, 87 per cent of women and young girls are trafficked for the purpose of sexual exploitation (UNODC 2006). It is a problem that has particularly affected parts of Asia. An estimated 5,000 to 7,000 Nepali girls and women, for example, are trafficked each year primarily to India (Crawford 2009).

As far as development is concerned, a number of competing gender perspectives have emerged. Modernization theorists have associated economic development with the emancipation of women from their traditional roles. In this view, patriarchal control and the subjugation of women is one of the key hierarchies that flourishes in traditional societies. The growth of market-based, capitalist relations brings with it, by contrast, a powerful drive towards individualism, valuing people less in terms of status and tradition and more in terms of their contribution to the productive process. This is reflected in the emergence of more egalitarian family structures in which all family members participate in a wide range of family functions. Opportunities for women to gain an education and enter careers also expand, as modernization creates the need for a more skilled and literate workforce. It is therefore little surprise that in the UN's ranking of countries on the basis of the **Gender Inequality Index** (GII), developed countries consistently outperform developing ones (see Table 17.1). In short, gender equality marches hand in hand with modernity.

From a feminist perspective, however, this conception of 'modernity' is constructed on the basis of essentially masculine norms. As already examined, this applies to economic liberalism, and it is therefore also evident in the idea of 'development as growth'. A further feminist concern has been that orthodox approaches to development have failed to recognize the extent to which poverty is 'feminized'. As Abbott *et al.* (2005) put it: 'Women make up half the world's population, perform two-thirds of the world's working hours, receive one-tenth of the world's income and own only one-hundredth of the world's property'. Some 70 per cent of the world's poor are women. Sen (1990) sought to highlight the degree to which female poverty is disregarded by pointing out that 'more than 100 million women are missing'. The 'missing women' he referred to are evident in population statistics that show that men outnumber women in parts of the world like South Asia and Africa, despite the fact that the normal tendency would be for women to slightly outnumber men (although, at birth, boys outnumber girls everywhere in the world, women tend to outnumber men in adult society because of their greater life expectancy). By some estimates, 50 million women are 'missing' in India alone. Such trends therefore reveal higher death rates among women and girls compared with men and boys in certain parts of the world. Part of the explanation for this is the preference of some parents, motivated by economic and/or cultural considerations, for boy children over girls, leading to the practice of sex-selective abortion or infanticide. This occurs in parts of East Asia and South Asia, and it is especially evident in China, linked to its 'one child' policy, and in some Indian states. In other cases, higher rates of disease and mortality amongst women and girls result from a failure to

● **People-trafficking**: The movement of persons, based on deception and coercion, with the purpose of exploiting them, usually through their sale into sexual or other forms of slavery.

● **Gender Inequality Index**: A measure, used by the UN, of the loss in human development as a result of gender inequality, taking account of three dimensions: reproductive health, empowerment and the labour market.

Table 17.1 Top ten and bottom ten countries in the GII league tables

Gender Inequality Index

1. Netherlands	= 139. Mauritania
2. Sweden	= 139. Sierra Leone
= 3. Switzerland	141. Mali
= 3. Denmark	142. Central African Republic
5. Norway	143. Liberia
= 6. Finland	144. Congo (DRC)
= 6. Germany	145. Saudi Arabia
8. Slovenia	146. Niger
9. France	147. Afghanistan
10. Iceland	148. Yemen

Source: UNDP 2013.

give them the same level of medical care, food and social services as boys and men. This misallocation of resources is generally worse in rural areas and particularly severe for late-born girls, and even worse for girls with elder sisters. Families with scarce resources may choose to care for boys over girls because of the expectation that boys will grow up to be wage earners or family workers, whereas girls are less likely to earn an income and, where **dowry systems** exist, may be viewed as a burden.

On the other hand, postcolonial feminists in particular have criticized the image of women in the developing world as victims – poor, under-educated, oppressed and disempowered. Women, they argue, often play a leading role in development and poverty reduction initiatives, especially when these initiatives are based on local ownership and reject top-down, technocratic models of development. Amongst the development initiatives that have placed particular emphasis on the role of women has been the expansion of **microcredit**. Often seen to have originated with the Bangladesh-based Grameen Bank, which, together with its founder Muhammad Yunus (see p. 384), was awarded the Nobel Peace Prize in 2006, microcredit has the advantage that it is an effective way of helping very poor families to form self-help groups to establish small businesses or advance agricultural or rural projects. The World Bank estimates that about 90 per cent of microcredit borrowers are women. This has major benefits for poor communities as women are more likely to invest their credit rather than spend it on themselves, and they have a better record of repayment than men. India and Bangladesh have been the main beneficiaries of such development initiatives, but they can also be found in countries ranging from Bosnia-Herzegovina and Russia to Ethiopia, Morocco and Brazil. However, the 'microcredit revolution' may also have drawbacks. Critics, for instance, have argued that microcredit schemes have sometimes led governments to scale back social provision, that repayment rates may be high, that they may create long-term dependency on external capital, and that, although they are often designed to empower women, an infusion of cash into the local economy may only increase dowry payments.

● **Dowry system**: The practice of making payments in cash or goods to a bridegroom's family, along with the bride.

● **Microcredit**: Very small loans for business investment, often given to people who cannot access traditional credit.

SUMMARY

- Feminism can broadly be defined as a movement for the social advancement of women. However, it has taken a wide range of forms, with distinctions particularly being made between feminist traditions orientated around the goal of gender equality and those that place a greater emphasis on women being 'woman-identified'.

- The 'gender lens' of empirical feminism is primarily concerned to 'add women' to existing analytical frameworks, especially in the attempt to tackle gender gaps between women and men. Making feminist sense of international politics therefore means recognizing the previously invisible contributions that women make to shaping world affairs.

- The 'gender lens' of analytical feminism is concerned, by contrast, to highlight the gender biases that pervade the theoretical framework and key concepts of mainstream international theory, and particularly realism. These are deconstructed to reveal masculinist biases that, in turn, help to legitimize gendered hierarchies and perpetuate the marginalization of women.

- Feminists have drawn attention to the gendered character of states and nations. Patriarchal biases within the state dictate that states will be competitive and at least potentially aggressive, while nations and nationalism are commonly entangled with gendered images that may place a special emphasis on female 'purity'.

- Feminists have been critical of the conventional notion of national security, seeing the broader idea of human security as a better means of highlighting women's concerns. War is often also viewed as a gendered phenomenon, reflecting tendencies such as the prevalence of men in senior positions in political and military life, and the impact of myths about masculinity and militarism and about the need for male 'warriors' to protect women and children.

- Feminist theorizing on economic issues has tended to stress the ways in which the sexual division of labour serves the economic interests of capitalism, as well as the extent to which the conceptual framework of conventional political economy has been constructed on a masculinist basis. Such ideas have influenced feminist thinking about both globalization and development.

Questions for discussion

- How did feminism's 'second wave' differ from its 'first wave'?

- Why have some feminists rejected the goal of gender equality?

- Why is the distinction between 'sex' and 'gender' so important in feminist theory?

- Is 'gender mainstreaming' an effective strategy for tackling gender injustice?

- Are the key concepts of mainstream international theory based on masculinist assumptions?

- What implications do feminists draw from the gendered character of nations and states?

- Why and how have feminists criticized the conventional idea of national security?

- Why have feminists argued that war and gender are intrinsically linked?

- Has economic globalization benefited, or harmed, the lives of women?

Further reading

Enloe, C., *The Curious Feminist: Searching for Women in a New Age of Empire* (2004). A stimulating series of essays that uncover the various and significant ways in which women participate in international politics.

Peterson, V.S. and A.S. Runyan, *Global Gender Issues in the New Millennium* (2010). An accessible and comprehensive introduction to gender issues in global politics.

Shepherd, L. J., *Gender Matters in Global Politics* (2010). A very useful collection of essays that examine the gendered character of a wide range of aspects of global politics.

Tickner, J. A., *Gendering World Politics: Issues and Approaches in the Post-Cold War Era* (2001). An influential survey of feminist approaches to international relations that highlights issues such as human rights and globalization.

 ONLINE RESOURCES AVAILABLE

Links to relevant web resources can be found on the *Global Politics* website

CHAPTER 18

International Organization and the United Nations

'More than ever before in human history, we share a common destiny. We can master it only if we face it together.'

KOFI ANNAN, 'Message for the New Millennium' (1999)

PREVIEW   The growth in the number and importance of international organizations has been one of the most prominent features of world politics, particularly since 1945. Some of these are high profile bodies such as the United Nations, the World Bank, the World Trade Organization and the International Monetary Fund, while others are lesser known but still play key roles in particular fields. By providing a framework for cooperative problem-solving amongst states, international organizations have modified traditional power politics without, at the same time, threatening the emergence of a global or regional superstate. However, the phenomenon of international organization also raises a number of important questions. For example, what factors and forces help to explain the emergence of international organizations? Do such bodies genuinely reflect the collective interests of their members, or are they created by and for powerful states? To what extent can international organizations affect global outcomes? Many of these questions, however, are best addressed by considering the case of the world's leading international organization, the United Nations. The UN (unlike its predecessor, the League of Nations) has established itself as a truly global body, and is regarded by most as an indispensable part of the international political scene. Its core concern with promoting international peace and security has been supplemented, over time, by an ever-expanding economic and social agenda. Has the UN lived up to the expectations of its founders, and could it ever? What factors determine the effectiveness of the UN, and how could it be made more effective?

KEY ISSUES
- What is international organization?
- Why are international organizations created?
- What have been the implications of the growth in international organization?
- How effective has the UN been in maintaining peace and security?
- What impact has the UN had on economic and social issues?
- What challenges confront the UN, and how should it respond to them?

INTERNATIONAL ORGANIZATION

Rise of international organization

The earliest embryonic international organizations were created after the Napoleonic Wars. These included the Congress of Vienna (1814–15), which established the Concert of Europe which continued until WWI. The number and membership of such organizations gradually increased during the nineteenth and early twentieth centuries, 49 of them being in existence in 1914. Following the end of WWI, just as after the Napoleonic Wars, there was a surge in new international organizations. By 1929 and the onset of the world economic crisis, their number had reached an inter-war peak of 83. The end of WWII marked a new boom, with the number of international organizations soaring to 123 by 1949, with new organizations including the United Nations (see p. 456) and the institutions of the Bretton Woods system (examined in Chapter 19). This reflected not only an awareness of growing interdependencies amongst states, linked to concerns over power politics, economic crises, human rights violations, developmental disparities and environmental degradation, but also the emerging hegemonic role of the USA, which saw the pursuit of US national interests and the promotion of international cooperation as mutually sustaining goals. By the mid-1980s, the total number of international organizations had reached 378, with the average membership per organization standing at over 40 (compared with 18.6 in 1945 and 22.7 in 1964). Although their number subsequently declined, largely due to the dissolution of Soviet bloc organizations at the end of the Cold War, this masks a substantial growth in international agencies and other institutions, as the number of bodies spawned by international organizations themselves has continued to grow. However, international organizations take a wide variety of forms. The most common bases for categorizing international organizations are the following:

- *Membership* – whether they have a restricted or universal membership
- *Competence* – whether their responsibilities are issue-specific or comprehensive
- *Function* – whether they are programme organizations or operational organizations
- *Decision-making authority* – whether they are examples of intergovernmentalism (see p. 466) or supranationalism (see p. 465).

The significance of the phenomenon of international organization has, nevertheless, been hotly disputed. For instance, while some see international organizations as little more than mechanisms for pursuing traditional power politics by other means, others claim (or warn) that they contain the seeds of supranational or world government (see p. 464). The relationship between international organization and global governance (see p. 462) has also been the subject of debate. Although the rise of international organization is sometimes seen as evidence of the emergence of a global governance system, global governance is a wider and more extensive phenomenon than international organization. In particular, global governance encompasses a range of informal as well as formal processes and also involves a wider array of actors, including national governments, non-governmental organizations (NGOs) (see p. 10), citizens' movements, transnational corporations (TNCs) (see p. 94) and global markets. Nevertheless, international organizations are often a key, if not *the* key element in global governance arrangements, in that the process of cooperative problem-solving that lies at the heart of global governance is usually facilitated by international organizations (Weiss and Kamran 2009). In that sense, international organizations are the vital formal or institutional face of global governance. (The nature of global governance is discussed at greater length in Chapter 19.)

Why are international organizations created?

There has been much political and academic debate about the forces and processes through which international organizations have been brought into being. The political debate reflects disagreements between liberals, realists and others about, amongst other things, whether the impulse to create international organizations stems from the collective interests of states generally, or primarily from powerful states or even a regional or global hegemon (see Hegemonic stability theory, p. 236). Such disagreements have profound implications for the nature and legitimacy of international organizations. Liberals argue that international organizations tend to reflect the collective interests of states, based on a recognition of what Keohane and Nye (1977) called 'complex interdependence' (see p. 7) and an awareness of mutual vulnerabilities that affect powerful and weak states alike. International organizations therefore operate essentially as neutral umpires or referees, capable of standing above, and even, to some extent, imposing order on, the incipient power politics of the state-system. Realists, by contrast, argue that power politics operates in and through international organizations, which are viewed more as appendages of the state-system, or simply as instruments controlled by powerful states, and do not constitute a separate (and perhaps morally superior) realm. The relationship between international organizations and power politics is also reflected in debate between neorealists and neoliberals over whether states are primarily concerned with 'relative' gains or 'absolute' gains (see p. 443).

Nevertheless, there is a further range of debates about the motivations and processes through which integration and institution building at an international level has been brought about. Three main theories have been advanced: federalism, functionalism and neofunctionalism. Federalism (see p. 133) refers to a territorial distribution of power through which sovereignty (see p. 4) is shared between central (national or international) bodies and peripheral ones. From the federalist perspective, international organizations are a product of conscious decision-making by the political elites, usually seeking to find a solution to the endemic problems of the state-system, and especially the problem of war. If war is caused by sovereign states pursuing self-interest in a context of anarchy, peace will only be achieved if states transfer at least a measure of their sovereignty to a higher, federal body. Functionalism, by contrast, views the formation of international organizations as an incremental process that stems from the fact that a growing range of government functions can be performed more effectively through collective action than by individual states. Integration is thus largely determined by a recognition of growing interdependence in economic and other areas. As David Mitrany (1966) puts it, 'form follows functions', in which 'form'

Robert Keohane (born 1941)

US international relations theorist. With his long-time collaborator, Joseph S. Nye (see p. 222), Keohane questioned some of the core assumptions of realist analysis in *Transnational Relations and World Politics* (1971), highlighting the increasing importance of non-state actors and of economic issues in world affairs. In *Power and Interdependence: World Politics in Transition* (1977) Keohane and Nye set out the theory of 'complex interdependence' as an alternative to realism, based on the trend towards international cooperation and the growing significance of international regimes. Since the publication of *After Hegemony* (1984), however, Keohane has attempted to synthesize structural realism and complex interdependence, creating a hybrid dubbed either 'modified structural realism' or 'neoliberal institutionalism'. His other major works include *International Institutions and State Power* (1989) and *Power and Interdependence in a Partially Globalized World* (2002).

represents institutional structures and 'functions' denotes the key activities of government. Such thinking was, in due course, revised by the idea of neofunctionalism, which sought to explain how international cooperation tends to broaden and deepen through a process of **spillover**. As these theories of institution building have largely been developed as a means of explaining the process of regional integration, and sometimes specifically European integration, they are discussed in greater detail in Chapter 20.

THE UNITED NATIONS

From the League to the UN

The United Nations is, without doubt, the most important international organization created to date. Established though the San Francisco Conference (April–June 1945), it is the only truly global organization ever to be constructed, having a membership of 193 states and counting. The principal aims of the UN, as spelled out by its founding Charter, are as follows:

- To safeguard peace and security in order 'to save succeeding generations from the scourge of war'
- To 'reaffirm faith in fundamental human rights'
- To uphold respect for international law
- To 'promote social progress and better standards of life'.

However, the UN was not the first organization that was constructed to guarantee world peace; its predecessor, the League of Nations, had been founded at the Paris Peace Conference of 1919 with very similar goals, namely to enable **collective security**, to arbitrate over international disputes and to bring about disarmament. The League of Nations was inspired by US President Woodrow Wilson's Fourteen Points, established as the basis for long-term peace in post-WWI Europe (see Woodrow Wilson, p. 445). The League, nevertheless, suffered

● **Spillover**: The dynamic process whereby integration in one policy area tends to 'spill over' into other areas, as new goals and new pressures are generated.

● **Collective security**: The idea or practice of common defence, in which a number of states pledge themselves to defend each other, based on the principle of 'all for one and one for all' (see p. 447)

Focus on . . .
Relative or absolute gains?

How much scope is there for international cooperation between and amongst states? This has long been an issue of debate between realists and liberals, the former believing that the struggle for power leaves little or no scope for cooperation between states, while the latter hold that cooperation can triumph over conflict because of an underlying harmony of interests amongst states. Since the 1980s, this issue has particularly divided neorealists and neoliberals, but the terms of the debate have changed. Neorealists have insisted that states are preoccupied with making 'relative' gains (improvements in a state's position relative to other states). In this view, anarchy makes states fear for their survival, and because power is the ultimate guarantor of survival, they constantly monitor their position in the international power hierarchy. Countries will only be prepared to cooperate if they believe that cooperation will bring about relative gains, and they will forego cooperation if they fear that their gains will be less than those of other countries. Country A would thus refuse to enter into a trade agreement with country B, even though it is likely to bring profit, if it calculates that country B's profits will be greater. Power, in this sense, is zero-sum game – one state's gain is another state's loss.

Neoliberals, on the other hand, argue that the neorealist position is simplistic. While not rejecting the concerns about relative gains (because they accept assumptions about state egoism), they hold that states may be more concerned about making 'absolute' gains (improvements in a state's position in absolute terms). This may occur, for instance, because states are confident about their survival and so can be more relaxed about their power relative to other states; because they judge that other states' intentions are peaceful regardless of their relative capabilities; or because, in reality, states have multiple relationships with multiple states, making calculations about relative gains simply impractical. If states are prepared to cooperate so long as this promises to deliver absolute gains, the scope for cooperation at an international level is considerable.

from major defects, which the later architects of the UN tried to take fully into account. In particular, the League never genuinely lived up its name; it was never properly a 'league of nations'. Some major states did not join, most notably the USA, through the refusal of the isolationist Congress to ratify US membership, while others left. Germany joined in 1926, only to leave after the Nazis came to power in 1933. Japan abandoned the League in 1933 after criticism of its occupation of Manchuria, while Italy walked out in 1936 after criticism of its invasion of Abyssinia. The Soviet Union, which entered the League in 1933, was expelled in 1939 following its attack on Finland. Moreover, the League lacked effective power. It could only make recommendations, not binding resolutions; its recommendations had to be unanimous; and anyway, no mechanism existed for taking military or economic action against miscreant states. As a result, the League of Nations stood by, largely powerless, as Germany, Italy and Japan embarked on aggressive wars during the 1930s and the events that would lead to the outbreak of WWII unfolded (as examined in Chapter 2).

It was no coincidence that the League of Nations and the United Nations were both set up in the aftermath of world wars. The key goals of both organizations were the promotion of international security and the peaceful settlement of disputes. In the case of the UN, this occurred in a context of an estimated

INTERNATIONAL ORGANIZATION

Realist view

Realists are deeply sceptical about international organizations. They view such bodies as largely ineffective, and also question their authority. The weakness of international organizations derives from the fact that international politics continues to be characterized by a quest for power amongst all states, reflected in the pursuit of relative gains. If world politics is shaped by a struggle for power rather than a harmony of interests, there is little scope for the levels of cooperation and trust that would allow international organizations to develop into meaningful and significant bodies. In addition, the growth of international organizations is usually deemed to be undesirable because of its implications for sovereignty. Any form of international organization therefore tends to erode the authority of the nation-state. However, realists do not completely discount the role of international organizations. Neorealists, for example, have drawn attention to the relationship between international organization and hegemony (see p. 228). As hegemonic states possess such superior power, they are the only states that can tolerate the relative gains of other states so long as they are making absolute gains themselves. The effectiveness of international organizations is therefore closely linked to the emergence of a global hegemon – the UK in the eighteenth and nineteenth centuries, and the USA since 1945 and, more particularly, since 1990. Nevertheless, the disproportionate burden that such powers shoulder may contribute to their long-term decline.

Liberal view

Liberals have been amongst the most committed supporters of international organizations. This is reflected in the ideas of liberal institutionalism. From the institutionalist perspective, states cooperate because it is in their interest to do so. This does not imply that state interests are always harmoniously in agreement, but only that there are important, and growing, areas of mutual interest where cooperation amongst states is rational and sensible. International organizations are therefore a reflection of the extent of interdependence in the global system, an acknowledgement by states that they can often achieve more by working together than by working separately. In areas of mutual interest, states' desire to make absolute gains usually wins out over concerns about relative gains. Neoliberal institu-

tionalists, nevertheless, acknowledge that the existence of complex interdependence among states does not automatically result in the creation of international organizations. Cooperation may be hard to achieve when, despite the existence of common interests, states feel they have an incentive to defect from an agreement or fear that other states may defect. One of the purposes of international organizations is therefore to reduce the likelihood of this happening, by both building trust between and amongst states and accustoming them to rule-governed behaviour. As such considerations apply to all states, regardless of where they stand within a hierarchy of power, liberals question the realist belief that successful international institutions require the participation of a hegemonic state.

Critical views

Social constructivists challenge both neorealist and neoliberal accounts of international organization on the grounds that, despite their differences, they assume that states are rational actors guided by objective interests. This discounts the role of ideas and perceptions. The state-system is an arena of inter-subjective interaction. Levels of cooperation within the international system therefore depend on how states construe their own identities and interests as well as the identities and interests of other states. These, moreover, change due to membership of, and interactions that take place within, international organizations, meaning that international organizations themselves are essentially ideational constructs. Other critical theories advance critiques of international organization that stress the degree to which international structures reflect, and, to some extent, exist to consolidate, the wider inequalities and imbalances of the global system. Frankfurt critical theorists, for example, emphasize that bodies such as the World Bank (see p. 380) and the IMF (see p. 475) have internalized a neoliberal agenda, and so act in the interests of global capitalism. Feminists, for their part, highlight the gendered construction of international organizations, reflecting both the traditional domination of elite men and the internalization of masculinist ideas and policy approaches. In this respect, green politics is often an exception. Many greens looked to international organization, and even some form of world government, to provide a solution to the 'tragedy of the commons' (see p. 395).

Woodrow Wilson (1856–1924)

US President, 1913–21. The son of a Presbyterian minister, Wilson was the president of Princeton University, 1902–10, before serving as the Democratic Governor of New Jersey, 1911–13, and being elected President in 1912. Wilson initially kept the USA out of WWI, but felt compelled to enter the war in April 1917 to make the world 'safe for democracy'. Wilson's idealistic internationalism, sometimes called 'Wilsonianism', was most clearly reflected in the Fourteen Points he laid out in a speech to Congress in January 1918, as the basis for an enduring peace. These expressed the ideas of national self-determination, open agreements and an end to secret diplomacy, freedom of trade and navigation, disarmament and collective security achieved through a 'general association of nations'. Wilsonian liberalism is usually associated with the idea that a world of democratic nation-states, modelled on the USA, is the surest means of preventing war.

civilian and military death toll of around 67 million and the radical dislocation of global and national economies in WWII, to say nothing of the Great Depression which had contributed to a significant sharpening of international tensions during the 1930s. The early origins of the UN, indeed, emerged during the war itself, taking the form of an alliance of 26 states which pledged themselves to defeat the Axis powers through the Declaration of United Nations on 1 January 1942. As with the League, the USA took a leading role in the process, with President Franklin D. Roosevelt pushing for the creation of the UN during the final years of the war. The basic blueprint for the new international organization was drawn up in August 1944 at Dumbarton Oaks, Washington, DC, by delegates from the USA, the Soviet Union, China and the UK. The UN Charter was signed in San Francisco on 26 June 1945, with the UN officially coming into existence on 24 October (since known as UN Day).

The UN is a sprawling and complex organization, described by its second Secretary-General, Dag Hammarskjöld, as 'a weird Picasso abstraction'. Its size and complexity has enabled the UN to respond to myriad interests and to address an ever-widening global agenda, but it has also resulted in an organization that is highly cumbersome, often conflict-ridden and, some say, is doomed to inefficiency. At its heart, the UN is a hybrid body, configured around competing concerns: the need to accept the realities of great power politics and to acknowledge the sovereign equality of member states. This has created, in a sense, two UNs, one reflected in the Security Council, the other in the General Assembly. The Security Council is the most significant UN body. It is responsible for the maintenance of international peace and security, and is dominated by the P-5, its permanent veto powers – the USA, Russia (until 1991, the Soviet Union), China (until 1971, the Republic of China or 'Taiwan'), the UK and France. The General Assembly, on the other hand, is a deliberative body that represents all members of the UN equally. Whereas the Council is criticized for being poorly representative and dominated by great powers (see Reforming the Security Council? p. 457), the Assembly, in a sense, is over-representative, a highly decentralized body that often serves as little more than a propaganda arena. This divi-

Focus on . . .
How the United Nations works

The Security Council: This is charged with the maintenance of international peace and security, and so is responsible for the UN's role as negotiator, observer, peacekeeper and, ultimately, peace enforcer. The Council has the power to pass legally-binding resolutions, to suspend or expel members, to impose economic sanctions and to take military action to maintain or restore peace and security. The Security Council has fifteen members. The Big Five (or P-5) – the USA, Russia, China, the UK and France – are permanent 'veto powers', meaning that they can block decisions made by other members of the Council. The other ten members are non-permanent members elected for two years by the General Assembly, in line with an established, if imperfect, regional balance.

The General Assembly: This is the main deliberative organ of the UN, sometimes dubbed the 'parliament of nations'. The Assembly consists of all members of the UN, each of which has a single vote. The Assembly can debate and pass resolutions on any matter covered by the Charter, and has a specific responsibility to examine and approve the UN's budget, determine the members' contributions, and elect, in conjunction with the Security Council, the UN Secretary-General and the judges of the International Court of Justice. Important decisions in the Assembly must be carried by a two-thirds majority, but, crucially, these decisions are recommendations rather than enforceable international law. The Assembly neither has a legislative role nor does it oversee or scrutinize, in any meaningful sense, the Security Council or the Secretariat.

The Secretariat: This services the other principal organs of the UN and administers the programmes and policies laid down by them. Although its main activities are located in the UN's headquarters in New York, it has offices all over the world and a total staff of about 40,000. At its head is the Secretary-General, who functions as the public face of the UN as well as its chief administrative officer. Appointed by the Assembly on the recommendation of the Security Council for a five-year, renewable term, the Secretary-General deals with a multifaceted bureaucracy staffed by civil servants from myriad states and cultures, and tries to maintain the UN's independence, often in a context of rivalry amongst P-5 states. Nevertheless, Secretaries-General have some capacity to influence the status and policy direction of the organization.

The Economic and Social Council: This consists of fifty-four members elected by the General Assembly. Its chief role is to coordinate the economic and social work of the UN and the UN family of organizations. This involves overseeing the activities of a large number of programmes, funds and specialized agencies. These include the so-called 'three sisters' – the World Bank, the IMF and the WTO – and also bodies such as the International Labour Organization (ILO), the World Health Organization (WHO), the United Nations Educational, Scientific and Cultural Organization (UNESCO) and the United Nations Children's Fund (UNICEF). The expansion of the UN's economic and social institutions occurred largely along functionalist lines, bodies being created or further developed as specific economic and social problems emerged.

sion between the two bodies became increasingly clear from the 1960s onwards as a result of the growing influence of newly-independent, developing countries in the Assembly, and the effective retreat of the P-5 to the Council. However, by no means do these two bodies make up the entirety of the UN. In addition to the Secretariat, the UN family consists of a sprawling range of funds, agencies and programmes that are responsible, at least in theory, to the Economic and Social Council (ECOSOC).

CONCEPT

Promoting peace and security

Banishing the 'scourge of war'?

Collective security

Collective security is the theory or practice of states pledging to defend one another in order to deter aggression or to punish a transgressor if international order has been breached. Its key idea is that aggression can best be resisted by united action taken by a number of states, this being the only alternative to the insecurity and uncertainty of power politics. Successful collective security depends on three conditions. First, the states must be roughly equal, or at least there must be no preponderant power. Second, *all* states must be willing to bear the cost and responsibility of defending one another. Third, there must be an international body that has the moral authority and political capacity to take effective action.

The principal aim of the UN is 'to maintain international peace and security' (Article 1), with responsibility for this being vested in the Security Council. Indeed, the performance of the UN can largely be judged in terms of the extent to which it has saved humankind from deadly military conflict. This, nevertheless, is difficult to judge. On the one hand, the fact that the two world wars of the twentieth century have not been followed by World War III has sometimes been seen as the supreme achievement of the UN (as well as demonstrating a clear advance on the performance of the League of Nations). On the other hand, realist theorists in particular have argued that the absence of global war since 1945 has had little to do with the UN, being more a consequence of the 'balance of terror' that developed during the Cold War as a nuclear stalemate developed between the USA and the Soviet Union. Ultimately, how global and regional conflict would have developed and whether 'cold' wars would have become 'hot' ones in the absence of the UN, is an unanswerable question. It is, nevertheless, evident that the UN has only had limited and intermittent success in establishing a system of collective security that can displace a reliance on violent self-help.

The capacity of the UN to enforce a system of collective security is severely limited by the fact that it is essentially a creature of its members: it can do no more than its member states, and particularly the permanent members of the Security Council, permit. As a result, its role has been confined essentially to providing mechanisms that facilitate the peaceful resolution of international conflicts. Even in this respect, however, its record has been patchy. There have been undoubted successes, for example in negotiating a ceasefire between India and Pakistan in 1959, maintaining peace in 1960 in the Belgian Congo (later Zaire, now DRC) and mediating between the Dutch and the Indonesians over West Irian (New Guinea) in 1962. However, for much of its history, the UN was virtually paralyzed by superpower rivalry. The Cold War ensured that, on most issues, the USA and the Soviet Union (the P-2) adopted opposing positions, which prevented the Security Council from taking decisive action.

This was compounded by two other factors. First, the use by the P-5 of their veto powers dramatically reduced the number of threats to peace and security or incidents of aggression that the Security Council could take action over. In practice, until the People's Republic of China replaced Taiwan in 1971, voting in the Security Council on controversial issues generally resulted in a clash between the Soviet Union and the other members of the P-5 (the P-4). During the Cold War, the Soviet Union was the most frequent user of the veto, exercising it on no fewer than 82 occasions between 1946 and 1955. After first using its veto in 1970, however, the USA has assumed this role. Second, despite the provision in the UN Charter for the setting-up of the Military Staff Committee as a subsidiary body of the Security Council, resistance amongst the P-5 has prevented the UN from developing its own military capacity. This has meant that when the UN has authorized military action it has either been subcontracted, for example, to US-led forces (Korean War and Gulf War) or to regional bodies such as NATO (Kosovo) or the African Union (Darfur), or it has been carried out by a multinational force of 'blue helmets' or 'blue berets' contributed by member states. Thus, one of the key conditions for an effective collective security system – the availability of permanent UN troops to enforce its will – has remained unfulfilled.

During much of the Cold War, then, the UN was characterized by deadlock and paralysis. The only occasion on which the Security Council agreed on measures of military enforcement was in relation to the Korean War in 1950, but the circumstances surrounding this were exceptional. UN intervention in Korea was only possible because the Soviet Union had temporarily withdrawn from the Council, in protest against the exclusion of 'Red China' (the People's Republic of China). This intervention, anyway, merely fuelled fears that the UN was western-dominated. The only times that non-military enforcement measures were employed were against two international pariahs, Rhodesia and South Africa. Economic sanctions were imposed on Rhodesia in 1966, on the grounds that the white minority regime's unilateral declaration of independence constituted a threat to peace. An arms embargo was imposed on the apartheid regime in South Africa in 1977, following the suppression of unrest in black townships the previous year. Otherwise, war and conflict proceeded essentially without UN involvement. The Suez crisis of 1956 was significant because, although the UK and France used their vetoes for the first time, to block a US resolution condemning Israeli, British and French action, diplomatic pressure from the USA and Soviet support for the Nasser regime quickly brought about a humiliating withdrawal. This demonstrated that some members of the P-5 were clearly more equal than others. During the Cuban missile crisis of 1962, as the world grew close to nuclear war, the UN was a powerless spectator. It was also unable to prevent the Soviet invasions of Hungary (1956), Czechoslovakia (1968) and Afghanistan (1979), or to curtail the USA's escalating military involvement in Vietnam during the 1960s and 1970s. Similarly, the UN had only a very limited influence on the succession of Arab–Israeli wars (see Key events: The Arab–Israeli conflict, p. 208).

The end of the Cold War was the beginning, many hoped, of a new chapter for the UN. For so long marginalized by superpower antagonism, the UN suddenly assumed a new prominence as the instrument through which an effective system of collective security could be brought about. For instance, the use by the P-5 of their veto power declined significantly, only being used 13 times between 1996 and 2006. The UN's intervention in the Gulf War of 1991, being only the second time (after Korea) that the UN authorized large-scale military action, seemed to demonstrate a renewed capacity to fulfil its obligation of deterring aggression and maintaining peace, as did the USA's decision not to pursue fleeing Iraqi troops into Iraq for fear of acting outside the authority of the UN. Indeed, a new era of UN activism appeared to be a major component of the 'new world order', as announced by President Bush Snr. Since 1990, the Security Council has approved non-military enforcement measures on numerous occasions – for instance, in relation to Afghanistan, Angola, Ethiopia and Eritrea, Haiti, Iraq, Rwanda, Somalia, the former Yugoslavia and so on – and measures of military enforcement, usually linked to **peacekeeping** operations (as discussed in the next section), have become much more common.

However, early hopes for a UN-dominated 'new world order' were quickly disappointed. This was evident not only in sometimes high-profile peacekeeping failures, as in Rwanda and the former Yugoslavia, but, most significantly, in the USA's decision to go ahead with the invasion of Iraq in 2003, despite opposition

● **Peacekeeping**: A technique designed to preserve the peace when fighting has been halted, and to assist in implementing agreements achieved by the peacemakers (see p. 451)

- The United Nations is a misnamed organization. As all representation at the UN is through national governments, its members are clearly not 'nations' but 'states'. Apart from the obvious problem with the alternative title – The 'United States' – the stress on 'nations' implies the participation, or at least consent, of peoples or national populations, and not just of their leaders. It suggests, indeed, that the national governments that comprise the UN are popularly-based, when, in fact, the existence of sustainable democracy has never been a criterion for membership of the UN, and would, if ever applied, substantially reduce the size of the UN (as well as cause deep conflict over the meaning of 'democracy').

Deconstructing . . .

THE 'UNITED NATIONS'

- The notion that the members of the UN are 'united' also raises questions. United nations would act with a single voice and on the basis of common interests. The term implies that at the heart of the UN is a cosmopolitan project, reflected in the desire to construct an organization that would in some way stand *above* national interests and concerns. Not only is this unrealistic (as the UN is very much a creature of its members, and the UN Charter firmly enshrines a commitment to national sovereignty), but it may also be thought to be undesirable (as it suggests that the UN is a proto-world government).

from leading members of the Security Council. During the post-Cold War period, the UN has been forced to confront a range of new problems and conflicts. These include the reluctance of states whose security is no longer threatened by East–West rivalry to commit resources to the cause of collective security or for the defence of states on the other side of the globe. Moreover, the emergence of what seemed to be a unipolar world order threatened to sideline the UN just as effectively as did Cold War bipolarity (see p. 223), as shown by the willingness of the USA and its allies to invade Iraq in 2003 without clear Security Council approval. The Syrian civil war nevertheless highlights how emerging multipolarity (see p. 237) may also act as a constraint on the UN (see p. 450). Finally, the international political focus has itself shifted. The UN's role used to be to keep the peace in a world dominated by conflict between communism and capitalism. Now it is forced to find a new role in a world structured by the dynamics of global capitalism, in which conflict increasingly arises from imbalances in the distribution of wealth and resources. This has meant that the UN's role in promoting peace and security has been conflated with the task of ensuring economic and social development, the two being merged in the shift from 'traditional' peacekeeping to 'multidimensional' or 'robust' peacekeeping.

Syria and the United Nations

Events: The conflict in Syria escalated quickly after the Syrian Army was deployed to suppress demonstrations against the regime of President Basher Assad, which had started in March 2011 and were linked to the wider Middle Eastern protest movement known as the Arab Spring (see p. 211). Within months, the conflict developed into a highly complex and intractable civil war, involving at least four main elements. The Syrian Army was supported by the Shabiha, pro-government militias drawn largely from Assad's Alawite minority group, and, after 2013, the Lebanon-based, Shi'a Islamic militant group, Hezbollah. The loose-knit, western-backed Free Syrian Army constituted the chief opposition force, but foreign al-Qaeda-linked militants gradually assumed an increasingly prominent role, while Syrian Kurds, long-time opponents of the Assad regime, established semi-autonomy in the northeast of the country. For over two years, the United Nations was effectively sidelined as the Syrian civil war turned into the bloodiest conflict of the twenty-first century to date. Nevertheless, following the sarin nerve gas attack on a suburb of Damascus in August 2013, the UN Security Council voted the following month to eliminate Syria's entire stockpile of chemical weapons by mid-2014, although the resolution did not threaten automatic punitive action against the Assad government if it did not comply.

Significance: The lack of effective UN intervention to end Syria's civil war, or to reduce the scale of the bloodshed (accepting that the decommissioning of the Syria's chemical weapons will not, in itself, accomplish either of these goals), can be explained by one key factor. This was the absence of a consensus in the UN Security Council over Syria, a situation that once again underlines the extent to which the UN is a creature of the Security Council's veto powers, as well as the capacity of disagreement within the Security Council to paralyse the organization. While the USA, France and the UK broadly aligned themselves with the Syrian rebels, in the hope that the fall of Assad would usher in a regime that is pro-western, democratically-based and less hostile to Israel, Russia and China consistently backed the Syrian government, blocking any draft resolution that condemned its part in the conflict, proposed that Assad should step down or threatened to impose sanctions on Syria. Russia's relations with Syria are particularly significant in this respect. Syria is Russia's key ally in the Middle East, having close military, economic and political ties that date back at least to the Assad family's seizure of power in 1971.

The chemical attack near Damascus in August 2013 nevertheless created circumstances that resulted in the UN taking a more prominent role in Syria, through the Security Council resolution on chemical weapons and its implementation by UN weapons inspectors. However, this development was by no means automatic or inevitable. The USA's initial reaction to the chemical attack, supported by France and, initially, by the UK, was to threaten to carry out a 'limited and tailored' military strike against the Syrian government, indicating that it would be willing to carry out this attack without Security Council approval. Such action threatened to further sideline the UN, in a manner reminiscent of the 2003 US invasion of Iraq, and to seriously damage US–Russian relations. The turnabout in the situation occurred when, in early September, Russia called on Syria to divest itself of its chemical weapons, initiating weeks of intense diplomacy between Russia and the USA, though which the text of eventually-successful Security Council resolution was negotiated. Acting through the mechanism of the UN in these circumstances satisfied Russia's desire to prevent military action being taken against the Assad regime, as well as the USA's wish to respond to the chemical attack without carrying out an intervention that would have had uncertain political, military and strategic outcomes.

From peacekeeping to peace-building

The term 'peacekeeping' is not found in the UN Charter. Nevertheless, over the years, peacekeeping has come to be the most significant way in which the UN has fulfilled its responsibility to maintain international peace and security. Falling somewhere between the UN's commitment to resolve disputes peacefully through means such as negotiation and mediation (Chapter Six) and more forceful actions to maintain security (Chapter Seven), peacekeeping was described by the second UN Secretary-General, Dag Hammarskjöld, as belonging to 'Chapter Six and a Half'. Between 1948 and 2013, the UN carried out 67 peacekeeping operations. In 2013, 15 of them remained active, involving 78,000 troops, some 12,500 uniformed police and about 1,800 military observers, drawn from 116 countries. In addition, the UN's peacekeeping operations were supported by about 5,000 international civilian personnel, 11,700 local civilian personnel and over 2,000 volunteer workers. During 2012–13, the budget for UN peacekeeping operations was about $7.33 billion.

Classical or 'first generation' UN peacekeeping involved the establishment of a UN force placed between the parties to a dispute once a ceasefire had been implemented. In 1948, UN peacekeepers were used to monitor the truce after the first Arab–Israeli War, and the following year a UN military observer group was deployed to monitor the ceasefire in the Kashmir region following large-scale killings that had occurred in the aftermath of the partition of India and Pakistan. The despatching of a 6,000-strong multinational peacekeeping force to act as a physical barrier between Israel and Egypt following the Suez crisis of 1956, and to facilitate the withdrawal of UK and French forces from the area, is often viewed as the prototype of 'first generation' peacekeeping. The 'blue helmets' only remained with the agreement of host states, and their purpose was to provide a shield against future hostilities rather than to resolve the deeper sources of the conflict or enforce a permanent settlement. In a context of East–West rivalry, a strict reliance on neutrality and impartiality, monitoring post-conflict situations rather than influencing them, appeared to be the only way in which the UN could contribute to the maintenance of peace.

However, the traditional approach to peacekeeping became increasingly unsustainable in the post-Cold War period, especially as the number of UN peacekeeping operations increased significantly. This increase came about both as a result of an upsurge in civil strife and humanitarian crises of various kinds, a consequence, in part, of the fact that declining superpower influence allowed ethnic and other divisions to rise to the surface, and of a new-found unanimity on the Security Council that created a bias in favour of intervention. No less importantly, the task of peacekeeping became more complex and difficult due to the changing nature of violent conflict. As interstate war became less frequent and civil war became more common, more conflicts were entangled with ethnic and cultural rivalries and endemic socio-economic divisions. This was reflected in two developments from the 1990s onwards. First, as peacekeepers were increasingly being dispatched to conflict zones in which violence remained an ongoing threat, if not a reality, there was greater emphasis on 'robust' peacekeeping, sometimes portrayed as **peace enforcement**. Second, as conflict situations became more complex, there was a recognition, over time, that the design and focus of peacekeeping operations had to keep up. This led to the advent of

---

CONCEPT

Peacekeeping

Peacekeeping is defined by the UN as 'a way to help countries torn by conflict create conditions for sustainable peace'. It is therefore essentially a technique designed to preserve the peace, however fragile, where fighting has been halted, and to assist in implementing agreements achieved by the peacemakers. 'Traditional' or classical peacekeeping amounts to monitoring and observing the peace process in post-conflict situations, with peacekeepers being deployed after a ceasefire has been negotiated and with no expectation of fighting except in the case of self-defence. This form of peacekeeping is consensual and requires the consent of the host state, its advantage being that the ability to report impartially on adherence to a ceasefire builds trust between previously warring states or groups.

● **Peace enforcement**: Coercive measures, including the use of military force, used to restore peace and security in situations where acts of aggression have taken place.

'multi-dimensional' peacekeeping, which includes, in addition to implementing a comprehensive peace agreement, the use of force to achieve humanitarian ends, the provision of emergency relief and steps towards political reconstruction. The emphasis therefore shifted from peacekeeping to peace-building.

Does UN peacekeeping work?

How successful has multidimensional peacekeeping in the post-Cold War period been? UN peacekeeping has been both effective and cost-effective when compared with the costs of conflict and the toll in lives and economic devastation (Collier and Hoeffler 2004). A study by the Rand Corporation in 2007 which analyzed eight UN-led peacekeeping operations determined that seven of them had succeeded in keeping the peace and six of them had helped to promote democracy (Dobbins 2007). These cases included the Congo (DRC), Cambodia, Namibia, Mozambique, El Salvador, East Timor, Eastern Slavonia and Sierra Leone. However, there have been a number of peacekeeping failures, notably in Rwanda, Somalia and Bosnia. UN peacekeepers were little more than spectators during the genocidal slaughter in Rwanda in 1994. UN-backed US intervention in Somalia led to humiliation and withdrawal in 1995, with warlord conflict continuing unabated. The Bosnian-Serb military in 1995 carried out the worst mass murder in Europe since WWII in the 'safe area' of Srebrenica, which had been under the protection of a UN battalion of Dutch peacekeepers. Some have seen such events as evidence of the pitfalls of intervention in alien places lacking civil order and legitimate political institutions. Others, nevertheless, argue that they highlight flaws and failings within the UN system. Failings on the ground have included the lack of a clear mission, and especially serious gaps between the mandate for intervention and the security challenges confronting peacekeepers, the varying quality of peacekeeping forces and a confused chain of command, and a general reliance on 'deterrence by presence', reflected in a reluctance to use force in the face of peace-breakers who use force freely and criminally. Failings at a higher level have been associated with a lack of political will, and conflicting priorities and agendas, in the Security Council and amongst other member states.

However, there is also evidence that the UN has learned lessons. Ever since the 1992 UN report, *An Agenda for Peace*, there has been an acknowledgement that peacekeeping alone is not enough to ensure lasting peace. The growing emphasis on peace-building reflects a desire to identify and support structures that will tend to strengthen and solidify peace in order to avoid a relapse into conflict, helping to establish 'positive' peace. Although the military remain the backbone of most peacekeeping operations, the many faces of peacekeeping now include administrators and economists, police officers and legal experts, de-miners and electoral observers, and human rights monitors and specialists in civil affairs and governance. In 2005, the UN Peacebuilding Commission was established as an advisory subsidiary body of the General Assembly and the Security Council. Its purpose is to support peace efforts in countries emerging from conflict, by bringing together all relevant actors (including international donors, the international financial institutions, national governments and troop-contributing countries), marshalling resources, and advising on and proposing integrated strategies for post-conflict peace-building and recovery.

Although, being advisory, the Peacebuilding Commission can accomplish little through its own efforts, the greater emphasis within the UN on peace-building is an acknowledgement that classical peacekeeping is effectively obsolete and that peace enforcement is always difficult and may only be possible under specific conditions (see Is humanitarian intervention justified?, p. 335). Peace-building, however, is a holistic exercise that straddles the UN 'harder' and 'softer' sides, its concern with promoting peace and security fusing with its commitment to economic and social development.

Promoting economic and social development

From the outset, the architects of the UN recognized the interconnectedness of economic and political issues. This largely reflected an awareness of the links between the economic turmoil of the Great Depression and the rise of political extremism and the growth of international conflict The UN Charter thus committed the organization to promoting 'social progress and better standards of life'. However, in its early phase, the UN's concerns with economic and social issues extended little beyond post-war reconstruction and recovery, in Western Europe and Japan in particular. A major shift in favour of the promotion of economic and social development was nevertheless evident from the 1960s onwards. This was a consequence of three factors. First, and most importantly, the process of decolonization and the growing influence of developing states within the ever-expanding UN focused more attention on the unequal distribution of wealth worldwide. The North–South divide (see p. 367) thus came to rival the significance of East–West rivalry within the UN. Second, a greater awareness of interdependence and the impact of globalization from the 1980s onwards meant that there was both an increased acceptance that economic and social problems in one part of the world have implications for other parts of the world, and that patterns of poverty and inequality are linked to the structure of the global economy. Third, as acknowledged by the transition from peacemaking to peace-building, the rise of civil war and ethnic strife underlined the fact that peace and security, on the one hand, and development, justice and human rights (see p. 311) on the other, are not separate agendas.

The UN's economic and social responsibilities are discharged by a sprawling and, seemingly, ever-enlarging array of programmes, funds and specialized agencies, supposedly coordinated by ECOSOC. Its main areas are human rights (discussed in Chapter 13), development and poverty reduction (discussed in Chapter 15) and the environment (discussed in Chapter 16). As far as development is concerned, the principal vehicle responsible for global development policy is the UN Development Programme (UNDP), created in 1965. The UNDP has a presence in more than 170 countries, working with them on their own solutions to global and national development challenges; it also helps developing countries attract and use aid effectively. Annual Human Development Reports (HDRs) focus the global debate on key development issues, providing new measurement tools (such as the Human Development Index or HDI), undertaking innovative analysis and often advancing controversial policy proposals. By focusing on the notions of 'human development' (see p. 363) and 'human security' (see p. 430), the UNDP has also fostered innovative thinking about poverty and deprivation, moving away from a narrowly economic defini-

History of the United Nations

1944	Dumbarton Oaks conference (the USA, the Soviet Union, the UK and China) sets down the general aims and structure of the future UN.
1945	UN Charter approved in San Francisco by 50 states (Poland was not represented but signed the Charter later to become one of UN's 51 original members).
1946	Trygve Lie (Norway) appointed Secretary-General.
1948	Universal Declaration of Human Rights adopted.
1950	Security Council approves military action in Korea.
1950	UN High Commissioner for Refugees (UNHCR) established.
1953	Dag Hammarskjöld (Sweden) appointed Secretary-General.
1956	First UN peacekeeping force sent to the Suez Canal.
1960	UN operation in the Congo established to oversee the transition from Belgian rule to independence.
1961	U Thant (Burma) appointed Secretary-General.
1964	UN peacekeepers sent to Cyprus.
1965	UN Development Programme (UNDP) founded.
1968	General Assembly approves the Treaty on the Non-Proliferation of Nuclear Weapons (NPT).
1971	People's Republic of China replaces the Republic of China (Taiwan) at the UN Security Council.
1972	First UN environment conference is held in Stockholm, leading to the establishment of the UN Environment Programme (UNEP).
1972	First UN conference on women in Mexico City, inaugurates International Women's Year.
1972	Kurt Waldheim (Austria) appointed Secretary-General.
1982	Javier Pérez de Cuéllar (Peru) appointed Secretary-General.
1990	UNICEF convenes the World Summit for Children.
1992	Boutros Boutros-Ghali (Egypt) appointed Secretary-General.
1992	The 'Earth Summit' in Rio approves a comprehensive plan to promote sustainable development.
1992	Security Council issues 'An Agenda for Peace', highlighting new approaches to peacemaking, peacekeeping and peace-building.
1997	Kofi Annan (Ghana) appointed Secretary-General.
2000	General Assembly adopts the Millennium Development Goals (see p. 382).
2002	International Criminal Court (ICC) established (see p. 158).
2005	UN Peacekeeping Commission is established.
2007	Ban Ki-moon (South Korea) appointed Secretary-General.

tion of poverty. In 1994, Secretary-General Boutros Boutros-Ghali issued *An Agenda for Development* (to complement *An Agenda for Peace*, two years earlier), which attempted to establish a coordinated programme for sustainable development (see p. 397) in an era of globalization and in the light of the end of the Cold War.

However, by the late 1990s, concerns about deepening global inequality, and especially the plight of sub-Saharan Africa, produced growing anxiety about the impact of the UN's development programmes. The 1999 *Human Development Report*, for example, noted that while the top fifth of the world's people in the richest countries enjoyed 82 per cent of the expanding export trade, the bottom fifth enjoyed barely more than 1 per cent (UNDP 1999). The desire to reinvigorate the UN's Development Programme led to the unveiling in 2000 of the Millennium Development Goals (MDGs) (see p. 382). These set a target of 2015 for, among other things, halving extreme poverty, halting the spread of HIV/AIDS and providing universal primary education. The UN's 2012 progress report on the achievement of the MDGs concluded that meeting the goals by 2015 was 'challenging but possible', with key causes of slower progress including natural disasters and the global financial crisis. Despite frustrations and difficulties, it is nevertheless clear that the UN has done more than any other organization or single state to alleviate the economic and social problems of developing countries (Hanhimäki 2008).

Future of the UN: challenges and reform

The UN is no stranger to controversy and criticism. Given the breadth and audacity of the UN's core mission, a gap between expectations and performance is inevitable. However, the nature of the challenges facing the organization has changed significantly over time. How will the UN fare as the twenty-first century unfolds? The major factor that shapes the influence that the UN wields is the global distribution of power. For much of the twentieth century, the UN was hamstrung by Cold War bipolarity. The high point of its influence came in the early to mid-1990s, and coincided with a relatively brief period of cooperation and agreement among P-5 states following the end of the Cold War. This, nevertheless, left the UN heavily dependent on the sole remaining superpower, the USA, creating the danger that US hegemony would render the UN a mere tool of US foreign policy, to be used, abused or ignored as Washington saw fit. On the other hand, the growing trend towards multipolarity, reflected, in particular, in the rise of China but also in the growing influence of powers such as India, Brazil and South Africa, is certain to have an impact on the UN. The nature of this impact is difficult to determine, however. In one view, a more even distribution of global power is likely to favour multilateralism and encourage states to rely more heavily on a system of collective security, facilitated by the UN, rather than on violent self-help. In the alternative view, multipolarity is likely to be associated with increased conflict and greater instability, in which case the future history of the UN may replicate that of the League of Nations, as intensifying great power rivalry makes the task of international mediation and negotiation increasingly difficult and perhaps impossible. In either event, the shifting location of global power is certain to keep the issue of the reform of the Security Council firmly on the agenda.

GLOBAL ACTORS . . .

THE UNITED NATIONS

Type: Intergovernmental organization • **Established:** 1945 • **Location:** New York
Membership: 193 countries

The United Nations was established as the successor to the League of Nations when fifty states met in San Francisco to agree the terms of the UN Charter. The UN has five major organs (see How the UN works, p. 446):

- The General Assembly
- The Security Council
- The Secretariat
- The International Court of Justice
- The Economic and Social Council.

The UN family also includes a range of specialized agencies, funds and programmes, including the IMF, the World Bank, the World Health Organization (WHO), the UN Educational, Scientific and Cultural Organization (UNESCO) and the UN Children's Fund (UNICEF).

Significance: The United Nations is a genuinely global body that has a unique international character. On the basis of its founding Charter, the organization can take action, in theory, in an unlimited range of areas. The UN is active in areas such as the environment, refugee protection, disaster relief, counterterrorism, disarmament, human rights, economic and social development and so on. However, its key role is widely accepted to be the maintenance of international peace and security, particularly as carried out through the Security Council's ability to issue binding resolutions, backed up, at least in theory, by the

ability to impose non-military and military sanctions in the event of non-compliance. This makes the UN the primary source of international law (see p. 339).

During the Cold War, the UN was routinely paralyzed by superpower rivalry that led to deadlock in the Security Council, a consequence of the veto powers of its permanent members. A further difficulty was that the UN was never able to develop an armed force of its own, so that it has always had to rely on troops supplied by individual member states. Its impact on matters of peace and security was therefore strictly limited. The end of the Cold War, however, produced optimism about the capacity of an activist UN to preside over a 'new world order'. The UN approved the US-led expulsion of Iraq from Kuwait in the Gulf War of 1991, and, in a few short years, the number of UN peacekeeping operations had doubled, and the annual budget for peacekeeping had quadrupled. Hopes for a more effective UN in the post-Cold War period were, however, dashed, largely by a declining willingness of states, freed from East–West tensions, to accept neutral, multilateral intervention, and by the eroding support, both financial and military, of the USA. Despite some genuine successes in peacekeeping (such as in Mozambique and El Salvador) and in peace-building (East Timor), the UN's reputation was badly damaged by its failure to prevent

large-scale slaughter in Rwanda and Bosnia in the mid-1990s.

The UN nevertheless continues to exert significant 'soft' power, particularly in the developing world, where it is viewed as the leading institution providing support for economic and social development. The UN remains the only international organization that approximates to a form of global governance, providing, at minimum, a framework through which the international community can address concerns ranging from peace and security, disarmament and non-proliferation to environmental protection, poverty reduction, gender equality and emergency relief. In view of the UN's unique role and moral authority, few would disagree with the view that if it did not exist it would need to be invented. However, the UN has been subject to a variety of criticisms. Most damningly, the UN has been portrayed as entirely non-legitimate, a proto-world government that has no democratic credentials and which, over time, has come to pay less respect to national sovereignty. Others claim that it is little more than a debating society, due to the fact that it can do no more than its member states, and particularly the P-5, allow it to do. Further criticisms focus on the convoluted and deeply bureaucratic nature of the organization itself, and its tendency towards inefficiency and mismanagement, exposed not least by the 2003 Oil-for-Food scandal.

Focus on . . .
Reforming the UN Security Council?

Why has there been pressure to reform the UN Security Council? And why has such reform been so difficult to bring about? Calls for the reform of the Security Council focus on two key, if interrelated, issues: the veto powers of its permanent members, and their identity. Permanent membership and the power to veto Council decisions means that the UN is dominated, as far as the core issue of peace and security is concerned, by great power politics. Some UN members are clearly more equal than others. The requirement of unanimity amongst P-5 states has also effectively neutered the UN as the basis for collective security, apart from exceptional circumstances (Korea and the Gulf War). Moreover, the membership of P-5 is widely seen to be outdated, reflecting the great powers of the immediate post-1945 period, not even the superpower politics of the Cold War period. If the Council is to have permanent members, few would challenge the right of the USA, China or Russia (at least in terms of its nuclear capability) to be among them, but France and the UK have long ceased to be states of first-ranking status. At different times, cases have been made out for the inclusion of Japan and Germany, in view of their economic strength, and, more recently, for emerging powers such as India, Brazil, Nigeria, Egypt and South Africa. Certainly, the existing membership reflects a regional imbalance, with no representation for Africa or for Latin America among its permanent members. The case for a revised membership is that a more represen-tative and up-to-date Council would enjoy wider support and influence, helping to make the UN a more effective peacemaker and peacekeeper.

However, the prospect of the reform of the Security Council is remote, with the veto being the major obstacle standing in the way. Veto status could not be removed without the unanimous agreement of the P-5 states, and it is unlikely that any of them would voluntarily abandon their privileged position. Moreover, the continued existence of permanent veto powers is, anyway, a (possibly vital) way of ensuring that the UN retains the support of the world's leading states. The enlargement or change in membership of the P-5 is also difficult to bring about. In the first place, it is highly likely to be opposed, and blocked, by existing P-5 states, especially the most vulnerable ones, France and the UK. Other P-5 members may also fear the different configuration of interests and influences that a reformed Council might bring about. Furthermore, there is significant resistance outside the P-5 to the candidacy of particular would-be members. For example, many European states oppose the inclusion of Germany; South Africa opposes the inclusion of Nigeria and vice versa; Argentina opposes the inclusion of Brazil and so on. Finally, a revised membership may require the introduction of regular membership reviews, as the distribution of global power is always changing.

A further issue is that the security challenges facing the modern UN are vastly different from those in earlier decades. Amongst other things, these include the threat of nuclear terrorism, the problem of state collapse and the disruption caused by the spread of infectious diseases. The changing nature of war and armed conflict raises particular difficulties for the UN in its peacekeeping and peace-building roles. Not only do the rise of identity wars and the links between civil strife, humanitarian and refugee crises and endemic crime make sustainable peace difficult to achieve, but they also strain the relationship between the quest for global justice and respect for state sovereignty. The case of Darfur, in the 2000s, shows how UN intervention to keep the peace and provide humanitarian aid can be blocked by an unwilling host government. Nevertheless, if the UN

Debating . . .
Is the UN obsolete and unnecessary?

The UN has long been a controversial body. Although for almost six decades the states that comprise the UN have come to value and need the organization, major and sometimes fundamental criticisms continue to be levelled at the United Nations and its composite bodies.

FOR

A proto-world government. The UN is fundamentally flawed because it was designed as a supranational body whose role is to police the international system. The UN therefore has all the drawbacks of a would-be world government – a lack of legitimacy, accountability and democratic credentials. Not only does the UN interfere in the affairs of nation-states (as is demonstrated by its declining support for state sovereignty), but it also disrupts the workings of the balance-of-power system, thereby endangering peace and stability.

Irrelevant debating society. For many, the chief problem with the UN is its ineffectiveness rather than its capacity to meddle in world affairs. As is commonly pointed out, there have been more wars since the creation of the UN than there had been before, and the organization is routinely sidelined as major world events unfold. The Security Council is commonly paralyzed by the difficulty of passing resolutions and achieving both regional acceptance and the support of the USA before action can be taken.

Lack of moral compass. In this view, the UN, at its creation, had a clear moral focus, derived from the fight against fascism: the need to defend human rights and fundamental freedoms. However, as the UN expanded and became a genuinely global body, it drifted towards a kind of moral relativism in which it seeks to be all things to all members. The UN's record on standing up to dictators, condemning human rights violations and intervening to prevent genocide and other comparable acts is therefore poor.

Outdated and unreformable. There is common agreement that the UN is in pressing need of reform, but it is not clear that such reform can be brought about. The reform of the Security Council is impossible to achieve because of the veto powers of its permanent members. The organization itself is simply dysfunctional – sprawling and complex and fraught with duplication and overlaps. Moreover, attempts to streamline the organization seem to make matters worse not better.

AGAINST

An indispensable body. For all its flaws and failings, one central fact must be borne in mind: the world is a safer place with the UN than it would be without it. Although the UN will never be able to prevent all wars and resolve all conflicts, it provides an indispensable framework for cooperation, should the international community choose to use it. The UN serves, however imperfectly, to increase the chances that international conflict can be resolved without the resort to war and, if war breaks out, that military conflict will quickly lead to peacemaking and peace-building.

Peacekeeping successes. Highly-publicized peacekeeping 'failures' have distorted the image of the UN's effectiveness in keeping the peace. Most studies show that UN peacekeeping operations are more often successful than unsuccessful. At an operational level, there are clearly functions that the UN is better at performing than any other body, including small-scale peacekeeping, the provision of humanitarian aid and the monitoring of elections. The shift towards multidimensional peacekeeping has also been beneficial.

New agendas and new thinking. The UN did not fossilize around its initial mission, but it has, rather, succeeded in adapting and redefining itself in the light of new global challenges. Not only has the UN developed into the leading organization promoting economic and social development worldwide, but it has also helped to shape the agenda as far as new global issues are concerned, ranging from climate change and gender equality to population control and dealing with pandemics.

Mend it, don't end it. Despite its imperfections, it is absurd to suggest that the UN is unreformable. The operational and strategic approach to peacekeeping and the provision of humanitarian aid have both improved significantly in recent years, and further reforms could undoubtedly be introduced. For example, UN agencies could be better coordinated; the UN could confer legitimacy on international action, rather than always implementing action itself; and relationships with regional organizations could be strengthened.

accepts a 'responsibility to protect', it is difficult to see where intervention will end. The UN, in addition, faces a continuing problem of who will foot the bill for its activities. While UN peacekeeping, development and other activities tend, remorselessly, to expand, major donor states have become more reluctant to keep up with their financial contributions, partly using these as levers to influence policy within the organization. At the end of 2006, member states owed the UN $2.3 billion, with the USA accounting for 43 per cent of this amount. How can the UN put its finances on a sounder footing without curtailing necessary work, and how can the link between budgetary contributions and policy influence within the UN be broken?

In the light of these challenges, the issue of UN reform has become increasingly prominent. In the late 1990s, the then-Secretary-General, Kofi Annan, embarked on an overarching reform programme which aimed to improve the coordination of the UN's economic and social arrangements and to strengthen the norms of the multilateral system. However, most would argue that this process remains incomplete and needs to be applied to a much broader range of UN activities. However, other important areas of reform are in peace operations, development and human rights. The 2000 Brahimi Report on Peacekeeping made a major contribution to reviewing UN peace operations, and provided the backdrop for the creation of the UN Peacebuilding Commission in 2005. An area of particular concern has been the need for the UN to have a 'rapid deployment capacity', the ability to send peacekeepers to different corners of the globe at short notice with the resources to act swiftly and effectively. The absence of such a capacity has often meant that UN peacekeepers are deployed late and are called upon to police highly difficult situations. The chief reform challenge facing the UN's development activities continues to be how to improve coordination and reduce overlaps and duplication amongst the plethora of development-orientated bodies within the UN's 'dysfunctional family'. The goal of 'delivering as one' has been recognized within the UN, but the task of translating this into practice, in order to increase efficiency and reduce administrative costs has yet to be achieved. In relation to human rights, the UN has been highly successful in creating a detailed body of international human rights legislation, and also in producing bodies that can observe and authoritatively report on adherence to global human rights norms. However, given the range of interests that operate in and through the UN, it has been less easy to ensure that these bodies act in a robust way. The much criticized Commission on Human Rights may have been replaced by the Human Rights Council, but as its unwillingness to criticize Sri Lanka in 2009 for the conduct of its civil war against the Tamil Tigers demonstrated, serious human rights violations can still escape sanction.

SUMMARY

- An international organization is an institution with formal procedures and a membership comprising three or more states. These bodies can be thought of as instruments through which states pursue their own interests, as arenas that facilitate debate, and as actors that can affect global outcomes.

- International organizations are created out of a composite of factors. These include the existence of inter-dependencies among states which encourage policy-makers to believe that international cooperation can serve common interests, and the presence of a hegemonic power willing and able to bear the costs of creating, and sustaining, an international organization.

- The United Nations is the only truly global organization ever constructed. The UN is nevertheless a hybrid body, configured around the competing need to accept the realities of great power politics and to acknowledge the sovereign equality of member states. This, in effect, has created the 'two UNs'.

- The principal aim of the UN is to maintain international peace and security, with responsibility for this being vested in the Security Council. However, the UN has been restricted in carrying out this role particularly by the veto powers of the P-5 and the lack of an independent military capacity. The UN's mixed performance in the area of peacekeeping has led to an increasing emphasis, instead, on the process of peace-building.

- The UN's economic and social responsibilities are discharged by a sprawling and, seemingly, ever-enlarging array of programmes, funds and specialized agencies. Its main areas are human rights, development and poverty reduction, and the environment. Such widening concerns have ensured strong support for the UN, particularly across the developing world.

- The UN faces a range of important challenges and pressures for reform. These include those generated by the changing location of global power in an increasingly multipolar world, those associated with criticisms of the composition and powers of the Security Council, and those related to the UN's finances and organization.

Questions for discussion

- How do international organizations differ from states?
- How are international organization and global governance linked?
- Are international organizations merely mechanisms for pursuing state interests by other means?
- Is a hegemonic power necessary for the creation of international organizations?
- To what extent are international organizations ideational constructs?
- Why has the UN been more successful than the League of Nations?
- Why has the UN only had limited success in establishing a system of collective security?
- How and why has the UN's approach to peace-keeping evolved?
- How effective has the UN been in discharging its economic and social responsibilities?
- Why is it so difficult to reform the Security Council?

Further reading

Armstrong, D., L. Lloyd and J. Redmond, *International Organisation in World Politics* (2004). An introduction to the history of modern international organization that places a particular emphasis on the development of the UN.

Gareis, S.B., *The United Nations: An Introduction* (2012). A concise analysis of the UN, its structure and work, its impact and its likely role and future prospects.

Rittberger, R., B. Zangl and A. Kruck, *International Organization: Polity, Politics and Policies* (2012). A systematic theoretical and empirical introduction to the evolution, structure and policies of international organizations.

Weiss, T.G., *What's Wrong with the United Nations (and How to Fix It)* (2009). A stimulating examination of the UN's alleged ills and of possible cures.

 ONLINE RESOURCES AVAILABLE

Links to relevant web resources can be found on the *Global Politics* website

CHAPTER 19

Global Governance and the Bretton Woods System

'The market is a good servant but a bad master.'

Economics maxim (sometimes applied to money)

PREVIEW

The issue of global governance has received growing attention, particularly since the 1990s. This has occurred for a number of reasons. The end of the Cold War meant that increased expectations fell on international organizations in general and on the United Nations in particular. Accelerated globalization stimulated discussions about the relationship between trends in the world economy and the institutional frameworks through which it is supposedly regulated. And there has been a general recognition that a growing number of worldwide problems are beyond the capacity of individual states to solve on their own. However, hovering somewhere between a Westphalian world of sovereign states and the fanciful idea of world government, global governance is profoundly difficult to analyze and assess. How is global governance best understood? Does it actually exist, or is global governance merely an aspiration? The arena in which global governance is most advanced is nevertheless the field of economic policy-making. This stems from the 1944 Bretton Woods agreement, which sought to establish the architecture for the postwar international economic order by creating three new bodies: the IMF, the World Bank and GATT (later replaced by the World Trade Organization), collectively known as 'the Bretton Woods system'. This system, however, has evolved significantly over time, as it has adapted to the changing pressures generated by the world economy. From an initial concern with postwar reconstruction in Europe and later development in the Third World, its key institutions were drawn into deeper controversy from the early 1970s onwards as they were converted to an agenda of economic liberalization and became inextricably linked to the forces of neoliberal globalization. What factors lie behind the creation of the Bretton Woods system, and how did its mission subsequently change? Have the Bretton Wood institutions been a force for good or for ill?

KEY ISSUES

- What is global governance?
- Is global governance a myth or a reality?
- How and why was the Bretton Woods system established
- How were the Bretton Woods institutions converted to economic liberalization?
- Why have the Bretton Woods institutions attracted so much criticism?
- What does the 2007–09 global crisis tell us about the need for global economic governance?

CONCEPT

Global governance

Global governance is a broad, dynamic and complex process of interactive decision-making at the global level that involves formal and informal mechanisms as well as governmental and non-governmental bodies. States and governments remain the primary institution for articulating public interests and those of the global community as a whole, but global governance also involves intergovernmental and, sometimes, supranational bodies. Global policy is made by a system of horizontal and vertical interactions in which officials in different branches of government work with counterparts in other countries as well as with activists, scientists, bankers and others outside government. The term 'global governance' is sometimes used more narrowly to refer to the institutions through which these interactions takes place.

GLOBAL GOVERNANCE

Global governance has been described as the 'collection of governance-related activities, rules and mechanisms, formal and informal, existing at a variety of levels in the world today' (Karns and Mingst 2009). As such, it refers to a wide variety of cooperative problem-solving arrangements whose common character- istic is that they facilitate 'governance' (see p. 130), in the sense of the *coordina- tion* of social life, rather than 'government', meaning ordered rule operating through a system of enforceable decisions. Such arrangements have become an increasingly prominent feature of global politics since the end of the Cold War, particularly in response to, but also, to some extent, in an attempt to shape, the process of globalization (see p. 8). Global governance is nevertheless a complex phenomenon that defies simple definitions or explanations. In the first place, it is commonly confused with international organization (see p. 440), to such an extent that global governance is sometimes, in effect, used as a collective term to describe the international organizations currently in existence. Although global governance and international organization are not synonyms, an important aspect of the emergence of global governance has been the growth in the number and importance of international organizations. Furthermore, as a set of processes through which states cooperate without, it seems, abandoning sover- eignty (see p. 4), global governance is a difficult phenomenon to categorize. In particular, how can global governance be distinguished from other models of world politics?

What global governance is, and is not

Global governance can be understood as a broad, dynamic and complex process of interactive decision-making at the global level. But what does this mean? What are the characteristic features of global governance? Perhaps the best way to define global governance is to highlight similarities and differences between it and alternative configurations of world politics, notably:

- International anarchy
- Global hegemony
- World government.

International anarchy

International anarchy has been the conventional model for understanding inter- national politics, its origins dating back to the emergence of the Westphalian state-system in the seventeenth century. It is also one of the core assumptions of realist theory. From this perspective, the central feature of the international system is the *absence* of a supranational authority capable of regulating the behaviour of states. States are thus sovereign entities, forced to rely on self-help for survival and security. The international system thus tends to be dynamic and prone to conflict, especially as a result of the fear and uncertainty that derive from the security dilemma (see p. 19). However, international anarchy is not necessarily characterized by unending chaos and disorder. Rather, periods of peace and at least relative order may develop, particularly when a balance of power (see p. 262) emerges that discourages states from pursuing their aggressive ambitions. Moreover, the prospect of war is diminished to the extent that states seek to maximize security (the avoidance of war) rather than to maximize power (gains made through conquest and expansion) (see Offensive or defensive realism? p. 240).

Does international anarchy still reign? The main weakness of this model is that, since 1945, countries in various parts of the world have, with the help of international organizations, demonstrated a capacity for sustainable cooperative behaviour based on norms and rules that increase levels of trust and reciprocity (see p. 344). The level of cooperation achieved by the European Union, for instance, defies the assumptions of realist theory. It is widely argued, therefore, that the international system has developed into an international society (see p. 9), meaning that international anarchy has developed into what Bull ([1977] 2002) called an 'anarchical society'. Yet, self-help and power politics have not been banished altogether. For instance, international relations across much of the Middle East are still best understood in balance-of-power terms, with 9/11 widely being interpreted as marking a return to traditional geopolitics (see p. 414). Realist theorists, moreover, challenge the idea that an international order can be constructed that permanently transcends the logic of power politics.

Global hegemony

Realists have always acknowledged that some measure of organization is imposed on the state system by the fact that there is a hierarchy of states. Although states are formally equal in terms of their entitlement to sovereign jurisdiction, they are highly unequal in terms of their resources and capacities. Powerful states therefore impose their will on weak states, not least through imperialism (see p. 28). The notion of global hegemony merely takes this idea of international order imposed 'from above' one step further. A hegemonic power is one that possesses pre-eminent military, economic and ideological resources and so is able to impose its will within a region (a regional hegemon) or worldwide (a global hegemon). Such a strongly asymmetrical distribution of power may lead to hostility and resentment but, more commonly, will encourage weaker states to 'bandwagon' in the hope of gaining security and other rewards. Global hegemony may therefore be consistent with international order, particularly when the hegemon is able to deliver collective goods such as a stable financial system, a dependable international currency and, acting as the 'world's police officer', the ability to resolve regional and other conflicts.

Many have argued that hegemony (see p. 228) provides the key to understanding modern global politics. The USA, having displaced the UK as the hegemonic power in the western hemisphere in 1945, became a global hegemon as a result of the end of the Cold War and the demise of the Soviet Union. Such a view also suggests that the growth of international organizations since 1945 was less a reflection of a greater willingness amongst states generally to cooperate, but more a manifestation of the USA's ability to accumulate 'structural' power. However, although the USA played a pivotal role in the construction of the leading institutions of global governance (the UN (see p. 456), the World Bank (see p. 380), the International Monetary Fund (IMF) (see p. 475) and the World

Trade Organization (see p. 537)), and has also given consistent encouragement to the process of European integration, it is simplistic to see international institutions at large as nothing more than a mechanism through which the USA pursues its national interests. This, for example, can be seen in the often difficult relationship the USA has with the UN. Moreover, the USA's global dominance, as well as its leadership over the institutions of global governance, may well be fading through the emergence of a multipolar world order, as discussed in Chapter 9.

World government

Of all the models of global politics considered here, world government corresponds least well to the structures and processes of the modern global system. Global governance could even be described as international cooperation in the absence of world government. The idea of world government has, indeed, become distinctly unfashionable. However, this was not always the case. The notion of world government has featured large in the history of international relations thought, dating back to Zeno and Marcus Aurelius in ancient Greece and Rome. Hugo Grotius (see p. 341) argued in favour of a system of law that would be binding on all peoples and all nations, while Immanuel Kant (see p. 15) asserted that 'perpetual peace' could be delivered through a federation of free states bound together by the conditions of universal hospitality (although this by no means constituted a simple plan for world government). The founding visions of both the League of Nations (1919–46) and the UN were constructed around a world government ideal, while support for federal world government has been expressed by people as varied as Albert Einstein (1879–1955), Winston Churchill (1874–1965), Bertrand Russell (1872–1970) and Mahatma Gandhi (see p. 268). The logic behind the idea of world government is the same as that which underlies the classic liberal justification for the state – social contract theory. Just as the only means of ensuring order and stability amongst individuals with differing interests is the establishment of a sovereign state, the only way of preventing conflict between self-interested states is to create a supreme world power (Yunker 2007). However, such a prospect is now widely considered to be both unrealistic and undesirable.

World government is unrealistic because there are no discernable indications that states, or peoples, are willing to give up their sovereignty to a global state or world federation. As even within one continent, as the European experience demonstrates (examined in Chapter 20), the emergence of transnational political identities is always likely to lag well behind progress in transnational institution-building. This suggests that if world government were ever to be established, it would be likely to take the form of a world empire (the clearest example perhaps being the Roman Empire), an extreme and institutionalized form of global hegemony. World government has been deemed to be undesirable for at least four reasons. First, it creates the prospect of unchecked – and uncheckable – power, meaning that it would degenerate into global despotism. Second, in view of the cultural, language, religious and other differences, it is likely that local or regional political allegiances will always remain stronger than global ones. Third, it is difficult to see how effective democratic accountability could operate within a system of world government. Fourth, many liberal theorists have abandoned the idea of

CONCEPT

World government

World government is the idea of all of humankind united under one common political authority. All conceptions of world government are based on the centralization of authority in a supranational body which would possess legislative and executive power. However, there are two quite different models of world government. In the *unitary* model, a 'cosmopolis', or world state, would enjoy a monopoly of the legitimate use of force and establish a strictly hierarchical world order. In the *federal* model, a central authority would be vested with autonomous authority over the rule of law and the maintenance of order, while the constituent units (previously states) retain control over local and domestic matters.

(see p. 348)

CONCEPT

Supranationalism

Supranationalism is the existence of an authority that is higher than that of the nation-state and capable of imposing its will on it. Supranationalism thus transfers sovereignty and decision-making authority from constituent states to an international or regional organization. This can occur through the establishment of an international federation, in which sovereignty is shared between central and peripheral bodies, a process often referred to as pooling sovereignty. The advance of supranationalism is seen as part of the general integrative trend within global politics. However, critics of supranationalism, especially realists, claim that it represents a threat not only to sovereignty, but also to national identity and democracy, perhaps even containing the seeds of world government.

world government on the grounds that the success of global governance and the spread of moral cosmopolitanism (as opposed to world state cosmopolitanism) show how problems such as war, global poverty and environmental degradation can be tackled without the need for a global state. However, although world government is now rarely deemed to be a meaningful political project, the principle of supranationalism that underpins it has undoubtedly acquired growing significance. For instance, the supranational authority that is vested in the UN Security Council (through its powers in relation to peace and security matters under Article 25 of the UN Charter), the International Court of Justice (see p. 348) and the International Criminal Court, and in certain EU institutions (see p. 504), contains at least some world government features.

Contours of global governance

While world government has increasingly been viewed as an outmoded, if not a deeply unattractive idea, the alternative notion of global governance has attracted growing attention. Global governance is more a *field* than an object of study: although it can be associated with particular institutions and identifiable actors, it is essentially a process or a complex of processes. Simply put, global governance is the management of global policies in the absence of a central government. As such, it differs from international anarchy, in that it involves a level of sustained cooperation and a preference for collective action which is impossible in a self-help system. States in a global governance system cooperate voluntarily, recognizing that it is in their interest to do so. Global governance has therefore emerged out of an acceptance by states that in a growing number of policy areas the problems they confront cannot be effectively addressed by individual states acting alone. Global governance differs from global hegemony and world government, in that each of the latter presupposed the existence of a supranational authority. It can therefore be described as a system of 'cooperation under anarchy' (Oye 1986). Global governance thus implies that international anarchy can be overcome without founding a world government or having to endure a world hegemonic order (see Table 19.1). The key features of global governance include the following:

- *Polycentrism* – Despite the UN's overarching role within the modern global governance system, global governance is multiple rather than singular, having different institutional frameworks and decision-making mechanisms in different issue areas.
- *Intergovernmentalism* – States and national governments retain considerable influence within the global governance system, reflecting international organizations' general disposition towards consensual decision-making and their weak powers of enforcement.
- *Mixed actor involvement* – In addition to states and international organizations, global governance embraces NGOs, TNCs and other institutions of global civil society (see p. 156), the blurring of the public/private divide meaning that the distinction between the state and civil society in domestic politics is absent in global decision-making.
- *Multilevel processes* – Global governance operates through interaction between groups and institutions at various levels (municipal, provincial,

national, regional and global), with no single level enjoying predominance over the others.

● *Deformalization* – Global governance tends to operate through norm-based and informal international regimes (see p. 71) rather than through formal and legally constituted bodies.

Global governance: myth or reality?

How far does modern world politics conform to the features of a global governance system? Liberal theorists in particular have argued that there is an unmistakable, and perhaps irresistible, trend in favour of global governance. The growth of international organizations provides both evidence of a greater willingness amongst states to cooperate and engage in collective action, and fosters further cooperation by strengthening trust amongst states, accustoming them to rule-governed behaviour. In the sense that global governance is closely linked to globalization, its salience may fluctuate, but is likely to grow over time as the tendency towards interdependence (see p. 7) and interconnectedness, once established, is difficult to reverse. This is demonstrated by developments ranging from international migration and global terrorism to transnational criminal organizations and global pandemics. However, the extent to which the world as a whole has become orderly and norm-governed should not be exaggerated. It is more accurate to refer to an emerging global governance *process* rather than an established global governance system. Moreover, the norms and rules of global governance are much better established in some parts of the world than in others. For instance, Europe has been portrayed by Cooper (2004) as the heart of the so-called 'postmodern' world by virtue of the EU's success in pooling sovereignty and banishing balance-of-power politics. Europe, nevertheless, is an exception and many parts of the world are still little affected by international norms and rules, as demonstrated by the existence of 'rogue' states (see p. 231) and pariah states.

GLOBAL ECONOMIC GOVERNANCE: THE EVOLUTION OF THE BRETTON WOODS SYSTEM

The trend towards global governance has been particularly evident in the sphere of economic policy-making. This is because economics is the most obvious area of interdependence amongst states, and the area where the failure of international cooperation can cause the clearest damage. Since 1945, a system of global economic governance has emerged through a thickening web of multilateral agreements, formal institutions and informal networks, with the most important institutions being those established by the Bretton Woods agreement, negotiated just before the end of World War II. The major factor behind the agreement was the desire not to return to the economic instability and sometimes chaos of the interwar period. Such concerns were made especially pressing by the recognition of the role that unemployment and economic insecurity had played in the rise of fascism and the circumstances that had led to WWII (as discussed in Chapter

CONCEPT

Multilateralism

Multilateralism can broadly be defined as a process that coordinates behaviour among three or more countries on the basis of generalized principles of conduct (Ruggie 1992). For a process to be genuinely multilateral, it must conform to three principles. These principles are non-discrimination (all participating countries must be treated alike), indivisibility (participating countries must behave as if they were a single entity, as in collective security (see p. 447)) and diffuse reciprocity (obligations among countries must have a general and enduring character, rather than being examples of one-off cooperation). Multilateralism may be informal, reflecting the acceptance of common norms and rules by three or more countries, but more commonly it is formal, in which case multilateralism equals institutionalism.

Table 19.1 Competing models of global politics

	No supranational authority	Supranational authority
No binding norms and rules	International anarchy	Global hegemony
Binding norms and rules	Global governance	World government

Source: Adapted from Rittberger *et al.* (2012).

2). The chief lesson of the Great Depression of the 1930s was therefore that so-called 'beggar-thy-neighbour' policies of **protectionism** were economically self-defeating and politically dangerous. However, such tendencies could only be countered if a framework of norms, rules and understandings could be established that enabled states to cooperate over economic matters and avoid the pitfalls of the 'welfare dilemma'.

Making of the Bretton Woods system

In August 1944, the USA, the UK and forty-two other states met at the UN Monetary and Financial Conference at the small resort town of Bretton Woods, New Hampshire, to formulate the institutional architecture for the postwar international financial and monetary system. The most significant outcome of the Bretton Woods process was the establishment of three new bodies, in due course collectively known as the 'Bretton Woods system'. These bodies were:

- The International Monetary Fund (IMF), which came into operation in March 1947
- The International Bank for Reconstruction and Development (IBRD), better known as the World Bank, which came into operation in June 1946
- The General Agreement on Tariffs and Trade (GATT), which was replaced by the World Trade Organization (WTO) in 1995. Although GATT is usually seen as part of the Bretton Woods system, it was created by the UN Conference on Trade and Employment and came into operation in January 1948.

The Bretton Woods agreement is a clear example of the multilateralism that was to become increasingly prominent in the post-1945 period. However, it would be a mistake to portray Bretton Woods simply in terms of multilateralism and the recognition of mutual interests. This would be to ignore the crucial role played by the USA, which emerged from WWII as the world's predominant military and economic power. Not only was the conference initiated by the USA and took place on US soil, but the USA was the leading force in the negotiation, effectively dictating some key outcomes. The USA's priorities in relation to Bretton Woods were twofold. First, having massively increased its industrial output

● **Protectionism**: The use of tariffs, quotas and other measures to restrict imports, supposedly to protect domestic industries.

Focus on . . .
A welfare dilemma?

Why is it difficult for states to cooperate over economic matters? Just as the security dilemma (see p. 19) helps to explain why and how security issues tend to breed distrust, fear and conflict among states, the welfare dilemma shows how this can also apply to welfare and economic relations. The welfare dilemma arises in an international economy in which each country can, without the intervention of a central authority, decide its own trade and monetary policies (Rittberger and Zangl 2006). In this context, each country may try to increase its share of the economic pie by, for example, raising tariffs (taxes on imports), imposing import restrictions, or devaluing its currency (making its exports cheaper and imports more expensive). Such attempts to prosper by 'beggaring-thy-neighbour' are nevertheless likely to have long-term costs, as other states reciprocate in kind, reducing the size of the overall economic cake. In highlighting the clash between the interests of individual states and the well-being of the community of states collectively, the welfare dilemma resembles the thinking behind the 'tragedy of the commons' (see p. 395), which explains obstacles to international cooperation over environmental matters.

However, the challenges implied by the welfare dilemma are, in some senses, less severe than those posed by the security dilemma or the 'tragedy of the commons'. This helps to explain why, since 1945, international cooperation has often progressed further and faster in economic areas than in any other area. Why does this happen? In the first place, states are usually more concerned in economic matters with absolute gains rather than relative gains (see Relative or absolute gains? p. 443). This applies because, unlike growing military disparities, widening economic disparities generally do not pose a threat to the survival of a state. Second, trust and transparency are easier to develop in matters of economic cooperation, where tariffs and other forms of protectionism are more difficult to conceal than the development of new weapons systems. Third, the costs involved in economic cooperation are relatively small (foregoing the opportunity to 'beggar-thy-neighbour'), particularly by comparison with some forms of environmental cooperation, notably those linked to climate change, as discussed in Chapter 16.

through rearmament and the expansion of exports in the run-up to, and during, the war years, re-establishing full employment in a way that Roosevelt's New Deal had failed to do, the USA needed to ensure that domestic growth levels could be sustained in the postwar period. This required the construction of an open and stable international economic system. Second, US thinking was shaped by a growing awareness of the threat posed by the Soviet Union and the need to contain the spread of communism. This encouraged the USA to seek ways of promoting reconstruction and recovery in war-ravaged Europe, as well as, over time, in defeated Germany and Japan.

At the centre of the Bretton Woods system was a new monetary order, overseen by the IMF, which sought to maintain stable **exchange rates**. This was achieved by fixing all currencies to the value of the US dollar, which acted as a 'currency anchor', with the US dollar being convertible to gold at a rate of $35 per ounce. The World Bank and GATT complemented the new international monetary order, by establishing, respectively, a new international financial order and a new international trading order. The main responsibility of the World Bank was to provided loans for countries in need of reconstruction and devel-

● **Exchange rate**: The price at which one currency is exchanged for another.

opment, while GATT, which existed more as a multilateral agreement than as an international organization, sought to advance the cause of **free trade** by bringing down tariff levels. Between them, these bodies established a form of proto-global economic governance, based on a framework of norms and rules that would guide the future economic relationships among states.

But what was the thinking behind the Bretton Woods system? Bretton Woods certainly reflected an underpinning faith in liberal economic theories, notably about the virtues of an open and competitive international economy. However, the fact that the institutional arrangements had to be put in place to, in a sense, 'police' the international economy and ensure stability reflected grave doubts about classical political economy and especially the doctrine of *laissez-faire* (see p. 106). The key idea of classical political economy is the belief that unregulated market competition tends towards long-term equilibrium. The economy thus works best when left alone by government, and this supposedly applies at the international level as well as at the national level. Bretton Woods, on the other hand, was shaped by the fear that an unregulated international economy is inherently unstable and crisis-prone, tendencies most dramatically demonstrated by the Great Depression itself. In line with the ideas of J. M. Keynes (see p. 108), markets therefore had to be 'managed'. The growing influence of such thinking in domestic politics was reflected in the postwar period in the gradual adoption by all industrialized states of Keynesian techniques of economic management, in which fiscal policy (government spending and taxation) was used to deliver growth and keep unemployment low. Bretton Woods reflected an attempt to establish a Keynesian-style regulative framework for the international economy. In that this acknowledged only the limited benefits of market competition, it has been described as a form of **embedded liberalism**, as opposed to 'pure' liberalism (Ruggie 1998).

Nevertheless, the exact form of the institutional framework agreed at Bretton Woods was also crucially shaped by the priorities and concerns of the USA. This was particularly evident in the defeat of Keynes' proposals, as head of the UK negotiating team at Bretton Woods, for a radical change in international monetary and financial arrangements. Keynes, rather misleadingly dubbed 'the intellectual godfather of the IMF', proposed the construction of a global bank, called the International Clearing Union, which would issue its own currency, known as the bancor. The radical aspect of these proposals was that the Clearing Union would have been able permanently to alter the **terms of trade** between creditor countries and debtor countries in the international economy, by imposing conditions on the former as well as the latter. Countries with a trade surplus would have to increase the value of their currencies, thereby boosting imports and making exports less competitive. In addition, Keynes proposed that capital should be allowed to flow into, but not out of, countries with a trade deficit, in the hope of stimulating growth and increasing the value of their exports. The rejection of these proposals for a more egalitarian international economic order by the USA, the world's leading creditor country, meant that no limits were placed on the surpluses that successful exporters could accumulate and that the entire burden for addressing **balance-of-payments** deficits was placed on debtor countries. Critics of global economic governance have argued that this introduced structural inequalities and imbalances into the management of the world economy.

● **Free trade**: A system of trading between states that is unrestricted by tariffs or other forms of protectionism.

● **Embedded liberalism**: A form of liberalism that seeks to reconcile the efficiency of markets with the broader values of social community.

● **Terms of trade**: The balance between import prices and export prices.

● **Balance of payments**: The balance of transactions conducted between a country and other countries, taking account of visible trade (exports and imports), invisible trade (services) and capital flows in the form of investments and loans.

GLOBAL ECONOMIC GOVERNANCE

Realist view

The realist stance on global economic governance is shaped by mercantilism and the belief that the world economy is essentially an arena of competition amongst states, each seeking to maximize its wealth and relative power. Economics is therefore largely explained in political terms. For realists, the combination of state egoism and international anarchy ensure that, in most circumstances, the scope for cooperation amongst states in economic affairs is very limited. This only alters, however, with the emergence of a hegemonic power, a state whose dominant military and economic position means that its interests are inextricably linked to those of the liberal world economy itself. As explained by hegemonic stability theory (see p. 236), a hegemon is necessary for the creation and full development of a liberal world economy because it is the only power that is willing and able to establish and enforce its basic rules. The Great Depression of the 1930s thus persisted as long as it did largely because the UK, as a fading hegemon, was no longer willing or able to re-establish economic stability (Kindleberger 1973). By the same token, the establishment of the Bretton Woods system marked the emergence of the USA as a hegemonic power. From the realist perspective, the breakdown of the system in the early 1970s reflected either the decline of US hegemony, or the emergence of the USA as a 'predatory hegemon'.

Liberal view

The liberal position on global economic governance is based on faith in the market and in untrammelled competition. As the workings of impersonal market forces draw resources towards their most profitable use and establish conditions of long-run equilibrium, it follows that any obstacle to the unfettered operation of markets should be ruled out. Such a stance could imply hostility towards any form of economic governance, whether operating on a national or global level. Nevertheless, most liberals accept the need for economic governance so long as it promotes, rather than restricts, openness and free competition. The emergence of a framework of global economic governance therefore reflected a recognition that, in conditions of economic interdependence, states have a mutual interest in upholding agreed norms and rules. The nature of these norms and rules is crucial,

however. From the perspective of economic liberalism, the Bretton Woods system was defective from the outset, because it set out to regulate a liberal economic order, not least though fixed exchange rates, that works best when it is free and unregulated. The breakdown of the Bretton Woods system thus reflected not the decline in US hegemony but fundamental flaws in the architecture of the Bretton Woods system itself. By comparison, the shift towards neoliberalism brought about by the emergence of the Washington consensus from the 1980s onwards marked the triumph of liberalism over the quasi-mercantilism of Bretton Woods.

Critical views

The two main critical approaches to global economic governance have been advanced from the perspectives, respectively, of social constructivism and neo-Marxist or post-Marxist theory. Social constructivists, such as Ruggie (1998, 2008), have emphasized the extent to which policies and institutional frameworks designed to regulate the world economy have been shaped by historical and sociological factors. The Bretton Woods system, thus, did not merely reflect a reconfiguration of state power and interests, but also a changing pattern of social expectations, norms and economic ideas in the form of 'embedded liberalism', which had come to be widely shared amongst industrialized states. Similarly, the later adoption of the Washington consensus owed a great deal to the growing hegemonic influence of neoliberal ideology, which helped to embed a belief in global markets. Neo-Marxists, such as world-systems theorists, and post-Marxist critical theorists have, for their part, challenged the liberal assumption that the institutions of global economic governance are neutral in the sense that they reflect the interests of all groups and all states (Soederberg 2006). Instead, they are constructed in line with the dominant interests in the global capitalist system: the USA as the leading capitalist state, transnational corporations (TNCs) (see p. 94) and banking conglomerates, and so on. For world-system theorists, the institutions of global economic governance have presided over a significant transfer of wealth and resources from 'peripheral' areas of the world economy to 'core' areas (Wallerstein 1984).

Fate of the Bretton Woods system

For at least two decades the Bretton Woods system appeared to be a remarkable success. Instead of the end of WWII and the consequent drop in military expenditure bringing back, as some had feared, the dark days of the Great Depression, it heralded the onset of the 'long boom' of the postwar period, the longest period of sustained economic growth the world economy had ever experienced. During the 'golden age' of the 1950s and 1960s, OECD member states consistently achieved average growth rates of 4–5 per cent per year. For many, this was a testament to the new stability in the world economy ushered in by Bretton Woods and the benefits of its mixture of free trade, free capital movement and stable currencies. How far Bretton Woods contributed to the economic boom of the postwar period is, however, a matter of debate. Many, for example, have argued that 'national' Keynesianism, through which governments stimulated domestic growth by running permanent budget deficits, had a greater impact than 'international' Keynesianism (Skidelsky 2009). Radical theorists, for their part, linked the long boom to the establishment of a 'permanent arms economy', a kind of 'military Keynesianism', in which the principal motor for growth was high and sustained military expenditure, legitimized by the Cold War (Oakes 1944). On the other hand, the economic stability of the period was perhaps not so much a product of a new era of multilateral governance but, rather, of the overwhelming economic dominance of the USA and the dollar. The USA contained, in 1950, some 60 per cent of all the capital stock across the industrialized world and was responsible for about 60 per cent of all industrial output. What thus made the Golden Age unusual was the USA's capacity to manage the world economy in its own interests. The Bretton Woods system has therefore been seen as an expression of US hegemony.

However, the long boom of the postwar period started to peter out in the late 1960s, leading to the 'stagflation' of the 1970s, in which economic stagnation and rising unemployment was linked to high inflation. The US economy was especially troubled by these difficulties, attempting to cope with spiralling spending at home and abroad, and, for the first time since 1945, facing increasingly stiff foreign competition. In 1971, the USA abandoned the system of fixed exchange rates, signalling, in effect, the end of the Bretton Woods system in its original form. The institutions set up as part of the Bretton Woods agreement nevertheless survived the transition from fixed to floating exchange rates, although their role and future policy focus initially remained unclear. In this context, the leaders and finance ministers of the major industrialized countries started to meet on a regular basis to discuss monetary issues and other matters related to the world economy. By 1975, this had led to the formation of the Group of Seven, or G-7 (see p. 472). The economic slowdown in the 1970s also weakened, and in some cases reversed, GATT's progress in reducing trade barriers, with industrialized countries in particular pushing-up **non-tariff barriers**. The resentment that this generated amongst developing countries, combined with recession, lead to growing support for a **'New International Economic Order'** (NIEO). Attempts to establish a NIEO nevertheless made little headway, a clear demonstration of where the balance of power in the world economy lay. Instead, during the 1980s, the institutions of global economic governance were reorientated around the ideas of the 'Washington consensus' (see p. 96). This, in effect, meant that a system based on embedded liberalism finally gave way to one based on neoliberalism (see p. 93).

● **Non-tariff barriers**: Rules, regulations or practices that hinder imports through, for instance, the procurement policies of governments, systematic border delays, or complex health and national standards.

● **New International Economic Order**: Proposals for the reform of the world economy to provide better protection for developing countries by, amongst other things, altering the terms of trade, strengthening regulation and nationalizing foreign enterprises.

Focus on . . .
The G-7/8: an abandoned project?

What has been the role and significance of the G-7/8, and why has it declined in importance? The Group of Seven (G-7) emerged out of a series of informal meetings of the finance ministers of the world's leading industrialized states (USA, France, Germany, the UK, Japan, Italy and Canada) that began in 1973. These took place against the backdrop of the collapse of the Bretton Woods system and the oil crisis of 1973. In 1975, the meetings were formalized and were expanded to include annual summit meetings of heads of government. When Russia was included in the heads of government meetings in 1997, the G-7 became the Group of Eight (G-8), although the G-7 framework survived for the finance ministers' meetings, as Russia was never included in these. The principal role of the G-7/8 was to ensure the overall coordination of the system of global economic governance. In this respect, the G-7/8 had some noted successes. For example, in the late 1970s, it persuaded West Germany and Japan to reflate their economies in return for US commitments to tighten fiscal policy to reduce inflation; it helped to break a log-jam that was threatening the Uruguay Round of WTO negotiations; and, in 2005, the G-8 agreed a bold scheme for debt relief for the world's poorest countries.

Nevertheless, over time, the G-7/8 served as a less and less effective mechanism for coordinating the system of global economic governance. In large part, this occurred because the advent of accelerated globalization in the 1980s, coupled with the shift in economic orthodoxy away from Keynesian managerialism and towards free-market thinking, left little scope or purpose for global macroeconomic policy. The perception that the G-7/8 was unable or unwilling to deal effectively with issues such as poverty and global inequality, trade policy and climate change, meant that G-8 summits in particular became an increasing focus of anti-globalization protest, especially at Genoa in 2001. Its effectiveness was further restricted by disagreements among G-8 leaders and its need to rely on consensus-building. However, the most serious limitation of the G-7/8 was that as the distribution of power within the global economy shifted towards emerging economies, its legitimacy was fatally compromised. Despite attempts to broaden the G-8 by including the so-called Outreach Five (China, Brazil, India, Mexico and South Africa), the use of the G-20 (see p. 121) as the principal vehicle for addressing the 2007–09 global financial crisis confirmed that G-7/8 had been replaced as the key forum for global economic decision-making.

EVALUATING GLOBAL ECONOMIC GOVERNANCE

The International Monetary Fund

The IMF was set up to oversee the new monetary order that had been established by the Bretton Woods agreement. Its chief purpose was to encourage international cooperation in the monetary field by removing foreign exchange restrictions, stabilizing exchange rates and facilitating a multilateral payment system between member countries. Member countries were committed to a system of fixed, but adaptable, exchange rates, with the IMF acting as a kind of 'currency buffer', granting loans to countries experiencing temporary balance-of-payments deficits. The system of fixed exchange rates established by Bretton Woods was based on the **gold exchange standard**, with the US dollar acting as an anchor. Its supposed advantage was that international business would flourish in conditions of stability, safe from the fear of currency fluctuations which would, in turn, alter the value of imports and exports. An element of flexibility was nevertheless introduced to this system by the fact that currency values could deviate from the rate fixed in relation to the US dollar by up to 1 per cent, meaning that in relation to other countries there could be deviations of up to 2 per cent. In the case of severe balance-of-payments instability, however, currencies could be **devalued**, although members of the IMF accepted that this was a strategy of the last resort.

The transition in the early 1970s from fixed to floating exchange rates fundamentally altered the function of the IMF. Abandoning its role as a 'currency buffer', the IMF increasingly focused on lending to the developing world and, after the end of the Cold War, to post-communist states, or **transition countries**. A particular concern of the IMF was to prevent financial crises, such as those in Mexico in 1982, Brazil in 1987, East Asia in 1997–98 and Russia in 1998, from spreading and threatening the entire global financial and currency system. The most controversial aspect of the loans that the IMF provided was that 'conditionalities' were attached to them. From the 1980s onwards, these conditions were shaped in line with the thinking of the Washington consensus, which required recipient countries to introduce 'structural adjustment' programmes (see p. 378) shaped by a faith in market fundamentalism. This led to a 'one size fits all' application of a neoliberal template based on the control of inflation ahead of other economic objectives, the immediate removal of barriers to trade and the flow of capital, the liberalization of the banking system, the reduction of government spending on everything except debt repayment, and the privatization of assets that could be sold to foreign investors.

Although structural adjustment programmes sometimes produced the required benefits, as in the case of South Korea, they often inflicted more harm than good on developing and transition countries. This occurred because of the destabilizing impact of 'shock therapy' market reforms which, by reducing government spending and rolling back welfare provision, increased poverty and unemployment, while economic openness exposed fragile economies to intensified foreign competition and expanded the influence of foreign banking and corporate interests. IMF-led structural adjustment thus often deepened, rather than reduced, economic crises in Asia, Russia and elsewhere, and, according to Joseph Stiglitz (see p. 474), it did so because the IMF responded, at heart, to the 'interests and ideology of the Western financial community'. The IMF, indeed, has been a focus of the wider criticism of global economic governance that it is an instrument of powerful economic interests in Northern economies, such as TNCs and international banking conglomerates, especially those linked to the USA, meaning that it is systematically biased against the interests of the developing world. The IMF's close relationship with the US government is illustrated not only by its location in Washington, DC and the fact that its deputy head, the First Deputy Managing Director, is always an American, but also by the allocation of voting rights on its Board of Governors in line with the size of a country's economy, which gives the USA an effective veto as most decisions require an 85 per cent majority.

● **Gold exchange standard**: A payments system in which currencies are valued in terms of a currency that is itself on the 'gold standard' (its currency can be exchanged for gold).

● **Devaluation**: The reduction in the official rate at which one currency is exchanged for another.

● **Transition countries**: Former Soviet bloc countries that are in the process of transition from central planning to market capitalism.

Joseph Stiglitz (born 1943)

Nobel Prize-winning US economist. The chair of President Clinton's Council of Economic Advisors, 1995–97, and chief economist of the World Bank, 1997–2000, Stiglitz is best known for his critical views on global economic governance and on globalization. In *Globalization and its Discontents* (2002), Stiglitz argued that the IMF had imposed policies on developing countries that often exacerbated, rather than relieved, balance-of-payments crises, being designed more to help banking and financial interests in the developed world than to alleviate poverty. In *Making Globalization Work* (2006), he linked globalization to 'Americanization', environmental degradation, a 'roll-back' of democracy and a widening of development disparities, calling instead for stronger and more transparent international institutions to expand economic opportunities and prevent financial crises. Stiglitz's other main works include *Whither Socialism?* (1996), *The Roaring Nineties* (2003) and *Freefall* (2010).

The IMF, by general agreement, has been slower to respond to criticism than its partner in promoting development, the World Bank. Nevertheless, in 2006 the IMF changed its governance to enhance the role of developing countries in its decision-making processes, a trend that was taken further in 2008 in the wake of the global financial crisis. The 2007–9 crisis, indeed, has effectively reformulated the mission of the IMF, making it less the arbiter of fiscal and macroeconomic rectitude in the developing world and more an instrument of global financial surveillance, designed to prevent crises rather than merely containing them. To be effective in this new role, however, the IMF would need to be significantly reformed, as discussed in the final section of this chapter.

The World Bank

The World Bank is, in a sense, the partner organization of the IMF. Both organizations were created by the Bretton Woods agreement, are housed in the same building in Washington, DC, have very similar weighted voting systems that take account of countries' strength in the global economy, and, particularly in the 1980s and 1990s, they shared a common neoliberal ideological orientation, shaped by the Washington consensus. Nevertheless, while the IMF and, for that matter, GATT/WTO have been primarily concerned to establish a regulative framework for international economic relations, the World Bank has an essentially redistributive function. This initially concentrated on assisting postwar recovery in Europe, but, from the 1960s onwards, increasingly focused on the developing world and, after the collapse of communism, transition countries. It does this by providing low interest loans to support major investment projects, as well as by providing technical assistance. How it has done this has changed significantly over time, however. During its early phase of so-called 'modernization without worry', it mainly supported large infrastructure projects in areas such as energy, telecommunications and transport. However, following the appointment in 1968 of Robert McNamara, a former US Secretary of Defence, as president of the World Bank, its priorities shifted towards projects dealing with basic needs

GLOBAL ACTORS . . .

INTERNATIONAL MONETARY FUND

Type: Intergovernmental organization • **Established:** 1947 • **Location:** Washington, DC
Membership: 188 states

The International Monetary Fund (IMF) was created as part of the 1944 Bretton Woods agreement. It was charged with overseeing the international monetary system to ensure exchange rate stability and encouraging members to eliminate restrictions on trade and currency exchange. This role ended with the collapse of the Bretton Woods system in 1971, with the IMF's role switching in the following decade to helping countries deal with the consequences of floating exchange rates and the oil crises of 1973 and 1979. From the early 1980s onwards, the IMF increasingly focused on supporting developing countries afflicted with debt crises and, in due course, transition countries. In its wider role, the IMF is responsible for managing financial crises and helping to ensure that national or regional crises do not develop into global crises. The IMF is a specialized agency of the United Nations (see p. 456), but has its own charter, governing structure and finances. Its highest decision-making body is the Board of Governors, on which voting rights reflect the relative economic strength of member states.

Significance: In its initial mission as the guarantor of exchange rate stability, the IMF was highly successful for at least two decades, helping to contribute to the sustained economic growth that the industrialized world experienced in the early post-1945 period. Moreover, the collapse of this system with the transition, in the early 1970s, from fixed to floating exchange rates had little to do with the ineffectiveness of the IMF as a body, although it may have reflected the long-term unsustainability of its initial mission. The IMF, nevertheless, became an increasingly controversial institution from the 1980s onwards. This was because it linked the provision of loans to developing and transition countries to conditions for 'structural adjustment' that reflected an unqualified faith in free markets and free trade. Supporters of the IMF argue that, despite short-term instability and insecurities, an adjustment to an open and market-based economy is the only reliable road to long-term economic success. Other strengths of the IMF are that it will often provide loans to countries that can find no other source of finance, and that its interest rates may be more competitive than those otherwise available. The IMF also provides extensive information services, not least reviewing and making recommendations about the economic health and stability of member states.

However, the IMF has been subject to often severe criticism. Radicals and many sympathetic to the anti-capitalist movement (see p. 74) have seen the IMF, and global economic governance generally, as the political arm of neoliberal globalization, forcing poor and vulnerable countries to accept a US business model that better caters to the needs of western banks and corporations than it does to long-term development needs. The fact that IMF intervention has often caused more problems that it has solved stems, critics argue, from its flawed development model, which fails to recognize the possibility of market failure or the drawbacks of economic openness. The IMF has also been viewed as an enemy of democracy and human rights (see p. 311), on the grounds that it has often provided support for military dictatorships, especially ones that were politically close to the USA or linked to western interests. Free-market economists have criticized the IMF, both on the grounds that 'structural adjustment' programmes are artificial and do not take account of the need for the development of an entrepreneurial culture and values, and on the grounds that particular 'remedies', such as devaluation and tax increases, may undermine market responsiveness. In the wake of the 2007–9 global financial crisis, the IMF was roundly criticized for not having prevented the crisis by highlighting the instabilities and imbalances that led to it. This led to calls for the reform of the IMF, particularly to strengthen its ability to regulate the global financial system. However, this has so far resulted in little more than a minor adjustment of voting rights in favour of developing states.

and what were perceived as the underlying causes of poverty, which drove the bank into areas such as population control, education and human rights.

However, the replacement of McNamara by A. W. Clausen in 1980 and the appointment of Ann Krueger as chief economist of the Bank in 1982, both critics of established approaches to development funding and more sympathetic towards market-orientated thinking, led, over the following decade, to a narrowly-focused concern with IMF-style structural adjustment policies. An emphasis on deregulation and privatization, and a stress on export-led growth rather than protectionism, often led to an increase, not a reduction, in poverty in Latin America, Asia and sub-Saharan Africa. World Bank adjustment programmes were usually wider in scope than those promoted by the IMF, having a more long-term development focus. However, in emphasizing the need to promote growth by expanding trade, particularly through the export of cash crops, the World Bank helped to maintain dependency and poverty. Development disparities thus became entrenched, and during the 1990s even widened, through a structural imbalance in trade that allowed developed countries to grow rich by selling high-price, capital-intensive goods, while developing countries sold low-price, labour-intensive goods, often in highly volatile markets. In this way, the World Bank, together with the IMF, presided over a substantial transfer of wealth from peripheral areas of the world economy to its industrialized core (Thurow 1996).

However, although the World Bank has remained faithful to the neoliberal paradigm that underpinned the Washington consensus, since the early 1990s it has responded to criticism from both without and within and accepted the need for reform. This has involved a greater awareness of the environmental costs of industrialization, urbanization and major infrastructure projects, helping to convert the Bank to the idea of sustainable development (see p. 397). A growing emphasis on good governance and anti-corruption policies also reflects a repudiation of the dogma of minimal government, based on the recognition that the state plays an essential role not only in ensuring civil order and containing criminal violence, but also in providing at least basic social protections. Furthermore, World Bank poverty reduction programmes have, since 2002, been increasingly formulated through negotiations with recipient countries, accepting the need for higher levels of local control and accountability and for projects to be better tailored to local needs. This has been reflected in a growing emphasis on 'partnership'. The desire to demonstrate a greater willingness to take on board the ideas of the developing world, particularly in the light of the 2007–09 global crisis, led the Bank in the spring of 2010 to boost its capital by $86 billion, the first increase in 20 years, and to allocate an additional seat on its Board of Directors to sub-Saharan Africa. The voting power of developing countries was also increased to 47 per cent, with the aim of increasing it to 50 per cent over time.

The World Trade Organization

The World Trade Organization was formed in 1995 as a replacement for GATT, established in 1947. However, GATT only emerged as the basis of the postwar international trading order as a result of the failure to establish the International Trade Organization (ITO). The ITO had been proposed in 1945 by the UN Economic and Social Council, and would have constituted a fully-fledged international organization, comparable with the IMF and the World Bank, with powers more in line with those of the later WTO. Its implementation was nevertheless abandoned once President Truman failed to submit its founding treaty, the Havana Charter (1948), to the US Senate for approval, fearing that the Senate would regard the organization as a threat to US sovereignty. In essence, GATT was an agreement amongst member countries to apply the multilateral principles of non-discrimination and reciprocity to matters of trade. This was guaranteed by the requirement that each country had to concede **most favoured nation** status to all trading partners. No trading partner could therefore be treated more favourably than any other.

The GATT trade regime was nevertheless limited in a number of ways. In the first place, GATT existed only as a set of norms and rules, acquiring the semblance of an institutional character only with the establishment in 1960 of the GATT Council. Its focus, moreover, was restricted to the reduction of tariff barriers against imported manufactured goods. Not only did this mean that agriculture and the growing service sector of the economy were largely off the agenda as far as GATT was concerned, but it also meant that GATT had a limited capacity to check the growth of 'non-tariff barriers'. GATT's procedures for settling disputes between trading partners were also weak. Nevertheless, within these parameters, GATT was highly successful. During its fifth, sixth and seventh rounds of negotiation in particular – the Kennedy Round, the Tokyo Round and the Uruguay Round – tariffs on manufactured goods were brought down so substantially that, in practical terms, they had almost been eradicated. Whereas average tariffs on the import value of goods in 1947 had stood at 40 per cent, this had been reduced to about 3 per cent by 2000. The final three GATT negotiating rounds had, further, made some progress in tackling non-tariff barriers, such as 'dumping' (flooding a market with large quantities of cheap exports in order to weaken the domestic industry), and had started to deal with a wider range of subjects, such as services, intellectual property, textiles and agriculture.

Nevertheless, the overall limitations of GATT became increasingly apparent during the Uruguay Round, which concluded in 1993 with the proposal to establish the WTO. In many ways, the emergence of the WTO was a response to the changing imperatives of the international trading system in the 1980s, linked to the wider triumph of neoliberalism and the acceleration of globalization. This created stronger pressure to advance the cause of free trade through a more powerful trade organization with broader responsibilities, something akin to the ILO that never was. The broader responsibilities of the WTO were achieved through incorporation not merely of a renegotiated GATT (sometimes called GATT 1994, as opposed to the original GATT 1947), and its framework of agreements concerning manufactured goods, but also agreements on the trade in services (GATS) and on the protection of intellectual property (TRIPS). This broadening was also evident in the formal recognition of 'new' or hidden protectionism in the form of non-tariff barriers that had particularly bedevilled international trade since the 1970s. The WTO is stronger than GATT, particularly in the field of dispute settlement. Under GATT, the settlement of disputes required the agreement of all members of a disputes panel, which comprised the members of the GATT Council, as well as the parties to the dispute itself. Under the WTO, by contrast, settlement judgements in the case of disputes can only be rejected if they are opposed by *all* members of the Dispute Settlement Body, to which *all*

● **Most favoured nation**: A designation given to a country which is thereby entitled to all and any favourable trading terms that apply to other countries.

GATT/WTO negotiating rounds

1947	23 countries sign the GATT treaty, which comes into force on 1 January 1948.
1949	Second GATT round held at Annecy, France.
1950	Third GATT round held at Torquay, the UK.
1955–6	Fourth GATT round held at Geneva, Switzerland.
1960–2	Fifth GATT round, called the Dillon Round after US Secretary of Treasury Douglas Dillon.
1964–7	Kennedy Round – achieves tariff cuts worth $40 billion of world trade.
1973–9	Tokyo Round – achieves tariff reductions worth more than $300 billion and reductions in non-tariff barriers.
1986–93	Uruguay Round – trading system extended into areas such as services and intellectual property; rules covering agriculture and textiles reformed; and agreement to create the World Trade Organization, established in 1995.
2001	Doha Round launched by the WTO.

member states belong. In effect, this has made the WTO the primary instrument of international law (see p. 339) in the area of trade.

However, the rules of the new organization were also shaped by the interests of key parties to the Uruguay Round negotiations. The decision to include agriculture and textiles within the WTO's responsibilities was a concession made to developing countries, which were also in the forefront of campaigning to bring non-tariff barriers within the regime, particularly as these had often been erected by developed countries. On the other hand, developed countries had been particularly keen to extend the trading regime to include services, as their economies were becoming increasingly service-orientated, with manufacturing being increasingly transferred from the developed world to the developing world. Furthermore, although agriculture was formally brought into the WTO regime, the agreement on agriculture was weak and allowed considerable scope for continued agricultural protection, a matter of particular concern for the USA and European Union. In some respects, the WTO appears to be a more democratic body than the IMF or the World Bank. Decisions are made within the WTO on a 'one country, one vote' basis, and usually require only a simple majority. These rules, in theory, give considerable weight to the views of developing countries, which constitute more than two-thirds of the WTO's members. However, the WTO is a highly controversial organization, which has often been the primary target of anti-globalization or anti-capitalist protests, as in the case of the 1999 Battle of Seattle.

Critics of the WTO argue that subtle biases operate within the decision-making structures that systematically favour developed countries over developing ones. These include a general emphasis on consensus-based decision-making, which tends to disadvantage developing countries which may have no permanent representation at the WTO's Geneva headquarters or have delegations much smaller then those of developed countries, or they may be excluded from the club-like meetings that are usually dominated by developed countries. Similarly, developed countries are much more likely to bring issues before the dispute settlement panel, and are more likely to offer to serve as 'third parties', able to influence the dispute settlement process, whereas the bulk of allegations of unfair trading practices are made against developing countries. Such subtle biases and the general lack of transparency and accountability in its decision-making processes have led to the WTO being described as a 'rich man's club'. However, the economic rise of China, which became a WTO member in 2001, and the growing influence of emerging economies such as India, Brazil, Egypt and South Africa, has started to alter balances within the WTO. This has been demonstrated in particular by the stalling of the Doha Round of negotiations, which were initiated in 2001 but which were suspended in 2009, largely due to disagreement over agriculture and textiles, where the USA and the EU were unwilling to abandon protectionism. Nevertheless, the main ideological debate about the benefits or otherwise of the WTO centres on its underpinning philosophy of free trade. While some argue that free trade brings prosperity to all and, in the process, makes war less likely, others view fair trade as blatantly unfair and a cause of structural inequality.

REFORMING THE BRETTON WOODS SYSTEM?

Global economic governance and the 2007–9 crisis

There is nothing new about concern over the performance of global economic governance. The institutional architecture was put in place to address the problems exposed by the economic turmoil of the 1930s, and yet financial and economic crises have occurred on a fairly regular basis since the 1960s, and, indeed, have become increasingly frequent and more serious since the 1980s. After both the Asian financial crisis of 1997–8 and the dot-com crisis of 2000 in particular, criticisms were voiced about the failure of the global economic governance system to provide adequate warnings by highlighting, in advance, key instabilities and crisis tendencies. In the case of the Asian crisis, IMF intervention was seen by some to have made the crisis more severe, not less severe. Moreover, intellectual and academic arguments about the growing and uncontained instabilities in the global economy had been gathering strength for some time. For instance, Susan Strange (1986, 1998) had highlighted the dangers of what she called 'casino capitalism', in which the unregulated dynamics of global capital movements allowed what she called 'mad money' to surge around the world in speculative bursts, creating unsustainable 'bubbles' and dramatic crises (see Chapter 4, for a discussion of the crises of modern global capitalism). Similarly, a string of high profile economic commentators, including Joseph

Debating . . .
Does free trade ensure prosperity and peace?

Although free trade has been an issue of debate since the nineteenth century, in modern global politics it is largely associated with the WTO's commitment to a *laissez-faire* paradigm of free trade. Does free trade bring prosperity for all and reduce the likelihood of war, or does it lead to unfairness and put national security at risk?

YES

Benefits of specialization. The key economic argument in favour of free trade, which can be traced back to the ideas of Adam Smith (see p. 88) and David Ricardo (1772–1823), is the theory of comparative advantage (sometimes known as 'comparative costs'). This suggests that international trade benefits all countries because it allows each country to specialize in the production of the goods and services that it is best suited to produce (in view of its natural resources, climate, skills, size of population and so on). Free trade thus draws economic resources, at the international level, to their most profitable use, and so delivers general prosperity.

Efficiency and choice. Free trade brings further economic advantages. These include that specialization enables production to be carried out on a larger scale and therefore offers the prospect of greater efficiency. Economies of scale, for instance, can be gained through the greater use of the division of labour, the ability to buy raw materials or components more cheaply and the lower cost of overheads. In addition, consumers benefit both because they have a wider choice of goods, including foreign-produced goods as well as domestically produced goods, and because more intense competition, particularly from more efficient and low-cost producers, tends to keep prices down.

Peace and cosmopolitanism. The central political argument in favour of free trade is that it helps to underpin international peace and harmony. This occurs for two reasons. First, in leading to greater economic interdependence, it pushes up the material cost of international conflict and makes warfare between trading partners virtually unthinkable. Second, economic links and intercourse between countries cannot but lead to greater understanding between them and strengthened respect for each other's distinctive cultures and national traditions. Protectionism, by contrast, is associated with war, because countries that seek resources but cannot acquire them through trade are inclined to resort to expansionism and conquest.

NO

Free trade as neo-colonialism. Free trade benefits industrialized and economically advanced countries at the expense of poor and developing ones. This is why the cause of free trade has been advanced most forcefully by dominant powers within the world economy, notably the UK in the nineteenth century and the USA since the mid-twentieth century. Such countries benefit from the reduction of trade barriers because it gives them access to larger markets for their goods whilst, at the same time, keeping the price of raw materials and other imported goods low. Developing countries, for their part, are disadvantaged by being forced to serve the needs of the world economy. This locks them in to the production of food and raw materials, thereby preventing them from making further economic progress.

Development through protectionism. Without rejecting the wider advantages of international trade, there are clearly a number of circumstances in which protectionism is economically beneficial. The most obvious of these is in the early stages of economic development, which can be distorted or stunted by unfair competition from stronger economies. Exposing fragile economies and so-called 'infant' industries to the full force of international competition simply ensures that they never develop, hence the need for the strategic use of protectionist measures to create a domestic economic environment more favourable to growth.

National security protectionism. The core political argument against free trade is that not all industries are alike in terms of their strategic significance. In short, national security trumps economic efficiency. This applies most obviously in the case of agriculture, where states have been anxious to avoid a dependency on other states for the supply of foodstuffs in case such supplies are curtailed through international crises or war. The same argument also applies in the case of vital natural resources, with a growing emphasis being placed on the need for protectionism to ensure 'energy security'.

Stiglitz, Paul Krugman (see p. 110) and George Soros (see p. 110), have highlighted the dangers implicit in the dogma of market fundamentalism that underpinned neoliberal globalization and helped to shape the Washington consensus. Nevertheless, nothing came of these warnings and criticisms, largely because they occurred against the backdrop of three decades of growth in the global economy and because the crises that had occurred predominantly affected emerging or transition economies, rather than those at the core of the world economy.

However, the global financial crisis of 2007–9 posed a series of deeper and more challenging problems. In the first place, it was deeper than the previous crises of modern global capitalism (see p. 109), amounting to the most severe downturn in the world economy since the 1930s. According to the World Bank, global GDP fell in 2009 by 1.7 per cent, the first decline in world output on record, and the volume of world trade dropped by 6.1 per cent, leading to this being dubbed the 'Great Recession' (as opposed to the Great Depression of the 1930s). Second, although its severity varied from country to country and from region to region, its impact was genuinely global, in that it affected virtually every country in the world. Third, instead of occurring in emerging or transition economies, it originated within the beating heart of finance capitalism, the USA (Seabrooke and Tsingou 2010). In this light, and especially after the remarkable events of September 2008, when stock markets around the world plummeted and global capitalism appeared to be on the brink of collapse, it is not surprising that the 2007–9 crisis and the related Great Recession led to calls for the urgent reform of the architecture of global economic governance (see p. 482). Initially at least, this was often expressed in calls for a 'new Bretton Woods'.

But what would a new Bretton Woods look like? There is no single model of reformed global economic governance, but rather a number of models. Indeed, perhaps the only thing these competing models have in common is that none of them envisages a fully-fledged return to Bretton Woods. None of them, in other words, proposes the re-establishment of a dollar-based gold exchange standard, if only because a return to fixed exchange rates is widely deemed to be unfeasible in modern, globalized economic circumstances. From the market fundamentalist perspective, moreover, the most appropriate response to the crisis has been, in effect, to do nothing. In this view, financial and economic crises are a small price to pay for roughly thirty years of sustained growth in the world economy, and, anyway, any attempt to strengthen national or global regulation will only make matters worse not better. On the other hand, for regulatory liberals, who draw on Keynesian or other insights about the fallibility of markets, what is needed is specific reforms of the global financial architecture, as well as new regulatory regimes at the domestic level (Gamble 2009). From this perspective, reform has to focus on curbing the excesses of neoliberalism, something that is impossible while the Washington consensus, even in its modified form, remains dominant. A variety of reforms have therefore been proposed, particularly in relation to the IMF and the World Bank. These include changing voting allocations and decision-making processes to increase the political influence of developing countries and weaken links between these bodies and Northern countries and interests; strengthening their ability to support countries adversely affected by debt and crises; and bolstering their capacity to oversee and regulate the world economy, with a view to preventing, rather than merely responding to, future crises.

Global economic governance and the 'Great Recession'

Events: At the height of the global financial crisis in September 2008, as banking crises erupted in the USA, the UK and elsewhere, and stock markets went into freefall worldwide, business and consumer confidence collapsed, giving rise to the most severe global recession since the Great Depression of the 1930s. During 2008–9, in what was later dubbed the 'Great Recession', most developed economies contracted and growth rates fell significantly across the developing world. The International Labour Organization estimated that global unemployment increased by 14 million people in 2008 alone. The G-20 (see p. 121) quickly became the leading mechanism through which the international community attempted to manage its response. In Washington in November 2008, and at their April 2009 London Summit, the G-20 countries committed themselves to an integrated strategy, which involved substantial and speedy cuts in interest rates (monetary stimulus), the boosting of domestic demand by economically advanced states (fiscal stimulus) and an agreement to resist pressure to increase tariffs and return to economic nationalism. In Seoul in November 2010, the G-20 pledged to reform the IMF, both by strengthening the voice and representation of the developing world within the organization and by tightening the IMF's surveillance of national and global economic circumstances.

Significance: For many, the 2007–9 global financial crisis highlighted the spectacular failure of global economic governance, whose key institutions had, because of their commitment to neoliberal economics, presided over an inadequate system of banking and financial regulation. Similarly, the Great Recession has demonstrated that the world lacks an appropriate and effective mechanism for responding to crises. The consensus over macroeconomic policy that had been fashioned at Washington and London broke down at the 2010 Toronto G-20 Summit, as a growing number of countries, concerned about rising debt levels, embraced austerity policies rather than sustained fiscal and monetary expansion, as advocated by Obama and the USA. From 2011 onwards, a new phase in the crisis also emerged through an escalating sovereign debt crisis in Europe (see p. 112). Although the IMF shared with the EU responsibility for international bail-outs to Greece, Portugal, Spain and other countries, it showed both a lack of leadership and an inability to come

up with fresh ideas (particularly about how to address debt challenges without damaging growth), allowing the response to the eurozone crisis to be largely dictated by a German-dominated EU. Furthermore, not only has the much-vaunted reform of the IMF failed to materialize beyond a minor adjustment of quota shares and increased funding, but the organization is increasingly looking like an irrelevant Euro-Atlantic body in a global economy in which power is shifting to China and other emerging states.

Nevertheless, if the Great Recession was a 'stress test' for global economic governance, the system may have come out of it in surprisingly good shape (Drezner, 2012). This is demonstrated by the fact that while the percentage drop in global industrial output and world trade levels at the start of the 2008 crisis were more severe than the fall-offs following the Wall Street Crash of 1929, the post-2008 rebound was significantly more robust. Four years after the onset of the Great Recession, global industrial output was 10 per cent higher than when the recession began; in contrast, four years after the onset of the Great Depression, industrial output was only two-thirds of the pre-crisis level (Eichengreen and O'Rourke, 2012). After 2008, there was a much higher level of international cooperation than in the 1930s, born out of a keener awareness of mutual vulnerabilities (possibly, thanks to globalization) and more robust than expected US leadership. Amongst the manifestations of this was concerted resistance to 'beggar-thy-neighbour' protectionism. By 2012, trade flows were thus 5 per cent higher than in 2008, while four years after the 1929 Crash they remained 25 per cent lower than pre-crisis levels.

Focus on . . .
The BRICs: the 'rise of the rest'?

How influential are the BRICs group of countries? Does the rise of the BRICs mark a decisive shift in the global balance of power and the end of US hegemony? The term 'BRICs' was coined in 2001 in a report by Goldman Sachs, the investment bank, to highlight the growing significance of four large, fast-growing economies – Brazil, Russia, India and China. Initial predictions of the growing economic might of the BRICs suggested that they would exceed the combined strength of the G-7 countries by the middle of the twenty-first century, although this has been repeatedly revised and could occur as early as 2021. In addition to highlighting a shift in the power balances of the global economy, with most of the growth in world output now coming from developing, transitional and emerging economies, the 'rise of the rest' (Zakaria 2009) has a growing political dimension. Initiated by Russia, BRICs foreign ministers' meetings, and sometimes heads of states' meetings have been occurring since 2006. The main goals of these BRICs meetings have been to counter-balance the USA by ensuring better representation for themselves – through, for instance, the G-20 and the Financial Stability Board – and by expanding the influence of the global South, allowing the BRICs to be portrayed as the 'guardian of the interests of developing countries'. Some, therefore, view the rise of the BRICs as a major challenge to the US-dominated liberal western order.

However, the significance of the rise of the BRICs may have been overstated. In the first place, no concrete agenda for changing the global economic governance system has emerged from BRICs meetings, still less a vision of what a post-western economic order might look like. Indeed, far from overthrowing the established order, the BRICs appear to be more intent on strengthening their position within it, enabling them to establish a partnership with the USA rather than indulging in 'hard' balancing. Second, the capacity of the BRICs to act as a single entity is severely restricted by political, ideological and economic differences amongst its members. Brazil and India are democracies, while China and Russia are authoritarian and practise a form of state capitalism. Similarly, while Brazil and Russia are commodity exporters, specializing, respectively, in agriculture and natural resources, India, which specializes in services, and China, which specializes in manufacturing, are both commodity importers. Frictions from persistent Sino-Russian and Sino-Indian rivalry are likely significantly to impede the construction of an anti-US alliance, even if one were thought to be desirable. Third, the BRICs is a forum with highly unequal members. Although Russia may be its most assertive political voice, China is easily its dominant economic force. The principal significance of the BRICs may be less that it reflects the common interests of 'the rest' and more that it is a device through which China can engage in 'soft' balancing with the USA without risking direct confrontation.

More radical proposals for reform have also been advanced, however. Cosmopolitan liberals have called not for the reform of the existing architecture of global economic governance but for an entirely new form of global governance to replace deeply flawed bodies such as the IMF, the World Bank and the WTO. New global architecture would have to be constructed on a more inclusive basis, taking much fuller account of the views and ideas of global civil society, and it would need to be orientated around the principle of 'cosmopolitan democracy' (Held 1995). For anti-capitalists, however, the problems exposed by the financial crisis and the Great Recession go deeper still. Rather than highlighting flaws or failings in the framework of global economic governance, they reflected the imbalances and inequalities of the global economy itself. What is required, from this perspective, is therefore a substantial redistribution of wealth and power both within national societies and within the global economy (Monbiot 2004).

However, apart from the rising significance of the G-20, and the declining importance of the G-7/8, as a mechanism for developing and coordinating strategy related to the world economy, the institutional response to the 2007–9 crisis, particularly at the global level, has been modest. The three pillars of global economic governance have survived the crisis, just as they survived the end of the Bretton Woods system, and although there has been some adjustment in the allocation of voting rights within the IMF and World Bank in favour of developing countries, fundamental power balances within these bodies remain substantially unchanged. The chief institutional development has been the establishment in April 2009 of the Financial Stability Board (FSB) as the successor to the Financial Stability Forum, a proposal that came out of the 2009 G-20 London summit. The purpose of the FSB is to coordinate at the global level the work of national financial authorities and international standard-setting bodies and to promote the implementation of effective regulatory, supervisory and other financial sector policies. The creation of the FSB as potentially the fourth pillar of the architecture of global economic governance is, in effect, an acknowledgement that even a reformed IMF is unlikely to be an effective mechanism for alerting policy-makers at national, regional and global levels to structural instabilities in their economies, helping thereby to prevent future crises. Nevertheless, although FSB member countries include all the G-20 major economies, as well as other developed or emerging economies, it affords the mass of the world's developing countries no representation whatsoever.

Obstacles to reform

It may not be possible for some time to make a judgement about how the architecture of global economic governance has responded to the 2007–09 global crisis. After all, in the case of both the Great Depression of the 1930s and the stagflation crisis of the 1970s, about a decade elapsed before an institutional response emerged, in the form of Bretton Woods and the Washington consensus, respectively. Nevertheless, the predominant response to date has been: 'business as usual'. How can this be explained? In the first place, the initial management of the crisis by the G-20, coordinating swift action at the domestic level to salvage the banking system and push though Keynesian-style reflationary policies, appeared to be effective. In particular, G-20 action managed to counter pressure for a resort to national protectionism, creating optimism that the global downturn, though severe, would be shorter than had been feared at the outset. A further but crucial factor has been the changing balance of power within the world economy. The decisive moments in the development of global economic governance – the making of Bretton Woods in 1944 and the transition to the Washington consensus in the mid 1980s – were both expressions of the USA's hegemonic power. Although the USA, under Obama, initially took a leading role in formulating the G-20's response to the crisis, and also shouldered significant responsibility for promoting domestic reflation, the USA no longer has the ability to re-orientate, still less reformulate, the global economic governance system at will (always assuming that it had the desire to do so). Any such development would, in future, be significantly influenced by the views, interests and requirements of new powers, especially China, but also India, Russia and Brazil, sometimes collectively referred to as the BRICs group of countries (see p. 483). Emerging economic multipolarity (see p. 237) is likely to ensure that any change to global economic governance will be gradual and incremental, effectively ruling out the kind of comprehensive and radical restructuring that can only be brought about through the existence of a global hegemon.

SUMMARY

- Global governance is a broad, dynamic and complex process of interactive decision-making at the global level. It hovers somewhere between the Westphalian state-system and the fanciful idea of world government. Although it involves binding norms and rules, these are not enforced by a supranational authority.

- Liberal theorists argue that there is an unmistakable, and perhaps irresistible, trend in favour of global governance, reflecting the growing interdependence and a greater willingness of states to engage in collective action. However, global governance is more an emerging process than an established system.

- The trend towards global governance has been particularly prominent in the economic sphere, where it has been associated with the Bretton Woods system that emerged in the aftermath of WWII. This system was based on three bodies: the International Monetary Fund, the World Bank and the General Agreement on Tariffs and Trade, replaced by the World Trade Organization in 1995.

- The Bretton Woods system initially supervised the world economy largely though the maintenance of stable exchange rates. This system nevertheless broke down in the early 1970s as floating exchange rates replaced fixed exchange rates, starting the process through which the Bretton Woods institutions were converted to the cause of economic liberalization.

- The IMF, the World Bank and the World Trade Organization have each, in their different ways, been drawn into controversy through their association with the processes of neoliberal globalization. Although supporters argue that they have contributed to a remarkable expansion of the global economy, critics claim that they have deepened global disparities and helped to produce an inherently unstable financial order.

- The 2007–09 global financial crisis has raised pressing concerns about the effectiveness of global economic governance, leading to calls for reform. However, major obstacles stand in the way of reform, not least the continuing dominance, in many countries, of neoliberal principles and the more diffuse location of global power.

Questions for discussion

- How, and to what extent, does global governance differ from international anarchy?
- Could global governance ever lead to world government?
- How does global governance blur the public/private divide?
- How far does modern world politics operate as a functioning global governance system?
- Why is global governance most advanced in the economic sphere?
- What was the thinking behind the creation of the Bretton Woods system?
- Is the IMF merely an instrument of powerful economic interests in Northern economies?
- How successful has the World Bank been in helping the world's poor?
- Is the global trading system crated by the WTO fair and effective?
- How has the 2007–09 crisis affected the processes of global economic governance?

Further reading

Goldin, I., *Divided Nations: Why Global Governance is Failing and What We Can Do About It* (2013). A stimulating examination of the defects of the current global governance system, from the perspective of an 'optimist'.

Karns, M. and K. Mingst, *International Organizations: The Politics and Processes of Global Governance* (2009). An authoritative introduction to the challenges of global governance and the role and performance of international organizations.

Peet, R., *Unholy Trinity: The IMF, World Bank and WTO* (2009). A critical examination of the birth, development and performance of the key Bretton Woods organizations.

Whitman, J. (ed.), *Global Governance* (2009). A very useful collection of essays that examine the nature and implications of global governance.

ONLINE RESOURCES AVAILABLE

Links to relevant web resources can be found on the *Global Politics* website

CHAPTER 20

Regionalism and Global Politics

'Europe has never existed . . . one has genuinely to create Europe.'

JEAN MONNET (1888–1979)

PREVIEW   The common assertion that world politics is being reconfigured on global lines has increasingly been challenged by the rival image of an emerging 'world of regions'. In this view, regionalism is both the successor to the nation-state and an alternative to globalization. Since 1945, regional organizations have sprung up in all parts of the world. The first phase of this process peaked in the 1960s, but the advance of regionalism has been particularly notable since the late 1980s. This has given rise to the phenomenon of the 'new' regionalism. Whereas earlier forms of regionalism had promoted regional cooperation, and even integration, over a range of issues – security, political, economic and so on – the 'new' regionalism has been reflected in the creation of regional trade blocs, either the establishment of new ones or the strengthening of existing ones. Some even believe that this is creating a world of competing trading blocs. But what are the main forces driving regional integration? Is regionalism the enemy of globalization, or are these two trends interlinked and mutually reinforcing? Does the advance of regionalism threaten global order and stability? Without doubt, the most advanced example of regionalism anywhere in the world is found in Europe. The European Union (EU) has engaged in experiments with supranational cooperation that have involved political and monetary union as well as economic union. In the process, it has developed into a political organization that is neither, strictly speaking, a conventional international organization nor a state, but has features of each. How is the EU best understood? To what extent does the EU constitute an effective global actor, or even a superpower? And is the European experience of integration unique to Europe itself, or does it constitute a model for the rest of the world to follow?

KEY ISSUES
- What is regionalism, and what are the main forms it has taken?
- Why has regionalism grown in prominence?
- What is the relationship between regionalism and globalization?
- How does regionalism in Europe differ from regionalism in other parts of the world?
- What is the nature and significance of European integration?

REGIONS AND REGIONALISM

Nature of regionalism

Regionalism (see p. 489), broadly, is a process through which geographical regions become significant political and/or economic units, serving as the basis for cooperation and, possibly, identity. Regionalism has two faces, however. In the first, it is a sub-national phenomenon, a process of **decentralization** that takes place *within* countries. This applies, for example, in the case of states that practise **federalism**. These states include the USA, Brazil, Pakistan, Australia, Mexico, Sweden, Nigeria, Malaysia and Canada. Sub-national regionalism is also found in states that practise **devolution**, such as Spain, France and the UK. The second face of regionalism is transnational rather than sub-national. In this, regionalism refers to a process of cooperation or integration *between* countries in the same region of the world. It is with this form of regionalism – regionalism in world politics – that this chapter is concerned.

Nevertheless, sub-national and transnational regionalism may not be as distinct as they appear. First, all forms of regionalism exhibit the same core dynamic, in the form of a relationship between the centre and the periphery, and thus between the forces of unity and diversity. Second, **centralization** within a system of transnational regionalism can lead to a process of state formation, from which a system of sub-national regionalism may emerge. In this sense, the creation of the United States of America may be the most dramatic historical example of the significance of regionalism. Once the 13 former British colonies in North America had gained sovereign independence through victory in the War of Independence (1776), they formed a **confederation**, first in the form of the Continental Congresses (1774–81), and then under the Articles of Confederation (1781–9). However, in the hope of gaining greater external influence and better coordinating their internal relations, these former colonies joined together and founded the United States of America, achieved in 1789 through the ratification of the US Constitution. The USA, in turn, became the world's first federal state. US regionalism subsequently became a model for other sub-national regional projects, but it has also inspired some transnational projects, notably in Europe through the idea of a 'United States of Europe'. Third, the distinction between sub-national and transnational regionalism may be blurred by the fact that sub-national regions sometimes have a transnational character, in that they cross state borders and may thus affect relations between states. For instance, the Kurdish region in the Middle East includes eastern Turkey, northern Iraq and parts of Syria and Iran, creating migratory flows and giving rise to forms of separatist nationalism. Links between the economies of San Diego, California, and Tijuana, Mexico, have also created a form of microregional integration that exists at a different level from US–Mexican regional cooperation through the North American Free Trade Agreement (NAFTA) (Breslin 2010).

An ongoing problem with regionalism has nevertheless been the difficulty of establishing the nature and extent of a region. What is a 'region'? On the face of it, a region is a distinctive geographical area. Regions can therefore be identified by consulting maps. This leads to a tendency to identify regions with continents, as applies in the case of Europe (through the European Union (EU) (see p. 509)), Africa (through the African Union (AU)) and America (through the

● **Decentralization**: The expansion of local autonomy through the transfer of powers and responsibilities away from national bodies.

● **Federalism**: A territorial distribution of power based on a sharing of sovereignty between central (national or international) bodies and peripheral ones (see p. 133)

● **Devolution**: The transfer of power from central government to subordinate regional institutions that, unlike federal institutions, have no share in sovereignty.

● **Centralization**: The concentration of political power or government authority at the centre.

● **Confederation**: A qualified union of states in which each state retains independence, typically guaranteed by unanimous decision-making.

CONCEPT

Regionalism

Regionalism is the theory or practice of coordinating social, economic or political activities within a geographical region comprising a number of states. On an institutional level, regionalism involves the growth of norms, rules and formal structures through which coordination is brought about. On an affective level, it implies a realignment of political identities and loyalties from the state to the region. The extent of regional integration may nevertheless range from cooperation amongst sovereign states on the basis of intergovernmentalism (see p. 466) to the transfer of authority from states to central decision-making bodies, in accordance with supranationalism (see p. 465).

Organization of American States). However, many regional organizations are sub-continental, such as the Association of South-East Asian Nations (ASEAN), the Southern African Customs Union and the Central American Common Market, while others are transcontinental, such as Asia-Pacific Economic Cooperation (APEC) and the North Atlantic Treaty Organization (NATO) (see p. 259). An alternative basis for regional identity is socio-cultural, reflecting similarities of religion, language, history or even ideological belief amongst a number of neighbouring states. Cultural identity is particularly important in the case of bodies such as the Arab League and the Nordic Council, and it may also apply in the case of the EU, where membership requires an explicit commitment to liberal-democratic values. In this view, a region may even be the geographical expression of a civilization, as implied by Huntington's 'clash of civilizations' thesis. However, economic integration in particular has often focused on establishing cooperation among countries that were formerly hostile to one another or which are divided in terms of their cultural or ideological identity. Indeed, if a culturally-based sense of belonging were viewed as an essential feature of a region, no 'regions' could be found anywhere in the world, as no regional organization, including the EU, has come close to rivalling, still less supplanting, a political identification with the nation-state.

The matter is further complicated, though, by the fact that regional identities (insofar as they exist) are often multiple and overlapping. For example, is Mexico part of North America (by virtue of being a member of NAFTA), part of Central America (by virtue of pre-colonial cultural inheritance), part of Latin America (by virtue of its language, culture and history of Spanish colonization), or part of Asia-Pacific (by virtue of its membership of APEC)? The answer, of course, is that it is all of these things. Regional identities are not mutually exclusive, nor are they (thankfully, for regionalism) incompatible with national identity. In the final analysis, regions are politically and socially constructed. Like the nation, the region is an 'imagined community' (Anderson 1983). Ultimately, 'Europe', 'Africa', 'Asia', and 'Latin America' are ideas, not concrete geographical, political, economic or cultural entities. Being political constructs, regions are almost endlessly fluid, capable of being redefined and reshaped, both as the extent and purposes of cooperation change over time, and as new members join or existing members leave. This also explains why regional identities are often contested. Competing models or 'projects' of regional integration may surface among, for example, different states, different political groups, or between economic and political elites and the wider population.

Finally, regionalism takes different forms depending on the primary areas over which neighbouring states choose to cooperate. Three types of regionalism can thus be identified:

- Economic regionalism
- Security regionalism
- Political regionalism.

Economic regionalism refers to the creation of greater economic opportunities through cooperation among states in the same geographical region. It is the primary form of regional integration, and it has become more so since the advent of so-called 'new' regionalism in the early 1990s, manifested in the growth of regional trade blocs and the deepening of existing trade blocs. This surge has continued unabated, so that, by 2005, only one WTO member – Mongolia – was not party to a regional trade agreement (RTA). By February 2010, 462 RTAs had been notified to GATT/World Trade Organization (WTO) (see p. 475). In most cases, these trade agreements establish **free trade areas**, but in other cases they may establish **customs unions** or **common markets**. Such agreements are accepted by the WTO as the only exception to its principle of equal treatment for all trading partners, based on granting all WTO members 'most favoured nation' status.

Security regionalism refers to forms of cooperation designed to protect states from their enemies, both neighbouring and distant ones. Regional integration may thus give rise what Karl Deutsch (1957) called a **'security community'**. This applies in two ways. First, regional bodies seek to enmesh their members within a system of 'peace through cooperation', in which ever deeper levels of interdependence and integration, particularly over economic matters, make war between member states unthinkable. One of the key motivations behind the formation of the European Coal and Steel Community (ECSC) in 1952, and the European Economic Community (EEC) in 1958 was to prevent a future war between France and Germany. The other security motivation behind regional cooperation is the desire to gain protection against a common external enemy. European integration was thus seen as a means of safeguarding Europe from the threat of Soviet expansionism; ASEAN's original role involved providing mutual defence against communism; and the Southern African Development Coordination Conference provided protection against apartheid-era South Africa. Security regionalism is also evident in the global trend in favour of regional peacekeeping (see p. 451). This has been evident, for example, in the significant contributions of military and police personnel from a wide range of Asia-Pacific countries which have carried out operations in Cambodia, 1992–93, and East Timor, 1999–2002, and the use of military personnel from the Economic Community of West African States (ECOWAS) to restore peace and stability to Liberia, 1990–8.

Political regionalism refers to attempts by states in the same area to strengthen or protect shared values, thereby enhancing their image and reputation and gaining a more powerful diplomatic voice. This was a significant factor in the construction of organizations such as the Council of Europe, which was created in 1949 with the aim of creating a common democratic and legal area throughout the continent of Europe, ensuring respect for human rights, democracy and the rule of law. The Arab League was formed in 1945 to 'draw closer the relations between member states and coordinate collaboration between them, to safeguard their independence and sovereignty, and to consider in a general way the affairs and interests of Arab countries'. The Organization of African Unity (OAU) was founded in 1963 to promote self-government, respect for territorial boundaries, and to promote social progress throughout the African continent. The OAU was replaced by the African Union in 2002. However, distinctions between economic, security and political forms of regionalism can also be misleading. Although certain regional organizations are clearly designed with a specific purpose in mind, to which they have remained faithful over time, most regional bodies are complex and evolving institutions that involve themselves in economic, strategic and political matters. For example, although the African

● **Free trade area**: An area within which states agree to reduce tariffs and other barriers to trade.

● **Customs union**: An arrangement whereby a number of states establish a common external tariff against the rest of the world, usually whilst abolishing internal tariffs.

● **Common market**: An area, comprising a number of states, within which there is a free movement of labour and capital, and a high level of economic harmonization; sometimes called a 'single' market.

● **Security community**: A region in which the level of cooperation and integration amongst states makes war or the use of large-scale violence unlikely, if not impossible.

Union is a political body that encompasses the Pan-African Parliament and the African Court of Justice, it also fosters economic integration within sub-regions, engages in development issues and tries to combat AIDS in Africa, and intervenes militarily in regional conflicts, as, for instance, it has done since 2005 in the Darfur region of Sudan.

Why regionalism?

In many ways, explanations of the rise of regionalism overlap with those related to the wider phenomenon of international organization (see Approaches to international organization, p. 444). However, the tendency towards regional integration, and particularly European experiments with supranational cooperation, have stimulated a particular theoretical debate about the motivations and processes through which integration and institution-building at the international level are brought about. Three main theories have been advanced:

- Federalism
- Functionalism
- Neofunctionalism.

Federalism

Federalism is the earliest theory of regional or even global integration, being advocated from the eighteenth century onwards by political thinkers such as G. W. F. Hegel (1770–1831) and Jean-Jacques Rousseau (1712–78), and drawing inspiration from its use in domestic politics as a device for reconciling tensions between the centre and the periphery. As an explanation for regional or international cooperation, federalism relies on a process of conscious decision-making by the political elites. The attraction of international federations is that they appear to offer a solution to the endemic problems of the state-system, and especially the problem of war. If war is caused by sovereign states pursuing self-interest in a context of anarchy, peace will only be achieved if states transfer at least a measure of their sovereignty (see p. 4) to a higher, federal body. This is often referred to as **pooled sovereignty**. The federalist vision of 'unity through diversity' is achieved by a system of shared sovereignty between international and national bodies and undoubtedly had a powerful impact on the founders of the European Communities, expressed, in the words of the Treaty of Rome (1957), in the desire to establish 'an ever closer union'. However, federalism has had relatively little impact on the wider process of integration or on the trend towards global governance. This is both because federalist projects have been too ambitious, if not utopian, in that they require states voluntarily to sacrifice sovereignty, and because enthusiasm for federalist projects has invariably been confined to political and intellectual elites, while political nationalism has continued to hold sway over the wider public.

Functionalism

Even in the case of the European project, federalist thinking quickly gave way to a functionalist road to integration. The key idea of **functionalism** is expressed in

● **Pooled sovereignty**: The sharing of decision-making authority by states within a system of international cooperation, in which certain sovereign powers are transferred to central bodies.

● **Functionalism**: The theory that government is primarily responsive to human needs; functionalism is associated with incremental steps towards integration, within specific areas of policy-making, at a pace controlled by constituent states.

Table 20.1 Key regional organizations and groupings of the world

Region	Regional organizations	Date founded	Number of member states
Africa	African Union (AU)	2002	54
	Central African Customs and Economic Union	1966	6
	Economic Community of West African States (ECOWAS)	1975	15
	Economic Community of Central African States (ECCAS)	1983	6
	Arab Maghreb Union	1988	5
	Southern African Development Community (SADC)	1992	15
	Southern African Customs Union (SACU)	1910	5
America	North American Free Trade Agreement (NAFTA)	1994	3
	Mercosur (Southern Cone Common Market)	1991	6
	Organization of American States (OAS)	1948	35
	Central American Common Market (CACM)	1960	5
	Andean Group	1969	4
	Latin American Integration Association (LAIA)	1980	14
Asia	The Association of South-East Asian Nations (ASEAN)	1967	10
	ASEAN Regional Forum (ARF)	1994	27
	East Asian Summit (EAS)	2005	18
	South Asian Association for Regional Cooperation (SAARC)	1985	7
	Gulf Cooperation Council (GCC)	1981	6
	Shanghai Cooperation Organization (SCO)	2001	6
	Economic Cooperation Organization (ECO)	1985	10
Asia-Pacific	Asia-Pacific Economic Cooperation (APEC)	1989	21
	Pacific Economic Cooperation Council (PECC)	1980	26
	Pacific Islands Forum	1971	15
Eurasia	Eurasian Economic Community (EAEC)	2000	6
	Black Sea Economic Cooperation (BSEC)	1992	12
Europe	European Union (EU)	1952	28
	Council of Europe (CoE)	1949	47
	Nordic Council	1952	8 *
	Benelux Economic Union	1958	3
Euro-Atlantic	North Atlantic Treaty Organization (NATO)	1949	28
	Organization for Security and Cooperation in Europe (OSCE)	1973	57

* including 3 autonomous territories.

David Mitrany's (1966) formulation: 'form follows function'. In this view, cooperation only works when it is focused on specific activities (functions) that would be performed more effectively through collective action than by individual states. This, then, creates pressure to construct institutional structures (forms) that would facilitate such cooperation in these areas. European integration very clearly followed a functionalist path, as it tended to focus on the promotion of economic cooperation, seen by states as the least controversial but most necessary form of integration. Functionalists have generally had high expectations about the extent to which integration and international cooperation are possible, believing that political loyalties can relatively easily be transferred away from nation-states (see p. 168) towards new functional organizations as the latter are seen to be effective in delivering goods and services. However, the weakness of functionalism is that it overemphasizes the willingness of states to hand over their responsibilities to functional bodies, especially in areas that are political rather than technical. Furthermore, there is little evidence that international organizations are capable of acquiring a level of popular legitimacy that rivals the nation-state, regardless of their functional importance.

Neofunctionalism

As a result of these deficiencies a growing emphasis has therefore been placed on what is called **neofunctionalism**. In the writings in particular of Haas (1964), neofunctionalism recognizes the limitations of the traditional functionalist idea that integration is largely determined by a recognition of growing interdependence in economic and other areas. Instead, it places greater emphasis on the interplay between economics and politics. From this perspective, functional cooperation tends to produce transnational constituencies of advocates for still closer cooperation, creating a dynamic that leads to wider political integration. This process is known as **spillover**. Through its emphasis on elite socialization and the notion that the integration process can be recast and redefined over time, neofunctionalism resembles some of the ideas of constructivist theorists. Nevertheless, its drawback is that it is usually narrowly linked to the process of European integration, and there is little to suggest that the European neofunctionalist path is being pursued by other regional organizations, still less by the institutions of global governance. Indeed, some have seen neofunctionalism more a description of European experience rather than as a theory of international organization.

Nevertheless, since the mid-1970s, disillusionment has grown with the bold claim of neofunctionalism that power politics is in the process of being replaced by new forms of supranational governance. This was, in part, because empirical developments seemed to render neofunctionalism implausible. Not only has it appeared that other forms of regionalism have been unwilling to follow Europe's example of federal-type integration, but hopes for an 'ever closer union' within Europe have been dashed by the continued relevance of the state and the persistence of nationalist allegiances. In this context, many have sought to explain inter-state cooperation in other ways, through an emphasis, for example, on interdependence (see p. 7), multilateralism (see p. 467), international regimes (see p. 71) or global governance (see p. 462). At any rate, the idea of a deeply rooted and perhaps irresistible dynamic in favour of integration has largely been

● **Neofunctionalism**: A revision of functionalism that recognizes that regional integration in one area generates pressures for further integration in the form of 'spillover'.

● **Spillover**: A process through which the creation and deepening of integration in one economic area creates pressure for further economic integration, and, potentially , for political integration.

KEY THEORISTS IN REGIONAL INTEGRATION

David Mitrany (1888–1975)

A Romanian-born UK historian and political theorist, Mitrany was the leading exponent of functionalism in international politics. His 'functionalist-sociological' approach emphasized that international cooperation would begin over specific transnational issues and then develop into a wider process. As 'functional' bodies proved to be more effective than national government, the state-system would develop into a 'working peace system'. Mitrany's major writings include *A Working Peace System* (1966) and *The Functionalist Theory of Politics* (1975).

Karl Deutsch (1912–92)

A Czech-born US political scientist, Deutsch challenged the traditional realist image of international relations by emphasizing how regional integration can modify the impact of international anarchy. 'Amalgamation', through the construction of a single decision-making centre, would nevertheless be less common than 'integration', which allows sovereign states to interact within a 'pluralist security community'. Deutsch's major works in this field include *Political Community in the North Atlantic Area* (1957) and *Nation-Building* (1966).

Ernst Haas (1924–2003)

A German-born US international relations theorist, Haas is best known as one of the founders of neofunctionalism, or 'federalism by instalments', particularly as applied to European integration. He argued that the process of 'spillover' would lead political actors progressively to shift their loyalties, expectations and activities from the nation-state towards a 'new larger centre'. However, Haas became disenchanted with neofunctionalism in the 1970s. His main works include *Beyond the Nation-State* (1964) and *Tangle of Hopes* (1969).

abandoned as the role of specific historical factors has been recognized. For example, the process of decolonization in Africa and Asia in particular contributed to the first wave of regionalism that peaked in the 1960s, as newly independent states tended to see regionalism as a mechanism for establishing settled relationships amongst themselves as well as with their former colonial power. A second factor is under-development and poor economic performance, encouraging states to view closer regional cooperation as a means of stimulating growth and gaining protection against intensifying international competition. This has been particularly evident in the complex, and sometimes contradictory, relationship between regionalism and globalization (see p. 8).

Regionalism and globalization

Since the late 1980s, there has been a clear and continuing resurgence in regionalism, often seen as regionalism's 'second coming' and associated with what is called the 'new' regionalism. But what was new about the new regionalism? New regionalism is essentially economic in character, and it largely takes the form of the creation of regional trade blocs. These trade blocs, moreover, operate very clearly as regional spaces through which states can interact, rather than being drawn into EU-style supranational experiments. Between 1990 and 1994, GATT was informed of 33 regional trading arrangements, nearly one third of those that had been negotiated since 1948. The Asia-Pacific Economic Cooperation was created in 1989 and has expanded from 12 members to 21 (including Australia, China, Russia, Japan and the USA), encompassing, collectively, countries that account for 40 per cent of the world's population and over 50 per cent of global GDP. In 1991, the signing of the Treaty of Asuación led to the formation of Mercosur, which links Argentina, Brazil, Paraguay, Uruguay and Venezuela with Chile, Columbia, Ecuador, Peru and Bolivia as associate members, constitutes Latin America's largest trade bloc. The year 1992 saw the signing of NAFTA, which came into force in 1994, linking Canada, Mexico and the USA. 1993 witnessed both the ratification of the Treaty of European Union (the TEU or Maastricht Treaty), which transformed the European Community into the European Union, and the introduction of the ASEAN Free Trade Area. 1994 saw an agreement to build the Free Trade Area of the Americas, as a proposed extension to NAFTA, designed eventually to encompass North and South America.

This surge of economic regionalism was driven by a variety of often disparate factors. In the first place, it reflected the wider acceptance of export-led economic strategies across the developing world, as more countries were inclined to follow the lead, first, of Japan and later of the Asian 'tiger' economies. Second, the end of the Cold War encouraged former communist countries to view economic integration as a means of supporting and consolidating their transition to the market economy, a development that later gave rise to the eastward expansion of the EU (see p. 510). Third, the establishment of the WTO and the growing influence of other institutions of global economic governance persuaded many countries that regionalism was a way of gaining greater influence within multilateral bodies. Fourth, the USA's transition from being a sponsor of regionalism to being an active participant gave the process considerable additional impetus. Finally, and underlying all the other factors, was the acceleration of globalization in the 1980s and 1990s. Regionalism became increasingly attractive as rapidly expanding global capital flows and an increasing trend towards transnational production patterns appeared to undermine the viability of the state as an independent economic unit. Regionalism was thus reborn as a mechanism through which states could manage the effects of globalization. However, there is significant debate about how regional integration has been used in these circumstances, and therefore about the implications of regionalism for globalization.

As Bhagwati (2008) put it, are regional trade blocs 'building blocks' or 'stumbling blocks' within the global system? How does the regional interact with the global? One face of economic regionalism has been essentially defensive, in that regional bodies have sometimes embraced protectionism as a means of resisting the disruption of economic and possibly social life through the impact of intensifying global competition. This gave rise to the idea of the region as a fortress, as in the once-fashionable notion of 'fortress Europe'. The near-simultaneous creation of NAFTA, the formation of the EU and the development of an ASEAN Free Trade Area have, for instance, been understood in these terms, creating a spectre of a world of competing regional blocs. In some cases, defensive region-alism has been a bottom-up process, driven by sub-national or transnational interest groups, such as agricultural interests across the EU and in the USA. A particularly significant concern within the EU has been to protect the European social model, characterized by comprehensive welfare provision, from a 'race to the bottom' ignited by neoliberal globalization.

Nevertheless, 'new' regionalism has been motivated by competitive impulses, and not merely protectionist ones. In these cases, countries have formed regional blocs not so much to resist global market forces but, rather, to engage more effec-tively with them. Although states have wished to consolidate or expand trading blocs in the hope of gaining access to more assured and wider markets, they have not turned their backs on the wider global market. This is evident in the growth of cross-regional interaction and attempts to influence the WTO and other bodies. The fortress model of regional integration has been weakened by the fact that regionalism has tended to march hand in hand with economic liberaliza-tion. In embracing the market, competition and entrepreneurialism, regional trade blocs have tended to be open and outward-looking, interested in engaging in global, not merely regional, free trade. In balancing competing impulses towards defence and competition, regional blocs have functioned more as filters, resisting particular threats to internal interests and priorities, rather than as fortresses. Nevertheless, the steady growth of regional trade agreements has meant that, instead of a common, global free trade system, there is a bewildering array of complex and overlapping bilateral and regional arrangements, each with conflicting and contradictory provisions, an arrangement that Bhagwati (2008) called the 'spaghetti bowl' system.

Regional integration outside Europe

Although new regionalism in particular has affected all parts of the world, it has not done so evenly. Some parts of the world have spawned more ambitious proj-ects of regional integration than others, and their levels of success or failure have varied considerably.

Regionalism in Asia

The most important regional initiatives to have emerged in Asia have come out of the Association of South-East Asian Nations (ASEAN). ASEAN was estab-lished in 1967 by Indonesia, Malaysia, the Philippines, Singapore and Thailand, with Negara Brunei Darussalam (1984), Vietnam (1995), Laos and Burma (1997) and Cambodia (1999) joining subsequently. ASEAN was a product of the Cold War period, its initial interests focusing mainly on security matters, espe-cially those linked to settling intra-regional disputes and resisting superpower influence. However, the organization moved steadily towards cooperation on economic and trade matters, leading in 1992 to the agreement to establish the ASEAN Free Trade Area, due to be completed by 2007. This was complemented by the growth of political regionalism, in the form of an emphasis on 'Asian values' (discussed in Chapter 8), sometimes portrayed as the 'ASEAN way', although enlargement and other developments have meant that this has become, over time, a more marginal and contested aspect of the ASEAN project. The

Debating . . .
Does the advance of regionalism threaten global order and stability?

The expansion and deepening of regionalism is widely accepted as one of the most prominent features of modern global politics. However, while some view a 'world of regions' as a recipe for conflict and instability, others argue that regionalism will promote security and widen prosperity.

YES

Regional egoism. Regionalism has not altered the essentially conflictual nature of world politics. Instead, power politics within the state-system is in the process of being replaced by power politics within a regional system. This occurs for two reasons. First, as realists emphasize, human nature has not changed. Thus, if regions are displacing states as the key units of global politics, state egoism is being reborn as regional egoism. Second, the essentially anarchical character of the global system means that if survival and security cannot be secured through the mechanism of the state, they must be secured through regional action. 'Fortress' regionalism will thus, perhaps inevitably, develop into aggressive regionalism, or even hegemonic regionalism.

Cultural or civilizational conflict. A further reason for inter-regional conflict is cultural difference, an idea expressed most graphically in the notion of the 'clash of civilizations'. In this view, regional integration is significantly motivated by the existence of shared values, traditions and beliefs, helping to explain why regional integration has therefore progressed further and faster in areas with a common cultural and ideological inheritance. This nevertheless implies suspicion of, and possibly hostility towards, regions of the world with different values, cultures and traditions. A world of regions is therefore a world of rival value systems and incompatible understandings, a recipe for conflict and global disorder.

Ever-deepening integration. Regionalism is driven by a logic that fosters progressively deeper levels of integration, making regional bodies both increasingly inward-looking and conflict-ridden. Neofunctionalist spillover will inevitably turn economic integration into political integration. Most clearly demonstrated by the example of European integration, but destined to be followed by other regions, this will create a widening gulf between a regionalized elite and increasingly marginalized and resentful general public, still wedded to national symbols and identities. This gulf is likely to fuel political extremism, particularly amongst those who feel disenfranchised by the regionalization process.

NO

Nationalism trumps regionalism. Predictions about the growth of inter-regional conflict are greatly overblown. The reality is that regionalism complements, rather than transcends, the state-system. States are, and will remain, the principal actors on the world stage, as no regional or global body can match the nation-state's capacity to generate political allegiance and civic identity. Supranational regionalism has therefore failed to materialize, regional bodies operating more like political spaces within which states cooperate on matters of mutual interest. With the possible exception of the EU, regional bodies have not achieved the level of integration necessary to become global actors on the world stage in their own right.

The global dominates the regional. The idea that regional blocs are stumbling blocks to globalization, implying that the global economy will increasingly become an arena of regional competition, is difficult to sustain. If regional integration has largely been dictated by the logic of interdependence, the recognition that states in the modern world must work together to tackle common problems, this implies that cooperation must extend beyond the region and encompass inter-regional and even global cooperation. Issues such as climate change, free trade, development disparities and international security cannot simply be addressed at a regional level. This forces regional bodies to be open and outward-looking, acting as stepping stones to higher levels of cooperation.

Limits of regionalism. Significant obstacles stand in the way of deep regional integration. These include the fact that as it is difficult to create democratically accountable regional organizations, such bodies tend to enjoy limited popular support. Furthermore, the harmonization of economic rules and arrangements can perhaps only be taken so far. This is evident in the difficulty of establishing common or single markets, in which genuinely free trade and the free movement of labour and capital ultimately require, as the EU recognized, a single currency and common interest rates. This level of harmonization nevertheless leads to over-rigid economic arrangements that are, sooner or later, doomed to collapse.

integration process was nevertheless given renewed impetus from the late 1990s onwards, both by the vulnerabilities exposed by the Asian financial crisis of 1997–8 and by the need to cooperate and compete effectively with the rapidly rising economic powers of China and India. This led to initiatives such as the proposed creation of the ASEAN Economic Community, due to be completed by 2015, which has led some to draw parallels with the EU and the process of European integration (see p. 499). In addition, attempts to foster political and economic dialogue with major powers, notably the 'big three' Asia-Pacific powers, the USA, China and Japan, were stepped up. Particular emphasis in this respect has been placed on strengthening ASEAN's relationship with China. In 2002, for instance, China and ASEAN agreed to create between them the world's largest free trade area, which would encompass over 2 billion people and which came into effect at the beginning of 2010.

ASEAN has also sought to promote wider regional cooperation, in a number of ways. These include the ASEAN Regional Forum (ARF), established in 1994, which aims to build confidence and enhanced dialogue on security matters amongst Asia-Pacific countries. As of 2013, the ARF had 27 members. The ASEAN Plus Three grouping, created in 1997, has deepened cooperation between the ASEAN ten and China, Japan and South Korea. One of its most important achievements was the Chiang Mai Initiative of 2000, under which the ASEAN Plus Three countries launched a multilateral arrangement of currency swaps designed to provide protection against future financial crises. ASEAN also plays a leading role in the East Asia Summit (EAS), which has been held annually since 2005 and includes, as well as the ASEAN countries, China, Japan, South Korea, India, Australia and New Zealand. However, regional integration in Asia has not simply been confined to ASEAN or to ASEAN-related initiatives. Important non-ASEAN initiatives have been promoted by the Asia-Pacific Economic Cooperation and, increasingly, by China. China's most important regional initiative has been the Shanghai Cooperation Organization (SCO). The SCO was founded in 2001 by the leaders of China, Kazakhstan, Kyrgyzstan, Russia, Tajikistan and Uzbekistan, the first four of which had been members of the Shanghai Five, established in 1996. Formed primarily to foster cooperation in Central Asia over security matters, notably those linked to terrorism (see p. 291), separatism and political extremism, the SCO's activities have subsequently expanded into the areas of military, economic and cultural cooperation. Some have nevertheless suggested that behind the SCO's engagement with traditional forms of regionalism lies a more serious geopolitical agenda: the desire to counter-balance US and NATO influence across the Eurasian landmass and particularly in resource-rich and strategically important Central Asia.

Regionalism in Africa

Although most states in Africa are committed to regionalism as part of the solution to their profound economic, political and social problems, the advance of regional integration has been hampered by the combined impact of poverty, political instability, border disputes and political and economic differences amongst African countries. Early experiments in regionalism in Africa emerged out of the politics of anti-colonialism, and were often based on pre-existing colonial arrangements. The French West African Federation was thus transformed,

Focus on ...

Regionalism in Asia: replicating European experience?

Are there parallels between regionalism in Asia and regionalism in Europe? Is ASEAN in the process of becoming an Asian version of the EU? Since the late 1990s, ASEAN has developed in ways that have encouraged commentators to draw comparisons with the process of European integration. This has happened particularly due to the ambitions set out at the ninth ASEAN summit meeting of heads of government, in Bali in 2003, to establish an 'ASEAN Community'. In language reminiscent of the TEU, this involves 'three pillars': the ASEAN Economic Community, the ASEAN Political-Security Community and the ASEAN Socio-Cultural Community. The economic aspect of this intensified cooperation is especially important because of the perception that ASEAN has only had limited success in creating a genuine free trade area. The ASEAN Economic Community aims to create a 'seamless production base' and an integrated market among member countries. In a process due to be completed by 2015, remaining tariffs within ASEAN are scheduled to be eliminated, together with a large number of non-tariff barriers; trade in services will be fully liberalized and barriers to flows of capital and skill labour will be relaxed in all economic sectors.

However, significant differences exist between ASEAN and the EU as models of regional integration, and these seem set to continue. In particular, ASEAN is geared to the establishment of a free trade area, with even the

goal of a common external tariff (which would make ASEAN a fully-fledged customs union) some way from being achieved. The EU, by contrast, has gone much further, by establishing a single market and subsequently embracing monetary union. Most importantly, ASEAN has remained firmly intergovernmental in character and has not engaged in EU-style experiments in supranational governance, its long-standing emphasis on state sovereignty impeding the construction of a more centralized decision-making framework.

How can differences between ASEAN and the EU be explained? In the first place, ASEAN embraces greater economic and political diversity than does the EU (for instance, Singapore and Burma represent radically different forms and levels of economic development). Second, as the largest economies in the region, notably China, Japan, India and South Korea, remain outside ASEAN, the association's emphasis tends to be placed more on sponsoring wider cooperation than on consolidating its internal market. Third, as an association of relatively equal countries, ASEAN lacks a major power, or powers, that could drive the integration process in the way that France and Germany have done in Europe. Fourth, ASEAN's project of regional integration has never been fuelled by the same level of political urgency as was injected into the European project by the pressing need to overcome Franco-German hostility and thus to prevent future world wars.

after independence, into the West African Economic and Monetary Union. In the case of the Southern African Customs Union, which was created in 1910 and claims to be the earliest customs union ever established, regional bodies created in the colonial period survived in a reinvented form once independence had been achieved. The Southern African Development Community (SADC) was founded in 1992, as the successor to an earlier nine-member body that had been formed in 1980 to promote economic cooperation amongst southern African states and reduce their dependence on apartheid-era South Africa. Having expanded to include all 15 southern African states (South Africa, for instance, joined in 1995), SADC is committed both to deepening economic integration and to extending economic integration into political and security areas. The two most significant examples of regionalism in Africa are nevertheless the African Union (AU), which came into being in 2002 as a replacement for the Organization of African Unity (OAU), and the Economic Community of West African States (ECOWAS).

The AU constitution, modelled on that of the EU, envisages a much more ambitious organization than its predecessor. The OAU had been created in 1963 with the intention of ending colonialism and supporting political liberation. Its agenda subsequently broadened through initiatives such as the establishment in 1993 of the African Economic Community, and agreement in 2001 on the New Partnership for Africa's Development (NEPAD), a programme of measures designed to alleviate poverty and promote constructive engagement with globalization. However, these economic initiatives have brought few concrete benefits, in part because of continuing and deep disagreements about the extent to which Africa should adopt an orthodox, market-orientated approach to development. Uncertainty about whether the AU should abandon its anti-western rhetoric and build partnerships with the West on matters such as dealing with war crimes and genocide (see p. 333) have also limited the AU's ability to exercise leadership in Africa over issues such as democracy, human rights (see p. 311) and the rule of law.

ECOWAS is the largest sub-regional organization established in Africa, comprising 15 states with a combined population of nearly 200 million. However, its impact on the economic performance of member states has been negligible, due to factors such as political instability and widespread corruption in the region, allied to ECOWAS's weak infrastructure and lack of political will. Although ECOWAS's involvement in the 1990s in internal conflicts in Liberia and Sierra Leone through its peacekeeping force divided opinion and eventually led to its replacement by UN peacekeepers, Ghana and Nigeria have subsequently moved to enhance the region's peacekeeping capabilities.

Regionalism in the Americas

The Americas have witnessed multiple, and often competing, levels of regionalism, reflecting, in large part, the geographical, cultural and political importance of sub-continental regions. The most important example of regionalism in North America was the formation in 1994 of NAFTA, through which the USA, Canada and Mexico agreed to build a free trade area. This has a combined GDP of $17.3 trillion and a population of 462 million. Formed in part as a response to the growing pace of economic integration, NAFTA was intended to provide the basis for a wider economic partnership covering the whole western hemisphere, expressed through the 1994 agreement to build a Free Trade Area of the Americas (FTAA). However, the aims of NAFTA are modest by comparison with those of the EU. Its chief goals have been to phase out tariffs on agricultural and a variety of manufacturing goods, to allow banks and other financial institutions access to wider markets, and to allow lorry drivers to cross borders freely. NAFTA is a much looser body than the EU, having strictly intergovernmental decision-making processes and, to date, successfully resisting neofunctional pressures for cooperation on trade to spill over into economic or political areas. NAFTA, nevertheless, remains a controversial issue in the USA, where its critics have accused it of facilitating the export of manufacturing jobs to Mexico. However, deeper problems include large disparities in wealth, education and economic structure between the USA and Canada, on the one hand, and Mexico on the other, and significant gaps in mutual knowledge and understanding amongst the citizens of the three countries. As far as the proposed FTAA is concerned, negotiations to establish this have faltered, largely due to tensions between developed and developing countries similar to those that impede the completion of the Doha Round of WTO negotiations, as discussed in Chapter 19.

The most important trading bloc in South America is Mercosur, which expanded through an agreement in 1994 to link the economies of Argentina, Brazil, Venezuela, Paraguay, Uruguay and Bolivia as full members, with Chile, Colombia, Ecuador and Peru as associate members. The main aims of Mercosur are to liberalize trade amongst its members, establishing a customs union (in which the associate members do not participate) and helping to coordinate economic policies within the region. From the outset, it embraced 'open regionalism' and engaged in market-orientated strategies, as advised by the WTO and other bodies. The Mercosur countries enjoyed dramatic growth in intra-regional trade as well as in their trade with the rest of the world during 1991–96. However, since then, trade levels have grown much more slowly, affected, in part, by financial crises in Brazil and Argentina. A deeper long-term problem within Mercosur is the tensions that derive from the fact that Brazil, with 79 per cent of the organization's total population and 71 per cent of its GDP, dwarfs other members, including Argentina.

EUROPEAN INTEGRATION

The 'European idea' (broadly, the belief that, regardless of historical, cultural and language differences, Europe constitutes a single political community) was born long before 1945. Before the Reformation of the sixteenth century, common allegiances to Rome invested the Papacy with supranational authority over much of Europe. Even after the European state-system came into existence, thinkers as different as Rousseau, the socialist Saint-Simon (1760–1825) and the nationalist Mazzini (1805–72) championed the cause of European cooperation, and in some cases advocated the establishment of Europe-wide political institutions. However, until the second half of the twentieth century such aspirations proved to be hopelessly utopian. Since WWII, Europe has undergone a historically unprecedented process of integration, aimed, some argue, at the creation of what Winston Churchill in 1946 called a 'United States of Europe'. Indeed, it has sometimes been suggested that European integration provides a model of political organization that would eventually be accepted worldwide as the deficiencies of the nation-state become increasingly apparent.

It is clear that this process was precipitated by a set of powerful, and possibly irresistible, historical circumstances in post-1945 Europe. The most significant of these were the following:

● The need for economic reconstruction in war-torn Europe through cooperation and the creation of a larger market
● The desire to preserve peace by permanently resolving the bitter Franco-German rivalry that caused the Franco-Prussian War (1870–1), and led to war in 1914 and 1939

Jean Monnet (1888–1979)

French economist and administrator. Monnet was largely self-taught. He found employment during WWI coordinating Franco-British war supplies, and he was later appointed Deputy Secretary-General of the League of Nations. He was the originator of Winston Churchill's offer of union between the UK and France in 1940, which was abandoned once Pétain's Vichy regime had been installed. Monnet took charge of the French modernization programme under de Gaulle in 1945, and in 1950 he produced the Schuman Plan, from which the European Coal and Steel community and the European Economic Community were subsequently developed. Although Monnet rejected intergovernmentalism in favour of supranational government, he was not a formal advocate of European federalism.

- The recognition that the **'German problem'** could be tackled only by integrating Germany into a wider Europe
- The desire to safeguard Europe from the threat of Soviet expansionism and to mark out for Europe an independent role and identity in a bipolar world order
- The wish of the USA to establish a prosperous and united Europe, both as a market for US goods and as a bulwark against the spread of communism
- The widespread acceptance, especially in continental Europe, that the sovereign nation-state was the enemy of peace and prosperity.

To some extent, the drift towards European integration was fuelled by an idealist commitment to internationalism (see p. 67) and the belief that international organizations embody a moral authority higher than that commanded by the state. This was evident in the federalist dream of an integrated Europe that was espoused by, for example, Jean Monnet and Robert Schuman (1886–1963). Early dreams of a federal Europe in which the sovereignty of the European states would be pooled came to nothing, however. Instead, a functionalist road to unity was followed. This is why the European project tended to focus on the means of promoting economic cooperation, seen by states as the least controversial but most necessary form of integration. The European Coal and Steel Community (ECSC) was founded in 1952 on the initiative of Monnet, advisor to the French foreign minister, Schuman. Under the Treaty of Rome (1957), the European Economic Community (EEC) came into existence. This was committed to the establishment of a common European market and the broader goal of an 'ever closer union among the peoples of Europe'. The EEC was incorporated into the European Community (EC) in 1967 and eventually into the European Union (EU) in 1993. But what kind of organization is the EU, and how much influence does it exert?

- **German problem**: The structural instability in the European state-system caused by the emergence of a powerful and united Germany.

What is the EU?

The EU is a very difficult political organization to categorize. Is it a state (see p. 118), perhaps even a 'superstate'? Is it an international organization, and, if so, what kind of international organization? Is the EU merely an arena or space

History of the European Union

1951	The Treaty of Paris establishes the European Coal and Steel Community (ECSC), which begins work the following year, with France, Germany, Italy and the Benelux countries as members.
1957	The Treaty of Rome provides for the establishment, the next year, of the European Economic Community (EEC) and the European Atomic Energy Community (Euratom).
1967	European Community (EC) is created through the merging of the ECSC, the EEC and Euratom.
1973	Denmark, Ireland and the UK join the EC.
1981	Greece joins the EC.
1986	Portugal and Spain join the EC.
1986	The Single European Act (SEA) prepares for the establishment of a common market (completed in 1992) and abolishes national vetoes in a host of areas.
1993	The Treaty of European Union (TEU or the Maastricht Treaty) is ratified, bringing the European Union (EU) into existence and preparing for monetary union.
1995	Austria, Finland and Sweden join the EU.
1997	The Treaty of Amsterdam is signed, paving the way for the eastward expansion of the EU and further reducing the influence of the national veto.
1999	The euro comes into effect as the official currency of 11 member states, with national currencies being replaced by euro notes and coins in 2002.
2001	The Treaty of Nice is signed, helping to ensure the effective functioning of the new Union with extra members; it comes into force in 2003.
2004	10 new states join the EU, bringing its membership to 25 countries.
2004	The Constitutional Treaty is signed, but withdrawn in 2005, following its rejection by the Netherlands and France.
2007	Bulgaria and Romania join, bringing the membership to 27.
2009	The Treaty of Lisbon is ratified as a modified version of the Constitutional Treaty, introducing new decision-making arrangements within the Union.
2010	European sovereign debt crisis (also known as the eurozone crisis) begins with EU–IMF bail-outs for Greece and Ireland.
2013	Croatia joins, bringing the membership to 28.

Focus on . . .
How the European Union works

- **The Council**: Informally called the Council of Ministers, this is the decision-making branch of the EU, and comprises ministers from the 28 states, who are accountable to their own assemblies and governments. The presidency (vested in a country, not a person) of the Council rotates amongst member states every six months. Important decisions are made by unanimous agreement, and others are reached through qualified majority voting or by a simple majority (*intergovernmental body*).
- **The European Council**: Informally called the European Summit, this is made up of the presidents or prime ministers of each member state, accompanied by their foreign ministers, and a permanent, full-time President of the European Council (since 2009, Herman Van Rompuy). The European Council meets four times a year and provides strategic leadership for the EU (*intergovernmental body*).
- **The European Commission**: Based in Brussels, with a staff of some 20,000 people, the Commission is the executive-bureaucratic arm of the EU. It is headed by 28 Commissioners and a President (José Manuel Barroso's term of office as President began in 2004). The Commission proposes legislation, is a watchdog that ensures that the EU's treaties are respected, and is broadly responsible for policy implementation (*supranational body*).

- **The European Parliament**: Usually located in Strasbourg, the EP is composed of 766 Members of the European Parliament (MEPs), who are directly elected every five years. MEPs sit according to political groups rather than their nationality. The Lisbon Treaty made the EP a stronger lawmaker, giving it equal rights with the Council in 40 areas. However, its major powers (to reject the European Union's budget and dismiss the European Commission) are too far-reaching to exercise (*supranational body*).
- **The European Court of Justice**: Based in Luxembourg, the ECJ interprets, and adjudicates on, EU law and treaties. There are 28 judges, one from each member state, and 8 advocates general, who advise the Court. As EU law has primacy over the national law of EU member states, the Court can disapply domestic laws. A Court of First Instance handles certain cases brought by individuals and companies (*supranational body*).
- **The European Central Bank**: Located in Frankfurt, the ECB is the central bank for Europe's single currency, the euro. The ECB's main task is to maintain the euro's purchasing power and thus price stability in the euro area. The eurozone comprises the 19 EU countries that have introduced the euro since 1999 (*supranational body*).

within which member states can interact, or has it become a meaningful actor in its own right? These questions are best considered by examining, first, the internal structure of the EU and then its relationship with the outside world. One of the difficulties with understanding the structure of the EU is that it has been substantially reshaped and institutionally redesigned on a number of occasions since the establishment of the ECSC in 1952. Not only has the ECSC given way to the EEC, the EC and, in due course, the EU, but other changes have, for example, seen the creation of a single market (through the Single European Act (SEA) in 1986), **monetary union** (agreed by the TEU in 1993) and the establishment of the EU as a single legal entity (through the Lisbon Treaty in 2009). Most significantly, the EEC/EC/EU has gone through a substantial process of widening and deepening. It has widened as the original Six (France, Germany, Italy, the Netherlands, Belgium and Luxembourg) became, over time, 28 (see Map 20.1),

● **Monetary union**: The establishment of a single currency within an area comprising a number of states.

and it has deepened as successive waves of integration have transferred certain areas of decision-making authority from member states to EU bodies.

In strict terms, the EU is no longer a confederation of independent states operating on the basis of intergovernmentalism, as the EEC and the EC were at their inception. The sovereignty of member states was enshrined in the so-called 'Luxembourg compromise' of 1966. This accepted the general practice of unanimous voting in the Council of Ministers (now known as the Council), and granted each member state an outright veto on matters threatening vital national interests. However, this confederal image of the EU has become difficult to sustain for at least three reasons. In the first place, starting with the SEA and continuing with each of the subsequent major treaties – the TEU, Amsterdam, Nice and Lisbon – the practice of **qualified majority voting**, which allows even the largest state to be outvoted in the Council, has been applied to a wider range of policy areas. This has progressively narrowed the scope of the national veto, which, in turn, circumscribes state sovereignty. Second, this trend has been compounded by the fact that EU law is binding on all member states. This, indeed, is one of the key differences between the EU and other international organizations. The EU has a body of law which supersedes national law in areas where the EU has 'competence', a position backed up by rulings from the European Court of Justice. The creation of this body of law has involved the voluntary surrender of powers by member states in a broad range of policy areas, and the development of a new level of legal authority to which the member states are subject (McCormick 2005). Third, and linked to this, the powers of certain EU bodies have expanded at the expense of national governments. The result is a political body that is a complex blend of intergovernmental and supranational features.

Nevertheless, although the EU has done much to realize the Treaty of Rome's goal of establishing 'an ever closer union', moving well beyond Charles de Gaulle's and Margaret Thatcher's vision of a confederation of independent states, it stops short of realizing a 'United States of Europe'. While the EU has not created a federal Europe, still less a European 'superstate', the superiority of European law over the national law of the member states perhaps suggests that it is accurate to talk of a 'federalizing' Europe. A major check on centralizing tendencies within the EU has been respect for the principle of subsidiarity (see p. 506), embodied in the TEU, and the pragmatic approach to integration adopted by key states such as France and Germany. Decision-making within the 'New Europe' is increasingly made on the basis of multilevel governance (as discussed in Chapter 5), in which the policy process has interconnected sub-national, national, intergovernmental and supranational levels, the balance between them shifting in relation to different issues and policy areas. This image of complex policy-making is more helpful than the sometimes sterile notion of a battle between national sovereignty and EU domination. The desire to bring greater coherence and formality to this complex and sometimes inefficient policy process nevertheless gave rise to the idea of an EU Constitution, which would codify major rules and principles, incorporating and superseding all previous treaties. However, although the Constitutional Treaty, which would have established this Constitution, was approved by heads of state or government in 2004, it was not ratified because of referendum defeats in the Netherlands and France in 2005. Although many of the elements of the

● **Qualified majority voting**: A system of voting in which different majorities are needed on different issues, with states' votes weighted (roughly) according to size.

CONCEPT

Subsidiarity

Subsidiarity (from the Latin *subsidiarii*, meaning a contingent of supplementary troops) is, broadly, the devolution of decision-making from the centre to lower levels. However, it is understood in two different ways. In federal states such as Germany, subsidiarity is understood as a *political* principle that implies decentralization and popular participation, particularly through local and provincial institutions. The TEU thus declares that decisions should be 'taken as closely as possible to the citizens'. However, subsidiarity is also interpreted, usually by anti-federalists, as a *constitutional* principle that defends national sovereignty against the encroachment of EU institutions. In this light, the TEU declares that the EU should act only over matters that 'cannot be sufficiently achieved by the member states'.

Constitutional Treaty were incorporated into the Lisbon Treaty, which was ratified in 2009, this episode highlights the extent to which, despite decades of institutional deepening, EU member states continue to function as states, still orientated around issues of national interest.

The EU and the world

Although it is clear that the EU has an external policy, the extent of its international 'actorness' (its capacity to act within the global system as a single entity) has been a matter of considerable debate. The most crucial area here has been foreign and defence policy. In its early incarnations, foreign policy, and, for that matter, the wider issue of political union, played little part in the developing European project. The Treaty of Rome made no mention of foreign policy and the EEC focused essentially on economic policies and issues. Such initiatives as there were to promote political integration tended to be piecemeal and had little impact. For example, the European Defence Community was proposed in 1950, most actively by France, but it was widely viewed as a threat to the authority of NATO, and the idea was abandoned in 1954 when it was rejected by the French National Assembly. However, the notion of an EU foreign and defence policy resurfaced through the TEU, when the Common Foreign and Security Policy (CFSP) was established as 'pillar two' of the EU. Although the CFSP has only loosely defined goals, it was given significant impetus by the creation, in the Treaty of Amsterdam, of the new position of High Representative for foreign affairs, and by the high-profile appointment of Javier Solana, the former Secretary General of NATO, to this office.

The Common Foreign and Security Policy has had a number of achievements. These include the deployment of over two dozen missions of peacekeepers, police officers and civilians to troubled parts of the world, including Bosnia, Chad, Eastern Congo and the Aceh province of Indonesia. It has also engaged in international diplomacy, particularly the EU3's (The EU together with France, Germany and the UK) efforts to persuade Iran to abandon its uranium enrichment programme. However, failures have been more prominent than successes. When it comes to the most pressing international problems, such as Afghanistan, Pakistan and North Korea, the EU has either been largely invisible or absent. Although the EU's presence in Bosnia and Kosovo has helped to ensure peace, EU policy in the Balkans has become less resolute and coherent over time. Lacking a military force of its own, the EU was forced to leave the resolution of the 1999 Kosovo crisis to US-led NATO forces. When the USA and most EU states recognized the independence of Kosovo in 2008, five EU states failed to, shattering the hard-won united approach to the Balkans that had been forged in the 1990s. Similarly, Slovenia is blocking Croatia's accession to the EU because of a border dispute, while Greece is thwarting Macedonia's progress towards membership because of its name (Macedonia is also a region in northern Greece).

The impediments to developing an effective common foreign and defence policy within the EU are many and various. In the first place, there are permanent tensions between member states that have an 'Atlanticist' approach to foreign policy, such as the UK, and those that have a 'Europeanist' approach, especially France. For the former, any EU defence policy, particularly the development of an EU military arm, must occur *within*, not outside or as an alterna-

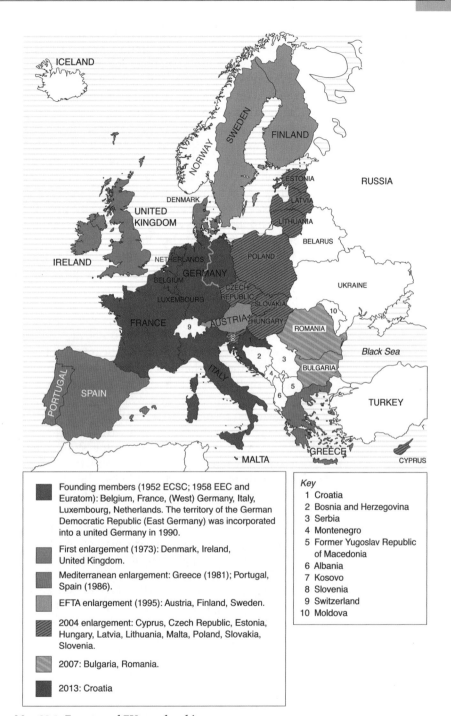

Map 20.1 Europe and EU membership

Source: Based on the map in Nugent (2004).

tive to, the framework of NATO. Second, member states have generally been much more reluctant to support political integration, rather than economic integration, and this especially applies in the case of foreign and defence policy. As the core purpose of the state is to ensure the 'high politics' of security and survival, independent control over foreign and defence affairs is widely viewed as the most important dimension of state sovereignty. Third, Europe's ability to develop an effective external presence has long been hampered by confusion about who represents the EU. As Henry Kissinger put it, 'Who do I call when I want to call Europe?' In the case of foreign and defence policy the EU has traditionally been represented by the 'troika', made up of the High Representative for foreign affairs, the European Commissioner for External Affairs and the foreign minister of the state currently holding the presidency of the Council. The confusions implicit in this arrangement were recognized by the creation, in the Lisbon Treaty, of the post of High Representative for Foreign Affairs and Security Policy. However, the appointment of the relatively inexperienced Catherine Ashton as the first post-holder suggests that this office may not fulfil the expectations of those who devised it. Fourth, an effective common defence policy requires levels of funding that few member states are prepared to support, particularly since the global financial crisis of 2007–9. It also needs a standardization of equipment and, ideally, a single, harmonized defence industry, which is a long way from being achieved and may, anyway, be impossible.

Nevertheless, the EU's external presence in economic affairs, particularly in trade matters, is much clearer. Because the EU is a customs union with a common commercial policy and a common external tariff, the Commission, rather than member states, conducts trade relations with outside parties. These include trade agreements with virtually all parts of the world and negotiations with GATT and, more recently, the WTO. The Commission also negotiates economic cooperation arrangements with other regional trading blocs as well as with individual states, an example being the biennial Asia-Europe Meeting. An additional aspect of the EU's external presence is over aid and development. Motivated both by the fact that key EU member states – notably the UK, France and Belgium – were once major imperial powers, and an awareness that the global South constitutes a particularly important market for EU exports, the EU has become the single biggest source of official development assistance in the world, collectively accounting, for instance, for just over half the total of $52 billion given in 2001. Most EU aid goes to sub-Saharan Africa, but an increasing proportion is going to Latin America. The EU also provides extensive emergency humanitarian aid and is, after the USA, the second largest provider of food aid in the world.

The EU in crisis?

Pronouncements about the stalling of the European project, and even predictions about the EU unravelling, have occurred throughout the history of the EEC/EC/EU. For some, the failure of the EU has always been just a matter of time. In this view, the level of diversity within the EU, in terms of history, traditions, language and culture, means that the EU can never match the capacity of the nation-state to engender political allegiance and act effectively on the world stage. However, two issues have proved to be particularly problematical in the

THE EUROPEAN UNION

Type: Regional organization • **Established:** 1993 • **Principal location:** Brussels
Membership: 28 states • **Population:** 510 m

The European Union was formed in 1993, through the ratification of the Treaty of European Union (TEU), a successor institution to the ECSC, the EEC and the EC. The EU is a unique international organization, in that it combines intergovernmental and supranational features. Its member states remain independent sovereign nations but 'pool' their sovereignty in order to gain a strength and world influence none of them could have on their own. The EU comprises four main bodies:

- The Council (which represents member states and is the main decision-making body; heads of state or government meet up to four times a year as the 'European Council')
- The European Commission (which represents the interests of the EU as a whole, initiates legislation and acts as the EU's executive arm)
- The European Parliament (a directly elected body that carries out scrutiny and oversight functions)
- The Court of Justice (which interprets and applies EU law).

The EU comprises three 'pillars': pillar one encompasses the existing Communities (the ECSC, the EEC and Euratom); the second and third pillars for foreign and defence policy and justice and home affairs respectively, are areas of intergovernmental cooperation. Within the EU, citizens enjoy common citizenship rights,

including the right to live, work and, if resident, be politically active anywhere within the Union.

Significance: The EU is the most advanced example of regional integration found anywhere in the world. With a population of over half a billion people, it is the third largest political unit in the world after China and India, and about 40 per cent larger than the USA. The EU is undoubtedly an economic super-power. It accounts for more than 23 per cent of world GDP, higher than that of the USA, and it produces more than one-quarter of global merchandize trade. The European single market was completed in 1993, with a single currency, the euro, coming into existence in 1999. Of the EU's 28 member states, 19 belong to the eurozone. For these reasons, the EU is sometimes seen as a major challenger to US hegemony. No longer in need of the security umbrella that the USA provided during the Cold War period, there is evidence that the EU and the USA increasingly view the world from different perspectives (Kagan 2004). Supporters of the EU highlight a variety of advantages. These include that it has brought peace and political stability to a continent that was the crucible of both WWI and WWII; that it encourages European people to rise above narrow and insular nationalism; that pooled sovereignty has given EU states greater influence in the world than they would have had acting alone; and that economic union and the

single market have boosted economic performance and widened opportunities.

However, although the EU's economic power cannot be doubted, it remains a weak global actor in other respects. Efforts to establish an effective Common Foreign and Security Policy have made limited progress, meaningful cooperation in these areas being particularly difficult to bring about. Divisions amongst member states have often weakened and sometimes paralyzed the EU over major global issues, examples including the EU's response to the 'war on terror', relations with China, especially over matters such as human rights and Tibet, and relations with Russia, notably on issues of trade and energy dependency. Some argue that the EU is fundamentally unsound and in danger of unravelling. Critics have pointed out, variously, that national, language and cultural differences may make it impossible for EU bodies to establish genuine political allegiances; that the 'democratic deficit' within the EU can never be overcome; that there may be irresolvable tension between the goals of widening and deepening; and that integration has been largely driven by political elites and corporate interests, which have run ahead of European populations. The EU may also not represent a viable economic model, either because its high level of social provision makes it globally uncompetitive or because the single currency may prove to be unworkable in the long term (see p. 511).

The EU expands to the east

Events: On 1 May 2004, the EU carried out an enlargement on a scale totally unprecedented in its history.
Whereas previous enlargements had led, at most, to
three new members joining, this enlargement involved
ten new members, turning an EU of 15 states into one
with 25 members. What was also notable was that, with
the exception of Malta and Cyprus, these new members
were former communist states of central and eastern
Europe. Three of them – Estonia, Latvia and Lithuania –
had been former Soviet republics, while the other five –
the Czech Republic, Hungary, Poland, Slovakia and
Slovenia – had been part of the Soviet bloc (in the
Soviet era, the Czech Republic and Slovakia had formed
a single country, Czechoslovakia, and Slovenia had been
a republic of Yugoslavia). This process was taken further
on 1 January 2007, when two other former Soviet bloc
states, Bulgaria and Romania, joined. Croatia's accession in
2013 brought the membership of the EU to 28.

Significance: The EU's expansion into eastern Europe has
been significant for a variety of reasons. In the first place,
it had a profound impact on the geopolitical restructuring
of Europe. It completed the process initiated by the
collapse of communism through the Eastern European
Revolutions of 1989–91, by bringing about the reunifica-
tion of Europe after decades of division by the Iron
Curtain. In so doing, EU membership played an important
role in supporting the politico-economic transformation of
eastern Europe. By fulfilling the 'Copenhagen criteria',
established in 1993 for any new members of the EU, the
accession states of central and eastern Europe demonstrated their support for democracy, the rule of law,
human rights and the protection of minorities, whilst also
committing themselves to market economics and accepting the established EU aims of political, economic and
monetary union. After 2004–7, then, the spread of liberal
democracy into eastern Europe became an unstoppable
process. Second, eastward expansion also affected the
balances within the EU and its general orientation. In
particular, the EU has been less able to function as a 'West
European club', dominated by the Franco-German axis and
with large states generally able to push through their preferences. Instead, the voice of smaller states has greatly
increased, meaning, in part, that the EU has placed greater
emphasis on providing support for economic and social
development. In some senses, the centre of gravity of the
EU has shifted eastwards, as attention has been given to
further eastward expansion, with Turkey, Macedonia,

Serbia and Croatia being amongst the countries interested
in joining, and the relationship between the EU and Russia
has become an issue of increasing importance.

Third, eastward expansion has had an effect on the
economic performance of the EU. On the one hand, by
increasing the population of the EU by 20 per cent, it has
created a larger internal market, providing an economic
boost for all member states, which will increase as new
members become economically successful. On the other
hand, large differences in living standards and economic
performance between existing members (the EU-15) and
the accession states, and the fact that the transition from
central planning to market economics is still an ongoing
process, have created economic challenges for the EU. For
instance, eastward expansion only increased the EU's GDP
by 5 per cent, and it placed considerable pressures on the
EU-15, which have provided about 90 per cent of revenues
for the EU as a whole since 2007. Finally, expansion has
had a significant impact on the decision-making processes
of the EU. Quite simply, the wider the range of national
and political interests that have to be satisfied, the more
difficult it is for the EU to make decisions and to pursue
coherent strategies. For many, the widening of the EU has
placed substantial restrictions on its deepening. This led to
attempts to establish more streamlined, centralized decision-making processes through a proposed EU
Constitution. Nevertheless, this proved to be impossible to
introduce in a more decentralized and, in certain respects,
more divided EU, the Constitutional Treaty being withdrawn after its rejection by the Netherlands and France,
and replaced by the more modest Lisbon Treaty. Some
therefore argue that expansion has rendered the original
goal of 'an ever closer union' impossible.

Focus on . . .

The euro: a viable currency?

The decision to press ahead with monetary union was one of the key features of the TEU negotiated in 1992. The euro (originally called the European Currency Unit or ecu) was introduced in 1999, with coins and bank notes entering circulation on 1 January 2002. The original 12 members of the eurozone later expanded to 19. The euro has developed into the world's second largest reserve currency, after the US dollar, and since 2009 the euro has surpassed the dollar in terms of the value of its bank notes and coins in circulation in the world.

The chief arguments in favour of monetary union are that it is the logical extension of the introduction of a European single market, and that it promises to boost levels of intra-European trade, thereby promoting prosperity. It does this both by reducing the costs associated with currency exchange and by strengthening competitiveness, as customers can more easily assess the relative prices of goods or services anywhere within the eurozone. A regional currency is likely to be stronger and more stable than a collection of national currencies, both because it is less susceptible to speculative attacks and because individual countries are no longer able to gain advantage over other countries by devaluing their currencies.

However, critics of the euro have argued that it is a triumph of political ambition over economic reality. In the first place, a successful single currency requires that differences in competitiveness and living standards between the different regions of the single currency zone are relatively modest. This was never the case with the eurozone, which included countries like Greece and Portugal that have still relatively underdeveloped industrial economies. Similarly, the free movement of people within the eurozone, a necessary condition to cope with growth disparities across the region, has been impaired by still important social, cultural and national differences. A key source of vulnerability within the eurozone has always been that a single currency requires a common interest rate, in this case set by the European Central Bank. However, a 'one size fits all' interest rate does not, and cannot, take account of differences in economic performance across the eurozone, meaning that national economies are unable to use monetary policy to address their economic difficulties. These problems were compounded by the fact that eurozone rules about levels of government spending and the size of deficits had not been rigorously applied. While some have argued that the eurozone crisis that erupted in 2010 highlights the inherent, and perhaps fatal, flaws of monetary union, others have pointed out the crisis exposed problems that were neither manifest nor life-threatening before the Great Recession occurred. (Baldwin and Vines 2012).

early twenty-first century. The first is EU enlargement and its implications. A significant part of the success of the early process of European integration stemmed from the fact that the original Six were bound together by powerful historical, political and economic factors, not least the overriding desire to ensure peace and stability between France and Germany and the wish of smaller, neighbouring states to participate in the benefits that might flow from Franco-German rapprochement. However, enlargement has reshaped the European project at each stage, sometimes through the incorporation of countries that had a weaker commitment to the European ideal (such as the UK and Denmark) and, on other occasions, through the incorporation of economically less prosperous countries of southern Europe (Spain, Portugal and Greece). Nevertheless, no enlargements have been as ambitious and significant as those that saw the eastward expansion of the EU during 2004–13 (see p. 510). In some respects, these enlargements were the crowning achievement of the EU, in that they underpinned and, in a sense, completed the politico-economic transformation of central and eastern Europe, marking the Europe-wide triumph for liberal democracy. However, they also caused profound difficulties, not least by permanently shifting the balance between unity and diversity within the EU firmly in favour of diversity. If the EU can no longer be 'managed' through deals done between a relatively small number of large states (notably France and Germany, but also, to some extent, the UK), the prospect of effective decision-making and coherent thinking within the EU has perhaps been lost forever. If the EU has a future, it may be less as an economic and political union, and more as a 'multi-speed' Europe or a two-tier or even three-tier Europe.

The second key challenge facing the EU is economic rather than political. Although economic union has, by common consent, been more successful than political union, there are reasons to believe that the EU's continued economic success is by no means assured. The EU's share of world trade and production are set to diminish, a trend widely associated with the determination of influential member states to maintain social protections and welfare provision in the face of growing global competitive pressures. These long-term problems were compounded by the 2007–9 global financial crisis, which had more serious implications for EU economies than it did, for instance, for emerging economies such as China, India and Brazil. The global recession led to spiralling sovereign debt in many parts of the EU, but particularly in Greece, Spain, Portugal, Ireland and, to some extent, Italy within the eurozone, and in the UK outside the eurozone. Such debt crises, often linked to banking crises, led to bail-outs by the EU, the IMF and the European Central Bank for Greece (2010 and 2012), Ireland (2010), Portugal (2011), Spain (2012) and Cyprus (2013).

This **eurozone crisis** threatens to have profound and far-reaching implications, however. For instance, it highlighted lax regulation within the eurozone itself, which, far from making weaker economies more competitive, had served as a kind of shelter under which states mainly in southern Europe had used low interest rates to fuel asset bubbles without reforming their economies. At the very least, this implied a much greater emphasis, within the eurozone but also beyond, on fiscal rectitude, cutting levels of government spending, particularly by scaling back welfare and reducing the size of the public sector. This not only implies that if the single currency is to survive, economic decision-making must be more centralized, monetary union leading to **fiscal union**, but also that, in an age of debt and austerity, social tensions and political instabilities are likely to become more commonplace (see p. 112). A further implication of the euro crisis is its effect on Germany. Germany is both the largest economy within the EU and the lynchpin of integration, in that, perhaps more than any other state, Germany has traditionally viewed EU interests as identical with its national interests. However, Germany's role in bailing out Greece and other states has raised serious questions in Germany about its responsibilities within the eurozone and even about its commitment to the single currency. At the same time, the crisis has significantly bolstered Germany's position within the eurozone, and within the wider EU, the size and underlying strength of its economy allowing it, in effect, to dictate how particular crises are managed and resolved.

● **Eurozone crisis**: A combined sovereign debt and banking crisis within the eurozone, underpinned by low growth and declining competitiveness..

● **Fiscal union**: The establishment of coordinated tax and spending policies within an area comprising a number of states.

SUMMARY

- Regionalism is a process through which geographical regions become significant political and/or economic units, serving as the basis for cooperation and, possibly, identity. Regionalism takes different forms depending on whether the primary areas for cooperation are economic, security or political.

- The tendency towards regional integration, and particularly European experiments with supranational cooperation, have stimulated theoretical debate about the motivations and processes through which integration and institution-building at the international level are brought about. Federalism, functionalism and neofunctionalism are the main theories of regional integration.

- 'New' regionalism is essentially economic in character, usually taking the form of the development of regional trade blocs. However, while some see these trade blocs as the building blocks of globalization, enabling states to engage more effectively with global market forces, others see them as stumbling blocks, defensive bodies designed to protect economic or social interests from wider competitive pressures.

- Although forms of regionalism have emerged in Asia, Africa and the Americas, regional integration has been taken furthest in Europe, precipitated by a particular, and possibly unique, set of historical circumstances. The product of this process, the EU, is nevertheless a very difficult political organization to categorize.

- The EU's capacity to act within the global system as a single entity has been enhanced by attempts to develop a common foreign defence policy. Nevertheless, tensions between 'Atlanticists' and 'Europeanists', sensitivity about the implications of security regionalism for NATO and the EU's relationship with the USA, and anxieties about the erosion of state sovereignty each help to explain why progress on this issue has been slow.

- After the renewed impetus that was injected into European integration in the 1980s and 1990s, concerns have emerged about the stalling of the European project. These have been associated with tensions between the goals of widening and deepening, about the EU's declining global competitiveness, and about whether or not monetary union can be made to work in the long run.

Questions for discussion

- What is a 'region'?
- How may sub-national regionalism be linked to regionalism as an international phenomenon?
- What different forms can economic regionalism take?
- Why has political regionalism generally made less progress than economic regionalism or security regionalism?
- How, and to what extent, has regionalism impeded the advance of globalization?
- What was new about 'new' regionalism?
- Are there parallels between regionalism in Europe and regionalism in Asia?
- How is European integration best explained?
- Is it possible to resolve the tensions within the EU between the goals of widening and deepening?
- How significant is the EU as a global actor?
- Is the process of European integration in danger of unravelling?

Further reading

Beeson, M., *Regionalism and Globalization in East Asia: Politics, Security and Economic Development* (2014). An examination of the complex relationship between regionalism and globalization in an East Asian context.

Fawn, R. (ed.), *Globalising the Regional, Regionalising the Global* (2009). An authoritative collection of essays that examine theoretical and thematic approaches to regionalism, including six regional case studies.

Paupp, T., *The Future of Global Relations: Crumbling Walls, Rising Regions* (2009). An analysis of the prospects for resistance to US hegemony through the creation of a cooperative world order based on regionalism.

Rosamond, B., *Theories of European Integration* (2000). A succinct, authoritative and accessible analysis of the main theoretical debates generated by the European process of European integration.

ONLINE RESOURCES AVAILABLE

Links to relevant web resources can be found on the *Global Politics* website

CHAPTER **21** **Why Theory Matters**

'In theory, theory and practice are the same. In practice, they are not.'

Attributed to ALBERT EINSTEIN

PREVIEW   Theory is unavoidable in the study of global politics. We have no choice about engaging with theory because, put most simply, facts do not speak for themselves. If we try to make sense of the world simply by looking at it, our understanding is overwhelmed by the complexity and sheer weight of the information confronting us. Theory thus invests apparently shapeless and confusing reality with meaning, and it does so, most obviously, by highlighting how and why events happen. However, theory is not just an explanatory tool; it can also be a simplifying device, a means of uncovering prejudice or bias, a guide to action and so on. But none of these uses of theory is straightforward. For instance, how does theory allow us to analyze events, rather than merely describe them? In what ways does theory uncover supposedly 'hidden' processes and structures? How far can, or should, theory be used as a guide to political practice? Nevertheless, recognizing what theory can do for us does not, in itself, help us to choose which theory to use. What constitutes 'good' theory? On what grounds can one theory be preferred to another theory? Finally, the growing prominence in recent years of theoretical frameworks such as constructivism, critical theory, feminism and poststructuralism has intensi- fied debate about the nature and role of theory. This has raised deeper and, at times, philosophically challenging questions about matters such as the value of theoretical frameworks or 'paradigms', the extent to which 'reality' exists separate from our perception of it, the relationship between theorizing and political activity, and the status and role of normative theory.

KEY ISSUES

- Why is theory important?
- How can theories be evaluated?
- Are theoretical paradigms enlightening or constraining?
- Do theories, in effect, 'construct' the world?
- Are theories always 'political'?
- How can theory link what *is* to what *ought to be*?

THE IMPORTANCE OF THEORY

The key substantive theories of global politics are examined in Chapter 3, as well as in the 'Approaches' boxes that can be found in each chapter. The present chapter returns to the issue of theory, but for a different purpose. Its aim is to examine how, and how far, theory contributes to our understanding of global politics. Why do we need theory, and what can it do for us? An indication of the role and importance of theory can be gained by reflecting on the difference between academic study and journalism. Journalism sets out to provide an account of what has happened; it aims, in effect, to answer the question: who did what to whom, when and how? Journalism can therefore be seen as, at best, the 'first rough draft of history'. Academic study, by contrast, seeks to be more reflective and analytical. It is concerned not just with the surface of events, but with the deeper layers of meaning that underlie them; and theory is the means through which these layers are uncovered and investigated. Theory thus allows us to analyse, explain, interpret and evaluate, and not just describe. But there is considerable debate about how theory can, and should, be used.

Uses of theory

The academic study of international politics has been defined, through its history, by theoretical developments. Born in the aftermath of WWI, the discipline's early years were dominated by liberal internationalism (see p. 67) and the attempt to change the world for the better by removing the blight of war. However, liberal internationalist theories were subject to a growing realist critique in the years leading up to WWII, creating the discipline's first 'great debate' between liberalism and realism (see p. 516). As the Cold War took shape during the 1950s, this debate was won decisively by realism. By the 1970s, the dominant realist paradigm (see p. 524) came under sustained attack from both liberals and radicals, mainly Marxists. The resulting debate, usually dubbed the 'inter-paradigm debate', stimulated developments within both realism and liberalism, giving rise to neorealism and neoliberalism, and thus the 'neo-neo debate'. Since the 1980s, often stimulated by the fall of communism and the end of the Cold War, international theory has been significantly enriched, but it has also become more deeply fragmented, due to growing interest in a series of theoretical 'new voices'. These included constructivism (see p. 75), postcolonialism (see p. 200), poststructuralism and green politics, as well as theoretical frameworks with a deeper history, such as critical theory and feminism. Nevertheless, as these developments have unfolded, theory has performed not a single function but, rather, a range of functions, the most important of which include the following:

- Analyzing and explaining events
- Simplifying the world
- Widening and/or sharpening our perceptual field
- Defining our ethical horizons
- Providing a guide to action.

Analyzing and explaining events

If we look at the world without the benefit of theory we are likely to see, as the historian Arnold Toynbee (1889–1975) is reputed to have said, just 'one damned

Focus on . . .
International relations: the 'great debates'

The academic discipline of international relations (frequently shortened to IR) emerged in the aftermath of World War I (1914–18), an important impetus being the desire to find ways of establishing enduring peace. The central focus of the discipline was on the study of the relations of states, and those relations were traditionally understood primarily in diplomatic, military and strategic terms. However, the nature and focus of the discipline has changed significantly over time, not least through a series of so-called 'great debates'.

- The first 'great debate' took place between the 1930s and 1950s, and was between liberal internationalists, who emphasized the possibility of peaceful cooperation, and realists, who believed in inescapable power politics. By the 1950s, realism had gained ascendancy within the discipline.

- The second 'great debate' took place during the 1960s, and was between **behaviouralists** and traditionalists over whether it is possible to develop objective 'laws' of international relations.
- The third 'great debate', sometimes called the 'inter-paradigm debate', took place during the 1970s and 1980s, and was between realists and liberals, on the one hand, and Marxists on the other, who interpreted international relations in economic terms.
- The fourth 'great debate' started in the late 1980s, and was between positivists and so-called post-positivists over the relationship between theory and reality. This reflected the growing influence within IR of a range of 'new' critical perspectives, such as constructivism, critical theory, poststructuralism, postcolonialism, feminism and green politics.

thing after another'. In its most common use, theory is an analytical tool, a means not only of describing events, but also of explaining why they happened. Theory does this by providing an account of **causality**. By uncovering causal relationships, or 'chains of events', order and shape is imposed on a world that might otherwise seem to be made up of a series of random occurrences. For instance, the democratic peace thesis (see p. 69) alerts us to patterns in the occurrence of war and peace, whereby wars very rarely (and, some argue, never) take place between democratic states. *Who*, *what* and *when* questions then allow us to ask *why* questions; in this case, about the likely reasons for the absence of war between democracies. Do democracies not fight each other because they are democracies, or because of other factors (such as their level of economic development). If democracy promotes peace (at least, among democracies themselves), what is it about democratic rule that deters war – the impact of public opinion, ingrained habits of non-violent conflict resolution, shared values between democratic states, or what? Or does the alleged link between democracy and peace merely reflect a tendency among states to define their enemies as non-democratic?

For theorists who emphasize structure rather than agency (see p. 76), causality is sometimes elaborated into 'laws' of social or political development, suggesting that the social sciences resemble the natural sciences in being characterized by inevitable and predictable patterns of behaviour. Such a tendency is most clearly associated with orthodox Marxism and the belief that, driven by contra-

● **Behaviouralism**: The belief that social theories should be constructed only on the basis of observable behaviour, providing quantifiable data for research.

● **Causality**: The relationship between an event or set of circumstances (the cause) and another event or set of circumstances (the effect), in which the latter is a consequence of the former.

dictions that are found in all class societies, history develops through a series of predictable stages, and is destined to culminate in the establishment of a classless communist society. Such **determinism** has nevertheless become distinctively unfashionable, not only because it is incompatible with the idea of free will, but also because of the growing recognition that, in an interdependent world in which 'everything affects everything else', linear causal relationships are increasingly unreliable.

Simplifying the world

The second role played by theory is to simplify the world by providing conceptual **models**. A model is generally thought of as a representation of something, usually on a smaller scale, as in a dolls house or a toy airplane. In this sense, the purpose of the model is to resemble the original object as faithfully as possible. However, conceptual models need not in any way resemble the object they are being used to understand. It would be absurd, for instance, to insist that a computer model of the economy should bear a physical resemblance to the economy itself. Rather, conceptual models are analytical tools; their value is that they are devices through which meaning can be imposed on what would otherwise be a bewildering and disorganized collection of facts. As such, the primary functions of theory are selection (choosing what to look at, and what to ignore) and prioritization (deciding what is more significant and what is less significant).

This can be illustrated by Kenneth Waltz's *Theory of International Politics* (1979), the seminal work of neorealism or 'structural realism'. Waltz sought to overcome the limitations of classical realism by placing realist theory on a firmer, scientific basis. He did this by constructing a conceptual model of international politics based on three key assumptions. First, in the absence of a supreme or unchallengeable power, the international system functions as a 'self-help' system, in which states are forced to prioritize survival and security over all other goals. Second, states are the most important actors in the international system. Third, states are rational actors, in the sense that they choose amongst alternative courses of action on the basis of which best corresponds to their consistent and ordered preferences. On this basis, Waltz argued, amongst other things, that great-power war would tend to be more frequent in an international system characterized by multipolarity (see p. 237) rather than bipolarity (see p. 223), as the latter is more likely to generate a stable balance of power that discourages risk-taking and adventurism amongst states. However, it is vital to remember that conceptual models are, at best, simplifications of the reality they seek to explain. They are simply devices for drawing out understanding; they do not constitute reliable knowledge, in themselves. For this reason, it is better to think of conceptual models not as being 'true' or 'false', but merely as more or less 'useful'.

Widening or sharpening our perceptual field

The first two roles of theory are associated with **explanatory theory**, sometimes called 'empirical' theory. Explanatory theories comprise causal propositions or conceptual models that can be tested against 'hard' evidence; that is, data that exists separately of our perception of it. By contrast, when theory is used as a means of widening or sharpening our perceptual horizons, the theory in ques-

● **Determinism**: The belief that human actions and choices are entirely conditioned by external factors; determinism implies that free will is a myth.

● **Model**: A theoretical representation of empirical data that aims to advance understanding by highlighting significant relationships and interactions.

● **Explanatory theory**: Theory that seeks to make sense of events, developments and issues in the 'real world', by advancing generalized causal propositions.

tion is **interpretive theory**, sometimes called 'constitutive' theory. Interpretive theory emphasizes that human reflection is a social process, and treats the 'real world' as a series of competing truths and interpretations. Is this sense, theories are 'lenses' on the world, sometimes referred to as 'world-views'. But why do we need theory to widen or sharpen our perceptual field? The first reason is that if we try to see the world simply 'as it is' – that is, without the benefit of theory – we see what we expect to see, what we think we will see. All observation is therefore selective. The benefit of theory is that it alerts us to relationships, processes and structures of which we may previously have been unaware. For example, looking at the world through a 'feminist lens' not only means recognizing the previously 'invisible' contribution women make to shaping world politics, but it also allows us to see how world affairs might look if women's values and concerns were treated as of central importance. This enables us to generate new insights into issues ranging from globalization and development to security, war and armed conflict (as discussed in Chapter 17).

The second way in which theory can sharpen our perceptual field is by making us aware of 'hidden' prejudices and **biases**. The choice between a view of the world that is informed by theory and one that is *a*theoretical is a myth: all perception involves interpretation. The question that remains is whether we are aware of these interpretations and consciously acknowledge them. Theory, in this sense, is a device for self-reflection and critique; it is a means of uncovering 'taken-for-granted' assumptions and understandings about world politics. Once again, feminism has been influential in this respect. Beyond seeking to make women visible in discussions about world affairs, feminists have tried to expose the degree to which mainstream thinking about such matters is '**gendered**'. Feminists have, for instance, argued that conventional conceptions of security, based as they are on realist assumptions about the need for 'national security' and the importance of military-based 'hard' power, are indicative of a 'masculinist' mindset.

Defining our ethical horizons

In its fourth function, theory relates less to our ability to 'make sense' of events, developments and circumstances, and more to how we should react to them in ethical or even emotional terms. This is the realm of **normative theory**. Although empirical and normative theorizing appear to be quite different from one another, the former dealing with *facts* (empirical evidence) while the latter deals with *values* (ethical beliefs), in practice they are closely connected. All major theories of international or global politics have important empirical *and* normative dimensions (Reus-Smit and Snidal 2010). Indeed, it is difficult to imagine how theorizing about world affairs could be purely empirical in character, lacking a normative dimension altogether (something that even applies to realist theory, as discussed later in the chapter). Social activity of any kind raises moral questions because it has consequences for other human beings, challenging us to reflect on whether an activity or set of social arrangements is right or wrong, good or bad. This is particularly the case in the study of global politics, because, in considering matters such as war and peace, global poverty, international aid, climate change, humanitarian intervention and terrorism, it addresses issues whose implications for human well-being are difficult to exaggerate. Nevertheless, there are significant debates about the prominence of, and the

● **Interpretive theory**: Theory that imposes meaning on events or issues, in an attempt to understand, rather than explain, the world (see p. 519).

● **Bias**: Sympathies or prejudices that (often unconsciously) affect human judgement; bias implies distortion..

● **Gendered**: The tendency to reflect the experiences, prejudices or orientations of one gender more than the other; bias in favour of one gender.

● **Normative theory**: Theory that prescribes values and standards of conduct, what 'ought to be' rather than what 'is'.

Focus on ...
'Explaining' and 'understanding' the fall of communism

'Explaining' and 'understanding' have been portrayed as alternative ways of making sense of the world (Hollis and Smith 1991). Explaining refers to attempts to uncover the *cause* (or causes) of events, making use of methods derived from the natural sciences. As explaining focuses on facts, evidence that is external to the actors involved, it can be viewed as an 'outside' story. Understanding refers to attempts to uncover the *meaning* of events, from the perspective of the actors involved. As understanding focuses on perceptions, motivations and beliefs, it can be viewed as an 'inside' story. Despite their different emphasis, explaining and understanding both offer fertile ways of making sense of the events, and, arguably, should be used in combination.

In the case of the fall of communism in the revolutions of 1989–91 (see p. 43), one of the key 'outside' stories was the widening economic gulf, since the 1960s, between the US-led West and the Soviet-led East. This, in turn, may be explained by factors such as the (perhaps fatal) structural flaws of Soviet-style central planning, the chaotic nature of the Gorbachev's economic reforms, and the tendency of 'accelerated' globalization to bolster growth rates in the West. However, these 'outside' developments also had an important 'inside' component, particularly in the form of rising frustration and discontent across much of the communist world due to a growing desire for western-style living standards and political freedom.

An alternative 'outside' story of the fall of communism stresses how the dynamics of Cold War bipolarity generated recurrent tension between the USA and the Soviet Union, helping to explain why President Reagan initiated the 'Second' Cold War in the early 1980s. This forced the Soviet Union into an unsustainable increase in military spending, so putting its economy under further pressure. Nevertheless, account should also be taken of the 'inside' story of the launch of the 'Second' Cold War, focusing not least on Reagan's perception of the Soviet Union as an 'Evil Empire'.

status that should be accorded, normative theory within the field of global politics, as well as about the proper relationship between what 'is' and what 'ought to be'. These issues are discussed in the final section of the chapter.

Providing a guide to action

In its final function, theory is prescriptive: it sets out how we should act in the world, and so links theory firmly to practice. This use of theory relies on a combination of normative and explanatory theorizing. Normative theory is used to establish a desired outcome, based on an evaluation of the rightness or wrongness of an action, policy, institution or practice. Explanatory theory is then used to highlight, by drawing attention to causal relationships, how the desired outcome can most reliably be brought about. An emphasis on the practical implications of theory has been one of the distinguishing features of the discipline of international relations, which has long been concerned with the 'policy relevance' of academic research, even advocating the idea of theory-informed policy-making. International relations was born in the aftermath of WWI, predominantly committed to liberal internationalist thinking that was designed to prevent future wars. Classical realism took shape in the writings of E. H. Carr (see p. 34) and others, who criticized the liberal world order of the inter-war period, and especially the reliance on international bodies such as the League of Nations, arguing that such policies made future major wars more likely, if not inevitable. The onset of the Cold War gave realism greater prominence within the discipline, first through classical realism and later in the form of neorealism, its power-politics theories helping to legitimize the USA's nuclear build-up and the policy of containment.

However, attempts by theorists to intervene in policy debates have by no means always been successful, and theorists and policy-makers have sometimes openly disagreed with one another, as when a collection of prominent realist theorists publicly criticized the Bush administration's conduct of the 'war on terror' and, especially, the 2003 invasion of Iraq (see p. 521). Nevertheless, the gap between theorists and practitioners of international politics has grown noticeably since the end of the Cold War. This has occurred, in part, because the rise of 'new' voices such as constructivism, critical theory, feminism and post-structuralism has meant that the idea of theory-informed policy-making has become distinctly less fashionable. Not only has theory increasingly been seen as a device for interpreting, rather than explaining, the world, but theorists have also become more concerned that participation in policy networks may compromise their academic independence. Such a stance on policy-making should, nevertheless, not be taken to imply that critical theorists insist on a strict distinction between theory and practice. Many critical theorists, indeed, see this as a false dichotomy, emphasizing that research, study and theorising are, in themselves, forms of political practice. This is why they have sometimes been inclined to view theory as a form of **praxis**.

Which theory is best?

What is the nature of 'good' theory? Can theories be meaningfully compared with one another and, if so, on what basis? From the perspective outlined in Thomas Kuhn's pioneering *The Structure of Scientific Revolutions* (1962), any attempt to show that one theory is better than another is, ultimately, a pointless exercise. Kuhn argued that the history of science is characterized by alternating 'revolutionary' and 'normal' phases. In the former, competition between rival theories means that progress is not made in terms of the accumulation of knowledge because protagonists are primarily concerned with establishing theoretical dominance. In the latter, a single paradigm achieves ascendancy over its rivals, but, while the stock of knowledge is then able to increase, this only occurs within the parameters of the established paradigm. As the search for knowledge only takes place *within* a paradigm, there is no external or objective criteria against which rival intellectual frameworks can be evaluated. Rival theories are therefore **incommensurable**. They do not provide competing accounts of the *same* world; in effect, they 'see' *different* worlds, and use different languages to describe those worlds. Rival theories, therefore, 'talk past each other'.

Those who use theory in an interpretive or a normative sense generally agree with the above reservations. In the absence of a reliable, objective standpoint from which theories can be judged, the task of choosing a preferred theory is likely to have more to do with political belief or ideological commitment than it does with evidence-based analysis. However, those who use theory in an explanatory sense would profoundly disagree. For them, theories are commensurable and one theory can be shown to be better than another. But what criteria

● **Praxis**: Free creative activity; reflection and action that seek to transform the world by challenging oppression.

● **Incommensurability**: An inability to compare or judge between rival beliefs or propositions, because of the absence of common features.

Theorists take on the White House

Events: On 26 September 2002, as the Bush administration in the USA was stepping up preparations for the invasion of Iraq, 33 international relations scholars, most of whom identified themselves as realists, signed a *New York Times* advertisement warning that 'War with Iraq is *not* in America's national interest'. The signatories included prominent figures such as Kenneth Waltz (see p. 63), John Mearsheimer (see p. 241), Robert Jervis and Steven Walt. Their key point was that military force should not be used in these circumstances as Iraq posed no immediate threat to the USA. Other concerns that were raised included that the justifications being advanced for an invasion (that Iraq possessed WMD and that the Saddam Hussein regime had links to terrorist groups) were, at best, unproven; that an invasion could cause regional instability and would divert resources from the more important campaign against al-Qaeda; and that, without a plausible exit strategy, war against Iraq may involve significant costs for both invading forces and neighbouring states, whilst increasing anti-Americanism around the globe. Such warnings nevertheless came to nothing, as the Iraq invasion duly went ahead in March 2003.

Significance: On the face of it, the warnings issued by the realist scholars were remarkably prescient. Not only did the claims about WMD and terrorist links prove to be bogus, but, despite the speedy overthrow of the Saddam Hussein regime, hopes for the establishment of a non-sectarian democracy were soon abandoned as the Iraq War spiralled into a complex counter-insurrectionary struggle, becoming the largest, most costly and (apart from Afghanistan) the longest use of armed force by the USA since the Vietnam War. In addition to the 4,421 US service personnel who had been killed by August 2010, when the US combat mission ended, estimates of Iraqi deaths (both civilian and military) due to violence related to the war have been put as high as 600,000. Realist critics of the war nevertheless argued that even had it not proved to be so problematic, the Iraq War would still have been unnecessary. At a deeper level, realists used the Iraq War to draw attention to the danger that a hegemonic USA was over-reaching itself, risking provoking opposition by its heavy-handed use of power.

However, it is by no means clear that the Iraq War demonstrates that foreign policy-makers should listen more closely to advice from the academy. In the first place, the Iraq War may have been a product of too much theory, not too little theory. The military assertiveness of the Bush administration was influenced, in large part, by a form of republican liberalism (or 'hard' Wilsonianism) that suggested that the spread of US-style democracy across the Middle East was the surest way of bringing peace and stability to that troubled region, even if this occurred through 'regime change'. The charge against the Bush administration, then, was not that it ignored the advice of theorists, but that it listened to the *wrong* theorists; in particular, it listened to neoconservative politicians and advisors rather than to realist academics (Mearsheimer 2005). Second, even if it were possible to determine which is the 'best' theory, it would by no means be easy to derive clear-cut policy strategies from a particular theory. This is because, in view of their breadth and complexity, all theoretical traditions embody some measure of ambiguity. The Iraq War, for instance, could be said to have reflected, rather than clashed with, realist principles, insofar as it was designed to deter challenges to the USA by redressing the image of a weakened post-9/11 USA. Finally, as realists claim to see the world 'as it is', rather than as they would 'like it to be', it could be argued that such a stark gap between theory and practice raises questions about the value of the realist project itself.

characterize 'good' theory? The standard criteria that are used in the social sciences include the following:

- Correspondence to reality
- Explanatory power
- Parsimony and elegance
- Logical coherence.

Correspondence to reality

The ultimate test of any theory is conventionally taken to be how well it explains events in the real world, an idea often dubbed the **correspondence theory of truth**. When they are constructed, theories amount to mere '**propositions**'. Propositions only become fully-fledged theories when they have been tested against a selected body of evidence. As global politics is clearly not a laboratory science, this suggests that arguments should be tested against the historical record. For example, neorealist stability theory (see p. 57) can be tested by, amongst other things, examining whether there is historical evidence that periods dominated by two great powers or power blocs are more peaceful and stable than other periods. Explanatory theories also stand or fall on the basis of future developments. The standing of neorealist stability theory will therefore be crucially affected by whether or not, as the twenty-first century unfolds, emerging multipolarity is associated with fluidity and instability, with great powers becoming increasingly restless and ambitious. Although correspondence with historical evidence is sometimes said to verify a theory, the fact that subsequent developments may always disprove it indicates that the scientific basis for any theory is, as Karl Popper (1959) pointed out, that it is falsifiable. Quite simply, if it is not possible to prove that a theory is incorrect, the theory has no value. However, the correspondence theory of truth depends entirely on whether 'the facts' can be reliably established, suggesting that they exist in an objective sense separate from our values and assumptions. In this light, it is worth remembering how far the 'historical record' is based on selection and prioritization, and the extent to which history is written by the victors rather than the vanquished, to say nothing about being rewritten by succeeding generations.

Explanatory power

Some theories are more effective in explaining events than other theories. But what would great explanatory power consist of? Explanatory power is not a single or straightforward attribute but refers, rather, to a variety of qualities. These include the range and complexity of phenomena that a theory is capable of explaining. Good theories are therefore usually taken to have a high level of generality; they have greater value because they have a significant scope and do not just apply to particular events or specific circumstances. Moreover, effective explanations are often said to have predictive power, providing a fuller and more detailed account of likely future developments. In that sense, explanations and predictions parallel one another, both consisting of a set of causal relationships. Apart from anything else, theories from which clear and detailed predictions can be derived contain grounds on which they can also be falsified. Finally, explana-

---

CONCEPT

Pragmatism

Pragmatism refers generally to a concern with practical circumstances rather than with theoretical beliefs, with what can be achieved in the real world, as opposed to what should be achieved in an ideal world. As a philosophical doctrine (most commonly associated with philosophers such as William James (1842–1910) and John Dewey (1859–1952), pragmatism holds that the meaning of and justification for beliefs should be judged by their practical consequences. Though, by definition, a pragmatic style of politics is non-ideological, it does not amount to unprincipled opportunism. As a political doctrine, pragmatism suggests a cautious attitude towards change that rejects sweeping reforms and revolution as a descent into the unknown.

● **Correspondence theory of truth**: The theory that propositions are true if, and only if, they correspond with the facts.

● **Proposition**: A statement that affirms or denies something, which may be either true or false; 'what is asserted'.

tory power is sometimes linked to a theory's internal fertility, the ability of a theory to be refined and expanded to make it relevant to a wider range of phenomena, or its capacity to generate a flow of interesting questions.

Parsimony and elegance

Good theories are often taken to be spare or sparse, the oft-repeated advice to theorists being to 'keep it simple'. A parsimonious theory, especially one that is elegant, in the sense of being simple and intellectually pleasing, has the advantage that it is clear, concise and intelligible. By contrast, complex theories, ones that contain a significant number of variable factors or qualifying conditions, are not only more difficult to comprehend, but also, in a sense, say less. Examples of parsimonious theory include **rational choice theory** and neorealism. Both of these are based on first principles. In the case of rational choice theory, individual actors, seen as the basic units of analysis, are taken to be rational, efficient and instrumental utility-maximizers. In the case of neorealism, such thinking, largely derived from neo-classical economics, is used to explain the behaviour of states in the international system. And yet, parsimony in theorizing is by no means an unambiguous good. For one thing, although concision and elegance may make a theory more attractive as an explanatory device, they do so only by increasing the theory's level of abstraction and reducing its reference to the real world. For another, simplicity is only of value in theorizing if the reality we wish to analyze is itself simple, something that can very seldom be said to apply in the field of global politics. Simple theories are thus of limited value in explaining complex realities.

Logical coherence

A final feature of good theory is that its various parts should 'fit' together, in the sense of being internally consistent. If this is not the case, a theory risks contradicting itself, so providing for its own downfall. This, nevertheless, may be a difficult judgement to make as far as the main theoretical traditions, such as realism, liberalism and Marxism/critical theory, are concerned, as each of these consists of a range of sub-traditions and specific theories, each of which has its own emphasis and implications. Interdependence liberalism therefore differs, in certain respects, from republican liberalism and neoliberal institutionalism. In this light, it is perhaps better to think of theoretical traditions as being only *more or less* coherent, rather than as being rigorously consistent. Of greater concern, however, is that the drive for logical coherence is rooted in **rationalist** assumptions that may be unfounded. Traditional conservatives, for instance, challenge the notion that the world has a rational structure, arguing instead that it is 'boundless and bottomless', its deep complexity meaning that the world is largely beyond the capacity of the human mind to fathom (Oakeshott 1962). If this is the case, theory does little more than perpetuate the belief that we can explain what is, frankly, incomprehensible, leaving pragmatism (see p. 522) as the surest guide to action.

DEBATING THEORY

The arrival of theoretical 'new voices' in recent decades (constructivism, critical theory, feminism, poststructuralism and so on) has not merely created a broader

● **Rational choice theory**: An approach to analysis in which models are constructed based on procedural rule, usually about the rationally-self-interested behaviour of the individuals concerned.

● **Rationalism**: The belief that the world can be understood and explained through the exercise of human reason, based on the assumption that it has a rational structure.

● **Meta-theory**: Theory that reflects on the philosophical assumptions that underlie theories, dealing in particular with issues of ontology, epistemology and methodology.

● **Ontology**: The study of what the world consists of, and what its relevant features might be.

● **Epistemology**: (From the Greek episteme, meaning 'knowledge') The study of how we can come to have relevant insights about the world.

● **Methodology**: A mode of analysis or research, including the methods used to unearth data or evidence.

and more fragmented theoretical landscape for the study of world affairs, but it has also stimulated deeper reflection about the nature and role of theory itself. This is the realm of **meta-theory**, sometimes thought of a 'theory about theory'. Although meta-theory appears to be a highly abstract – threatening (some warn) to descend into a concern with theory *for its own sake* – in fact, it addresses some of the most interesting and important questions in political analysis. The most basic meta-theoretical concern is with the issue of **ontology**; that is, what exists in the world, what the world is made of. What do we think political reality looks like? Answering ontological questions is often seen to inform where we stand on the issue of **epistemology**; that is, what we can know about the world, and how we can know it. What is it possible to know about political reality? Answering epistemological questions, in turn, leads us to adopt a particular **methodology**; that is, a set of procedures for acquiring knowledge of the world, a way of knowing. How can we find out about political reality? In the study of world affairs, these and other issues have been raised by a series of debates. The most important debates include the following:

● Do paradigms enlighten or constrain?
● Is there a real world 'out there', or does everything exist, in a sense, in the mind?
● Can theories be neutral, or are they always *for* someone or some purpose?
● How should we link what *is* ('reality') to what *ought to be* ('utopia')?

Paradigms: enlightening or constraining?

As pointed out earlier, one of the implications of Thomas Kuhn's (1962) account of the history of science is that all knowledge is, and can only be, framed within a specific paradigm. As defined by Kuhn, a paradigm is 'the entire constellation of beliefs, values, techniques and so on shared by members of a given community'. Although Kuhn developed the concept of paradigm specifically in relation to the natural sciences, it has come to be widely applied to the social sciences. The major theoretical approaches to world affairs are thus commonly treated as paradigms, in the Kuhnian sense. The value of paradigms is that they help us to make sense of what would otherwise be an impenetrably complex reality. They define what is important to study and highlight significant trends, patterns and processes. In so doing, they draw attention to relevant questions and lines of enquiry, as well as indicate how the results of intellectual enquiry should be interpreted. What is more, as the limitations of an established paradigm are more widely recognized, not least through a growing recognition of anomalies that it is unable to explain, the search for knowledge can be dramatically reinvigorated by a **paradigm shift**, as the established paradigm breaks down and a new one is constructed in its place. This, for example, occurred in physics in the early twentieth century, through the transition from Newtonian mechanics to the ideas of quantum mechanics, made possible by the development of Einstein's theory of relativity. In economics, a similar process occurred during the 1970s and 1980s as Keynesianism was displaced by monetarism.

However, paradigms may also foster tunnel vision and hinder intellectual progress. Paradigms may limit our perceptual field, meaning that we 'see' only what our favoured paradigm shows us. Moreover, paradigms tend to generate

Postmodernism

'Postmodernism' is a controversial and confusing term that was first used to describe experimental movements in western arts, architecture and cultural development in general. As a tool of social and political analysis, postmodernism highlights the shift away from societies structured by industrialization and class solidarity to increasingly fragmented and pluralistic 'information societies', in which individualism replaces class, religious and ethnic loyalties. In philosophical terms, postmodernism is distinguished, above all, by its rejection of the idea of absolute and universal truth. Postmodernists, instead, place an emphasis on discourse and debate, embracing pluralism and difference, rather than seeking to banish or overcome them.

● **Paradigm shift**: The process through which the dominant paradigm within a field of knowledge is displaced by a rival paradigm.

● **Metanarrative**: A creed or ideology that is based on a universal theory of history which views society as a coherent totality.

● **Empiricism**: The belief that experience is the only basis for knowledge and, therefore, that all hypotheses and theories should be tested by observation

conformity amongst students and scholars alike, unable, or unwilling, to think outside the currently dominant (or fashionable) paradigm. An example of this came with the end of the Cold War, which, although it was the most significant event in world politics since 1945, appeared to take international relations scholars as much by surprise as it did other commentators (see p. 225). This occurred, at least in part, because neorealist and neoliberal thinking failed to draw attention to how far Soviet perceptions of the national interest had changed under Gorbachev. Apart from anything else, this shift meant that, in contrast to earlier uprisings in Hungary (1956) and Czechoslovakia (1968), the Soviet Union refused in 1989 to intervene in Eastern Europe to prop up crumbling communist regimes.

The field of global politics accentuates the drawbacks of paradigms because it is, by its nature, multifaceted and multidimensional, straining the capacity of any paradigm, or, for that matter, any academic discipline, to capture it in its entirety. Such a critical approach to 'paradigm thinking' (thinking firmly rooted in an established paradigm) has perhaps been taken furthest by postmodern theorists. The central theme of postmodernism was summed up by Jean-François Lyotard (1984) as 'incredulity towards **metanarratives**', the clearest examples of which are liberalism and Marxism. Metanarratives (which can be thought of as highly systematic and developed paradigms) emerged out of the sense of solidity and certainty that was generated by 'modern' societies which were structured by industrialization and strong class identities. Postmodernists argue that the emergence of increasingly fragmented and pluralistic 'postmodern' societies means that metanarratives have been rendered irrelevant. In their view, all knowledge is partial and local.

If paradigms are intellectual prisons, where does this leave us? Can we think *across* paradigms, or perhaps *beyond* paradigms? Certainly, in view of 'globalizing' tendencies in modern world politics, it is highly unlikely that a single paradigm – be it realism, liberalism, constructivism, feminism or whatever – is going to constitute the final word on any particular theme or issue. These paradigms, anyway, will be more or less relevant, or more or less persuasive, in relation to some issues rather than others. In considering paradigms, then, it is as unhelpful merely to select a theoretical 'box' within which to think as it is to adopt an 'anything goes' approach to theorizing that simply leads to incoherence. If no paradigm is capable, on its own, of fully explaining the almost infinitely complex realities it purports to disclose, cross-paradigm dialogue may offer the prospect of a fuller and clearer picture of world affairs. In this light, Sil and Katzenstein (2010) championed the cause of 'analytic eclecticism', an approach to research that is problem-driven rather than paradigm-driven, and is grounded in a pragmatic theory of knowledge. However, as long as paradigms survive, dialogue between them is constructive only if two conditions are met. First, competing paradigms must share sufficient common ground that they are commensurable. Second, dialogue must be conducted with open-mindedness rather than as a contest, something that is difficult to achieve as it requires, from the outset, an acceptance that one's chosen paradigm may be wrong.

All in the mind?

The conventional approach to theorizing draws its philosophical underpinning from the doctrine of **empiricism** (also known as 'naturalism'), which spread

CONCEPT

Positivism

Positivism is an intellectual movement that originated in nineteenth-century social science and early twentieth-century philosophy. Its key ideas are that science is the only reliable means of establishing knowledge, and that science can only deal with observable entities which can be directly experienced. Positivists argue that the methodology of the natural sciences can be applied to the study of society, in particular because human behaviour can be observed and objectively measured. Although positivism is sometimes equated with neorealism, its influence on the study of world affairs has extended more broadly to any attempt to build explanatory theory, whether or not this involves quantification.

from the seventeenth century onwards through the work of thinkers such as John Locke (1632–1704) and David Hume (1711–76). The doctrine of empiricism advanced the belief that experience is the only basis of knowledge, and that therefore all hypotheses and theories should be tested by a process of observation and experiment. By the nineteenth century, such ideas had developed into what became known as positivism, an intellectual movement particularly associated with the writings of Auguste Comte (1798–1857). This proclaimed that the social sciences and, for that matter, all forms of philosophical enquiry should adhere strictly to the methods of the natural sciences. As a methodological tradition, positivism was thus based on the following ontological and epistemological positions:

● There is a real world 'out there', independent of our experience of it
● This world consists of regularities and patterns, rather than random events
● Knowledge of these regularities and patterns can be gained through observation and experiment, what Comte called 'positive perception'
● A clear distinction exists between facts and values, between empirical and normative beliefs
● Empirical knowledge accumulates over time, both through the acquisition of new knowledge and the refinement of existing knowledge.

However, since the 1980s, positivist thinking about world affairs has been subject to criticism from a range of 'post-positivist' approaches. These include constructivism, critical theory, poststructuralism, postcolonialism and, in certain respects, feminism. What these approaches have in common is that they question the idea that there is a 'real world', separate from the beliefs, ideas and assumptions of the observer. As we observe the world, we are also in the process of imposing meaning upon it: we only ever see the world as we *think* it exists. Such an approach leads to a more critical and reflective view of theory, which is taken, in a sense, to 'construct' the world, rather than merely explain the world. Greater attention is therefore paid to the biases and hidden assumptions that are embodied in theory, implying that dispassionate scholarship may be an unachievable ideal (see p. 529).

Constructivism has been particularly influential in this respect, in that it challenges the tendency within mainstream realist and liberal theory to treat political actors as though they have fixed or objective interests or identities. Constructivists, rather, believe that account must also be taken of the normative, institutional, historical and other factors that shape how states see themselves and how they see each other. An example of this would be the stark difference in the way the USA reacts to UK nuclear weapons and how it reacts to North Korean nuclear weapons, given the perception of the UK as a 'friend' and of North Korea as an 'enemy' (Wendt 1995). The position of constructivism in the debate between positivism and post-positivism is nevertheless unclear, as constructivism itself is divided into two camps (Hopf 1998). 'Conventional' constructivists (also called 'mainstream' constructivists), such as Alexander Wendt (see p. 77) and Martha Finnemore (see p. 527), stress the importance in world politics of social concepts (like 'friend' and 'enemy'), but continue to adopt a positivist epistemology and explain the world largely in terms of cause-and-effect relationships. By contrast, 'critical' constructivists (also called 'radical' or 'postmodern' constructivists) reject

Martha Finnemore (born 1959)

A US international relations scholar. Finnemore helped to pioneer the use of constructivist analysis in international relations, especially in works such as *National Interests in International Society* (1996) and *The Purpose of Intervention* (2003). In the former, Finnemore challenged the tendency of neorealism and neoliberalism to treat state interests as though they are both stable and roughly identical, consisting of some combination of power, security and wealth. Instead, she highlighted the extent to which state interests are defined and redefined by the dense network of transnational and international social relations of which they are a part. In the latter work, Finnemore examined how the purposes for which states use military intervention have changed over some four centuries, giving particular attention to the growing significance of new norms about who is human and how we should treat 'strangers'.

the idea of objective knowledge, and question the notion that social relationships can be explained in terms of discrete 'causes' and 'effects'.

Although the ontological divide between positivists and post-positivists is ultimately unbridgeable, as the two positions are based on mutually exclusive assumptions, the two approaches may nevertheless aspire to similar goals. For instance, post-positivists may agree with positivists that there is a real world 'out there', resisting the stark division between **objectivism** and **subjectivism**. The major difference between them may be epistemological rather than ontological, as it relates to the reliability of our knowledge of the world. While post-positivists may, like positivists, pursue objectivity, not least through attempts to expose bias, they insist that the search for unchallengeable, rock-solid foundations for knowledge will always be fruitless.

For some purpose?

Post-positivist theorizing about world affairs has acquired a distinctive emphasis within critical theory. Critical theorists reject the idea of value-free social science on the grounds that, as knowledge is inherently political, theoretical debates are basically political debates. This stance is reflected in Robert Cox's (1981) much quoted observation that 'theory is always *for* someone and *for* some purpose'. Such a position is rooted in Marx's (see p. 72) theory of ideology. Marx used the term 'ideology' to refer to the ideas of the economically dominant class (the bourgeoisie), emphasizing that the purpose of these ideas was to manipulate and delude the oppressed class (the proletariat), preventing them from recognizing the fact of their own exploitation. Ideology therefore promotes 'false consciousness'. Marx nevertheless believed that his own ideas (portrayed by his friend and collaborator Friedrich Engels (1820–95) as 'scientific socialism') peeled off these layers of manipulation by exposing the exploitative nature of the capitalist system, so helping to bring the proletariat to revolutionary **class consciousness**. From the Marxist perspective, our theories, ideas and beliefs are therefore always politically engaged because they are linked to class interests: they either serve to uphold the class system or to overthrow it.

● **Objectivism**: Judgements that pertain to objects, in which case truth can be independently distinguished from falsehood.

● **Subjectivism**: Judgements that pertain to subjects (persons), which are neither true or false but relate to feelings, taste or morality.

● **Class consciousness**: A Marxist term denoting an accurate awareness of class interests, transforming a class in-itself into a class for-itself.

THEORY

Realist view

In view of their core focus on 'reality' (the world 'as it is') and their deep scepticism towards ideals and principles (the world 'as it ought to be'), realists traditionally 'travelled light' in theoretical terms. Classical realism thus set out to explain recurrent patterns of state interaction largely in terms of an unsentimental view of human nature (even if this was sometimes portrayed less as a theory and more as a 'fact of life'). Within classical realism, theoretical belief has always been balanced against pragmatism, reflected in a stress on statecraft and on subjective evaluations of international relations made by state leaders. However, the advent of neorealism marked the emergence of a more systematic, rigorous and structural approach to theory within realism. Heavily influenced by positivist models, particularly as used in economics, its pioneering work, Waltz's (1979) *Theory of International Politics*, set out to produce nothing less than a science of world politics. In this, states are compelled to act in certain ways by the structure of the international system. Abiding realist concerns about normative theory reflect not so much a rejection of morality (after all, few realists question the moral priority of the national interest) but, rather, a distaste for 'moralism', which places respect for ethical principles above all other considerations and blinds state leaders to the messy realities of the world. For realists, not only should morality never be an absolute guide to political practice, but it should also always be judged in relation to a particular time, place and national context.

Liberal view

Liberalism's strong emphasis on theory reflects the fact that its origins in the Enlightenment imbued it with a faith in scientific rationality, freedom and progress. As liberals believe in universal moral and rational principles, the explanatory and normative dimensions of theory are usually taken to be intertwined, although the balance between them has varied over time. Early liberal theorizing about international relations, in the years following WWI, drew heavily on idealism (see p. 65), and was shaped, above all, by the attempt to find a solution to the problem of war. However, as liberal thinking about international relations was eclipsed by realist thinking during the Cold War period, liberalism progressively disengaged from idealism, its normative agenda being significantly narrowed in the process.

This became particularly apparent during the 1970s and 1980s with the rise of neoliberal institutionalism, which adopted a clearly social-scientific methodology. The 'neo-neo' debate was therefore conducted *within* a positivist framework, neorealists and neoliberals subscribing to common ontological and epistemological assumptions. The end of the Cold War nevertheless encouraged liberals to re-embrace normative theory more explicitly, notably though a stress on human rights (see p. 311). However, this 'normative turn' did not amount to a full return to idealism, as it was also accompanied by a greater emphasis within liberalism on the construction of explanatory theories grounded in testable propositions.

Critical views

Critical perspectives on world affairs have stimulated a major reappraisal of the nature and role of theory. This has happened, most importantly, through the attempt to go beyond the positivism of mainstream realist and liberal theory. By emphasizing the role of consciousness in shaping social conduct, post-positivist perspectives used theory not so much as a tool for explaining the world, in an objective sense, but as a device for broadening and/or sharpening our perception of the world, implying that theory has an essentially constitutive or interpretive role. The extent of ontological and epistemological agreement among (and, sometimes, within) critical perspectives should not be over-stated, however. For instance, while 'conventional' constructivists (such as Wendt (see p. 77)) seek to probe the inter-subjective content of events and episodes, but within a social-scientific methodology, 'critical' constructivists either (in common with postmodernists) deny the existence of a real world 'out there', or argue that it is buried under so many layers of conceptual and contextual meaning that we can never gain access to it. The shift to post-positivism has also allowed a greater emphasis to be placed on the normative dimension of theory, albeit in different ways. Thus, whereas constructivism has been used to show how states may transcend a narrow perception of self-interest, Frankfurt School critical theory has focused on uncovering structures of oppression and injustice in world politics; and feminism has attempted, among other things, to challenge an established gender order that excludes women from moral status.

Focus on ...

Can the study of global politics be value-free and dispassionate?

Those who champion the cause of neutral and dispassionate scholarship in global politics advance at least three arguments. In the first place, they hold that there is a strict distinction between political analysis and political advocacy, the motive for the former being a desire to understand and explain the political world (to 'make sense' of things), rather than to reshape the world in line with one's values or personal preferences. Political convictions are therefore put to one side, recognizing how they can blind people to 'inconvenient' truths. Second, education and the rigour of academic study are themselves a training-ground in dispassionate scholarship, encouraging students to distance themselves, over time, from allegiances and biases that derive from social and family background, Third, and most important, the possibility of neutral scholarship is founded on a commitment to, and belief in, 'scientific' objectivity. In this view, scientific method (involving the use of observation, measurement and experimentation) is the only approach to knowledge that can reliably distinguish between truth and falsehood, and it does this by insisting that propositions are verified or falsified by comparing them with what we know of the 'real world'. Such an approach to knowledge is applicable not only to global politics, but to all fields of learning.

However, while natural scientists may be able to approach their studies from an objective and impartial standpoint, this may be impossible in global politics. Politics, at all levels, addresses questions about the society in which we live and have grown up. Family background, social experience, economic position, political sympathies and so on therefore build into each of us ingrained preconceptions about the political world we are seeking to study. Indeed, perhaps the greatest threat to reliable knowledge comes not from bias, as such, but from a failure to acknowledge bias, reflected in bogus claims to academic neutrality. Such concerns have been deepened by doubts about the possibility of scientific objectivity derived from an awareness that there may be more than one way in which the world can be understood. From this perspective, there is no single, overarching truth about the 'real world' out there, separate from the beliefs, ideas and assumptions of the observer. If the subject (the student of global politics) cannot in any reliable way be distinguished from the object (the political world), then dispassionate scholarship must be treated as, at best, an unachievable ideal.

Influenced by the work of Antonio Gramsci (see p. 73) and of leading figures from the Frankfurt School of critical theory, Cox (1981) developed this analysis into a distinction between 'critical theory' and what he called 'problem-solving theory'. Problem-solving theory tends to legitimize prevailing social and political structures, because, as Cox put it, it 'takes the world as it finds it'. As it does not establish a position outside of prevailing power structures from which they can be critically evaluated, it accepts, rather than questions, the global status quo. In being used to 'solve problems', such theory therefore serves to ensure the 'smooth working' of the existing order. The classic examples of problem-solving theory are neorealism and neoliberalism, both of which are used to diffuse conflicts, tensions and crises within the established world order. By contrast, all forms of critical theory tend to have an emancipatory orientation. They seek to oppose the dominant forces and structures in modern world affairs, and are usually aligned to the interests of marginalized or oppressed groups. For Cox (2008), the purpose of studying world politics is to bring about basic change in the structure of world power, in line with priorities such as ensuring the survival of the

CONCEPT

Utopianism

A utopia is literally an ideal or perfect society. Utopianism is often used as a pejorative term, implying deluded or fanciful thinking, a belief in an unrealistic and unachievable goal. Realists have referred to liberal internationalism as 'utopianism', in this sense. However, the term can be used in the positive sense to refer to a style of political theorizing that develops a critique of the existing order by constructing a model of an ideal or perfect alternative (examples including anarchism and Marxism). Utopian theories are usually based on (realistic or unrealistic) assumptions about the scope for human self-development. Utopias are usually characterized by the abolition of want, the absence of conflict and the avoidance of oppression and violence.

biosphere, avoiding nuclear war, moderating the gap between the rich and the poor, and protecting the most vulnerable people.

This view of theory has also attracted criticism, however. In the first place, there appears to be tension between critical theory's commitment to serving the interests of the marginalized and oppressed, which must surely be founded on the ability to uncover reliable, if not objective, knowledge, and the adoption of a post-positivist methodology that casts serious doubt over the notion of objective truth. This tension, indeed, may be traced back to Marx's assertion that all belief systems are ideological (and therefore false), except his own. Some critical theorists may nevertheless argue that their purpose is not so much to establish objective solutions to the problems of the marginalized, as to recognise their experience and perspective and to give them a political voice, enabling them to develop solutions of their own.

Second, even if it is accepted that all theory is entangled with politics, judgements about which political purposes are 'emancipatory' and which are 'oppressive' may, in the absence of agreed or objective standards, be little more than a matter of personal preference or subjective ideological orientation. This can be seen, for example, in debates about the benefits of free trade (see p. 480). Third, the project of changing the world 'for the good', especially through radical social upheavals, has, at best, a patchy record. It is notable, for instance, that the scholars of the Frankfurt School deliberately retreated from political activism and concentrated instead on theory, in large part because of their distaste for 'actually-existing' socialism, in the form of the Soviet Union and the communist bloc. In other words, emancipatory theory may not always lead to emancipatory practice.

Between utopia and reality?

The status and role of normative theory in the study of world affairs has long been a matter of dispute. Normative concerns dominated the academic study of world affairs in its early years, as attempts were made to find a solution to the problem of war, inspired by a tradition of 'idealist' (see p. 65) theorizing that derived from the ideas of thinkers such as Thomas Aquinas (see p. 261) and Immanuel Kant (see p. 15). In the aftermath of WW II, however, normative theory became distinctly unfashionable, being pushed to the margins of academic interest. This occurred, first, because the rise of realism was accompanied by a critique of normative theory, sometimes dubbed 'utopianism', which held that it had contributed to the resurgence of great-power rivalry that eventually led to war in 1939. In this view, an unrealistic faith in the capacity of states to cooperate through bodies such as the League of Nations had blinded policymakers to the threat posed by rising and ambitious powers. Second, attempts, since the 1960s, to develop a 'science' of international politics strengthened the idea that facts are firmly distinct from values, suggesting that the search for truth should not be 'contaminated' by ethical considerations. Since the 1980s, nevertheless, normative theory has once again gained prominence, partly as a result of frustration with the 'amoral' power-politics theories that had dominated the Cold War period. The prospect of radically re-orientating world order as the shadow of superpower rivalry faded also helped to generate growing interest in the doctrine of human rights (see p. 311) and associated ideas such as cosmopolitanism (see p. 21) and international justice.

CONCEPT

Communitarianism

Communitarianism is, broadly, the belief that the self or person is constituted through the community, in the sense that individuals are shaped by the communities to which they belong and owe them a debt of respect and consideration. As a school of thought, communitarianism emerged in the 1980s and 1990s as a critique of liberalism, highlighting the damage done to the public culture by an over-emphasis on individual rights and freedoms. In the study of world politics, communitarianism is usually linked with nationalism, and especially the idea that morality is fashioned by the distinctive history, culture and traditions of particular nations, rather than by universal principles such as human rights. Communitarianism and cosmopolitanism are thus rival normative theories.

● **Realistic utopia**: An ideal of a society whose members enjoy just and peaceful relations, but which is sufficiently close to the 'real' world to be attainable.

Nevertheless, as discussed earlier, the apparently strict divide between explanatory theory and normative theory is misleading. Empirical analysis is invariably motivated, at some level, by normative concerns, implying that the 'is' and the 'ought' are intertwined. If people were unconcerned about the level of violence and suffering in the world, why would they study, for instance, the causes of war or the incidence of poverty? All theoretical traditions within the field of global politics are therefore shaped by normative goals. For example, although realists have firmly rejected the idea that foreign policy should be guided by ethical objectives, they have done so largely because of their assessment that 'hard-headed' foreign policy better serves the national interest. The choice is thus not between embracing or rejecting normative theory, but between different models of ethics, in particular between those based on communitarianism and those based on cosmopolitanism. Moreover, ethical speculation about world affairs cannot but address issues related to political 'reality', implying that normative theory always has an empirical dimension. For example, the (normative) commitment to reduce global poverty is invariably linked to (empirical) attempts to understand the causes of poverty and how it can be reduced or ended.

However, debate has surrounded the exact nature of the link between normative and empirical thinking. While normative aspirations have to be sufficiently bold to be appealing and desirable, they must also be politically feasible. In that sense, 'utopia' must be linked to 'reality', but is the notion of a '**realistic utopia**' meaningful? In *The Laws of the People* (1999), John Rawls outlined what he claimed was a realistic utopia. This took the form of a peaceful and cooperative international order, in which moral ambition was limited to a number of specific goals, including the elimination of unjust war and oppression, the removal of religious persecution and restrictions on freedom of conscience, and an end to genocide and mass murder. Rawls claimed that this vision fell within the limits of 'practical political possibility' because it was based on minimal standards of human rights and involved no requirement for wholesale economic redistribution. For Jürgen Habermas (2010), a realistic utopia could be constructed in the form of a 'democratically constituted world society', in which human rights would be enforceable. Habermas nevertheless acknowledged that democracy cannot operate meaningfully at a level beyond the nation-state, and accepted that global governance (see p. 462) could never develop into anything more than a 'negotiating system' which ensures fair bargaining amongst interested parties and networks. However, the drawback of any supposed realistic utopia is that it can be criticized from both sides. Realistic utopias may be condemned for being so utopian they are politically unfeasible, or for being so realistic they are fatally morally compromised.

SUMMARY

- Theory has a range of uses and a number of dimensions. Its uses include analyzing and explaining events, simplifying the world, widening and/or sharpening our perceptual field, defining our ethical horizons, and providing a guide to action. Although distinct explanatory, interpretive and normative dimensions of theory can be identified, these sometimes overlap.

- Attempts to establish 'good' theory are sometimes dismissed as pointless, on the grounds that rival theories are incommensurable. However, others argue that theories can be evaluated using the standard criteria employed in the social sciences. These include a theory's correspondence to reality, its explanatory power, its parsimony and elegance, and its logical coherence.

- Paradigms aid understanding in that they define what is important to study, draw attention to significant trends, patterns and processes, and highlight relevant questions and lines of enquiry. However, paradigms may also limit our perceptual field, meaning that we 'see' only what our favoured paradigm shows us.

- Positivists proclaim that the social sciences should adhere strictly to the methods of the natural sciences, based on the possibility of establishing objective knowledge. Post-positivists question whether there is a real world 'out there', separate from our beliefs, ideas and assumptions about it. We therefore only see the world as we *think* it exists.

- Critical theorists reject the idea of value-free social science on the grounds that knowledge is inherently political, in which case theoretical debates are basically political debates. Such thinking has been criticized for, amongst other things, failing to show how we can make reliable judgements about the (alleged) political purposes of theory.

- The notion of a 'realistic utopia' may allow us to reconcile normative theory with empirically-based explanatory theory. However, realistic utopias may fall between two stools, being either so utopian they are politically unfeasible or so realistic they are fatally morally compromised.

Questions for discussion

- Why is theory unavoidable?
- How does theory allow us to analyze, rather than just describe, world affairs?
- How can theory be used to widen and deepen our perceptions?
- Does theory constitute a sound guide to action?
- Is it possible to 'prove' that one theory is better than another?
- Is all knowledge framed within a paradigm?
- Do the attractions of thinking 'across' paradigms outweigh the drawbacks?
- Is there a real world 'out there', and, if so, how do we know?
- Is neutral and dispassionate scholarship possible?
- How and why are empirical and normative theory intrinsically linked?
- Is the notion of a 'realistic utopia' meaningful or helpful?

Further reading

Jørgensen, K. E., *International Relations Theory: A New Introduction* (2010). An account of the main theoretical traditions of international relations, which introduces students to the activity of 'doing' theory.

Moses, J. W. and T. Knutsen, *Ways of Knowing: Competing Methodologies in Social and Politics Science* (2012). A clear and accessible introduction to competing naturalist (positivist) and constructivist methodologies in the social sciences

Reus-Smit, C. and D. Snidal, *The Oxford Handbook of International Relations* (2010). A stimulating collection of essays that both explore the complex links between theory, method and political practice, and provide a comprehensive overview of international theories.

Savigny, H. and L. Marsden, *Doing Political Science and International Relations: Theories in Action* (2011). An innovative text that examines how a wide range of theoretical perspectives illuminate key issues in global as well as domestic politics.

ONLINE RESOURCES AVAILABLE

Links to relevant web resources can be found on the *Global Politics* website

CHAPTER 22

Images of the Global Future

'And in today already walks tomorrow.'

SAMUEL TAYLOR COLERIDGE (1875–1912)

PREVIEW

Theories can help us to understand the world. But as the preceding chapters make clear they have significant limitations in helping us to predict the likely shape of global politics in the twenty-first century. A useful starting point for such a discussion is perhaps provided by a range of sometimes stark, even dramatic, images, which academics, policy analysts or political commentators have advanced, often with the explicit intention of predicting the global future. Frequently having an impact well beyond academic circles, and influencing popular discourse about world affairs, these have, amongst other things, announced the arrival of a 'borderless world', proclaimed the 'end of history', predicted an emerging 'clash of civilizations' and announced the birth of the 'Chinese century'. Such images have been thrown up by the shifts and deep transformations that have occurred in global politics in recent decades – the advance of globalization, the end of the Cold War, the advent of global terrorism and so forth. As old certainties have been thrown into question and the contours of global politics have become more indistinct, a thirst has grown for pithy explanations and neat hypotheses – that is, for images. What trends do these images highlight, and how persuasive are they as visions of the global future? These images nevertheless raise still larger questions, notably about whether we can ever know the future, and, if so, how far into the future we can see. Although greater resources than ever before are currently devoted to forecasting economic, financial and other matters (not least the weather), there is little evidence that we are much better off as a result. Are these efforts worthwhile? Or do they merely sustain delusions about the extent and reliability of human knowledge?

KEY ISSUES

- How do images help us understand reality?
- What role does image play in global politics?
- What have been the most influential images of modern global politics?
- What have been the key strengths and weaknesses of these images?
- Can images help to uncover the global future?
- Is it possible to know the future?

IMAGES AND REALITY

An image is a representation or likeness of an individual, a group or a thing (an institution, event, system and so on). As such, images are nothing more than illusions or constructs of our mind. However this does not mean that images are of 'inner' significance only. Images may play an important role in building up knowledge and understanding, and they may feature as a significant component in explaining the behaviour of global actors. As far as developing knowledge is concerned, images play a much wider role than is commonly assumed. This can be seen, for example, in the processes through which scientific knowledge has developed. The notion that scientists develop understanding only through a strict process of experimentation designed to distinguish subjective elements (such as bias or wishful-thinking) from 'hard' objective knowledge is quite misleading. Charles Darwin's theory of 'natural selection' (the basis of modern biology), Albert Einstein's theory of relativity (the basis of modern atomic and sub-atomic physics), Alfred Wegener's theory of plate tectonics (which explains movements on the Earth's surface), and Georges Lemaître's theory of the 'big bang' (which provides a model of the origins of the universe), are all examples of scientific 'discoveries' that could not, because of their nature, have emerged through the use of the experimental method alone. Instead, each of them originated as an image, an image that commended itself on the grounds that it appeared to make elegant sense of an otherwise baffling reality. Only later, and sometimes only partially, did experimentation provide support for these images. As Einstein put it, 'Imagination is more important than knowledge'.

As the basis for explaining the behaviour of actors on the world stage, image is important in shaping both how people see themselves and how they see others. This is perhaps most clear in relation to nationalism and the role of national image. In his seminal work on the subject, Boulding (1956) highlighted the crucial importance that national image plays in processes such as conflict resolution and peacebuilding. Prefiguring the ideas of later constructivists, he suggested that it is what we think the world is like, not what it is really like, that determines our behaviour. Thus, it is one nation's image of the hostility or friendliness of another, not its 'real' hostility or friendliness, which determines its reaction to it. In Boulding's view, the image can therefore be thought of as the 'total cognitive, affective and evaluative structure of the behavioural unit'; in effect, its internal view of itself and the universe it operates in. However, national images are not fixed and unchanging; rather, governments and political leaders actively engage in remodelling and reshaping national images both for domestic consumption and to project these on the world stage. This process of image projection can clearly be seen in the case of international summits, conferences and major sporting events. For instance, the 2008 Beijing Olympics was used to project an image of a creative, modern and above all successful China, marking, in effect, China's 'coming out' as a power of the first order. This was evident in the huge resources that were ploughed into the opening and closing ceremonies, the construction of some 31 state-of-the-art sporting venues and substantial related infrastructural development (including the renovation of Beijing airport with the addition of the new Terminal 3, the world's largest airport terminal), and the meticulous preparation of Chinese athletes for the Olympics (China's 51 gold medals topped the medals table and eclipsed the USA for the first time).

The emphasis on the role and significance of image in modern global politics has perhaps been taken furthest by poststructuralist theorists. James Der Derian (2009), for instance, examined the processes and influences that have helped to fashion the chimera of high-tech, low-risk 'virtuous war', and how this image has helped to shape the direction of US foreign policy, particularly in the post-9/11 period. Abandoning the outdated idea of the military-industrial complex, Der Derian highlighted the role of what he called the 'new military-industrial-media-entertainment network', which operates though the exposure of modern warfare on television, Hollywood war movies, military war games, computer video games and the like, in creating the vision of bloodless, humanitarian, hygienic wars. The moral danger of this is that as 'the virtual' and 'the virtuous' are conflated, people's attitudes to war cease to be shaped by the often profound and widespread human costs of 'real' warfare. The political danger of virtuous war is that it can draw policy-makers into foreign involvements massively over-confident about the efficacy of modern military technology and seriously unaware of the strategic and other complexities that military conflict often involves. For Der Derian, virtuous war took centre stage in the 2003 'shock and awe' invasion of Iraq, but this was nevertheless followed by a protracted counter-insurgency war for which the USA was not fully prepared.

CONTENDING IMAGES OF THE GLOBAL FUTURE

However, images are not only significant in structuring how states interact with one another and approach issues of war and peace. They are also used as wider explanatory tools, graphic ways of highlighting important trends and developments in global politics. In recent decades, myriad such images have been thrown up, as international relations scholars, social scientists, policy advisors, journalists and sometimes politicians have competed to imprint their own understanding of global politics on the academic and wider public imagination. Indeed, debate on global politics has increasingly been orientated around such images and counter-images, providing a seductively neat way of encapsulating where one stands on the major issues of the day. Although there are no reliable criteria for determining the relative importance of these images, some of the most influential include the following:

- A borderless world
- A world of democracies
- Civilizations in conflict
- A Chinese century
- The growth of international community
- The rise of the global South
- The coming environmental catastrophe
- Towards cosmopolitan democracy.

A borderless world?

The image of a borderless world surfaced in the writings of Ohmae (1990). It is an image that captures the key ideas of the hyperglobalist model of globalization (see p. 8). This portrays globalization as a profound, even revolutionary set of economic, cultural, technological and political shifts that have dramatic implications for the state and conventional notions of sovereignty (see p. 4). As globalization advances, increased cross-border flows of people, goods, money, technology and ideas weaken the state as a territorial entity and significantly undermine the capacity of national governments to control what goes on within their borders. What would a borderless world look like? Most importantly, it would be a world of global interconnectedness and 'accelerated' interdependence. For hyperglobalists, the emergence of an interlocking global economy creates the prospect of prosperity for all. Economic resources will be drawn towards their most profitable use, regardless of where in the world that might be, and material disparities will diminish as all countries and areas that participate in the global economy gain benefit, creating the 'great convergence' (Mahbubani 2013). In this respect, the substantial shift that has occurred in favour of free trade since the end of WWII, brought about in part through the work of bodies such as the World Trade Organization (see p. 537), has helped to make the rich richer but also the poor less poor. The political implications of a borderless world would be no less significant, however. In particular, in line with the ideas of commercial or interdependence liberalism, global free trade, transnational production and trans-world investment flows create the prospect of widespread and enduring peace. Not only would the economic cost of war in such a context be unacceptably high, but intensified economic and financial interconnectedness would build increased international understanding, even cosmopolitanism (see p. 21).

How persuasive is this image? The chief problem of the hyperglobalist model of world politics is that it overstates the extent to which the advance of globalization weakens states and renders national borders irrelevant. As discussed in Chapter 5, the much heralded rise of 'post-sovereign governance', in which the state has been so 'hollowed out' that it has become, in effect, redundant, has failed to emerge. States have been transformed by conditions of advanced globalization; they have not been consigned to the dustbin of history. Indeed, globalization may, in some ways, have strengthened the state, which, as states such as China and Russia have demonstrated, has gained renewed importance as an agent of modernization. To the extent that states, and therefore the state-system, continue to exert influence, global politics will remain a battlefield between the forces of interdependence and the forces of anarchy, with the latter stubbornly refusing to succumb to the former. Furthermore, the idea that the borderless world would be characterized by harmony, peace and prosperity is open to doubt for at least two reasons. In the first place, globalization has bred a cultural and political backlash, perhaps reflecting the politico-cultural limits to globalization. This is evident in the extent to which the rise of ethnic nationalism and religious fundamentalism (see p. 199) has occurred as a reaction against the imposition of alien and threatening values and practices. Second, it is by no means clear that a borderless world would be one in which everyone wins, participating in a rising but shared prosperity. Instead, as market-based economic systems have always generated structural disparities, it is more likely that any transition from national capitalism to global capitalism will reshape these disparities rather than abolish them altogether.

GLOBAL ACTORS . . .

THE WORLD TRADE ORGANIZATION

Type: Intergovernmental organization • **Established:** 1995 • **Location:** Geneva, Switzerland
Membership: 159 member states

The World Trade Organization (WTO) was created on January 1, 1995 as a replacement for the General Agreement on Tariffs and Trade (GATT). It was a product of the Uruguay Round of trade negotiations, 1986-93. The key aim of the WTO is to uphold the principles of the multilateral trading system. Above all, the WTO is a negotiating forum, a place where member governments attempt to sort out the trade problems they face with each other. The organization is run by its member governments: all major decisions are made by the membership as a whole. Decisions are normally taken by consensus. In this respect, the WTO differs from UN bodies such as the World Bank (see p. 380) and the IMF (see p. 475), which both have executive boards to direct the executive officers of the organization, as well as a system of weighted voting that favours the major industrial countries.

Significance: Supporters of the WTO argue that it has played a key role in supporting trade liberalization, thus making a major contribution to promoting sustainable growth in the world economy. This is largely based on the belief that free and open trade is mutually beneficial to the countries that engage in it. Trade liberalization sharpens competition, fosters innovation and breeds success for all. Unlike the World Bank and the IMF, the WTO also has a strongly democratic culture based on consensus-

building amongst all member governments. WTO rules are enforced by the members themselves under agreed procedures that they have negotiated. When sanctions are imposed, these are authorized by the membership as a whole. This ensures that the views and interests of developing countries are fully taken into account, both because of their numerical strength (developing states constitute about two-thirds of WTO members) and because of a growing emphasis on the idea of trade-orientated development. Of particular importance to the WTO's effectiveness is its disputes settlement process, widely seen as an advance on GATT's. Under GATT, there was no fixed timetable for settling disputes, rulings were easy to block, and many cases dragged on inconclusively for a long time. The WTO, by contrast, has a more structured process and places greater emphasis on prompt settlement. Most disputes are nevertheless settled 'out of court' through informal consultations, with only just over a third of cases being resolved by the Dispute Settlement Body.

The WTO has nevertheless been a highly controversial organization. Many of its critics focus on its basic principles, arguing that, far from bringing benefit to all, trade liberalization is responsible for structural inequalities and the weakening of workers' rights and environmental protection. This derives both from the tendency of industrially and technologically advanced countries to

gain most from international trade (as they gain access to larger markets without exposing themselves to greatly intensified competition) and because free-trade rules make it more difficult for states to maintain social and environmental protections. Furthermore, the WTO's emphasis on consensus-building means that its decision-making processes lack transparency and therefore accountability. A second criticism dismisses WTO democracy as a sham. Developed countries allegedly enjoy a range of advantages within the WTO over developing ones. These include that consensus decision-making is biased in favour of states that have sizeable, well resourced and permanent representation in Geneva, meaning that the WTO is often characterized as a 'rich man's club'. A third criticism highlights the weakness of the WTO, and specifically its inability to reconcile strongly-held opposing views. This is evident in the near-collapse of the Doha Round of negotiations, which commenced in 2001. Negotiations have stalled because of disagreements, mainly over agricultural subsidies, between, on the one hand, developing countries and emerging economies, including China, and developed countries on the other hand. Such a failure has enabled the USA and the EU to maintain agricultural protectionism, while penalizing developing countries and the world's poor, who will benefit most from reducing barriers and subsidies in farming.

A world of democracies?

The image of a world of democracies is rooted in republican liberalism, and has a history that can be traced back to seventeenth and eighteenth century ideas about the contractual basis of government power. In its modern version, it highlights a supposedly irresistible trend in favour of democratic governance and against autocracy and authoritarianism. According to 'end of history' theorists such as Francis Fukuyama (see p. 539), democracy, or more accurately, liberal democracy (see p. 189), represents the determinate end-point of human history. This is supposedly because it both offers all members of society the prospect of social mobility and material security, and allows citizens the opportunity for personal self-development without the interference of the state. For Fukuyama and theorists such as Doyle (1986, 1995), the principal outcome of the inexorable trend towards democracy is the general spread of peace, and certainly the declining likelihood of large-scale conflict between states. This prediction is based on the 'democratic peace' thesis (see p. 69), in which the decline of war amongst democratic states over time is explained in terms of the homogenization of values that occurs as states converge towards liberal-democratic norms. Historical evidence for the alleged trend in favour of democracy has been advanced by Huntington (1991), who drew attention to three 'waves' of democratization. The first occurred between 1828 and 1926 and involved countries such as the USA, France and the UK; the second occurred between 1943 and 1962 and involved ones such as West Germany, Italy, Japan and India; and the third began in 1974 with the overthrow of right-wing dictatorships in Greece, Portugal and Spain, the retreat of the generals in Latin America, and, most significantly, the collapse of communism from 1989 onwards. By 2003, 63 per cent of states, accounting for about 70 per cent of the world's population, exhibited some of the key features of democratic governance.

The idea that the state-system will be transformed through the trend in favour of democracy has nevertheless attracted criticism. For example, the 'end of history' thesis had hardly been outlined before the end of communism threw up very different, and somewhat less optimistic, images. The East European Revolutions of 1989–91 unleashed ancient hatreds, not least through the break-up of Yugoslavia in the 1990s, and produced an explosion of crime and corruption, sometimes linked to the 'shock therapy' transition to market capitalism, suggesting the re-emergence of chaos and instability rather than a long-term trend towards peace. This implied that the main significance of the collapse of communism and the end of the Cold War may not be the opportunity it provided for a new wave of democratization, but rather that it marked the transition from a stable, bipolar world order to one characterized by inherently unstable multipolarity (see p. 237) (Mearsheimer 1990). Further doubts about the idea of a world of democracies and the prospect of a 'democratic peace' have emerged from the growing significance of non-democratic states on the world stage. In their different ways, China and Russia are perhaps demonstrating that authoritarianism has certain advantages over democracy. These may include the success of state capitalism as an economic model in which the strengths of the market are balanced against a strong state, which undertakes long-term planning and reduces the instabilities associated with US-style enterprise capitalism. Similarly, authoritarian states may be in a better position than democratic states

Francis Fukuyama (born 1952)

US social analyst and political commentator. Fukuyama was born in Chicago, USA, the son of a Protestant preacher. He was a member of the Policy Planning Staff of the US State Department before becoming a consultant for the Rand Corporation. A staunch Republican, he came to international prominence as a result of his article 'The End of History?' (1989), which he later developed into *The End of History and the Last Man* (1992). These claimed that the history of ideas had ended with the recognition of liberal democracy as 'the final form of human government'. In *Trust* (1996) and *The Great Disruption* (1999), Fukuyama discussed the relationship between economic development and social cohesion, highlighting contrasting forms of capitalist development. In *The Origins of Political Order* (2011), he examined the paths that different societies have taken to reach their current form of political order.

to implement the tougher policies that the challenges of climate change may throw up. Finally, Kagan (2008) sought to revise the optimism embodied in the 'end of history' thesis by announcing the 'return of history'. This suggests that twenty-first century global politics will be characterized not by a democratic peace, but by rivalry between democratic states (especially the USA) and authoritarian states (notably China and Russia).

Civilizations in conflict?

The idea of civilizations in conflict emerged in the aftermath of the Cold War, through the clash of civilizations thesis developed in the writings of Samuel Huntington (see p. 540). At the core of this thesis was the assertion that twenty-first century world order would be characterized by growing tension and conflict, but that this conflict will be cultural in character, rather than ideological, political or economic. A new era of global politics have therefore emerged in which civilization would be the primary force, a civilization being 'culture writ large'. For Huntington, the emerging 'world of civilizations' would comprise nine major civilizations – western, Sinic or Chinese, Japanese, Hindu, Islamic, Buddhist, African, Latin American and Orthodox Christian. As discussed in Chapter 8, Huntington (1993, 1996) assumed that, as these civilizations are based on irreconcilable values, rivalry and conflict among them is inevitable, with particular emphasis being placed on the likelihood of conflict between China (wedded to distinctive Sinic cultural values despite rapid economic growth) and the West, and the West and Islam. He also identified the potential for conflict between the West and 'the Rest', possibly spearheaded by an anti-western alliance of Confucian and Islamic states. As such, the image of civilizations in conflict offers an alternative to state-centric realism (even though Huntington acknowledged that civilizations operate through allegiances to 'core' states, in which case nation-states would remain the principal actors in world affairs) and provides a stark contrast to the liberal images of a borderless world or a world of democracies.

This image of global politics undoubtedly had its greatest impact in the aftermath of the September 11 terrorist attacks (see p. 20), when 'global' or 'Islamist'

Samuel P. Huntington (1927–2008)

US academic and political commentator. Huntington made influential contributions to three fields: military politics, strategy and civil/military relations; US and comparative politics; and the politics of less developed societies. In *The Third Wave* (1991), he coined the notion of 'waves of democratization' and linked the process of democratization after 1972 to earlier waves, in 1828–1926 and 1943–62. His most widely discussed work, *The Clash of Civilizations and the Making of World Order* (1996), advanced the controversial thesis that in the twenty-first century conflict between the world's major civilizations would lead to warfare and international disorder. In *Who Are We?* (2004) Huntington discussed the challenges posed to the USA's national identity by large-scale Latino immigration and the unwillingness of Latino communities to assimilate into the language and culture of majority society.

terrorism was widely interpreted as a civilizational phenomenon, a manifestation of growing hostility between Islam and the West. Such thinking also shaped the 'war on terror' (see p. 230), at least in its early incarnations. However, the image of civilizations in conflict has also attracted much criticism. For example, objections have been raised about the so-called 'tectonic' model of civilizations on which it is based, which portrays cultures as rigid and homogenous, clearly distinct from one another. In reality, civilizations or cultures are more often complex, fragmented and open to external influence. The notion of inevitable civilizational conflict is also undermined by significant historical evidence of people from different cultures, religions or ethnic groups living together in conditions of at least relative peace and harmony. Moreover, when conflict does occur, it is by no means clear that it genuinely has a cultural or civilizational character. Islamist terrorism, for example, may be better understood as a violent response to political conditions and crises that have found expression in a politico-cultural ideology, rather than as a manifestation of a resurgent Islamic world. Finally, the image of implacable civilizational conflict is undermined by countervailing global trends towards interdependence and homogenization. This is evident in the tendency of globalization to ensure that, regardless of their contrasting political and cultural identities, states in different parts of the world increasingly resemble one another in terms of economic values and practices, and in widening and, to some extent, cross-cultural support for the doctrine of human rights (see p. 311)

A Chinese century?

The twentieth century was commonly portrayed as the 'American century', in an attempt to highlight the hegemonic role of the USA, first, after WWII, as the leading state in the capitalist West, and, after the end of the Cold War, as the sole remaining superpower. Although the notion of US decline had been fashionable during the 1970s and 1980s (Kennedy 1989), it returned with greater force in the early years of the twenty-first century, usually linked to the idea that the world was witnessing a general shift in power from a US-led West to Asia, and especially to China. This notion is frequently captured in the image of the twenty-first century as the 'Chinese century', China being the new global hegemon. The chief basis for this image is China's remarkable record of sustained economic growth dating back to the 1980s, which, by 2010, had turned China into the world's second largest economy, seemingly fast closing on the USA. China's economic emergence is also matched by its growing diplomatic self-confidence and burgeoning structural power. However, the idea of the Chinese century is associated with two, starkly different images. In the first, the rise of China is linked to the prospect of intensified international conflict and a greater likelihood of war. Offensive realists in particular argue that the transfer of hegemony is rarely accomplished peacefully, both because the new hegemon is likely to seek a military and strategic status that matches its new-found economic dominance, and because the old hegemon is unlikely easily to be reconciled to its loss of status and position (see p. 243). In the second image, however, the Chinese century is stable and peaceful. Such expectations are substantially based on the belief that globalization alters how states define the national interest (see p. 135) and interact with one another. In this view, China may be a global hegemon of a new kind, one that is prepared permanently to place economic considerations ahead of strategic ones. Similarly, the USA may be reconciled to its loss of hegemony (see p. 228) by the fact that it would relieve it of the burden of global leadership.

Nevertheless, the idea of the inexorable rise of China, which underpins both of these images, may prove to be a delusion. Although China has experienced growth rates of about 8-10 per cent for some three decades, this process started from a very low base and still leaves China decades away from equalling the USA's level of technological development and its military power. Moreover, there is no assurance that China's economic rise will continue smoothly during the twenty-first century. Significant doubts have been expressed about the long term compatibility of its Stalinist political structures (dominated by the 25-strong Politburo and the about 200-strong Central Committee of the Chinese Communist Party) and the burgeoning capitalism that is transforming China's economy and social system. Moreover, Chinese economic success has largely been based on a combination of cheap labour and cheap exports, made possible by a seemingly endless supply of workers from the impoverished countryside. As this ends, as, despite a population of 1.3 billion, it inevitably must, China will be forced to restructure its economic model around generating growth more from domestic demand than from exports, and by shifting from cheap manufacturing to more sophisticated, high technology production. How easily this can be accomplished nevertheless remains to be seen.

The growth of international community?

The idea of the 'international community' has its origins in the notion of 'international society', which may have been prefigured by Grotius's (see p. 341) belief that war can only be justified if its causes and conduct conform to the principles of justice. The key assumption made by modern international society theorists is that, while states are, and will remain, egoistical and power-seeking, relations among them have come to be structured to a significant degree by cultural cohesion and social integration. The international system is, thus, a 'society of states', not, as realists argue, a 'system of states'. The image of the international community nevertheless takes this process a stage further, in that, whereas society suggests regular patterns of interaction between and amongst its members, community implies ties of affection and mutual respect. The term international community therefore creates the image of a collection of states acting in concert as a single, unified entity. Although the term has long been used in international politics (for example, through the idea that international organizations express the 'will of the international community'), the notion of international community gained greater impetus from the 1990s onwards. This reflected both the fact that the end of superpower rivalry offered new opportunities for international cooperation and that the trend towards global interdependence was widely seen to have political and security implications, not just economic ones. In the light of the 1991 Gulf War and the wider use of humanitarian intervention (see p. 326), the then-UK Prime Minister Tony Blair (2004) thus drew attention to what he called the 'doctrine of international community'. Under this, the international community has a right, even a duty or responsibility, to get actively involved in other people's conflicts, thereby setting aside the norm of non-interference that has for so long been considered a key principle of international order.

Is the growth of international community a continuing trend, and does it offer the prospect of a safer and more just world? Realist critics of the notion have always argued that it over-emphasizes the degree to which states are able to set aside considerations of narrow self-interest for the wider benefits this may bring. Indeed, international community may simply be a bogus idea, one that attempts to give the self-seeking behaviour of states the stamp of moral authority. A postcolonial critique of international community has also been developed. From this perspective, the idea that certain, usually western, states can assume the mantle of the international community, claiming the authority to 'sort out' less favoured parts of the world can be seen as an example of Eurocentrism. Forcible intervention on allegedly humanitarian grounds and, for that matter, other forms of interference in the developing world, such as international aid, can therefore be viewed as a continuation of colonialism by other means. Finally, even if international community is a meaningful and worthwhile idea, states may only be willing and able to act as a single, unified entity in very particular historical circumstances. Strengthened interest in international community during the 1990s may therefore be nothing more than a reflection of the unusual set of circumstances that defined the early post-Cold War period.

The rise of the global South?

The economic emergence of China, and the general shift of global power away from the West and towards Asia, may be part of a still larger process: a realignment in the relationship between the global North and the global South. The idea of the North-South divide (see p. 367) dates back to the early 1980s and the recognition of structural inequalities in the global economy between the high-wage, high-investment industrialized North and the low-wage, low-investment and predominantly rural South. The image of the North-South divide has nevertheless already lost much of its relevance. This started to occurred in the 1970s and 1980s, through the rise of the 'tiger' economies of East and Southeast Asia, and it has continued through the economic emergence of states such as China, India and Brazil and other emerging economies. Significant parts of the global

KEY THEORISTS OF INTERNATIONAL SOCIETY

Hedley Bull (1932–1985)

An Australian international relations theorist, Bull's *The Anarchical Society* ([1977] 2012) famously distinguished between a 'system of states' and a 'society of states'. He advanced a neo-Grotian approach to theory and practice, in which international society amounts to a real but fragile normative order, based on the institutions of the balance of power, international law, diplomacy, war and the great powers. Bull (1966) also acknowledged that international society may tend towards either solidarism or pluralism, depending on the extent to which states operate cohesively and pursue shared goals. His other major works include *The Control of the Arms Race* (1961) and *Justice in International Relations* (1984).

Martin Wight (1913–72)

A UK international relations theorist, Wight's best known book, *International Theory: The Three Traditions* (1991), advanced the idea that international theory can be divided into the 'three Rs' – realism, revolutionism and rationalism. While realism views international politics as a zero-sum struggle for power, revolutionism highlights deep tension between the dynamics of the state-system and the real interests of individual citizens. Rationalism stands between these extremes, advancing the idea that, as social creatures, humans forge societies that are regulated by reciprocal rights and obligations. International society is therefore neither chaotic and necessarily violent nor blissfully peaceful.

Terry Nardin (born 1942)

A US political scientist and academic, Nardin's *Law, Morality and the Relations of States* (1983) advanced a pluralist model of international society, based on a 'practical', rather than a 'purposive', association of states. Drawing on the ideas of the UK political philosopher, Michael Oakeshott (1901–90), he argued that international society provides rules that enable its member states to coexist and to interact with one another in a peaceful and orderly fashion, despite being committed to different cultures, ways of life, and political systems. Nardin is particularly interested in the tensions between sovereignty and legitimacy. His other main works include *The Ethics of War and Peace* (1998) and *The Philosophy of Michael Oakeshott* (2001).

See also **Michael Walzer** (p. 265)

South are therefore making substantial progress in reducing poverty and bringing about economic development, demonstrating that not all relationships between the North and the South are based on power and dependency. The rise of the South, however, goes well beyond the BRICs countries (see p. 463), with developing states such as Turkey, Mexico, Thailand and Indonesia also becoming leading actors on the world stage (UNDP 2013). Optimism about this also extends to Africa, where economies are growing, wars are ending and the blight of HIV/AIDS is starting to be brought under control. More broadly, demographic trends support such predictions: most of the world's population lives in the global South and these populations are much younger than those in the fast-ageing North.

How would the rise of the global South affect global politics? There are, basically, optimistic and pessimistic visions of the rise of the global South. The optimistic vision suggests that, just as the emergence of the Asian 'tigers', and later of China, India and Brazil, helped to fuel global growth, providing the North with new markets as well as with cheaper manufactured goods, the rise of Africa and of other still 'under-developed' parts of the South will have the same implications. Not only will the global economy expand, but the benefits of this will be more equally distributed, apart from anything else relieving Northern countries of the need to provide aid and to write off debt. The pessimistic vision suggests that if Southern countries ever reach living standards remotely approaching those of the developed North, they will create demand for food, energy and water so vast that other parts of the world will not be able to meet them in the long term.

However, many doubt whether the rise of the South will occur in the first place. As far as neo-Marxist world-system theorists are concerned, the under-development of the South will continue so long as the global capitalism remains unreformed, structural inequalities being intrinsic to the system itself. A further problem lies in the South's exposure to environmental threats and particularly climate change. Europe, the USA and Japan may be rich enough to adapt to climate change, paying ever higher prices for dwindling oil reserves and exporting their environmental problems by shifting polluting industries to poorer countries. However, Southern countries may not be able to avoid environmental constraints so easily, either because they are too poor (like most African countries), or simply too large (China, India and Brazil). A final problem is that the South may turn on itself. This could happen, for example, if Africa's dependency on the North is replaced by a dependency on China in particular, as 'new' colonialism sweeps the continent in a search for minerals and other vital natural resources.

The coming environmental catastrophe?

Environmental activists have long argued that the world is effectively sleepwalking into ecological disaster. Although the list of environmental threats to the planet is long – deforestation and particularly the loss of the rain forests; the pollution of the seas including the deep oceans; the decline in biodiversity as species become extinct at an accelerating rate, and so on – by common consent, the most serious of these is climate change, or global warming. Two broad obstacles prevent the international community from taking effective action over climate change. The first is the intrinsic problem that individual states will always tend to put their national interest before the common good of the international community, as suggested by the idea of the 'tragedy of the commons' (see p. 395). Such difficulties are all the more acute when deep tensions between developed and developing states over the issue are taken into account. The second obstacle is the sheer scope and scale of the task in hand, and the political, economic and personal costs that substantial and worldwide cuts in greenhouse gas emissions would involve. Not only does tackling climate change require a wholesale restructuring of economies that have been founded on carbon-based production, but radical environmentalists argue that reduced gas emissions can only be achieved by consuming less, and thus accepting more meagre living standards. If these obstacles are not overcome, the consequences may be catastrophically serious – longer and more intense heat waves in many parts of the world; an increased likelihood of floods and drought; the melting of the Arctic ice cap; the rise in sea levels; more regular and stronger hurricanes and other storms; and damage to ecosystems and the loss of agricultural production.

Nevertheless, there are those who argue that the spectre of environmental catastrophe, conjured up by environmentalists, has been greatly exaggerated, preventing a balanced appraisal of the costs of climate change and its possible solutions. Even if the views of climate change deniers (who reject the very idea of anthropocentric or human-induced global warming) are disregarded, climate change may not be as important as many have argued. For example, Bjørn Lomborg (2007), the controversial Danish political scientist, relegated climate change to fifteenth place on his list of the most important problems in the world, placing it beneath communicable diseases, a lack of clean drinking water and malnutrition. Lomborg argued that many environmental indicators are getting better, not worse, and that although climate change is a genuine global problem, we need to think carefully about the costs and benefits of tackling it. In particular, it would be more cost-effective to alleviate the suffering of present generations, by, for example, reducing poverty and the spread of HIV/AIDS, than it would be to reduce the impact of global warming on future generations who will be, anyway, much wealthier than present generations. Such a view generally favours adaptation strategies to climate change over mitigation strategies, on the grounds that the former are substantially cheaper and easier to implement.

Towards cosmopolitan democracy?

The idea of 'cosmopolitan democracy' (Held 1995) emerged out of debates about the nature and future direction of global governance (see p. 462). Although it recognized that the trend towards global governance was profound and probably irresistible, it highlighted a major defect in the emerging global governance system, namely a lack of democratic participation and accountability. The novel aspect of this idea was that it suggested that the project of democratization, which has traditionally focused on domestic politics, can and should be refocused on global political institutions. However, this is not to argue in favour of world government (see p. 464) or a global state, as most advocates of cosmopolitan democracy favour a multilevel system of post-sovereign governance, in which supra-state bodies, state-level bodies and sub-state bodies interact without any of them exercising final authority. The argument in favour of cosmopolitan democracy is based on the assumption that domestic democracy (democracy that operates only at state and sub-state levels) is no longer adequate, largely because globalization has 'hollowed out' the state and strengthened transnational processes. But what would cosmopolitan democracy look like? For Held (1995), it would involve the establishment of a 'global parliament', reformed and more accountable regional and global political bodies, and the 'permanent shift of a growing proportion of a nation state's coercive capability to regional and global institutions'. Monbiot (2004), for his part, proposed the creation of a popularly elected world parliament, containing 600 representatives, each with a constituency of about 10 million people, many of which would straddle national borders.

However, the idea of cosmopolitan democracy has been criticized as both unachievable and undesirable. Realists regard any project of political cosmopolitanism, whether democratic or non-democratic, as unfeasible, because effective power continues to reside with states, and states will be unwilling to relinquish it. States, and especially major states, will therefore block any trend towards global democracy, or ensure that any 'alternative' bodies that may be created will be peripheral to global decision-making and lack credibility. In a wider sense, the egalitarian thrust implicit in the idea of cosmopolitan democracy is simply out of step with the deep economic, political and military disparities of the existing global system. However, even if democratic global institutions could be established, they may suffer from a number of drawbacks. In the first place, the 'gap' between popularly-elected global political institutions and ordinary citizens around the world would mean that any idea that these institutions are democratic would be mere pretence. Communitarian and multiculturalist thinkers have added to this critique by pointing out that cosmopolitan democracy would be unable to articulate the views and interests of ethnically- or culturally-based communities. Finally, cosmopolitan democracy assumes the existence of a global citizenry, whose values and sensibilities somehow transcend those of the nation-state. As nationalism is showing little sign of succumbing to cosmopolitanism, it is difficult to see how cosmopolitan democracy could be anything other than a creature of 'globalized' political elites.

AN UNKNOWABLE FUTURE?

Images, however, are not predictions – even though many of those considered above have been advanced as models of a likely, or perhaps inevitable, future. The value of examining images arises less from the insight they give us into the shape of the global future and more from their ability to highlight important trends in the global present. The one thing that these images share is that they will each, in their different ways, be confounded by events; each of them will be wrong, at least in the form in which they have been advanced. This is because history has a seemingly inexhaustible capacity to surprise us, to defy predictions, however prescient or insightful they may at first have appeared. Images such as the 'end of history' and the 'clash of civilizations' stimulated enormous interest and debate when they were initially advanced, but each later came to attract more criticism than applause. Similarly, widespread and confident predictions in the 1980s that Japan was destined for global leadership (China, at the time, being barely considered) appeared to be absurd barely a decade later. Moreover, when major historical developments, such as the collapse of communism, the growth of religious fundamentalism or the advent of transnational terrorism, do occur, they appear to come almost out of the blue, and only start to make sense in retrospect.

Why is it so difficult to predict the future? Is the future unknowable? One problem is that most attempts to forecast the future are based on extrapolations from present trends, and these are inherently unreliable. This is evident in weather forecasting but it also applies in the area of economic forecasting, where universities, banks, professional organizations, national governments and bodies such as the IMF devote huge resources and often massive computing power to the attempt to make predictions about the economy as a whole or in part. And yet, events such as the 2007–9 global financial crisis still took the vast majority of commentators and analysts working in the field by surprise. In fact, the one thing that we can be certain of is that current trends will not continue, unchanged, into the future, as even the most cursory awareness of past trends will confirm.

A further problem is that our knowledge of the present is always limited. However refined and sophisticated our theories and models are, they can never fully capture the almost infinite complexities of the real world. In other words, we operate on the cusp between the known and the unknown. Donald Rumsfeld, the then US Defence Secretary, expressed this in 2002 in pointing out the following: 'There are known knowns; there are things that we know we know. There are known unknowns; that is to say, there are things that we know we don't know. But there are also unknown unknowns; there are things that we don't know we don't know'. Although much derided at the time for this statement (not least for his tortured expression), Rumsfeld's notion of 'unknown unknowns' brilliantly conveys why future events will always defy predictions: the basis for these predictions is always flawed, and we do not know how flawed or where these flaws might be. Such problems are, indeed, more acute the larger the scale of our thinking. This is because, as chaos theorists emphasize, complex systems contain such a large number of elements that interactions between and among them defy our understanding, giving events a seemingly random character. If this applies to politics at every level, it must be particularly true, in view of its heightened complexities, of global politics. The global future must therefore ever remain a surprise. All we can speculate about is what kind of surprise it will be.

SUMMARY

- An image is a representation or likeness of an individual, a group or a thing (an institution, event, system and so on). As such, images are nothing more than illusions or constructs of our mind. However, images may play an important role in building up knowledge and understanding by imposing meaning on an otherwise shapeless reality.

- As the basis for explaining the behaviour of actors on the world stage, image is important in shaping both how people see themselves and how they see others. This is perhaps most clear in relation to nationalism and the role of national image. The emphasis on the role and significance of image in modern global politics has nevertheless been taken furthest by poststructuralist theorists.

- Images may also serve as wider explanatory tools, graphic ways of highlighting important trends and developments in global politics. Influential images of modern global politics have highlighted trends such as the declining significance of national borders, the spread of democracy, the growth of cultural conflict, the rise of China, the increasing importance of international community, the emergence of the global South, the greater likelihood of environmental catastrophe and the democratization of international organizations.

- The value of examining images arises less from the insight they give us into the shape of the global future and more from their ability to highlight important trends in the global present. The one thing that these images share is that they will each, in their different ways, be confounded by events.

- The future is unknowable, in part, because extrapolations from present trends are always incorrect due to the fact trends inevitably, sooner or later, diverge from their course. Moreover, our knowledge of the present is always limited, a problem that is more acute the larger the scale of our thinking, because of the greater number of factors that may influence outcomes. This implies that the future of global politics is, and must remain, unknowable.

Questions for discussion

- Is it possible, ultimately, to distinguish between image and reality?

- What role may national image play in conflict resolution and peacebuilding?

- To what extent is the modern world borderless?

- Is there an inevitable global trend in favour of democracy?

- To what extent is modern conflict cultural or civilizational in character?

- Will the twenty-first century be the Chinese century?

- Is the international community a force for global justice and security?

- Can the global South ever escape from dependency on the North?

- Have the negative consequence of climate change been over-played or under-played?

- Is the future inherently unknowable?

- Do attempts to predict future trends in global politics have any value?

Further reading

Cohen-Tanugi. L., *The Shape of the World to Come: Charting the Geopolitics of the New Century* (2009). A stimulating discussion of the transformation of world affairs by globalization, the changing world order and other developments.

Kegley, C. W. and G. A. Raymond, *The Global Future: A Brief Introduction to World Politics* (2011). An exploration of key trends and transformations in twenty-first century world politics.

Paul, T. V. and J. A. Hall (eds), *International Order and the Future of World Politics* (1999). A thought-provoking collection of essays that reflect on future trends in world politics.

Snow, D. M., *The Shape of the Future: World Politics in a New Century* (1998). A discussion of the political, economic and military dimensions of the emergent international system.

ONLINE RESOURCES AVAILABLE

Links to relevant web resources can be found on the *Global Politics* website

Bibliography

Abbott, P., C. Wallace and M. Tyler *et al.* (2005) *An Introduction to Sociology: Feminist Perspectives*. London: Routledge.

Ackerly, B. and J. True (2010) *Doing Feminist Research in Political and Social Science*. Basingstoke: Palgrave Macmillan.

Albert, M., L.-E. Cederman and A. Wendt (eds) (2010) *New Systems Theories of World Politics*. Basingstoke: Palgrave Macmillan.

Agnew, J. (1994) 'The Territorial Trap: The Geographical Assumptions of International Relations Theory', *Review of International Political Economy*, 1(1).

Albrow, M. (1996) *The Global Age: State and Society Beyond Modernity*. Cambridge: Polity Press.

Allison, G. (1971) *Essence of Decision*. Boston, MA: Little, Brown.

Allison, G. (2004) *Nuclear Terrorism: The Ultimate Preventable Catastrophe*. New York: Times Books.

Alston, P. (1990) 'The Fiftieth Anniversary of the Universal Declaration of Human Rights', in J. Berting, P. R. Baeher, J. H. Bergers, C. Flinterman, B. de Klerk, R. Kroes, C. A. van Minnen and K. Vanderwal (eds), *Human Rights in a Pluralist World*. London: Meckler.

Altheide, D. (2006) *Terrorism and the Politics of Fear*. Lanham, MD: AltaMira Press

Amin, S. (1997) *Imperialism and Unequal Development*. New York: Monthly Review Press.

Amin, S. (2008) *The World We Wish to See: Revolutionary Objectives in the Twenty-First Century*. New York: Monthly Review Press.

Anand, D. (2007) 'Anxious Sexualities: Masculinity, Nationalism and Violence', *The British Journal of Politics and International Relations*, 9(2).

Anderson, B. (1983) *Imagined Communities: Reflections on the Origins and Spread of Nationalism*. London: Verso.

Anderson, B. (1998) *The Spectres of Comparison: Nationalism, Southeast Asia and the World*. London: Verso.

Anderson, B. (2005) *Under Three Flags: Anarchism and the Anti-colonial Imagination*. London: Verso.

Angus, I. (2008) 'The Myth of the Tragedy of the Commons', *Monthly Review*, August.

Annan, K. (1999) 'Two Concepts of Sovereignty', *The Economist*, 18 September.

Antony, A. (2005) *Imperialism, Sovereignty and the Making of International Law*. Cambridge: Cambridge University Press.

Archibugi, D. and D. Held (eds) (1995) *Cosmopolitan Democracy: An Agenda for a New World Order*. Cambridge: Polity Press.

Armstrong, D., L. Lloyd and J. Redmond (2004) *International Organisation in World Politics*. Basingstoke: Palgrave Macmillan.

Ash, T. G. (2005) *Free World: Why a Crisis of the West Reveals the Opportunity of Our Time*. Harmondsworth: Penguin.

Axelrod, R. (1984) *The Evolution of Cooperation*. New York: Basic Books.

Azzam, M. (2008) 'Understanding al Qa'eda', *Political Studies Review*, 6(3).

Baev, P. K. (2003) 'Examining the 'Terrorism-War' Dichotomy in the 'Russian-Chechnya Case', *Contemporary Security Policy* , 24(2).

Bales, K. (2003) 'Because She Looks Like a Child', in B. Ehrenreich and A. R. Hochschild (eds) *Global Women*. London: Granta Books.

Baldwin R. and D. Vines (eds) (2012) *Rethinking Global Economic Governance in the Light of the Crisis: New Perspectives on Economic Policy Foundations*. London: Centre for Economic Policy Research.

Ball, P. (2004) *Critical Mass: How One Thing Leads to Another*. London: Arrow Books.

Barber, B. (2003) *Jihad vs McWorld*. London: Corgi Books.

Barnett, M. and R. Duvall (eds) (2005) *Power in Global Governance*. Cambridge: Cambridge University Press.

Basch, L. , N. Glick Schiller and C. Blanc-Szanton (1994) *Nations Unbound: Transnational Projects, Post-colonial Predicaments, and De-territorialized Nation-states*. Geneva: Gordon & Breach.

Bauman, Z. (1994) *Modernity and the Holocaust*. Cambridge: Polity Press.

Bauman, Z. (1998) *Globalization: The Human Consequences*. Cambridge: Polity Press.

Bauman, Z. (2000) *Liquid Modernity*. Cambridge: Polity Press.

Bauman, Z. (2007) *Liquid Times: Living in an Age of Uncertainty*. Cambridge: Polity Press.

Baylis, J., S. Smith and P. Owens (eds) (2008) *The Globalization of World Politics*. Oxford: Oxford University Press.

Beck, U. (1992) *The Risk Society: Towards a New Modernity*. London: Sage.

Beck, U. (2000) *The Brave New World of Work*. Cambridge: Cambridge University Press.

Beck, U. (2006) *Power in the Global Age*. Cambridge: Polity Press.

Beck, U. (2009) *World at Risk*. Cambridge and Malden, MA: Polity Press.

Beck, U. and E. Beck-Gernsheim (2002) *Individualization: Individualized Individualism and its Social and Political Consequences*. London: Sage.

Beeson, M. (2014) *Regionalism and Globalization in East Asia: Politics, Security and Economic Development*. Basingstoke: Palgrave Macmillan.

Beeson, M. and N. Bisley (eds) (2013) *Issues in 21st Century World Politics*. Basingstoke: Palgrave Macmillan.

Beevor, A. (2002) *Berlin: The Downfall 1945*. London: Penguin.

Bell, D. (ed.) (2010) *Ethics and World Politics*. Oxford: Oxford University Press.

Bell, S. and A. Hindmoor (2009) *Rethinking Governance: The Centrality of the State in Modern Society*. Cambridge and New York: Cambridge University Press.

Bellamy, A. (2006) *Just Wars: From Cicero to Iraq*. London: Polity Press.

Bentham, J. (1968) *The Works of Jeremy Bentham*. Oxford: Clarendon Press.

Berman, P. (2003) *Terror and Liberalism*. New York: W. W. Norton & Co.

Bernanke, B. (2004) *Essays on the Great Depression*. Princeton: Princeton University Press.

Betsill, M., K. Hochstetler and D. Stevis (eds) (2006) *International Environmental Politics*. Basingstoke: Palgrave Macmillan.

Bhagwati, J. (2004) *In Defence of Globalization*. Oxford: Oxford University Press.

Bhagwati, J. (2008) *Termites in the Trading System*. Oxford: Oxford University Press.

Bisley, N. (2007) *Rethinking Globalization*. Basingstoke: Palgrave Macmillan.

Blainey, G. (1988) *The Causes of War*. New York: Free Press.

Blair, T (2004) 'Doctrine of the International Community', in I. Stelzer (ed.) (2004) *Neoconservatism*. London: Atlantic Books.

Bloom, M. (2007) *Dying to Kill: The Allure of Suicide Terror*. New York: Columbia University Press.

Bobbitt, P. (2002) *The Shield of Achilles: War, Peace, and the Course of History*. New York: Alfred A. Knopf.

Bohne, E. (2010) *The World Trade Organization: Institutional Development and Reform*. Basingstoke: Palgrave Macmillan.

Bookchin, M. (1975) *Our Synthetic Environment*. London: Harper & Row.

Bookchin, M. (1982) *The Ecology of Freedom: The Emergence and Dissolution of Hierarchy*. Palo Alto: Cheshire.

Bookchin, M. (1995) *Re-enchanting Humanity: A Defence of the Human Spirit Against Antihumanism, Misanthropy, Mysticism and Primitivism*. New York: Continuum International Publishing.

Bookchin, M. (2006) *The Ecology of Freedom*. New York: AK Press.

Booth, K. and N. Wheeler (2008) *The Security Dilemma: Fear, Cooperation and Trust in World Politics*. Basingstoke: Palgrave Macmillan.

Boulding, K. (1956) *The Image: Knowledge in Life and Society*. Ann Arbor, MI: University of Michigan Press.

Boulding, K. (1966) 'The Economics of the Coming Spaceship Earth', in H. Jarrett (ed.) *Environmental Quality in a Growing Economy*. Baltimore: Johns Hopkins Press.

Brass, P. A. (2003) *The Production of Hindu-Muslim Violence in Contemporary India*. Washington, DC: University of Washington Press.

Braybrooke, D. and C. Lindblom (1963) *A Strategy of Decision: Policy Evaluation as a Political Process*. New York: Collier Macmillan.

Brenner, N. (2004) *New State Spaces: Urban Governance and the Rescaling of Statehood*. Oxford: Oxford University Press.

Breslin, S. (2010) 'Regions and Regionalism in World Politics' in M. Beeson and N. Bisley (eds), *Issues in 21st Century World Politics*. Basingstoke: Palgrave Macmillan.

Brett, E. (2009) *Reconstructing Development Theory*. Basingstoke: Palgrave Macmillan.

Brown, C. and K. Ainley (2009) *Understanding International Relations*. Basingstoke: Palgrave Macmillan.

Brown, G. W. (2008) 'Moving from Cosmopolitan Legal Theory to Legal Practice', *Legal Studies*, 28(3).

Brown, M. B. (1995) *Models in Political Economy: A Guide to the Arguments* (2nd edn). Harmondsworth: Penguin.

Brown, M. E. (ed) (1998) *Theories of War and Peace*. Cambridge, MA: The MIT Press

Buchanan, A. (2007) *Justice, Legitimacy, and Self-Determination: Moral Foundations for International Law*. New York: Oxford University Press.

Bull, H. (1961) *The Control of the Arms Race: Disarmament and Arms Control in the Missile Age*. New York: Praeger.

Bull, H. (1966) 'The Grotian conception of international society', in H. Butterfield and M. Wight (eds) *Diplomatic Investigations*. London: Allen & Unwin.

Bull, H. (1984) *Justice in International Relations: The Hagey Lectures*. Waterloo, Ontario: University of Waterloo.

Bull, H. (2012) *The Anarchical Society: A Study of Order in World Politics*. Basingstoke: Macmillan.

Burchill, S., A. Linklater, R. Devetak, J. Donnelly, T. Nardin, M. Paterson, C. Reus-Smit and J. True (2013) *Theories of International Relations*. Basingstoke: Palgrave Macmillan.

Burke, J. (2007) *Al-Qaeda: The True Story of Radical Islam*. Harmondsworth: Penguin.

Burke, J. (2012) *The 9/11 Wars*. London and New York: Penguin Books.

Burton, J. (1972) *World Society*. London and New York: Cambridge University Press.

Buruma, I. and A. Margalit (2004) *Occidentalism: A Short History of Anti-Westernism*. London: Atlantic Books.

Butko, J. (2009) 'Four Perspectives on Terrorism: Where They Stand Depends on Where You Sit', *Political Studies Review*, 7(2).

Buzam, B. (2004) *From International to World Society?* Cambridge: Cambridge University Press.

Byers, M. (ed.) (2000) *The Role of Law in International Politics: Essays in International Relations and International Law*. Oxford: Oxford University Press.

Caney, S. (2005) *Justice Beyond Borders: A Global Political Theory*. Oxford: Oxford University Press.

Capra, F. (1975) *The Tao of Physics*. Boston: Shambhala.

Capra, F. (1976) *The Web of Life*. London: Flamingo; New York: Anchor/Doubleday.

Capra, F. (1982) *The Turning Point*. New York: Simon & Schuster.

Capra. F. (2003) *The Hidden Connections*. London: HarperCollins.

Caprioli, M. and M. Boyer (2001) 'Gender, Violence and International Crisis', *The Journal of Conflict Resolution*, 45(4).

Carr, E. H. (1939) *The Twenty Years' Crisis 1919–39*. London: Macmillan.

Carr, N. (2008) 'Is Google Making Us Stupid?' in *The Atlantic Magazine*, July/August.

Carr, N. (2010) *The Shallows: What the Internet is Doing to our Brains*. New York: Norton.

Carson, R. (1962) *The Silent Spring*. Boston, MA: Houghton Mifflin.

Carter, A., J. Deutch and P. Zelikow (1998) 'Catastrophic Terrorism', *Foreign Affairs*, 77(6).

Casey, T. (2011) *The Legacy of the Crash: How the Financial Crisis Changed America and Britain*. Basingstoke and New York: Palgrave Macmillan.

Castells, M. (1996) *The Rise of the Network Society*. Oxford: Blackwell.

Castells, M. (2001) *The Internet Galaxy: Reflections on the Internet, Business and Society*. Oxford: Oxford University Press.

Castells, M. (2004) *The Internet Galaxy: Reflections on the Internet: Business and Society*. Oxford: Oxford University Press.

Castells, M. (2009) *Communication Power*. New York: Oxford University Press.

Castles, S., H. de Haas and M.J. Miller (2013) *The Age of Migration: International Population Movements in the Modern World*. Basingstoke: Palgrave Macmillan.

Cerny, F. G. (2010) 'Globalization and Statehood', in M. Beeson and N. Bisley (eds), *Issues in 21st Century World Politics*. Basingstoke: Palgrave Macmillan.

Chenoy, A. (2002) 'The Politics of Gender in the Politics of Hatred', *Aman Ekta Manchin Manch Digest*, 3.

Chomsky, N. (1999) *The New Military Humanism: Lessons from Kosovo*. Monroe, ME: Common Courage Press.

Chomsky, N. (2003) *Hegemony or Survival: America's Quest for Global Dominance*. New York: Henry Holt & Company.

Chowdhry, G. and S. Nair (eds) (2002) *Postcolonialism and International Relations: Race, Gender and Class*. London: Routledge.

Chua, A. (2003) *World on Fire: How Exporting Free Market Democracy Breeds Ethnic Hatred and Global Instability*. London: Heinemann.

Clarke, J. J. (1997) *Oriental Enlightenment: The Encounter Between Asian and Western Thought*. London and New York: Routledge.

Clausewitz, K. von ([1831]1976} *On War*. Princeton: Princeton University Press.

Cockayne, J. (2010) 'Crime, Corruption and Violent Economies', in M. Bardel and A. Wennman (eds) *Ending Wars, Consolidating Peace; Economic Perspectives*. International Institute of Strategic Studies.

Cohen, R. and P. Kennedy (2013) *Global Sociology*. Basingstoke: Palgrave Macmillan.

Cohen-Tanugi, L. (2009) *The Shape of Things to Come: Charting the Geopolitics of the New Century*. New York: Columbia University Press.

Collier, P. (2007) *The Bottom Million: Why the Poorest Countries are Failing and What can be Done about it*. Oxford and New York: Oxford University Press.

Collier, P. and A. Hoeffler (2004) 'Greed and Grievance in Civil Wars', *Oxford Economic Papers*, 56(4).

Cooper, R. (2004) *The Breaking of Nations: Order and Chaos in the Twenty-first Century*. London: Atlantic Books.

Copeland, T. (2001) 'Is the New Terrorism Really New? An Analysis of the New Paradigm for Terrorism', *Journal of Conflict Studies*, 11(2).

Corbett, P. (1956) *Morals, Law and Power in International Relations*. Los Angeles: J. R. and D. Hayes Foundation.

Cornia, G. A. (2003) 'The Impact of Liberalization and Globalization on Within-Country Income Inequality', *Economic Studies*, 49(4).

Cornia, G. A. and J. Court (2001) *Inequality, Growth and Poverty in the Era of Liberalization and Globalization*. Helsinki: UNU World Institute for Development Economics Research.

Cowen, N. (2001) *Global History: A Short Overview*. Cambridge and Malden, MA: Polity Press.

Cox, R. (1981) 'Social Forces, States and World Orders: Beyond International Relations Theory', *Millennium*, 10(2).

Cox, R. (1987) *Production, Power and World Order: Social Forces in the Making of History*. New York: Columbia University Press.

Cox, R. (1993) 'Structural Issues in Global Governance: Implications for Europe', in S. Gill (ed.) *Gramsci, Historical Materialism and International Relations*. Cambridge: Cambridge University Press.

Cox, R. (1994) 'Global Restructuring: Making Sense of the Changing International Political Economy', in R. Stubbs and G. Underhill (eds) *Political Economy and the Changing Global Order*. Oxford: Oxford University Press.

Cox, R. (2010) 'The Point is not just to Explain the World but Change It', in C. Reus-Smit and D. Snidal (eds) *The Oxford Handbook on International Relations*. Oxford: Oxford University Press.

Cox, R. (with T. Sinclair) (1996) *Approaches to World Order*. Cambridge: Cambridge University Press.

Cox, R. and H. Jacobson (1972) *Anatomy of Influence: Decision Making in International Organization*. Newhaven, CT: Yale University Press.

Cox, S. (1985) 'No Tragedy of the Commons', *Environmental Ethics* 7.

Crawford, M. (2009) *Sex Trafficking in South Asia: Telling Maya's Story*. London: Routledge.

Crenshaw, M. (ed.) (1983) *Terrorism, Legitimacy and Power*. Middletown: Wesleyan University Press.

Daalder, I. and J. Savrides (2012) 'NATOs Victory in Libya', *Foreign Affairs*, 91/2.

Daly, H. (ed.) (1973) *Towards a Steady-State Economy*. San Francisco: Freeman.

Daly, H. and J. Cobb (1990) *For the Common Good: Redirecting the Economy towards Community, the Environment and a Sustainable Future*. London: Greenprint.

Dedeoglu, B. (2003) 'Bermuda Triangle: Comparing Official Definitions of Terrorist Activity', *Terrorism and Political Violence*. 15(3).

Deffeyes, K. (2006) *Beyond Oil: The View from Hubbert's Peak*. New York: Hill & Wang.

Der Derian, J. (20091) *Virtuous War: Mapping the Military-Industrial-Media-Entertainment Network. London: Routledge.* Boulder, CO: Westview Press.

Der Derian, J. and M. Shapiro (eds) (1989) *International/Intertextual: Postmodern Readings in World Politics*. Lexington MA: Lexington Books.

Dernhard Gareis, S. (2012) *The United Nations: An Introduction*. Basingstoke and New York: Palgrave Macmillan.

Derrida, J. (1976) *Of Grammatology*. Baltimore and London: Johns Hopkins University.

Dessler, A. and E. Parson (2010) *The Science and Politics of Global Climate Change*. Cambridge: Cambridge University Press.

Deutsch, K. (1957) *Political Community and the North Atlantic Area*. Princeton: Princeton University Press.

Devarajan, S. and W. Fengler (2013) 'Africa's Economic Boom' *Foreign Affairs*, 92/3.

Dobbins, J. (2007) 'A Comparative Evaluation of United Nations Peacekeeping', Rand Corporation.

Donnelly, J. (2000) *Realism and International Relations*. Cambridge: Cambridge University Press.

Donnelly, J. (2013) *Universal Human Rights in Theory and Practice*. Ithaca: Cornell University Press.

Dower, N. (1998) *World Ethics: The New Agenda*, Edinburgh: Edinburgh University Press.

Dower, N. (2003) *An Introduction to Global Citizenship*. Edinburgh: Edinburgh University Press.

Downs, A. (1957) *An Economic Theory of Democracy*. New York: Harper & Row.

Doyle, M. (1986) 'Liberalism and World Politics', *American Political Science Review*, 80.

Doyle, M. (1995) 'Liberalism and World Politics Revisited', in C. W. Kegley (ed.) *Controversies in International Relations Theory*. New York: St. Martin's Press.

Drezner, D. (2012) *The Irony of Global Economic Governance: The System Worked*. Council of Foreign Relations.

Dunne, T. and N. J. Wheeler (eds) (1999) *Human Rights in Global Politics*. Cambridge: Cambridge University Press.

Durkheim, E. (1997) *Suicide*. New York: Free Press.

Easterly, W. (2001) 'IMF and World Bank Structural Adjustment Programs and Poverty', paper prepared for the World Bank February 2001.

Easterly, W. (2006) *The Elusive Quest for Growth: Economists' Adventures and Misadventures in the Tropics*. Cambridge, MA and London: MIT Press.

Ehrenreich, B. (1999) 'Fukuyama's Follies: So What If Women Rule the World', *Foreign Affairs*, January/February.

Ehrenreich, B. and A. R. Hochschild (2003) *Global Women: Nannies, Maids and Sex Workers in the New Economy*. London: Granta Books.

Eichengreen, D. and K. O'Rourke (2012) 'A Tale of Two Depressions and a Redux', *Vox EU.Org*.

Elliott, L. (2004) *The Global Politics of the Environment*. Basingstoke: Palgrave Macmillan.

Elshtain, J. B. (1981) *Public Man, Private Women: Women in Social and Political Thought*. Oxford: Martin Robertson and Princeton: Princeton University Press.

Elshtain, J. B. (1987) *Women and War*. New York: Basic Books.

Elshtain, J. B. (2003) *Just War Against Terror: The Burden of American Power in a Violent World*. New York: Basic Books.

Elshtain, J. B. (2008) *Sovereignty: God, State, and Self*. New York: Basic Books.

Emmott, B. (2009) *Rivals: How the Power Struggle between China, India and Japan will shape our Next Decade*. London and New York: Penguin Books.

English, R. (2009) *Terrorism: How to Respond*. Oxford: Oxford University Press.

Enloe, C. (1989) *Bananas, Beaches and Bases: Making Feminist Sense of International Politics*. London: Pandora Books.

Enloe, C. (1993) *The Morning After: Sexual Politics at the End of the Cold War*. Berekley: University of California Press.

Enloe, C. (2000) *Manoeuvres: The International Politics of Militarizing Women's Lives*. Berekley: University of California Press.

Enloe, C. (2004) *The Curious Feminist: Searching for Women in a New Age of Empire*. Berekley: University of California Press.

Evans, G., and J. Newham (eds) (1998) *The Penguin Dictionary of International Relations*. Harmondsworth: Penguin.

Falk, R. (1991) 'The Terrorist Foundations of Recent US Foreign Policy', in A. George (ed.) *Western State Terrorism*. Cambridge: Polity Press.

Fawn, R. (2009) *Globalising the Regional, Regionalising the Global*. Cambridge: Cambridge University Press.

Field, A. (2009) 'The 'New Terrorism': Revolution or Evolution?', *Political Studies Review*, 7(2).

Finnemore, M. (1996) *National Interests in International Society*. Ithaca, NY: Cornell University Press.

Finnemore, M. (2003) *The Purpose of Intervention: Changing Beliefs about the Use of Force*. Ithaca: Cornell University Press.

Fischer, F. (1968) *Germany's Aims in the First World War*. New York: W. W. Norton.

Forsythe, D. P. (2006) *Human rights in International Relations*. Cambridge University Press.

Fox, W. (1990) *Towards a Transpersonal Ecology: Developing the Foundations for Environmentalism*. Boston, MA: Shambhala.

Franck, T. M. (1990) *The Power of Legitimacy Among Nations*. New York: Oxford University Press.

Friedman, E. (1995) 'Women's Human Rights: The Emergence of a Movement', in Peters, J. and A. Wolper (eds) *Women's Rights, Human Rights: International Feminist Perspectives*. London & New York: Routledge.

Friedman, M. (1962) *Capitalism and Freedom*. Chicago: Chicago University Press.

Friedman, T. (2006) *The World is Flat*. New York: Farrer, Straus & Giroux.

Fromm, E. (1941) *Fear of Freedom*. London: Ark.

Frowe, H. (2011) *The Ethics of War and Peace: An Introduction*. London and New York: Routledge.

Fukuyama, F. (1989) 'The End of History', *The National Interest*, 16.

Fukuyama, F. (1991) *The End of History and the Last Man*. London: Hamish Hamilton.

Fukuyama, F. (1998) 'Women and the Evolution of World Politics', *Foreign Affairs*, September/October.

Fukuyama, F. (2005) *State-Building: Governance and World Order in the Twenty-First Century*. London: Profile Books.

Galbraith, J. K. (1963) *American Capitalism: The Concept of Countervailing Power*. Harmondsworth: Penguin.

Galbraith, J. K. (1992) *The Culture of Contentment*. London: Sinclair Stevenson.

Galbraith, J. K. (2009) *The Great Crash, 1929*. London and New York: Penguin.

Gallie, W. B. (1955/56) 'Essentially Contested Concepts', *Proceedings of the Aristotelian Society*, Vol. 56.

Gamble, A. (2009) *The Spectre at the Feast: Capitalist Crisis and the Politics of Recession*. Basingstoke: Palgrave Macmillan.

Gareis, S. R. (2012) *The United Nations: An Introduction*. Basingstoke and New York: Palgrave Macmillan.

George, S. (1976) *How the Other Half Dies: The Real Reasons for World Hunger*. Harmondsworth: Penguin.

George, S. (1988) *A Fate Worse than Debt*. New York: Grove Weidenfeld.

George, S. (2004) *Another World is Possible, If …* London: Verso.

Giddens, A. (1990) *The Consequences of Modernity*. Cambridge: Polity Press.

Giddens, A. (1994) *Beyond Left and Right: The Future of Radical Politics*. Cambridge: Polity Press.

Gilbert, P. (2003) *New Terror, New Wars*. Edinburgh: Edinburgh University Press.

Gilpin, R. (1987) *The Political Economy of International Relations*. Princeton: Princeton University Press.

Gilpin, R. (2005) 'Conversations in International Relations: Interview with Robert Gilpin', *International Relations*, 19.

Goldin, I. (2013) *Divided Nations: Why Global Governance is Failing and What we can Do About It*. Oxford and New York: Oxford University Press

Goldstein, J. (2001) *War and Gender: How Gender Shapes the War System and Vice Versa*. Cambridge: Cambridge University Press.

Goodin, R. (2006) *What's Wrong with Terrorism?* Cambridge: Polity Press.

Gramsci, A. (1971) *Selections from the Prison Notebooks*. London: Lawrence & Wishart.

Gray, C. (1997) *Postmodern War: The New Politics of Conflict*. New York: Guilford Press.

Gray, C. (2005) *Peace, War, and Computers*. New York and London: Routledge.

Gray, C. (2008) *International Law and the Use of Force*. Oxford: Oxford University Press.

Greenspan, A. (2007) *The Age of Turbulence: Adventures in a New World*. New York: Penguin Press.

Greig, A., D. Hulme and M. Turner (2007) *Challenging Global Inequality: Development Theory and Practice in the 21st Century*. Basingstoke: Palgrave Macmillan.

Griffiths, M. (ed.) (1999) *Fifty Key Thinkers in International Relations*. London and New York: Routledge.

Griffiths, M. (2011) *Rethinking International Relations Theory*. Basingstoke: Palgrave Macmillan.

Griffiths, M. and T. O'Callaghan (eds) (2002) *International Relations: The Key Concepts*. London and New York: Routledge.

Grovogui, S. (1996) *Sovereigns, Quasi-Sovereigns, and Africans: Race and Self-Determination in International Law*. Minneapolis: University of Minnesota Press.

Guardiola, Rivera, O. (2010) *What if Latin America Ruled the World?* London: Bloomsbury.

Gutman, R. and D. Rieff (eds) (1999) *Crimes of War: What the Public Should Know*. New York: W. W. Norton.

Haas, E. (1964) *Beyond the Nation-State: Functionalism and International Organization*. Stanford: Stanford University Press.

Haass, R. (2008) 'The Age of Nonpolarity: What will Follow US Dominance?', *Foreign Affairs*, May/June.

Habermas, J. (2001) *The Postnational Constellation: Political Essays*. Cambridge, MA: MIT Press.

Habermas, J. (2006) *The Divided West*. Cambridge: Polity Press.

Habermas, J. (2010) 'The Concept of Human Dignity and the Realistic Utopia of Human Rights', *Metaphilosophy*, 41.4.

Hall, P. and D. Soskice (eds) (2001) *Varieties of Capitalism: The Institutional Foundations of Comparative Advantage*. Oxford: Oxford University Press.

Hanhimäki, J. (2008) *The United Nations: A Very Short Introduction*. Oxford: Oxford University Press.

Haq, M. ul (1976) *The Poverty Curtain*. New York: Columbia University Press.

Haq, M. ul (1996) *Reflections on Human Development*. Oxford: Oxford University Press.

Hardin, G. (1968) 'The Tragedy of the Commons', *Science*, 162.

Hardin, G. (1974) 'Living on a Lifeboat', *Bioscience*, 24(10).

Harvey, D. (1990) *The Condition of Postmodernity: An Enquiry into the Origins of Cultural Change*. Malden, MA and Oxford: Blackwell.

Harvey, D. (2007) *A Brief History of Neoliberalism*. Oxford and New York: Oxford University Press.

Harvey, D. (2009) *Cosmopolitanism and the Geography of Freedom*. New York: Columbia University Press.

Hay, C. (2002) *Political Analysis: A Critical Introduction*. Basingstoke: Palgrave Macmillan.

Hay, C. (ed.) (2010) *New Directions in Political Science: Responding to the Challenges of an Interdependent World*. Basingstoke: Palgrave Macmillan.

Hay, C., M. Lister and D. Marsh (eds) (2006) *The State: Theories and Issues*. Basingstoke: Palgrave Macmillan.

Hearn, J. (2006) *Rethinking Nationalism: A Critical Introduction*. Basingstoke and New York: Palgrave Macmillan.

Hehir, A. (2013) *Humanitarian Intervention: An Introduction*. Basingstoke: Palgrave Macmillan.

Hehir, A., N. Kuhrt and A. Mumford (eds) (2013) *International Law, Security and Ethics: Policy Changes in the 9/11 World*. London and New York: Routledge.

Heinberg, R. (2006) *The Oil Depletion Protocol: A Plan to Avert Oil Wars, Terrorism and Economic Collapse*. Gabriola Island, BC: New Society Publishers.

Held, D. (1995) *Democracy and the Global Order: From the Modern State to Cosmopolitan Governance*. Cambridge: Polity Press.

Held, D. and A. Kaya (eds) (2006) *Global Inequality: Patterns and Explanations*. Cambridge: Polity.

Held, D. and A. McGrew (2007) *Globalization/Anti-globalization: Beyond the Great Divide*. Cambridge and Malden, MA: Polity Press.

Held, D., A. McGrew, D. Goldblatt and J. Perraton (1999) *Global Transformations*. Cambridge: Polity Press.

Held, V. (2005) *The Ethics of Care: Personal, Political, and Global*. New York: Oxford University Press.

Herring, E. (ed) (2000) *Preventing the Use of Weapons of Mass Destruction. Journal of Strategic Studies*, 23(1).

Hertz, N. (2002) *The Silent Takeover*. London: Arrow.

Heywood, A. (2013) *Politics*. Basingstoke: Palgrave Macmillan.

Hill, C. (2003) *The Changing Politics of Foreign Policy*. Basingstoke: Palgrave Macmillan.

Hirst, P. and G. Thompson (1999) *Globalization in Question*. Cambridge: Polity Press.

Hobsbawm, E. (1983) 'Inventing Traditions', in E. Hobsbawm and T. Ranger (eds) *The Invention of Traditions*. Cambridge: Cambridge University Press.

Hobsbawm, E. (1992) *Nations and Nationalism since 1780*. Cambridge: Cambridge University Press.

Hobsbawm, E. (1994) *Age of Extremes: The Short Twentieth Century 1914–1991*. London: Michael Joseph.

Hobsbawm, E. (2006) *Globalization, Democracy and Terrorism*. London: Abacus.

Hoffman, B. (2006) *Inside Terrorism*. New York: Columbia University Press.

Hollis, M. and S. Smith (1991) *Explaining and Understanding International Relations*. Oxford and New York: Oxford University Press.

Holmes, R. (ed.) (1990) *Non-violence in Theory and Practice*, Belmont, CA: Wadsworth Publishing Co.

Honderich, T. (1989) *Violence for Equality: Inquiries in Political Philosophy*. London: Routledge.

Hopf, T. (1998) 'The Promise of Constructivism in International Relations theory', *International Security*, 23(1).

Howard, M. (1983) *Clausewitz*. Oxford: Oxford University Press.

Howard, M. (2002) *The Invention of Peace and the Reinvention of War*. London: Profile Books.

Huntington, S. (1991) *Third Wave: Democratization in the Late Twentieth Century*. Norman, OK. and London: University of Oklahoma Press.

Huntington, S. (1993) *The Clash of Civilizations, Foreign Affairs*, 72(3).

Huntington, S. (1996) *The Clash of Civilizations and the Remaking of World Order*. New York: Simon & Schuster.

Huntington, S. (2004) *Who Are We? The Challenges to America's National Identity*. New York: Simon & Schuster.

Hutton, W. (2007) *The Writing on the Wall: China and the West in the 21st Century*. London: Little, Brown.

Hymans, J. (2006) *The Psychology of Nuclear Proliferation*. Cambridge: Cambridge University Press.

Ignatieff, M. (2004) *The Lesser Evil: Political Ethics in an Age of Terror*. Edinburgh: Edinburgh University Press.

Inglehart, R. (1977) *The Silent Revolution: Changing Values and Political Styles Amongst Western Publics*. Princeton: Princeton University Press.

Inglehart, R. (1990) *Cultural Shift in Advanced Industrial Society*. Princeton: Princeton University Press.

Jackson, R. (2009) 'The Study of Terrorism after 11 September 2001: Problems, Challenges and Future Developments', *Political Studies Review*, 7(2).

Jackson, R. and S. J. Sinclair (2012) *Contemporary Debates on Terrorism*. London: Routledge.

Jackson, R. and G. Sørensen (2012) *Introduction to International Relations: Theories and Approaches*. Oxford: Oxford University Press.

Jackson, R., M. Smyth, J. Gunning and L. Jarvis (2011) *Terrorism: A Critical Introduction*. Basingstoke: Palgrave Macmillan.

Janis, I. L. (1982) *Groupthink: Psychological Studies of Policy Decisions and Fiascos*. Boston, MA: Houghton Mifflin.

Jervis, R. (1968) 'Hypotheses on Misperception', *World Politics*, 20.

Jervis, R. (1976) *Perception and Misperception in International Politics*. Princeton: Princeton University Press.

Jervis, R. (1990) *The Meaning of Nuclear Revolution: Statecraft and the Prospect of Armageddon*. Ithaca: Cornell University Press.

Jessop, B. (2002) *The Future of the Capitalist State*. Cambridge: Polity Press.

Jones, A. (2008) *Crimes Against Humanity: A Beginner's Guide*. Oxford: Oneworld Publications.

Jørgensen, K. E. (2010) *International Relations Theory: A New Introduction*. Basingstoke and New York: Palgrave Macmillan.

Kagan, R. (2004) *Paradise and Power: America and Europe in the New World Order*. London: Atlantic Books.

Kagan, R. (2008) *The Return of History: And the End of Dreams*. New York: Alfred A. Knopf.

Kahn, H. (1960) *On Thermonuclear War*. Princeton: Princeton University Press.

Kaldor, M. (2003) *Global Civil Society: An Answer to War*. Cambridge: Polity Press.

Kaldor, M. (2007) *Human Security: Reflections on Globalization and Intervention*. Cambridge: Polity Press.

Kaldor, M. (2012) *New Wars and Old Wars: Organized Violence in a Global Era*. Cambridge: Polity Press.

Kang, D. (2002) *Crony Capitalism: Corruption and Development in South Korea and the Philippines*. Cambridge: Cambridge University Press.

Karns, M. and K. Mingst (2009) *International Organizations: The Politics and Processes of Global Governance*. Boulder, CO: Lynne Rienner Publishers.

Kay, J. (2004) *The Truth About Markets: Why Some Nations are Rich but Others Remain Poor*. Harmondsworth: Penguin.

Keane, J. (2003) *Global Civil Society?* Cambridge and New York: Cambridge University Press.

Kedourie, E, (1966) *Nationalism*. London: Hutchinson.

Kegley, C. W. and G. A Raymond (2011) *The Global Future: A Brief Introduction to World Politics*. Boston, MA: Wadsworth.

Kennedy, C. and T. Waldman (2013) 'Ways of War in the 21st Century', in M. Beeson and N. Bisley (eds) *Issues in 21st Century World Politics*. Basingstoke and New York: Palgrave Macmillan.

Kennedy, P. (1989) *The Rise and Fall of Great Powers: Economic Change and Military Conflict from 1500 to 2000*. London: Fontana.

Keohane, R. (1986) 'Reciprocity in International Relations', *International Organization*, 40(1).

Keohane, R. (1989) 'International Relations Theory: Contributions of a Feminist Standpoint', *Millennium*, 18.

Keohane, R. (1998) 'Beyond Dichotomy: Conversations between International Relations and Feminist Theory', *International Studies Quarterly*, 42.

Keohane, R. and J. Nye (1977) *Power and Interdependence: World Politics in Transition*. Boston: Little Brown.

Kepel, G. (2004) *The War for Muslim Minds: Islam and the West*. Cambridge MA and London: Belknap Press.

Kepel, G. (2006) *Jihad: The Trial of Political Islam*. London: I. B. Tauris.

Keynes, J. M. ([1936] 1963) *The General Theory of Employment, Interest and Money*. London: Macmillan.

Kilkullen, D. (2005) 'Countering Global Insurgency', *Journal of Strategic Studies*.

Kilkullen, D. (2009) *The Accidental Guerrilla: Fighting Small Wars in the Midst of a Big One*. Oxford: Oxford University Press.

Kilkullen, D. (2010) *Counter Insurgency*. Melbourne: Scribe.

Kindleberger, C. (1973) *The World in Depression, 1929-1939*. Berkeley: University of California Press.

Klare, M. (2001) *Resource Wars: The New Landscape of Global Conflict*. New York: Henry Holt & Company.

Klare, M. (2008) *Rising Powers, Shrinking Planet: How Scarce Energy is Creating a New World Order*. Oxford: Oneworld Publications.

Klein, N. (2000) *No Logo*. London: Flamingo.

Klein, N. (2008) *The Shock Doctrine*. Harmondsworth: Penguin.

Kolko, G. (1985) *Anatomy of a War; Vietnam, the United States, and the Modern Historical Experience*. New York: The New Press

Koskenniemi, M. (2006) *From Apology to Utopia: The Structure of International Legal Argument*. Cambridge: Cambridge University Press.

Kosko, B. (1994) *Fuzzy Thinking: The New Science of Fuzzy Logic*. London: HarperCollins.

Kristof, N. D. and S. WuDunn (2010) *Half the Sky: How to Change the World*. London: Virago.

Kristol, W. and R. Kagan (2004) 'National Interest and Global Responsibility', in I. Stelzer (ed.) *Neoconservatism*. London: Atlantic Books.

Krugman, P. (2007) *The Conscience of A Liberal*. New York: W.W. Norton & Company.

Krugman, P. (2008) *The Return of Depression Economics and the Crisis of 2008*. London: Penguin.

Kuhn, T. (1962) *The Structure of Scientific Revolutions*. Chicago: Chicago University Press.

Kymlicka, W. (1999) 'Misunderstanding Nationalism', in R. Beiner (ed.) *Theorizing Nationalism*. Albany, NY: SUNY Press.

Laclau, E. and C. Mouffe (1985) *Hegemony and Socialist Strategy: Towards a Radical Democratic Politics*. London: Verso.

Laferrière and P. Stoett (1999) *International Relations Theory and Ecological Thought: Towards and Synthesis*. London and New York: Routledge.

Lal, D. (2004) *In Praise of Empire: Globalization and Order*. Basingstoke: Palgrave Macmillan.

Laqueur, W. (1977) *Terrorism*. London: Weidenfeld & Nicholson.

Laqueur, W. (1987) *The Age of Terrorism*. Boston, MA: Little, Brown.

Laqueur, W. (1996) 'Postmodern Terrorism', *Foreign Affairs*, 75 (5).

Laqueur, W. (1999) *The New Terrorism*. Oxford: Oxford University Press.

Layard, R. (2006) *Happiness: Lessons from a New Science*. Harmondsworth: Penguin.

Lenin, V. I. (1970) *Imperialism: The Highest Stage of Capitalism*. Moscow: Progress Publishers.

Leopold, A. (1968) *Sand County Almanac*. Oxford: Oxford University Press.

Lewis, B. (2004) *The Crisis of Islam: Holy War and Unholy Terror*. New York: Random House.

Lifton, R. J. and R. A. Falk (1982) *Indefensible Weapons: The Political and Psychological Case Against Nuclearism*. New York: Basic Books.

Lindblom, C. (1959) 'Science of Muddling Through', *Public Administration Review*, 19.

Linklater, A. (1990) *Beyond Realism and Marxism: Critical Theory and International Relations*. Basingstoke: Palgrave Macmillan.

Linklater, A. (1998) *The Transformation of Political Community: Ethical Foundations of a Post-Westphalian Era*. Columbia: University of South Carolina Press.

Lomborg, B. (2007) *Cool It: The Skeptical Environmentalist's Guide to Global Warming*. New York: Knopf Publishing Group.

Lomborg, B. (2010) *Smart Solutions to Climate Change*. Cambridge: Cambridge University Press.

Lorenz, K. (1966) *On Aggression*. London: Methuen.

Lovelock, J. (1979) *Gaia: A New Look at Life on Earth*. Oxford: Oxford University Press.

Lovelock, J. (1989) *The Ages of Gaia: A Biography of our Living Earth*. Oxford: Oxford University Press.

Lovelock, J. (2006) *Revenge of Gaia: Why the Earth is Fighting Back, and How we can Save Humanity*. Santa Barbara, CA: Allen Lane.

Luban, D. (1985) 'Just War and Human Rights', in C.R. Beitz *et al.* (eds), *International Ethics*. Princeton: Princeton University Press.

Luttlak, E. (2001) *Strategy: The Logic of War and Peace*. Cambridge MA and London: The Belknap Press.

Lutz, E. and C. Reiger (eds) (2009) *Prosecuting Heads of State*. Cambridge and New York: Cambridge University Press.

Lyotard, J.-F. (1984) *The Postmodern Condition: A Report on Knowledge*. Minneapolis: University of Minnesota Press.

Mabee, B. (2013) *Understanding American Power: The Changing World of US Foreign Policy*. Basingstoke and London: Palgrave Macmillan.

MacKinnon, C. (1989) *Towards a Feminist Theory of the State*. Cambridge, MA: Harvard University Press.

Mahbubani, K. (2013) *The Great Convergence: Asia, The West and the Logic of One World*. New York: PublicAffairs.

Marcuse, H. (1964) *One Dimensional Man: Studies in the Ideology of Advanced Industrial Society*. Boston, MA: Beacon.

Marx, K. (1968) *Marx and Engels: Selected Works*. London: Lawrence & Wishart.

Marx, K. (1971) *Grundrisse*. London: Macmillan.

Marx, K. and F. Engels (1976) *The Communist Manifesto*. Harmondsworth: Penguin.

Maslow, A. (1943) 'A Theory of Human Motivation', *Psychological Review*, 50.

Maslow, A. (1970) *Motivation and Personality*. New York: Harper & Row.

Mastanduno, M. (1991) 'Do Relative Gains Matter? America's Response to Japanese Industrial Policy', *International Security*, 16.

McCormick, R. (2005) *Understanding the European Union: A Concise Introduction*. Basingstoke: Palgrave Macmillan.

Meadows, D. H., D. L. Meadows, D. Randers and W. Williams (1972) *The Limits to Growth*. London: Earth Island.

Mearsheimer, J. (1990) 'Back to the Future: Instability after the Cold War', *International Security*, 15(1).

Mearsheimer, J. (2001) *The Tragedy of Great Power Politics*. New York: W. W. Norton.

Mearsheimer, J. (2005) 'Realism is Right', *The National Interest*, Fall.

Mearsheimer, J. (2006) 'China's Unpeaceful Rise', *Current History*, (April).

Mearsheimer, J. and S. Walt (2007) *The Israel Lobby and US Foreign Policy*. New York: Farrar, Straus & Giroux.

Merchant, C. (1983) *The Death of Nature*. New York: Harper & Row.

Merchant, C. (1992) *Radical Ecology: The Search for a Liveable World*. London and New York: Routledge.

Milanovic, B. (2005) *Worlds Apart: Measuring International and Global Inequality*. Princeton: Princeton University Press.

Miller, D. (2007) *National Responsibility and Global Justice*. Oxford: Oxford University Press.

Millett, K. (1970) *Sexual Politics*. New York: Doubleday.

Mitrany, D. (1966) *A Working Peace System: An Argument for the Functional Development of International Organization*. Chicago: University of Chicago Press.

Monbiot, G. (2004) *The Age of Consent: A Manifesto for a New World Order*. London: Harper Perennial.

Moon, K. (1997) *Sex Amongst Allies: Military Prostitution in US-Korea Relations*. New York: Columbia University Press.

Morgenthau, H. (1946) *Scientific Man Versus Power Politics*. Chicago: Chicago University Press.

Morgenthau, H. (1948) *Politics Among Nations: The Struggle for Power and Peace*. New York: Knopf.

Morgenthau, H. (1951) *In Defence of the National Interest: A Critical Examination of American Foreign Policy*. New York: Knopf.

Morgenthau, H. (1960) *The Purpose of American Politics*. New York: Knopf.

Moser, C. and F. Clark (eds) (2001) *Victims, Perpetrators or Actors? Gender, Armed Conflict and Political Violence.* London: Zed Books Ltd.

Moses, J. and T. Knutsen (2007) *Ways of Knowing: Competing Methodologies in Social and Political Research.* Basingstoke: Palgrave Macmillan.

Naess, A. (1973) 'The shallow and the deep, long-range ecological movement: a summary', *Inquiry,* 16.

Naess, A. (1989) *Ecology, Community and Lifestyle.* Cambridge: Cambridge University Press.

Nardin, T. (2001) *The Philosophy of Michael Oakeshott.* Pennsylvania, PA: Pennsylvania State University Press.

Narliker, A. 2005) *The World Trade Organization: A Very Short Introduction.* Oxford: Oxford University Press.

Narveson, J. (1970) 'Pacificism: a philosophical analysis', in R. Wasserstrom (ed.) *War and Morality*, Belmont, CA: Wadsworth Publishing Co.

Nagel. T. (2005) 'The Problem of Global Justice', *Philosophy and Public Affairs,* 33.

Norberg, J. (2003) *In Defence of Global Capitalism.* Washington, DC: CATO Institute.

Norris, R. and H. Kristensen (2010) 'Global nuclear inventories, 1945-2010', *Bulletin of the Atomic Scientists*, July/August.

Nugent, N. (2004) *The Government and Politics of the European Union.* Basingstoke and New York: Palgrave Macmillan.

Nye, J. S. (1988) *Nuclear Ethics.* New York: Free Press.

Nye, J. S. (1990) *Bound to Lead: The Changing Nature of American Power.* New York: Basic Books.

Nye, J. S. (2002) *The Paradox of American Power.* New York: Oxford University Press.

Nye, J. S. (2005) *Soft Power.* New York: PublicAffairs.

Nye, J. S. (2008a) *Understanding International Conflict: An Introduction to Theory and History.* London: Longman.

Nye, J. S. (2008b) *The Powers to Lead: Soft, Hard, and Smart.* New York: Oxford University Press.

O'Brien, R. and M. Williams (2013) *Global Political Economy: Evolution and Dynamics.* Basingstoke: Palgrave Macmillan.

O'Neill, O. (1996) *Towards Justice and Virtue: A Constructive Account of Practical Reasoning.* Cambridge: Cambridge University Press.

Oakes, W. (1944) 'Towards a Permanent Arms Economy?', *Politics*, February.

Oakeshott. M. (1962) *Rationalism in Politics and Other Essays.* London: Methuen.

Ohmae, K. (1990) *The Borderless World: Power and Strategy in the Interlinked Economy.* London: Fontana.

Ohmae, K. (1995) *The End of the Nation State: The Rise of Regional Economies.* New York: Free Press.

Orford, A. (2003) *Reading Humanitarian Intervention.* Cambridge: Cambridge University Press.

Osborne, D. and T. Gaebler (1992) *Reinventing Government.* New York: Addison-Wesley.

Ostrom, E. (1990) *Governing the Commons: The Evolution of Institutions for Collective Action.* Cambridge: Cambridge University Press.

Oye, K. (1986) *Cooperation under Anarchy.* Princeton: Princeton University Press.

Pape, R. (2005) *Dying to Win: The Strategic Logic of Suicide Terrorism.* New York: Random House.

Parekh, B. (2000) *Rethinking Multiculturalism: Cultural Diversity and Political Theory.* Basingstoke: Palgrave Macmillan.

Parekh, B.(2008) *A New Politics of Identity: Political Principles for an Interdependent World.* Basingstoke and New York: Palgrave Macmillan.

Parmar, I. and M. Cox (eds) (2010) *Soft Power and US Foreign Policy.* London: Routledge.

Paul, T. V. and J. A. Hall (1999) *International Order and the Future of World Politics.* Cambridge: Cambridge University Press.

Paupp. T. (2009) *The Future of Global Relations: Crumbling Walls, Rising Regions*. Basingstoke: Palgrave Macmillan.

Peet, R. (2009) *Unholy Trinity: The IMF, World Bank and WTO*. New York: Zed Books.

Perkovich, G. and J. M. Acton (2008) *Abolishing Nuclear Weapons*. Abingdon: Routledge.

Peterson, V. S. (1992) *Gendered States: Feminist (Re)Visions of International Relations Theory*. Boulder, CO: Lynne Rienner Publishers.

Peterson, V. S. and A. S. Runyan (2010) *Global Gender Issues in the New Millenium*. Boulder, CO: Westview Press.

Phillips, A. (2010) 'Transnational Terrorism', in M. Beeson and N. Bisley (eds) *Issues in 21st Century World Politics*. Basingstoke: Palgrave Macmillan.

Pierre, J. and B. G. Peters (2000) *Governance, Politics and the State*. Basingstoke: Palgrave Macmillan.

Piore, M. and C. Sabel (1984) *The Second Industrial Divide: Possibilities for Prosperity*. New York: Basic Books.

Pogge, T. (2008) *World Poverty and Human Rights: Cosmopolitan Responsibilities and Reforms*. Cambridge: Polity Press.

Popper, K. (1959) *The Logic of Scientific Discovery*. London: Hutchinson & Co.

Pryke, S. (2009) *Nationalism in a Global World*. Basingstoke: Palgrave Macmillan.

Przeworski, A. (ed.) (2000) *Democracy and Development: Political Institutions and Well-Being in the World, 1950-1990*. New York: Cambridge University Press.

Przeworski, A. and J. R. Vernon (2000) 'The Effect of IMF Structural Adjustment Programs on Economic Growth', *Journal of Development Economics*, 62.

Putnam, R. (2000) *Bowling Alone: The Collapse and Revival of American Community*. New York: Simon & Schuster.

Rabkin, J. (2005) *Law Without Nations? Why Constitutional Government Requires Sovereign States*. Princeton: Princeton University Press.

Ralston Saul, J. (2009) *The Collapse of Globalism*. New York: Atlantic Books.

Ramo, J. (2004) *The Beijing Consensus*. London: The Foreign Policy Centre.

Ravenhill, J. (ed.) (2011) *Global Political Economy*. Oxford and New York: Oxford University Press.

Rawls, J. (1999) *The Law of Peoples*. Cambridge, MA: Harvard University Press.

Reinicke, W. H. and F. M. Deng (eds) (2000) *Critical Choices: The United Nations, Networks and the Future of Global Governance*. Ottawa, Canada: International Development Research Centre.

Reus-Smit, C. and D. Snidal (2010) *The Oxford Handbook of International Relations*. Oxford and New York: Oxford University Press.

Reus-Smit, C. and D. Snidal (2010) 'Between Utopia and Reality: The Practical Discourses of International Relations', in C. Reus-Smit and D. Snidal (eds) *Oxford Handbook of International Relations*. Oxford: Oxford University Press.

Riddell, R. (2007) *Does Foreign Aid Really Work?* Oxford: Oxford University Press.

Rittberger, V., B. Zangl and A. Kruck (2012) *International Organization: Polity, Politics and Policies*. Basingstoke: Palgrave Macmillan.

Ritzer, G. (1993) *The McDonaldization of Society: An Investigation into the Changing Character of Social Life*. Thousand Oaks, CA: Pine Forge Press.

Robertson, R. (1992) *Globalization: Social Theory and Global Culture*. London: Sage.

Rodin, D. (2002) *War and Self Defence*. Oxford: Oxford University Press.

Rosamond, B. (2000) *Theories of European Integration*. Basingstoke: Palgrave Macmillan.

Rosenau, J. N. (1990) *Turbulence in World Politics: A Theory of Change and Continuity*. Princeton: Princeton University Press.

Rosenau, J. (1997) *Along the Domestic-Foreign Frontier: Exploring Governance in a Turbulent World*. Cambridge: Cambridge University Press.

Rosenau, J. (2003) *Distant Proximities: Dynamics Beyond Globalization*. Princeton, NJ: Princeton University Press.

Rostow, W. W. (1960) *The Stages of Economic Growth: The Non-Communist Manifesto.* Cambridge: Cambridge University Press.

Roszak, T. (1994) *A Cult of Information: The Folklore of Computers and the True Art of Thinking.* London: Paladin Books.

Roy, O. (1994) *The Failure of Political Islam.* Cambridge, MA: Harvard University Press.

Ruggie, J. (1992) 'Multilateralism: The Anatomy of an Institution', *International Organization,* 46.

Ruggie, J. (1998) *Constructing the World Polity: Essays on International Institutionalization.* London: Routledge.

Ruggie, J. (2008) (ed.) *Embedding Global Markets: An Enduring Challenge.* Aldershot, UK and Burlington, VT: Ashgate Publishing Company.

Ruggie, J. (ed.) (1993) *Multilateralism Matters: The Theory and Praxis of an International Form.* New York: Columbia University Press.

Ruthven, M. (2005) *Fundamentalism: The Search for Meaning.* Oxford: Oxford University Press.

Sachs, J. (2005) *The End of Poverty: Economic Possibilities for our Time.* Harmondsworth: Penguin.

Sachs, J. (2008) *Common Wealth: Economics for a Crowded Planet.* Harmondsworth: Penguin.

Sageman, M. (2004) *Understanding Terror Networks.* Philadelphia, PA: University of Pennsylvania Press.

Sageman, M. (2008) *Leaderless Jihad: Terror Networks in the Twenty-First Century.* Philadelphia, PA: University of Pennsylvania Press.

Said, E. (1993) *Culture and Imperialism.* New York: Alfred A. Knopf.

Said, E. (2003) *Orientalism.* Harmondsworth: Penguin.

Samarasinghe, V. (2009) *Female Sex Trafficking in Asia: The Resilience of Patriarchy in a Changing World.* London: Routledge.

Sandel, M. (1982) *Liberalism and the Limits of Justice.* Cambridge: Cambridge University Press.

Sassen, S. (1988) *The Mobility of Capital and Labour.* Cambridge: Cambridge University Press.

Sassen, S. (2001) *The Global City: New York, London, Tokyo.* Princeton: Princeton University Press.

Sassen, S. (2006) *Territory, Authority, Rights: From Medieval to Global Assemblages.* Princeton: Princeton University Press.

Savigny, H. and L. Marsden (2011) *Doing Political Science and International Relations.* Basingstoke and New York: Palgrave Macmillan.

Schmid, A., and A. Jongman (1988) *Political Terrorism: A New Guide to Actors, Authors, Concepts, Databases, Theories and Literature.* Oxford: North Holland.

Schmitt, C. (1996) *The Concept of the Political.* Chicago: University of Chicago Press.

Scholte, J. A. (1993) *International Relations of Social Change.* Buckingham: Open University Press.

Scholte, J. A. (2005) *Globalization: A Critical Introduction.* Basingstoke: Palgrave Macmillan.

Schumpeter, J. (1942) *Capitalism, Socialism and Democracy.* London: Allen & Unwin.

Schumpeter, J. (1954) *History of Economic Analysis.* Oxford: Oxford University Press.

Seabrooke, L. and E. Tsingou (2010) 'Responding to the Global Credit Crisis: The Politics of Financial Reform', *The British Journal of Politics and International Relations,* 12/(2).

Sen, A. (1981) *Poverty and Famine: An Essay on Entitlements and Deprivation.* Oxford: Clarendon Press.

Sen, A. (1990) 'More than a hundred million women are missing', *The New York Review of Books,* 37(20).

Sen, A. (1999) *Development as Freedom.* Oxford: Oxford University Press.

Sen, A. (2006) *Identity and Violence: The Illusion of Destiny.* London and New York: Penguin.

Sen, A. (2009) *The Idea of Justice.* London: Allen Lane.

Shaw, M. (2003) *International Law.* Cambridge: Cambridge University Press.

Shepherd, L. J. (2009) 'Gender, Violence and Global Politics', *Political Studies Review*, 7(2).

Shepherd, L. J. (2010) *Gender Matters in Global Politics*. London and New York: Routledge.

Shimko, K. L. (2008) *International Relations: Perspectives and Controversies*. Boston, MA: Houghton Mifflin.

Shiva, V. (1993) *Monocultures of the Mind: Biodiversity, Biotechnology and Agriculture*. New Delhi: Zed Press.

Shiva V. (1999) *Stolen Harvest: The Hijacking of the Global Food Supply*. Cambridge, MA: Southend Press.

Shue, H. (1996) *Basic Rights: Subsistence, Affluence and US Foreign Policy*. Princeton: Princeton University Press.

Shultz, G. P. and W. J. Perry, H. Kissinger and S. Nunn (2007) 'A World Free of Nuclear Weapons', *The Wall Street Journal*, January 4.

Sil, R. and J. Katzenstein (2010) *Beyond Paradigms: Analytic Eclecticism in Study of World Politics*. Basingstoke: Palgrave Macmillan.

Simon, H. (1983) *Models of Bounded Rationality – Vol. 2*. Cambridge, MA: MIT Press.

Singer, M. and A. Wildavsky (1993) *The Real World Order: Zones of Peace / Zones of Turmoil*. Chatham, NJ: Chatham House Publishers.

Singer, P. (1993) *Practical Ethics*. Cambridge: Cambridge University Press.

Singer, P. (2002) *One World: The Ethics of Globalization*. Newhaven CT and London: Yale University Press.

Skidelsky, R. (2009) *Keynes: The Return of the Master*. London: Allen Lane.

Smith, A. D. (1986) *The Ethnic Origin of Nations*. Oxford: Blackwell.

Smith, A. D. (1991) *National Identity*. London: Penguin.

Smith, A. D. (1995) *Nations and Nationalism in a Global Era*. Cambridge: Polity Press.

Smith, M. E. (2010) *International Security: Politics, Policy, Prospects*. Basingstoke: Palgrave Macmillan.

Smith, R. (2006) *The Utility of Force: The Art of War in the Modern World*. Harmondsworth: Penguin.

Smith, S. (1995) 'The Self-Image of a Discipline: A Genealogy of International Relations Theory', in K. Booth and S. Smith (eds) *International Relations Theory Today*. Cambridge: Cambridge University Press.

Smith, S., A. Hadfield and T. Dunne (eds) (2012) *Foreign Policy: Theories, Actors, Cases*. Oxford: Oxford University Press.

Snow, D. M. (1998) *The Shape of the Future: World Politics in a New Century*. New York: M. E. Sharpe.

Soederberg, S. (2006) *Global Governance in Question: Empire, Class and the New Commonsense in Managing North-South Relations*. London: Pluto Press.

Solingen, E. (2007) *Nuclear Logics: Contrasting Paths in East Asia and the Middle East*. Princeton: Princeton University Press.

Sørensen, G. (2004) *The Transformation of the State: Beyond the Myth of Retreat*. Basingstoke and New York: Palgrave Macmillan.

Soros, G. (2000) *Open Society: The Crisis of Global Capitalism Reconsidered*. London: Little Brown.

Soros, G. (2008) *The New Paradigm for Financial Markets: The Credit Crisis of 2008 and What it Means*. New York: PublicAffairs.

Spellman W. (2006) *A Concise History of the World Since 1945*. Basingstoke and New York: Palgrave Macmillan.

Spencer, P. and H. Wollman (2002) *Nationalism: A Critical Introduction*. London and Thousand Oaks, CA: Sage.

Sprinzak, E. (2001) 'The Lone Gunmen', *Foreign Policy*, 127.

Squires, J. (1999) *Gender in Political Theory*. Cambridge: Polity Press.

Steans, J. (1998) *Gender and International Relations: An Introduction*. Cambridge: Polity Press.

Steans, J., L. Pettiford, T. Diez and I. El-Anis (2010) *An Introduction to International Relations Theory: Perspectives and Themes*. Harlow: Pearson Education Limited.

Steger, M. (2003) *Globalization: A Very Short Introduction*. Oxford: Oxford University Press.

Stein, A. (1990) *Why Nations Cooperate: Circumstance and Choice in International Relations*. Ithaca: Cornell University Press.

Stelzer, I (ed,) (2004) *Neoconservatism*. London: Atlantic Books.

Stiglitz, J. (1996) *Whither Socialism?* Cambridge, MA: MIT Press

Stiglitz, J. (2002) *Globalization and its Discontents*. New York: W.W. Norton.

Stiglitz, J. (2003) *The Roaring Nineties*. New York: W.W. Norton.

Stiglitz, J. (2005) *Fair Trade for All: How Trade Can Promote Development*. Oxford: Oxford University Press.

Stiglitz, J. (2006) *Making Globalization Work*. London: Penguin Books.

Stiglitz, J. (2010) *Freefall: America, Free Markets, and the Sinking of the World Economy*. New York: W.W. Norton & Company.

Stoessinger, J. G. (2005) *Why Nations Go to War*. Belmont. CA: Wadsworth.

Strange, S. (1986) *Casino Capitalism*. Oxford: Basil Blackwell.

Strange, S. (1988) *States and Markets*. London: Pinter.

Strange, S. (1996) *The Retreat of the State: The Diffusion of Power in the World Economy*. Cambridge: Cambridge University Press.

Strange, S. (1998) *Mad Money: When Markets Outgrow Governments*. Manchester: Manchester University Press.

Suganami, H. (1996) *On the Causes of War*. Oxford: Clarendon Press.

Sutherland, C. (2012) *Nationalism in the Twenty-First Century: Challenges and Responses*. Basingstoke and New York: Palgrave Macmillan.

Sylvester, C. (1994) *Feminist Theory and International Relations in a Postmodern Era*. Cambridge: Cambridge University Press.

Taylor, C. (1994) *Multiculturalism and 'The Politics of Recognition'*. Princeton: Princeton University Press.

Thakur, R. (2006) *The United Nations, Peace and Security: From Collective Security to the Responsibility to Protect*. Cambridge: Cambridge University Press.

Thurow, L. (1996) *The Future of Capitalism: How Today's Economic Forces Shape Tomorrow's World*. London: Penguin Books.

Tickner, J. A. (1987) *Self-Reliance Versus Power Politics*. New York: Columbia University Press.

Tickner, J. A. (1988) 'Hans Morgenthau's Principles of Political Realism: A Feminist Reformulation', *Millennium*, 17(3).

Tickner, J. A. (1992) *Gender in International Relations: Feminist Perspectives on Achieving Global Security*. New York: Columbia University Press.

Tickner, J. A. (1992a) 'On the Fringes of the Global Economy', in R. Tooze and C. Murphy (eds), *The New International Political Economy*. Boulder, CO: Lynne Rienner.

Tickner, J. A. (1997) 'You just don't understand', *International Studies Quarterly*, 41.

Tickner, J. A. (2001) *Gender in World Politics: Issues and Approaches in the Post-Cold War Era*. New York: Columbia University Press.

Tickner, J. A. (2002) 'Feminist Perspectives on 9/11', *International Studies Perspectives*, 3(4).

Tobin, J. (1955) 'A Dynamic Aggregative Model', *Journal of Political Economy* 63.(2).

Tobin, J. (1969) 'A General Equilibrium Approach to Monetary Theory', *Journal of Money, Credit and Banking* 1.1 (1).

Tormey, S. (2004) *Anti-Capitalism: A Beginner's Guide*. Oxford: Oneworld Publications.

Townsend, C. 2002) *Terrorism: A Very Short Introduction*. Oxford: Oxford University Press.

True, J. (2009) 'Feminism', in S. Burchill *et al.* (eds) *Theories of International Relations*. Basingstoke: Palgrave Macmillan.

Truong, T., S. Wieringa and A. Chhachhi (2007) *Engendering Human Security: Feminist Perspectives*. London: Zed Books.

UNDP (2005) *UN Human Development Report*. New York: Oxford University Press.

UNDP (2006) *UN Human Development Report*. New York: Oxford University Press.

UNDP (2007) *UN Human Development Report*. New York: Oxford University Press.

UNDP (2008) *UN Human Development Report*. New York: Oxford University Press.

UNDP (2009) *UN Human Development Report*. New York: Oxford University Press.

UNDP (2010) *UN Human Development Report*. New York: Oxford University Press.

UNDP (2011) *UN Human Development Report*. New York: Oxford University Press.

UNDP (2013) *UN Human Development Report*. New York: Oxford University Press.

UNODC (2006) *Trafficking in Persons: Global Patterns*. Vienna: UN High Commission for Refugees.

van Creveld, M. (1991) *The Transformation of War*. New York: Free Press.

van Creveld, M. (2000) *The Art of War: War and Military Thought*. London: Cassell.

van Kersbergen, K. (1995) *Social Capitalism: A Study of Christian Democracy and the Welfare State*. London: Routledge.

Vanderheiden, S. (2008) 'Two Conceptions of Sustainability', *Political Studies* 56(2).

Vasak, K. (1977) 'Human Rights: A Thirty-Year Struggle', *UNESCO Courier 30:11*. Paris: UNESCO.

Vincent, J. (1986) *Human Rights and International Relations*. Cambridge: Cambridge University Press.

Wallerstein, I. (1974) *The Modern World System*. New York: Academic Press.

Wallerstein, I. (1984) *The Politics of the World Economy: States, Movements and Civilizations*. Oxford: Polity Press.

Waltz, K. (1959) *Man, the State, and War*. New York: Columbia University Press.

Waltz, K. (1979) *Theory of International Politics*. Reading, MA: Addison-Wesley.

Waltz, K. (1986) 'Reflections on Theory of International Politics', in R. Keohane (ed.) *Neo-Realism and Its Critics*. New York: Columbia University Press.

Waltz, K. (1990) 'Realist Thought and Neorealist Theory', *Journal of International Affairs*, 44(1).

Waltz, K. (2002) 'Structural Realism After the Cold War', in G. Ikenberry (ed.) *America Unrivalled: The Future of the Balance of Power*. Ithaca and London: Cornell University Press.

Waltz, K. (2012) 'Why Iran should get the Bomb', *Foreign Affairs*, July/August.

Walzer, M. (1977) *Just and Unjust Wars: A Moral Argument with Historical Illustrations*. New York: Basic Books.

Walzer, M. (1983) *Spheres of Justice: A Defence of Pluralism and Equality*. New York: Basic Books.

Walzer, M. (1994) *Thick and Thin: Moral Argument at Home and Abroad*. Chicago: Notre Dame Press,

Walzer, M. (2004) *Arguing about War*. London: Yale University Press.

Walzer. M. (2007) 'Political Action: The Problem of Dirty Hands', in D. Miller (ed.) *Thinking Politically: Essays in Political Theory*. Newhaven: Yale University Press.

Ward, B. and R. Dubois (1972) *Only One Earth*. Harmondsworth: Penguin; New York: New American Library.

Weber, M. (1948) *From Max Weber: Essays in Sociology*. London: Routledge & Kegan Paul.

Weiss, G, and A. Kamran (2009) 'Global Governance as International Organization', in J. Whitman (ed.) *Global Governance*. Basingstoke: Palgrave Macmillan.

Weiss, T. G. (2007) *Humanitarian Intervention: Ideas in Action*. Cambridge: Polity Press

Weiss, T. G. (2009) *What's Wrong with the United Nations (and How to Fix It)*. Cambridge and Malden, MA: Polity Press.

Wendt, A. (1987) 'The Agent-Structure Problem in International Relations Theory', *International Organization*, 41.

Wendt, A. (1992) 'Anarchy is what States make of it: The Social Construction of Power Politics', *International Organization*, 46(2).

Wendt, A. (1995) 'Constructing International Politics'. In *International Society*, 20.

Wendt, A. (1999) *Social Theory of International Politics*. Cambridge: Cambridge University Press.

Wheeler, N. (2000) *Saving Strangers: Humanitarian Intervention in International Society.* Oxford: Oxford University Press.

Whitman, J. (ed.) *Global Governance.* Basingstoke: Palgrave Macmillan.

Wight, M. (1991) *International Theory: The Three Traditions.* Leicester: Leicester University Press.

Wilkinson, P. (2003) 'Why Modern Terrorism? Differentiating Types and Distinguishing Ideological Motivations', in C. Kegley Jr (ed.) *The New Global Terrorism: Characteristics, Causes and Controls.* Upper Saddle River, NJ: Prentice Hall.

Wilkinson, P. (2006) *Terrorism Versus Democracy.* London and New York: Routledge.

Wilkinson, R. and K. Pickett (2010) *The Spirit Level: Why Equality is Better for Everyone.* Harmondsworth: Penguin.

Williamson, J. (1990) *Latin American Adjustment: How Much Has Happened?* Washington, DC: Institute for International Economics.

Williamson, J. (1993) 'Democracy and the 'Washington Consensus', *World Development,* 21 (8).

Willis, K. (2011) *Theories and Practices of Development.* London and New York: Routledge.

Wohlforth, W. (1993) *Elusive Balance: Power and Perception during the Cold War.* Ithaca, NY: Cornell University Press.

Wolf, M. (2005) *Why Globalization Works.* Newhaven, CT: Yale University Press.

Woods, N. (2006) *The Globalizers: The IMF, the World Bank, and their Borrowers.* Ithaca: Cornell University Press.

World Bank (2010) *Global Economic Prospects 2009: Forecast Update.*

World Economic Forum (2007) *The Global Gender Gap Report 2007.*

Yergin, D. (1980) *Shattered Peace: Origins of the Cold War and the National Security State.* Harmondsworth: Penguin.

Young, A., J. Duckett and P. Graham (eds) (2010) *Perspectives on the Global Distribution of Power.* Exceptional special edition of *Politics,* 30(1).

Young, I. (1995) *Justice and the Politics of Difference.* Princeton: Princeton University Press.

Young, J. W. and G. Kent (2004) *International Relations Since 1945: A Global History.* Oxford: Oxford University Press.

Young, R. (2003) *Postcolonialism: A Very Short Introduction.* Oxford: Oxford University Press.

Yunker, J. (2007) *Political Globalization: A New Vision of World Government.* Lanham, MD: University Press of America.

Yuval-Davis, N. (1997) *Gender and Nation.* London: Sage

Yuval-Davis, N. and F. Anthias (eds) (1989) *Woman, Nation-State.* London: Macmillan.

Zakaria, F. (1998) *From Wealth to Power.* Princeton: Princeton University Press.

Zakaria, F. (2009) *The Post-American World.* New York: W.W. Norton & Co.

Index

Numbers in **bold** refer to boxed information.
Numbers in *italics* refer to terms defined in the margin.
f = figure, n = note, t = table